ALGORITHMS & DATA STRUCTURES

Algorithms & Data Structures

Editor:

Ivan Stanimirović, Ph.D.

ArclerPress

www.arclerpress.com

Algorithms & Data Structures

Editor: Ivan Stanimirović, Ph.D.

© 2017 Arcler Press LLC
708 3rd Avenue, 6th Floor
New York
NY 10017
United States of America
www.arclerpress.com

ISBN: 978-1-68094-463-1

Library of Congress Control Number: 2016951158

Arcler Press LLC publishes wide variety of books and eBooks. For more information about Arcler Press and its products, visit our website at www.arclerpress.com

Contents

List of Contributors

Markus Rupp
TU Wien, Institute of Telecommunications, Gusshausstr. 25, 1040 Vienna, Austria

Xinghua Liu
Department of Auto, School of Information Science and Technology, University of Science and Technology of China, Anhui 230027, China

Enrique Baeyens
Instituto de las Tecnologías Avanzadas de la Producción (ITAP), Universidad de Valladolid, Paseo del Cauce 59, 47011 Valladolid, Spain

Alberto Herreros
Instituto de las Tecnologías Avanzadas de la Producción (ITAP), Universidad de Valladolid, Paseo del Cauce 59, 47011 Valladolid, Spain

José R. Perán
Centro Tecnológico Cartif, Parque Tecnológico de Boecillo 205, 47151 Bocillo, Spain

Daniel R. Page
Department of Computer Science, Western University, London, ON N6A5B7, Canada

Roberto Solis-Oba
Department of Computer Science, Western University, London, ON N6A5B7, Canada

Xianglei Xing
College of Automation, Harbin Engineering University, Harbin 150001, China

Sidan Du
School of Electronic Science and Engineering, Nanjing University, Nanjing 210046, China

Kejun Wang
College of Automation, Harbin Engineering University, Harbin 150001, China

Alfredo Cuzzocrea
DIA Department, University of Trieste and ICAR-CNR, Trieste 34127, Italy

Yibing Li
College of Information and Communication Engineering, Harbin Engineering University, Harbin 150001, China

Xueying Diao
College of Information and Communication Engineering, Harbin Engineering University, Harbin 150001, China

Ge Dong
College of Information and Communication Engineering, Harbin Engineering University, Harbin 150001, China

Fang Ye
College of Information and Communication Engineering, Harbin Engineering University, Harbin 150001, China

Alfredo Cuzzocrea
DIA Department, University of Trieste and ICAR-CNR, Trieste 34127, Italy

Mirel Cosulschi
Department of Computer Science, University of Craiova, Craiova 200585, Romania

Roberto de Virgilio
Dipartimento di Informatica e Automazione, Universitá Roma Tre, Rome 00146, Italy

Fan Jiang
Department of Computer Science, University of Manitoba, Winnipeg, MB, R3T 2N2, Canada

Carson K. Leung
Department of Computer Science, University of Manitoba, Winnipeg, MB, R3T 2N2, Canada

Michael Charles Davis
Organisation Européene pour la Recherche Nucléaire (CERN), Route de Meyrin 385, 1217 Meyrin, Switzerland

Zhanyu Ma
Pattern Recognition and Intelligent Systems (PRIS) Lab, Beijing University of Posts and Telecommunications (BUPT), 100876 Beijing, China

Weiru Liu
School of Electrical and Electronic Engineering and Computer Science, Queen's University Belfast, University Road, Belfast BT7 1NN, UK

Paul Miller
School of Electrical and Electronic Engineering and Computer Science, Queen's University Belfast, University Road, Belfast BT7 1NN, UK

Ruth Hunter
Centre for Public Health, Queen's University Belfast, University Road, Belfast BT7 1NN, UK

Frank Kee
Centre for Public Health, Queen's University Belfast, University Road, Belfast BT7 1NN, UK

Lei Feng
College of Computer and Information Science, Southwest University, Chongqing 400715, China

Guoxian Yu
College of Computer and Information Science, Southwest University, Chongqing 400715, China
Key Laboratory of Symbolic Computation and Knowledge Engineering of Ministry of Education, Jilin University, Changchun 130012, China

Guillermo M. Mallén-Fullerton
Engineering Department, Universidad Iberoamericana Ciudad de México, Prolongación Paseo de la Reforma 880, Lomas de Santa Fe, Distrito Federal 01219, Mexico

J. Emilio Quiroz-Ibarra
Universidad Iberoamericana Ciudad de México, DCI, Prolongación Paseo de la Reforma 880, Lomas de Santa Fe, Distrito Federal 01219, Mexico

Antonio Miranda
Physics and Mathematics Department, Universidad Iberoamericana Ciudad de México, Prolongación Paseo de la Reforma 880, Lomas de Santa Fe, Distrito Federal 01219, Mexico

Guillermo Fernández-Anaya
Physics and Mathematics Department, Universidad Iberoamericana Ciudad de México, Prolongación Paseo de la Reforma 880, Lomas de Santa Fe, Distrito Federal 01219, Mexico

Natarajan Meghanathan
Computer Science, Jackson State University, Jackson, MS 39217, USA; Tel.: +1-601-979-3661

Bastien Cazaux
LIRMM, CNRS and Université de Montpellier, 161 rue Ada, 34095 Montpellier Cedex 5, France
Institut de Biologie Computationnelle, CNRS and Université de Montpellier, 860 rue Saint Priest, 34095 Montpellier Cedex 5, France

Eric Rivals
LIRMM, CNRS and Université de Montpellier, 161 rue Ada, 34095 Montpellier Cedex 5, France
Institut de Biologie Computationnelle, CNRS and Université de Montpellier, 860 rue Saint Priest, 34095 Montpellier Cedex 5, France

Sanguthevar Rajasekaran
Dept. of Computer Science and Engineering, Univ. of Connecticut, Storrs, CT, USA

Marius Nicolae
Dept. of Computer Science and Engineering, Univ. of Connecticut, Storrs, CT, USA

Khalid A. Alsatami
Department of Mathematics, College of Science, Qassim University, Buraydah 51452, Saudi Arabia

Hong-Jian Lai
Department of Mathematics, West Virginia University, Morgantown, WV 26506, USA

Xindong Zhang
College of Mathematics Sciences, Xinjiang Normal University, Urumqi 830054, China

Ashish Kumar Das
Department of Mathematics, North-Eastern Hill University, Permanent Campus, Shillong, Meghalaya 793022, India

Deiborlang Nongsiang
Department of Mathematics, North-Eastern Hill University, Permanent Campus, Shillong, Meghalaya 793022, India

Srinivasa Rao Kola
Department of Mathematical and Computational Sciences, National Institute of Technology Karnataka, Karnataka 575025, India

Pratima Panigrahi
Department of Mathematics, Indian Institute of Technology Kharagpur, Kharagpur 721302, India

Medha Itagi Huilgol
Department of Mathematics, Bangalore University, Central College Campus, Bangalore 560001, India

Md. Forhad Hossain
Department of Computer Science and Engineering, Bangladesh University of Engineering and Technology, Dhaka 1000, Bangladesh

Md. Momin Al Aziz
Department of Computer Science and Engineering, Bangladesh University of Engineering and Technology, Dhaka 1000, Bangladesh

M. Kaykobad
Department of Computer Science and Engineering, Bangladesh University of Engineering and Technology, Dhaka 1000, Bangladesh

Preface

Asymptotic algorithm analysis is a methodology which has been given a lot of attention recently. Several methods of asymptotic analysis are considered to estimate the resource consumption of an algorithm, giving an assessment if a proposed algorithm can meet the resource constraints for a problem before the implementation. Processing nodes of the binary and non-binary trees in an organized manner is investigated using various algorithms. Several methods for implementing binary trees and their nodes are given. Issues relating to the design of algorithms and data structures for disk-based applications are solved, as well as problems of searching data stored in lists and tables. Algorithms for solving some problems related to finding shortest routes in a graph and the minimum-cost spanning tree, are applied to determine lowest-cost connectivity in a network.

The initial five chapters of this book considers asymptotic algorithm analysis and provide various algorithms, such as modification of LMS algorithm, a direct search algorithm is proposed for minimizing an arbitrary function, etc. The following nine chapters present generative algorithms for random graphs, trees and big data. The remaining content of this book focuses on the advances of specific methods and algorithms in the field of data structures, especially in graph theory.

The mean square convergence of the LMS algorithm is investigated for the large class of linearly filtered random driving processes, containing the following contributions: (i) The parameter error vector covariance matrix can be decomposed into two parts, (ii) The impact of additive noise is shown to contribute only to the modal space of the driving process independently from the noise statistic and thus defines the steady state of the filter.

The certain and uncertain neutral systems with time-delay and saturating actuator are considered. In order to analyse and optimize the system, auxiliary functions are presented based on additive decomposition approach and the relationship among them is discussed. As the novel stability criterion, two sufficient conditions are obtained for asymptotic stability of the neutral systems. Furthermore, the stability analysis algorithm and optimality algorithm are introduced to optimize the result.

A direct search algorithm is proposed for minimizing an arbitrary real valued function. The algorithm uses a new function transformation and three simplex-based operations. The function transformation provides global exploration features, while the simplex-based operations guarantees the termination of the algorithm and provides global convergence to a stationary point if the cost function is differentiable and its gradient is Lipschitz continuous. The algorithm's performance has been extensively tested using benchmark functions and compared to some well-known global optimization algorithms.

In the pursuit of finding subclasses of the makespan minimization problem on unrelated parallel machines that have approximation algorithms with approximation ratio better than 2, the graph balancing problem has been of current interest. In the graph balancing problem each job can be non-preemptively scheduled on one of at most two machines with the same processing time on either machine. A 3/2 -approximation algorithm for the graph balancing problem is presented.

Recently manifold learning has received extensive interest in the community of pattern recognition. Despite their appealing properties, most manifold learning algorithms are not robust in practical applications. This problem is addressed in the context of the Hessian locally linear embedding (HLLE) algorithm and propose a more robust method, called RHLLE, which aims to be robust against both outliers and noise in the data. Specifically, a fast outlier detection method for high-dimensional datasets is proposed. Then, a local smoothing method is employed to reduce noise.

Nowadays, a leading instance of big data is represented by Web data that lead to the definition of so-called big Web data. In order to process such kind of big data, MapReduce, an open source computational framework specifically tailored to big data processing, has emerged during the last years as the reference implementation for this critical setting. In line with this trend, an approach is presented for efficiently implementing traversals of large-scale Resource Description Framework (RDF) graphs over MapReduce that is based on the Breadth First Search (BFS) strategy for visiting (RDF) graphs to be decomposed and processed according to the MapReduce framework.

Big data are everywhere as high volumes of varieties of valuable precise and uncertain data can be easily collected or generated at high velocity in various real-life applications. Embedded in these big data are rich sets of useful information and knowledge. To mine these big data and to discover useful information and knowledge, a data analytic algorithm is presented. This algorithm manages, queries, and processes uncertain big data in cloud environments. More specifically, it manages transactions of uncertain big data, allows users to query these big data by specifying constraints expressing their interests, and processes the user-specified constraints to discover useful information and knowledge from the uncertain big data.

Generative algorithms for random graphs have yielded insights into the structure and evolution of real-world networks. A generative model for random graphs with discrete vertex labels and numeric edge weights is developed. The weights are represented as a set of Beta Mixture Models (BMMs) with an arbitrary number of mixtures, which are learned from real-world networks. Therefore, a Bayesian Variational Inference (VI) approach is proposed, which yields an accurate estimation while keeping computation times tractable.

Aggregation delay is the minimum number of time slots required to aggregate data along the edges of a data gathering tree (DG tree) spanning all the nodes in a wireless sensor network (WSN). A benchmarking algorithm is proposed to determine the minimum possible aggregation delay for DG trees in a WSN. It is shown that the minimum aggregation delay for a DG tree depends on the underlying design choices (bottleneck node-weight based or bottleneck link-weight based) behind its construction.

Some properties of a graph which is constructed from the equivalence classes of nonzero zero-divisors determined by the annihilator ideals of a poset are studied. In particular, it is demonstrated how this graph helps in identifying the annihilator prime ideals of a poset that satisfies the ascending chain condition for its proper annihilator ideals.

An m-distant tree T is a tree in which there is a path of maximum length such that every vertex in is at the most distance from. This path is called a central path. For every tree, there is an integer such that is an m-distant tree. The radio number of some m-distant trees is determined for any positive integer, and as a consequence of it, the radio number of a class of 1-distant trees is found.

The concept of distance degree regular (DDR) graphs denotes the graphs for which all vertices have the same distance degree sequence. By definition, a DDR graph must be a regular graph, but a regular graph may not be DDR. A graph is distance degree injective (DDI) graph if no two vertices have the same distance degree sequence. DDI graphs are highly irregular, in comparison with the DDR graphs. In this book, an exhaustive review of the two concepts of DDR and DDI graphs is conducted, starting with an insight into all distance related sequences and their applications. All the related open problems are listed.

Editor
Ivan Stanimirović, Ph.D.

CHAPTER 1

ASYMPTOTIC EQUIVALENT ANALYSIS OF THE LMS ALGORITHM UNDER LINEARLY FILTERED PROCESSES

Markus Rupp

TU Wien, Institute of Telecommunications, Gusshausstr. 25, 1040 Vienna, Austria

ABSTRACT

While the least mean square (LMS) algorithm has been widely explored for some specific statistics of the driving process, an understanding of its behavior under general statistics has not been fully achieved. In this paper, the mean square convergence of the LMS algorithm is investigated for the large class of linearly filtered random driving processes. In particular, the paper contains the following contributions: (i) The parameter error vector covariance matrix can be decomposed into two parts, a first part that exists in the modal space of the driving process of the LMS filter and a second part, existing in its orthogonal complement space, which does not contribute to the performance measures (misadjustment, mismatch) of the algorithm. (ii) The impact of additive noise is shown to contribute only to the modal space of the driving process independently from the noise statistic and thus defines the steady state of the filter. (iii) While the previous results have been derived with some approximation, an exact solution for very long filters is presented based on a matrix equivalence property, resulting in a new conservative stability bound that is more relaxed than previous ones. (iv) In particular, it will be shown that the joint fourth-order moment of the decorrelated driving process is a more relevant parameter for the step-size bound rather than, as is often believed, the second-order moment. (v) We furthermore introduce a new correction factor accounting for the influence of the filter length as well as the driving process statistic, making our approach quite suitable even for short filters. (vi) All statements are validated by Monte Carlo simulations, demonstrating the strength of this novel approach to independently assess the influence of filter length, as well as correlation and probability density function of the driving process.

INTRODUCTION

The well-known least mean square (LMS) algorithm [1] is the most successful of all adaptive algorithms. In its normalized version (NLMS), it can be found by the million in electrical echo compensators [2], in telephone switches, and also in the form of adaptive equalizers [3]. No other adaptive algorithm has been so successfully placed in commercial products.[1] With a fixed step-size, starting at initial value $\mathbf{w}_0$, the LMS algorithm is given by

$$e_k = d_k - \mathbf{u}_k{}^T\mathbf{w}_k = v_k + \mathbf{u}_k{}^T(\mathbf{w} - \mathbf{w}_k) \qquad (1)$$

$$\mathbf{w}_{k+1} = \mathbf{w}_k + \mu\mathbf{u}_k e_k \;;k = 0,1,2,.. \qquad (2)$$

Citation: Markus Rupp, Asymptotic equivalent analysis of the LMS algorithm under linearly filtered processes, EURASIP Journal on Advances in Signal Processing, December (2016), 2016:18, DOI: 10.1186/s13634-015-0291-1

Here, a reference model $d_k=\mathbf{w}^T\mathbf{u}_k+v_k$ has been introduced, as is common for a system identification problem, assuming that an optimal solution $\mathbf{w}\in IR^{M\times 1}$ exists. It is further assumed that the observed system output is additively disturbed by real-valued, zero-mean, noise $v_k \in IR$ of variance σ_v^2. The regression vector is $\mathbf{u}_k\in IR^{M\times 1}$, with M denoting the order of the filter. The algorithm starts with an initial value of $\mathbf{w}_0$, trying to improve its estimate $\mathbf{w}_k\in IR^{M\times 1}$ with every time instant k. All signals are formulated as real-valued (i.e., $\in IR$), which makes the derivations easier to follow. Although, in most cases, it is straightforward to extend the results to complex-valued processes if difficulties arise, results for the complex-valued case will be pointed out.

While deterministic approaches have proven l_2 stability for any kind of driving signal $\mathbf{u}_k$[4–7], results from stochastic approaches are restricted to specific classes of random processes (unfiltered independent identically distributed (IID) [8], Gaussian [9, 10], and spherically invariant random processes (SIRP) [11]). A recent historical overview is provided in [12]. Nevertheless, such stochastic analysis is useful since it provides information about how the speed of convergence and the steady-state error depend on the step-size μ. The resulting stability bounds [8–11, 13] are typically conservative:

$$\mu_{\text{classic}} \leq \frac{2}{3\text{tr}[\mathbf{R}_{\text{uu}}]} \tag{3}$$

and are based on fourth-order moments of Gaussian variables, which in turn can be expressed as second-order moments of the autocorrelation matrix $\mathbf{R}_{uu}=E[\mathbf{u}_k\mathbf{u}_k^T]$. Furthermore, the derivation of this bound for stability in the mean square sense is based on the so-called independence assumption (IA), an assumption that also will be applied throughout this article.

In Section 2, it is demonstrated that an initial parameter error vector covariance matrix is forced by the LMS algorithm to remain a member of the modal space of $\mathbf{R}_{uu}$. However, this rule is not true in a strict sense for arbitrary driving processes and requires some mild approximations to make it a more general statement.

In Section 3, our considerations are complemented by analyzing the steady-state behavior of the algorithm and finally we link all these elements to a strong statement about a large class of linearly filtered random processes of the moving average type. This class naturally includes linearly filtered IID processes but it is even possible to include some particular statistically dependent terms, meaning that SIRPs are also covered. A crucial parameter to describe dynamical as well as stability behavior turns out to be the joint fourth-order moment $m_x^{(2,2)} = E\left[x_k^2 x_l^2\right]$; for $l \neq k$ of the corresponding decorrelated (white)[2] driving process. In the case of very long filters, it turns out that even the mild approximations of the driving process are no longer required and thus less conservative step-size bounds are obtained. This is reported in Section 4. Finally, a validation of the theoretical statements is provided in Section 5by Monte Carlo simulations. Some conclusions in Section 6 round up the paper.

Notation: To further facilitate the reading of the article, a list of commonly used variables and terms is provided in Table 1. The notation $A[x_k]$ is used to describe a linear operator on a scalar input and $A[\mathbf{x}_k]$ on a vector input. As the linear operator $A[\cdot]$ in our contribution is limited to a linear time-invariant filter, it can equivalently be described by a convolution $A[x_k] = \sum_{m=0}^{P} a_m x_{k-m}$ with the coefficients a_m describing the impulse response of the filter. Consequently, $A[\mathbf{x}_k] = \sum_{m=0}^{P} a_m \mathbf{x}_{k-m}$. Equivalently, such a convolution can be described by a linear transformation applying an upper right Toeplitz matrix $\mathbf{A}\in IR^{M\times(M+P)}$ to an input vector $\mathbf{x}_k \in IR^{(M+P)\times 1}$. In this case, the output vector $\mathbf{u}_k=\mathbf{A}\mathbf{x}_k$ is of dimension $IR^{M\times 1}$. If the vector $\mathbf{x}_k=[x_k,x_{k-1},\ldots x_{k-M-P+1}]^T$ exhibits a shift property, so does the corresponding output $\mathbf{u}_k=[u_k,u_{k-1},\ldots su_{k-M+1}]^T$. The variable x_k will be denoted for describing a white process throughout the paper while u_k will denote the corresponding filtered process throughout this paper. Furthermore, two other linear operators on square matrices will be used: (1) $\Lambda=\text{diag}[\mathbf{L}]$ on a matrix $\mathbf{L}$ results in a diagonal matrix Λ whose diagonal entries are identical to the diagonal of **L**and all other entries are zero; (2) $\text{tr}[\mathbf{L}]$ on a matrix $\mathbf{L}$ results in the trace of the matrix, i.e., $\text{tr}[\mathbf{L}] = \sum_{m=1}^{M} \mathbf{L}_{mm}$. The symbol ⊗ denotes a tensor or Kronecker product.

Table 1. List of commonly used terms for filters of length M

Variable	Dimension	Meaning
d_k	IR	Desired output of unknown system
$\mathbf{w}$	$IR^{M\times 1}$	Impulse response of unknown system
$\mathbf{w}_k$	$IR^{M\times 1}$	Estimate of **w**
$\mathbf{u}_k$	$IR^{M\times 1}$	Regression vector
u_k	$IR^{1\times 1}$	Elements of the regression vector
v_k	IR	Additive noise
$\mathbf{R}_{uu}$	$IR^{M\times M}$	Autocorrelation matrix of $\mathbf{u}_k$
Λ_u	$IR^{M\times M}$	Diagonal matrix=$\mathbf{Q}\mathbf{R}_{uu}\mathbf{Q}^T$

$\mathbf{K}_k$	$\mathrm{IR}^{M\times M}$	Covariance matrix of $\mathbf{w}-\mathbf{w}_k$
x_k	IR	White generating process
$m_x^{(2)}$	IR	Second-order moment of x_k
$m_x^{(2,2)}$	IR	Joint fourth-order moment of x_k
μ	IR	Step-size
$\mathbf{A}$	$\mathrm{IR}^{M\times(M+P)}$	upper right Toeplitz matrix
$\mathbf{I}$	$\mathrm{IR}^{M\times M}$	Identity matrix of dimension M
$\mathbf{I}_P$	$\mathrm{IR}^{P\times P}$	Identity matrix of dimension P
$\mathbf{1}$	$\mathrm{IR}^{M\times 1}$	Vector with ones as entries

MODAL SPACE OF THE LMS ALGORITHM

Let us consider the classical LMS analysis [8, 10], utilizing the IA as stated in the introduction:

Independence assumption (IA): The regression vector $\mathbf{u}_k$ is statistically independent of the past regression vectors, i.e., $\{\mathbf{u}_{k-1},\mathbf{u}_{k-2},\ldots,\mathbf{u}_0\}$.

This assumption was introduced by Ungerboeck [8] and thoroughly investigated by Mazo [14] in the context of adaptive equalizers. A consequence of such an assumption is that parameter estimate $\mathbf{w}_k$ (as well as parameter error vector $\tilde{\mathbf{w}}_k = \mathbf{w} - \mathbf{w}_k$) is independent of $\mathbf{u}_k$ and thus $E[\mathbf{u}_k\mathbf{u}_k^T(\mathbf{w}-\mathbf{w}_k)(\mathbf{w}-\mathbf{w}_k)^T\mathbf{u}_k\mathbf{u}_k^T]=E[\mathbf{u}_k\mathbf{u}_k^T E[(\mathbf{w}-\mathbf{w}_k)(\mathbf{w}-\mathbf{w}_k)^T]\mathbf{u}_k\mathbf{u}_k^T] = E[\mathbf{u}_k\mathbf{u}_k^T\mathbf{K}_k\mathbf{u}_k\mathbf{u}_k^T]$ where the parameter error vector covariance matrix

$$\mathbf{K}_k = E\left[(\mathbf{w}-\mathbf{w}_k)(\mathbf{w}-\mathbf{w}_k)^T\right] \tag{4}$$

was applied.[3] In the literature, $\tilde{\mathbf{w}}_k$ is also often referred to as weight error vector, $\mathbf{w}_k$ as weight estimate, and $\mathbf{K}_k$ as weight error vector covariance matrix. The IA holds exactly for the linear combiner case in which the succeeding regression vectors are statistically independent of each other (see, for example, in multiple sidelobe canceller (MSLC) applications [15]) while in practice, the LMS algorithm is mostly run on transversal filters in which the regression vectors exhibit a shift dependency. Note that we will consider the shift structure of the regression vector that is $\mathbf{u}_k=[u_k,u_{k-1},\ldots,u_{k-M+1}]^T$ only for its generation process, as it will be generated by linearly filtering random processes over time. The IA in the derivations for analyzing the algorithm will however be required which is not a contradiction to the generation process. The major advantage of the IA is that the evolution of the parameter error covariance matrix $\mathbf{K}_k$ can be computed and thus the learning curves of the algorithm, i.e., its learning behavior, can be derived. This knowledge also provides the steady-state values and, furthermore, the derivation of practical step-size bounds.

Note that some analyses in the past have attempted to overcome the independence assumption; good overviews on techniques can be found in [16, 17]. In [17, 18], the authors have assumed small step-sizes (much smaller than the largest possible step-size) so that the updates are mostly static compared to the rapid changes in the signals. This approach, however, basically leads to first-order results as the LMS algorithm then behaves similarly to the steepest decent algorithm. In [19, 20], Douglas et al. solved the problem by introducing a linearly filtered moving average (MA) process and formulating all terms in the evolution of the covariance matrix $\mathbf{K}_k$ explicitly. While the outcomes obtained are precise, the method relies on symbolic computation (MAPLE) and results, even for small problems (filter order M<10), in a very large set of linear equations. The method only provides numerical terms that neither give much insight into the functionality of the algorithm nor provide general analytical statements. Also, the approach in [21, 22] follows along such lines, however with imposing the IA, where a large set of linear equations (of the order $M^2\times M^2$) is required to be computed due to terms of the form $\mathbf{u}_k\mathbf{u}_k^T \otimes \mathbf{u}_k\mathbf{u}_k^T$ and then analyzed. Similar to the previous idea, this method also does not provide analytical insight and becomes tedious if not infeasible for correlated signals as well as large matrices. Finally, Butterweck [18, 23–25] has introduced a novel idea based on wave propagation. He showed that for very long filters ($M\rightarrow\infty$), the derivation does not require the classic IA. However, several other signal conditions are required (e.g., Gaussian driving process, small step-size, infinite filter order M). Our results in Section 4 will be compared to his results when stability conditions for very long filters are derived. Finally, it should be mentioned that neither do the deterministic approaches [4, 5, 7] require the IA in order to derive step-size bounds, but as in the case of other contributions, they are unable to provide learning curves or steady-state values without imposing the IA. Experimental results have shown that utilizing the IA in FIR filter structures may lead to poor learning behavior estimates under strongly correlated processes but surprisingly accurate values for steady-state values of the parameter covariance matrix. The IA therefore is still frequently used in current analyses of gradient-type algorithms, see, for example, recent publications [3, 26, 27]. Note that our analysis is also based on an infinite filter length approach but different to others, we quantify the error term related to the filter length which allows us to provide rather accurate results even for short filters (e.g., M=10).

In this paper, the classic stochastic approaches from Horowitz and Senne [9] and Feuer and Weinstein [10] are pursued and extended in numerous directions, relying on a general MA driving process similar to that proposed in [19, 20]. Symmetric matrices as they appear in the form of the parameter error vector covariance matrix $\mathbf{K}_k$ can be decomposed into two complementary subspaces (see [28] and Appendix 1 for details), namely

$$\mathbf{K}_k = b_0\mathbf{I}+b_1\mathbf{R}_{\mathrm{uu}}+\ldots+b_{M-1}\mathbf{R}_{\mathrm{uu}}^{M-1}+\mathbf{K}_k^{\perp} = P(\mathbf{R}_{\mathrm{uu}})+\mathbf{K}_k^{\perp}. \tag{5}$$

Here, $P(\mathbf{R}_{\mathrm{uu}})$ denotes a polynomial in $\mathbf{R}_{\mathrm{uu}}$ and $\mathbf{K}_k^{\perp}$ is an element of its orthogonal complement, i.e., everything in $\mathbf{K}_k$ that cannot be approximated by $P(\mathbf{R}_{\mathrm{uu}})$. Note that the impact of the complement space is only evident in the trace but not in the matrix itself: $\mathbf{K}_k^{\perp}\mathbf{R}_{\mathrm{uu}}^{l} \neq \mathbf{0}$ while $\mathrm{tr}[\mathbf{K}_k^{\perp}\mathbf{R}_{\mathrm{uu}}^{l}] = 0$. It turns out that only members in subspace $P(\mathbf{R}_{\mathrm{uu}})$ contribute to the error performance measures (see Eq. (42) for mismatch: $\mathrm{tr}\left[\mathbf{K}_k\mathbf{R}_{\mathrm{uu}}^{0}\right]$; see (43) for misadjustment: $\mathrm{tr}[\mathbf{K}_k\mathbf{R}_{\mathrm{uu}}]$) of the algorithm as only terms of $\mathrm{tr}\left[\mathbf{K}_k\mathbf{R}_{\mathrm{uu}}^{l}\right]$ are of interest while the complementary part $\mathrm{tr}[\mathbf{K}_k^{\perp}\mathbf{R}_{\mathrm{uu}}^{l}] = 0$ and thus does not contribute to the performance measures.

In a first step, the following equation

$$\begin{aligned}\mathbf{K}_1 &= E\left[\left(\mathbf{I}-\mu\mathbf{u}_0\mathbf{u}_0^T\right)\mathbf{K}_0\left(\mathbf{I}-\mu\mathbf{u}_0\mathbf{u}_0^T\right)^T\right]\\ &= \mathbf{K}_0-\mu\mathbf{R}_{\mathrm{uu}}\mathbf{K}_0-\mu\mathbf{K}_0\mathbf{R}_{\mathrm{uu}}+\mu^2E\left[\mathbf{u}_0\mathbf{u}_0^T\mathbf{K}_0\mathbf{u}_0\mathbf{u}_0^T\right]+\mu^2\mathbf{R}_{\mathrm{uu}}\sigma_v^2\end{aligned} \tag{6}$$

is obtained. Let us start with an example to illustrate its behavior.

Example: A general $\mathbf{K}_0$ will be a linear combination as shown in (5). Take, for example, a fixed system $\mathbf{w}$ to be identified. In this case, $\mathbf{K}_0=\mathbf{w}\mathbf{w}^T$. This value can be decomposed into $P(\mathbf{R}_{\mathrm{uu}})$ in the modal space of $\mathbf{R}_{\mathrm{uu}}$ and a component $\mathbf{K}^{\perp}$ from its orthogonal complement. This also allows the description of the evolution of the individual components; starting with $\mathbf{K}_k = \mathbf{K}_k^{\parallel}+\mathbf{K}_k^{\perp}$, with $\mathbf{K}_k^{\parallel} \in \mathcal{R}_{\mathrm{u}}$ and $\mathbf{K}_k^{\perp} \in \mathcal{R}_{\mathrm{u}}^{\perp}$, a set of equations is obtained

$$\begin{aligned}\mathbf{K}_{k+1}^{\parallel} &= \mathbf{K}_k^{\parallel}-\mu\mathbf{R}_{\mathrm{uu}}\mathbf{K}_k^{\parallel}-\mu\mathbf{K}_k^{\parallel}\mathbf{R}_{\mathrm{uu}}\\ &\quad+\mu^2\left(2\mathbf{R}_{\mathrm{uu}}\mathbf{K}_k^{\parallel}\mathbf{R}_{\mathrm{uu}}+\mathbf{R}_{\mathrm{uu}}\mathrm{tr}\left[\mathbf{K}_k^{\parallel}\mathbf{R}_{\mathrm{uu}}\right]\right)+\mu^2\mathbf{R}_{\mathrm{uu}}\sigma_v^2.\end{aligned} \tag{7}$$

$$\mathbf{K}_{k+1}^{\perp} = \mathbf{K}_k^{\perp}-\mu\mathbf{R}_{\mathrm{uu}}\mathbf{K}_k^{\perp}-\mu\mathbf{K}_k^{\perp}\mathbf{R}_{\mathrm{uu}}+2\mu^2\mathbf{R}_{\mathrm{uu}}\mathbf{K}_k^{\perp}\mathbf{R}_{\mathrm{uu}}. \tag{8}$$

Parameter error covariance matrix $\mathbf{K}_k = \mathbf{K}_k^{\parallel}+\mathbf{K}_k^{\perp}$ thus evolves into a new matrix $\mathbf{K}_{k+1} = \mathbf{K}_{k+1}^{\parallel}+\mathbf{K}_{k+1}^{\perp}$ in which its part $\mathbf{K}_k^{\parallel}$ from R_{u} stays in the modal space and appears as new part $\mathbf{K}_{k+1}^{\parallel}$, contributing to learning performance terms. Similarly, the perpendicular term $\mathbf{K}_k^{\perp}$ stays in the complement space as $\mathbf{K}_{k+1}^{\perp}$ and will thus not contribute to the algorithm's performance curves under the trace operation. The noise contributes only to the modal space. This makes it possible to formulate an initial first statement for Gaussian driving processes.

Lemma 2.1.

Assume the driving process to be a correlated Gaussian process with autocorrelation matrix $\mathbf{R}_{\mathrm{uu}}$. Under the IA, the initial parameter error vector covariance matrix $\mathbf{K}_0$ of the LMS algorithm evolves (1) into a polynomial in $\mathbf{R}_{\mathrm{uu}}$ of the modal space of $\mathbf{R}_{\mathrm{uu}}$, solely responsible for the mismatch and the misadjustment of the algorithm, and (2) a part in its orthogonal complement which has no impact on the performance measures.

Note that the correlated Gaussian case has been solved for a while [9, 10], typically resulting in a matrix evolution as presented in (7), see, e.g., [13, 29]. However, the term ((8) has never been studied at all. Including uncorrelated IID or SIRP processes required modifications of the method [11, 30]. With the proposed method, we will be able to include arbitrary correlated processes within the same framework.

As such example presented above is somewhat intuitive for the particular case of a Gaussian driving process, what can be said about larger classes of driving processes is of interest. To achieve this goal, a number of considerations with respect to the driving process are required.

Driving process: The properties of Lemma 2.1 are not only maintained by Gaussian random processes but also by a much larger class of driving processes. It will be shown that these properties hold for random processes that are constructed by a linearly filtered white zero-mean random process $u_k = A[x_k] = \sum_{m=0}^{P} a_m x_{k-m}$, whose only conditions are that:

Driving process assumptions (A1a):

$$m_x^{(2)} = E\left[x_k^2\right] = 1 \tag{9}$$

$$m_x^{(2,2)} = E\left[x_k^2 x_l^2\right] \le c_2 < \infty; k \neq l \tag{10}$$

$$m_x^{(4)} = E\left[x_k^4\right] \le c_3 < \infty \tag{11}$$

$$m_x^{(1,1,1,1)} = E\left[x_k x_l x_m x_n\right] = 0; k \neq l \neq m \neq n \tag{12}$$

$$m_x^{(2,1,1)} = E\left[x_k^2 x_m x_n\right] = 0; k \neq m \neq n \tag{13}$$

$$m_x^{(1,3)} = E\left[x_k x_l^3\right] = 0; k \neq l \tag{14}$$

$$m_x = E[x_k] = 0. \tag{15}$$

Note that the conditions are shown for real-valued processes; for complex-valued processes, they need to be adjusted. The last four conditions (12)–(15) are listed here for completeness. They exclude processes that do not have a zero mean in some sense and have been assumed, although not often explicitly mentioned, in most of the literature. Linearly filtering such processes will preserve the zero-mean properties (12)–(15). These processes certainly include not only real-valued Gaussian and SIRP $\left(3m_x^{(2,2)} = m_x^{(4)} = 3\right)$ and complex-valued Gaussian and SIRP $\left(2m_x^{(2,2)} = m_x^{(4)} = 2\right)$, processes, but also IID processes $\left(m_x^{(2,2)} = \left(m_x^{(2)}\right)^2\right)$. Once vectors $\mathbf{x}_k = [x_k, x_{k-1}, \ldots, x_{k-N+1}]^T$ have been constructed, the following second- and fourth-order expressions are found:

$$E\left[\mathbf{x}_k \mathbf{x}_k^T\right] = \mathbf{I}_N, \tag{16}$$

$$E\left[\mathbf{x}_k \mathbf{x}_k^T \mathbf{x}_k \mathbf{x}_k^T\right] = \left(m_x^{(4)} + (N-1) m_x^{(2,2)}\right) \mathbf{I}_N. \tag{17}$$

Correspondingly, the linearly filtered vectors read

$$\mathbf{u}_k = \mathbf{A}\mathbf{x}_k = \begin{bmatrix} a_0 & a_1 & \ldots & a_P & & & \\ & a_0 & a_1 & \ldots & a_P & & \\ & & \ddots & & \ddots & & \\ & & & a_0 & a_1 & \ldots & a_P \end{bmatrix} \mathbf{x}_k \tag{18}$$

with an upper right Toeplitz matrix $\mathbf{A}$ of dimension $M \times N = M \times (M+P)$. The impulse response of the coloring filter is given by $a_0, a_1, \ldots a_P$ and appears on every row of $\mathbf{A}$ starting with a_0 on its main diagonal. In general, the driving process vector $\mathbf{x}_k$ is longer than $\mathbf{u}_k$, depending on the order P of the impulse response.

However, in order to guarantee independence of vectors $\mathbf{u}_k, \mathbf{u}_{k-1}, \ldots$ we have to impose a second condition on the driving process:

Driving process assumptions (A1b): Assume the driving process u_k being generated by a linearly filtered process x_k as described above. We furthermore have to assume that at each time instant k, a new statistically independent process $\left\{x_l^{(k)}\right\}$ is being generated whose values are processed from $l=k-N+1\ldots k$ to generate $\mathbf{u}_k$. For two different time instants k_1 and k_2, we assume that their joint pdfs are statistically independent, i.e.,

$$f_{\left\{\mathbf{x}_l^{(k_1)}\right\}, \left\{\mathbf{x}_l^{(k_2)}\right\}} = f_{\left\{\mathbf{x}_l^{(k_1)}\right\}} f_{\left\{\mathbf{x}_l^{(k_2)}\right\}} \tag{19}$$

Note that Assumption A1b is sufficient to avoid the IA but not required. On the other hand, dropping A1b requires the IA to ensure the results of the paper hold. To facilitate reading, we will drop the notation $\mathbf{x}_l^{(k)} \to \mathbf{x}_l$. With such assumptions, we are now ready for our first general statement.

Lemma 2.2.

Assume driving process $u_k = A[x_k]$ to originate from a linearly filtered white random process x_k so that $\mathbf{u}_k = \mathbf{A}\mathbf{x}_k$ with $\mathbf{x}_k = [x_k, x_{k-1}, \ldots, x_{k-N+1}]^T$, where $\mathbf{A}$ denotes an upper right Toeplitz matrix with the correlation filter impulse response and x_k satisfies conditions (9)–(17). The initial parameter error vector covariance matrix $\mathbf{K}_0 = \mathbf{K}_0^{\|} + \mathbf{K}_0^{\perp}$ of the LMS algorithm essentially (with error of order $O(\mu^2)$) evolves into a polynomial in $\mathbf{A}\mathbf{A}^T$ in the modal space of $\mathbf{R}_{uu}$ while terms in its orthogonal complement $\mathbf{K}^{\perp}$ either remain there or die out.

Note that this formulation may imply that this is only true for linearly filtered processes of the moving average (MA) type. As no condition on the order P of such a process is imposed, P (and thus N=M+P) can become arbitrarily large (e.g., P→∞) and thus autoregressive processes (AR) or combinations (ARMA) can also be resembled as well (e.g., see [13] (chapter 2.7)).

Proof.

The proof proceeds in two steps: first, rewriting (6) for $\mathbf{K}_0=\mathbf{I}$ in order to discover the most important terms and mathematical steps based on a simpler formulation and then refining the arguments for arbitrary values of $\mathbf{K}_k$ to $\mathbf{K}_{k+1}$.

For $\mathbf{K}_0=\mathbf{I}$ and recalling that $\mathbf{R}_{uu}=E[\mathbf{u}_k\mathbf{u}_k^T]=\mathbf{A}E[\mathbf{x}_k\mathbf{x}_k^T]\mathbf{A}^T=\mathbf{A}\mathbf{A}^T$, the following is obtained:

$$\mathbf{K}_1 = \mathbf{I} - 2\mu\mathbf{A}\mathbf{A}^T + \mu^2\mathbf{A}E\left[\mathbf{x}_k{\mathbf{x}_k}^T\mathbf{A}^T\mathbf{A}\mathbf{x}_k{\mathbf{x}_k}^T\right]\mathbf{A}^T + \mu^2\sigma_v^2\mathbf{A}\mathbf{A}^T. \quad (20)$$

On the main diagonal of the M×M matrix $\mathbf{A}\mathbf{A}^T$, identical elements are found: $\sum_{i=0}^{P}|a_i|^2$, thus, $\mathrm{tr}[\mathbf{A}\mathbf{A}^T] = M\sum_{i=0}^{P}|a_i|^2$, with P denoting the filter order of the MA process.

Due to properties (9)–(17) of driving process $x_k \in \mathrm{IR}$

$$E\left[\mathbf{x}_k{\mathbf{x}_k}^T\mathbf{L}\mathbf{x}_k{\mathbf{x}_k}^T\right]_{ij} = \begin{cases} m_x^{(2,2)}(\mathbf{L}_{ij}+\mathbf{L}_{ji}) & ;i\neq j \\ m_x^{(4)}\mathbf{L}_{ii} + m_x^{(2,2)}\sum_{k\neq i}\mathbf{L}_{kk} & ;i=j \end{cases}$$

$$E\left[\mathbf{x}_k{\mathbf{x}_k}^T\mathbf{L}\mathbf{x}_k{\mathbf{x}_k}^T\right] = m_x^{(2,2)}(\mathbf{L}+\mathbf{L}^T) + m_x^{(2,2)}\mathrm{tr}[\mathbf{L}]\,\mathbf{I}_{M+P} + \left(m_x^{(4)} - 3m_x^{(2,2)}\right)\mathrm{diag}[\mathbf{L}] \quad (21)$$

is found, where diag[**L**] denotes a diagonal matrix with the diagonal terms of a matrix **L** as entries. When $x_k \in \mathrm{IC}$, a slightly different result is obtained:

$$E\left[\mathbf{x}_k{\mathbf{x}_k}^H\mathbf{L}\mathbf{x}_k{\mathbf{x}_k}^H\right] = m_x^{(2,2)}\mathbf{L} + m_x^{(2,2)}\mathrm{tr}[\mathbf{L}]\,\mathbf{I}_{M+P} + \left(m_x^{(4)} - 2m_x^{(2,2)}\right)\mathrm{diag}[\mathbf{L}]. \quad (22)$$

For spherically invariant random processes (including Gaussian), the term (m(4)x−3m(2,2)x)(mx(4)−3mx(2,2)) $\left(m_x^{(4)} - 3m_x^{(2,2)}\right)$ for real-valued signals, or for complex-valued signals, vanishes and thus the problem can be solved classically.

In our particular case, $\mathbf{L}=\mathbf{A}^T\mathbf{A}\in\mathbf{R}^{(M+P)\times(M+P)}$ with $\mathrm{tr}[\mathbf{A}^T\mathbf{A}]= M\sum_{i=0}^{P}|a_i|^2$ and $\mathrm{diag}[\mathbf{A}\mathbf{A}^T]= \sum_{i=0}^{P}|a_i|^2\mathbf{I}_{M+P} = \frac{1}{M}\mathrm{tr}[\mathbf{A}^T\mathbf{A}]\,\mathbf{I}_{M+P}$.

There still remains one problematic term, however: diag[$\mathbf{A}^T\mathbf{A}$]. At this point, the following is proposed:

Asymptotic equivalence:

$$\lim_{M\to\infty}\frac{1}{M}\left\|\mathrm{diag}\left[\mathbf{A}^T\mathbf{A}\right]-\frac{\mathrm{tr}\left[\mathbf{A}^T\mathbf{A}\right]}{M}\mathbf{I}_{M+P}\right\|_F=0$$

with an identity matrix $\mathbf{I}_{M+P}$ of the corresponding dimension. Note that the equivalence would hold exact even for small dimensions if it had the term diag[$\mathbf{A}\mathbf{A}^T$] instead of diag[$\mathbf{A}^T\mathbf{A}$]. The asymptotic equivalence can be interpreted as replacing each of the diagonal elements of $\mathbf{A}^T\mathbf{A}$ by their average value $\frac{1}{M}\mathrm{tr}\left[\mathbf{A}^T\mathbf{A}\right]$. Consider the relative difference matrix

$$\Delta_\epsilon = \left(\frac{\mathrm{tr}[\mathbf{A}^T\mathbf{A}]}{M}\right)^{-1}\left[\mathrm{diag}[\mathbf{A}^T\mathbf{A}] - \frac{\mathrm{tr}[\mathbf{A}^T\mathbf{A}]}{M}\mathbf{I}_{M+P}\right] = \frac{M}{\mathrm{tr}[\mathbf{A}^T\mathbf{A}]}\mathrm{diag}[\mathbf{A}^T\mathbf{A}] - \mathbf{I}_{M+P} \quad (23)$$

of dimension (M+P)×(M+P). Its P diagonal terms at the beginning and end of the diagonal remain unequal to zero while those terms in the middle (whose range can be substantially large if M>P) are zero. The first P elements on the diagonal are, for example, given by $\Delta\varepsilon,ii = -\sum_{m=i}^{P}|am|^2 / \sum_{m=0}^{P}|am|^2$; I = 1..P. If M≫P, the next elements are all zero and finally, the last P elements are the first in backward notation. In case P>M/2, the zero elements do not occur. We can conclude from the construction of the diagonal elements $\mathbf{\Delta}_{\varepsilon,ii}$ that they are all in the interval (−1,0], or alternatively $\|\mathbf{\Delta}_\varepsilon\|_\infty \leq 1$, where we have applied a max norm. Note that for white processes $a_0=1$ and $a_i=0;i=1,2,\ldots$, thus $\|\mathbf{\Delta}_\varepsilon\|_\infty=0$.

It is worth comparing the long filter derivations by Butterweck [24] that exclude border effects at the beginning and ending of the matrices. Our approximation can therefore be interpreted as being along the same lines of approximations, only originating from a different approach. We however are able to quantify the error term which will further be helpful. Note that in Section 4, this approximation will be dropped entirely for large values of M for different reasons. With this error term $\mathbf{\Delta}_\varepsilon$ for real-valued driving processes,

$$E\left[\mathbf{x}_k\mathbf{x}_k^T\mathbf{A}^T\mathbf{A}\mathbf{x}_k\mathbf{x}_k^T\right] = 2m_{\mathrm{x}}^{(2,2)}\mathbf{A}^T\mathbf{A} + \left(m_{\mathrm{x}}^{(2,2)} + \left(m_{\mathrm{x}}^{(4)} - 3m_{\mathrm{x}}^{(2,2)}\right)/M\right)\mathrm{tr}[\mathbf{A}^T\mathbf{A}]\,\mathbf{I}_{M+P} + \left(m_{\mathrm{x}}^{(4)} - 3m_{\mathrm{x}}^{(2,2)}\right)\mathrm{tr}[\mathbf{A}^T\mathbf{A}]\,\Delta_\epsilon$$
$$= 2m_{\mathrm{x}}^{(2,2)}\mathbf{A}^T\mathbf{A} + \gamma_{\mathrm{x}}m_{\mathrm{x}}^{(2,2)}\mathrm{tr}[\mathbf{A}^T\mathbf{A}]\,\mathbf{I}_{M+P} + (\gamma_{\mathrm{x}} - 1)m_{\mathrm{x}}^{(2,2)}\mathrm{tr}[\mathbf{A}^T\mathbf{A}]\,\Delta_\epsilon, \qquad (24)$$

is obtained with a newly introduced pdf shape correction value

$$\gamma_{\mathrm{x}} = 1 + \left(\frac{m_{\mathrm{x}}^{(4)}}{m_{\mathrm{x}}^{(2,2)}} - 3\right)\frac{1}{M}, \qquad (25)$$

a value that depends on the statistic of random process x_k. The term $\frac{m_{\mathrm{x}}^{(4)}}{m_{\mathrm{x}}^{(2,2)}} - 3$ is similar to the excess kurtosis $\frac{E[|x-m_{\mathrm{x}}|^4]}{E[|x-m_{\mathrm{x}}|^2]^2} - 3 = \frac{m_{\mathrm{x}}^{(4)}}{\left(m_{\mathrm{x}}^{(2)}\right)^2} - 3$. Processes with negative excess kurtosis are often referred to as sub-Gaussian processes while a positive excess kurtosis leads to so-called super-Gaussian processes. This (slightly abused) terminology will be used correspondingly to discriminate the term $\frac{m_{\mathrm{x}}^{(4)}}{m_{\mathrm{x}}^{(2,2)}} - 3$. Thus, sub-Gaussian processes in this sense take on γ_{x} values smaller than one while super-Gaussian processes have values larger than one. However, it is also noted that our approximation error $\mathbf{\Delta}_\varepsilon$ only has an impact when $\gamma_{\mathrm{x}} \neq 1$, which vanishes not only for Gaussian pdfs but also with decreasing step-size μ (which comes along naturally with growing filter order M). If comparing the approximation term $(\gamma_{\mathrm{x}} - 1)m_{\mathrm{x}}^{(2,2)}\mathrm{tr}[\mathbf{A}^T\mathbf{A}]\,\Delta_\epsilon$ with $\gamma_{\mathrm{x}}m_{\mathrm{x}}^{(2,2)}\mathrm{tr}[\mathbf{A}^T\mathbf{A}]\,\mathbf{I}_{M+P}$, we recognize that the approximation is of order 1/M smaller, thus diminishes with higher filter order.

Note further that the term in the LMS algorithm where the asymptotic equivalence applies is proportional to μ^2. It thus has no impact for small step-sizes but certainly is expected to have one on the stability bound. A first conclusion, therefore, is that the error on the parameter error vector covariance matrix due to this approximation is of order $O(\mu^2)$. Note that the step-size being small is not to be interpreted as small relative to the step-size at the stability bound but small in absolute terms, i.e., $\mu \ll 1$, which is certainly given for long filters as $\mu \sim 1/M$. The consequence that the applied approximation is negligible for small step-sizes (large filter order M) as well as for Gaussian-type processes is reflected in Lemma 2.2 by the wording "essentially." This means that in extreme cases (large μ (small M) and far from Gaussian), a very small proportion can indeed leak into the complementary space. At the first update with $\mathbf{K}_0=\mathbf{I}$,

$$\mathbf{K}_1 = \mathbf{I} - 2\mu\mathbf{A}\mathbf{A}^T + 2\mu^2 m_{\mathrm{x}}^{(2,2)}(\mathbf{A}\mathbf{A}^T)^2 + \mu^2 m_{\mathrm{x}}^{(2,2)}\gamma_{\mathrm{x}}\mathrm{tr}[\mathbf{A}^T\mathbf{A}]\,\mathbf{A}\mathbf{A}^T + \mu^2\mathbf{A}\mathbf{A}^T\sigma_v^2 + \mathcal{O}(\mu^2) \qquad (26)$$

is obtained, a polynomial in $\mathbf{A}\mathbf{A}^T$.

Now, the proof starts for general updates from $\mathbf{K}_k$ to $\mathbf{K}_{k+1}$. While the first terms that are linear in μ are straightforward, the quadratic part in μ needs further attention.

$$E\left[\mathbf{u}_k\mathbf{u}_k^T\mathbf{K}_k\mathbf{u}_k\mathbf{u}_k^T\right] = \mathbf{A}E\left[\mathbf{x}_k\mathbf{x}_k^T\mathbf{A}^T\mathbf{K}_k\mathbf{A}\mathbf{x}_k\mathbf{x}_k^T\right]\mathbf{A}^T$$
$$= m_{\mathrm{x}}^{(2,2)}\mathbf{A}\left(2\mathbf{A}^T\mathbf{K}_k\mathbf{A} + \mathrm{tr}\left[\mathbf{A}\mathbf{A}^T\mathbf{K}_k\right]\right)\mathbf{A}^T + \left(m_{\mathrm{x}}^{(4)} - 3m_{\mathrm{x}}^{(2,2)}\right)\mathbf{A}\mathrm{diag}\left[\mathbf{A}^T\mathbf{K}_k\mathbf{A}\right]\mathbf{A}^T. \qquad (27)$$

Here, the same asymptotic equivalence concept as used above is imposed, i.e., diag[$\mathbf{A}^T\mathbf{K}_k\mathbf{A}$]≈tr[$\mathbf{A}\mathbf{A}^T\mathbf{K}_k$]$\mathbf{I}_{M+P}$/M resulting in

$$E\left[\mathbf{u}_k\mathbf{u}_k{}^T\mathbf{K}_k\mathbf{u}_k\mathbf{u}_k{}^T\right] = 2m_\mathrm{x}^{(2,2)}\mathbf{A}\mathbf{A}^T\mathbf{K}_k\mathbf{A}\mathbf{A}^T + \gamma_\mathrm{x} m_\mathrm{x}^{(2,2)}\mathbf{A}\mathbf{A}^T\mathrm{tr}\left[\mathbf{A}\mathbf{A}^T\mathbf{K}_k\right] + \mathcal{O}(\mu^2) \tag{28}$$

and eventually obtaining

$$\mathbf{K}_{k+1} = \mathbf{K}_k - \mu\mathbf{A}\mathbf{A}^T\mathbf{K}_k - \mu\mathbf{K}_k\mathbf{A}\mathbf{A}^T + \mu^2 m_\mathrm{x}^{(2,2)}\left(2\mathbf{A}\mathbf{A}^T\mathbf{K}_k\mathbf{A}\mathbf{A}^T + \gamma_\mathrm{x}\mathbf{A}\mathbf{A}^T\mathrm{tr}\left[\mathbf{A}\mathbf{A}^T\mathbf{K}_k\right]\right) + \mu^2\sigma_v^2\mathbf{A}\mathbf{A}^T + \mathcal{O}(\mu^2). \tag{29}$$

This can now be split into two parts, one in its modal space $\mathbf{K}^{\|}$ and in its orthogonal complement $\mathbf{K}^{\perp}$ as in (7) and (8) above, and the following is obtained:

$$\mathbf{K}_{k+1}^{\|} = \mathbf{K}_k^{\|} - \mu\mathbf{A}\mathbf{A}^T\mathbf{K}_k^{\|} - \mu\mathbf{K}_k^{\|}\mathbf{A}\mathbf{A}^T + \mu^2 m_\mathrm{x}^{(2,2)}\left(2\mathbf{A}\mathbf{A}^T\mathbf{K}_k^{\|}\mathbf{A}\mathbf{A}^T + \gamma_\mathrm{x}\mathbf{A}\mathbf{A}^T\mathrm{tr}\left[\mathbf{A}\mathbf{A}^T\mathbf{K}_k^{\|}\right]\right) + \mu^2\sigma_v^2\mathbf{A}\mathbf{A}^T + \mathcal{O}(\mu^2) \tag{30}$$

$$= \mathbf{K}_k^{\|} - 2\mu\mathbf{A}\mathbf{A}^T\mathbf{K}_k^{\|} + \mu^2 m_\mathrm{x}^{(2,2)}\left(2[\mathbf{A}\mathbf{A}^T]^2\,\mathbf{K}_k^{\|} + \gamma_\mathrm{x}\mathbf{A}\mathbf{A}^T\mathrm{tr}\left[\mathbf{A}\mathbf{A}^T\mathbf{K}_k^{\|}\right]\right) + \mu^2\sigma_v^2\mathbf{A}\mathbf{A}^T + \mathcal{O}(\mu^2), \tag{31}$$

$$\mathbf{K}_{k+1}^{\perp} = \mathbf{K}_k^{\perp} - \mu\mathbf{A}\mathbf{A}^T\mathbf{K}_k^{\perp} - \mu\mathbf{K}_k^{\perp}\mathbf{A}\mathbf{A}^T + 2\mu^2 m_\mathrm{x}^{(2,2)}\mathbf{A}\mathbf{A}^T\mathbf{K}_k^{\perp}\mathbf{A}\mathbf{A}^T + \mathcal{O}(\mu^2). \tag{32}$$

The consequence of this statement is that the parameter error vector covariance matrix is forced by the driving process to remain only in the modal space of the latter. This is not only true for its initial values but also at every time instant k. The components of the orthogonal complement either remain there or die out. This statement will be addressed later in greater detail in the context of step-size bounds for stability. Note also that for complex-valued processes, the only difference in (29) is the occurrence of $\mathbf{A}\mathbf{A}^H\mathbf{K}_k\mathbf{A}\mathbf{A}^H$ rather than $2\mathbf{A}\mathbf{A}^T\mathbf{K}_k\mathbf{A}\mathbf{A}^T$.

LEARNING AND STEADY-STATE BEHAVIOR

As we have already recognized, independent of its statistics, the additional noise term also lies in the modal space of the driving process and thus is entirely responsible for the learning and steady-state behavior. Components of the orthogonal complement thus die out as long as $0<\mu<1/\left[m_x^{(2,2)}\lambda_{\max}\right]$, $\lambda_{\max}$ denoting the largest eigenvalue of $\mathbf{R}_{uu}$[4]. As we will see later, the step-size bound for the component $\mathbf{K}^{\|}$ of the modal space is smaller and thus all terms in the orthogonal complement will die out for the step-size range of interest. The learning behavior is thus typically derived based on the modal space, i.e., the terms on the main diagonal of $K_k^{\|}$. To obtain this, we start with (30) and transform the modal matrices by a unitary matrix $\mathbf{Q}\mathbf{K}_k^{\|}\mathbf{Q}^T = \Lambda_{K_k}$ and $\mathbf{Q}\mathbf{A}\mathbf{A}^T\mathbf{Q}^T = \mathbf{Q}\mathbf{R}_{uu}\mathbf{Q}^T = \Lambda_u$. We can now apply a vectorization $\Lambda_\mathrm{u}\mathbf{1} = \lambda_\mathrm{u}$, $\Lambda_{K_k}\mathbf{1} = \lambda_{K_k}$ and obtain the evolution in the modal space as

$$\lambda_{K_{k+1}} = \underbrace{\left[\mathbf{I} - 2\mu\Lambda_\mathrm{u} + \mu^2 m_\mathrm{x}^{(2,2)}\left(\Lambda_\mathrm{u}^2\right) + \lambda_\mathrm{u}\lambda_\mathrm{u}^T\right]}_{\mathbf{B}}\lambda_{K_k}. \tag{33}$$

The eigenvalues of matrix $\mathbf{B}$ define the learning speed, in particular the largest eigenvalue $\lambda_{\max}(\mathbf{B}(\mu))$. We call

$$\mu_\mathrm{opt} = \arg\min_{\mu}\lambda_{\max}(\mathbf{B}(\mu)) \tag{34}$$

the optimal step-size, causing fastest convergence.

Steady-state behavior: From **I**–**B**, steady-state values such as misadjustment can be computed. As terms in the orthogonal complement die out, $K_\infty = \lim_{k\to\infty} K_k$ is expected to exist only in the modal space of $\mathbf{R}_{uu}$. Compute the steady-state solution for $k\to\infty$ and, omitting the approximation error terms $O(\mu^2)$ in the following for simplicity,

$$\begin{aligned}\mathbf{K}_\infty &= \mathbf{K}_\infty - 2\mu\mathbf{A}\mathbf{A}^T\mathbf{K}_\infty + \mu^2\sigma_v^2\mathbf{A}\mathbf{A}^T \\ &\quad + \mu^2 m_{\mathrm{x}}^{(2,2)}\left(2(\mathbf{A}\mathbf{A}^T)^2\mathbf{K}_\infty + \gamma_{\mathrm{x}}\mathbf{A}\mathbf{A}^T\mathrm{tr}\left[\mathbf{A}\mathbf{A}^T\mathbf{K}_\infty\right]\right)\end{aligned} \tag{35}$$

is obtained, or equivalently

$$\begin{aligned}&\left[2\mathbf{A}\mathbf{A}^T - 2\mu m_{\mathrm{x}}^{(2,2)}(\mathbf{A}\mathbf{A}^T)^2\right]\mathbf{K}_\infty - \mu m_{\mathrm{x}}^{(2,2)}\gamma_{\mathrm{x}}\mathrm{tr}\left[\mathbf{A}\mathbf{A}^T\mathbf{K}_\infty\right] \\ &\qquad \mathbf{A}\mathbf{A}^T = \mu\sigma_v^2\mathbf{A}\mathbf{A}^T.\end{aligned} \tag{36}$$

Since $\mathbf{K}_\infty$ exists only in the modal space of $\mathbf{AA}^T$, diagonalizing both by the same unitary matrix leads to $\mathbf{QK}_\infty\mathbf{Q}^T = \Lambda_K$ and $\mathbf{QAA}^T\mathbf{Q}^T = \Lambda_u$.

$$2\Lambda_{\mathrm{u}}\Lambda_K - \mu m_{\mathrm{x}}^{(2,2)}\left(2\Lambda_{\mathrm{u}}^2\Lambda_K - \gamma_{\mathrm{x}}\Lambda_{\mathrm{u}}\mathrm{tr}[\Lambda_{\mathrm{u}}\Lambda_K]\right) = \mu\sigma_v^2\Lambda_{\mathrm{u}}. \tag{37}$$

Stacking the diagonal values of the matrices into vectors: $\Lambda_u\mathbf{1} = \lambda_u, \Lambda_K\mathbf{1} = \lambda_K$, $\lambda_u = [\lambda_1, \lambda_2, \ldots, \lambda_M]^T$, the following is obtained

$$\left[2\Lambda_{\mathrm{u}} - 2\mu m_{\mathrm{x}}^{(2,2)}\Lambda_{\mathrm{u}}^2 - \mu m_{\mathrm{x}}^{(2,2)}\gamma_{\mathrm{x}}\lambda_{\mathrm{u}}\lambda_{\mathrm{u}}^T\right]\lambda_K = \mu\sigma_v^2\lambda_{\mathrm{u}}. \tag{38}$$

resulting in the well-known form [11] [Eq. (3.15)]:

$$\begin{aligned}\lambda_K &= \mu\sigma_v^2\left[2\Lambda_{\mathrm{u}} - 2\mu m_{\mathrm{x}}^{(2,2)}\Lambda_{\mathrm{u}}^2 - \mu m_{\mathrm{x}}^{(2,2)}\gamma_{\mathrm{x}}\lambda_{\mathrm{u}}\lambda_{\mathrm{u}}^T\right]^{-1}\lambda_{\mathrm{u}} \\ &= \beta_\infty\left[2\Lambda_{\mathrm{u}} - 2\mu m_{\mathrm{x}}^{(2,2)}\Lambda_{\mathrm{u}}^2\right]^{-1}\lambda_{\mathrm{u}},\end{aligned} \tag{39}$$

with the abbreviation

$$\beta_\infty = \frac{2\mu\sigma_v^2}{2 - \mu m_{\mathrm{x}}^{(2,2)}\gamma_{\mathrm{x}}\sum_i \frac{\lambda_i}{1\;\mu m_{\mathrm{x}}^{(2,2)}\lambda_i}}, \tag{40}$$

obtained by employing the matrix inversion lemma [13]: $\left[P(\Lambda_u) + \lambda_u\lambda_u^T\right]^{-1}\lambda_u = 1/\left[1 + \lambda_u^T P^{-1}(\Lambda_u)\lambda_u\right]P^{-1}(\Lambda_u)\lambda_u$ The final steady-state system mismatch is thus given by

$$M_S = \mathrm{tr}[\mathbf{K}_\infty] = \|\lambda_K\|_1 = \mathbf{1}^T\lambda_K \tag{41}$$

$$= \frac{\mu\sigma_v^2\sum_i\frac{1}{1-\mu m_{\mathrm{x}}^{(2,2)}\lambda_i}}{2 - \mu m_{\mathrm{x}}^{(2,2)}\gamma_{\mathrm{x}}\sum_i\frac{\lambda_i}{1-\mu m_{\mathrm{x}}^{(2,2)}\lambda_i}} \tag{42}$$

and the misadjustment

$$\mathcal{M} = \frac{\mathrm{tr}[\mathbf{K}_\infty\mathbf{R}_{\mathrm{uu}}]}{\sigma_v^2} = \frac{\lambda_{\mathrm{u}}^T\lambda_K}{\sigma_v^2} = \frac{\mu\sum_i\frac{\lambda_i}{1-\mu m_{\mathrm{x}}^{(2,2)}\lambda_i}}{2 - \mu m_{\mathrm{x}}^{(2,2)}\gamma_{\mathrm{x}}\sum_i\frac{\lambda_i}{1-\mu m_{\mathrm{x}}^{(2,2)}\lambda_i}}, \tag{43}$$

the only difference with classic solutions for SIRPs [11] being the term γ_x that contains influences of the fourth-order moments m_x^4 and $m_x^{(2,2)}$ as well as $m_x^{(2,2)}$ explicitly.

For complex-valued driving processes, the final steady-state system mismatch is given correspondingly by

$$M_S = \frac{\mu\sigma_v^2\sum_i\frac{1}{2-\mu m_{\mathrm{x}}^{(2,2)}\lambda_i}}{1 - \mu m_{\mathrm{x}}^{(2,2)}\gamma_{\mathrm{x}}\sum_i\frac{\lambda_i}{2-\mu m_{\mathrm{x}}^{(2,2)}\lambda_i}} \tag{44}$$

and the misadjustment

$$\mathcal{M} = \frac{\mu \sum_i \frac{\lambda_i}{2-\mu m_x^{(2,2)}\lambda_i}}{1-\mu m_x^{(2,2)} \gamma_x \sum_i \frac{\lambda_i}{2-\mu m_x^{(2,2)}\lambda_i}}. \tag{45}$$

Stability bounds: The step-size bound can now be derived either from (42) or by means of Gershgorin's circle theorem from the largest eigenvalue of matrix **B** in (33). The result is identical whichever way is used and conservative for real-valued x_k:

$$0 < \mu \le \frac{2}{m_x^{(2,2)}\left(2\lambda_{\max} + \gamma_x \mathrm{tr}[\mathbf{R}_{uu}]\right)}. \tag{46}$$

Depending on the statistic of the driving process, a more or less conservative bound is obtained. It is worth distinguishing sub- and super Gaussian cases. For sub-Gaussian distributions, $\gamma_x<1$, the bound grows while for super-Gaussian distributions, $\gamma_x>1$, the bound decreases. The step-size bound thus varies with the distribution type by approximately $\mathrm{tr}[\mathbf{R}_{uu}]$ in the bound (46). For SIRPs (and thus Gaussian) distributions, as well as for very long filters, $\gamma_x=1$ and thus

$$0 < \mu \le \frac{2}{3m_x^{(2,2)}\mathrm{tr}[\mathbf{R}_{uu}]} \le \frac{2}{m_x^{(2,2)}\left(2\lambda_{\max} + \mathrm{tr}[\mathbf{R}_{uu}]\right)}. \tag{47}$$

This result is identical to (3) for Gaussian processes as $m_x^{(2,2)}=1$. For complex-valued processes x_k, the bounds are obtained in a very similar way, simply replacing the term $2\lambda_{\max}$ with $\lambda_{\max}$.

For a real-valued statistically white driving process, an exact bound without Gershgorin's theorem can be computed, leading to

$$0 < \mu_{\text{white}} \le \frac{2}{m_x^{(2,2)}\mathrm{tr}[\mathbf{R}_{uu}]\left(\gamma_x + 2/M\right)}, \tag{48}$$

thus also a significantly larger bound than (3), but still dependent on the distribution by the value of γ_x.

Such a result, in particular the lower 2/3 bound in (47) and (3), originating from the correlation of the random process, is conservative. Note that the largest eigenvalue $\lambda_{\max}$ is related to the maximal magnitude of the correlation filter, i.e., $\lambda_{\max} \ge \max_\Omega |A(e^{j\Omega})|^2$ with equality approaching for $M\to\infty$. Thus, for very long filters, the energy ($\mathrm{tr}[\mathbf{R}_{uu}]$) will not be entirely concentrated around its peak magnitude, unless we intended to build an oscillator. With this argument, the term $\lambda_{\max}$ can be omitted for the long filter (see also [29] Eq. (10.4.40)), and a much larger bound is obtained:

$$0 < \mu_{\text{long}} \le \frac{2}{m_x^{(2,2)}\mathrm{tr}[\mathbf{R}_{uu}]}. \tag{49}$$

We will return to the discussion of stability bounds in the context of simulation results in Section 5.

VERY LONG ADAPTIVE FILTERS

An analysis for very long filter orders M has been considered by Butterweck [18, 23–25], however, in the context of avoiding the IA. The previously introduced term $\gamma_x = \left(1+\left(m_x^{(4)}/m_x^{(2,2)}-3\right)/M\right)$ already hints towards $\gamma_x=1$ for very large filter orders M. But note that the derivation in the previous sections required a further asymptotic equivalence result that can be traded against a much simpler asymptotic equivalence result for the long filter case. This will provide us with a second opinion at least for the special case of very long filters that should be in agreement with our findings so far.

The main reason for eliminating our first asymptotic equivalence lies in the fact that for very long linear filters, it is well known that Toeplitz matrices **A** behave in an asymptotically equivalent manner to circulant matrices [31], say **C**. Rather than $\mathbf{A}\mathbf{A}^T$, now, $\mathbf{C}\mathbf{C}^T=\mathbf{R}_{uu}$ and the diagonalization is achieved by DFT matrices $\mathbf{F}\in\mathbb{C}^{M\times M}$: $\mathbf{C} = \mathbf{F}^H \Lambda_u^{1/2}\mathbf{F}$ and thus $\mathbf{F}^H\Lambda_u\mathbf{F}=\mathbf{R}_{uu}$.

Theorem 4.1.

Assuming driving process $u_k = C[x_k]$ to originate from a linearly filtered white random process x_k according to (9)–(17) by cyclic filtering, i.e., $\mathbf{u}_k=\mathbf{C}\mathbf{x}_k$ with circulant matrix $\mathbf{C}\in\mathbb{R}^{M\times M}$. Then, any initial parameter error covariance matrix $\mathbf{K}_0$ evolves only in the modal space of $\mathbf{R}_{uu}$, now defined by DFT matrices $\mathbf{F}\in\mathbb{C}^{M\times M}$.

Proof.

Following the fact that circulant matrices can be diagonalized by DFT matrices, say **F**, reconsider the term $E[\mathbf{u}_k\mathbf{u}_k^T\mathbf{K}_k\mathbf{u}_k\mathbf{u}_k^T]$, remembering that a process linearly filtered by a unitary filter **F** for very long filters preserves its properties (see Appendix 2 for proof) at the output of the filter. It is found that

$$\begin{aligned}
&E\left[\mathbf{u}_k\mathbf{u}_k{}^T\mathbf{K}_k\mathbf{u}_k\mathbf{u}_k{}^T\right]\\
&= \mathbf{C}E\left[\mathbf{x}_k\mathbf{x}_k{}^T\mathbf{C}^T\mathbf{K}_k\mathbf{C}\mathbf{x}_k\mathbf{x}_k{}^T\right]\mathbf{C}^T\\
&= \mathbf{F}^H\Lambda_u^{1/2}\mathbf{F}E\left[\mathbf{x}_k\mathbf{x}_k{}^T\mathbf{F}^H\Lambda_u^{1/2}\mathbf{F}\mathbf{K}_k\mathbf{F}^H\Lambda_u^{1/2}\mathbf{F}\mathbf{x}_k\mathbf{x}_k{}^T\right]\mathbf{F}^H\Lambda_u^{1/2}\mathbf{F}\\
&= \mathbf{F}^H\Lambda_u^{1/2}E\left[\mathbf{f}_k\mathbf{f}_k{}^H(\Lambda_u^{1/2}\mathbf{F}\mathbf{K}_k\mathbf{F}^H\Lambda_u^{1/2})\mathbf{f}_k\mathbf{f}_k{}^H\right]\Lambda_u^{1/2}\mathbf{F}\\
&= \mathbf{F}^H\Lambda_u^{1/2}E\left[\mathbf{f}_k\mathbf{f}_k{}^H\left(\Lambda_u^{1/2}\Lambda_{K_k}\Lambda_u^{1/2}\right)\mathbf{f}_k\mathbf{f}_k{}^H\right]\Lambda_u^{1/2}\mathbf{F}.
\end{aligned} \tag{50}$$

In the last line, we assumed that $\mathbf{K}_k$ is also circulant. But similar to the considerations in Section 2, we could start from an initial parameter error covariance matrix $\mathbf{K}_0$ that is not circulant, e.g., $\mathbf{K}_0=\mathbf{w}\mathbf{w}^T$. In this case, $\mathbf{K}_0$ can be separated in one part that lies in the modal space, defined by **F**, and one part from its complement space. As the part in the complement space is no longer excited, it will follow the evolution as described in (32) and dies out.

Note that the filter is now being formulated in terms of a complex-valued driving process $\mathbf{f}_k=\mathbf{F}\mathbf{x}_k$ even though $\mathbf{x}_k\in\mathbb{R}^{M\times 1}$. Noticing that the center term of the last equation is of diagonal form, and simplifying the terms to

$$E\left[\mathbf{f}_k\mathbf{f}_k{}^H\mathbf{L}\mathbf{f}_k\mathbf{f}_k{}^H\right] = m_{\mathrm{f}}^{(2,2)}\mathbf{L} + m_{\mathrm{f}}^{(2,2)}\mathrm{tr}[\mathbf{L}]\,\mathbf{I} + \left(m_{\mathrm{f}}^{(4)} - 2m_{\mathrm{f}}^{(2,2)}\right)\mathbf{L},$$
$$= m_{\mathrm{f}}^{(2,2)}\mathrm{tr}[\mathbf{L}]\,\mathbf{I} + m_{\mathrm{f}}^{(2,2)}\mathbf{L}, \tag{51}$$

with the particular solution $\mathbf{L} = \Lambda_{\mathrm{u}}^{1/2}\Lambda_{\mathbf{K}_k}\Lambda_{\mathrm{u}}^{1/2}$ and the property $\mathrm{tr}[\mathbf{L}] = \mathrm{tr}\left[\Lambda_{\mathrm{u}}^{1/2}\Lambda_{\mathbf{K}_k}\Lambda_{\mathrm{u}}^{1/2}\right] = \mathrm{tr}[\Lambda_{\mathrm{u}}\Lambda_{\mathbf{K}_k}]$. Note that $m_{\mathrm{f}}^{(4)} = 2m_{\mathrm{f}}^{(2,2)}$ as shown in Appendix 2, m_f denoting the corresponding moments of the driving process $\mathbf{f}_k$. The parameter error vector covariance matrix in transformed form $\Lambda_{\mathbf{K}_{k+1}} = \mathbf{F}\mathbf{K}_{k+1}\mathbf{F}^H$ now evolves as

$$\Lambda_{\mathbf{K}_{k+1}} = \Lambda_{\mathbf{K}_k} - 2\mu\Lambda_{\mathrm{u}}\Lambda_{\mathbf{K}_k} + \mu^2\sigma_v^2\Lambda_{\mathrm{u}}$$
$$+ \mu^2 m_{\mathrm{f}}^{(2,2)}\left(\mathrm{tr}[\Lambda_{\mathrm{u}}\Lambda_{\mathbf{K}_k}]\,\Lambda_{\mathrm{u}} + \Lambda_{\mathrm{u}}^2\Lambda_{\mathbf{K}_k}\right). \tag{52}$$

This shows that for very large filter orders, our previous considerations hold exactly and the parameter error vector covariance matrix $\mathbf{K}_k$ indeed remains in the modal space of the driving process u_k defined by the DFT matrices $\mathbf{F}\in\mathbb{C}^{M\times M}$.

Steady-state behavior: The steady-state values are obtained for $k\to\infty$, i.e.,

$$\Lambda_{\mathbf{K}} = \Lambda_{\mathbf{K}} - 2\mu\Lambda_{\mathrm{u}}\Lambda_{\mathbf{K}} + \mu^2\sigma_v^2\Lambda_{\mathrm{u}}$$
$$+ \mu^2 m_{\mathrm{f}}^{(2,2)}\left(\mathrm{tr}[\Lambda_{\mathrm{u}}\Lambda_{\mathbf{K}}]\,\Lambda_{\mathrm{u}} + \Lambda_{\mathrm{u}}^2\Lambda_{\mathbf{K}}\right) \tag{53}$$

$$2\Lambda_{\mathrm{u}}\Lambda_{\mathbf{K}} = \mu m_{\mathrm{f}}^{(2,2)}\left(\mathrm{tr}[\Lambda_{\mathrm{u}}\Lambda_{\mathbf{K}}]\,\Lambda_{\mathrm{u}} + \Lambda_{\mathrm{u}}^2\Lambda_{\mathbf{K}}\right) + \mu\sigma_v^2\Lambda_{\mathrm{u}}. \tag{54}$$

Reshaping the diagonal terms into vectors $\Lambda_{\mathbf{K}}\mathbf{1}=\lambda_{\mathbf{K}}$ leads to

$$2\Lambda_{\mathrm{u}}\lambda_{\mathbf{K}} = \mu m_{\mathrm{f}}^{(2,2)}\left[\lambda_{\mathrm{u}}\lambda_{\mathrm{u}}^T\lambda_{\mathbf{K}} + \Lambda_{\mathrm{u}}^2\lambda_{\mathbf{K}}\right] + \mu\sigma_v^2\lambda_{\mathrm{u}}. \tag{55}$$

and finally by applying the matrix inversion lemma

$$\lambda_{\mathbf{K}} = \beta_\infty\left[2\Lambda_{\mathrm{u}} - \mu m_{\mathrm{f}}^{(2,2)}\Lambda_{\mathrm{u}}^2\right]^{-1}\lambda_{\mathrm{u}}. \tag{56}$$

with

$$\beta_\infty = \frac{\mu\sigma_v^2}{1 - \mu m_{\mathrm{f}}^{(2,2)}\sum_i \frac{\lambda_i}{2-\mu m_{\mathrm{f}}^{(2,2)}\lambda_i}}. \tag{57}$$

The final steady-state system mismatch is thus given by

$$M_S = \mathrm{tr}[\mathbf{K}_\infty] = \mathbf{1}^T\lambda_{\mathbf{K}} = \frac{\mu\sigma_v^2\sum_i \frac{1}{2-\mu m_{\mathrm{f}}^{(2,2)}\lambda_i}}{1 - \mu m_{\mathrm{f}}^{(2,2)}\sum_i \frac{\lambda_i}{2-\mu m_{\mathrm{f}}^{(2,2)}\lambda_i}}, \tag{58}$$

and the misadjustment reads

$$\mathcal{M} = \frac{\mathrm{tr}[\mathbf{K}_\infty\mathbf{R}_{\mathrm{uu}}]}{\sigma_v^2} = \frac{\lambda_{\mathrm{u}}{}^T\lambda_{\mathbf{K}}}{\sigma_v^2} = \frac{\mu\sum_i \frac{\lambda_i}{2-\mu m_{\mathrm{f}}^{(2,2)}\lambda_i}}{1 - \mu m_{\mathrm{f}}^{(2,2)}\sum_i \frac{\lambda_i}{2-\mu m_{\mathrm{f}}^{(2,2)}\lambda_i}}. \tag{59}$$

Note that this result for the long filter depends only on the joint moment $m_f^{(2,2)}$ of the DFT of the driving process. As shown in the Appendix, for most distributions, this moment takes on the same value. This explains why the long LMS filter behaves more or less identically, independently of the driving process, as long as the correlation is the same. The interested reader may like to compare this with an older publication by Gardner [30] in which the very similar fourth-order moment $m_x^{(4)}$ was emphasized for purely white driving processes.

Stability bounds: The last equation in turn results in the conservative step-size bound

$$0 < \mu \leq \frac{1}{m_{\mathrm{f}}^{(2,2)}\mathrm{tr}[\mathbf{R}_{\mathrm{uu}}]} \leq \frac{2}{m_{\mathrm{f}}^{(2,2)}(\lambda_{\max} + \mathrm{tr}[\mathbf{R}_{\mathrm{uu}}])}. \tag{60}$$

The step-size bound for the very long filter appears considerably larger (by one third when compared to (47)) than that for short lengths. Following the same argument for long filters as at the end of the previous section, we can argue that λ_{max} is small compared to tr[$\mathbf{R}_{uu}$] and obtain the even larger bound

$$0 < \mu \leq \frac{2}{m_{\mathrm{f}}^{(2,2)}\mathrm{tr}[\mathbf{R}_{\mathrm{uu}}]}, \tag{61}$$

which is identical to (49) as for long filters m(2,2)x=m(2,2) fmx(2,2)=mf(2,2).

An alternative bound is also possible now. As the eigenvalues λ_i are simply originating from the circulant matrices **C** that linearly filter the driving process, they are obtained by a DFT on the filter matrices $\mathbf{CC}^T$, or equivalently correspond to the powers of the spectrum of u_k at equidistant frequencies $2\pi/M$, allowing an alternative bound for $\lambda_{max} \geq \max\Omega|C(e^{j\Omega})|^2$, both being identical for large M. For the long filter, we thus find

$$0 < \mu \leq \frac{2}{m_{\mathrm{f}}^{(2,2)} M \max_{\Omega} |C(e^{j\Omega})|^2} = \frac{2}{m_{\mathrm{f}}^{(2,2)} M \lambda_{\mathrm{max}}} \leq \frac{2}{m_{\mathrm{f}}^{(2,2)}\mathrm{tr}[\mathbf{R}_{\mathrm{uu}}]}. \tag{62}$$

This more conservative bound corresponds to the spectral variations in the driving process while the former bound including the trace term focuses more on the gain of the correlation filter. A similar (even more conservative) bound based on the power spectrum of the driving process has already been proposed by Butterweck [24] and reads in our notation

$$0 < \mu_{\text{Butterweck}} \leq \frac{1}{m_{\mathrm{x}}^{(2)} M \max_{\Omega} |C(e^{j\Omega})|^2}. \tag{63}$$

The bound was derived for the long filter without IA but under Gaussian processes for which $m_f^{(2,2)} = m_x^{(2)}$, following a wave-theoretical argument. As for long filters $\max\Omega|C(e^{j\Omega})|^2 = \lambda_{max}(\mathbf{CC}^H) = \|\mathbf{CC}^H\|_{2,\mathrm{ind}}$, Butterweck's result appears conservative. It is nevertheless reassuring to learn that classic matrix approaches lead to very similar results even though the Butterweck's analysis is based on Gaussian processes and thus the fourth-order moment $m_f^{(2,2)}$ is not accounted for. In particular, this plays a crucial role for non-Gaussian spherically invariant processes.

VALIDATION BY SIMULATION

In this section, we validate our theoretical findings in terms of convergence bounds and steady-state behavior of the LMS algorithm by Monte Carlo (MC) simulations. Table 2 below lists six typical zero-mean distributions and corresponding second- and fourth-order moments. The corresponding value before and after the DFT (top and bottom, respectively) is shown for each process. While the first line provides m_x terms, the second exhibits the corresponding m_f terms of the complex-valued process after the DFT, according to the relations described in Appendix 2. Note that the values m_f are provided for large values of the filter order M so that $\gamma_x=1$ (see also (76) in the Appendix). The first two are classic Gaussian distributions in either IR or IC. The next three are IID, whether bipolar, uniform, or a product of two independent Gaussian processes (Gauss^2). Finally, an SIRP originating from a mixture of two Gaussian processes is presented. While the first two IID processes are sub-Gaussian ($\gamma_x<1$), the last IID process as well as the SIRP are super-Gaussian ($\gamma_x>1$).

Table 2. Second- and fourth-order moments of various (decorrelated) distributions for large filter order M

Distribution	m(2)xmx(2)	m(2,2)xmx(2,2)	m(4)xmx(4)
Gauss ∈ IR	1	1	3
DFT of Gauss	1	1	2
Gauss ∈ IC	1	1	2
DFT of Gauss	1	1	2
IID bipolar ∈IR	1	1	1
DFT of IID bipolar	1	1	2
IID uniform ∈IR	1	1	1.8
DFT of IID uniform	1	1	2
IID Gauss^2 ∈IR	1	1	9
DFT of Gauss^2	1	1	2
K_0 SIRP ∈IR	1	3	9
DFT of K_0 SIRP	1	3	6

All MC simulations are run on linear combiners and thus satisfy the driving process assumptions A1a and A1b. The M taps of the system **w** to identify were selected randomly from N(0,1)N(0,1), a fresh selection being made for each MC run. Simulations were run with filter length M={10,100,400} and step-sizes μ={1,2,5,9,12,15,18,21,24,27,29}×1/[15M], thus ranging up to the largest possible stability bound 2/M. The driving process had unit variance $m_x^{(2)}=1$ and the additive noise was Gaussian with variance 10^{-4}.

In a first step, we analyzed the number of MC runs required for averaging in order to obtain consistent results. Here, the findings of [32] are a great help as they propose to analyze the mismatch fluctuations, defined as

$$\rho_k = \frac{\sqrt{\mathrm{var}\left\{||\tilde{\mathbf{w}}||_k^2\right\}}}{\mathrm{E}||\tilde{\mathbf{w}}||_k^2}, \tag{64}$$

a value that increases, when μ approaches the stability bound. Based on experiments with relatively large step-sizes, we decided that 1 000 MC runs provide sufficiently good results. For long filters, the fluctuations become considerably smaller, and 100 MC runs appear sufficient. We thus applied {1 000,1 000,100} averages for M={10,100,400}, respectively, to keep simulation times manageable. The observation $\bar{M}_S$ for the steady-state system mismatch is obtained by ensemble averaging over the number of MC runs and finally averaging the last 10 % values over time. As the numbers thus obtained are typically very close to the predicted values, the relative error in system mismatch $(M_S-\bar{M}_S)/M_S$ is computed and plotted as a percentage.

Experiment 1: In the first set of experiments, the white processes with properties in Table 2were the driving source. The outcome of such experiments provides a validation to the predicted steady-state behavior. For the long filter, (58) simplifies to

$$M_S = \frac{\mu M}{2-\mu M m_f^{(2,2)}}, \tag{65}$$

while (42) for the arbitrary LMS algorithm simplifies to the same expression with $m_x^{(2,2)}$ replacing $m_f^{(2,2)}$. This is in agreement with (76) (see Appendix 2) as for large filter order M; both terms become identical. Such simplified formula is often applied in practice. As we expect differences only if the step-size is large, the precision of the formula is investigated in this experiment.

Figure 1 presents the relative errors $1-\frac{\bar{M}_S}{M_S}$ obtained, in percentage terms when applying (65).

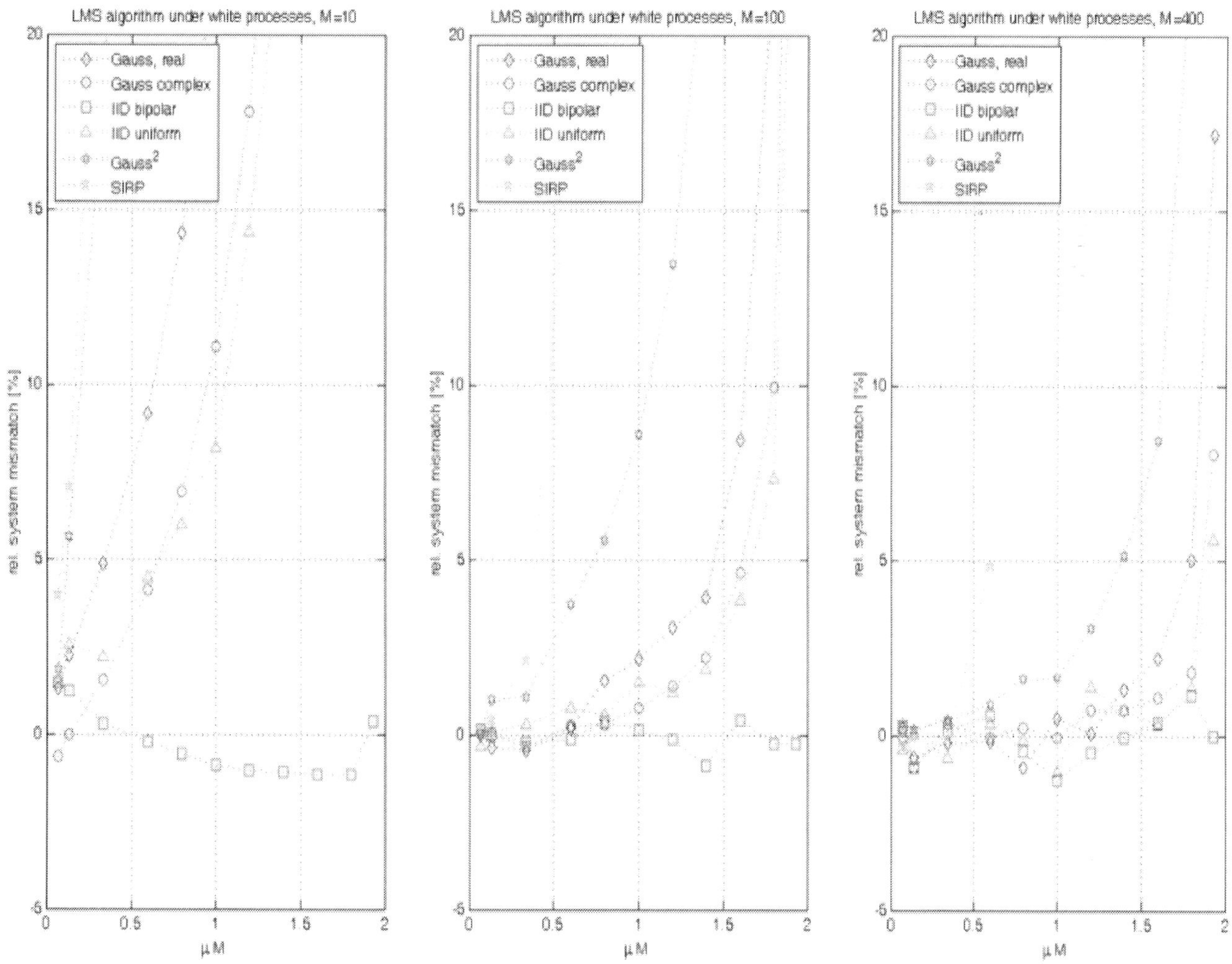

Figure 1. Relative system mismatch $(M_S-\bar{M}_S)/M_S$ in percent based on simplified formula for white driving processes with different filter lengths (M={10,100,400}).

The results are as follows:

1. In all distributions, the errors obtained for small step-sizes are very small, confirming our theoretical predictions.
2. The larger the filter length M, the smaller the errors. This is expected as formula (65) was not only derived for long filters but also for small step-sizes, which are unavoidable for large filter lengths.
3. Only in the case of M=10, for which a significant $\gamma_x \neq 1$ is expected, the errors are moderate to large compared to the other cases.
4. As expected, the errors are higher for processes that are the furthest from Gaussian (see, for example, Gauss^2) and of large μ (small filter length M). The results in the figure clearly show the impact of our asymptotic equivalence assumption, as the mismatch decreases with smaller step-sizes (which is a consequence of higher filter order M).
5. Even for the SIRPs, our prediction is excellent. Note, however, that this depends very much on how an SIRP is modeled. A K_0 SIRP is generated by a product process of a Gaussian process with a random variable that is itself Gaussian distributed. If this RV, serving as the standard deviation of the process and defining its variance, is kept constant for each simulation run, the ensemble average will not converge. As the RV can take on arbitrarily large values (high energy driving process), the adaptation process can become extremely slow for some runs due to its fixed step-size. But even worse, as there is a finite probability that the variance of this process is below any bound, a fixed step-size is then too large for these runs to become stable. Such SIRP processes are only possible in the context of the normalized LMS (NLMS) algorithm. The situation is considerably better if the RV that defines the variance of the random process is itself generated by a random process, producing a slight change at every time instant so as to slowly modify the signal's variance over time, as is commonly done to resemble speech signals with their slowly changing variance. Note that for SIRPs, $m_x^{(2,2)}=3$, restricting the step-size range considerably (the stability bound is roughly at $\mu_{\lim} M=2/3$).

The step-size range in Fig. 1 is limited to $\mu=\{1,\ldots,29\}\times 1/[15M]$. The problem with higher step-size values is that the fluctuations become larger and thus significantly longer averaging is required (see also [32] for explanations of this effect), this not being feasible. In particular for short filters (M=10), the convergence bounds are alternated by γ_x and thus the classical bound (3) is still too high. This can be observed very clearly for the IID Gauss^2 process, which leads to extremely high errors, when operating in close vicinity to the stability bound.

Experiment 2: We repeat the previous experiment, but we compare the results with the much more precise bound derived from (42) for a white driving process (real-valued):

$$M_S = \frac{\mu M \sigma_v^2}{2-\mu m_x^{(2,2)}(2+\gamma_x M)} = \frac{\mu M \sigma_v^2}{2-\mu m_x^{(2,2)}\left(M-1+\frac{m_x^{(4)}}{m_x^{(2,2)}}\right)}. \quad (66)$$

In case the process is complex-valued, the bound (44) simplifies to a similar expression as (66); just the term M−1 in the denominator is to be replaced by M−2.

Figure 2 depicts the results. The major difference now is that the precision becomes much higher even for those processes that are far away from Gaussian (for example Gauss^2). No matter what distribution or length of the filter, the error obtained remains below roughly 1 % as long as the step-size does not reach the stability bound.

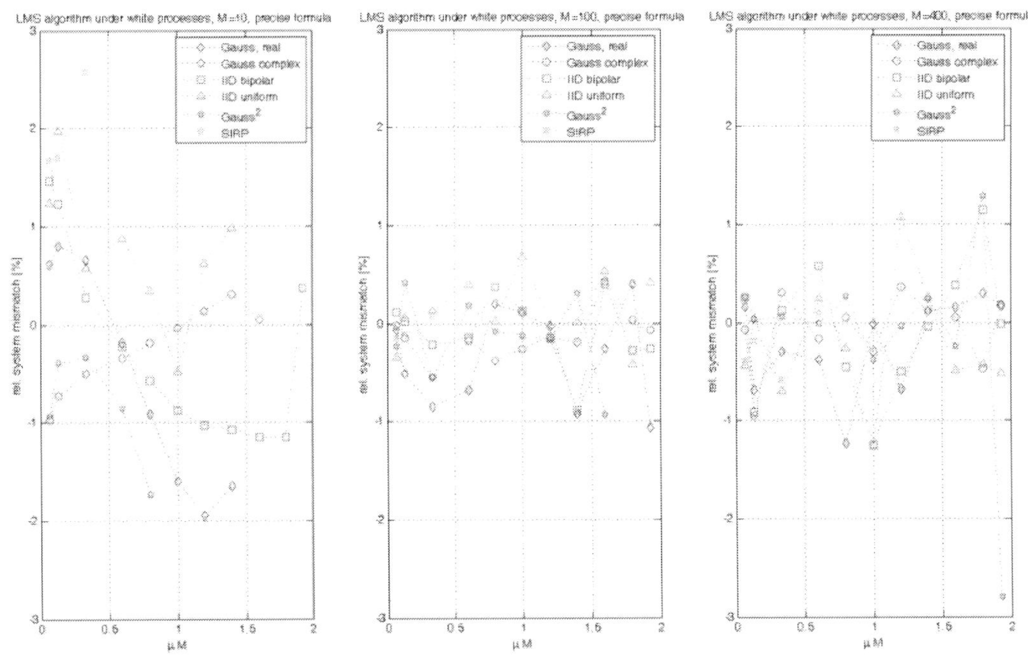

Figure 2. Relative system mismatch $(M_S - \bar{M}_S)/M_S$ in percent based on precise formula for white driving processes with different filter lengths (M={10,100,400}).

We compare now our observations for the predicted stability bound (48), which reads in our case for real-valued processes:

$$0 < \mu \leq \frac{2}{m_x^{(2,2)}\left(M - 1 + \frac{m_x^{(4)}}{m_x^{(2,2)}}\right)}. \qquad (67)$$

We recognize that for large M, we find μlimM=2/$m_x^{(2,2)}$, thus 2 in general and 2/3 for SIRPs. For small values of M, the situation is different and we obtain $\mu_{\lim}M=\{10/6=1.66,20/11=1.81,2,20/10.8=1.85,10/9=1.11,5/9=0.55\}$ for our six processes, an excellent agreement when compared to the left hand side of Fig. 2.

Experiment 3: In a last set of experiments, the previous simulation runs from Experiments 1 and 2 were repeated for correlated driving processes. We applied a linear filter with impulse response

$$a_k = 0.6 \times 0.8^k; \qquad k = 0, 1, \ldots \qquad (68)$$

on the six driving processes of the previous experiment. The so-obtained AR(1) process with unit gain exhibits a relatively high correlation as it is common in speech processes. If as in this case, the filter $A(q^{-1}) = \frac{0.6}{1-0.8q^{-1}}$ becomes very long (P→∞), the largest eigenvalue becomes small compared to tr[$\mathbf{R}_{uu}$]. Thus, the convergence bound for μ becomes practically 2/($m_f^{(2,2)}$ tr[$\mathbf{R}_{uu}$]), which agrees well with our simulation results. Note that such bound can be much larger as well as much smaller than the classic bound in (3), depending on the value of $m_f^{(2,2)}$. In Fig. 3, we compare our simulation results with the predicted values from (42) and (44), for real- and complex-valued processes, respectively. As before, we find excellent agreement in the order of 1 % error. For a small filter length M=10, the largest eigenvalue becomes λ_{max}=5.5 and the predicted stability bounds are reduced from $\mu_{\lim}M=\{1.66,1.81,2,1.85,1.11,0.55\}$ of the white driving processes to $\mu_{\lim}M=\{0.95,1.29,1.05,1.01,0.74,0.31\}$ which is well reflected in the simulation results. For larger filters, the stability bound moves towards $\mu_{\lim}M\rightarrow 2$ (2/3 for SIRP) for all processes, independent of the correlation. For M=400, the largest eigenvalue has only slightly increased to λ_{max}=8.9 and thus has little influence on the stability bound.

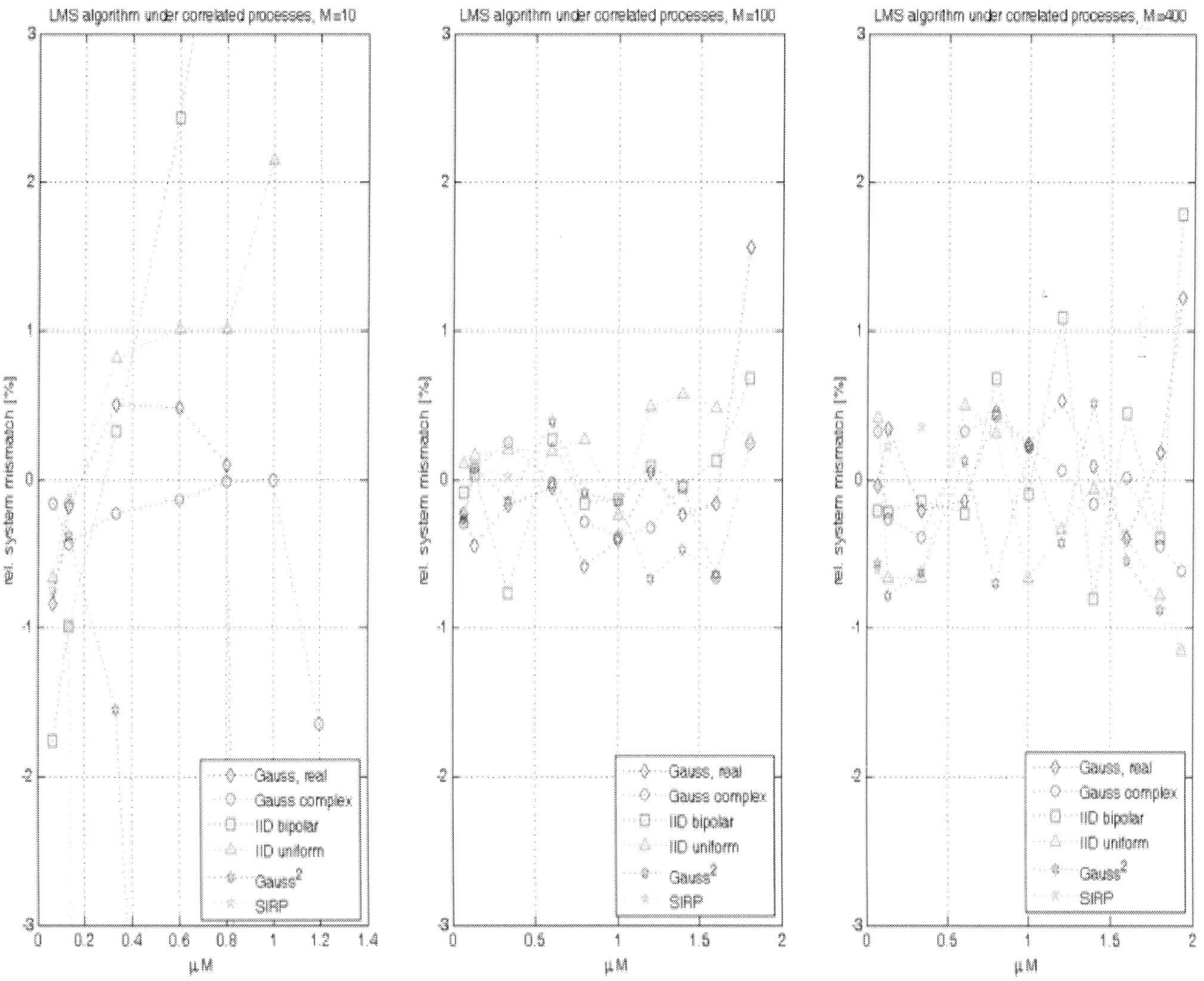

Figure 3. Relative system mismatch $(M_S - \bar{M}_S)/M_S$ in percent of correlated AR(1) driving processes.

We finally are interested in the fluctuations of the various runs (see [32]), defined in (64), which are evaluated at steady state now:

$$\rho = \lim_{k\to\infty} \rho_k = \lim_{k\to\infty} \frac{\sqrt{\operatorname{var}\left\{\|\tilde{\mathbf{w}}\|_k^2\right\}}}{\mathrm{E}\|\tilde{\mathbf{w}}\|_k^2}. \tag{69}$$

As expected, the fluctuations, depicted in Fig. 4, increase considerably only for step-sizes close to the stability bound. For the very long filter, such bound was correctly predicted in (61), independent of pdf and correlation.

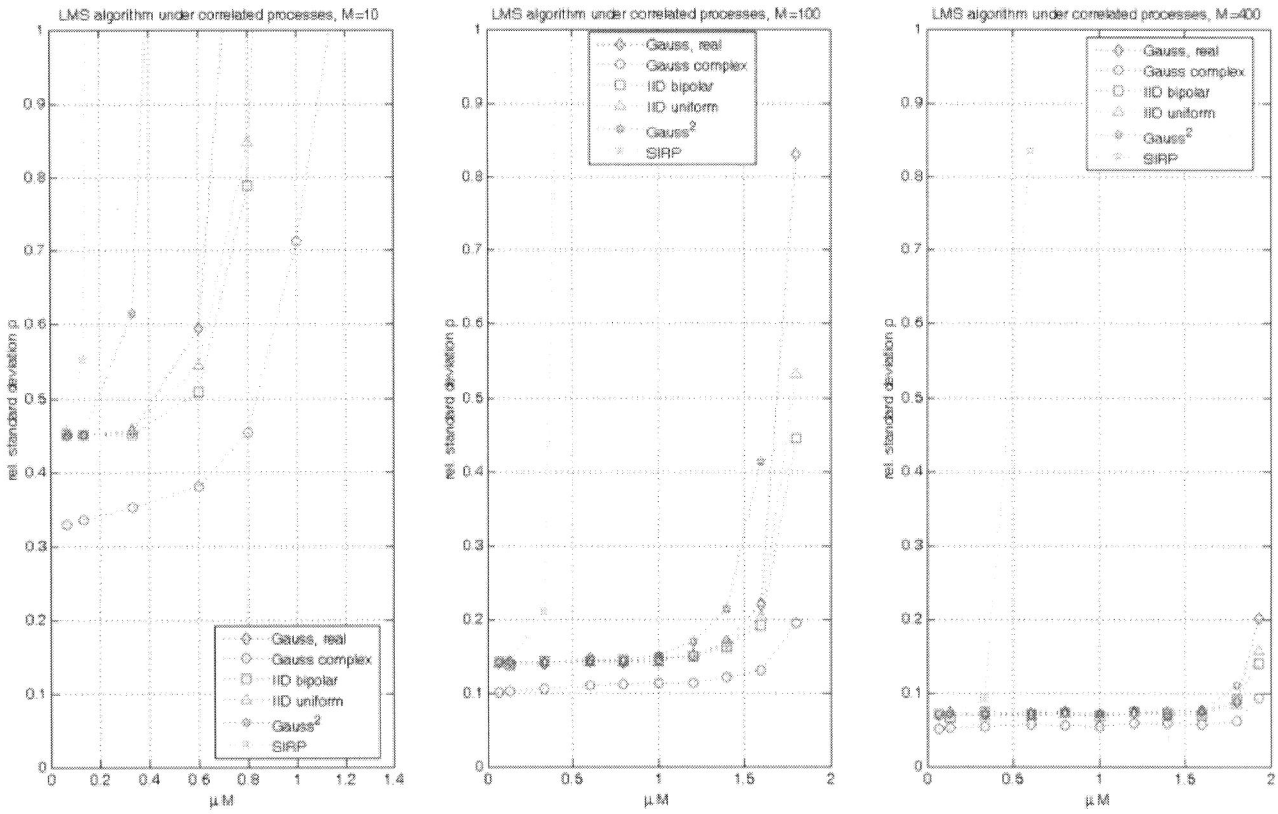

Figure 4. Fluctuations ρ as a function of μM for three different filter lengths (M={10,100,400}) of correlated AR(1) driving processes.

CONCLUSIONS

In this contribution, a stochastic analysis of second-order moments in terms of the parameter error covariance matrix has been shown for the LMS algorithm under the large class of linearly filtered random driving processes. While results were previously only known for a small number of statistics, this contribution deals with the large class of linearly filtered white processes with arbitrary statistics. Particularly interesting is the fact that the parameter error covariance matrix is essentially being forced to remain in the modal space of the driving process, defined by its autocorrelation matrix $\mathbf{R}_{uu}$. Such a property was shown to be independent of the correlation and the pdf of the driving process. Next to the independence assumption, an asymptotic equivalence is required for this derivation, producing minor errors only for large step-size (short filters) and pdfs that are far from Gaussian. The error term on the other hand also quantifies and allows to accurately predict the filter behavior even for small filters. Alternatively, for very long filters, an even simpler asymptotic equivalence guarantees exact results. The result for the very long filter is particularly interesting as it shows a more relaxed step-size bound compared to the short filter. Moreover, an alternative step-size bound that includes the maximum gain of the spectral filter rather than the trace of the autocorrelation matrix is provided, this potentially being a more practical solution. It is shown that the joint moment $m_x^{(2,2)}$ of the decorrelated process is more relevant than the term $m_x^{(2,2)}$ for the steady-state prediction even though it has no impact for most typical processes. Furthermore, a correction factor γ_x occurs in the step-size bound, describing the influence of having either short filters or non-Gaussian driving processes. These results may appear less practical than previous ones since more details regarding the statistics of the driving process now need to be known, but note that also for classic results, the second-order moments, i.e., the autocorrelation matrix, needed to be known a priori (or estimated). Bringing in more parameters is the price of having a more general form of theory.

ENDNOTES

[1] Naturally, the basic LMS algorithm requires modification to apply it successfully in various applications; we simply refer here to the entire family with similar algorithmic structure whose core elements are the LMS algorithm. Worth mentioning is in any case the normalized version NLMS of the LMS

algorithm that ensures independence of the input's signal power. Such small modification alone, however, already complicates the analysis substantially [11, 33]. Even for very long filters, non-Gaussian excitation such as speech signals can lead to severe problems [34] if no normalization is applied.

[2] The terms white and decorrelated will henceforth be used interchangeably.

[3] Note that the requirement of having statistically independent regression vectors is actually far too strong as we only need to ensure that $E[\mathbf{u}_k\mathbf{u}_k^T(\mathbf{w}-\mathbf{w}_k)(\mathbf{w}-\mathbf{w}_k)^T\mathbf{u}_k\mathbf{u}_k^T]=E[\mathbf{u}_k\mathbf{u}_k^T\mathbf{K}_k\mathbf{u}_k\mathbf{u}_k^T]$. One could also call it independence approximation and just require this property.

[4] The procedure for obtaining such result is the same as explained in the following paragraph for $\mathbf{K}^{\|}$, only much simpler, as the trace terms do not appear.

APPENDIX

Appendix 1: Decomposition of Symmetric Matrices

A problem in the derivation of the LMS behavior is that the covariance matrices as they appear for the parameter error vector $\mathbf{K}_k=E[(\mathbf{w}-\mathbf{w}_k)(\mathbf{w}-\mathbf{w}_k)^T]$ are in general not in the modal space of the driving process $\mathbf{u}_k=[u_k,u_{k-1},\ldots,u_{k-M+1}]^T$ with autocorrelation matrix $\mathbf{R}_{uu}=E[\mathbf{u}_k\mathbf{u}_k^T]=\mathbf{Q}\Lambda_u\mathbf{Q}^T$ thus

$$\mathbf{K}_k \neq b_0\mathbf{I} + b_1\mathbf{R}_{uu} + b_2\mathbf{R}_{uu}^2 + \ldots \tag{70}$$

Since the derivation of the LMS algorithm only requires that the trace of such matrices be known, it is sufficient to analyze only the algorithm's impact on the parameter error vector with respect to $\mathbf{R}_{uu}$. It is therefore proposed to decompose a given matrix $\mathbf{K}$ into a first part, i.e., in the modal space of the autocorrelation matrix $\mathbf{R}_{uu}$ of the driving process $\mathbf{u}_k$ and a second part in its orthogonal complement space, i.e.,

$$\mathbf{K} = b_0\mathbf{I}+b_1\mathbf{R}_{uu}+\ldots+b_{M-1}\mathbf{R}_{uu}^{M-1}+\mathbf{K}^{\perp} = P(\mathbf{R}_{uu})+\mathbf{K}^{\perp}. \tag{71}$$

Here, $P(\mathbf{R}_{uu})$ denotes a polynomial in $\mathbf{R}_{uu}$. Note that due to the Cayley-Hamilton theorem, an exponent larger than M−1, with M denoting the system order, is not required [28].

Lemma 1.

Any symmetric matrix $\mathbf{K}$ can be decomposed into a part from the subspace of a given modal space $\{\mathbf{I}, \mathbf{R}_{uu}, \mathbf{R}_{uu}^2, \ldots, \mathbf{R}_{uu}^{M-1}\}$ and its orthogonal complement subspace $\mathcal{R}_u^{\perp}$ for which $tr\left[\mathbf{K}^{\perp}\mathbf{R}_{uu}^{l}\right]=0$ for any value of l=0,1,2,....

Proof.

The optimal set of coefficients for approximating the symmetric matrix $\mathbf{K}$ is found by

$$\min_{\{b_0,b_1,..,b_{M-1}\}} \operatorname{tr}\left[(\mathbf{K}-P(\mathbf{R}_{uu}))(\mathbf{K}-P(\mathbf{R}_{uu}))^T\right], \tag{72}$$

which is a simple quadratic problem with linear solution:

$$\begin{bmatrix} M & \operatorname{tr}[\mathbf{R}_{uu}] & \ldots & \operatorname{tr}\left[\mathbf{R}_{uu}^{M-1}\right] \\ \operatorname{tr}[\mathbf{R}_{uu}] & \operatorname{tr}\left[\mathbf{R}_{uu}^{2}\right] & \ldots & \operatorname{tr}\left[\mathbf{R}_{uu}^{M}\right] \\ \operatorname{tr}[\mathbf{R}_{uu}^2] & \operatorname{tr}\left[\mathbf{R}_{uu}^{3}\right] & \ldots & \operatorname{tr}\left[\mathbf{R}_{uu}^{M+1}\right] \\ \vdots & & & \\ \operatorname{tr}\left[\mathbf{R}_{uu}^{M-1}\right] & \operatorname{tr}\left[\mathbf{R}_{uu}^{M}\right] & \ldots & \operatorname{tr}\left[\mathbf{R}_{uu}^{2M-2}\right] \end{bmatrix} \begin{bmatrix} b_0 \\ b_1 \\ b_2 \\ \vdots \\ b_{M-1} \end{bmatrix} = \begin{bmatrix} \operatorname{tr}[\mathbf{K}] \\ \operatorname{tr}[\mathbf{K}\mathbf{R}_{uu}] \\ \operatorname{tr}\left[\mathbf{K}\mathbf{R}_{uu}^2\right] \\ \vdots \\ \operatorname{tr}\left[\mathbf{K}\mathbf{R}_{uu}^{M-1}\right] \end{bmatrix} \tag{73}$$

The trace of $\mathbf{R}_{uu}^0=\mathbf{I}$ is simply M, the system order. Due to the orthogonality property of the least squares solution, it is found that

$$\operatorname{tr}\left[\mathbf{K}^{\perp}\mathbf{R}_{uu}^{l}\right]=0, \tag{74}$$

for arbitrary values of l=0,1,2,....

As a further consequence terms of the form $\operatorname{tr}\left[\mathbf{R}_{uu}^{m}\mathbf{K}^{\perp}\mathbf{R}_{uu}^{l}\right]=0$, and thus $\mathbf{R}_{uu}^{m}\mathbf{K}^{\perp}\mathbf{R}_{uu}^{l}\in\mathcal{R}_u^{\perp}$, and any polynomial $P(\mathbf{R}_{uu})\in R_u$. Note that it is straightforward to extend the results to Hermitian matrices that occur for complex-valued processes.

Appendix 2: Relation to Higher Order Moments

Here, the second- and fourth-order moments are considered once a random process is Fourier-transformed by a unitary matrix **F**. Assume a random process x_k with the properties (9)–(17). Take M consecutive values of such process, build a vector $\mathbf{x}_k$, and convert it to its Fourier transform by $\mathbf{f}_k=\mathbf{F}\mathbf{x}_k$.

It is straightforward to show that the process f_k is zero mean if x_k is zero mean and, due to the unitary property of **F**, it is found that $m_{\mathrm{f}}^{(2)} = E[|f_k|^2] = 1$ as long as m(2)x=E[|xk|2]=1mx(2)=E[|xk|2]=1.

For the fourth-order moments, the expression $E[\mathbf{x}_k\mathbf{x}_k^T\mathbf{g}\mathbf{h}^H\mathbf{x}_k\mathbf{x}_k^T]$ is considered, where **g** and **h** are simply two different rows of **F**, thus $\mathbf{g}^H\mathbf{h}=\mathbf{g}^T\mathbf{h}=0$ and $\mathbf{g}^H\mathbf{g}=\mathbf{h}^H\mathbf{h}=1$. By $\mathbf{L}=\mathbf{g}\mathbf{h}^H$ in (21), it is found that

$$E\left[\mathbf{x}_k\mathbf{x}_k^T\mathbf{g}\mathbf{h}^H\mathbf{x}_k\mathbf{x}_k^T\right]=m_{\mathrm{x}}^{(2,2)}\left(\mathbf{g}\mathbf{h}^H+\mathbf{h}^*\mathbf{g}^T\right)+m_{\mathrm{x}}^{(2,2)}\mathrm{tr}[\,\mathbf{g}\mathbf{h}^H]\mathbf{I} + \left(m_{\mathrm{x}}^{(4)} - 3m_{\mathrm{x}}^{(2,2)}\right)\mathrm{diag}[\,\mathbf{g}\mathbf{h}^H]. \tag{75}$$

From here, the following can be computed:

$$\begin{aligned} m_{\mathrm{f}}^{(2,2)} &= E\left[\mathbf{g}^H\mathbf{x}_k\mathbf{x}_k^T\mathbf{g}\mathbf{h}^H\mathbf{x}_k\mathbf{x}_k^T\mathbf{h}\right] \\ &= m_{\mathrm{x}}^{(2,2)} + \left(m_{\mathrm{x}}^{(4)} - 3m_{\mathrm{x}}^{(2,2)}\right)\sum |g_i|^2|h_i|^2 \\ &= m_{\mathrm{x}}^{(2,2)} + \left(m_{\mathrm{x}}^{(4)} - 3m_{\mathrm{x}}^{(2,2)}\right)\frac{1}{M} \\ &= m_{\mathrm{x}}^{(2,2)}\left(1+\left(\frac{m_{\mathrm{x}}^{(4)}}{m_{\mathrm{x}}^{(2,2)}}-3\right)\frac{1}{M}\right) = m_{\mathrm{x}}^{(2,2)}\gamma_{\mathrm{x}}. \end{aligned} \tag{76}$$

The latter relation is simply due to the fact that each element of the DFT matrix **F** is a rotation scaled by $1/\sqrt{M}$. For M→∞, it is concluded that $m_f^{(2,2)} = m_x^{(2,2)}$. The result would not change if $\mathbf{x}_k \in$IC. It is in fact this equivalence that convinced us to use $m^{(2,2)}$ rather than $m^{(4)}$ in our formulations. Note also that the term γ_x from (25) shows up here again. It is thus the correction term for the joint fourth-order moment that only has an impact on small filter dimensions.

Similarly, for the fourth-order moment, select **g**=**h** and obtain $m_{\mathrm{f}}^{(4)} \le 2m_{\mathrm{x}}^{(2,2)} + \left(m_{\mathrm{x}}^{(4)} - 3m_{\mathrm{x}}^{(2,2)}\right)\frac{1}{M}$ and again for large $M,\, m_{\mathrm{f}}^{(4)} = 2m_{\mathrm{x}}^{(2,2)}$ remains, also independently of whether x_k is from IR or IC. Finally, $E[f_kf_lf_mf_m] \le \left(m_{\mathrm{x}}^{(4)} - 3m_{\mathrm{x}}^{(2,2)}\right)\frac{1}{M}$ once $k \ne l \ne m$ and thus for large M: $E[f_kf_lf_mf_m] \to 0$. The properties of the driving process are thus preserved under DFT for very long filters. Furthermore, regardless of the input process, after DFT of the long sequence, it is always found that $m_{\mathrm{f}}^{(4)} = 2m_{\mathrm{f}}^{(2,2)}$, which significantly simplifies subsequent analysis.

REFERENCES

1. B Widrow, ME Hoff Jr, in IRE WESCON Conv. Rec, Part 4. Adaptive switching circuits, (1960), pp. 96–104.
2. E Hänsler, G Schmidt, Acoustic Echo and Noise Control (John Wiley & Sons, Chichester, New York, Brisabne, Toronto, Singapore, 2004). M Rupp, Convergence properties of adaptive equalizer algorithms. IEEE Trans. Signal Process.59(6), 2562–2574 (2011).
3. AH Sayed, M Rupp, in Proc. SPIE 1995. A time-domain feedback analysis of adaptive gradient algorithms via the small gain theorem (San Diego, USA, 1995), pp. 458–469.
4. M Rupp, AH Sayed, A time-domain feedback analysis of filtered-error adaptive gradient algorithms. IEEE Trans. Signal Process.44(6), 1428–1439 (1996). doi:http://dx.doi.org/10.1109/78.506609.
5. AH Sayed, M Rupp, Error-energy bounds for adaptive gradient algorithms. IEEE Trans. Signal Process.44(8), 1982–1989 (1996). doi:http://dx.doi.org/10.1109/78.533719.
6. AH Sayed, M Rupp, in The DSP Handbook. Robustness issues in adaptive filtering (CRC PressFlorida, 1998).
7. G Ungerboeck, Theory on the speed of convergence in adaptive equalizers for digital communication. IBM J. Res. Dev.16(6), 546–555 (1972).
8. LL Horowitz, KD Senne, Performance advantage of complex LMS for controlling narrow-band adaptive arrays. IEEE Trans. Signal Process.29:, 722–736 (1981).
9. A Feuer, E Weinstein, Convergence analysis of LMS filters with uncorrelated Gaussian data. IEEE Trans. Acoust. Speech Signal Process.ASSP–33(1), 222–230 (1985).
10. M Rupp, The behavior of LMS and NLMS algorithms in the presence of spherically invariant processes. IEEE Trans. Signal Process.41(3), 1149–1160 (1993).
11. M Rupp, Adaptive filters: Stable but not convergent. EURASIP J. Adv. Signal Process. (2015).

12. S Haykin, Adaptive Filter Theory (Prentice–Hall, Inf. and System Sciences Series, Englewood Cliffs, NJ, 1986).

13. JE Mazo, On the independence theory of equalizer convergence. Bell Syst. Technical J.58(5), 963–993 (1979).

14. R Nitzberg, Normalized LMS algorithm degradation due to estimation noise. IEEE Trans. Aerospace Electron. Syst.AES-22(6), 740–750 (1986). doi:http://dx.doi.org/10.1109/TAES.1986.310809.

15. Macchi, Adaptive Processing (John Wiley & Sons, Chichester, New York, Brisabne, Toronto, Singapore, 1995).

16. V Solo, X Kong, Adaptive Signal Processing Algorithms. Prentice-Hall information and system sciences series (Prentice-Hall, Englewood Cliffs (NJ), USA, 1995).

17. H-J Butterweck, in International Conference on Acoustics, Speech, and Signal Processing (ICASSP-95), 2. A steady-state analysis of the LMS adaptive algorithm without use of the independence assumption, (1995), pp. 1404–1407. doi:http://dx.doi.org/10.1109/ICASSP.1995.480504.

18. SC Douglas, TH-Y Meng, in Proc. IEEE International Conf. on Acoustics, Speech, and Signal Processing. Exact expectation analysis of the LMS adaptive filter without the independence assumption (San Francisco, CA, 1992), pp. 61–64.

19. SC Douglas, W Pan, Exact expectation analysis of the LMS adaptive filter. IEEE Trans. Signal Process.43(12), 2863–2871 (1995). doi:http://dx.doi.org/10.1109/78.476430.

20. TY Al-Naffouri, AH Sayed, Transient analysis of data-normalized adaptive filters. IEEE Trans. Signal Process.51(3), 639–652 (2003). doi:http://dx.doi.org/10.1109/TSP.2002.808106.

21. AH Sayed, Fundamentals of Adaptive Filtering (John Wiley & Sons, Inc., Hoboken (NJ), USA, 2003).

22. H-J Butterweck, Iterative analysis of the steady-state weight fluctuations in LMS-type adaptive filters. IEEE Trans. Signal Process.47(9), 2558–2561 (1999).

23. H-J Butterweck, A wave theory of long adaptive filters. IEEE Trans. Circ. Syst. I: Fundamental Theory Appl.48(6), 739–747 (2001).

24. H-J Butterweck, Steady-state analysis of the long LMS adaptive filter. Signal Process. Elsevier. 91(4), 690–701 (2011). doi:http://dx.doi.org/10.1016/j.sigpro.2010.07.015.

25. SJM de Almeida, JCM Bermudez, NJ Bershad, A stochastic model for a pseudo affine projection algorithm. IEEE Trans. Signal Process.57:, 117–118 (2009).

26. HIK Rao, B Farhang-Boroujeny, Analysis of the stereophonic LMS/Newton algorithm and impact of signal nonlinearity on its convergence behavior. IEEE Trans. Signal Process.58(12), 6080–6092 (2010). doi:http://dx.doi.org/10.1109/TSP.2010.2074198.

27. M Rupp, H-J Butterweck, in Proc. of the 37th Asilomar Conference, 1. Overcoming the independence assumption in LMS filtering, (2003), pp. 607–611.

28. DG Manolakis, VK Ingle, SM Kogon, Statistical and Adaptive Signal Processing (Artech House, Boston, London, 2005).

29. WA Gardner, Learning characteristics of stochastic gradient descent algorithms: a general study, analysis and critique. Signal Process.6(2), 113–133 (1984).

30. RM Gray, Toeplitz and Circulant Matrices: A Review. Foundations and Trends in Communications and Information Theory, vol. 2 (Now publisher, Delft, 2006).

31. VH Nascimento, AH Sayed, On the learning mechanism of adaptive filters. IEEE Trans. Signal Process.48(6), 1609–1625 (2000). doi:http://dx.doi.org/10.1109/78.845919.

32. NJ Bershad, Analysis of the normalized LMS algorithm with Gaussian inputs. IEEE Trans. Acoust. Speech Signal Process.34(4), 793–806 (1986).

33. M Rupp, Bursting in the LMS algorithm. IEEE Trans. Signal Process.43(10), 2414–2417 (1995).

CHAPTER 2

ASYMPTOTIC STABILITY ANALYSIS AND OPTIMALITY ALGORITHM FOR UNCERTAIN NEUTRAL SYSTEMS WITH SATURATION

Xinghua Liu

Department of Auto, School of Information Science and Technology, University of Science and Technology of China, Anhui 230027, China

ABSTRACT

The certain and uncertain neutral systems with time-delay and saturating actuator are considered in this paper. In order to analyze and optimize the system, auxiliary functions are presented based on additive decomposition approach and the relationship among them is discussed. As the novel stability criterion, two sufficient conditions are obtained for asymptotic stability of the neutral systems. Furthermore, the paper gives the stability analysis algorithm and optimality algorithm to optimize the result. Finally, from the two-stage dissolution tank of solid caustic soda in a chemical plant, three numerical examples are implemented to show the effectiveness of the proposed method.

INTRODUCTION

Delay is often inevitable in various practical systems; examples include population ecology [1], steam or water pipes, heat exchanges [2], and many others [3–5]. In the control engineering language, these delays can be categorized as state delay, input or output delay (retarded systems), delay in the state derivative (neutral systems), and so forth. Guaranteeing the stability of systems with delay is one core design objective both in theory and in practice. Particularly, in terms of neutral systems, the focus has mainly been on systems with identical delays in neutral and discrete terms [6–10]. Results also exist that depend only on the size of the discrete delays but not on the size of the neutral delays [11–13].

Citation: Xinghua Liu, "Asymptotic Stability Analysis and Optimality Algorithm for Uncertain Neutral Systems with Saturation," ISRN Applied Mathematics, vol. 2014, Article ID 805798, 14 pages, 2014. doi:10.1155/2014/805798

Besides delays, the saturated controller is apt to cause instability as well. In the presence of actuator saturation, the problem of estimating asymptotic stability regions for linear systems subject to it has been studied by many researches in the past years in [14]. Generally speaking, the existing methods for estimating the stability regions for linear systems with saturating actuators are based on the concept of Lyapunov level set. LMI optimization-based approaches were proposed to estimate the stability regions by using quadratic Lyapunov functions and the Lur's-type Lyapunov functions in [15–19].

For the studies in response to both issues of delay and saturation, the sufficient conditions for systems with delay and saturated actuator are obtained in [18, 20–22]; Lyapunov-Krasovskii functional is employed to investigate the delay-dependent robust stabilization for uncertain neutral systems with saturated actuators in [20]; a controller is constructed in terms of linear matrix inequalities using descriptor model transformation in [18], just to name a few. However, this paper wants to provide a new method to find the system stability region and give the optimality algorithm to obtain the largest region in this method. Besides, it gives the application in the chemical process of the plant.

In this paper, a novel Lyapunov functional is proposed based on the delay-dividing approach, which leads to less conservative stability conditions for linear systems with time-delay and saturated actuator. This is done by introducing auxiliary functions based on the additive decomposition approach [23]. We also propose an algorithm to obtain the optimal auxiliary function. Finally, we design a two-stage dissolution tank of the chemical process by modeling it as a neutral delay system with actuator saturation and demonstrate the effectiveness of the proposed method.

Notations. $\star$ denotes the symmetric part to be a symmetric block matrix, $\mathbb{R}^n$ denotes the n dimensional Euclidean space, and $\mathbb{R}^{m\times n}$ is the set of all real $m\times n$ matrices. I is the identity matrix with proper dimensions. C_0 is the set of all continuous functions from $[-\tau, 0]$ to $\mathbb{R}^n$ where τ is a constant representing the neutral time-delay. A^T is the transpose of matrix A. $|A| = [|a_{ij}|]$, with $A = [a_{ij}]$. For real symmetric matrices X and Y, the notation $X\geq Y$ (respectively, $X>Y$) means that the matrix $X-Y$ is positive semidefinite (respectively, positive definite). $\lambda_{\max(\min)}(A)$ is the eigenvalue of matrix A with maximum (minimum) real part. $\|V\|$ is the Euclidean norm of vector V, $\|V\|=(V^TV)^{1/2}$, while $\|A\|$ is spectral norm of matrix A, $\|A\| = [\lambda_{\max}(A^TA)]^{1/2}$. ρ represents the domain of attraction. diag$\{\cdot\ \cdot\ \cdot\}$ denotes a block-diagonal matrix decided by the corresponding elements in the brace and finally $B(\rho) = \{y \in R^n : \|y\| \leq \rho\}$.

PROBLEM STATEMENT AND PRELIMINARIES

The following neutral system with time-delay and actuator saturation is considered:

$$\dot{x}(t) - D\dot{x}(t-\tau) = Ax(t) + Bx(t-h) + C\,\mathrm{Sat}(u(t)), \tag{1}$$

where $x(t) \in \mathbb{R}^n$ is the system state and $u(t)$ is the control input. $h > 0$ is the constant discrete time delay and $\tau>0$ is the constant neutral time-delay. A, B, C, and D are known real constant parameter matrices of appropriate dimensions with $\|D\| < 1$. Sat$(\cdot)$ is used to denote the standard saturation function defined for $u = [u_1, u_2,...,u_m]$:

$$\mathrm{Sat}(u) = [\mathrm{Sat}(u_1), \mathrm{Sat}(u_2), \ldots, \mathrm{Sat}(u_m)]^T,$$

$$\mathrm{Sat}(u_i) = \begin{cases} u_i^+ & \text{if } u_i > u_i^+ \\ u_i & \text{otherwise} \\ -u_i^+ & \text{if } u_i < -u_i^+. \end{cases} \tag{2}$$

The following linear state feedback is to be designed:

$$u(t) = -Kx(t), \tag{3}$$

where the linear state feedback gain $K = [K_1^T, K_2^T, \ldots, K_m^T]^T$; $K_i \in \mathbb{R}^n$ is an n-dimensional row vector.

Here we have slightly abused the notation by using Sat to denote both a scalar valued and a vector valued function. We have also assumed a unity saturation level for the saturation function without loss of generality.

Define $Dz(u(t)) = u(t) - \mathrm{Sat}(u(t))$ where $Dz(u(t)) = [dz(u_1), dz(u_2), \ldots, dz(u_m)]^T$ and

$$dz(u_i) = \begin{cases} u_i - u_i^+ & \text{if } u_i > u_i^+ \\ 0 & \text{otherwise} \\ u_i + u_i^+ & \text{if } u_i < -u_i^+. \end{cases} \tag{4}$$

The saturated system can now be written as follows:

$$\dot{x}(t) - D\dot{x}(t-\tau) = A_c x(t) + Bx(t-h) + CDz(Kx(t)), \tag{5}$$

where $A_c = A - CK$.

The neutral system (5) then leads to the following by model transformation:

$$\frac{d}{dt}[\mathscr{L}(x(t))] = \widehat{A}_c x(t) + CDz(Kx), \tag{6}$$

where $\widehat{A}_c = A_c + B = A + B - CK$ and $\mathscr{L}(x(t)) = x(t) - Dx(t-\tau) + B\int_{t-h}^{t} x(s)ds$.

The following definitions and lemmas are required before proceeding with the main contributions presented in the next section.

Definition 1 (see [24]). The operator $\mathscr{L} : C_0 \to \mathbb{R}^n$ is said to be stable if the zero solution of the homogeneous difference equation

$$\mathscr{L}(x(t)) = 0, \quad t \geq 0,$$

$$x_0 = \psi \in \{\varphi \in C_0 : \mathscr{L}\varphi = 0\} \tag{7}$$

is uniformly asymptotically stable. The stability of operator $\mathscr{L}$ is necessary for the stability of neutral system (1) with (3), which is always satisfied when $\||h|B| + D\| < 1$.

Lemma 2 (see [24]). For any matrix $B, D \in \mathbb{R}^{m\times n}$, if $\||h|B| + D\| < 1$, then the operator $\mathscr{L} : C_0 \to \mathbb{R}^n$ with

$$\mathscr{L}(x(t)) = x(t) + B\int_{t-h}^{t} x(s)\,ds - Dx(t-\tau) \tag{8}$$

is stable.

Lemma 3 (see [25]). Let $U \in \mathbb{R}^{n\times n}$ and $V \in \mathbb{R}^{n\times n}$, and let $x \in \mathbb{R}^n$. Then we have

$$x^T UVx \leq \|UV\|\, x^T x \leq \|U\|\,\|V\|\, x^T x,$$

$$2x^T UVx \leq x^T\left(\frac{1}{\gamma}UU^T + \gamma V^T V\right)x, \quad \forall\gamma > 0. \tag{9}$$

Definition 4 (see [23]). Auxiliary functions $W_1(\rho_1)$ and $W_2(\rho_2)$ are described in the following

$$W_1(\rho_1) = \begin{cases} \sum_{i=1}^{m}\left(1 - \frac{u_i^+}{\|K_i\|\rho_1}\right)^2 K_i^T K_i & \text{if } \|K_i\|\rho_1 > u_i^+, \\ 0 & \text{otherwise,} \end{cases}$$

$$W_2(\rho_2) = \begin{cases} \sum_{i=1}^{m}\left(\frac{\rho_2}{4u_i^+}\right)^2 \left(K_i^T K_i\right)^2 & \text{if } \|K_i\|\rho_2 > u_i^+, \\ 0 & \text{otherwise.} \end{cases} \tag{10}$$

MAIN RESULTS

In this section, we firstly construct the auxiliary functions $W_3(\rho_3)$, $W_4(\rho_4)$, . . . , $W_n(\rho_n)$ using the geometric method and with them present a new delay-dependent stabilization criterion. Then the relationship between those auxiliary functions is explored which helps to obtain the optimal $W(\rho_i)$.

Consider the polynomial function $y = ax^n$ which is tangent with saturated function $y = x - u_i^+$ in positive axis. a can be firstly determined by the geometric relation and auxiliary polynomial functions can be obtained.

Let

$$y = ax^n,$$

$$y = x - u_i^+. \tag{11}$$

The slope of polynomial function $y = ax^n$ equals to 1 at the tangent point. Thus we have

$$\dot{y} = anx^{n-1} = 1. \tag{12}$$

It can be determined by solving the resulting equations simultaneously and we obtain

$$a = \left(\frac{n-1}{u_i^+}\right)^{n-1}\frac{1}{n^n}. \tag{13}$$

Noting in the polynomial function, we replace x with u_i here so that they have the same independent variable with $d(u_i)$. Consider

$$y = \left(\frac{n-1}{u_i^+}\right)^{n-1}\frac{1}{n^n}u_i^n. \tag{14}$$

Thus we compare the nonlinear function $d(u_i)$ with the polynomial function above. For simplicity, we consider the cases n=2 and n=3. As shown in Figure 1, the graphics of quadratic and cubic polynomial functions are above the graphic of $|d(u_i)|$.

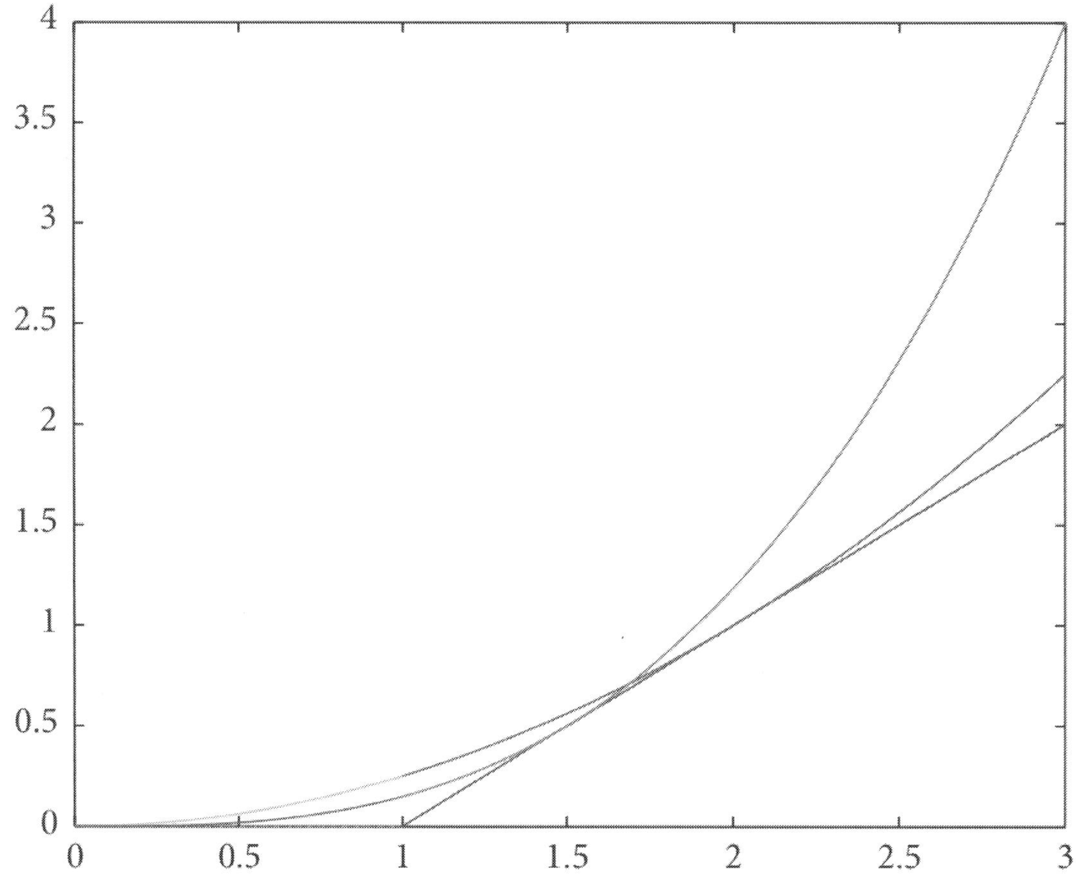

Figure 1: Two polynomial functions are $y=\left(1/4u_i^+\right)u_i^2$ and $y=\left(4/27\right)\left(1/4u_i^+\right)^2 u_i^3$ (when $u_i^+=2$) and the piecewise linear function is $dz(u_i)$.

Furthermore, according to the nature of the polynomial function when $n = 4, 5, \ldots$, the graphic of function $y=\left((n-1)/u_i^+\right)^{n-1}\left(1/n^n\right)u_i^n$ is also above the graphic of $|dz(u_i)|$. So we have the following inequality:

$$|dz(u_i)| \leq \left(\frac{n-1}{u_i^+}\right)^{n-1} \frac{1}{n^n} u_i^n, \tag{15}$$

where $n = 2, 3, 4, \ldots$.

Lemma 5. When $n = 2, 3, 4, \ldots$, the following inequality holds:

$$Dz^T(Kx(t))\,Dz(Kx(t)) \leq x^T W_n(\rho_n)\,x, \tag{16}$$

where

$$W_n(\rho_n) = \begin{cases} \sum_{i=1}^{m} \left(\frac{(n-1)\rho_n}{n^{n/(n-1)}u_i^+}\right)^{2n-2} \left(K_i^T K_i\right)^n & if\ \|K_i\|\rho_n > u_i^+ \\ 0 & otherwise. \end{cases} \tag{17}$$

Proof. From (15) we obtain that

$$
\begin{aligned}
Dz^{T}(Kx)\,Dz(Kx) &= \sum_{i=1}^{m} dz^{2}(u_i) \\
&\le \sum_{i=1}^{m}\left(\frac{n-1}{u_i^{+}}\right)^{2n-2}\frac{1}{n^{2n}}u_i^{2n} \\
&\le \sum_{i=1}^{m}\left(\frac{n-1}{u_i^{+}}\right)^{2n-2} \\
&\quad \times \frac{1}{n^{2n}}x^{T}K_i^{T}K_i x\cdots x^{T}K_i^{T}K_i x \\
&\le \sum_{i=1}^{m}\left(\frac{n-1}{u_i^{+}}\right)^{2n-2} \\
&\quad \times \frac{1}{n^{2n}}\left\|xx^{T}\right\|^{n-1}x^{T}K_i^{T}K_i\cdots K_i^{T}K_i x \\
&\le \sum_{i=1}^{m}\left(\frac{n-1}{u_i^{+}}\right)^{2n-2}\frac{1}{n^{2n}}\rho_n^{2n-2}x^{T}\left(K_i^{T}K_i\right)^{n}x \\
&\le x^{T}W_n(\rho_n)\,x.
\end{aligned}
\tag{18}
$$

This completes the proof.

Asymptotic Stability for Certain Neutral System

Theorem 6. The neutral system with time-delay and actuator saturation as described in (1) and (3) is asymptotic stability if $\|h|B| + D\| < 1$ and there exist scalars $\gamma_i > 0$, $i = 1, 2, 3$, $P > 0$, $\widehat{P} > 0$, $Q = [Q_{ij}]_{2\times 2}$, $Q_{ij} > 0$, $R = [R_{ij}]_{2\times 2}$, $R_{ij} > 0$, $T_i > 0$ ($i = 1, 2, 3, 4, 5, 6$), and $\tilde{T}_i > 0$ ($i = 3, 4$) such that the following symmetric linear matrix inequality holds:

$$
\Phi = \begin{bmatrix}
\Phi_{11} & \Phi_{12} & 0 & \Phi_{14} & \Phi_{15} & \Phi_{16} & 0 \\
\star & \Phi_{22} & \Phi_{23} & 0 & 0 & 0 & 0 \\
\star & \star & \Phi_{33} & 0 & 0 & 0 & 0 \\
\star & \star & \star & \Phi_{44} & \Phi_{45} & 0 & 0 \\
\star & \star & \star & \star & \Phi_{55} & 0 & 0 \\
\star & \star & \star & \star & \star & \Phi_{66} & 0 \\
\star & \star & \star & \star & \star & \star & \Phi_{77}
\end{bmatrix} < 0,
\tag{19}
$$

where

$$
W_n(\rho) = \begin{cases}
\displaystyle\sum_{i=1}^{m}\left(\frac{(n-1)\rho_n}{n^{n/(n-1)}u_i^{+}}\right)^{2n-2}\left(K_i^{T}K_i\right)^{n} & if\ \ \|K_i\|\rho_n > u_i^{+}, \\
0 & otherwise,
\end{cases}
$$

$$
\begin{aligned}
\Phi_{11} &= \widehat{A}_c^{T}P + P\widehat{A}_c + \frac{1}{\gamma_1}\widehat{P} + (\gamma_1+\gamma_2+\gamma_3)\left\|C^{T}C\right\|W_i(\rho_i) \\
&\quad + Q_{11} + R_{11} + T_1 + T_2 + \frac{h^2}{2}\left(\tilde{T}_3 + T_5\right) + \frac{\tau^2}{2}\left(\tilde{T}_4 + T_6\right),
\end{aligned}
$$

$$\Phi_{22} = Q_{22} - Q_{11},$$

$$\Phi_{33} = -Q_{22} - T_1,$$

$$\Phi_{44} = R_{22} - R_{11},$$

$$\Phi_{55} = \frac{1}{\gamma_2} D^T \widehat{P} D - R_{22} - T_2,$$

$$\Phi_{66} = \frac{1}{\gamma_3} B^T \widehat{P} B - T_3,$$

$$\Phi_{77} = -T_4,$$

$$\Phi_{12} = Q_{12},$$

$$\Phi_{14} = R_{12},$$

$$\Phi_{15} = -\widehat{A}_c^T PD,$$

$$\Phi_{16} = \widehat{A}_c^T PB,$$

$$\Phi_{23} = -Q_{12},$$

$$\Phi_{45} = -R_{12}. \tag{20}$$

Proof. Define a legitimate Lyapunov functional candidate as follows:

$$V(x(t)) = V_1(x(t)) + V_2(x(t)) + V_3(x(t)) + V_4(x(t)) + V_5(x(t)) + V_6(x(t)), \tag{21}$$

where

$$V_1(x(t)) = \mathscr{L}^T(x(t)) P \mathscr{L}(x(t)),$$

$$V_2(x(t)) = \int_{t-(h/2)}^{t} \begin{bmatrix} x(s) \\ x\left(s - \frac{h}{2}\right) \end{bmatrix}^T \begin{bmatrix} Q_{11} & Q_{12} \\ \star & Q_{22} \end{bmatrix} \times \begin{bmatrix} x(s) \\ x\left(s - \frac{h}{2}\right) \end{bmatrix} ds + \int_{t-(\tau/2)}^{t} \begin{bmatrix} x(s) \\ x\left(s - \frac{\tau}{2}\right) \end{bmatrix}^T \times \begin{bmatrix} R_{11} & R_{12} \\ \star & R_{22} \end{bmatrix} \begin{bmatrix} x(s) \\ x\left(s - \frac{\tau}{2}\right) \end{bmatrix} ds,$$

$$V_3(x(t)) = \int_{t-h}^{t} x^T(s) T_1 x(s)\, ds + \int_{t-\tau}^{t} x^T(s) T_2 x(s)\, ds,$$

$$V_4(x(t)) = \int_{t-h}^{t} \left[\int_s^t x^T(s_1)\, ds_1\right] T_3 \left[\int_s^t x(s_2)\, ds_2\right] ds,$$

$$V_5(x(t)) = \int_{t-\tau}^{t} \left[\int_s^t x^T(s_1)\, ds_1\right] T_4 \left[\int_s^t x^T(s_2)\, ds_2\right] ds, \tag{22}$$

$$V_6(x(t)) = \frac{1}{2}\int_{t-h}^{t}(s-t+h)^2 x^T(s)\,T_5 x(s)\,ds$$

$$+\frac{1}{2}\int_{t-\tau}^{t}(s-t+\tau)^2 x^T(s)\,T_6 x(s)\,ds, \tag{23}$$

where $P > 0$, $Q = [Q_{ij}]_{2\times 2}$, $Q_{ij} > 0$, $R = [R_{ij}]_{2\times 2}$, $R_{ij} > 0$, and $T_i > 0$, $i = 1, 2, 3, 4, 5, 6$.

Then

$$\dot V(x(t)) = \dot V_1(x(t)) + \dot V_2(x(t)) + \dot V_3(x(t))$$

$$+\dot V_4(x(t)) + \dot V_5(x(t)) + \dot V_6(x(t)). \tag{24}$$

By (19)-(22), we obtain that

$$\dot V_1(x(t)) = 2\left\{x^T(t) - x^T(t-\tau)D^T + \left[\int_{t-h}^{t} x^T(s)\,ds\right]B^T\right\}$$

$$\times P\left[\widehat{A}_c x(t) + CDz(Kx)\right]$$

$$= 2x^T P\widehat{A}_c x + 2x^T PCDz(Kx) - 2x^T \widehat{A}_c^T PDx(t-\tau)$$

$$- 2x^T(t-\tau)D^T PCDz(Kx)$$

$$+ 2x^T(t)\widehat{A}_c^T PB\left[\int_{t-h}^{t} x(s)\,ds\right]$$

$$+ 2\left[\int_{t-h}^{t} x^T(s)\,ds\right]B^T PCDz(Kx)$$

$$\le x^T\left[\widehat{A}_c^T P + P\widehat{A}_c + \frac{1}{\gamma_1}\widehat{P}\right.$$

$$\left. + (\gamma_1 + \gamma_2 + \gamma_3)\left\|C^T C\right\| W_i(\rho_i)\right] x$$

$$+ \frac{1}{\gamma_2}x^T(t-\tau)D^T\widehat{P}Dx(t-\tau)$$

$$+ \frac{1}{\gamma_3}\left[\int_{t-h}^{t} x^T(s)\,ds\right]B^T\widehat{P}B\left[\int_{t-h}^{t} x(s)\,ds\right]$$

$$- 2x^T(t)\widehat{A}_c^T PDx(t-\tau)$$

$$+ 2x^T(t)\widehat{A}_c^T PB\left[\int_{t-h}^{t} x(s)\,ds\right], \tag{25}$$

where $\widehat{P} > 0$, since $\widehat{P} = P^2$. Consider

$$\dot{V}_2(x(t)) = \begin{bmatrix} x(t) \\ x\left(t-\frac{h}{2}\right) \end{bmatrix}^T \begin{bmatrix} Q_{11} & Q_{12} \\ \star & Q_{22} \end{bmatrix} \begin{bmatrix} x(t) \\ x\left(t-\frac{h}{2}\right) \end{bmatrix}$$

$$- \begin{bmatrix} x\left(t-\frac{h}{2}\right) \\ x(t-h) \end{bmatrix}^T \begin{bmatrix} Q_{11} & Q_{12} \\ \star & Q_{22} \end{bmatrix} \begin{bmatrix} x\left(t-\frac{h}{2}\right) \\ x(t-h) \end{bmatrix}$$

$$+ \begin{bmatrix} x(t) \\ x\left(t-\frac{\tau}{2}\right) \end{bmatrix}^T \begin{bmatrix} R_{11} & R_{12} \\ \star & R_{22} \end{bmatrix} \begin{bmatrix} x(t) \\ x\left(t-\frac{\tau}{2}\right) \end{bmatrix}$$

$$- \begin{bmatrix} x\left(t-\frac{\tau}{2}\right) \\ x(t-\tau) \end{bmatrix}^T \begin{bmatrix} R_{11} & R_{12} \\ \star & R_{22} \end{bmatrix} \begin{bmatrix} x\left(t-\frac{\tau}{2}\right) \\ x(t-\tau) \end{bmatrix},$$

$$\dot{V}_3(x(t)) = x^T(t)T_1x(t) - x^T(t-h)T_1x(t-h)$$

$$+ x^T(t)T_2x(t) - x^T(t-\tau)T_2x(t-\tau),$$

$$\dot{V}_4(x(t)) = -\left[\int_{t-h}^{t} x^T(s_1)\,ds_1\right] T_3 \left[\int_{t-h}^{t} x(s_2)\,ds_2\right]$$

$$+ \int_{t-h}^{t} x^T(t)T_3\left[\int_{s}^{t} x(s_2)\,ds_2\right] ds$$

$$+ \int_{t-h}^{t} \left[\int_{s}^{t} x(s_2)\,ds_2\right] T_3x(t)\,ds$$

$$= -\left[\int_{t-h}^{t} x^T(s_1)\,ds_1\right] T_3 \left[\int_{t-h}^{t} x(s_2)\,ds_2\right]$$

$$+ \int_{t-h}^{t} (s-t+h)\,x^T(t)T_3x(s)\,ds$$

$$+ \int_{t-h}^{t} (s-t+h)\,x^T(s)T_3x(t)\,ds$$

$$= -\left[\int_{t-h}^{t} x^T(s_1)\,ds_1\right] T_3 \left[\int_{t-h}^{t} x(s_2)\,ds_2\right]$$

$$- \int_{t-h}^{t} (s-t+h)\left(T_3x(t) - T_5x(s)\right)^T$$

$$\times T_5^{-1}\left(T_3x(t) - T_5x(s)\right) ds$$

$$+ \frac{h^2}{2} x^T(t)T_3T_5^{-1}T_3x(t)$$

$$+ \int_{t-h}^{t} (s-t+h)\,x^T(s)T_5x(s)\,ds$$

$$\leq -\left[\int_{t-h}^{t} x^T(s_1)\,ds_1\right] T_3 \left[\int_{t-h}^{t} x(s_2)\,ds_2\right]$$

$$+\frac{h^2}{2} x^T(t)\,\tilde{T}_3 x(t)$$

$$+\int_{t-h}^{t} (s-t+h)\,x^T(s)\,T_5 x(s)\,ds, \tag{26}$$

where $\tilde{T}_3 > 0$, since $\tilde{T}_3 = T_3 T_5^{-1} T_3$.

Similarly we have

$$\dot{V}_5(x(t)) \leq -\left[\int_{t-\tau}^{t} x^T(s_1)\,ds_1\right] T_4 \left[\int_{t-\tau}^{t} x(s_2)\,ds_2\right]$$

$$+\frac{\tau^2}{2} x^T(t)\,\tilde{T}_4 x(t)$$

$$+\int_{t-\tau}^{t} (s-t+\tau)\,x^T(s)\,T_6 x(s)\,ds, \tag{27}$$

where $\tilde{T}_4 > 0$, since $\tilde{T}_4 = T_4 T_6^{-1} T_4$. Consider

$$\dot{V}_6(x(t))$$

$$= \frac{1}{2} h^2 x^T(t)\,T_5 x(t) - \int_{t-h}^{t} (s-t+h)\,x^T(s)\,T_5 x(s)\,ds$$

$$+\frac{1}{2}\tau^2 x^T(t)\,T_6 x(t) - \int_{t-\tau}^{t} (s-t+\tau)\,x^T(s)\,T_6 x(s)\,ds. \tag{28}$$

Substituting these into (24), the time-derivative of V has new upper bound as follows:

$$\dot{V}(x(t)) \leq \xi^T(t)\,\Phi\,\xi(t), \tag{29}$$

where

$$\xi^T(t) = \left[x^T(t)\;\; x^T\left(t-\frac{h}{2}\right)\;\; x^T(t-h)\;\; x^T\left(t-\frac{\tau}{2}\right)\;\; x^T(t-\tau)\;\; \int_{t-h}^{t} x^T(s)\,ds\;\; \int_{t-\tau}^{t} x^T(s)\,ds\right]; \tag{30}$$

Φ is defined as stated in (19)

If linear matrix inequality (19) is feasible, then we can get $\dot{V}((t)) < 0$, for all $x \in B(\rho)$. Therefore, if constant scalar h, constant parameter matrices B, D such that $\|h|B| + D\| < 1$ and there exist $P > 0$, $\tilde{P} > 0$, $Q = [Q_{ij}]_{2\times 2}$, $Q_{ij} > 0$, $R = [R_{ij}]_{2\times 2}$, $R_{ij} > 0$, $T_i > 0$ ($i = 1, 2, 3, 4, 5, 6$), and $\tilde{T}_i > 0$ ($i = 3, 4$) satisfying (19) for real scalars $\gamma_i > 0$ ($i = 1, 2, 3$), from Hale and Verduyn Lunel [24], we can draw the neutral system which can be described by (1) and (3) is asymptotic stability. This completes the proof.

***Remark** 7.* $W(\rho_i)(i = 1, 2, \ldots, n)$ are created by the parameter ρi which is a measure tool for domain of attraction. With these functions, we obtain the novel stability criterion. However, in Theorem 6 we need to look for the largest value of ρ_i with the optimal $W(\rho_i)$. These can be seen in Section 3.3 below.

Remark 8. Remark 8. Theorem 6 gives a delay-dependent stability criterion for neutral system with (1) and (3) using a delay-dividing approach. The delay differential conditions in other works, such as in [26], are usually more strict. These facts mean that our result is less conservative than some previous approaches.

The delay-dependent stability criterion for system (1) with $\tau\equiv h$ is presented in the following corollary.

Corollary 9. The neutral systems (1) and (3) with $\tau \equiv h$ are asymptotic stability if $\|h|B|+D\| < 1$ and there exist $P > 0$, $\hat{P} > 0$, $Q = [Q_{ij}]_{2\times 2}$, $Q_{ij} > 0$, $T_i > 0$ $(i = 1, 2, 3)$, and $\tilde{T}_2 > 0$ such that the following symmetric linear matrix inequality holds for real constant scalars $\gamma_i > 0$, $i = 1, 2, 3$:

$$\overline{\Phi} = \begin{bmatrix} \overline{\Phi}_{11} & \overline{\Phi}_{12} & \overline{\Phi}_{13} & \overline{\Phi}_{14} \\ \star & \overline{\Phi}_{22} & \overline{\Phi}_{23} & 0 \\ \star & \star & \overline{\Phi}_{33} & 0 \\ \star & \star & \star & \overline{\Phi}_{44} \end{bmatrix} < 0, \tag{31}$$

where $W_i(\rho_i)$, $i = 1, 2, 3, \ldots, n$, are defined as before. Consider

$$\overline{\Phi}_{11} = \widehat{A}_c^T P + P\widehat{A}_c + \frac{1}{\gamma_1}\widehat{P} + (\gamma_1 + \gamma_2 + \gamma_3)\left\|C^T C\right\| W_i(\rho_i$$
$$+ Q_{11} + T_1 + \frac{h^2}{2}\left(\widetilde{T}_2 + T_3\right),$$
$$\overline{\Phi}_{22} = Q_{22} - Q_{11},$$
$$\overline{\Phi}_{33} = \frac{1}{\gamma_2} D^T\widehat{P}D - Q_{22} - T_1,$$
$$\overline{\Phi}_{44} = \frac{1}{\gamma_3} B^T\widehat{P}B - T_2,$$
$$\overline{\Phi}_{12} = Q_{12},$$
$$\overline{\Phi}_{13} = -\widehat{A}_c^T PD,$$
$$\overline{\Phi}_{14} = \widehat{A}_c^T PB,$$
$$\overline{\Phi}_{23} = -Q_{12}. \tag{32}$$

Proof. Define a legitimate Lyapunov functional candidate as

$$V(x(t)) = V_1(x(t)) + V_2(x(t)) + V_3(x(t)) + V_4(x(t)) + V_5(x(t)), \tag{33}$$

where

$$V_1(x(t)) = \mathscr{L}^T(x(t))\, P\mathscr{L}(x(t)),$$
$$V_2(x(t)) = \int_{t-(h/2)}^{t} \begin{bmatrix} x(s) \\ x\left(s-\frac{h}{2}\right)\end{bmatrix}^T \begin{bmatrix} Q_{11} & Q_{12} \\ \star & Q_{22}\end{bmatrix} \begin{bmatrix} x(s) \\ x\left(s-\frac{h}{2}\right)\end{bmatrix} ds,$$
$$V_3(x(t)) = \int_{t-h}^{t} x^T(s)\, T_1 x(s)\, ds,$$
$$V_4(x(t)) = \int_{t-h}^{t}\left[\int_s^t x^T(s_1)\, ds_1\right] T_2 \left[\int_s^t x(s_2)\, ds_2\right] ds,$$
$$V_5(x(t)) = \frac{1}{2}\int_{t-h}^{t} (s-t+h)^2 x^T(s)\, T_3 x(s)\, ds, \tag{34}$$

where $P > 0$, $Q = [Q_{ij}]_{2\times 2}$, $Q_{ij} > 0$, and $T_i > 0$, $i = 1, 2, 3$.

According to (34) we obtain

$$\dot{V}_1(x(t)) \leq x^T\left[\widehat{A}_c^T P + P\widehat{A}_c + \frac{1}{\gamma_1}\widehat{P} + (\gamma_1+\gamma_2+\gamma_3)\left\|C^T C\right\| W_i(\rho_i)\right]x + \frac{1}{\gamma_2}x^T(t-h)D^T\widehat{P}Dx(t-h) + \frac{1}{\gamma_3}\left[\int_{t-h}^{t} x^T(s)\,ds\right]B^T\widehat{P}B\left[\int_{t-h}^{t} x(s)\,ds\right] - 2x^T(t)\widehat{A}_c^T PDx(t-h) + 2x^T(t)\widehat{A}_c^T PB\left[\int_{t-h}^{t} x(s)\,ds\right], \quad (35)$$

where $\widehat{P}>0$, since $\widehat{P}=P^2$. Consider

$$\dot{V}_2(x(t)) = \begin{bmatrix} x(t) \\ x\left(t-\frac{h}{2}\right)\end{bmatrix}^T \begin{bmatrix} Q_{11} & Q_{12} \\ \star & Q_{22}\end{bmatrix}\begin{bmatrix} x(t) \\ x\left(t-\frac{h}{2}\right)\end{bmatrix} - \begin{bmatrix} x\left(t-\frac{h}{2}\right) \\ x(t-h)\end{bmatrix}^T \begin{bmatrix} Q_{11} & Q_{12} \\ \star & Q_{22}\end{bmatrix}\begin{bmatrix} x\left(t-\frac{h}{2}\right) \\ x(t-h)\end{bmatrix},$$

$$\dot{V}_3(x(t)) = x^T(t)T_1x(t) - x^T(t-h)T_1x(t-h),$$

$$\dot{V}_4(x(t)) \leq -\left[\int_{t-h}^{t} x^T(s_1)\,ds_1\right]T_2\left[\int_{t-h}^{t} x(s_2)\,ds_2\right] + \frac{h^2}{2}x^T(t)\widetilde{T}_2x(t) + \int_{t-h}^{t}(s-t+h)x^T(s)T_3x(s)\,ds, \quad (36)$$

where $\tilde{T}_2>0$, since $\tilde{T}_2=T_2T_3^{-1}T_2$. Consider

$$\dot{V}_5(x(t)) = \frac{1}{2}h^2x^T(t)T_3x(t) - \int_{t-h}^{t}(s-t+h)x^T(s)T_3x(s)\,ds. \quad (37)$$

Then, the time-derivative of V has new upper bound as follows:

$$\dot{V}(x(t)) = \dot{V}_1(x(t)) + \dot{V}_2(x(t)) + \dot{V}_3(x(t)) + \dot{V}_4(x(t)) + \dot{V}_5(x(t)) \leq \bar{\xi}^T(t)\bar{\Phi}\bar{\xi}(t), \tag{38}$$

where $\bar{\Phi}$ is defined as stated in (31) and

$$\bar{\xi}^T(t) = \left[x^T(t) \;\; x^T\left(t - \frac{h}{2}\right) \;\; x^T(t-h) \;\; \int_{t-h}^{t} x^T(s)\,ds\right]. \tag{39}$$

The corollary can then be proved following [24].

Asymptotic Stability for Uncertain Neutral System

Consider the following uncertain neutral system with time-delay and actuator saturation:

$$\dot{x}(t) - D\dot{x}(t-\tau) = (A + \Delta A(t))x(t) + Bx(t-h) + (C + \Delta C(t))\,\mathrm{Sat}(u(t)), \tag{40}$$

where $\Delta A(t)$ and $\Delta C(t)$ stand for the uncertainties. For simplicity, the constant parameter matrices A, B, C, and D are square matrices. The spectral norm bound of the unknown uncertainties is

$$\|\Delta A(t)\| \leq \alpha, \quad \|\Delta C(t)\| \leq \beta, \quad \forall t \geq 0. \tag{41}$$

Using the nonlinear function $D(\cdot)$, rewrite the uncertain neutral system as follows:

$$\dot{x}(t) - D\dot{x}(t-\tau) = (A_c + \Delta A(t) - \Delta C(t)K)x(t) + Bx(t-h) + (C + \Delta C(t))Dz(Kx(t)), \tag{42}$$

where Ac is defined as the same with certain neutral system with time-delay and actuator saturation. In particular, when $\|\Delta(t)\| = 0$ and $\|\Delta C(t)\| = 0$, the uncertain neutral system becomes the certain case.

Similarly, we employ the operator $\mathscr{L} : C_0 \rightarrow \mathbb{R}^n$ with

$$\mathscr{L}(x(t)) = x(t) + B\int_{t-h}^{t} x(s)\,ds - Dx(t-\tau). \tag{43}$$

The following transformed system is then obtained:

$$\frac{d}{dt}\mathscr{L}(x(t)) = \bar{A}_c x(t) + (C + \Delta C(t))Dz(Kx(t)), \tag{44}$$

where $\bar{A}_c = A_c + \Delta A(t) - \Delta C(t)K = A + B - CK + \Delta A(t) - \Delta C(t)K$.

Theorem 10. The uncertain neutral system in (40) with feedback control (3) is asymptotic stability if $\||h|B| + D\| < 1$ and there exist scalars $\gamma_i > 0$, $i = 1, 2, 3, 4, 5, 6$, $P > 0$, $\tilde{P} > 0$, $Q = [Q_{ij}]_{2\times 2}$, $Q_{ij} > 0$, $R = [R_{ij}]_{2\times 2}$, $R_{ij} > 0$, $T_i > 0$ ($i = 1, 2, 3, 4, 5, 6$), and $\tilde{T}_i > 0$ ($i = 3, 4$) such that the following symmetric linear matrix inequality holds:

$$\Xi = \begin{bmatrix} \Xi_{11} & \Xi_{12} & 0 & \Xi_{14} & \Xi_{15} & \Xi_{16} & 0 \\ \star & \Xi_{22} & \Xi_{23} & 0 & 0 & 0 & 0 \\ \star & \star & \Xi_{33} & 0 & 0 & 0 & 0 \\ \star & \star & \star & \Xi_{44} & \Xi_{45} & 0 & 0 \\ \star & \star & \star & \star & \Xi_{55} & 0 & 0 \\ \star & \star & \star & \star & \star & \Xi_{66} & 0 \\ \star & \star & \star & \star & \star & \star & \Xi_{77} \end{bmatrix} < 0, \tag{45}$$

where

$$\begin{aligned}
\Xi_{11} &= \widehat{A}_c^T P + P\widehat{A}_c + \frac{1}{\gamma_1}\widehat{P} + \frac{1}{\gamma_2}\widehat{P} \\
&\quad + (\gamma_1 + \gamma_3 + \gamma_5)\left(\alpha^2 + 2\alpha\beta\,\|K\| + \beta^2\|K\|^2\right) I \\
&\quad + (\gamma_2 + \gamma_4 + \gamma_6)\left(\beta^2 + 2\beta\,\|C\| + \|C\|^2\right) W_i(\rho_i) \\
&\quad + Q_{11} + R_{11} + T_1 + T_2 + \frac{h^2}{2}\left(\widetilde{T}_3 + T_5\right) + \frac{\tau^2}{2}\left(\widetilde{T}_4 + T_6\right), \\
\Xi_{22} &= Q_{22} - Q_{11}, \\
\Xi_{33} &= -Q_{22} - T_1, \\
\Xi_{44} &= R_{22} - R_{11}, \\
\Xi_{55} &= \left(\frac{1}{\gamma_3} + \frac{1}{\gamma_4}\right) D^T\widehat{P}D - R_{22} - T_2, \\
\Xi_{66} &= \left(\frac{1}{\gamma_5} + \frac{1}{\gamma_6}\right) B^T\widehat{P}B - T_3, \\
\Xi_{77} &= -T_4, \\
\Xi_{12} &= Q_{12}, \\
\Xi_{14} &= R_{12}, \\
\Xi_{15} &= -\widehat{A}_c^T PD, \\
\Xi_{16} &= \widehat{A}_c^T PB, \\
\Xi_{23} &= -Q_{12}, \\
\Xi_{45} &= -R_{12}.
\end{aligned} \tag{46}$$

Proof. Define the legitimate Lyapunov functional candidate as

$$\begin{aligned} V(x(t)) &= V_1(x(t)) + V_2(x(t)) + V_3(x(t)) \\ &\quad + V_4(x(t)) + V_5(x(t)) + V_6(x(t)), \end{aligned} \tag{47}$$

where $V_1(x(t))$, $V_2(x(t))$, $V_3(x(t))$, $V_4(x(t))$, $V_5(x(t))$, and $V_6(x(t))$ are the same as in Theorem 6.

The time-derivative of $(x(t))$ along the trajectories of closed system (44) is given by the following:

$$\dot{V}(x(t)) = \dot{V}_1(x(t)) + \dot{V}_2(x(t)) + \dot{V}_3(x(t)) + \dot{V}_4(x(t)) + \dot{V}_5(x(t)) + \dot{V}_6(x(t)). \tag{48}$$

Then

$$\begin{aligned}
\dot{V}_1(x(t)) = 2\Big\{&x^T(t) - x^T(t-\tau)D^T \\
&+ \left[\int_{t-h}^{t} x^T(s)\,ds\right]B^T\Big\} \\
&\times P\left[\overline{A}_c x(t) + (C+\Delta C)Dz(Kx)\right] \\
= {}& 2x^T P\overline{A}_c x + 2x^T P(C+\Delta C)Dz(Kx) \\
&- 2x^T\overline{A}_c^{\,T} PDx(t-\tau) - 2x^T(t-\tau)D^T \\
&\times P(C+\Delta C)Dz(Kx) \\
&+ 2x^T(t)\overline{A}_c^{\,T} PB\left[\int_{t-h}^{t} x(s)\,ds\right] \\
&+ 2\left[\int_{t-h}^{t} x^T(s)\,ds\right]B^T P(C+\Delta C)Dz(Kx) \\
= {}& 2x^T P\widehat{A}_c x + 2x^T P(\Delta A - \Delta CK)x \\
&+ 2x^T P(C+\Delta C)Dz(Kx) \\
&- 2x^T(t-\tau)D^T P\widehat{A}_c x(t) \\
&- 2x^T(t-\tau)D^T P(\Delta A - \Delta CK)x \\
&- 2x^T(t-\tau)D^T P(C+\Delta C)Dz(Kx) \\
&+ 2\left[\int_{t-h}^{t} x^T(s)\,ds\right]B^T P\widehat{A}_c x
\end{aligned}$$

$$
\begin{aligned}
& - 2x^T (t-\tau) D^T P (\Delta A - \Delta C K) x \\
& - 2x^T (t-\tau) D^T P (C + \Delta C) Dz (Kx) \\
& + 2 \left[\int_{t-h}^{t} x^T (s)\, ds \right] B^T P \widehat{A}_c x \\
& + 2 \left[\int_{t-h}^{t} x^T (s)\, ds \right] B^T P (\Delta A - \Delta C K) x \\
& + 2 \left[\int_{t-h}^{t} x^T (s)\, ds \right] B^T P (C + \Delta C) Dz (Kx) \\
\leq\ & x^T \left[\widehat{A}_c^T P + P \widehat{A}_c \right] x - 2x^T (t) \widehat{A}_c^T P D x (t-\tau) \\
& + 2x^T (t) \widehat{A}_c^T P B \left[\int_{t-h}^{t} x (s)\, ds \right] \\
& + \frac{1}{\gamma_1} x^T \widehat{P} x + \gamma_1 x^T (\Delta A - \Delta C K)^T (\Delta A - \Delta C K) x \\
& + \frac{1}{\gamma_2} x^T \widehat{P} x + \gamma_2 D z^T (Kx) (C + \Delta C)^T \\
& \times (C + \Delta C) Dz (Kx) \\
& + \frac{1}{\gamma_3} x^T (t-\tau) D^T \widehat{P} D x (t-\tau) \\
& + \gamma_3 x^T (\Delta A - \Delta C K)^T (\Delta A - \Delta C K) x \\
& + \frac{1}{\gamma_4} x^T (t-\tau) D^T \widehat{P} D x (t-\tau) \\
& + \gamma_4 D z^T (Kx) (C + \Delta C)^T (C + \Delta C) Dz (Kx) \\
& + \frac{1}{\gamma_5} \left[\int_{t-h}^{t} x^T (s)\, ds \right] B^T \widehat{P} B \left[\int_{t-h}^{t} x (s)\, ds \right] \\
& + \gamma_5 x^T (\Delta A - \Delta C K)^T (\Delta A - \Delta C K) x \\
& + \frac{1}{\gamma_6} \left[\int_{t-h}^{t} x^T (s)\, ds \right] B^T \widehat{P} B \left[\int_{t-h}^{t} x (s)\, ds \right]
\end{aligned}
$$

$$
\begin{aligned}
&+ \gamma_6 Dz^T(Kx)(C+\Delta C)^T(C+\Delta C)Dz(Kx) \\
&\leq x^T \Bigg\{ \left(\widehat{A}_c^T P + P\widehat{A}_c\right) \\
&\quad + \left[\frac{1}{\gamma_1}\widehat{P} + \gamma_1\left(\alpha^2 + 2\alpha\beta\|K\| + \beta^2\|K\|^2\right)I\right] \\
&\quad + \left[\frac{1}{\gamma_2}\widehat{P} + \gamma_2\left(\beta^2 + 2\beta\|C\| + \|C\|^2\right)W_i(\rho)\right] \\
&\quad + \gamma_3\left(\alpha^2 + 2\alpha\beta\|K\| + \beta^2\|K\|^2\right)I \\
&\quad + \gamma_4\left(\beta^2 + 2\beta\|C\| + \|C\|^2\right)W_i(\rho_i) \\
&\quad + \gamma_5\left(\alpha^2 + 2\alpha\beta\|K\| + \beta^2\|K\|^2\right)I \\
&\quad + \gamma_6\left(\beta^2 + 2\beta\|C\| + \|C\|^2\right)W_i(\rho_i)\Bigg\} x \\
&+ x^T(t-\tau)\left(\frac{1}{\gamma_3}D^T\widehat{P}D + \frac{1}{\gamma_4}D^T\widehat{P}D\right)x(t-\tau) \\
&+ \left[\left[\int_{t-h}^{t} x^T(s)\,ds\right]\left[\frac{1}{\gamma_5}B^T\widehat{P}B + \frac{1}{\gamma_6}B^T\widehat{P}B\right]\right. \\
&\times \left[\left[\int_{t-h}^{t} x(s)\,ds\right] - 2x^T(t)\widehat{A}_c^T PDx(t-\tau)\right. \\
&+ 2x^T(t)\widehat{A}_c^T PB\left[\left[\int_{t-h}^{t} x(s)\,ds\right],\right.
\end{aligned}
\tag{49}
$$

where $\widehat{P} > 0$, since $\widehat{P} = P^2$.

$\dot{V}_2(x(t)), \dot{V}_3(x(t)), \dot{V}_4(x(t)), \dot{V}_5(x(t))$, and $V_6(x(t))$ are obtained similarly as in Theorem 6. Substituting these into (48), the time-derivative of V has new upper bound as follows:

$$
\dot{V}(x(t)) \leq \xi^T(t)\,\Xi\,\xi(t), \tag{50}
$$

where

$$
\xi^T(t) = \left[x^T(t)\;\; x^T\left(t-\frac{h}{2}\right)\;\; x^T(t-h)\;\; x^T\left(t-\frac{\tau}{2}\right)\;\; x^T(t-\tau)\;\; \int_{t-h}^{t} x^T(s)\,ds\;\; \int_{t-\tau}^{t} x^T(s)\,ds\right]; \tag{51}
$$

Ξ is defined as stated in (45).

If linear matrix inequality (45) is feasible, then $\dot{V}((t)) < 0$, for all $x \in B(\rho)$. The theorem can then be proved following [24].

Theorem 10 provides new asymptotic stability conditions for the uncertain neutral systems in (40) and (3). The following corollary is presented as a special case of the theorem.

Corollary 11. The uncertain neutral system in (40) and (3) with $\tau \equiv h$ is asymptotic stability if $\|h|B| + D\| < 1$ and there exist $P > 0$, $\hat{P} > 0$, $Q = [Q_{ij}]_{2\times 2}$, $Q_{ij} > 0$, $T_i > 0$ $(i = 1, 3)$, and $\tilde{T}_2 > 0$ such that the following symmetric linear matrix inequality holds for real constant scalars $\gamma_i > 0$, $i = 1, 2, 3, 4, 5, 6$:

$$\overline{\Xi} = \begin{bmatrix} \overline{\Xi}_{11} & \overline{\Xi}_{12} & \overline{\Xi}_{13} & \overline{\Xi}_{14} \\ \star & \overline{\Xi}_{22} & \overline{\Xi}_{23} & 0 \\ \star & \star & \overline{\Xi}_{33} & 0 \\ \star & \star & \star & \overline{\Xi}_{44} \end{bmatrix} < 0, \tag{52}$$

where $W_i(\rho)$, $i = 1, 2, 3, \ldots, n$ are defined as before and

$$\begin{aligned} \overline{\Xi}_{11} &= \widehat{A}_c^T P + P\widehat{A}_c + \frac{1}{\gamma_1}\hat{P} + \frac{1}{\gamma_2}\hat{P} \\ &\quad + (\gamma_1 + \gamma_3 + \gamma_5)\left(\alpha^2 + 2\alpha\beta\|K\| + \beta^2\|K\|^2\right) I \\ &\quad + (\gamma_2 + \gamma_4 + \gamma_6)\left(\beta^2 + 2\beta\|C\| + \|C\|^2\right) W_i(\rho_i) \\ &\quad + Q_{11} + T_1 + \frac{h^2}{2}\left(\tilde{T}_2 + T_3\right), \\ \overline{\Xi}_{22} &= Q_{22} - Q_{11}, \\ \overline{\Xi}_{33} &= \left(\frac{1}{\gamma_3} + \frac{1}{\gamma_4}\right) D^T \hat{P} D - Q_{22} - T_1, \\ \overline{\Xi}_{44} &= \left(\frac{1}{\gamma_5} + \frac{1}{\gamma_6}\right) B^T \hat{P} B - T_2, \\ \overline{\Xi}_{12} &= Q_{12}, \\ \overline{\Xi}_{13} &= -\widehat{A}_c^T P D, \\ \overline{\Xi}_{14} &= \widehat{A}_c^T P B, \\ \overline{\Xi}_{23} &= -Q_{12}. \end{aligned} \tag{53}$$

Proof. Choose a legitimate Lyapunov functional candidate as

$$\begin{aligned} V(x(t)) &= V_1(x(t)) + V_2(x(t)) \\ &\quad + V_3(x(t)) + V_4(x(t)) + V_5(x(t)) \end{aligned} \tag{54}$$

which are the same as (34).

$\dot{V}_1(x(t))$ can be evaluated similarly as in Theorem 10 and Corollary 9. The proof can be readily obtained.

The Algorithm with $W_2(\rho_2)$ and the Algorithm to Solve the Optimal $W_i(\rho_i)$.

From Definition 4, it is seen that $W_1(\rho 1)$ are different from $W_2(\rho_2)$, $W_3(\rho_3)$, and $W_4(\rho_4)$, . . . , $W_n(\rho_n)$. We compare between $W_2(\rho_2)$, $W_3(\rho_3)$, and $W_4(\rho_4)$, . . . , $W_n(\rho_n)$ and intend to reduce the conservativeness of the result. To that end, we should obtain ρ_2 in the first place. In what follows we present the stability analysis algorithm with $W_2(\rho_2)$ to solve ρ_2.

Step 1. Give α, β, K.

Step 2. Set positive values γ_i ($i = 1, 2, 3, 4, 5, 6$).

Step 3. Initialize ρ_2.

Step 4. With $W_2(\rho_2)$, solve linear matrix inequality (45) by Matlab LMI Toolbox.

Step 5. If the solution satisfies the stability condition, go to Step 6; otherwise, reduce ρ_2 and go to Step 3.

Step 6. Increase ρ_2 and go to Step 3.

Step 7. End.

Remark 12. The above algorithm is stated with respect to uncertain systems (40) and (3). Other cases can be dealt with similarly.

After defining ρ_2, we replace $W_2(\rho_2)$ by $W_i(\rho_i)$ to reduce the conservativeness. We analyze these functions $W_2(\rho_2)$, $W_3(\rho_3)$, $W_4(\rho_4), \ldots, W_n(\rho_n)$ and find the optimal $W_i(\rho_i)$ to obtain the maximum ρ_i among $\rho_2, \rho_3, \ldots, \rho_n$.

Theorem 13. Given $W_2(\rho_2)$, $W_3(\rho_3)$, $W_4(\rho_4), \ldots, W_n(\rho_n)$, if there exists $j \leq n$, such that $\rho_{j-1} \geq \rho_k$ and $\|W_j(\rho_{j-1})\| \leq \|W_k(\rho_k)\|$, for all $k = 2, 3, \ldots, j-1$, then we have

$$\frac{\|K_i\| \rho_{j-1}}{u_i^+} \leq f_k(j), \quad \forall k = 2, 3, \ldots, j-1, \tag{55}$$

where ρ_j is the domain attraction obtained by $W_j(\rho_j)$ and

$$f_k(j) = \frac{(k-1)^{(k-1)/(j-k)}}{k^{k/(j-k)}} \times \frac{j^{j/(j-k)}}{(j-1)^{(j-1)/(j-k)}}. \tag{56}$$

Proof. Recall the definition of $W(\rho_j)$, we know it can be expressed in the following equality:

$$W_j(\rho_j) = \sum_{i=1}^{m} \left(\frac{(j-1)\rho_j}{j^{j/(j-1)} u_i^+} \right)^{2j-2} (K_i^T K_i)^j. \tag{57}$$

If we have $\rho_{j-1} \geq \rho_k$, for all $k = 2, 3, \ldots, j-1$, then from the above equality we obtain

$$\|W_k(\rho_k)\| \leq \left\|W_k(\rho_{j-1})\right\|, \quad \forall k = 2, 3, \ldots, j-1. \tag{58}$$

With regard to $W(\rho_{j-1})$, we have

$$\begin{aligned} W_j(\rho_{j-1}) &= \sum_{i=1}^{m} \left(\frac{(j-1)\rho_{j-1}}{j^{j/(j-1)} u_i^+} \right)^{2j-2} (K_i^T K_i)^k (K_i^T K_i)^{j-k} \\ &= \sum_{i=1}^{m} \left[\frac{(k-1)\rho_{j-1}}{k^{k/(k-1)} u_i^+} \right]^{2k-2} (K_i^T K_i)^k (K_i^T K_i)^{j-k} \\ &\quad \times \left(\frac{\rho_{j-1}}{u_i^+} \right)^{2(j-k)} \frac{k^{2k}}{(k-1)^{2k-2}} \frac{(j-1)^{2j-2}}{j^{2j}} \\ &= \|K_i\|^{2(j-k)} \left(\frac{\rho_{j-1}}{u_i^+} \right)^{2(j-k)} \\ &\quad \times \frac{k^{2k}}{(k-1)^{2k-2}} \frac{(j-1)^{2j-2}}{j^{2j}} W_k(\rho_{j-1}). \end{aligned} \tag{59}$$

If we have $\|W(\rho_{j-1})\| \leq \|W_k(\rho_k)\|$, then we can obtain

$$\left\|W_j\left(\rho_{j-1}\right)\right\| = \left\|K_i\right\|^{2(j-k)}\left(\frac{\rho_{j-1}}{u_i^+}\right)^{2(j-k)}\frac{k^{2k}}{(k-1)^{2k-2}} \times \frac{(j-1)^{2j-2}}{j^{2j}}\left\|W_k\left(\rho_{j-1}\right)\right\| \leq \left\|W_k\left(\rho_k\right)\right\|. \tag{60}$$

By (58), we have

$$\left(\frac{\left\|K_i\right\|\rho_{j-1}}{u_i^+}\right)^{2(j-k)}\frac{k^{2k}}{(k-1)^{2k-2}}\frac{(j-1)^{2j-2}}{j^{2j}} \leq 1, \tag{61}$$

where $j = 3, 4, 5, \ldots$, and $k = 2, 3, \ldots, j-1$.

Then we easily obtain

$$\frac{\left\|K_i\right\|\rho_{j-1}}{u_i^+} \leq f_k(j) = \frac{(k-1)^{(k-1)/(j-k)}}{k^{k/(j-k)}} \times \frac{j^{j/(j-k)}}{(j-1)^{(j-1)/(j-k)}} \tag{62}$$

which completes the proof.

Remark 14. Theorem 13 provides us a criterion to find the optimal $W(\rho_j)$. That is, if condition (55) cannot be satisfied, the procedure to find the optimal one should be ended. For example, when ρ_4 is obtained, we compute $\left\|K_i\right\|\rho_4/u_i^+$ and the following inequalities need to be satisfied:

$$\frac{\left\|K_i\right\|\rho_4}{u_i^+} \leq f_2(5), \quad \frac{\left\|K_i\right\|\rho_4}{u_i^+} \leq f_3(5), \quad \frac{\left\|K_i\right\|\rho_4}{u_i^+} \leq f_4(5). \tag{63}$$

Otherwise, the algorithm terminates with ρ_4.

The following optimality algorithm is used to obtain the optimal $W(\rho_n)$.

Step 1. Set positive value δ (small value, for example, 10^{-5}).

Step 2. Solve ρ_2 based on the above stability analysis algorithm with $W_2(\rho_2)$.

Step 3. Compute $\left\|K_i\right\|\rho_2/u_i^+$, if $\left(\left\|K_i\right\|\rho_2/u_i^+\right) - f_k(j) \leq f_2(3)$, then go to Step 4; otherwise, go to Step 7.

Step 4. Set $\rho_{j+1} = \rho_j$, repeat the stability analysis algorithm with $W_{j+1}(\rho_j)$ then obtain ρ_{j+1} iteratively.

Step 5. Compute $\left\|K_i\right\|\rho_{j+1}/u_i^+$, if

$$\frac{\left\|K_i\right\|\rho_{j+1}}{u_i^+} \leq f_k(j+2), \quad \left|\frac{\left\|K_i\right\|\rho_{j+1}}{u_i^+} - f_k(j+2)\right| > \delta, \quad \forall k = 2, 3, \ldots, j+1 \tag{64}$$

then go to Step 6; otherwise go to Step 7.

Step 6. Set $j = j+1$ and go to Step 4.

Step 7. End.

APPLICATION AND NUMERICAL EXAMPLES

The two-stage system has been applied to many factories worldwide. For the interest of efficiency, a lot of equipment such as converter, cylinder, and ejector is designed in the two-stage form. The natural, social, and economic systems also exhibit the two-stage mode. A typical example is the two-stage ditch design which is a conservation tool supported by the conservancy in

Indiana. The advantages of a two-stage ditch against the typical agricultural ditch include both improved drainage function and ecological function. The two-stage design improves ditch stability by reducing water flow and the need for maintenance, saving both labor and money.

Consider Figure 2 which shows two-stage dissolution tank in the chemical process. The solute in the hopper is transported by the conveyor belt and falls into DT1 within a certain time. The solute is part of the solution in DT1; then within a certain time the solution in DT1 and the undissolved solute flow into DT2 to continue to dissolve and dilute.

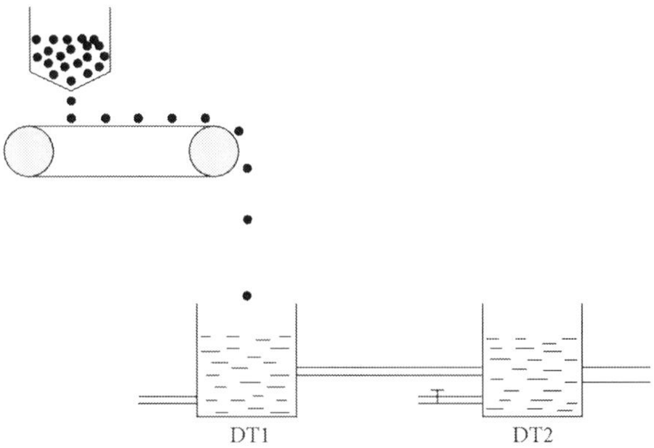

Figure 2: Two-stage dissolution tank.

Under normal circumstances, the dilute fluid flow of DT1 and the velocity of the conveyor belt are constant. The dilute fluid flow of DT2 is controllable. In practical system design, the pipeline of the DT2 dilute fluid is thin and the regulating action of DT2 is tiny, which can thus be represented by the saturating form Sat($u(t)$). Let $\lambda_1(t)$ and $\lambda_2(t)$ be the solution concentration of DT1 and DT2 and λ_{10} and λ_{20} the solution concentration of DT1 and DT2 when the system reaches an equilibrium, respectively. $x_1(t) = \lambda_1(t) - \lambda_{10}$ and $x_2(t) = \lambda_2(t) - \lambda_{20}$ are the considered system states and the dilute fluid flow into DT2 $u(t)$ is the control input. The latter is of the saturating form Sat($u(t)$) because the dilute fluid flow into DT2 $u(t)$ is a fine adjustment role. The chemical plant puts the solute into DT1 with constant speed; that is, the velocity of the conveyor belt is constant in a period of time interval. In addition, the velocity of the dilute fluid flow into DT1 is also constant in a period of time interval.

No Uncertainty Case

Example 1. The model for the above described system is

$$\dot{x}(t) - \begin{bmatrix} 0.2 & 0 \\ 0 & 0.2 \end{bmatrix} \dot{x}(t-\tau) = \begin{bmatrix} 1 & 1.5 \\ 0.3 & -2 \end{bmatrix} x(t) + \begin{bmatrix} 0 & -1 \\ 0 & 0 \end{bmatrix} x(t-h) \begin{bmatrix} 0 \\ 1 \end{bmatrix} \mathrm{Sat}(u(t)), \tag{65}$$

where the saturation limit is $u^+ = 15$. The discrete time-delay $h = 0.2$ and neutral time-delay $\tau = 0.4$.

It is seen that

$$\|h|B| + D\| = \left\| 0.2 \left| \begin{bmatrix} 0 & -1 \\ 0 & 0 \end{bmatrix} \right| + \begin{bmatrix} 0.2 & 0 \\ 0 & 0.2 \end{bmatrix} \right\| = 0.1047 < 1 \tag{66}$$

and the operator $u = -Kx = [-0.1325 \;\; 0.0153]\, x$ with

$$\mathscr{L}(x(t)) = x(t) + B \int_{t-h}^{t} x(s)\, ds - Dx(t-\tau) \tag{67}$$

is stable.

The following linear state feedback control is used and the same as [18]:

$$u = -Kx = \begin{bmatrix} -0.1325 & 0.0153 \end{bmatrix} x \tag{68}$$

To begin with the stability analysis algorithm, we have $\rho_2 = 161.73$, and compute $\|K\|\rho_2/u^+ = 1.4383$. It is seen that

$$1 < \frac{\|K\|\,\rho_2}{u^+} \le f_2(3) = \frac{27}{16} \doteq 1.6875. \tag{69}$$

According to the optimality algorithm, let initial data $\rho_3 = \rho_2$. Repeating the stability algorithm with $W_3(\rho_3)$, we obtain $\rho_3 = 163.46$. Similarly, we compute $\|K\|\rho_3/u+$ and $(\|K\|\rho_3/u^+) = 1.4537$.

It is seen that

$$\frac{\|K\|\,\rho_3}{u^+} < f_2(4) \doteq 1.5396, \qquad \text{but } \frac{\|K\|\,\rho_3}{u^+} > f_3(4) \doteq 1.4047 \tag{70}$$

which terminates the algorithm. In this example, we obtain that the optimal auxiliary function is $W_3(\rho_3)$. By Theorem 13, we must verify $\|W_3(\rho_3)\| \le \|W_2(\rho_2)\|$, which is true as $\|W_3(\rho_3)\| = 0.0017$ and $\|W_2(\rho_2)\| = 0.0023$. So we infer that $W_3(\rho_3)$ is the optimal auxiliary function among $W_2(\rho_2)$, $W_3(\rho_3)$, $W_4(\rho_4)$, . . . , $W_n(\rho_n)$ and ρ_3 is the largest one among $\rho_2, \rho_3, \rho_4, \ldots, \rho_n$.

The comparison of these results can be seen in Figure 3. Notice that ρ is not the domain of attraction.

We obtain the largest parameter ρ_i with optimal $W(\rho_i)$ to enlarge the stability region. Thus the chemical plant can make the conveyor belt and dilute fluid flow of DT1 speed up accordingly. In this way, this chemical plant can improve the production efficiency and reduce the cost of production.

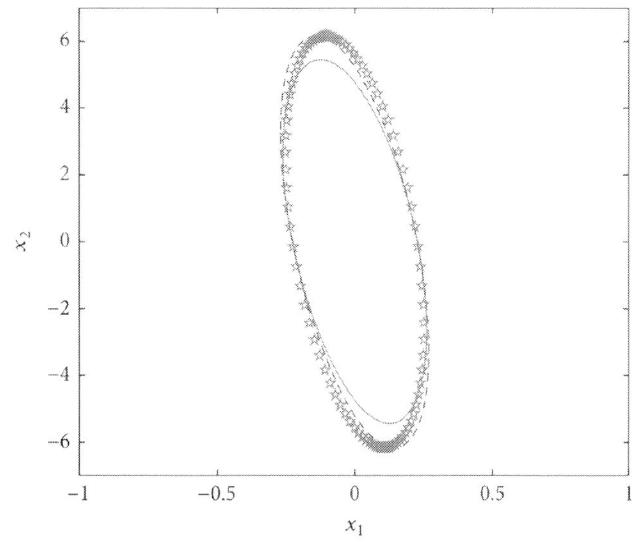

Figure 3: Attraction domain expanding schematic diagram: the largest parameter ρ_3 with optimal $W_3(\rho_3)$ is in red pentagram, with $W_2(\rho_2)$ in blue, and another one with $W_4(\rho_4)$ in red.

However, in some circumstances, we cannot enlarge the domain of attraction by replacing $W_2(\rho_2)$ with $W_i(\rho_i)$, $i = 3, 4, \ldots, n$. For example, let us see the following example.

Example 2. Consider the following linear neutral system with time-delay and actuator saturation:

$$\begin{aligned} \dot{x}(t) - \begin{bmatrix} 0.2 & 0 \\ 0 & 0.2 \end{bmatrix} \dot{x}(t-\tau) &= \begin{bmatrix} 0.1 & -0.1 \\ 0.1 & -3.0 \end{bmatrix} x(t) \\ &+ \begin{bmatrix} 0.5 & -1 \\ 0 & 0.5 \end{bmatrix} x(t-h) + \begin{bmatrix} 0.7 & 0 \\ 0 & 0.1 \end{bmatrix} \mathrm{Sat}(u(t)), \end{aligned} \tag{71}$$

where the saturation limit values are $u_1^+ = 10$ and $u_2^+ = 4$. The discrete time-delay $h = 0.2$ and neutral time-delay $\tau = 0.1$. Compute $\|h|B| + D\|$ and we also know that the operator $u = -Kx = -\begin{bmatrix} 0.8456 & 0.0627 \\ 0.0142 & 1.3754 \end{bmatrix} x.$ with

$$\mathscr{L}(x(t)) = x(t) + B\int_{t-h}^{t} x(s)\,ds - Dx(t-\tau) \tag{72}$$

is stable. Then we obtain the linear state feedback control without considering the saturation using optimal control law in [27]. Consider

$$u = -Kx = -\begin{bmatrix} 0.8456 & 0.0627 \\ 0.0142 & 1.3754 \end{bmatrix} x. \tag{73}$$

To begin with the stability analysis algorithm, we have $\rho_2 = 17.84$, and compute

$$\frac{\|K_1\|\,\rho_2}{u_1^+} = 1.5127, \qquad \frac{\|K_2\|\,\rho_2}{u_2^+} = 6.1780. \tag{74}$$

It is seen that

$$1 < \frac{\|K_1\|\,\rho_2}{u_1^+} \le f_2(3) = \frac{27}{16} \doteq 1.6875,$$

$$\text{but } \frac{\|K_2\|\,\rho_2}{u_2^+} > f_2(3) \tag{75}$$

which terminates the algorithm. So we infer that $W_2(\rho_2)$ is the optimal auxiliary function among $W_2(\rho_2)$, $W_3(\rho_3)$, $W_4(\rho_4)$, . . . , $W_n(\rho_n)$. ρ_2 has been the largest one among ρ_2, ρ_3, $\rho_{4,\dots,n}$ and we cannot maximize the value of ρ_i.

The comparison of these results can be seen in Figure 4.

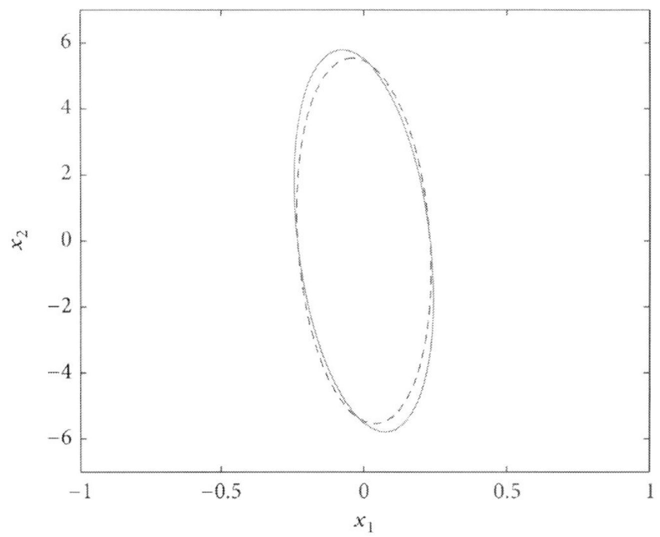

Figure 4: Attraction domain expanding schematic diagram: the largest parameter ρ_2 with optimal $W_2(\rho_2)$ is in red and another one with $W_3(\rho_3)$ in blue.

Uncertainty Case

In this subsection, we consider the existence of uncertainty due to outside interference. The numerical example demonstrates the effectiveness of the proposed algorithm.

Example 3. Consider system (65) with norm bounded uncertainties:

$$\|\Delta A(t)\| \le 0.1, \qquad \|\Delta B(t)\| \le 0.1. \tag{76}$$

It is known that this uncertainty decreases the initial state bound that guarantees the asymptotic stability of the system (65). To compare with the above case, the feedback control (68) is applied and we use (45) in Theorem10.

Using the stability analysis algorithm and the optimal algorithm, we see that $W_3(\rho_3)$ is the optimal auxiliary function among $W_2(\rho_2)$, $W_3(\rho_3)$, $W_4(\rho_4)$, . . . , $W_n(\rho_n)$. $\rho_3 = 43.57$ is the largest one among ρ_2, ρ_3, $\rho_{4,\dots,n}$. This is shown in Figure 5.

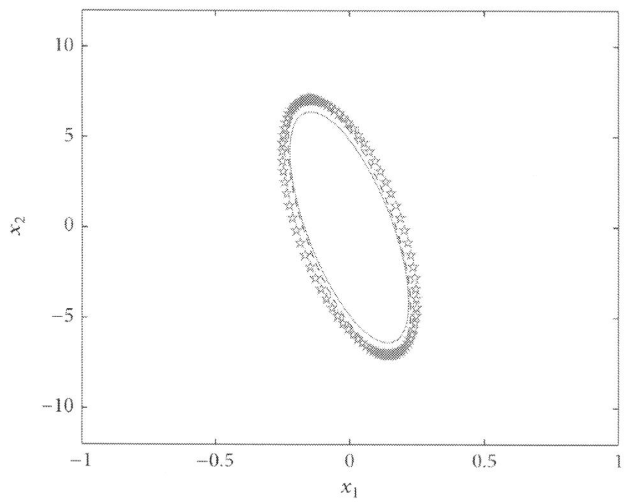

Figure 5: Attraction domain expanding schematic diagram: the largest parameter ρ_3 with optimal $W_3(\rho_3)$ is in red pentagram, with $W_2(\rho_2)$ in blue, and another one with $W_4(\rho_4)$ in red.

CONCLUSIONS

By model transformation and Lyapunov method, delay-dependent criteria for a class of uncertain neutral delay systems with saturation are derived in terms of the spectral radius and LMIs. Both conditions for asymptotic stability and algorithms are presented. These theoretical findings are successfully verified via a two-stage dissolution tank in the chemical plant. Potentially, the result is of great significance to the chemical production process.

ACKNOWLEDGMENTS

The author would like to thank the Associate Editor and the anonymous reviewers for their constructive comments and suggestions to improve the quality of the paper. This work was supported in part by the Fundamental Research Funds for the Central Universities.

REFERENCES

1. Y. Kuang, Delay Differential Equations with Applications in Population Dynamics, Academic Press, San Diego, Calif, USA, 1993.
2. V. B. Kolmanovskii and A. Myshkis, Applied Theory of Functional Differential Equations, Kluwer Academic Publishers, Dordrecht, The Netherlands, 1999.
3. J.-E. Feng and S. Xu, "Output feedback stabilization for a class of stochastic non-linear systems with delays in input," Asian Journal of Control, vol. 12, no. 1, pp. 110–115, 2010.
4. L. Dugard and E. I. Verriest, Stability and Control of Time-Delay Systems, Springer, London, UK, 1998.
5. S.-I. Niculescu, Delay Effects on Stability: A Robust Control Approach, vol. 269 of Lecture Notes in Control and Information Sciences, Springer, London, UK, 2001.
6. C.-H. Lien, "New stability criterion for a class of uncertain nonlinear neutral time-delay systems,"International Journal of Systems Science, vol. 32, no. 2, pp. 215–219, 2001.
7. C.-H. Lien, K.-W. Yu, and J.-G. Hsieh, "Stability conditions for a class of neutral systems with multiple time delays," Journal of Mathematical Analysis and Applications, vol. 245, no. 1, pp. 20–27, 2000.
8. E. Fridman, "New Lyapunov-Krasovskii functionals for stability of linear retarded and neutral type systems," Systems & Control Letters, vol. 43, no. 4, pp. 309–319, 2001.
9. J. D. Chen, C. H. Lien, K. K. Fan, and J. H. Chou, "Criteria for asymptotic stability of a class of neutral systems via a LMI approach," IEE Proceedings: Control Theory and Applications, vol. 148, no. 6, pp. 442–447, 2001.
10. Q.-L. Han, "Robust stability of uncertain delay-differential systems of neutral type," Automatica, vol. 38, no. 4, pp. 719–723, 2002.
11. D. Ivănescu, S.-I. Niculescu, L. Dugard, J.-M. Dion, and E. I. Verriest, "On delay-dependent stability for linear neutral systems," Automatica, vol. 39, no. 2, pp. 255–261, 2003.
12. Q.-L. Han, "On delay-dependent stability for neutral delay-differential systems," International Journal of Applied Mathematics and Computer Science, vol. 11, no. 4, pp. 965–976, 2001.
13. S.-I. Niculescu, "On delay-dependent stability under model transformations of some neutral linear systems," International Journal of Control, vol. 74, no. 6, pp. 609–617, 2001.
14. T. S. Hu and Z. L. Lin, Control Systems with Actuator Saturation: Analysis and Design, Birkhauser, Boston, Mass, USA, 2001.
15. C. Pittet, S. Tarbouriech, and C. Burgat, "Stability regions for linear systems with saturating controls via circle and Popov criteria," in Proceedings of the 36th IEEE Conference on Decision and Control, pp. 4518–4523, San Diego, Calif, USA, December 1997.
16. G. Scorletti, J. P. Folcher, and L. El Ghaoui, "Output feedback control with input saturations: LMI design approaches," European Journal of Control, vol. 7, no. 6, pp. 567–579, 2001.
17. H. Hindi and S. Boyd, "Analysis of linear systems with saturation using convex optimization," inProceedings of the 37th IEEE Conference on Decision and Control (CDC '98), pp. 903–908, Tampa, Fla, USA, December 1998.
18. J. M. Gomes da Silva, Jr., A. Seuret, E. Fridman, and J. P. Richard, "Stabilisation of neutral systems with saturating control inputs," International Journal of Systems Science, vol. 42, no. 7, pp. 1093–1103, 2011.
19. S. Srivastava and F. Jabbari, "Scheduled controllers for disturbance attenuation of systems with bounded inputs," in Proceedings of the American Control Conference, pp. 735–739, Chicago, Ill, USA, June 2000.
20. A. Haurani, H. H. Michalska, and B. Boulet, "Delay-dependent robust stabilization of uncertain neutral systems with saturating actuators," in Proceedings of the American Control Conference, pp. 509–514, Denver, Colo, USA, June 2003.

21. J.-J. Yan, J.-S. Lin, and T.-L. Liao, "Robust dynamic compensator for a class of time delay systems containing saturating control input," Chaos, Solitons & Fractals, vol. 31, no. 5, pp. 1223–1231, 2007.

22. P.-L. Liu, "Stabilization of input delay constrained systems with delay dependence," International Journal of Systems Science, vol. 26, no. 2, pp. 245–255, 1995.

23. J.-H. Kim and Z. Bien, "Robust stability of uncertain linear systems with saturating actuators," IEEE Transactions on Automatic Control, vol. 39, no. 1, pp. 202–207, 1994.

24. J. K. Hale and S. M. Verduyn Lunel, Introduction to Functional-Differential Equations, Applied Mathematical Sciences, Springer, New York, NY, USA, 1993.

25. H. B. Ji, Algebra Foundation of Control Theory, University of Science and Technology of China Press, Hefei, China, 2008.

26. W.-A. Zhang and L. Yu, "Delay-dependent robust stability of neutral systems with mixed delays and nonlinear perturbations," Acta Automatica Sinica, vol. 33, no. 8, pp. 863–866, 2007.

27. D. E. Kirk, Optimal Control Theory-An Introducion, Prentice-Hall, Englewood Cliffs, NJ, USA, 1970.

CHAPTER 3 A DIRECT SEARCH ALGORITHM FOR GLOBAL OPTIMIZATION

Enrique Baeyens[1], Alberto Herreros[1], and José R. Perán[2]

[1]Instituto de las Tecnologías Avanzadas de la Producción (ITAP), Universidad de Valladolid, Paseo del Cauce 59, 47011 Valladolid, Spain

[2]Centro Tecnológico Cartif, Parque Tecnológico de Boecillo 205, 47151 Bocillo, Spain

ABSTRACT

A direct search algorithm is proposed for minimizing an arbitrary real valued function. The algorithm uses a new function transformation and three simplex-based operations. The function transformation provides global exploration features, while the simplex-based operations guarantees the termination of the algorithm and provides global convergence to a stationary point if the cost function is differentiable and its gradient is Lipschitz continuous. The algorithm's performance has been extensively tested using benchmark functions and compared to some well-known global optimization algorithms. The results of the computational study show that the algorithm combines both simplicity and efficiency and is competitive with the heuristics-based strategies presently used for global optimization.

INTRODUCTION

An optimization problem consists of finding an element of a given set that minimizes (or maximizes) a certain value associated with each element of the set. In this paper, we are interested in minimizing the value of a real valued function defined over the n-dimensional Euclidean space. Without loss of generality, our problem is equivalent to minimizing a real valued function over the open unit n-box $(0,1)^n \subset \mathbb{R}^n$.

Let f denote a real function defined over the open unit n-box $(0,1)^n \subset \mathbb{R}^n$, and consider the following optimization problem:

$$\min\{f(x) : x \in (0,1)^n\} \quad (1)$$

Citation: Enrique Baeyens, Alberto Herreros, and José R. Perán. A Direct Search Algorithm for Global Optimization, Algorithms 2016, 9(2), 40; DOI: 10.3390/a9020040

The function to be minimized f is called the cost function and the unit n-box $(0,1)^n$ is the search space of the problem. Our aim is to obtain a point $x^* \in (0,1)^n$, such that the cost function f attains a minimum at x^*, *i.e.*, $f(x^*) \leq f(x)$, $\forall x \in (0,1)^n$. We shall make the following assumption:

***A*1:** The cost function f attains its minimum at a point of the search space.

If the function f is continuously differentiable in $(0,1)^n$, then:

$$\nabla f(x^*) = 0,\ x^* \in (0,1) \quad (2)$$

Many optimization methods make use of the stationarity Equation (2) to compute candidate optimizer points. These methods require the explicit knowledge of the gradient, but they do not guarantee that the point obtained is an optimizer, except for a pseudoconvex function.

We shall also make an additional assumption that will restrict our alternatives to design a procedure to compute the optimum.

A2: The gradient of the cost function is not available for the optimization mechanism.

Consequently, only function evaluations can be used to compute the minimum.

Remark 1. The problem Equation (1) is equivalent to unconstrained optimization. Consider the following unconstrained optimization problem:

$$\min\{f(\xi) : \xi \in \mathbb{R}^n\} \quad (3)$$

and let $\xi = [\xi_1 \xi_2 \cdots \xi_n]^T$ be the vector of variables of the cost function. The invertible transformation:

$$x_i = \frac{1}{1+e^{-\xi_i}} \quad (4)$$

transforms the real line into the unit interval. Consequently, we can convert an unconstrained minimization problem into an open unit n-box constrained minimization problem by transforming each of its variables. Similarly, the linear transformation:

$$x_i = \frac{\xi_i - a}{b - a} \quad (5)$$

converts the open interval (a,b) into the open unit interval. Consequently, both unconstrained and arbitrary open n-box optimization problems are included in our formulation. Furthermore, under Assumption A2 and by choosing appropriate values of a and b, the global minimum of function f is attained in an interior point of the open n-box $(a,b)^n$.

The rest of this paper is organized as follows. Section 2 is a review of the literature on direct search and global optimization algorithms. The direct search algorithm for global optimization is designed in Section 3. The algorithm makes use of a set of simplex-based operations for a transformed cost function. We begin by reviewing some basic results about n-dimensional simplices that will be used later to define the algorithm and study its properties. Then, we will introduce a transformation of the cost function that is crucial to improving the exploratory properties of the algorithm. Finally, we conclude this section by explaining the algorithm in detail and analyzing its convergence properties. In Section 4, an experimental study of the algorithm's performance is accomplished by using three well-known test functions. Its performance is also compared to other global optimization strategies. The conclusions are presented in Section 5.

DIRECT SEARCH METHODS AND GLOBAL OPTIMIZATION

A direct search method solves optimization problems without requiring any information about the gradient of the cost function [1,2]. Unlike many traditional optimization algorithms that use information about the gradient or higher derivatives to search for an optimal point, a direct search algorithm searches a set of points around the current point, looking for one where the value of the cost function is lower than the value at the current point. Direct search methods solve problems for which the cost function is not differentiable or not even continuous. Direct search optimization has been receiving increasing attention over recent years within the optimization community, including the establishment of solid mathematical foundations for many of the methods considered in practice [1,3,4,5,6,7]. These techniques do not attempt to compute approximations to the gradient, but rather, the improvement is derived from a model of the cost function or using geometric strategies. There exists a great number of problems in different fields, such as engineering, mathematics, physics, chemistry, economics, medicine, computer science or operational research, where derivatives are not available, but there is a need for optimization. Some relevant examples are: tuning of algorithmic parameters, automatic error analysis, structural design, circuit design, molecular geometry or dynamic pricing. See Chapter 1 of [6] for a detailed description of the applications.

Initially, direct search methods have been dismissed for several reasons [8]. Some of them are the following: they are based on heuristics, but not on rigorous mathematical theory; they are slow to converge and only appropriate for small-sized problems; and finally, there were no mathematical analysis tools to accompany them. However, these drawbacks can be refuted today. Regarding slow convergence, in practice, one only needs improvement rather than optimality. In such a case, direct methods can be a good option because they can obtain an improved solution even faster than local methods that require gradient information. In addition, direct search methods are straightforward to implement. If we not only consider the elapsed time for a computer to run, but the total time needed to formulate the problem, program the algorithm and obtain an answer, then a direct search is also a compelling alternative. Regarding the problem size, it is usually considered that direct search methods are best suited for problems with a small number of variables. However, they have been successfully applied to problems with a few hundred variables. Finally, regarding analytical tools, several convergence analysis studies for a direct search algorithm were published starting in the early 1970s [9,10,11,12]. These results prove that it is possible to provide rigorous guarantees of convergence for a large number of direct search methods [4], even in the presence of heuristics. Consequently, direct search methods are regarded today as a respectable choice, and sometimes the only option, for solving certain classes of difficult and practical optimization problems, and they should not be dismissed as a compelling alternative in these cases. Direct search methods are broadly classified into local and global optimization approaches.

Local Optimization Approaches

Since there does not exist a suitable algorithmic characterization of global optima, most optimizers are based on local optimization. The most important derivative-free local based methods are pattern search methods and model-based search methods. Pattern search methods perform local exploration of the cost function on a pattern (a set of points conveniently selected). The Hooke–Jeeves [13] method and the Nelder–Mead simplex method [14] are two well-known examples of pattern search local methods.

The method of Hooke and Jeeves consists of a sequence of exploratory moves from a base point in the coordinate directions, which, if successful, are followed by pattern moves. The purpose of an exploratory move is to acquire information about the cost function in the neighborhood of the current base point. A pattern move attempts to speed up the search by using the information already acquired about the function to identify the best search direction.

The Nelder–Mead simplex algorithm belongs to the class of simplex-based direct search methods introduced by Spendley*et al.* in [15]. This class of methods evolves a pattern set of $n + 1$ vectors on an n-dimensional search space that is interpreted as the vertex set of a simplex, *i.e.*, a convex n-dimensional polytope. Different simplex-based methods use different operators to evolve the vertex set. The Nelder–Mead algorithm starts by ordering the vertices of the simplex and uses five operators: reflection, expansion, outer contraction, inner contraction and shrinkage. At each iteration, only one of these operations is performed. As a result, a new simplex is obtained such that either contains a better vertex (a vertex that is better than the worst one and substitutes it) or has a smaller volume. From the point of view of the function value, every operator, except for the shrinkage, is productive and obtains a vertex that improves the worst one. The shrinkage operator reduces the volume of the simplex to guarantee algorithm termination. Unfortunately, the convergence of the Nelder–Mead simplex algorithm to a local minimizer is not guaranteed [16], and a number of modifications have been introduced to get convergence. Nevertheless, the Nelder–Mead simplex algorithm remains as one of the most popular direct search algorithms.

Model-based search methods are based on the idea of using function evaluations to compute a model of the cost function and to obtain derivative approximations from this model. Many model-based methods are trust-region algorithms [17] that interpolate the cost function in some region of appropriate shape and size to obtain a good approximation of the cost function that can later be easily optimized on that region. Typically, the model to be adjusted is a fixed-order polynomial, and the trust region is a sphere in some norm of the search space. The model function is sequentially optimized in the trust region, and the trust region is updated for the next iteration until the approximated model satisfies a first-order optimality condition. Model-based methods also include [18,19,20]. During the last decade, there has been a considerable amount of work to handle constraints in the field of direct search methods. New algorithms have been developed to deal with bounds and linear inequalities [21,22] smooth nonlinear constraints [23,24] or non-smooth constraints [25,26,27]. In this work, we do not deal with constraints. Our aim here is to develop a simple and efficient algorithm that improves the heuristics-based optimization methods that are presently used to obtain the global minimum in a multidimensional and multimodal continuous function.

Global Optimization Approaches

Local optimization methods are the best option for convex, or at least unimodal, optimization problems. However, most real-world problems are not convex, and the solution provided by a local method is not guaranteed to be global. Unfortunately, even if derivatives are available, it is not possible in general to prove that a local optimum is global. A rigorous global optimization algorithm for a multimodal cost function requires in-depth exploration of the search space, and this is only possible for functions with a small number of variables, because the computational time for space exploration increases exponentially with the dimension of the search space.

In order to circumvent the curse of dimensionality, many global optimization algorithms use random search [28] and heuristics [29,30]. Some successful classes of global optimization algorithms are simulated annealing algorithms [31], evolutionary algorithms [32], estimation of distribution algorithms [33], particle swarm optimization algorithms [34,35], differential evolution algorithms [36,37], tabu search algorithms [38,39] or ant colony optimization algorithms [40,41].

In recent years, there has been a great interest in derivative-free methods for global optimization; see the monographs [42,43,44,45,46] and the references therein. In particular, there are two classes of algorithms that are of special interest. The first class is Lipschitz optimization methods. Lipschitz methods substitute the cost function by an auxiliary function that underestimates it. The auxiliary function is linear piecewise and is obtained by partitioning the search space and repeatedly using the Lipschitz property [47,48,49,50]. An interesting Lipschitz method is DIRECT (DIviding RECTangles) that was introduced in [51]. In this method, the cost function is evaluated at several sample points by using all possible weights on local *versus* global search expressed by the Lipschitz constant. The DIRECT algorithm has gained popularity due to its simplicity. However, it has two weaknesses. First, it is slow in reaching the solution with high accuracy, and second, it spends an excessive number of evaluations exploring local minima. Some variants have been developed to improve these weaknesses [52,53,54,55].

Another class of global optimization methods uses a filled function to avoid local minima. The basic idea is to design an auxiliary function, called the filled function, such that when the algorithm reaches a local minimum, the minimization of the filled function provides a point that moves away from the basin of the local minimum. The filled function method was introduced by Ge [56,57]. It has had increasing interest in filled methods in the last few years [58,59,60].

A DIRECT SEARCH ALGORITHM FOR GLOBAL OPTIMIZATION

The direct search algorithm for global optimization proposed here has two main ingredients: a transformed cost function and a simplex-based mechanism to evolve the initial point. The transformed cost function improves global exploration, while the evolution mechanism guarantees the termination and global convergence to a stationary point. To the best of our knowledge, the transformed cost function has not been previously used in the literature, and it is a key ingredient of our approach, because it provides global exploration of the search space. The new algorithm is an efficient alternative to heuristics-based optimization methods for global optimization and preserves the convergence properties of a well-designed direct search method.

The algorithm makes use of an initial point that is allocated as a qualified vertex of an n-dimensional initial simplex. This simplex is evolved by a sequence of operations that depend on the value of the transformed cost function at each vertex. Each operation produces a similar simplex of a different size.

The sequence of operations is designed in such a way that the simplex tends to asymptotically collapse in a single point. The algorithm terminates when the simplex vertices are close enough to each other.

Before explaining the algorithm and its operators in detail, we shall review some basic geometric results about n-simplices. Later, we shall introduce the cost function transformation and its main properties.

Notation

A brief summary of the notation used in this paper is included next for quick reference.

Setofintegernumbersininterval $\mathcal{I}$: $\mathbb{Z}_{\mathcal{I}} := \{z \in \mathbb{Z} : z \in \mathcal{I}\}$
.

Closed convex hull of a set $\mathcal{A}$: $\mathbf{Co}(\mathcal{A})$.

Difference set $\mathcal{A}\backslash\mathcal{B} = \{x \in \mathcal{A} : x \notin \mathcal{B}\}$.

Larger integer less than or equal to x: $\lfloor x \rfloor$.

Inner product of Euclidean space: $\langle x, y\rangle = x^T y$.

p-norm of Euclidean space: $\|\mathbf{x}\|_p = \left(\sum_{i=1}^{n} |x_i|^p\right)^{\frac{1}{p}}, p \in \mathbb{Z}_{[1,\infty)}$.

∞-norm of Euclidean space: $\|\mathbf{x}\|_\infty = \lim_{p\to\infty} \|\mathbf{x}\|_p = \max\{|x_i| : \forall i\}$.

Review of the Basic Geometric Results about n-Simplices

Let $V=\{x_i : i \in \mathbb{Z}_{[0,n]}\}$ be a set of $n + 1$ affinely-independent points in $\mathbb{R}^n$, then the closed convex hull of V is an n-simplex Σ with vertex set V, and it is denoted as follows:

$$\Sigma = \mathrm{Co}(V) \tag{6}$$

Next, we introduce certain specific types of n-simplices that are non-standard in the literature.

Definition 1. (Right n-simplex). A right n-simplex has a vertex, such that the n edges intersecting at it are pairwise orthogonal. This vertex is called the right vertex.

Definition 2. (Isosceles right n-simplex). A right n-simplex, such that every edge intersecting at the right vertex has the same length Δ, is an isosceles right n-simplex of length Δ.

Definition 3. (Standard n-simplex). The standard n-simplex is an isosceles right n-simplex of unit length.

By locating the zero of $\mathbb{R}^n$ in the right vertex, the standard n-simplex Σ_n^0 is the n-dimensional polytope with vertex set $\mathcal{V} = \{\mathbf{b}_i \in \mathbb{R}^n : i \in \mathbb{Z}_{[0,n]}\}$ where b0 is the zero vector, and bi is the i-th element of the standard basis of $\mathbb{R}^n$. Alternatively, the standard n-simplex can be defined as the intersection of the closed unit ball in the one-norm of $\mathbb{R}^n$ and the non-negative orthant, *i.e.*, $\Sigma_n^0 = \{\mathbf{x} \in [0,1]^n : \|\mathbf{x}\|_1 \leq 1\}$.

The content of an n-dimensional object is the measure of the amount of space inside its boundary. For instance, the content of a two-simplex is its area, and the content of a three-simplex is its volume. It can be proven by induction that the content of a standard n-simplex is $\frac{1}{n!}$.

A regular n-box is an n-dimensional box with edges of equal length. If the content of an n-simplex is not zero, then a geometric object of nonzero content can fit in its interior. The following lemma provides the edge length of the maximum regular n-box that can fit in the interior of a standard n-simplex.

Lemma 1. *The regular n-box of maximum size that can be contained inside a standard n-simplex has edge length* $\frac{1}{n}$ *and content* $\left(\frac{1}{n}\right)^n$.

Proof. The standard n-simplex is given as $\Sigma_n^0 = \{\mathbf{x} \in [0,1]^n : \|\mathbf{x}\|_1 \leq 1\}$. The maximum n-box that can be allocated inside the standard n-simplex has a vertex in the origin, and it is oriented along the coordinate directions. The opposite vertex to the origin of this regular n-box has coordinates $x_i = \frac{1}{n}$ for $i \in \mathbb{Z}_{[1,n]}$; therefore, its edge length is $\frac{1}{n}$, and its content is $\left(\frac{1}{n}\right)^n$.

The edges that intersect at the right vertex of a standard n-simplex are oriented along the coordinate directions, so these edge directions define a nonnegative orthant. Any direction inside this orthant can be expressed by a nonnegative n-dimensional vector of unit norm, *i.e.*, $\langle d, d\rangle = 1$. A direction d forms angles θ_i with the coordinate directions whose cosines are called the directional cosines and are given by $\cos\theta_i = \langle d, b_i\rangle$. The following lemma proves that any direction d contained in the nonnegative orthant has at least one directional cosine that never is less than $\frac{1}{\sqrt{n}}$.

Lemma 2. *The smallest directional cosine of any direction contained in the orthant formed by the edges intersecting at the right vertex of a standard n-simplex is never less than* $\frac{1}{\sqrt{n}}$.

Proof. Without loss of generality, suppose that the right vertex is the zero point and that the edges are in the coordinate directions, characterized by the elements of the standard basis of $\mathbb{R}^n$, *i.e.*, b_i for $i \in \mathbb{Z}_{[0,n]}$. Consider the direction $\mathbf{d}^* = \left[\frac{1}{\sqrt{n}} \cdots \frac{1}{\sqrt{n}}\right]$ whose directional cosines are $\cos\theta_i^* = \langle \mathbf{d}^*, \mathbf{b}_i\rangle = \frac{1}{\sqrt{n}}$ for all $i \in \mathbb{Z}_{[1,n]}$. Suppose that unlike the lemma statement, there exists a direction d with unit norm $\langle d, d\rangle = 1$, such that $\cos\theta_i = \langle \mathbf{d}, \mathbf{b}_i\rangle < \frac{1}{\sqrt{n}}$ for all $i \in \mathbb{Z}_{[1,n]}$, then $\langle \mathbf{d}, \mathbf{d}\rangle < n\sum_{i\in\mathbb{Z}_{[1,n]}} \frac{1}{n} = 1$. This contradicts the fact that d has unit norm, and the lemma is proven.

A consequence of this lemma is that any direction contained in the nonnegative n-orthant always forms an angle less than $\frac{\pi}{2}$ radians with at least one of the coordinate directions that form the orthant. In addition, if we consider an arbitrary direction d $\in \mathbb{R}^n$, then there always exists an n-simplex similar to the standard n-simplex, such that the edge directions of its right vertex define an orthant, such that the smallest directional cosine is never less than $\frac{1}{\sqrt{n}}$. This

n-simplex is obtained by rotating ϖ radians the edges of the standard n simplex corresponding to the negative components of the direction vector d.

Function Transformation

A key ingredient of our direct search global optimization algorithm is a transformation of the cost function that improves its exploratory features, providing the capability of jumping out of local minimizers, while preserving termination and convergence properties.

Let $x \in \mathbb{R}^n$ be an n-dimensional vector; $\lfloor x \rfloor$ denotes the n-dimensional vector whose components are the greatest integers less than or equal to the components of x. The fractional part of x is denoted as frac(x) and is defined as follows:

$$\text{frac}(x) = x - \lfloor x \rfloor \quad (7)$$

Let ξ be an arbitrary n-dimensional vector of real numbers and P a positive integer. Let us introduce the following map:

$$x(\xi) = \text{frac}(P\xi) \quad (8)$$

This map is onto and transforms the n-dimensional Euclidean space $\mathbb{R}^n$ in the n-dimensional unit interval (0,1) n. Let f be the cost function of the minimization problem given in Equation (1) and introduce the following function transformation:

$$\varphi(\xi) := f(x(\xi)) = f(\text{frac}(P\xi)) \quad (9)$$

where P is a positive integer. Since the cost function f is not necessarily defined outside of the open unit n-box, the domain of the transformed cost function φ is:

$$\text{dom}\, \phi = \{\xi \in \mathbb{R}^n : P\xi \notin \mathbb{Z}^n\} \quad (10)$$

The reason is that if $P\xi \in \mathbb{Z}^n$, then frac($P\xi$) = 0, and f is not necessarily defined for $\xi = 0$.

The transformed function φ has certain interesting properties. The most important are the periodicity of period P^{-1} and piecewise continuity, both on each variable.

Lemma 3. *The transformed function* $\varphi(\xi) = f(\text{frac}(P\xi))$ *satisfies the following properties:*

- *The function* φ *is continuous for any* $\xi \in \mathbb{R}^n$*, such that* $P\xi \in (0,1)^n$.
- *Let* $\xi, \eta \in \mathbb{R}^n$ *be such that* $P\xi \in (0,1)^n$ *and* $P\eta \in \mathbb{Z}^n$*, then* $\varphi(\xi + \eta) = \varphi(\xi)$.

Proof. (i) If $P\xi \in (0,1)^n$, then frac($P\xi$) = $P\xi$ and $\varphi(\xi) = f(P\xi)$. Since f is continuous for any $x \in (0,1)$n, then φ is continuous for any $\xi \in \mathbb{R}^n$, such that $P\xi \in (0,1)^n$; (ii) If ξ and η are n-dimensional vectors, such that $P\xi \in (0,1)$n and $P\eta \in \mathbb{Z}^n$, respectively, then frac($P\eta$) = 0 and frac($P(\xi + \eta)$) = frac($P\xi$) = $P\xi$; consequently, $\varphi(\xi + \eta) = f(\text{frac}(P\xi)) = \varphi(\xi)$.

Let $x \in \mathbb{R}^n$ and $B_p(x)$ denote the following n-box:

$$\mathcal{B}_P(\mathbf{x}) = \{\xi \in \mathbb{R}^n : \lfloor P\xi \rfloor = \lfloor P\mathbf{x} \rfloor,\ P\xi \notin \mathbb{Z}^n\} \quad (11)$$

The transformed function φ is continuous on $B_p(x)$, and there always exists $\xi^* \in B_p(x)$, such that $\varphi(\xi^*) = \min\{\varphi(\xi) : \xi \in \text{dom}\,\varphi\}$. Note that the n-box B(x) is given by $B_p(x) = \{\xi = P^{-1}(z + \lfloor Px \rfloor) : z \in (0,1)^n\}$. If x = 0, then $B_p(0)$ is the fundamental n-box of the function φ, *i.e.*, $B_p(0) = (0,P-1)^n$. For another $x \in \mathbb{R}^n$, BP(x) is an n-box of length P^{-1}, where the function φ takes the same values as in the fundamental n-box $B_p(0)$. Note that there are P^n different n-boxes for $x \in (0,1)^n$; then, the function φ repeats P^n times in the unit n-box $(0,1)^n$.

Example 1. The function $f(x) = |x| - |\sqrt{x}\sin(3\pi x)|$, and the transformed function $\varphi(\xi) = f(\text{frac}(P\xi))$ for P = 10 are depicted for the open unit interval in Figure 1. The function f is continuous on the open unit interval (0,1) and has three local minima. The transformed function φ is periodic, of period $P^{-1} = 0.1$, and piecewise continuous on the open unit interval. The fundamental period of φ is B(0)=(0,0.1), and the function value repeats ten times on the unit interval. The function φ is continuous on each interval $B(x) = \{\xi : \lfloor 10\xi \rfloor = \lfloor 10x \rfloor, 10\xi \notin \mathbb{Z}\}$ for $x \in \mathbb{R}$, but discontinuous at the boundary points of these intervals, which are given by $\xi = 0.1k$ for any integer k. This discontinuity always occurs if $f(0 + \epsilon) \neq f(1 - \epsilon)$ for any $\epsilon > 0$, as occurs in this example and which is clearly visible in Figure 1. Moreover, the function φ is not necessarily defined for these points of discontinuity.

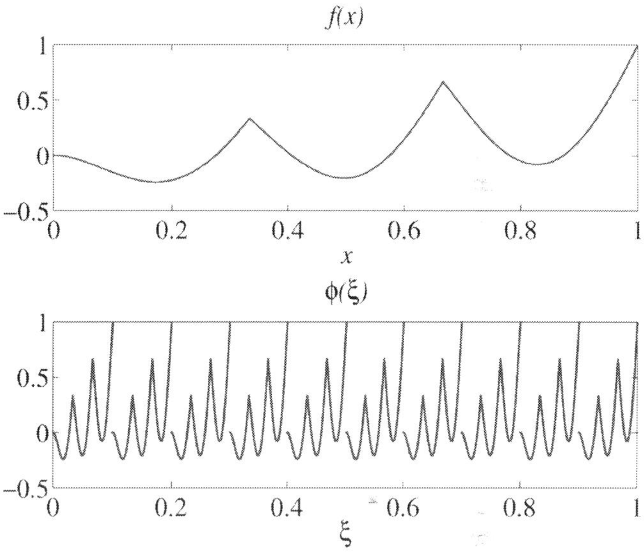

Figure 1. A continuous function $f(x) = |x| - |\sqrt{x}\sin(3\pi x)|$ with three local minima in the unit interval (0,1) and the corresponding transformed function $\phi(\xi) := f(\text{frac}(P\xi))$ where P = 10 for the same interval.

Consider the unconstrained optimization problem:

$$\min\{\phi(\xi) : \xi \in \text{dom}\,\varphi\} \quad (12)$$

The function φ has a global optimizer at ξ^* if $\phi(\xi^*) \leq \varphi(\xi)$ for all $\xi \in \text{dom}\,\varphi$. The following theorem proves that the transformed unconstrained minimization problem Equation (12) also provides the minimum value of the original optimization problem Equation (1).

Theorem 1. *Let f be a real value continuous function on the open unit n-box, and let* φ *be defined as* $\varphi(\xi) = f(\text{frac}(P\xi))$*, where P is a positive integer, then* $\lambda^* = \min\{f(x) : x \in (0,1)^n\}$ *if and only if* $\lambda^* = \min\{\varphi(\xi) : \xi \in \text{dom}\,\varphi\}$.

Proof. (If): Let x^* be such that $\lambda^* = f(x^*) = \min\{f(x) : x \in (0,1)^n\}$ and $\varphi(\xi) = f(\text{frac}(P\xi))$, where P is a positive integer; then define $\xi^* = P^{-1}(x^* + \eta)$ for any $\eta \in \mathbb{Z}^n$; then $\varphi(\xi^*) = f(x^*) = \lambda^*$. (Only if): Let ξ^* be such that $\lambda^* = \varphi(\xi^*) = \min\{\varphi(\xi) : \xi \in \text{dom}\varphi\}$; define $x^* = \text{frac}(P\xi^*)$; then $f(x^*) = \varphi(\xi^*) = \lambda^*$.

Theorem 1 allows us to obtain a global minimizer of the original function f on the open unit n-box by solving the unconstrained optimization problem (12). If we have a method that computes a global minimizer ξ^* of the unconstrained optimization problem (12), then $x^* = \text{frac}(P\xi^*) \in (0,1)^n$, and it satisfies $\varphi(\xi^*) = f(x^*)$.

The following lemma proves that any regular n-box of a size greater than or equal to P^{-1} always contains a point ξ^* that attains the global minimum of the unconstrained optimization problem (12).

Lemma 4. *Let* B *be a regular n-box of edge length* Δ_B, *such that* $P\Delta_B \geq 1$, *and let* $\lambda^* = \min\{f(x) : x \in (0,1)\}$*; then, the n-box* B *always contains a point* $\xi^* \in \mathbb{R}^n$, *such that* $\varphi(\xi^*) = \lambda^*$.

Proof. Let $x^* \in (0,1)^n$ be such that $f(x^*) = \lambda^* \leq f(x)$ for any $x \in (0,1)^n$, and let $\bar{\xi} \in B$, such that $\lfloor P\bar{\xi} \rfloor = \lfloor P\bar{\xi} + x^* \rfloor$. Consider the open n-box $B_P(\bar{\xi}) = \{\xi \in \mathbb{R}^n : \lfloor P\xi \rfloor = \lfloor P\bar{\xi} \rfloor, P\xi \notin \mathbb{Z}^n\}$, then $B_P(\bar{\xi})$ has edge length P^{-1}, and the point $\xi^* = P^{-1}(x^* + \lfloor P\bar{\xi} \rfloor)$ satisfies $\xi^* \in B(\bar{\xi}) \cap B$ and $\varphi(\xi^*) = f(x^*) = \lambda^*$.

We are also interested in determining the size of an n-simplex similar to the standard n-simplex that always contains a global minimizer of $\{\varphi(\xi) : \xi \in \text{dom } \varphi\}$. Since Lemma 4 establishes that such a point is always contained in a regular n-box of length not less than P^{-1}, then the solution is an isosceles right n-simplex that contains a regular n-box of length P^{-1}. From Lemma 1, this n-simplex has edge length nP^{-1} and content $P^{-n}/(n-1)!$. The following lemma states the result.

Theorem 2. *Let* Σ *be an isosceles right n-simplex of length* Δ, *such that* $P\Delta \geq n$, *and let* $\lambda^* = \min\{f(x) : x \in (0,1)^n\}$*; then, the n-simplex* Σ *always contains a point* $\xi^* \in \text{dom } \varphi$, *such that* $f(\text{frac}(\xi^*)) = \lambda^*$.

Proof. A regular n-box of edge length $\Delta_B = \Delta/n$ can be inscribed inside any isosceles right n-simplex of length Δ. Since $P\Delta \geq n$, then $P\Delta_B \geq 1$, and the theorem statement is a straightforward consequence of Lemma 4.

In the rest of this section, we shall design a direct search algorithm to obtain a solution for the optimization problem (1). We distinguish two algorithms, the basic algorithm and the complete algorithm. The basic algorithm is a simplex-based algorithm for the transformed cost function. An initial point is embedded at the right vertex of an isosceles right n-simplex of edge length Δ_0. This n-simplex evolves by a sequence of operations. As a result of each iteration, another n-simplex is obtained that is similar to the standard n-simplex and has the point with minimum value of the transformed cost function located in the right vertex. The edge length of the n-simplex decreases by a constant factor if no operations performed during the iteration produce a vertex with a smaller value of the transformed cost function. Whenever the edge length is no less than nP^{-1}, we say that the algorithm is in exploratory phase, because the n-simplex always contains a global minimizer of $\{\varphi(\xi) : \xi \in \text{dom } \varphi\}$. When the edge length of the n-simplex is less than nP^{-1}, then we say that the algorithm is in convergence phase, and it aims to approach a stationary point. Thus, the basic algorithm is designed to preserve the good properties of direct search algorithms, such as convergence to a stationary point, but increases the possibility to reach the global optimum at the end of the exploratory phase. Another feature of the basic algorithm is that there is no interruption or change from one phase to the other, it is a straightforward consequence of using the transformed cost function.

The Basic Algorithm

The basic algorithm is a simplex-based algorithm for the transformed optimization problem Equation (12). It performs a sequence of operations over an initial simplex until a termination condition is satisfied. The main operators of this algorithm are expansive translation, rotation and shrinkage. The expansive translation is performed after a sufficient decrease of the transformed cost function to ensure that the best point is located at the right vertex. The rotation operation provides exploration of the search space, and the shrinkage operator guarantees termination and global convergence to a stationary point of the transformed cost function. The global improvement is a consequence of using the transformed cost function Equation (8). A sufficient decrease condition of the cost function to accept a successful iteration is a key aspect to prove the termination and global convergence to a stationary point. The main components of the basic algorithm are explained below.

Function Transformation

The cost function transformation is given by:

$$\varphi(\xi) = f(\text{frac}(P\xi)) \quad (13)$$

This transformation aims to perform global improvement at each iteration $k \in \mathbb{Z}_{[0,\infty)}$ whenever the n-simplex has an edge length, such that $P\Delta_k \geq n$.

Initial Simplex

Let $\text{vset}(\xi, \Delta)$ where $\xi \in \mathbb{R}^n$ and $\Delta \in \mathbb{R}$ be defined as follows:

$$\text{vset}(\xi, \Delta) := \{\xi_i : \xi_i = \xi + \Delta b_i,\ i \in \mathbb{Z}_{[1,n]}\} \quad (14)$$

where b_0 is an n-dimensional zero vector and bi for $i \in \mathbb{Z}_{[1,n]}$ is the i-th element of the standard basis of $\mathbb{R}^n$. The initial n-simplex is obtained by varying an initial point at a distance Δ_0 in each coordinate direction, such that $P\Delta_0 > n$. Let $\xi_0 \in (0,1)^n$ be an initial point; then, the vertex set of the initial simplex is given by:

$$V_0 = \text{vset}(\xi_0, \Delta_0) \quad (15)$$

If the initial point ξ_0 is not provided as an input of the algorithm, then it can be randomly chosen. Consequently, the initial simplex is an isosceles right n-simplex with edge length Δ_0 and content $\frac{1}{n!}\Delta_0^n$ whose right vertex is indexed by zero.

Expansive Translation

This operation aims to position the point with lowest value of the transformed cost function found so far at the right vertex. Let V be the vertex set of an isosceles right n-simplex with edge length Δ, and let $\xi_i \in V$ be such that $\varphi(\xi_i) \leq \varphi(\xi_j)$ for $\xi_j \in V$; then, the expansive translation of the right n-simplex V with respect to the vertex i is given by the following expression:

$$\xi'_j = \xi_i + \rho(\xi_j - \xi_0),\ \xi_j \in \mathcal{V}$$

(16)

where $1 \leq \rho < \infty$. If the vertex set of the current simplex is given by V = vset(ξ_0, Δ), then the transformed n-simplex has the vertex set V′ = vset(ξ_j, Δ′), where Δ′ = ρΔ, and its edge length is |Δ′|. The new n-simplex, after the expansive translation, preserves its shape, but increases its content by a factor of ρ^n. From a practical point of view, it is convenient to choose the expansive factor close to one, but slightly greater, because this avoids obtaining candidate points that were already visited in previous iterations, in the next rotation operation.

Let c be an arbitrary positive constant; if $\varphi(\xi'_i) < \varphi(\xi_0) - c\Delta^2$ for some $\xi'_i \in V'$}, then the algorithm proceeds to a new iteration and performs an expansive translation operation. Otherwise, the algorithm executes a rotation operation.

The introduction of the positive term $c\Delta^2$ guarantees that the iteration is considered successful only if it provides a point with a sufficient decrease of the cost function.

Rotation

This operation produces a similar n-simplex, but where each edge is rotated ϖ radians with respect to the right vertex. A graphical interpretation is depicted in Figure 2.

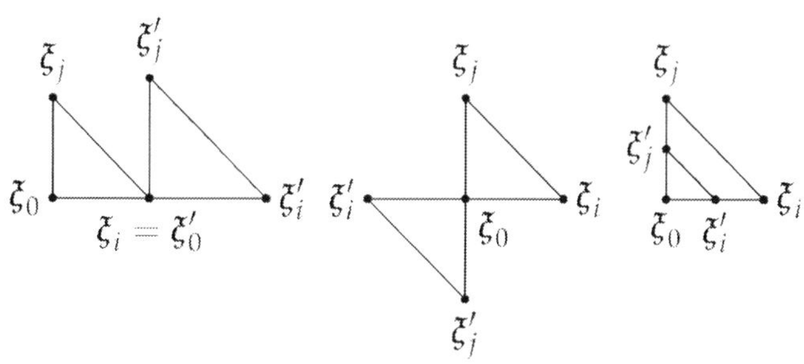

Figure 2. Graphical representation of the simplex translation, rotation and shrinking simplex operations for three points in R2. The initial vertex set is V = {ξ_0, ξ_i, ξ_j}, and the final vertex set is $\mathcal{V}' = \{\xi'_0, \xi'_i, \xi'_j\}$. The three operations produce similar simplices.

Let V denote the vertex set of an n-simplex. The vertices of the rotated n simplex are given by the following expression:

$$\xi'_j = \xi_0 - (\xi_j - \xi_0),\ \xi_j \in \mathcal{V} \tag{17}$$

If the vertex set of the current simplex is given by V = vset(ξ_0, Δ), then the transformed n-simplex has the vertex set V′ = vset(ξ_0, Δ′), where Δ′ = − Δ, and its edge length is |Δ′|. If $\varphi(\xi'_i) < \varphi(\xi_0) - c\Delta^2$ for some $\xi'_i \in V'$, then the rotation operation succeeds, and the algorithm proceeds to start a new iteration and performs an expansive translation operation. Otherwise, the rotation operation fails; the rotated vertex set is discarded; and the algorithm executes a shrinkage operation with the original vertex set V.

Shrinkage

This operation performs a contraction of the simplex by fixing the right vertex and placing the remaining vertices along the same directions, but at a distance that is reduced by a constant factor σ ∈ (0,1). A graphical interpretation of the shrinkage operation is depicted in Figure 2 for $\mathbb{R}^2$.

Let V denote the vertex set of an n-simplex. The vertices of the transformed n-simplex are given by:

$$\xi'_j = \xi_0 + \sigma(\xi_j - \xi_0),\ \xi_j \in \mathcal{V} \tag{18}$$

If the vertex set of the current simplex is given by V = vset(ξ_0, Δ), then the transformed n-simplex has the vertex set V′ = vset(ξ_0, Δ′), where Δ′ = σΔ, and its edge length is |Δ′|. After the shrinkage operation, the algorithm proceeds to start a new iteration by performing an expansive translation operation.

Sufficient Decrease Condition

The expansive translation and rotation operations are considered successful if some vertex of the transformed n-simplex satisfies the following sufficient decrease condition:

$\varphi(\xi'_i) < \varphi(\xi_0) - c\Delta^2$, for some $\xi'_i \in V'$

where c is a positive constant. This condition is key to proving the termination of the basic algorithm and global convergence to a stationary point. The constant c is arbitrary, but usually, a small value is chosen.

Stopping Criterion

The sufficient decrease condition and the shrinkage operation guarantee that the size of the n-simplex converges to zero. Consequently, a stopping criterion can be defined by taking a sufficiently small number ϵ > 0. Let |Δ| be the edge length of the n-simplex; then, the basic algorithm stops when the following condition is satisfied:

$$P|\Delta| \leq \epsilon \tag{19}$$

Space Transformation

The search space transformation is given by the map:

$$x(\xi) = \mathrm{frac}(P\xi) \tag{20}$$

Therefore, when the n-simplex with vertex set V reaches edge length Δ≤ϵ, the basic algorithm stops, and the point obtained is $\bar{\mathbf{x}} = \mathrm{frac}(P\bar{\xi})$, where $\bar{\xi} \in \arg\min\{\xi : \xi \in \mathcal{V}\}$; and it attains the function value $f(\bar{\mathbf{x}}) = \phi(\bar{\xi})$.

Implementation

An implementation of the basic algorithm in pseudocode is given in Algorithm 1.

Algorithm 1 Basic algorithm.

function BGDS(f, x_0)	
parameters: $\epsilon > 0$, $P \in \mathbb{N}$	
definitions: $s(\xi) := P\xi - \lfloor P\xi \rfloor$, $\phi(\xi) := f(s(\xi))$	
$z \leftarrow \text{rand}(\dim(x_0))$	
$\xi_0 \leftarrow (\lfloor Pz \rfloor + x_0)/P$	
$\epsilon \leftarrow \epsilon/P$	
$\xi \leftarrow \text{LDS}(\phi, \xi_0, \epsilon)$	▹ Local direct search
return $s(\xi)$	
end function	
function LDS(ϕ, ξ_0, ϵ)	
parameters: $\rho, \sigma, c \in \mathbb{R} : 1 \leq \rho, 0 < \sigma < 1, 0 < c, 0 < \Delta$	
definitions: $\text{vset}(\xi, \Delta) := \xi \in \mathbb{R}^n, \Delta \in \mathbb{R}\}$, $\text{vmin}(V) \in \text{argmin}\{\phi(\xi_i) : \xi_i \in V\}$	
$\xi \leftarrow \xi_0$	
$V \leftarrow \text{vset}(\xi, \Delta)$	
$\xi_{min} \leftarrow \text{vmin}(V)$	
while $\epsilon < \lvert\Delta\rvert$ **do**	
if $\phi(\xi_{min}) < \phi(\xi) - c\Delta^2$ **then**	▹ Expansive translation
$\xi \leftarrow \xi_{min}$	
$\Delta \leftarrow \rho\Delta$	
$V \leftarrow \text{vset}(x, \Delta)$	
$\xi_{min} \leftarrow \text{vmin}(V)$	
end if	
if $\phi(\xi) - c\Delta^2 \leq \phi(\xi_{min})$ **then**	▹ Rotation
$\Delta \leftarrow -\Delta$	
$V \leftarrow \text{vset}(\xi, \Delta)$	
$\xi_{min} \leftarrow \text{vmin}(V)$	
end if	
if $\phi(\xi) - c\Delta^2 \leq \phi(\xi_{min})$ **then**	▹ Shrinkage
$\Delta \leftarrow \sigma\Delta$	
$V \leftarrow \text{vset}(\xi, \Delta)$	
$\xi_{min} \leftarrow \text{vmin}(V)$	
end if	
end while	
return ξ_{min}	
end function	

Convergence of the Basic Algorithm

The basic algorithm has been designed to provide termination and improvement by performing a sequence of simplex transformations. If in addition, the cost function is differentiable and its gradient is Lipschitz continuous, then the basic algorithm converges to a stationary point.

Theorem 3. *Let f be the cost function of a minimization problem on the open unit n-box; then the basic algorithm always terminates. If, in addition, f is differentiable and its gradient Δf is Lipschitz continuous on the unit n-box, then the sequence of points generated at each iteration by the basic algorithm converges to a stationary point.*

Proof. Let S and U denote the index sets of successful and unsuccessful iterations of the basic algorithm, respectively. Let $\mathbf{x}_k = \mathrm{frac}(P\xi_k)$, then $f(\mathbf{x}_k) = \phi(\xi_k)$. If k ∈ S, then $f(\mathbf{x}_{k+1}) < f(\mathbf{x}_k) - c\Delta_k^2$ and $\Delta_{k+1} = \rho\Delta_k$, while if k ∈ U, then $f(\mathbf{x}_{k+1}) \geq f(\mathbf{x}_k) - c\Delta_k^2$ and $\Delta_{k+1} = \sigma\Delta_k$. Let us begin by proving that $\lim_{k\to\infty} |\Delta_k| = 0$. Suppose not; then, for any k ∈ $\mathbb{Z}_{[0,\infty]}$, there exists $\ell \geq k$, such that $\ell \in S$ because, if such an *l* does not exist, then the set of successful iterations would be finite, and when *k* approaches infinity, the update rule $\Delta_{k+1} = \sigma\Delta_k$ yields $\lim_{k\to\infty} |\Delta_k| = 0$. In addition, there exists $\underline{\Delta} > 0$, such that for each successful iteration $\ell \in \mathcal{S}, |\Delta_\ell| \geq \underline{\Delta}$ and:

$$f(\mathbf{x}_{\ell+1}) < f(\mathbf{x}_\ell) - c\Delta_\ell^2 \leq f(\mathbf{x}_\ell) - c\underline{\Delta}^2$$

However, since *l* approaches infinity, this implies that $f(\mathbf{x}_{\ell+1}) \to -\infty$, which contradicts the fact that the function *f* is bounded below on (0,1)n. Consequently, the boundedness of *f* implies that $\underline{\Delta} = 0$ and $\lim_{k\to\infty} |\Delta_k| = 0$. This proves the termination of the basic algorithm.

For the second part of the theorem, if *f* is continuous and differentiable on (0,1)n, then so is $\phi(\xi) = f(\mathrm{frac}(P\xi))$ on the *n*-box $\mathcal{B}_P(\mathbf{x}) = \{\xi \in \mathbb{R}^n : \lfloor P\xi \rfloor = \lfloor P\mathbf{x} \rfloor, P\xi \notin \mathbb{Z}^n\}$ for any $x \in \mathbb{R}^n$. Furthermore, if ∇*f* is Lipschitz continuous with constant *M* on $(0,1)^n$, then so is ∇ϕ in $B_p(x)$ with constant PM. Since we proved that $\lim_{k\to\infty} |\Delta_k| = 0,$ then there always exists a positive integer *L*, such that $\lfloor P\xi_k \rfloor = \lfloor P\xi_L \rfloor$ for any positive integer k > L. The basic algorithm searches points along the coordinate directions; then, from Lemma 2 and for any positive integer k>L, no matter the value of $\nabla\phi(\xi_k)$, there is always at least one (positive or negative) coordinate direction $\mathbf{d}_i \in \{\mathbf{b}_i, -\mathbf{b}_i\}$, such that:

$$\frac{1}{\sqrt{n}} \leq \cos\theta = \frac{\langle -\nabla\phi(\xi_k), \mathbf{b}_i \rangle}{\|\nabla\phi(\xi_k)\| \|\mathbf{d}_i\|}$$

or equivalently:

$$\frac{1}{\sqrt{n}} \|\nabla\phi(\xi_k) \leq -\langle \nabla\phi(\xi_k), \mathbf{d}_i \rangle \tag{21}$$

because $\|d_i\|=1$. For any unsuccessful iteration k ∈ U, $\phi(\xi_k + |\Delta_k|\mathbf{d}_k) \geq \phi(\xi_k) - c\Delta_k^2$, the mean value theorem establishes that:

$$\begin{aligned} -c\Delta_k^2 &\leq \phi(\xi_k + |\Delta_k|\mathbf{d}_i) - \phi(\xi_k) \\ &= \langle \nabla\phi(\xi_k + \alpha_k|\Delta_k|\mathbf{d}_i), \mathbf{d}_i \rangle |\Delta_k| \end{aligned}$$

for some $\alpha_k \in [0,1]$. Subtracting $\langle \nabla\phi(\xi_k), \mathbf{d}_i \rangle |\Delta_k|$ from both sides leads to:

$$-c\Delta_k^2 - \langle \nabla\phi(\xi_k), \mathbf{d}_i \rangle |\Delta_k| \leq \langle \nabla\phi(\xi_k + \alpha_k|\Delta_k|\mathbf{d}_i) - \nabla\phi(\xi_k), \mathbf{d}_i \rangle |\Delta_k|$$

Applying Equation (21) yields:

$$\frac{1}{\sqrt{n}} \|\nabla\phi(\xi_k)\| \leq \langle \nabla\phi(\xi_k + \alpha_k|\Delta_k|\mathbf{d}_i) - \nabla\phi(\xi_k), \mathbf{d}_i \rangle + c|\Delta_k|$$

Taking into account that φ is continuously differentiable in $B_p(\xi_k)$ and its gradient ∇ϕ is Lipschitz with constant PM in $B_p(\xi_k)$,

$$\frac{1}{\sqrt{n}} \|\nabla\phi(\xi_k)\| \leq PM\|\alpha_k\Delta_k\mathbf{d}_i\| + c|\Delta_k| \leq (PM + c)|\Delta_k|$$

because $\alpha_k \in (0,1)$ and $\|b_i\|=1$. Consequently,

$$\|\nabla\phi(\xi_k)\| \leq \sqrt{n}(PM+c)|\Delta_k|$$

and taking the limit when k approaches infinity, it is possible to conclude that:

$$\lim_{k\to\infty} \|\nabla\phi(\xi_k)\| \leq \sqrt{n}(PM+c) \lim_{k\to\infty} |\Delta_k| = 0, \text{ for } k \in \mathcal{U}$$

and finally, by making $x_k = \text{frac}(\xi_k)$:

$$\lim_{k\to\infty} \|\nabla f(\mathbf{x}_k)\| = P \lim_{k\to\infty} \|\nabla\phi(\xi_k)\| = 0, \text{ for } k \in \mathcal{U}.$$

Consequently, the sequence of points generated by the basic algorithm converges to a stationary point.

Remark 2. The basic algorithm can be applied to any cost function f, not necessarily continuous or differentiable in the search space $(0,1)^n$. For a continuous and differentiable function with a Lipschitz continuous gradient, the basic algorithm converges to a stationary point. If in addition the cost function is strictly convex, then the unique optimizer is a stationary point, and Theorem 3 guarantees that the basic algorithm converges to the unique optimizer. Note that we do not need to know the value of the Lipschitz constant M.

Example 2. The evolution of the basic algorithm for the function $f(x) = |x| - |\sqrt{x}\sin(3\pi x)|$ is depicted in Figure 3. The parameters of the algorithm are $P = 10^4$, $\sigma = 0.5$, $\rho = 1.05$, $c = 0.01$, $\epsilon = 10^{-4}$. Since this problem is unidimensional, the simplex is an interval. The left plots represent the vertex points of the simplex in the original space (above) and their corresponding function values (below) after each iteration. The right plots represent the values of the worst (above) and best (below) points of the simplex in the original space that were obtained during the execution of the algorithm. Note that the algorithm explores the whole range of the unit interval. This exploration is performed whenever the length of the simplex edge Δ_k satisfies $P\Delta_k \geq 1$, which corresponds to the exploratory phase of the algorithm. Once Δ_k is $P\Delta_k < 1$, then the algorithm enters the phase of convergence to a stationary point. In this example, the algorithm stops after 24 iterations. From Iterations 1 to 12, the algorithm is in the exploratory phase, and from Iterations 13 to 24, the algorithm is in the convergence phase to a stationary point. The point obtained corresponds to $f(0.1721) = -0.2422$, which is the global minimal value within the space tolerance ϵ.

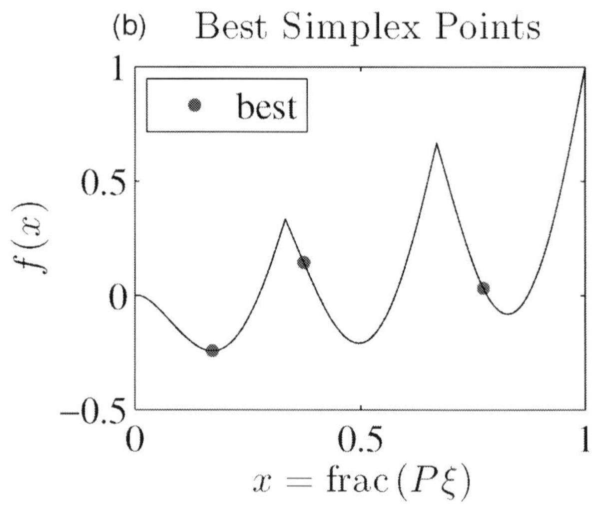

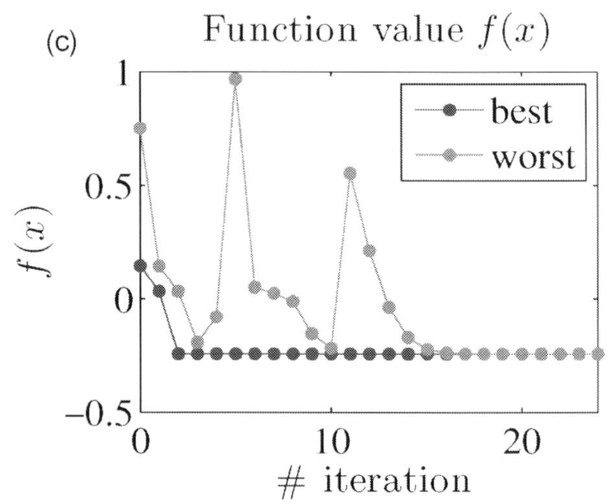

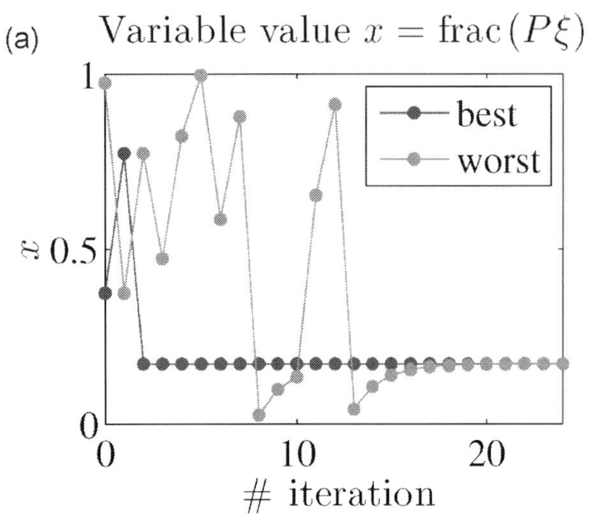

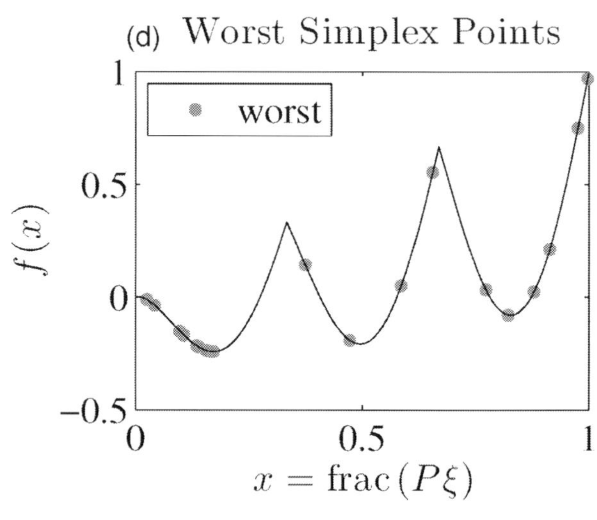

Figure 3. Evolution of the algorithm for $f(x) = |x| - |\sqrt{x}\sin(3\pi x)|$ and $x(\xi) = \text{frac}(P\xi)$. The parameters of the algorithm are $P = 10^4$, $\sigma = 0.5$, $\rho = 1.05$, $c = 0.01$, $\epsilon = 10^{-4}/P$.

The Complete Algorithm

The complete algorithm that we call GDS (an acronym for Global Direct Search), is obtained by repeating the basic algorithm a number of times. A single application of the basic algorithm may obtain the global optimum within a space tolerance only in easy problems. For more difficult optimization problems, a new execution of the basic algorithm, starting with the best point obtained in the previous execution, may improve the result. Each execution produces a local minimizer; however, if there are better points in some coordinate direction, the algorithm may jump to one of these points during the exploratory phase of a new execution. Unfortunately, not every optimization problem satisfies the property that, for any local minimizer, there are points in some coordinate direction where the cost function is improved. In such a case, a strategy that turns out to be more effective is to start from a new random initial point. The class of cost functions that we are facing is not usually known in advance, and we do not know which strategy is more appropriate for a new execution of the basic algorithm. A trade-off solution is to repeat the basic algorithm N times, but starting from a new random initial point after a number $R \leq N$ of repetitions.

Initial Point

Let N denote the total number of executions of the basic algorithm and R the number of repetitions without choosing a new initial point. Let $\bar{x}$ denote the point obtained in the previous execution of the basic algorithm and ξ_r a random vector in $(0,1)^n$ with a uniform probability distribution. The initial point for the n-th execution of the basic algorithm is obtained as follows:

$$\xi_0 = \begin{cases} \text{frac}(P^{-1}\text{int}(P\xi_r) + \bar{\mathbf{x}}) & \text{if } n \bmod (R+1) \neq 0 \\ \xi_r & \text{if } n \bmod (R+1) = 0 \end{cases} \tag{22}$$

where mod is the modulo operator that represents the remainder of the integer division of their arguments. Note that if $R = 0$, the initial point is always a random point; however, if $R = N$, the initial point is always the point obtained in the previous execution of the basic algorithm.

Best Point Storage

The minimum point found during the execution of the complete algorithm is preserved. The point obtained after each basic algorithm execution is compared to the best solution stored and, in the case of improvement, the new point replaces it. Let x denote the point obtained after the last execution of the basic algorithm and x_{min} the best point stored so far; the storage rule is:

$$\mathbf{x}'_{\text{min}} = \begin{cases} \bar{\mathbf{x}} & \text{if } f(\bar{\mathbf{x}}) < f(\mathbf{x}_{\text{min}}) \\ \mathbf{x}_{\text{min}} & \text{otherwise} \end{cases} \tag{23}$$

Implementation of the Complete Algorithm

An implementation of the complete algorithm GDS in pseudocode is given in Algorithm 2.

Algorithm 2 Complete algorithm GDS.

```
function GDS(f, x_0)
parameters: N, R ∈ ℕ, such that R ≤ N
x_min ← x_0
for k = 1 to N do
x ← x_min
if k mod(R +1) = 0 then
x ← r and(dim(x_0))
end if
x ← BGDS(f, x)          ▷ Basic global direct search
if f(x) < f(x_min) then
x_min ← x
end if
end for
return x_min
end function
```

EXPERIMENTAL STUDY

Test Functions

Global optimization is not a trivial problem. Theoretical results, such as the No Free Lunch (NFL) theorem [61], state that an efficient general-purpose universal optimization algorithm is not possible. In other words, this result says that one algorithm can outperform another only for a certain class of problems. It is a usual practice to analyze the performance of an optimization algorithm by using test functions. A large number of standard test functions have been used to study the performance of our direct search global optimization algorithm. In this section, we present the results for the 24 functions given in Table 1. These function are described in detail in [62]. The functions are classified into five groups: separable functions (func # 1.xx), functions with low or moderate conditioning (func # 2.xx), unimodal functions with high conditioning (func # 3.xx), multimodal functions with an adequate global structure (func # 4.xx) and multimodal functions with a weak global structure (func # 5.xx). All of the functions are scalable with the dimension. All of the functions are defined and can be evaluated over $\mathbb{R}^n$, and the search space is $[-5,5]^n$, where n is the dimension of the function domain. The global optimal value is attained in this search space.

Table 1. Description of the functions used in the experimental study.

Func #	Description
1.01	Sphere
1.02	Ellipsoid separable with monotone x-transformation, condition 1e + 06
1.03	Rastrigin separable with both x-transformations condition 10
1.04	Skew Rastrigin–Bueche separable, condition 10, skew-condition 100
1.05	Linear slope, neutral extension outside the domain (not flat)
2.06	Attractive sector function
2.07	Step-ellipsoid, condition 100
2.08	Rosenbrock, original
2.09	Rosenbrock, rotated
3.10	Ellipsoid with monotone x-transformation, condition 1e6
3.11	Discus with monotone x-transformation, condition 1e6
3.12	Bent cigar with asymmetric x-transformation, condition 1e6
3.13	Sharp ridge, slope 1:100, condition 10
3.14	Sum of different powers
4.15	Rastrigin with both x-transformations, condition 10
4.16	Weierstrass with monotone x-transformation, condition 100
4.17	Schaffer F7 with asymmetric x-transformation, condition 10
4.18	Schaffer F7 with asymmetric x-transformation, condition 1000
4.19	F8F2 composition of 2D Griewank–Rosenbrock
5.20	Schwefel x sin(x) with tridiagonal transformation, condition 10
5.21	Gallagher 101 Gaussian peaks, condition up to 1000
5.22	Gallagher 21 Gaussian peaks, condition up to 1000, 1000 for global opt
5.23	Katsuuras repetitive rugged function
5.24	Lunacek bi-Rastrigin, condition 100

Selection of the GDS Parameters

The performance of the GDS algorithm for different parameter values has been empirically analyzed by means of extensive computer studies. Our algorithm has been implemented in the scientific software MATLAB [63], and its performance has been successfully compared to the global optimization strategies that are implemented in the Global Optimization Toolbox of MATLAB. The GDS algorithm has a number of configurable parameters, and this comparative study allowed us to select a set of parameters that are appropriate for many problems. The expansive and contractive factors are set to $\rho = 1.05$ and $\sigma = 0.5$. It is convenient to take the expansive value slightly greater than one to avoid evaluating points already checked in previous iterations. However, large values of ρ usually produce slow convergence. Consequently, values in the interval [1.01,1.10] are usually a good option for most problems. Regarding the contractive factor σ, the closer to one, the larger the number of iterations of the basic GDS algorithm will be. From our experiments, $\sigma = 0.5$ is a convenient value that produces a satisfactory trade-off between the efficiency of the algorithm and the convergence time. The constant c of the sufficient decrease condition is chosen as c = 0.01. Any positive value of *c* provides the termination of the algorithm, but small values are recommended to improve the algorithm's performance during the initial iterations when Δ is large. The parameters *P* and *R* were fixed to P = 1000 and R = 5. These values were selected after a massive experimentation. In our experiments, we analyzed the mean value of the CPU time for one execution of the basic GDS algorithm for different values of the parameter *R*. The empirical results showed that the larger the value of *R*, the lower the CPU time for execution. This means that when *R* increases, the number of executions *N* can also be increased to a certain extent without compromising the total CPU time. The reduction is larger for smaller values of *R*, e.g., the reduction is about 40% from R = 0 to R = 1 and about 30% from R = 1 to R = 2. Since increasing *R* is also beneficial for functions that can be globally optimized along the coordinate directions, a good option that trades off between moderate CPU time and efficiency in computing the global optimum is to choose $R \in [2,10]$ and increase the number of repetitions of the basic algorithm *N* as much as possible, to maintain a moderate total CPU time. In fact, we have checked that a good selection of *P* and *R* could improve the results depending on the problem. However, since a practitioner usually does not know in advance what class its problem belongs to, it is important to fix a set of parameters that tradeoff for a large class of problems. In conclusion, the parameter values of the GDS algorithm for the experimental study were selected as P = 1000, R = 5, $\rho = 1.05$, $\sigma = 0.5$, c = 0.01 and N = 1e9, and the stopping criterion is the number of function evaluations.

Performance Evaluation

The evaluation of the GDS algorithm has been accomplished by solving the 24 functions in Table 1 using the fixed set of parameters values explained in the previous subsection. The performance of GDS is compared to DIRECT [51]. DIRECT is a deterministic global optimization algorithm based on the domain partition strategy. Each iteration includes two phases. The first phase identifies hyper-rectangles that potentially contain a global optima. In the second phase, the hyper-rectangles identified in the first phase are partitioned into smaller hyper-rectangles, and the cost function is evaluated at the centers of the hyper-rectangles. The convergence properties guarantee that if no termination criteria are included, DIRECT will exhaustively sample the domain. The implementation of DIRECT in MATLAB by Finkel [64] has been used in this study. The experiments have been performed in a laptop PC equipped with a dual core processor Intel (R) Core (TM) i5-3317U CPU @1.70 GHz running MATLAB R2014a under the Windows operating system.

The comparative study has been performed as follows: For both algorithms, GDS and DIRECT, a fixed number of function evaluations is used as a stopping condition, and the error in computing the global minimum value is obtained. Each problem has been solved 15 times, and the median of the error is tabulated for each function. The study has been accomplished for the 24 functions of Table 1 and for different dimensions of the function domain and different numbers of function evaluations. The default parameters of DIRECT [64] have been used, but using the number of function evaluations as stopping conditions.

In Table 2, the results for functions of dimensions five and 10 and a number of function evaluations equal to 10^3 and $10^4$are shown, while in Table 3, the same results are shown for dimensions 10 and 20 and 10^4 and 10^5 function evaluations. GDS and DIRECT obtained different results for different functions. In general, for a small number of function evaluations, DIRECT gets a smaller median of the error. However, as the number of function evaluations increases, the improvement in approaching the minimum value is higher in GDS. One of the outstanding features of GDS is its simplicity. This can be checked by comparing the CPU time with DIRECT. The CPU time for all of the problems, dimensions and function evaluations is much smaller for GDS; see Figure 4 and Figure 5. Note that GDS is more than 100-times faster than DIRECT for several functions of dimension 40 and 10^5 function evaluations.

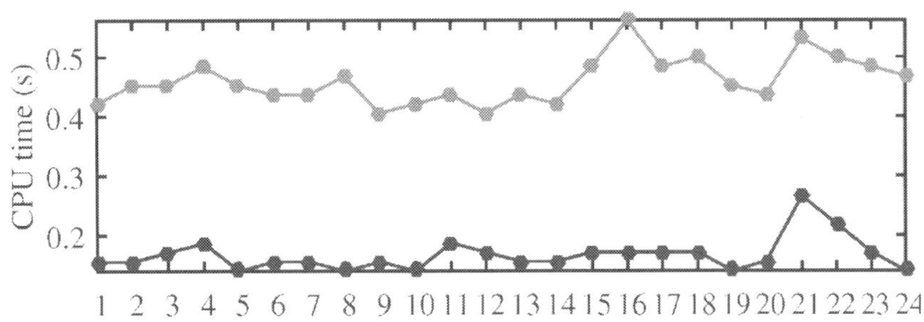

(a) Functions (1-24)

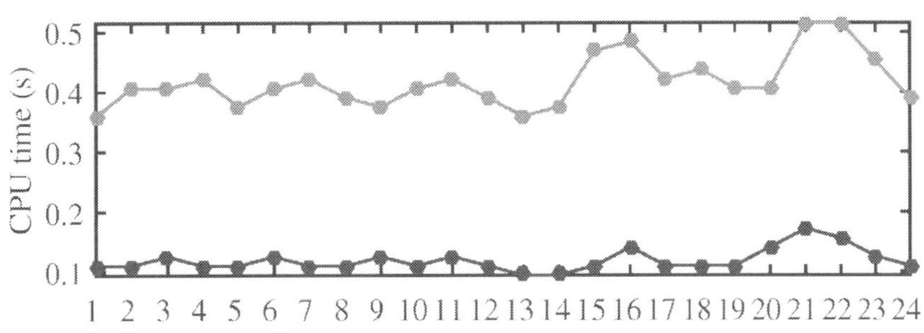

(b) Functions (1-24)

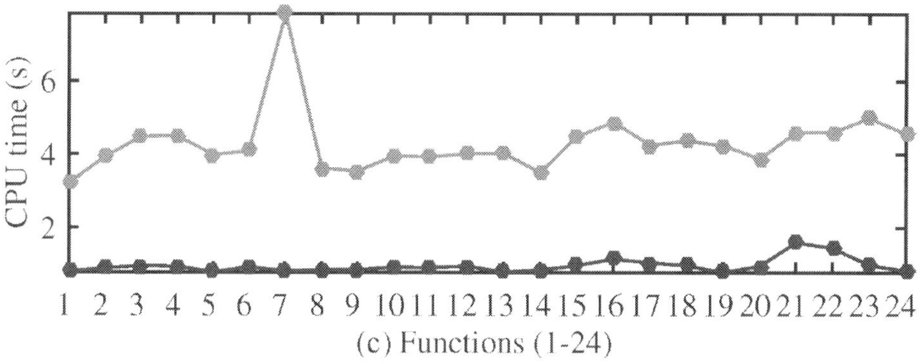

Figure 4. Comparative study of the CPU time of GDS (blue) and DIRECT (red) for solving 24 problems of dimension five (**a**) and dimension 10 (**b**) using 10^3 function evaluations (**c**) and 10^4 function evaluations (**d**).

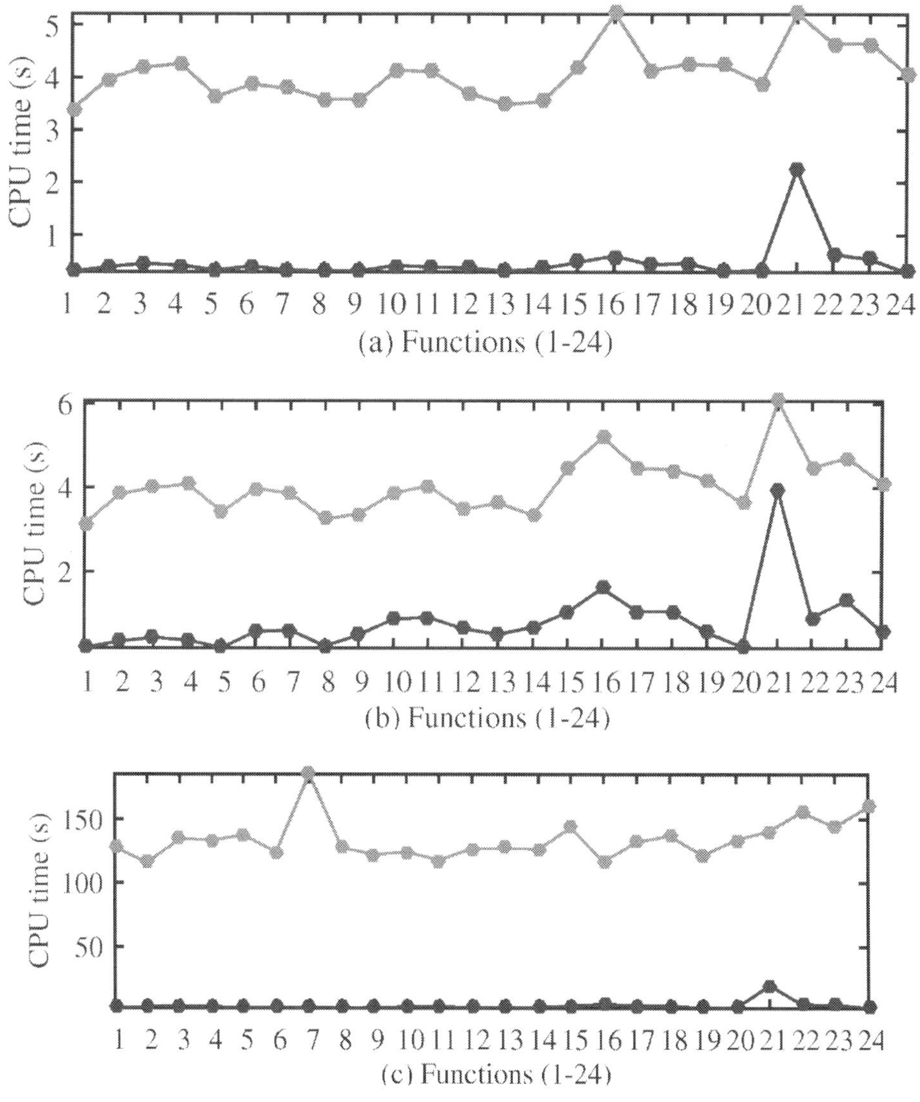

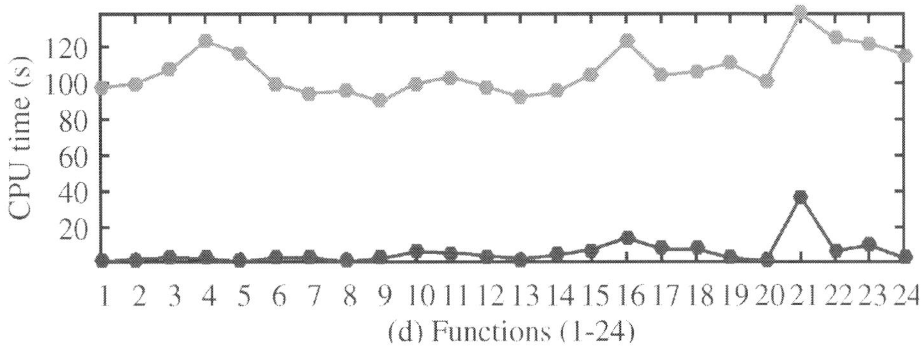

Figure 5. Comparative study of CPU time of GDS (blue) and DIRECT (red) for solving 24 problems of dimension 20 (**a**) and dimension 40 (**b**) using 10^4 function evaluations (**c**) and 10^5 function evaluations (**d**).

Table 2. Comparative study of the median of the error for problems of dimensions 5 and 10 and the number of evaluations 1e + 03 and 1e + 04.

Func	**GDS**	**DIRECT**	**GDS**	**DIRECT**	**GDS**	**DIRECT**	**GDS**	**DIRECT**
#	**dim = 5**	**nev = 1e+03**	**dim = 5**	**nev = 1e+04**	**dim = 10**	**nev = 1e+03**	**dim = 10**	**nev = 1e+04**
1.01	3.647e+01	5.094e-04	9.920e-09	1.347e-04	1.422e+02	1.862e-01	9.826e-09	1.076e-03
1.02	2.400e+06	2.044e+00	8.064e-06	3.053e-01	1.072e+07	1.475e+05	2.020e-05	2.129e+00
1.03	3.649e+02	7.015e+00	2.002e-02	5.970e+00	6.338e+02	4.234e+01	7.859e-02	1.692e+01
1.04	2.507e+02	1.249e+01	1.696e-02	6.967e+00	9.518e+02	5.252e+01	1.058e+00	2.274e+01
1.05	6.767e+01	1.643e-02	7.809e-05	1.643e-02	1.788e+02	2.271e+01	1.986e-04	1.909e-02
2.06	6.348e+04	2.306e+00	3.497e-07	7.272e-01	5.778e+05	2.520e+01	1.435e-01	1.185e+01
2.07	4.044e+00	6.738e-01	5.543e-01	5.216e-03	2.796e+01	6.227e+00	5.254e+00	1.815e+00
2.08	3.644e+04	2.107e+00	1.647e+00	1.794e-02	2.066e+05	9.353e+01	3.141e+00	8.302e+00
2.09	7.835e+03	5.858e-01	2.433e-01	2.747e-02	8.654e+04	1.551e+01	5.383e+00	6.010e+00
3.10	1.426e+05	8.102e+02	9.892e+02	3.345e+01	7.788e+06	1.312e+04	3.999e+03	1.640e+03
3.11	1.003e+02	1.997e+01	5.722e+01	4.615e+00	1.647e+06	5.343e+01	1.023e+02	3.198e+01
3.12	4.213e+07	6.904e+00	4.372e+00	2.012e-02	2.597e+08	1.284e+05	5.751e+00	7.904e-01
3.13	8.841e+02	2.545e+00	1.067e+00	5.285e-02	2.388e+03	9.999e+01	2.036e+00	6.097e+00
3.14	2.356e+01	8.957e-03	8.020e-04	7.238e-04	5.779e+01	2.685e-01	2.232e-03	1.452e-02
4.15	1.920e+02	7.971e+00	5.014e+00	2.988e+00	7.494e+02	5.364e+01	6.365e+01	1.991e+01
4.16	3.869e+00	6.053e-01	6.144e-01	4.247e-03	3.089e+01	5.140e+00	2.428e+00	5.762e-01
4.17	1.069e+01	1.104e-01	9.849e-01	6.272e-03	2.350e+01	1.457e+00	1.265e+01	9.732e-02
4.18	4.694e+01	2.134e-01	2.395e+00	2.908e-02	5.608e+01	6.410e+00	5.172e+01	4.363e-01
4.19	2.775e+00	8.478e-02	5.901e-01	4.858e-02	2.127e+01	1.990e-01	2.630e+00	1.620e-01
5.20	1.983e+04	1.265e+00	2.392e-01	8.295e-01	7.714e+04	2.707e+00	9.283e-01	1.829e+00
5.21	1.751e+01	2.052e-04	9.300e-01	6.972e-06	7.886e+01	2.338e+00	6.676e+00	2.239e-03
5.22	4.032e+01	6.928e-01	6.024e-02	2.746e-04	8.485e+01	1.651e+00	7.272e+00	6.928e-01
5.23	1.395e+00	9.682e-01	6.205e-01	8.782e-01	2.247e+00	1.438e+00	7.203e-01	9.066e-01
5.24	9.572e+01	2.122e+01	1.108e+01	1.071e+01	2.673e+02	7.556e+01	9.847e+01	6.139e+01

Table 3. Comparative study of the median of the error for problems of dimensions 20 and 40 and the number of evaluations 1e + 04 and 1e + 05.

Func	GDS	DIRECT	GDS	DIRECT	GDS	DIRECT	GDS	DIRECT
#	dim = 20	nev = 1e+04	dim = 20	nev = 1e+05	dim = 40	nev = 1e+04	dim = 40	nev = 1e+05
1.01	6.690e-2	1.456e-01	9.434e-09	2.626e-03	3.187e+02	2.533e+01	8.897e-09	5.976e-02
1.02	3.171e+03	1.570e+06	3.806e-05	3.471e+01	1.195e+07	2.904e+06	4.865e-02	2.904e+06
1.03	9.586e+00	5.187e+01	3.545e-02	3.620e+01	1.719e+03	5.029e+02	2.008e+00	9.027e+01
1.04	9.342e+00	6.536e+01	7.299e-02	6.174e+01	4.448e+03	5.542e+02	1.487e+00	1.165e+02
1.05	5.537e-01	3.190e+01	4.178e-04	2.201e-02	5.900e+02	3.495e+02	8.092e-04	4.421e+01
2.06	3.202e+01	6.464e+01	1.873e+00	3.152e+01	9.308e+05	1.415e+03	2.211e+00	1.177e+02
2.07	3.453e+01	1.654e+01	1.371e+01	6.260e+00	1.376e+02	1.234e+02	6.765e+01	4.261e+01
2.08	7.405e+01	6.866e+01	4.320e+00	3.332e+01	6.045e+05	7.049e+03	8.010e+01	1.602e+02
2.09	2.030e+01	5.129e+01	8.313e+00	3.241e+01	3.287e+05	2.260e+02	3.715e+01	1.424e+02
3.10	4.927e+04	1.210e+04	2.472e+03	4.680e+03	1.048e+07	2.325e+05	2.234e+04	6.582e+04
3.11	2.337e+02	8.049e+01	2.610e+02	6.898e+01	5.563e+02	1.885e+02	4.841e+02	1.792e+02
3.12	1.716e+04	1.010e+05	6.880e+00	1.499e+03	6.739e+08	2.964e+07	7.067e+00	1.240e+05
3.13	3.187e+01	1.404e+02	1.805e+00	1.050e+02	3.588e+03	9.766e+02	2.019e+00	1.607e+02
3.14	2.114e-02	2.780e-01	6.335e-04	8.335e-02	1.016e+02	6.893e+00	2.241e-03	3.609e-01
4.15	1.349e+03	1.125e+02	9.561e+01	6.304e+01	3.134e+03	4.190e+02	7.482e+02	2.579e+02
4.16	6.812e+00	5.866e+00	3.164e+00	3.113e+00	2.283e+01	1.475e+01	9.467e+00	8.788e+00
4.17	1.885e+01	1.854e+00	2.314e+01	4.799e-1	2.714e+01	5.368e+00	2.041e+01	1.716e+00
4.18	7.823e+01	5.327e+00	8.362e+01	1.387e+00	1.084e+02	2.034e+01	1.062e+02	8.653e+00
4.19	6.546e+00	2.504e-01	4.953e+00	2.307e-01	2.069e+01	2.504e-01	8.861e+00	2.504e-01
5.20	1.108e+00	1.973e+00	6.419e-01	1.837e+00	1.273e+05	2.104e+02	9.083e-01	2.075e+00
5.21	7.598e+00	5.096e-01	1.803e+00	1.227e-01	8.327e+01	7.596e+00	4.714e+00	1.086e+00
5.22	1.114e+01	2.024e+00	6.919e-01	7.305e-1	8.487e+01	1.260e+01	8.905e+00	6.475e+00
5.23	1.038e+00	1.229e+00	6.147e-01	1.175e+00	2.385e+00	2.263e+00	1.078e+00	1.798e+00
5.24	5.915e+02	1.532e+02	9.995e+01	1.532e+02	1.333e+03	3.299e+02	8.494e+02	3.055e+02

The results of a study of the GDS algorithm for functions of high dimension are presented in Figure 6. The GDS algorithm is executed on the functions 1.02, 1.02, 1.04 and 1.05 of dimensions 100 and 200 to search the global minimum. The error to the global minimum in the logarithmic scale and the CPU time are shown for 10^4, 10^5, 10^6 and 10^7. It is interesting to remark that the CPU time grows linearly with the dimension of the problem.

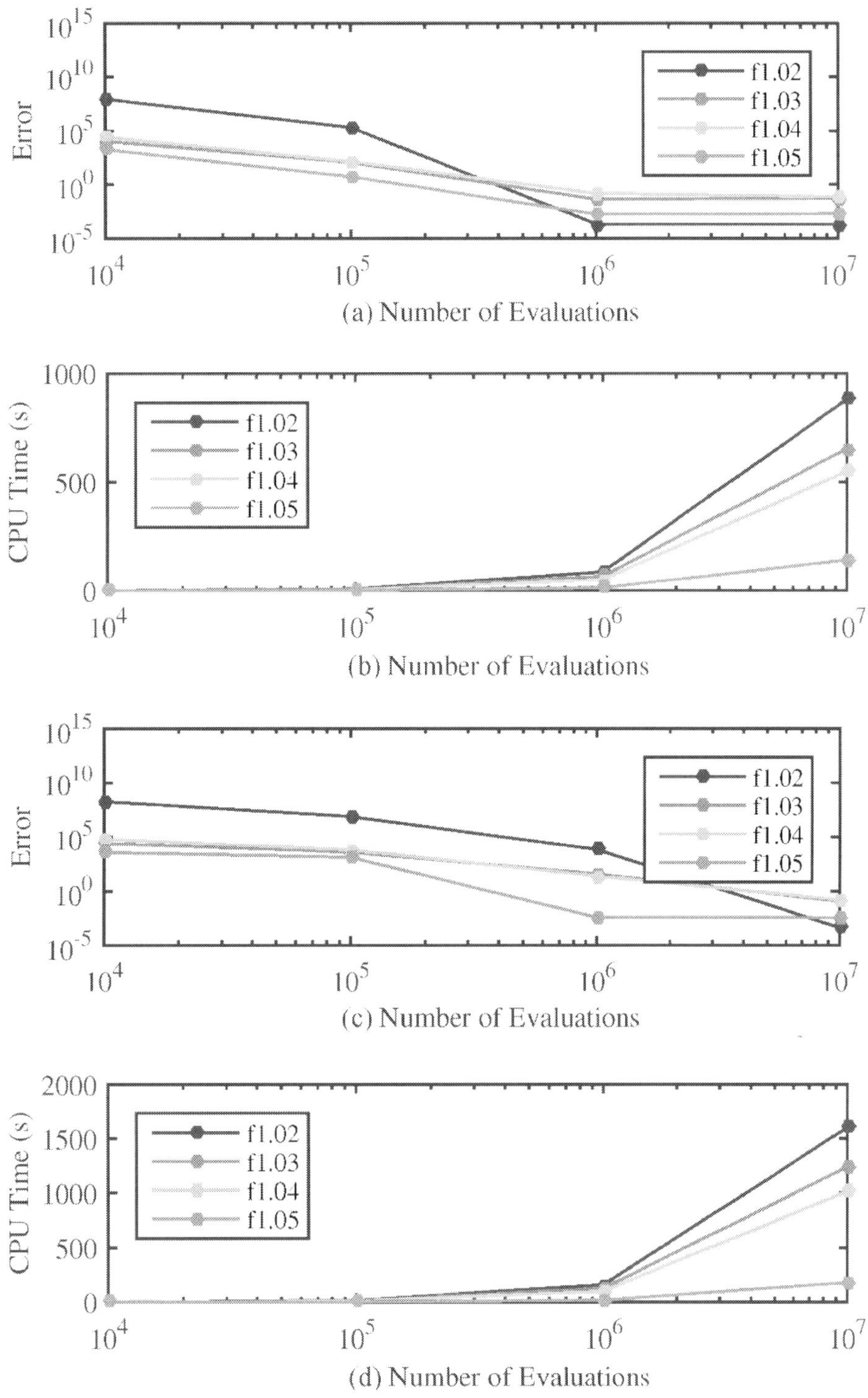

Figure 6. Study of the error to attain the global optimum (**a**) and CPU time (**b**) for functions of dimension 100 (**c**) and dimension 200 (**d**) using the GDS algorithm.

Since GDS is simple and computationally efficient, it can be successfully applied to problems of high dimensions where the number of function evaluations to obtain a good result is large for any direct search algorithm.

CONCLUSIONS

A direct search algorithm for the global optimization of multivariate functions has been reported. The algorithm performs a sequence of operations for an initial isosceles right n-simplex. The result of these operations is always a similar n-simplex of a different size. The operations depend on the values of the vertices of the n-simplex, where these values are computed using a transformed cost function that improves the exploratory features of the algorithm. The convergence properties of the algorithm have been proven. The results of an extensive experimental study demonstrate that the algorithm is capable of approaching the global optimum for black box problems with moderate computation time. It is competitive with most of the heuristic-based global optimization strategies presently used. Furthermore, it has been compared to DIRECT, a well-known Lipschitzian-based direct search algorithm. The new algorithm is very simple and computationally cost-effective and can be applied to problems of high dimension, because the empirical results demonstrate that its computation time increases linearly with the dimension of the problem. In future work, we plan to extend the algorithm to constrained optimization.

ACKNOWLEDGMENTS

The authors thank Instituto de las Tecnologías Avanzadas de la Producción (ITAP) for supporting the publication costs.

AUTHOR CONTRIBUTIONS

Enrique Baeyens and Alberto Herreros design the GDS algorithm and develop the experiments. José R. Perán analyzed the results. The three autors contributed equally to writing the paper.

REFERENCES

1. Lewis, R.M.; Torczon, V.; Trosset, M.W. Direct Search Methods: Then and Now. *J. Comput. Appl. Math.* 2000, *124*, 191–207.
2. Cohn, A.; Scheinberg, K.; Vicente, L. *Introduction to Derivative-Free Optimization*; MOS/SIAM Series on Optimization; SIAM: Philadelphia, PA, USA, 2009.
3. Pinter, J.D. Global Optimization: Software, Test Problems, and Applications. In *Handbook of Global Optimization*; Pardalos, P.M., Romeijn, H.E., Eds.; Kluwer Academic Publishers: Dordrecht, The Netherlands, 2002; Volume 2.
4. Kolda, T.G.; Lewis, R.M.; Torczon, V. Optimization by Direct Search: New Perspectives on Some Classical and Modern Methods. *SIAM Rev.* 2003, *45*, 385–482.
5. Neumaier, A. Complete Search in Continuous Global Optimization and Constraint Satisfaction. *Acta Numer.* 2004, *13*, 271–369.
6. Conn, A.R.; Scheinberg, K.; Vicente, L.N. *Introduction to Derivative-Free Optimization*; SIAM: Philadelphia, PA, USA, 2009; Volume 8.
7. Rios, L.M.; Sahinidis, N.V. Derivative-free optimization: A review of algorithms and comparison of software implementations. *J. Glob. Optim.* 2013, *56*, 1247–1293.
8. Swann, W.H. Direct Search Methods. In *Numerical Methods for Unconstrained Optimization*; Murray, W., Ed.; Academic Press: Salt Lake City, UT, USA, 1972; pp. 13–28.
9. Evtushenko, Y.G. Numerical methods for finding global extrema (case of a non-uniform mesh). *USSR Comput. Math. Math. Phys.* 1971, *11*, 38–54.
10. Strongin, R. A simple algorithm for searching for the global extremum of a function of several variables and its utilization in the problem of approximating functions. *Radiophys. Quantum Electron.* 1972, *15*, 823–829.
11. Sergeyev, Y.D.; Strongin, R. A global minimization algorithm with parallel iterations. *USSR Comput. Math. Math. Phys.* 1989, *29*, 7–15.
12. Dennis, J.E.J.; Torczon, V. Direct Search Methods On Parallel Machines. *SIAM J. Optim.* 1991, *1*, 448–474.
13. Hooke, R.; Jeeves, T. Direct search solution of numerical and statistical problems. *J. ACM* 1961, *8*, 12–229.
14. Nelder, J.A.; Mead, R. A Simplex Method for Function Minimization. *Comput. J.* 1965, *7*, 308–313.
15. Spendley, W.; Hext, G.R.; Himsworth, F.R. Sequential Application of Simplex Designs in Optimisation and Evolutionary Operation. *Technometrics* 1962, *4*, 441–461.
16. Lagarias, J.; Reeds, J.; Wright, M.; Wright, P. Convergence Properties of the Nelder-Mead Simplex Method in Low Dimensions. *SIAM J. Optim.* 1998, *9*, 112–147.
17. Conn, A.; Gould, N.; Toint, P. *Trust-Region Methods*; Society for Industrial and Applied Mathematics: Philadelphia, PA, USA, 2000.
18. Regis, R.; Shoemaker, C. Constrained global optimization of expensive black box functions using radial basis functions. *J. Glob. Optim.* 2005, *31*, 153–171.
19. Custodio, A.; Rocha, H.; Vicente, L. Incorporating minimum Frobenius norm models in direct search. *Comput. Optim. Appl.* 2010, *46*, 265–278.
20. Conn, A.; Le Digabel, S. Use of quadratic models with mesh-adaptive direct search for constrained black box optimization. *Optim. Methods Softw.* 2013, *28*, 139–158.
21. Lewis, R.; Torczon, V. Pattern search algorithms for bound constrained minimization. *SIAM J. Optim.* 1999, *9*, 1082–1099.
22. Lewis, R.; Torczon, V. Pattern search algorithms for linearly constrained minimization. *SIAM J. Optim.* 2000, *10*, 917–941.
23. Lewis, R.; Torczon, V. A globally convergent augmented Lagrangian pattern search algorithm for optimization with general constraints and simple bounds. *SIAM J. Optim.* 2002, *12*, 1071–1089.
24. Kolda, T.; Lewis, R.; Torczon, V. *A Generating Set Direct Search Augmented Lagrangian Algorithm for Optimization with a Combination of General and Linear Constraints*; Sandia National Laboratories: Livermore, CA, USA, 2006.
25. Audet, C.; Dennis, J.E. A pattern search filter method for nonlinear programming without derivatives. *SIAM J. Optim.*2004, *14*, 980–1010.
26. Abramson, M.; Audet, C.; Dennis, J. Filter pattern search algorithms for mixed variable constrained optimization problems. *Pac. J. Optim.* 2007, *3*, 477–500.
27. Dennis, J.; Price, C.; Coope, I. Direct search methods for nonlinearly constrained optimization using filters and frames.*Optim. Eng.* 2004, *5*, 123–144.
28. Solis, F.J.; Wets, R.J.B. Minimization by Random Search Techniques. *Math. Oper. Res.* 1981, *6*, 19–30.
29. Pearl, J. *Heuristics: Intelligent Search Strategies for Computer Problem Solving*; Addison-Wesley Longman Publishing Co., Inc.: Boston, MA, USA, 1984.
30. Michalewicz, Z.; Fogel, D.B. *How to Solve It: Modern Heuristics*, 2nd ed.; Springer: Berlin, Germany, 2004.
31. Kirkpatrick, S.; Gelatt, C.D.; Vecchi, M.P. Optimization by Simulated Annealing. *Science* 1983, *220*, 671–680.
32. Bäck, T. *Evolutionary Algorithms in Theory and Pratice*; Oxford University Press: New York, NY, USA, 1996.

33. Larrañaga, P.; Lozano, J.A. *Estimation of Distribution Algorithms: A New Tool for Evolutionary Computation*; Kluwer: Boston, MA, USA, 2002.
34. Kennedy, J.; Eberhart, R. Particle Swarm Optimization. In Proceedings of the 1995 IEEE International Conference on Neural Networks, Perth, Australia, 27 November–1 December 1995; Volume 4, pp. 1942–1948.
35. Poli, R.; Kennedy, J.; Blackwell, T. Particle swarm optimization. *Swarm Intell.* 2007, *1*, 33–57.
36. Storn, R.; Price, K. Differential Evolution—A Simple and Efficient Heuristic for global Optimization over Continuous Spaces. *J. Glob. Optim.* 1997, *11*, 341–359.
37. Chakraborty, U.K. *Advances in Differential Evolution*; Springer Publishing Company: Berlin, Germany, 2008.
38. Glover, F. Tabu Search—Part I. *ORSA J. Comput.* 1989, *2*, 190–206.
39. Glover, F.; Laguna, M. *Tabu Search*; Kluwer Academic Publishers: New York, NY, USA, 1997.
40. Dorigo, M.; Maniezzo, V.; Colorni, A. Ant system: Optimization by a colony of cooperating agents. *IEEE Trans. Syst. Man Cybern. Part B Cybern.* 1996, *26*, 29–41.
41. Dorigo, M.; Stützle, T. *Ant Colony Optimization*; Bradford Company: Scituate, MA, USA, 2004.
42. Paulavičius, R.; Žilinskas, J. *Simplicial Global Optimization*; Springer: Berlin, Germany, 2014.
43. Sergeyev, Y.D.; Strongin, R.G.; Lera, D. *Introduction to Global Optimization Exploiting Space-Filling Curves*; Springer: Berlin, Germany, 2013.
44. Strongin, R.G.; Sergeyev, Y.D. *Global Optimization with Non-Convex Constraints: Sequential and Parallel Algorithms*; Springer: Berlin, Germany, 2013.
45. Zhigljavsky, A.; Žilinskas, A. *Stochastic Global Optimization*; Springer: Berlin, Germany, 2008.
46. Zhigljavsky, A.A. *Theory of Global Random Search*; Springer: Berlin, Germany, 2012.
47. Shubert, B.O. A sequential method seeking the global maximum of a function. *SIAM J. Numer. Anal.* 1972, *9*, 379–388.
48. Sergeyev, Y.D.; Kvasov, D.E. Global search based on efficient diagonal partitions and a set of Lipschitz constants.*SIAM J. Optim.* 2006, *16*, 910–937.
49. Lera, D.; Sergeyev, Y.D. Lipschitz and Hölder global optimization using space-filling curves. *Appl. Numer. Math.* 2010,*60*, 115–129.
50. Kvasov, D.E.; Sergeyev, Y.D. Lipschitz global optimization methods in control problems. *Autom. Remote Control* 2013,*74*, 1435–1448.
51. Jones, D.R.; Perttunen, C.D.; Stuckman, B.E. Lipschitzian optimization without the Lipschitz constant. *J. Optim. Theory Appl.* 1993, *79*, 157–181.
52. Gablonsky, J.M.; Kelley, C.T. A locally-biased form of the DIRECT algorithm. *J. Glob. Optim.* 2001, *21*, 27–37.
53. Finkel, D.E.; Kelley, C. Additive scaling and the DIRECT algorithm. *J. Glob. Optim.* 2006, *36*, 597–608.
54. Paulavičius, R.; Sergeyev, Y.D.; Kvasov, D.E.; Žilinskas, J. Globally-biased Disimpl algorithm for expensive global optimization. *J. Glob. Optim.* 2014, *59*, 545–567.
55. Liu, Q.; Cheng, W. A modified DIRECT algorithm with bilevel partition. *J. Glob. Optim.* 2014, *60*, 483–499.
56. Ge, R.P. The theory of filled function-method for finding global minimizers of nonlinearly constrained minimization problems. *J. Comput. Math.* 1987, *5*, 1–9.
57. Ge, R.; Qin, Y. The globally convexized filled functions for global optimization. *Appl. Math. Comput.* 1990, *35*, 131–158.
58. Han, Q.; Han, J. Revised filled function methods for global optimization. *Appl. Math. Comput.* 2001, *119*, 217–228.
59. Liu, X.; Xu, W. A new filled function applied to global optimization. *Comput. Oper. Res.* 2004, *31*, 61–80.
60. Zhang, Y.; Zhang, L.; Xu, Y. New filled functions for nonsmooth global optimization. *Appl. Math. Model.* 2009, *33*, 3114–3129.
61. Wolpert, D.; Macready, W. No Free Lunch Theorems for Optimization. *IEEE Trans. Evol. Comput.* 1997, *1*, 67–82.
62. Hansen, N.; Finck, S.; Ros, R.; Auger, A. *Real-Parameter Black-Box Optimization Benchmarking 2009: Noiseless Functions Definitions*; Research Report RR-6829; INRIA: Rocquencourt, France, 2009.
63. Mathworks. *MATLAB User's Guide (R2010a)*; The MathWorks, Inc.: Natick, MA, USA, 2010.
64. Finkel, D.E. *DIRECT Optimization Algorithm User Guide*; Center for Research in Scientific Computation, North Carolina State University: Raleigh, NC, USA, 2003.

CHAPTER 4

A 3/2-APPROXIMATION ALGORITHM FOR THE GRAPH BALANCING PROBLEM WITH TWO WEIGHTS

Daniel R. Page and Roberto Solis-Oba

Department of Computer Science, Western University, London, ON N6A5B7, Canada

ABSTRACT

In the pursuit of finding subclasses of the makespan minimization problem on unrelated parallel machines that have approximation algorithms with approximation ratio better than 2, the graph balancing problem has been of current interest. In the graph balancing problem each job can be non-preemptively scheduled on one of at most two machines with the same processing time on either machine. Recently, Ebenlendr, Krčál, and Sgall (Algorithmica 2014, 68, 62–80.) presented a 7/4-approximation algorithm for the graph balancing problem. Let r, s $\in \mathbb{Z}^+$. In this paper we consider the graph balancing problem with two weights, where a job either takes r time units or s time units. We present a 3/2-approximation algorithm for this problem. This is an improvement over the previously best-known approximation algorithm for the problem with approximation ratio 1.652 and it matches the best known inapproximability bound for it.

INTRODUCTION

Let G = (V, E, p, q) be a weighted multigraph, where V is the set of vertices, E is the set of edges, p = (p_1, …, p|E|) are non-negative edge weights, and q = (q_1, …, q|V|) are the dedicated loads. A dedicated load qvof vertex v is the sum of the weights of self-loops incident on v in the multigraph; we assume the self-loops are removed from G. An orientation $\gamma : E \rightarrow V$ orients each edge e $\in$ E towards one of its endpoints. Given a weighted multigraph G, the graph balancing problem is to find an orientation γ where the maximum load of the vertices is minimized, where the load of a vertex v is defined as $q_v + \sum_{e|\gamma(e)=v}$ pe.

Citation: Daniel R. Page and Roberto Solis-Oba. A 3/2-approximation algorithm for the graph balancing problem with two weights, Algorithms 2016, 9(2), 38; DOI: 10.3390/a9020038

Let r, s $\in \mathbb{Z}^+$, where r < s. We focus on a special case of this problem we call the graph balancing problem with two weights (GBP2W), where the edges have either weight r or s and each dedicated load is of the form ar + bs for a, b $\in \mathbb{Z}^+ \cup \{0\}$.

The graph balancing problem is a special case of the makespan minimization problem on unrelated parallel machines ($R||C_{max}$ in Graham notation, see [1]). Presently, the best-known approximation algorithms for $R||C_{max}$ have approximation ratio 2. The first 2-approximation algorithm for $R||C_{max}$ was presented by Lenstra et al. [2], and in 2005 a (2 − 1/m)-approximation algorithm was given by Shchepin and Vakhania [3], where m is the number of machines. These 2-approximation algorithms utilize linear programming, but it is worth noting that there is a combinatorial 2-approximation algorithm by Gairing et al. [4] that employs generalized flow networks. Finding an approximation algorithm with approximation ratio better than 2 for $R||C_{max}$ is an important open problem in scheduling theory, and trying to get any further insight into the problem through the study of subclasses of $R||C_{max}$ has been of attention lately [5, 6, 7, 8, 9, 10, 11, 12, 13].

Recently, Ebenlendr et al. [7] gave a 7/4-approximation algorithm for the graph balancing problem. In addition, Ebenlendr et al. [14] showed that for $p < 3/2$, there is no p-approximation algorithm for the graph balancing problem when the edges of the multigraph have weight 1/2 or 1, unless P = NP. Note that this hardness result was also independently proven by Asahiro et al. [5, 15]. This matches the inapproximability bound for the makespan minimization problem on unrelated parallel machines given by Lenstra et al. [2], so, GBP2W is worth investigating due to being one of the simplest scheduling problems presently known to share inapproximability properties with $R||C_{max}$.

3/2-approximation algorithms have been presented for some special cases of GBP2W. The graph orientation problem with two weights is a NP-hard special case of GBP2W where G is simple, and every dedicated load $q_v = 0$. In [5, 15], Asahiro et al. gave two approximation algorithms that achieve the bound 3/2 for variants of the graph orientation problem with two weights: one called Cycle-Canceling when $r = 1$ and $s = 2$; and another called Refined Cycle-Canceling when $r = 1$ and $s = 3$. Later, Kolliopoulos and Moysoglou [9] gave a 3/2-approximation algorithm for GBP2W when $r = 1$ and $s = k$, where k is a positive integer (Theorem 4.1).

Most recently, Kolliopoulos and Moysoglou [9] presented a 1.652-approximation algorithm for GBP2W. Their approximation algorithm employs binary search, and for a given estimation of the optimal load T different approximation algorithms are used based on the values of the weights with respect to T. A core component of this approximation algorithm is a flow-network based approximation algorithm for the two-valued case of the restricted assignment problem introduced in the same paper. In this paper we present a 3/2-approximation algorithm for GBP2W. We adopt a technique of considering particular intervals for the weights during a binary search similar to that of by Kolliopoulos and Moysoglou to derive our 3/2-approximation algorithm.

To conclude this section, we outline the remainder of this paper. In Section 2, we present our contribution—a 3/2-approximation algorithm for GBP2W. After describing our algorithm, we give subroutines used by the algorithm and their correctness in Section 2.1, Section 2.2, Section 2.3 and Section 2.4, then prove our algorithm is indeed a 3/2-approximation algorithm for GBP2W in Section 2.5. In Section 3, we conclude our paper.

ALGORITHM

Similar to the algorithm by Lenstra et al. [2], our approximation algorithm uses an estimation T of the maximum load of a vertex in an optimal orientation as a parameter. The algorithm GB2W presented below as Algorithm 1 finds a solution of value at most 3T/2 if a solution of value at most T exists. We combine this algorithm with a binary search procedure to find the smallest value for T for which an orientation with load at most 3T/2 for the graph balancing problem with two weights is found: if for a given T the algorithm does not find a solution of value at most 3T/2 then the value of T is increased in the binary search; otherwise it is decreased. By the above property of our algorithm this smallest value of T must be less than or equal to the value of an optimum solution, hence our algorithm has approximation ratio 3/2.

The remainder of this section gives Lemmas 1–4 which provide the subroutines used by our algorithm, then in Theorem 5 we prove our algorithm is a 3/2-approximation algorithm for GBP2W. First, we present Lemma 1 which covers Step 4 of our algorithm. Note that in Step 1 the algorithm scales the weights so the estimation for the optimum load is $T = 1$. We define a big edge e to be an edge with weight $p_e > 1/2$; otherwise, we call an edge small. Let the value for an optimum solution for the problem be denoted as OPT. From this point forward, we assume that as edges are oriented in Steps 4–5.3, they are removed from G.

Algorithm 1: GB2W ($G = (V, E, p, q)$, T)

Input:

Multigraph G, value T.

Output:

An orientation γ for the edges in E with maximum vertex load at most 3T/2 or FAIL. If FAIL is returned there is no orientation for E with maximum vertex load T.

1. Divide edge weights and vertex dedicated loads by T; set T = 1.
2. **If** $s > 1$ or $q_v > 1$ for any $v \in V$ **then return** FAIL.
3. **If** $r, s \in (0, 1/2]$ **then** apply the algorithm by Lenstra et al. [2].
4. **If** $r, s \in (1/2, 1]$ **then** apply the algorithm given in Lemma 1.
5. **If** $r \in (0, 1/2]$ and $s \in (1/2, 1]$ we consider three subcases. Let $k = \lfloor 1/r \rfloor$, so $1/(k + 1) < r \leq 1/k$.

5.1.**If** $k/(k + 1) \leq s \leq 1$ **then** apply the algorithm in Lemma 2.

5.2.

If $(k - 1)/k \leq s < k/(k + 1)$ **then** apply the algorithm in Lemma 3.

5.3.**If** $1/2 < s < (k - 1)/k$ **then** apply the algorithm in Lemma 4.

6. **If** any of the algorithms used in Steps 3–5 reports FAIL or if the solution computed by them has value larger than 3/2 **then return** FAIL; otherwise **return** the solution computed in the above steps.

Step 4

Lemma 1. There is a polynomial-time algorithm for the graph balancing problem with two rational weights $r, s \in (1/2, 1]$that either finds a solution of value at most 1 or proves that OPT > 1.

Proof. Since $r, s \in (1/2, 1]$, each edge of G is a big edge. If there is an orientation for the edges with maximal load at most 1, then at most one edge can be oriented towards a given vertex. Therefore, if any connected component $C = (V_C, E_C)$ of G has $|E_C| > |V_C|$ then there is no solution for the graph balancing problem of value at most 1. The algorithm is as follows (Big_rs, Algorithm 2).

Algorithm 2: Big_rs ($G = (V, E, p, q)$)

Input:

Multigraph G.

Output:

An orientation γ for the edges in E with maximum vertex load at most 1 or FAIL. If FAIL is returned there is no orientation for E with maximum vertex load 1.

1. **If** any connected component $C = (V_C, E_C)$ of G has $|E_C| > |V_C|$, **then return** FAIL.
2. **While** G has cycles **do**

2.1.Find a cycle C′ of G.

2.2.Mark the vertices in C′ and orient the cycle in an arbitrary direction. Remove the edges in C′ from G.

3. **For** every maximal tree T in G **do**

3.1.**If** there is a vertex v in T with $q_v > 0$ or that is marked, **then** set v as the root of T

3.2.**else** choose any vertex v in T as the root.

3.3.Orient all the edges in T away from its root.

3.4.**If** any edge in T is oriented towards a vertex u with qu > 0 or that is marked **then return** FAIL.

4. **Return** orientation for the edges of G.

Multigraph G must have at most |V| edges, and an optimal orientation matches each edge to a unique vertex with no dedicated load. If a solution of value at most 1 exists, it must be found in Steps 2 and 3. The above algorithm runs in $O(|V| + |E|)$ time.

Step 5.1

Next, we consider the case handled in Step 5.1 of the algorithm, namely when $k/(k + 1) \leq s \leq 1$ and $k = \lfloor 1/r \rfloor$ so $1/(k + 1) < r \leq 1/k$. In Lemma 2, we utilize the property that $r + s > 1$, which means that if $OPT \leq 1$, then no small edge can be oriented with a big edge towards a given vertex without causing the maximal load to be greater than 1.

Lemma 2. For any $k \geq 2$, there is a polynomial-time algorithm for the graph balancing problem with two rational weights r, s, where $1/(k + 1) < r \leq 1/k$ and $k/(k + 1) \leq s \leq 1$ that either finds a solution of value at most 3/2 or proves that $OPT > 1$.

Proof. If $OPT \leq 1$, since $r + s > 1$, for any optimal orientation either at most a big edge is oriented towards a vertex, or at most k small edges are oriented towards a vertex. This property is natural to encode into a flow network. To find an orientation for the edges of the weighted multigraph G = (V, E, p, q), we use a multi-level flow network similar to that in [9].

We build a flow network N as follows. First, we consider the dedicated loads of the vertices. For each vertex $v \in V$, define a value $\beta_v \geq 0$ as follows: if $q_v \geq s$, set $\beta_v = k$; otherwise there is a non-negative integer p_v so that $q_v = p_v r$, assign $\beta_v = p_v$. The flow network will have a source α_1 and sink α_2. We will describe the network level by level. First, we have a level of nodes in the network called edge nodes. These are nodes corresponding to the edges in the multigraph. There are two types of edge nodes: big edge nodes for edges with weight s; and small edge nodes for those with weight r. From source α_1, add an arc from α_1 to each edge node, and set its capacity to k if it is to a big edge node, and 1 otherwise. The next level consists of buffer nodes, one for each vertex. The buffer nodes are added to prevent excess flow from being contributed by the big edge nodes. While this part of the network is not important for proving this lemma, it will be vital for how we later use this network in Lemma 3. For each big edge $\{u, v\} \in E$, add arcs with capacity k from its big edge node to buffer nodes u and v. For the next level of the network, create a vertex node that will correspond to each vertex in the multigraph. For each buffer node for $v \in V$, add an arc from its buffer node to its vertex node with capacity k. Next, for each small edge $\{u, v\} \in E$, include arcs with capacity 1 from its small edge node to vertex nodes u and v. Finally, for each vertex $v \in V$, add an arc from vertex node v to sink α_2 with capacity $k - \beta_v$. The resulting flow network is shown in Figure 1.

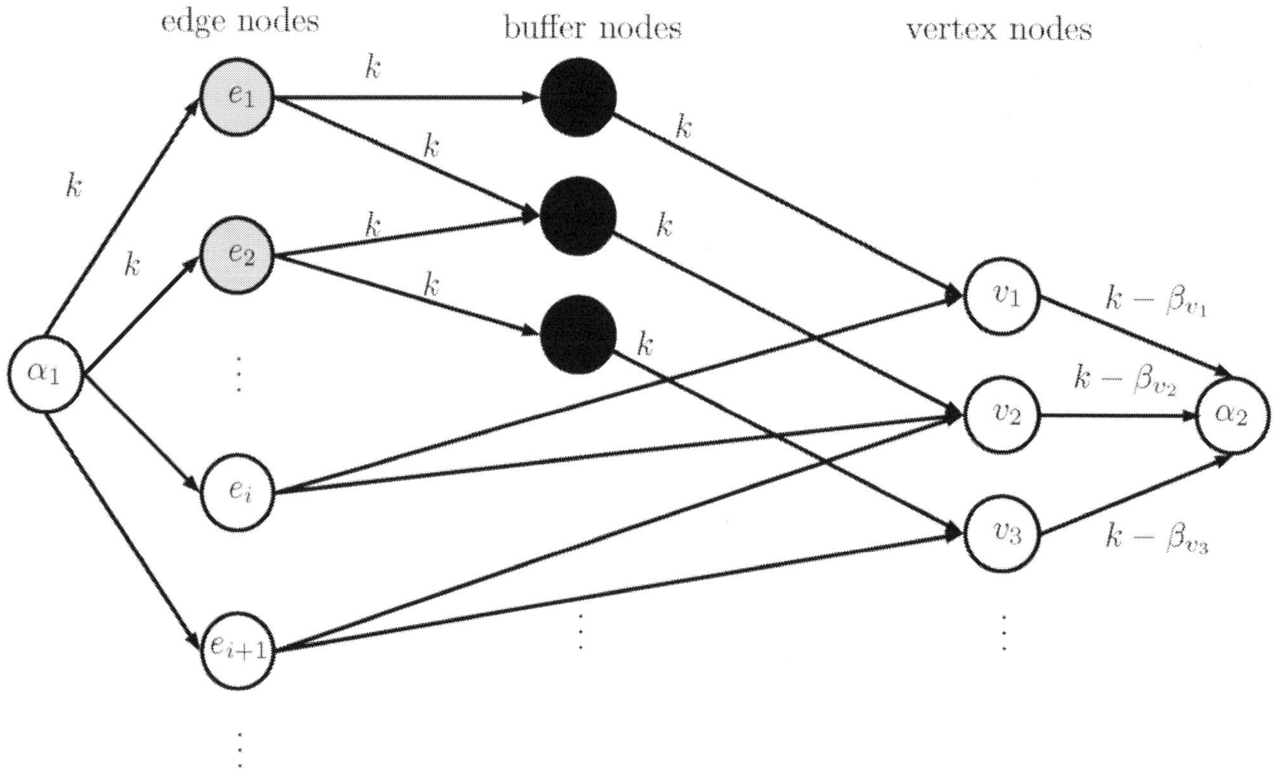

Figure 1. The flow network N for the case when $1/(k + 1) < r \leq 1/k$ and $k/(k + 1) \leq s \leq 1$. Shaded nodes represent big edge nodes, and each black node is a buffer node associated with one vertex node. Arcs that are unlabeled have flow capacity 1.

Before we proceed to describe the algorithm, we show that this network has the following property: if $OPT \leq 1$, an integral maximum flow on this network saturates all the arcs leaving source α_1. Consider any optimal orientation γ^*. Using γ^* we construct a flow function in which every small edge node receives 1 unit of flow, and each big edge node receives k units of flow from the source α_1. For each big edge $\{u_1, u_2\}$ of G with $\gamma^*(u_1, u_2) = u_1$, if u is the big edge node for $\{u_1, u_2\}$ send k units of flow from α1 to u, k units of flow from u to buffer node u_1, k units of flow from buffer node u_1 to vertex node u_1, and k units of flow from u_1 to the sink α_2. Similarly, for each edge $\{u_1, u_2\}$ represented by small edge node u and $\gamma^*(u_1, u_2) = u_1$, send 1 unit of flow from α_1 to u, from u to vertex node u_1, and from u_1 to α_2. It is not hard to see that this flow function is feasible and that no additional flow can be sent through the network.

Algorithm 3: BigSmall_rs $(G = (V, E, p, q))$

Input:

Multigraph G. Note that $k = \lfloor 1/r \rfloor$.

Output:

An orientation γ for the edges in E with maximum vertex load at most 3/2 or FAIL. If FAIL is returned there is no orientation for E with maximum vertex load 1.

1. Build the flow network N.
2. Compute an integral maximum flow f of N.
3. **If** all the arcs leaving the source are not saturated in f, **then return** FAIL.
4. Construct bipartite graph $G' = (V_{big} \cup V_{rec}, E')$, where V_{big} is the set of big edge nodes, V_{rec} is the set of buffer nodes that receive at least $\lceil k/2 \rceil$ units of flow from a big edge node, and
$$E' = \{(u, v) \mid u \in V_{big}, v \in V_{rec}, f(u, v) \geq \lceil k/2 \rceil\}.$$
5. Compute a matching on G' that matches each node in V_{big} with a unique vertex in V_{rec}.
6. **For each** arc (u, u_i) in the matching of Step 5, orient big edge u towards vertex u_i.
7. **For each** small edge node u and vertex node u_i with $f(u, u_i) = 1$, orient u towards u_i.
8. **Return** orientation for the edges of G.

The time complexity of algorithm BigSmall_rs (Algorithm 3) is polynomial. Now we prove that this algorithm finds an orientation with maximal load at most 3/2 if $OPT \leq 1$. If $OPT \leq 1$, then as shown above, every small edge node receives 1 unit of flow from α_1. By flow conservation, each small edge node u sends its one unit of flow to a vertex node u_i, and the algorithm orients small edge u towards vertex u_i. As a result, every small edge is oriented by the algorithm. What remains to be shown is that all the big edges are oriented. The orientation of each big edge is determined by the matching computed by the algorithm. We must show this matching exists. Consider any subset $V'_{big} \subseteq V_{big}$, and denote the neighborhood in G' of this subset of nodes as $N_G'(V'_{big})$. Note that $N_G'(V'_{big}) \subseteq V_{rec}$. To show the above matching exists, we prove $|V'_{big}| \leq |N_G'(V'_{big})|$. Two key observations are that the outdegree of every edge node is 2, and every big edge node is sent at most k units of flow. Furthermore, by flow conservation every big edge node must send at most k units of flow to the buffer nodes. We have two cases:

- If k is odd, a buffer node in $N_{G'}(V'_{big})$ can receive at least $\lceil k/2 \rceil$ units of flow from only one big edge node in V'_{big} because $k < 2 \cdot \lceil k/2 \rceil$. Furthermore, since $k - \lceil k/2 \rceil = \lfloor k/2 \rfloor < \lceil k/2 \rceil$, each big edge node in G' has degree 1. Hence, $|V'_{big}| = |N_{G'}(V'_{big})|$.
- If k is even, $\lceil k/2 \rceil = k/2$, and a buffer node can receive k/2 units of flow from at most two big edge nodes. Partition $N_{G'}(V'_{big})$ into two disjoint sets N_1 and N_2, where N_1 contains the buffer nodes that receive more than k/2 units of flow from a big edge node, and N_2 has the buffer nodes that receive k/2 units of flow from a big edge node. Similar to when k is odd, each big edge node in V'_{big} is adjacent to only one buffer node in N_1, and so each buffer node in N_1 has degree 1 in G'. This leaves $||V'_{big}| - |N_1||$ vertices adjacent to buffer nodes in N_2. The indegree of each buffer node in N_2 is at least one (and no more than 2), but the outdegree of every big edge node adjacent to the buffer nodes in N_2 is exactly 2. This implies that the $||V'_{big}| - |N_1|| \leq |N_2||$. Putting this together, $|V'_{big}| \leq |N_1| + |N_2| = |N_{G'}(V'_{big})|$.
- Since $|V'_{big}| \leq |N_{G'}(V'_{big})|$, by Hall's Theorem [16], a matching covering V_{big} exists. Hence, the algorithm computes an orientation if $OPT \leq 1$ and reports FAIL otherwise.
- Consider the orientation produced by the algorithm. If vertex v has $\beta_v = k$, then the edge from v to α_2 in N has capacity zero which implies that no edge is oriented towards v, so the load of v is $q_v \leq 1$. Next we check when v has $\beta_v = p_v < k$.
- First, let v be a vertex with a big edge oriented towards it. Since a big edge oriented towards v implies a big edge node sends at least $\lceil k/2 \rceil$ units of flow to the vertex node for v, at most $(k - p_v) - \lceil k/2 \rceil$ units of flow can be additionally sent to this vertex node by small edge nodes; hence at most $(k - p_v) - \lceil k/2 \rceil$ additional small edges are oriented towards v.
- Second, the capacity from any vertex node v to α_2 is $k - p_v$, so any vertex that is not assigned a big edge has at most $k - p_v$ small edges oriented towards it.

Hence, the load of a vertex v is at most

$$\begin{aligned} p_v r + \max\{r(k - p_v), s + r((k - p_v) - \lceil k/2 \rceil)\} \\ \leq \max\{rk, s + r(k - k/2)\} \\ \leq \max\{k/k, s + k/(2k)\} \\ \leq 1 + 1/2 = 3/2 \end{aligned}$$

Step 5.2

Next, we cover the case when $1/(k + 1) < r \leq 1/k$ and $(k - 1)/k \leq s < k/(k + 1)$. In this case, it is possible that $r + s \leq 1$. If $OPT \leq 1$, at most one big edge can be oriented along with one small edge toward the same vertex; we exploit this property below.

Lemma 3. For any $k \geq 2$, there is a polynomial-time algorithm for the graph balancing problem with two rational weights r, s, where $1/(k + 1) < r \leq 1/k$ and $(k - 1)/k \leq s < k/(k + 1)$ that either finds a solution of value at most 3/2 or proves that OPT > 1.

Proof. We consider two cases: $r + s > 1$, and $r + s \leq 1$. Assuming OPT ≤ 1, if $r + s > 1$ either at most one big edge is oriented towards a vertex or at most k small edges are oriented towards a vertex; apply Lemma 2 to obtain an orientation where each vertex has load at most 3/2, if such an orientation exists.

From this point forward, assume $r + s \leq 1$. Observe that $2r + s > 1$. If OPT ≤ 1, an optimal orientation either has at most a big edge oriented along with a small edge towards the same vertex, or at most k small edges are oriented towards a vertex. Like Lemma 2, compute a value β_v for the dedicated load of each $v \in V$. When $q_v \geq r + s$, set $\beta_v = k$. Otherwise, if $q_v \geq s$ set $\beta_v = k - 1$, and if not, assign $\beta_v = p_v$ where $q_v = p_v r$. The algorithm will build a modified version of the flow network N of Lemma 2, which we describe now. First, change the capacities on the arcs incident on the big edge nodes from k to $k - 1$. Second, for each $v \in V$, set the capacity of the arc from buffer node v to vertex node v to $k - 1$ instead of k. Leave the capacities from the vertex nodes to the sink α_2 as $k - \beta_v$. We show this flow network in Figure 2. It is straightforward to see that this modified network maintains the same property that all the arcs leaving $\alpha 1$ are saturated in an integral maximum flow if OPT ≤ 1.

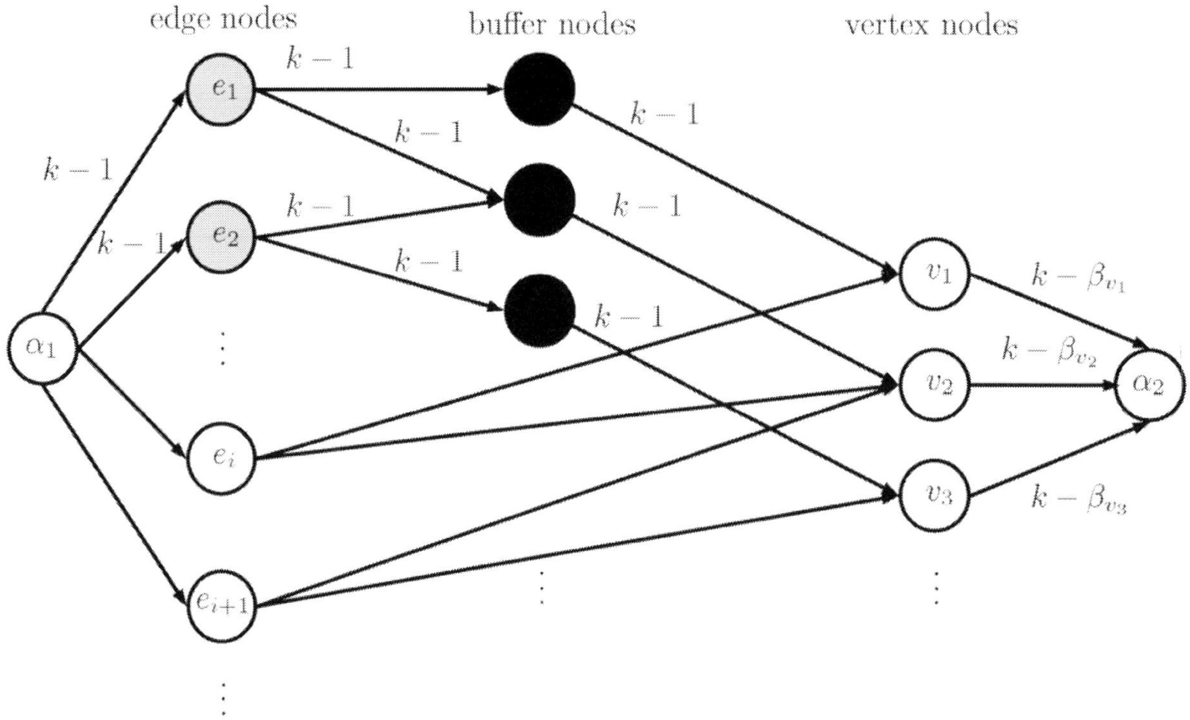

Figure 2. The modified flow network constructed for the case when $1/(k + 1) < r \leq 1/k$ and $(k - 1)/k \leq s < k/(k + 1)$. Shaded nodes represent big edge nodes, and every black node is a buffer node associated with a vertex node. Assume arcs that are unlabeled have flow capacity 1.

We modify the algorithm from Lemma 2 as follows. We refer the reader to BigSmall_rs (Algorithm 3). The modified flow network we described above is built for Step 1. Steps 2–3 are the same as before. In Step 4, when constructing the bipartite graph G′ between the big edge nodes and buffer nodes, V_{big} remains the same, but Vreccontains buffer nodes that receive instead at least $[(k - 1)/2]$ units of flow from a big edge node and

$$E' = \{(u, v) | u \in V_{big}, v \in V_{rec}, f(u, v) \geq [(k - 1)/2]\}$$

steps 5–8 remain the same as before. Since the capacities of the arcs leaving the buffer nodes and the incoming flow to the big edge nodes are one less than in the network in Lemma 2, one can show a matching on G′ exists if OPT ≤ 1 by replacing k with $k - 1$ and switching the even and odd cases of our original argument in Lemma 2.

Consider the load of a vertex v in the orientation produced by the algorithm. Clearly any vertex v with $q_v \geq r + s$ has $\beta_v = k$ and $k - \beta_v = 0$. No flow is sent to these vertex nodes, so the load of these vertices is at most 1. Now, examine vertices with $0 \leq q_v < r + s$. If $q_v \geq s$, then at most one additional small edge can be oriented towards v. Hence, the load of v when $q_v \geq s$ is at most $q_v + r \leq 1 + r \leq 3/2$ since $r \leq 1/2$. Finally, consider when $\beta_v = p_v$ and $q_v = p_v r < s$.

- Let v be a vertex with a big edge oriented towards it. At least $[(k - 1)/2]$ units of flow are sent from its big edge node to v. Then, at most $(k - p_v) - [(k - 1)/2]$ small edges can be oriented along with the big edge towards v.
- Let v not have a big edge oriented towards it. At most $k - p_v$ small edges are oriented towards v.

Therefore, the load of v is at most

$$\begin{aligned} p_v r + \max\{r(k - p_v), s + r((k - p_v) - [(k - 1)/2])\} \\ \leq \max\{rk, s + r(k - (k - 1)/2)\} \\ < \max\{k/k, k/(k + 1) + (k + 1)/2k\} \\ = k/(k + 1) + 1/(2k) + ½ \\ < (k + 1)/(k + 1) + 1/2 = 3/2 \end{aligned}$$

Step 5.3

For the final case in Step 5 of our algorithm, we apply a variant of the algorithm by Ebenlendr et al. [7]. First we give a brief explanation of their original algorithm that has approximation ratio 7/4.

Let E^B be the set of big edges and let $G^B = (V, E^B)$ be the subgraph of G consisting of big edges. If $OPT \leq 1$, every connected component of G^B with b vertices contains at most b edges, which implies that each component has at most one cycle. For each connected component, identify a cycle if it exists, then orient every big edge not in the cycle away from the cycle and remove each oriented edge. Add the weight of each oriented big edge to the dedicated load of the endpoint farther from the cycle. G^B is now a disjoint union of trees and cycles.

As shorthand, if v is a vertex and e is an edge, $v \in e$ means "v is incident to e". For any $T \subseteq G$, let

$L(T) = \{(v, e) \in V \times E \mid v \text{ is a leafo f} T, v \in e, \text{ and } e \in T\}$

where each (v, e) is called a leaf pair of T. Consider any tree $T \subseteq G^B$. Assuming $OPT \leq 1$, since T has one more vertex than edges, at most one edge in the set of leaf pairs can be oriented away from its leaf. This leads to what is called the tree constraint (Tree T) in linear program 1 (LP1) shown below, which is a relaxation of an integer program formulation of the graph balancing problem. A variable x_{ev} is defined for each edge $e \in E$ and endpoint v of e. If $x_{ev} = 1$, e is oriented towards v. If $0 < x_{ev} < 1$, we say that e is fractionally oriented towards v.

Linear program 1 (LP1)

$$x_{eu} + x_{ev} = 1 \quad \text{for all } e = \{u,v\} \in E$$

$$q_v + \sum_{e|v \in e} p_e x_{ev} \leq 1 \quad \text{for all } v \in V$$

$$\sum_{(v,e)\in L(T)} p_e x_{ev} \geq \sum_{(v,e)\in L(T)} p_e - 1 \quad \text{for each } T \subseteq G^B \qquad \text{(Tree } T\text{)}$$

$$x_{ev} \geq 0 \quad \text{for all } e \in E \text{ and } v \in e.$$

Solve LP1 to obtain a fractional solution x. As a brief remark, there can be exponentially many trees, but there is a separation oracle that can be used to solve LP1 in polynomial time with the ellipsoid method [7]. Let $E_x = \{e \in E \mid 0 < x_{eu} < 1 \text{ for } u \in e\}$. Also, let $G_x = (V, E_x)$ and $G_x^B = (V, E_x \cap E^B)$. If a feasible solution is not found for LP1, then $OPT > 1$.

The algorithm then considers fractionally oriented edges in G_x, and performs a rounding procedure to determine their final orientations. It is assumed that as edges are oriented, G_x and G_x^B are updated accordingly. If there is a vertex v of degree 1 in G_x and $0 < x_{ev} < 1$ for edge $e = \{u, v\}$ then

- Leaf assignment: if $p_e x_{eu} \leq 3/4$, e is oriented towards v;
- Tree assignment: if $p_e x_{eu} > 3/4$ note that e then is a big edge and the connected component of G_x^B containing e must be a tree T. Orient all edges in T away from v.

Finally, if no vertex v as above is found, then there must be a cycle. If so, perform a walk around the cycle changing the values x_{eu} of the edges in the cycle by the minimum amount δ that makes at least one of these values zero and the loads on the vertices remain unchanged. Note that when traversing G_x to find a cycle, big edges are taken in priority over small edges. This step is called rotation. The algorithm terminates once G_x no longer has an edge.

The rounding performed by a leaf assignment increases the load of a vertex u by at most 3/4 if the edge e under consideration is big or it increases by at most 1/2 if e is small. Furthermore, a tree assignment can increase the load of a vertex u by at most 1/4. A vertex u can have its load increased by either only one leaf assignment or by a tree assignment plus a leaf assignment involving a small edge. In either case the maximum load of a vertex is at most 7/4. Note that a rotation does not change loads.

Now we show how to modify this algorithm for our problem.

Lemma 4. For every positive integer $k \geq 2$, there is a polynomial-time algorithm for the graph balancing problem with two rational weights r, s, where $1/(k + 1) < r \leq 1/k$ and $1/2 < s < (k - 1)/k$ that either finds a solution of value at most3/2 or proves that $OPT > 1$.

Proof. We make the following modifications to the algorithm in [7]. Consider any tree $T \subseteq G^B$. Every big edge e has weight $p_e = s$, so we simplify the tree constraint to

$$\sum_{(v,e)\in L(T)} s x_{ev} \geq \left(\sum_{(v,e)\in L(T)} s \right) - s \Leftrightarrow \sum_{(v,e)\in L(T)} x_{ev} \geq |L(T)| - 1$$

Also, in the rounding procedure of [7] we change the leaf assignment and tree assignment:

- New leaf assignment: if $p_e x_{eu} \leq 1/2$, e is oriented towards v.
- New tree assignment: if $p_e x_{eu} > 1/2$, then e is a big edge and the connected component of G_x^B containing e is a tree T. Orient all edges in T away from v.

Use the algorithm of Ebenlendr et al. [7] with the above modifications. If no fractional solution is found then no orientation exists; report FAIL if this is the case. Since modifying the above threshold from 3/4 to 1/2 will still allow all fractionally oriented edges to be rounded, the algorithm still finds an orientation in polynomial time.

We can extend the arguments by Ebenlendr et al. [7] to show that the algorithm has approximation ratio 3/2 in our case. It is not hard to modify the proof of Theorem 1 in [7] to show that the following conditions are maintained by each vertex v ∈ V before and after each step in the rounding procedure.

The load of v is at most 3/2.

- If e ∈ G_x is incident on v, then v has load at most 1 + (s − 1/2).
- If e_B is a big edge in G_x^B incident on v, the load of v is at most 1.
- For any tree T that is a subgraph of G_x^B, the tree constraint (Tree T) is never violated.

For completeness we sketch a proof that the above conditions hold throughout the rounding procedure. At the beginning of the algorithm, after the modified LP1 is solved, all the conditions above are satisfied and the load of each vertex is at most 1. Next, we show conditions (1)–(4) are preserved for any vertex that changes its load during the rounding procedure.

- Tree assignment: In a tree assignment, only vertices in the tree T ⊆ G_x^B containing big edge e = {u, v} for which $p_e x_{eu} > 1/2$ and v is a leaf of T have their loads modified. Every vertex in T is incident with a big edge in G_x. Hence before this step is performed, by condition (3), each one of these vertices has load at most 1. Consider vertex u′ in T after the tree assignment has been performed. If u′ = v, the load of v is decreased as big edges are oriented away from v. If u′ ≠ v, there exists a path P in T from u′ to v. Say this path begins at edge e′. As P is a subtree of T, it must satisfy our tightened tree constraint of LP1 and so

$$x_{ev} + x_{e'u'} \geq |L(P)| - 1 = 2 - 1 = 1 \Leftrightarrow x_{e'u'} \geq (1 - x_{ev}) = x_{eu}$$

All the edges in P are big, so $sx_{e'u'} \geq sx_{eu} > 1/2$. Hence, the load of u′ increases by at most $s - sx_{e'u'} < s - 1/2$, and conditions (1) and (2) are satisfied for vertex u′. Note that since fractional edge assignments in T have been eliminated, u′ cannot be incident on a big edge following a tree assignment. Thus, condition (3) does not apply to this case and condition (4) is satisfied.

- Leaf assignment: In a leaf assignment, edges are oriented towards a leaf vertex. Say vertex v is a leaf. We consider two cases for edge e = {u, v} such that $p_e x_{eu} \leq 1/2$: $p_e > 1/2$, and $p_e \leq 1/2$.

If $p_e > 1/2$, then v is incident on a big edge and so by condition (3), the load of v is at most 1 before the leaf assignment. Since $p_e - x_{ev}p_e = x_{eu}p_e \leq 1/2$, then following the leaf assignment, the load of v is at most 1 + 1/2 = 3/2.

If $p_e \leq 1/2$, then $p_e = r$. By condition (2), before the leaf assignment the load of v is at most 1 + (s − 1/2). So after the leaf assignment the load of v is at most

$1 + (s - 1/2) + r \leq 1 + (k - 1)/k - 1/2 + 1/k = 3/2$

In any case, after a leaf assignment v is isolated in G_x, so conditions (1)–(4) are satisfied.

- Rotation: The rotation step does not change the vertex loads so conditions (1)–(3) hold. The argument showing that condition (4) holds is essentially the same as that in [7] and since it is a bit lengthy we omit it here.

Therefore, by condition (1), the load of a vertex is at most 3/2.

Proof of Approximation Algorithm

Finally we prove our algorithm is indeed a 3/2-approximation algorithm for GBP2W.

Theorem 5. There is a 3/2-approximation algorithm for the graph balancing problem with two weights.

Proof. Recall that in Step 1, algorithm GB2W scales the edge weights and vertex dedicated loads by T, then sets T = 1. Step 3 of algorithm GB2W invokes the algorithm of Lenstra et al. [2]. This algorithm finds a fractional solution using linear programming, and then it performs a two-step rounding procedure. If the value of an optimum solution is OPT ≤ 1, the first step guarantees that the load of any vertex is at most 1; the second step orients at most one more edge towards each vertex. Hence, either an orientation with maximum load 1 + max{r, s} ≤ 1 + 1/2 = 3/2 is found, or OPT > 1 or an orientation is not produced. For Steps 4 and 5 of algorithm GB2W, Lemmas 1–4 ensure that either a solution of value at most 3/2 is found or OPT > 1. Therefore, if OPT ≤ 1, Step 6 of the algorithm returns an orientation γ; otherwise it returns FAIL.

The binary search then is guaranteed to find a value T ≤ OPT and an orientation with load at most 3T/2. For a weighted multigraph G = (V, E, p, q), since OPT ≤ |E|s, the number of iterations of the binary search is at most O(log|E| + logs) and since algorithm GB2W has polynomial running time, the overall running time is also polynomial in the size of the input.

CONCLUSIONS

We have presented a 3/2-approximation algorithm for the graph balancing problem with two weights, which meets the best-known inapproximability bound 3/2. We hope our result further motivates other researchers to investigate the 3/2 to 2 inapproximability-to-approximation gap for the makespan minimization problem on unrelated parallel machines.

ACKNOWLEDGMENTS

The second author was partially supported by the Natural Sciences and Engineering Research Council of Canada, grant 04667-2015 RGPIN.

AUTHOR CONTRIBUTIONS

The results in this paper were developed by both authors. Daniel Page prepared the manuscript, and Roberto Solis-Oba commented and contributed to the preparation of the final manuscript.

REFERENCES

1. Graham, R.L.; Lawler, E.L.; Lenstra, J.K.; Kan, A.R. Optimization and approximation in deterministic sequencing and scheduling: A survey. Ann. Discrete Math. 1979, 5, 287–326.
2. Lenstra, J.K.; Shmoys, D.B.; Tardos, É. Approximation algorithms for scheduling unrelated parallel machines. Math. Program. 1990, 46, 259–271.
3. Shchepin, E.V.; Vakhania, N. An optimal rounding gives a better approximation for scheduling unrelated machines. Oper. Res. Lett. 2005, 33, 127–133.
4. Gairing, M.; Monien, B.; Woclaw, A. A faster combinatorial approximation algorithm for scheduling unrelated parallel machines. Theor. Comput. Sci. 2007, 380, 87–99.
5. Asahiro, Y.; Jansson, J.; Miyano, E.; Ono, H.; Zenmyo, K. Approximation algorithms for the graph orientation minimizing the maximum weighted outdegree. J. Comb. Optim. 2011, 22, 78–96.
6. Chakrabarty, D.; Khanna, S.; Li, S. On (1, ε)-restricted assignment makespan minimization. In Proceedings of the Twenty-Sixth Annual ACM-SIAM Symposium on Discrete Algorithms, San Diego, CA, USA, 4–6 January 2015; pp. 1087–1101.
7. Ebenlendr, T.; Krčál, M.; Sgall, J. Graph balancing: A special case of scheduling unrelated parallel machines. Algorithmica 2014, 68, 62–80.
8. Kangbok, L.; Leung, J.Y.-T.; Pinedo, M. A note on graph balancing problems with restrictions. Inf. Process. Lett.2009, 110, 24–29.
9. Kolliopoulos, S.G.; Moysoglou, Y. The 2-valued case of makespan minimization with assignment constraints.Inf. Process. Lett. 2013, 113, 39–43.
10. Page, D.R. Approximation algorithms for subclasses of the makespan problem on unrelated parallel machines with restricted processing times. SOP Trans. Appl. Math. 2015, 2, 20–27.
11. Svensson, O. Santa claus schedules jobs on unrelated machines. SIAM J. Comput. 2012, 41, 1318–1341.
12. Vakhania, N.; Hernandez, J.A.; Werner, F. Scheduling unrelated machines with two types of jobs. Int. J. Prod. Res. 2014, 52, 3793–3801.
13. Verschae, J.; Wiese, A. On the configuration-LP for scheduling on unrelated machines. J. Sched. 2014, 17, 371–383.
14. Ebenlendr, T.; krčál, M.; Sgall, J. Graph balancing: A special case of scheduling unrelated parallel machines. In Proceedings of the Nineteenth Annual ACM-SIAM Symposium on Discrete Algorithms, San Francisco, CA, USA, 20–22 January 2008; pp. 483–490.
15. Asahiro, Y.; Jansson, J.; Miyano, E.; Ono, H.; Zenmyo, K. Approximation algorithms for the graph orientation minimizing the maximum weighted outdegree. In Proceedings of the Third International Conference on Algorithmic Aspects in Information and Management, Portland, OR, USA, 6–8 June 2007; pp. 167–177.
16. Hall, P. On representatives of subsets. J. London Math. Soc. 1935, 10, 26–30.

CHAPTER 5

ROBUST HESSIAN LOCALLY LINEAR EMBEDDING TECHNIQUES FOR HIGH-DIMENSIONAL DATA

Xianglei Xing[1], Sidan Du[2], and Kejun Wang[1]

[1]College of Automation, Harbin Engineering University, Harbin 150001, China

[2]School of Electronic Science and Engineering, Nanjing University, Nanjing 210046, China

ABSTRACT

Recently manifold learning has received extensive interest in the community of pattern recognition. Despite their appealing properties, most manifold learning algorithms are not robust in practical applications. In this paper, we address this problem in the context of the Hessian locally linear embedding (HLLE) algorithm and propose a more robust method, called RHLLE, which aims to be robust against both outliers and noise in the data. Specifically, we first propose a fast outlier detection method for high-dimensional datasets. Then, we employ a local smoothing method to reduce noise. Furthermore, we reformulate the original HLLE algorithm by using the truncation function from differentiable manifolds. In the reformulated framework, we explicitly introduce a weighted global functional to further reduce the undesirable effect of outliers and noise on the embedding result. Experiments on synthetic as well as real datasets demonstrate the effectiveness of our proposed algorithm.

INTRODUCTION

Over the past 10 years, manifold learning has become a significant component of pattern recognition, machine learning, computer vision and robotics. A large number of nonlinear manifold learning methods have been proposed to discover the intrinsic structures of high-dimensional datasets, including Isometric feature mapping [1], Locally Linear Embedding (LLE) [2], Laplacian Eigenmaps (LE) [3], Local Tangent Space Alignment (LTSA) [4], Hessian eigenmaps or HLLE [5], Maximum Variance Unfolding (MVU) [6], Riemannian Manifold learning [7], Maximal linear embedding [8] and Fusion of Local Manifold learning methods (FLM) [9]. The discovered low-dimensional structures can be further used for classification, clustering, and data visualization. Most manifold learning algorithms assume that the sampled high-dimensional data reside on a smooth low-dimensional manifold. The basic manifold assumption [10] is also the key assumption in manifold classification [11, 12] and manifold clustering [13]. However, the basic assumption may be unsuitable for real applications since real-world data are often contaminated with outliers and noises due to human mistakes or imperfect sensors. Outliers are observations that deviate so much from the underlying manifold as to arouse suspicion that they were generated by a different mechanism [14]. The percentage of outliers in the whole dataset is usually small. Comparing to outliers, noises are observations that deviate a little from the underlying manifold, while the percentage of noises can be large. Outliers and noises puzzle the existing manifold learning algorithms; therefore, a robust design is

Citation: Xianglei Xing, Sidan Du, and Kejun Wang. Robust hessian locally linear embedding techniques for high-dimensional data, Algorithms 2016, 9(2), 36; DOI : 10.3390/a9020036

important to extend manifold learning to more realistic and challenging applications.

Some extensions have been proposed to improve the robustness of existing manifold learning algorithms. Chang and Yeung [15] attempt to address the outlier problem by proposing a robust version of LLE. RLLE adopts robust principal component analysis (RPCA) [16] to estimate the reliability score of each data point, then uses these reliable scores to detect outliers. Zhan and Yin [17] address this problem in the context of LTSA. RLTSA first performs RPCA to obtain local tangent coordinates; then using the result of RPCA, RLTSA minimizes the weighted local alignment error to obtain embedding result. Although some experimental results show that RLLE and RLTSA are robust against outliers, they still have some disadvantages: RPCA uses an iterative procedure to find the solution by starting from some estimates which is time consuming for high-dimensional data. Moreover, RLLE and RLTSA would fail when the dataset is corrupted by a large amount of small noises [18]. Zhang and Zha [18, 19] propose a local smooth method for noise reduction. It is based on a weighted version of PCA to regulate the input data locally. Although this procedure is efficient for noisy data, it is not suitable for outliers. Since pulling back the outliers requires multiple iterations, the local-smoothing procedure suffers from the "trim the peak and fill the valley" phenomenon for regions of the manifold where the curvature is large. Hein and Maier [20] present a manifold denoising algorithm based on a graph-based diffusion process of the point sample. The denoising algorithm can be used as a pre-processing step to improve the discriminative capacity of graph-based semi-supervised learning [21, 22]. However, since the diffusion process on the graph may concentrate the data into local clusters and change the local geometric structures of the original data, manifold denoising is not suitable for faithfully recovering the low-dimensional embedding. More recently, Gashler and Martinez [23] proposed a robust manifold learning method called CycleCut which is inspired by max-flow/min-cut methods for graph partitioning. The CycleCut algorithm can remove short-circuit connections and sever toroidal connections in a manifold. However, CycleCut cannot improve the stabilization of manifold learning algorithms, which means that CycleCut would also fail when the data have large amounts of small noises.

To our best knowledge, however, there is no extension of HLLE to address the outlier or noise problem. In this paper, we investigate the robust manifold learning problem in the context of HLLE and propose a robust version of HLLE algorithm called RHLLE. It is worthwhile to highlight our main contributions here:

1. We reformulate the original HLLE algorithm through the truncation function from differential manifold [24]. As far as we know, we are the first to explicitly relate the truncation function from differential manifold to a classical manifold learning method, *i.e.*, HLLE, to explain the connection between the local geometric object and the global geometric object of the manifold. With the help of this reformulation, we explicitly propose a weighted global functional to reduce the influence of outliers and noises.
2. We propose a fast outlier detection method based on robust statistics [25]. In contrast to the traditional RPCA-based algorithms, our method is much more efficient for high-dimensional datasets. Our proposed method can be successfully applied to the existing manifold learning algorithms to improve their robustness.
3. As reviewed in this section, the related works are suitable for either the outlier or noise problem. In contrast, our RHLLE algorithm is robust against both outliers and noises.

The rest of the paper is organized as follows: we first briefly review the original HLLE algorithm and reformulate it through the truncation function from the differential manifold in Section 2. The sensitivity of HLLE to outliers and noises is illustrated in Section 3. Section 4 gives the details of our proposed RHLLE algorithm. Experimental results are reported in Section 5 and Section 6 concludes.

REFORMULATING HLLE THROUGH TRUNCATION FUNCTION FROM DIFFERENTIAL MANIFOLD

Brief Review of Hessian LLE

Hessian LLE may be viewed as a modification of locally-linear embedding and its theoretical framework as a modification of the Laplacian eigenmap framework by replacing the Laplacian operator with the Hessian. HLLE is guaranteed to asymptotically recover the true manifold if the manifold is locally isometric to an open connected subset of $\mathbb{R}^d$ [5].

Consider a dataset *X*, which consists of *N* data points $x_1, x_2, \cdots, x_N$ in high-dimensional space $\mathbb{R}^D$, and hypothesize that they lie on a smooth manifold $M \subset \mathbb{R}^D$ of intrinsic dimensionality $d < D$. Let $X = [x_1, x_2, \cdots, x_N] \in \mathbb{R}^D \times N$ and $Y = [y_1, y_2, \cdots, y_N] \in \mathbb{R}d \times N$ denote the matrix of all sampled points and their embedding coordinates, respectively. The objective of a manifold-based dimensionality reduction algorithm is to recover the corresponding low-dimensional coordinates $y_i \in Y$ of each $x_i \in M$. In other words, we assume M is the image of some coordinate space $Y \subset \mathbb{R}^d$ under some smooth mapping $\psi : Y \to \mathbb{R}^D$. Because the mapping ψ is a locally-isometric embedding, the inverse mapping $\varphi = \psi - 1 : M \to \mathbb{R}^d$ provides a locally-isometric coordinate system on M. Let *x* be a fixed point in the interior of M, and Tx(M) be the tangent space defined at *x*. To define the Hessian, HLLE uses the orthogonal coordinates on the tangent space to compute the Hessian of a function $f : M \to \mathbb{R}$ that is C^2 near *x*. Suppose that the tangent coordinate of $x \in N(x)$ is given by *u*, where N(x) is the local patch built by the point *x* and its *k* nearest neighborhoods, $N(x) = \{x, x_1, \cdots, x_k\}$. Then the rule $g(u) = f(x) = f \circ \psi(u)$ defines a function $g : U \to R$, where *U* is the neighborhood of $u \in \mathbb{R}^d$ formed by the tangent coordinates of N(x). The Hessian of *f* at *x* in tangent coordinates can be defined as the ordinary Hessian of *g*:

$$(H_f^{tan})_{i,j}(x) = \frac{\partial}{\partial u_i}\frac{\partial}{\partial u_j}g(u)|_{u=\phi(x)} \tag{1}$$

Although different local coordinate systems give different tangent Hessians, all of these Hessians share the same Frobenius norm $\|H_f^{tan}(x)\|_F^2,$ so that the following quadratic form can be well defined:

$$\mathcal{H}(f) = \int_{\mathcal{M}} \|H_f^{tan}(x)\|_F^2 dx \quad (2)$$

where dx stands for the canonical measure corresponding to the volume form on M. The functional H(*f*)measures the average curviness of *f* over the manifold M.

The key result of Donoho and Grimes [5] is that, if M truly is locally-isometric to an open connected subset of $\mathbb{R}^d$, then H(*f*) has a (d + 1)-dimensional null space, consisting of the constant functions and a *d*-dimensional space of functions spanned by the original isometric coordinates. The HLLE algorithm adapts the basic structure of LLE to estimate the nullspace of the functional H(*f*), and has five steps :

1. Find nearest neighbors: For each data point xi, find the indices corresponding to the *k*-nearest neighbors in Euclidean distance. Let $N(x_i)$ denote the collection of those neighbors.
2. Obtain tangent coordinates: Perform a singular value decomposition on the points in $N(x_i)$, getting their tangent coordinates.
3. Develop Hessian estimator: Develop the infrastructure for least-squares estimation of the local Hessian operator Hi.
4. Develop quadratic form: Build a symmetric matrix $\bar{\mathcal{H}}$ having, in coordinate pair *ij*, the entry $\bar{\mathcal{H}}_{i,j} = \sum_l \sum_r ((H^l)_{r,i}(H^l)_{r,j})$. $\bar{\mathcal{H}}$ approximates the continuous operator H.
5. Compute the embedding from the estimated H functional: Perform an Eigen analysis of $\bar{\mathcal{H}}$ and choose *Y* to be the eigenvectors corresponding to the *d* smallest eigenvalues, excluding the constant eigenvector.

Reformulating Hessian LLE

The original implementation of HLLE lacks a straightforward interpretation about the construction of the approximated Hessian functional $\bar{\mathcal{H}}$ in Step 4. The original implementation also lacks an unambiguous explanation about the estimation of the local Hessian operator Hi in Step 3. Furthermore, it is time consuming to use SVD to compute the tangent coordinates for the high-dimensional data. In this subsection, we present an alternative way to formulate HLLE. The truncation function from differential manifold [24] is employed for relating the locality and the global structure of the manifold. In the given framework, a straightforward interpretation about the construction of the approximated Hessian functional explicitly appears. For completeness, we also give an unambiguous explanation about the estimation of the local Hessian operator and the tangent coordinates in this subsection. It is worth noting that Kim *et al.* [26] also propose a similar way to estimate the Hessian energy using the local tangent coordinates in the context of semi-supervised regression. The proposed work is focused on the context of dimensionality reduction while the work in [26] is focused on the context of semi-supervised regression. The essence of the two works in the estimation of the local Hessian operator and the tangent coordinates is the same. However, our expression and formulation is easier to follow. Recently, based on the local tangent coordinates, Lin *et al.* [27, 28] proposed a parallel vector field approach to approximate a second order operator, the connection Laplacian, which can also be used to approximate the Hessian operator.

In order to estimate the local tangent coordinates, we first perform PCA on the points in $N(x_i)$ and get *d* leading PCA eigenvectors $V^i = \{v_1^i, v_2^i, \ldots, v_d^i\},$ which correspond to an orthogonal basis of $T_{x_i}(\mathcal{M})$ (seen as a *d*-dimensional affine subspace of $\mathbb{R}^D$ that is tangent to M at x_i). The trick presented by Turk and Pentland for Eigen Faces [29] is employed for high-dimensional data. Then the local tangent coordinates $\{u_j^i\}_{j=1}^k$ of a point $x_i \in N(x_i)$ can be computed by projecting the local neighborhoods to this tangent subspace :

$$u_j^i = \langle V^i, x_j - x_i \rangle = (V^i)^T (x_j - x_i) \quad (3)$$

It is worth noting that we fix the origin of the tangent space at xi to be the data sample itself, while the original algorithm uses the mean of the neighborhood $N(x_i)$ of xi to be the origin of the tangent space. When the dataset is non-uniformly distributed or sparse, it is lack of enough data samples to form different neighborhoods in some regions. Therefore, the local tangent spaces computed for the data samples in these regions will become the same. As a consequence, the tangent coordinates of the data samples will be biased. According to [30], the above correction of the origin of the tangent space can overcome the drawbacks of tangent space approximation in dealing with sparse or non-uniformly distributed-data-manifolds.

In order to estimate the local Hessian operator, we first perform a second-order Taylor expansion at a fixed x_i on the smooth functions: $\{f(x_j)\}_{j=1}^k, f : \mathcal{M} \to \mathbb{R}$ that is C^2 near x_i.

$$f(x_j) = f(x_i) + (\nabla f)^T (x_j - x_i) + \frac{1}{2}(x_j - x_i)^T H_f^i (x_j - x_i) + O(\|x_j - x_i\|^3) \quad (4)$$

Recall that we have defined a function g : U → $\mathbb{R}$ which uses the local tangent coordinates and satisfies the rule $g(u) = f(x) = f \circ \psi(u)$ in Section 2.1. Together with $u_i^i = \langle V^i, x_i - x_i \rangle = 0,$ we have:

$$f(x_j) = g(u_j^i) = g(0) + (\nabla g)^T u_j^i + \frac{1}{2} u_j^{i\,T} H_f^i u_j^i + O(\|u_j^i\|^3) \quad (5)$$

Over the neighborhood of $u^i_{j'}$ we develop the operator bi that approximates the function g(uij) by its projection on the basis $U^i_j = \{1, u^i_{j1}, \ldots, u^i_{jd}, (u^i_{j1})^2, \ldots, (u^i_{jd})^2, \ldots, u^i_{j1} \times u^i_{j2}, \ldots, u^i_{jd-1} \times u^i_{jd}\}$, we have:

$$f(x_j) = g(u^i_j) = (b^i)^T \cdot U^i_j \tag{6}$$

Let $b^i = [g(0), \nabla g, h^i] \in R^{1+d+d(d+1)/2}$; then, $h_i \in \mathbb{R}^{d(d+1)/2}$ is the vector form of local Hessian matrix H^i_f over neighborhood $N(x_i)$. The least-squares estimation of the operator bi can be obtained by:

$$\underset{b^i}{\operatorname{argmin}} \sum_{j=1}^{k} (f(x_j) - \langle b^i, U^i_j \rangle)^2 \tag{7}$$

The least-squares solution is $b^i = (U^i)^\dagger f^i$, where $f^i = [f(x_1), \ldots, f(x_k)] \in \mathbb{R}^k$, $U^i = [U^i_1; U^i_2; \ldots; U^i_k] \in \mathbb{R}^{k \times (1+d+d(d+1)/2)}$ and $(U^i)^\dagger$ denotes the pseudo-inverse of U^i. Note that the last d(d + 1)/2 components of bi correspond to hi, which is the vector form of local Hessian matrix H^i_f. The local Hessian operator $H^i \in \mathbb{R}^{(d(d+1)/2) \times k}$ is constructed by the last d(d + 1)/2 rows of $(U^i)^\dagger$, and we have : $h^i = H^i \cdot f$. Therefore, the local quadratic form $\|H^{tan}_f(x_i)\|^2_F$ can be estimated with :

$$\|H^{tan}_f(x_i)\|^2_F = (h^i)^T(h^i) = (f^i)^T(H^i)^T(H^i)(f^i) \tag{8}$$

$\|H^{tan}_f(x_i)\|^2_F$ is a local object defined on the manifold, while $H(f)$ is a global object defined on the manifold. We use the truncation function from the differential manifold to connect them together. The truncation function is an important tool in the differential manifold to establish a relationship between the local and global properties of the manifold. Suppose U and V are two nonempty subsets of a smooth manifold M, where $\bar{V}$ is compact and $\bar{V} \subset U$ ($\bar{V}$ is the closure of V). Then the truncation function [24] is defined as a smooth function s : M → ℝ such that :

$$s(p) = \begin{cases} 1, & p \in V \\ 0, & p \notin U \end{cases} \tag{9}$$

The truncation function s can be discretely approximated by the 0-1 selection matrix $S^i \in \mathbb{R}^{N \times k}$ and an entry of S^i is defined as:

$$(S^i)_{pq} = \begin{cases} 1, & p = N_i\{q\} \\ 0, & p \neq N_i\{q\} \end{cases} \tag{10}$$

where $N_i = \{i_1, \cdots, i_k\}$ denotes the set of indices for the k-nearest neighborhood of data point x_i. Thus, the local object $f^i = [f(x^i_1), \ldots, f(x^i_k)] \in \mathbb{R}^k$ can be expressed by $f^i = (S^i)^T f$, where $f = [f(x_1), \ldots, f(x_N)] \in \mathbb{R}^N$ is a global object defined on the whole manifold.

By using the truncation function and its discrete approximation, together with Equation (8), the global functional H can be discretely approximated as follows :

$$\begin{aligned} \mathcal{H}(f) &= \int_{\mathcal{M}} \|H^{tan}_f(x)\|^2_F dx = \frac{1}{N}\sum_{i=1}^{N} \|H^{tan}_f(x_i)\|^2_F \\ &= \frac{1}{N}\sum_{i=1}^{N} (f^i)^T(H^i)^T(H^i)(f^i) = \frac{1}{N}\sum_{i=1}^{N} f^T S^i (H^i)^T(H^i)(S^i)^T f \\ &= f^T \bar{\mathcal{H}} f \end{aligned} \tag{11}$$

where $\bar{\mathcal{H}} = \frac{1}{N}\sum_{i=1}^{N} S^i(H^i)^T(H^i)(S^i)^T \in \mathbb{R}^{N \times N}$ is a sparse N × N matrix which approximates the continuous operator H. $\bar{\mathcal{H}}$ is also named alignment matrix in the algorithm of local tangent space alignment (LTSA) [4] and can be computed based on an iterative procedure:

$$\bar{\mathcal{H}}(N_i, N_i) \leftarrow \bar{\mathcal{H}}(N_i, N_i) + (H^i)^T(H^i) \tag{12}$$

where $i = 1, \cdots, N$ and $\bar{\mathcal{H}}$ is initialized by the zero matrix. Recall that N_i is the neighborhood index set with respect to the i-th point.

The global embedding coordinates $Y = [y_1, y_2, \ldots, y_N] \in \mathbb{R}^{d \times N}$ can be obtained by minimizing the functional H(f). Let $y = f = [f(x_1), \ldots, f(x_N)]$ be a row vector of Y. It is not hard to know that the embedding coordinates matrix Y is constructed with the eigenvectors corresponding to the d smallest eigenvalues, excluding the constant eigenvector, of $\bar{\mathcal{H}}$.

At the end of this section, we compare the original HLLE with our reformulated HLLE on four synthetic 2Dmanifolds. As we can see from Figure 1, the results derived by both methods are very similar on the "Swiss Roll with hole" and "S-curve" manifolds, and our reformulated HLLE performs better than the original HLLE on the "Uniform Swiss Roll" and "Punched Sphere" manifolds. The results show that our reformulated HLLE is equivalent to the original HLLE on the general situation, while our reformulated HLLE is superior to the original HLLE in the case when data samples are sparse or not evenly distributed. The reason behind this good performance is that we correct the origin of the tangent space at a point x_i from the mean of the neighborhood of x_i to the point x_i itself. This phenomenon is consistent with the research result of [30] because the local tangent spaces at sparse or not evenly-distributed regions, where there is a lack of data samples to form different neighborhoods, will become the same for two data points that are not adjacent to each other, if one uses the mean of the neighborhood of x_i (other than x_i itself) to be the origin of the tangent space.

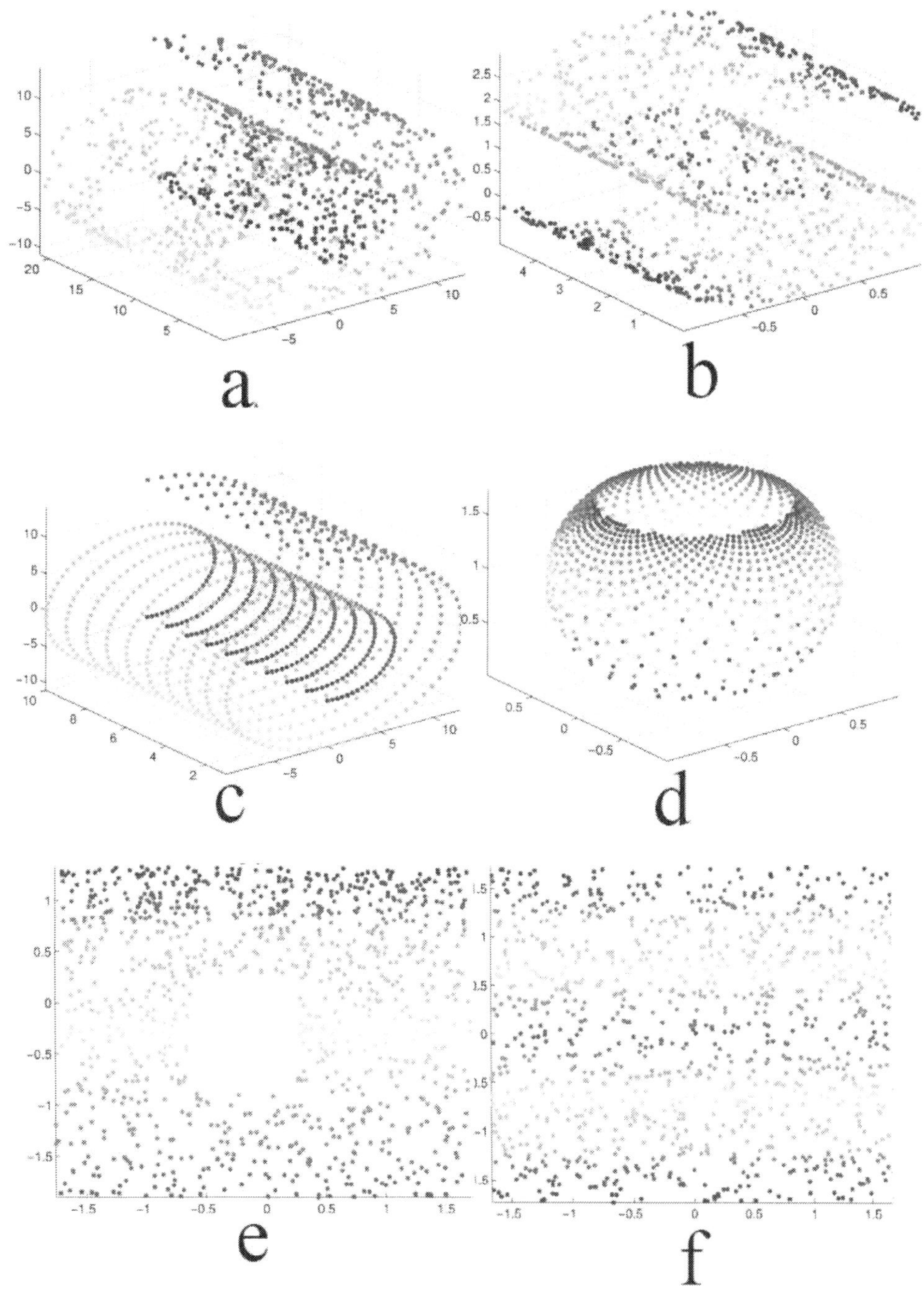

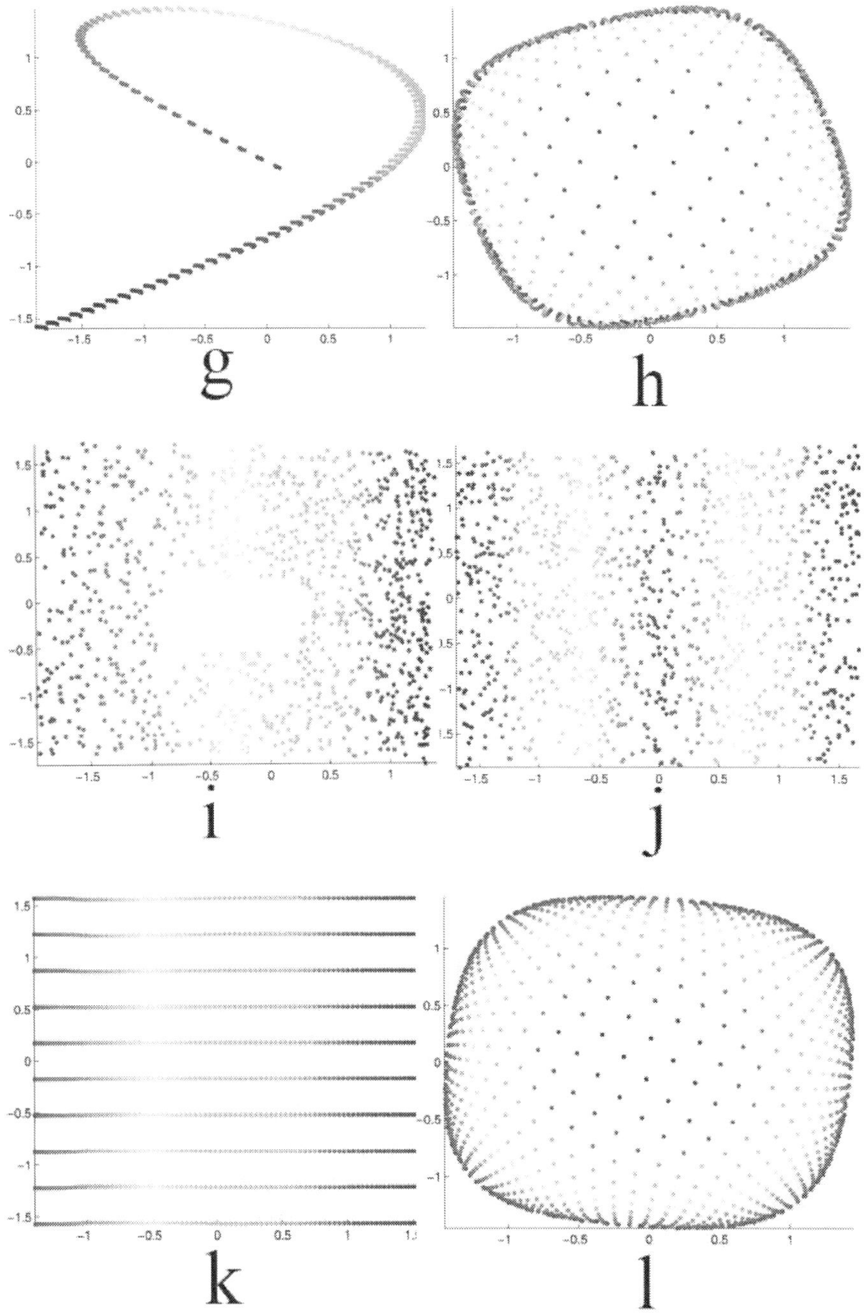

Figure 1. Embeddings of the synthetic 2D manifolds. (**a**) Swiss Roll with a hole; (**b**) S-curve; (**c**) Uniform Swiss Roll; (**d**) Punched Sphere. The first row shows the four manifolds, and the second (**e** – **h**) and third rows; (**i** – **l**) are the corresponding embedding results obtained by the original HLLE and our reformulated HLLE respectively. In all experiments, the number of data samples is 1000 and the number of nearest neighbors is fixed to k = 9.

SENSITIVITY OF HESSIAN LLE TO OUTLIERS AND NOISE

In this section, we use the "Swiss Roll with hole" dataset to illustrate how the HLLE result can be affected by outliers and noises in the data. There are 1500 samples in the dataset. We randomly select 150 samples (10%) and impose uniformly-distributed random noise with a large amplitude on them as outliers. We add Gaussian noise to the remaining 90% of the samples to simulate noise-corrupted data. Figure 2a plots these sample points, where the black points are the outliers and the colored points are the noise-corrupted data. As we can see from Figure 2g, due to outliers and noise, HLLE cannot recover the manifold structure well. In fact, the outliers and noise-corrupted points usually deviate from the smooth surface of the underlying manifold. Therefore, the dimension of the approximated local tangent space of the data points corrupted by the outliers or noises may be larger than the intrinsic dimension of the real manifold. Furthermore, the orientation of the approximated local tangent space of of the data points corrupted by the outliers or noise may deviate from the true one of the local manifold. As a result, the estimated local tangent space cannot catch the real local geometry of the manifold; hence, the local Hessian matrix, which uses the local tangent coordinates cannot reflect the local manifold structure well, leading to a large bias with respect to the true embedding result. Based on robust statistics, the RLLE algorithm can identify and remove the outliers successfully (see Figure 2b).

However, RLLE would fail when the data have a large amount of small noises (seeFigure 2h). In the next section, we present an approach to make HLLE more robust against both outliers and noises.

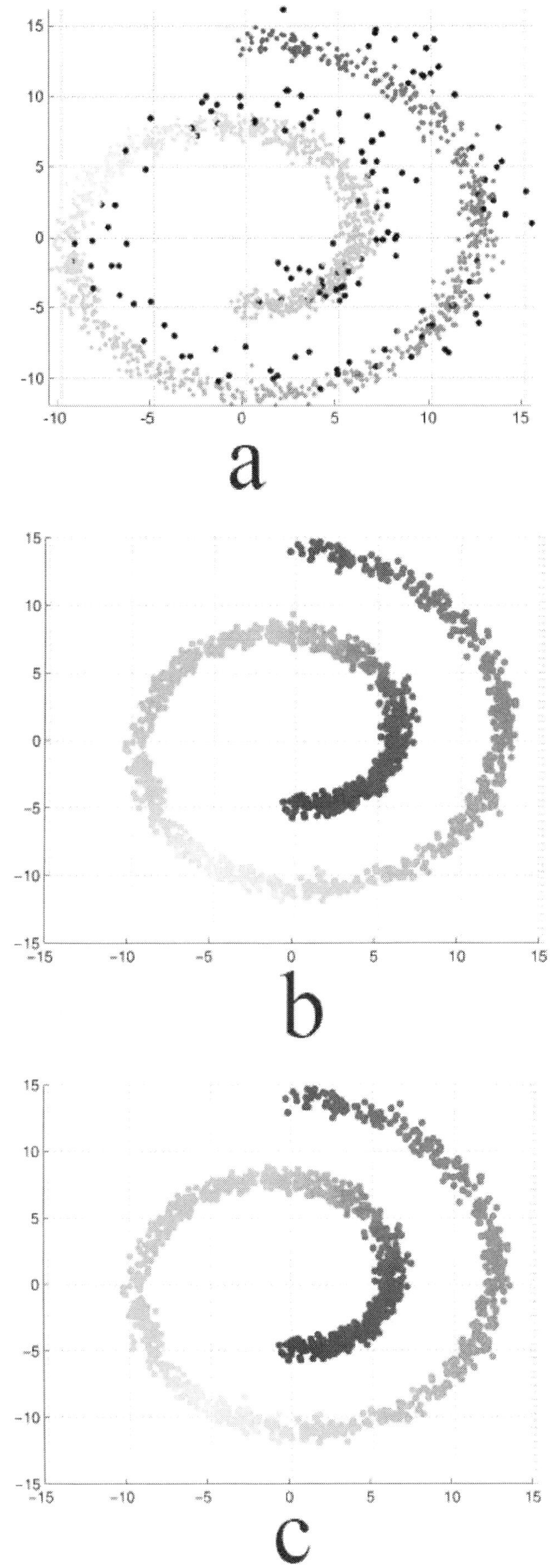

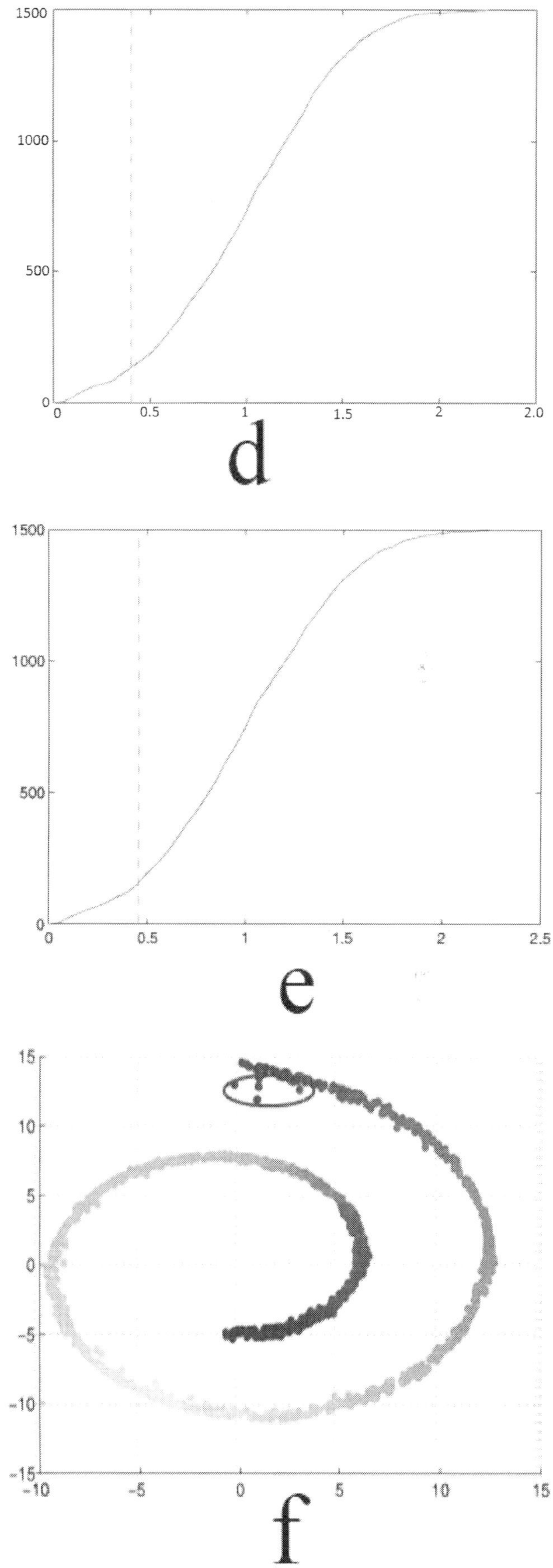

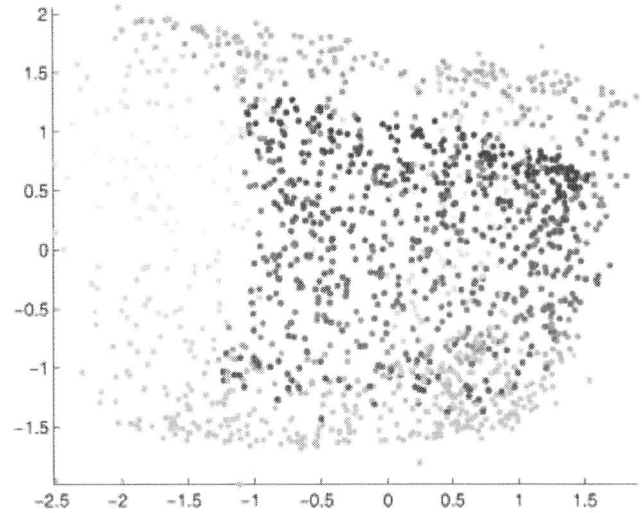

g

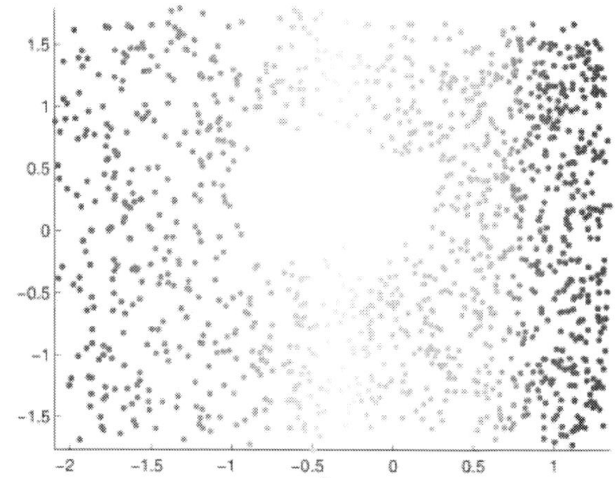

i

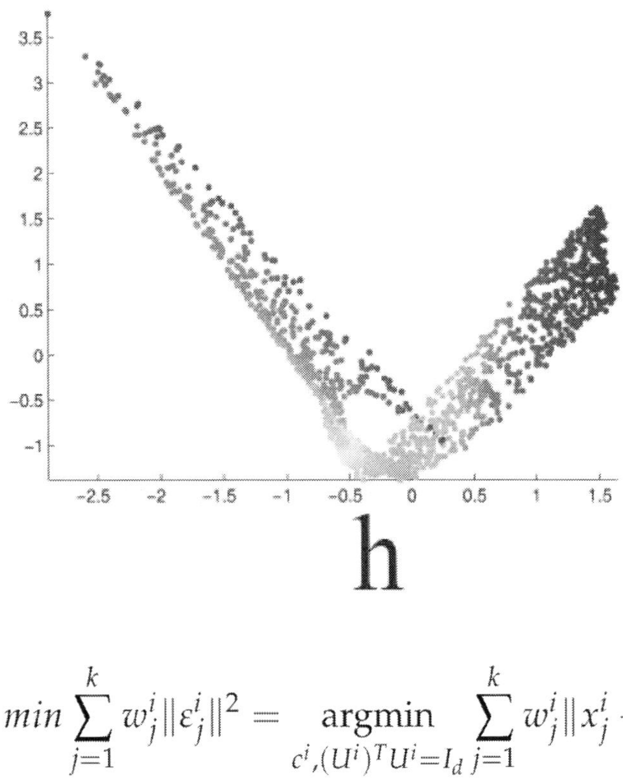

h

Figure 2. Results of HLLE, RLLE and RHLLE applied to the "Swiss roll with a hole" dataset with the existence of outliers and noises. (**a**) Dataset with outliers and noises; (**b**) Results of outlier removal using RLLE's method; (**c**) Results of outlier removal using RHLLE's method; (**d**) Cumulative distributions of reliability scores computed by the RLLE's method; (**e**) Cumulative distributions of reliability scores computed by the RHLLE's method; (**f**) Results of noise reduction with one iteration of local smoothing; (**g**) HLLE result; (**h**) RLLE result; (**i**) RHLLE result.

ROBUST HESSIAN LOCALLY LINEAR EMBEDDING

Robust PCA

In the original HLLE algorithm, the local tangent coordinates are obtained by performing PCA on each local patch. However, as is well known, PCA is quite sensitive to outliers. An iteratively-reweighted PCA algorithm, called Robust PCA (RPCA) [31], has been proposed to make PCA less sensitive to outliers. The optimization objective for the weighted PCA on the neighborhoods of x_i can be expressed as:

$$min \sum_{j=1}^{k} w_j^i \|\varepsilon_j^i\|^2 = \underset{c^i,(U^i)^T U^i = I_d}{\text{argmin}} \sum_{j=1}^{k} w_j^i \|x_j^i - c^i - U^i (U^i)^T (x_j^i - c^i)\|^2 \tag{13}$$

where $U^i \in \mathbb{R}^{D \times d}$ forms the orthonormal basis of the local tangent space of the point x_i, $c^i \in \mathbb{R}^D$ gives the displacement of the local tangent space, and the weights $w_j^i (j = 1, 2, \ldots, k)$ are fixed. The least squares solution of the problem is given by:

$$U^i = [u_1^i, \ldots, u_k^i], c^i = \frac{\sum_{j=1}^{k} w_j^i x_j^i}{\sum_{j=1}^{k} w_j^i} = \bar{x}_w \tag{14}$$

where $\{u_1^i, \ldots, u_k^i\}$ are the eigenvectors of the weighted sample covariance matrix :

$$S_w = \frac{1}{k} \sum_{j=1}^{k} w_j^i (x_j^i - \bar{x}_w)(x_j^i - \bar{x}_w)^T \tag{15}$$

Following the basic ideas from robust statistics, Robust PCA determines the weights w_j^i by the corresponding projection error ε_j^i:

$$w_j^i = \begin{cases} 1, & \varepsilon_j^i \leq \frac{1}{2}\bar{\varepsilon}^i \\ \frac{\bar{\varepsilon}^i}{2\varepsilon_j^i}, & \varepsilon_j^i > \frac{1}{2}\bar{\varepsilon}^i \end{cases} \tag{16}$$

where $\bar{\varepsilon}^i = \frac{1}{k}\sum_{k=1}^{1} \varepsilon_j^i$ is the mean value of the projection error of the k nearest neighbors of x_i. Then RPCA uses an iterative procedure to find the solution by starting from some initial estimates. The iterative procedure of RPCA can be summarized as follows [32]:

1. Perform PCA to compute the orthonormal basis matrix U^i and displacement c^i of the local tangent space. Set l = 0.
2. Repeat until convergence :

Compute

$$(\varepsilon_j^i)^l = x_j^i - (c^i)^l - (U^i)^l (U^i)^{lT} (x_j^i - (c^i)^l);$$

- Compute $(w_j^i)^l (j = 1, \ldots, k)$ according to (16), where $\varepsilon_j^i = (\varepsilon_j^i)^l$
- Compute the weighted least squares estimates $\left(U^i\right)^{(l+1)}$ and $\left(c^i\right)^{(l+1)}$ according to (14 15), where $w_j^i = \left(w_j^i\right)^l$
- If $\left\|\left(U^i\right)^{(l+1)} - \left(U^i\right)^l\right\| F < \epsilon$, return;

else $l = l + 1$.

Fast Outlier Identifying Algorithm

By setting an appropriate weight of each sample, Robust PCA can provide a measure of how likely each sample is coming from the underlying data manifold. With the help of Robust PCA, one can remove the outliers and obtain robust local tangent coordinates. However, the computational burden of RPCA is heavy for high-dimensional data. The bottleneck lies in the computation of the reconstruction error ε_j^i which depends on the matrix production $U^i(U^i)^T$. Since the iterative procedure of RPCA has to be executed for each sample point, and multiple iterations are usually needed. Suppose the average iterative time for each sample point is $\bar{L}$; then, the computational complexity for all reconstruction errors is $O(kN\bar{L}dD^2)$.

In this subsection, we propose a fast algorithm for outlier identifying and removal. Our basic idea is motivated by the following facts: (1) after convergence, RPCA will give a weighted sample mean, which approximates the mean of the clean samples among the k neighbors; (2) each iteration, RPCA uses the weight function from the robust statistics to perform M-estimation [25] for reducing the influence of possible outliers. Therefore, we can develop a two-step approach to approximate the original RPCA. Specifically, in sStep 1, we design an iterative algorithm with low computational complexity to compute the approximate mean of the clean samples among the *k* neighbors. In Step 2, we update the weights by the similar weight function from the robust statistics in one iteration.

Step 1

Since the objective of introducing the weights is to reduce the influence of possible outliers among the *k* neighbors, ideally we want to set the weights such that w_j^i is small if x_j^i is considered as an outlier. Note that the outliers are usually far from the mean of the subset of the *k* neighbors in which outliers have been removed. Conversely, the clean samples are much closer to the above mean than the outliers. Based on the above observation, we can choose the isotropic Gaussian exponential weights defined as:

$$w_j^i = \frac{exp(-\|x_j^i - \bar{x}_i\|^2/\sigma)}{\sum_{j=1}^{k} exp(-\|x_j^i - \bar{x}_i\|^2/\sigma)} \tag{17}$$

where $\bar{x}_i$ denotes an approximation of the mean of the clean sample points from the local patch, and σ is defined as the mean squared Euclidean distance of *k* nearest neighbors. With this definition, clean samples in the local patch have large weights, while outliers have small weights which decay exponentially with the distances to the mean of the clean samples.

In order to approximate the mean of the clean sample points from the local patch, we first choose $\bar{x}_i$ to be the mean of all the *k* samples from the local patch, including both the clean points and outliers. Then we update the mean $\bar{x}_i$ with the weighted sample mean vector:

$$\bar{x}_i^w = \sum_{j=1}^{k} w_j^i x_j^i \tag{18}$$

where w_j^i is computed by Equation (17). Then the mean $\bar{x}_i$ depends on the weights $w_j^i(j = 1, \ldots, k)$. However, as we can see from Equation (17), the weights in turn depend on the mean $\bar{x}_i$. Because of this cyclic dependency, we exploit an iterative procedure to find the solution. This iterative procedure can be summarized as follows:

1 Set the initial mean $\bar{x}_i^{(0)} = \frac{1}{k}\sum_{j=1}^{k} x_j^i$. Set l = 0.

2. Repeat until convergence:

a. Compute $w_j^i(j = 1, \ldots, k)$ according to Equation (17);

b. update the mean $\bar{x}_i^{(l+1)} = \sum_{j=1}^{k} (w_j^i)^l (\bar{x}_i^j)^{(l)}$

c. if $\|\bar{x}_i^{(l+1)} - \bar{x}_i^{(l)}\|_2 < \epsilon$ (we set $\epsilon = 0.01$ in our experiments), return;

else $l = l + 1$.

Step 2

After we obtain the iterative solution of $\bar{x}_i$, we further update the weights w_j^i based on the idea from robust statistics. Specifically, we perform weighted PCA and compute the reconstruction errors for all the k samples from the local patch. Then, we update the weights by the weight function defined as:

$$w_j^i = w(\varepsilon_j^i) = \frac{\rho'(\varepsilon_j^i)}{\varepsilon_j^i} = \begin{cases} 1, & \varepsilon_j^i \leq \frac{1}{2}c \\ \frac{c}{2\varepsilon_j^i}, & \varepsilon_j^i > \frac{1}{2}c \end{cases} \tag{19}$$

where $\rho'(\cdot)$ is the first derivative of $\rho(\cdot)$ which is called the Huber function [33] and defined as :

$$\rho(\varepsilon) = \begin{cases} \frac{1}{2}\varepsilon^2, & |\varepsilon| \leq c \\ c(|\varepsilon| - \frac{1}{2}c), & |\varepsilon| > c \end{cases} \tag{20}$$

where $c > 0$ is a user-defined parameter. In this paper, the value of c is set according to the mean value of the projection errors; thus, $c = \bar{\varepsilon}^i = \frac{1}{k}\sum_{k=1}^{1} \varepsilon_j^i$.

It is worth noting that the computational complexity of the iterative procedure in Step 1 of our proposed algorithm is about $O(kNLD)$, where L is the assumed average iterative times. It is much lower than the computational complexity of the iterative procedure in RPCA, which is $O(kNLdD^2)$. In Step 2, we update the weights in one iteration. This procedure has the complexity of $O(kNdD^2)$ which is 1/L of that of the RPCA algorithm. Therefore, comparing with the original RPCA, our proposed two-step approach can save the computation time effectively, especially for high-dimensional data (when D is large).

After performing our robust two-step algorithm on the local patch, each point x_j^i in it has an associated weight w_j^i. In order to identify the outliers, we compute the normalized weight as $(w_j^i)^* = w_j^i / \sum_{j=1}^k w_j^i$. For other points that are not in the local patch containing x_i, we set their normalized weight to 0. The normalized weights give us a measure on how likely each sample comes from the underlying data manifold that we can infer from the corresponding local patch. Then we can obtain the total reliability score of each point by summing up the normalized weights computed from all the local patches. The total reliability score of each point $x_j (j = 1, 2, \ldots, N)$ can be defined as:

$$s_j = \sum_{i=1}^{N} (w_j^i)^* \tag{21}$$

The total reliability score is very small for outliers, while the total reliability score of clean points is relatively large. Therefore, we can identify the outliers based on the reliability scores, *i.e.*, a point x_j is identified as an outlier if and only if $s_j \leq \alpha$ for some threshold $\alpha > 0$. Furthermore, we can plot the cumulative distributions of reliability scores for the dataset to make it easier to choose the appropriate value of α. Figure 2d, e show the cumulative distributions of reliability scores for the "Swiss roll with a hole" dataset, where the y-axis shows the frequency counts, the x-axis indicates the reliability scores computed by the RPCA algorithm and our fast approximate algorithm respectively. The vertical dashed lines indicate the α values used in our experiments (usually near a point at which the slope of the cumulative distribution curve has a large change). Figure 2b, c show the outlier removal results by the RPCA algorithm and our fast approximate algorithm respectively. As we can see from Figure 2b, c, both our fast approximate algorithm and the RPCA algorithm can be applied to identify and remove the outliers effectively.

Noise Reduction Using Local Linear Smoothing

When the data have a large amount of small noises, we employ the local linear smoothing [18] method for noise reduction. The local smoothing algorithm is similar in spirit to local polynomial smoothing applied in nonparametric regression [34]. The basic idea of local linear smoothing is to project each point x_i to an approximate tangent space computed by the weighted PCA. The main steps of local linear smoothing, for each iteration, are as follows [18]:

1. For each sample $x_i (i = 1, 2, \cdots, N')$, find the k nearest neighbors of x_i including itself: $X_i = [x_1^i, x_2^i, \ldots, x_k^i]$
2. Compute the weights $w_j^i (j = 1, \ldots, k)$ using an iterative weight selection procedure.
3. Compute an approximation of the tangent space at x_i by a weighted PCA according to Equation (13);
4. Project x_i to the approximate tangent subspace to obtain :

$$\hat{x}_i = \bar{x}_w^i + U^i (U^i)^T (x_i - \bar{x}_w^i)$$

As pointed out in [18], when increasing the number of iterations in local linear smoothing, local linear smoothing will suffer from the well-known "trim the peak and fill the valley" phenomenon [34] for regions of the manifold where the curvature is large. Bias correction can also alleviate this problem for some applications. However, bias-correction is also possible to overshoot the correction. Moreover, it is difficult to choose a suitable scaling parameter to balance between the bias-correction and the overshooting. Therefore, we employ for the local linear smoothing only one iteration in our algorithm. Figure 2f shows the result of the noise reduction using one iteration of local smoothing on the "Swiss roll with a hole" dataset whose outliers have been removed by our fast approximate algorithm. As we can see from this, most of the noise-corrupted points have been moved close to the underlying manifold surface, and only a few points in the blue ellipse still deviate from the manifold surface. Nevertheless, as we will present in the next subsection, our Robust HLLE algorithm can further reduce the undesirable effects of outliers and noises on the embedding result.

Robust Hessian Locally Linear Embedding

With the above preparation, we are now ready to present our main Robust Hessian locally linear embedding algorithm. We assumed that a dataset $X^{on} = [x_1^{on}, x_2^{on}, \ldots, x_{N_{all}}^{on}] \in \mathbb{R}^{D \times N}$ is sampled from a d-dimensional manifold M with the existence of outliers and noise-corrupted points. Our RHLLE algorithm can be formally stated as follows:

1. Perform the fast outlier identifying algorithm described in Section 4.2 on the dataset X^{on}, and obtain the d dataset $X^{or} = [x_1^{or}, x_2^{or}, \ldots, x_N^{or}]$ whose outliers have been removed.
2. Perform the local smoothing procedure described in Section 4.3 on the dataset X^{or}, and obtain the noise reduction dataset $X^{nr} = [x_1, x_2, \ldots, x_N]$.
3. Find the k nearest neighbors for each point $x_i \in X^{nr}$ as the HLLE algorithm does.

a. Compute the total reliability scores W_i^p for each local patch $N(x_i)$, and determine the reliable local patch subset RLP.

b. Compute the local tangent coordinates and the local Hessian operator Hi for each local patch $N(x_i) \in$ RLP as described in Section 2.2.

c. Compute the weighted global functional $\bar{\mathcal{H}}_w$ instead of the global functional in Equation (11) which measures the average "curviness" of the manifold M :

$$\bar{\mathcal{H}}_w = \sum_{\mathcal{N}(x_i) \in \mathcal{RLP}} W_i^p S^i (H^i)^T (H^i) (S^i)^T \tag{22}$$

d. Perform an Eigen analysis of $\bar{\mathcal{H}}_w$ and choose the low-dimensional embedding coordinates Y to be the eigenvectors of $\bar{\mathcal{H}}_w$ with d smallest eigenvalues, excluding the constant eigenvector.

Our RHLLE algorithm makes HLLE more robust from three aspects. In the first step of the algorithm, we use our proposed fast outlier identifying algorithm to remove the outliers. In the second step, we employ the local smoothing algorithm to reduce the influence of noise-corrupted data points. To further reduce the undesirable effects of outliers and noises on the embedding result, in the third step, we compute the local Hessian operators based on the selected reliable local patches and endow the reliable local patches with different weights to construct the weighted global functional.

In order to compute the total reliability scores W_i^p in Step 3 (b) of our RHLLE algorithm, we first compute the total reliability scores s_j for each point x_j according to Equation (21).

Then the total reliability scores W_i^p for each local patch $N(x_i)$ can be defined as follows:

$$W_i^p = \sum_{x_j \in \mathcal{N}(x_i)} s_j \tag{23}$$

The above total reliability scores W_i^p can be used to qualitatively classify the local patches into two classes: the reliable local patches and unreliable local patches. In the reliable local patch, clean data points are preponderant, in contrast, the unreliable local patch usually contains data points that diverge from the underlying manifold. Therefore, the total reliability score in the reliable local patch is much larger than that of the unreliable local patch. Following the ideas of robust statistics [25], we set the threshold value to be $\theta = \frac{1}{2N} \sum_{i=1}^{N} W_i^p$; then, the reliable local patch subset can be formally defined as:

$$\mathcal{RLP} = \{\mathcal{N}(x_i) : W_i^p \geq \theta\} \tag{24}$$

At the end of this subsection, we compare our RHLLE algorithm to the RLLE [15] and RLTSA [17] algorithms. All these methods develop the corresponding weighted cost function instead of the original one to reduce the undesirable effect of outliers or noises. However, there are three significant differences among them. Firstly, both RLLE and RLTSA use RPCA technique to identify the outliers, while our RHLLE develops a fast algorithm to identify the outliers. Our proposed fast algorithm is robust and can save much time, especially for high-dimensional data. Secondly, our RHLLE employs the local smoothing technique to reduce the influence of small noises, while the RLLE and RLTSA algorithms will fail when the dataset has large amounts of small noises. Furthermore, RLLE incorporates the reliability score of each point as weight into the reconstruction function to further reduce the influence of outliers. Whereas in RLTSA and our RHLLE, the undesirable effect of outliers and noise is further reduced by incorporating the total reliability scores of each reliable local patch as weight into the global functional.

EXPERIMENTS

In this section, we apply our RHLLE algorithm to both synthetic datasets and real-world datasets to test its performance.

Synthetic Data

We apply our RHLLE to datasets that have been commonly used by other researchers: Swiss roll (Figure 3), S-curve (Figure 4) and helix manifold (Figure 5). For each manifold, we add uniformly distributed random noise with large amplitude to a small percentage of the data to simulate the dataset with outliers; we add Gaussian noise to a large percentage of the data to simulate the noise-corrupted dataset. Table 1 shows the parameter settings used in these synthetic data experiments. The parameters include the dimensionality of the ambient space D, the dimensionality of the intrinsic dimensionality of the nonlinear manifold d, the number of nearest neighbors k, the number of the data points, the percentage of the outliers, the percentage of the noise-corrupted points, the amplitude of the outliers and the standard deviation of the Gaussian noise.

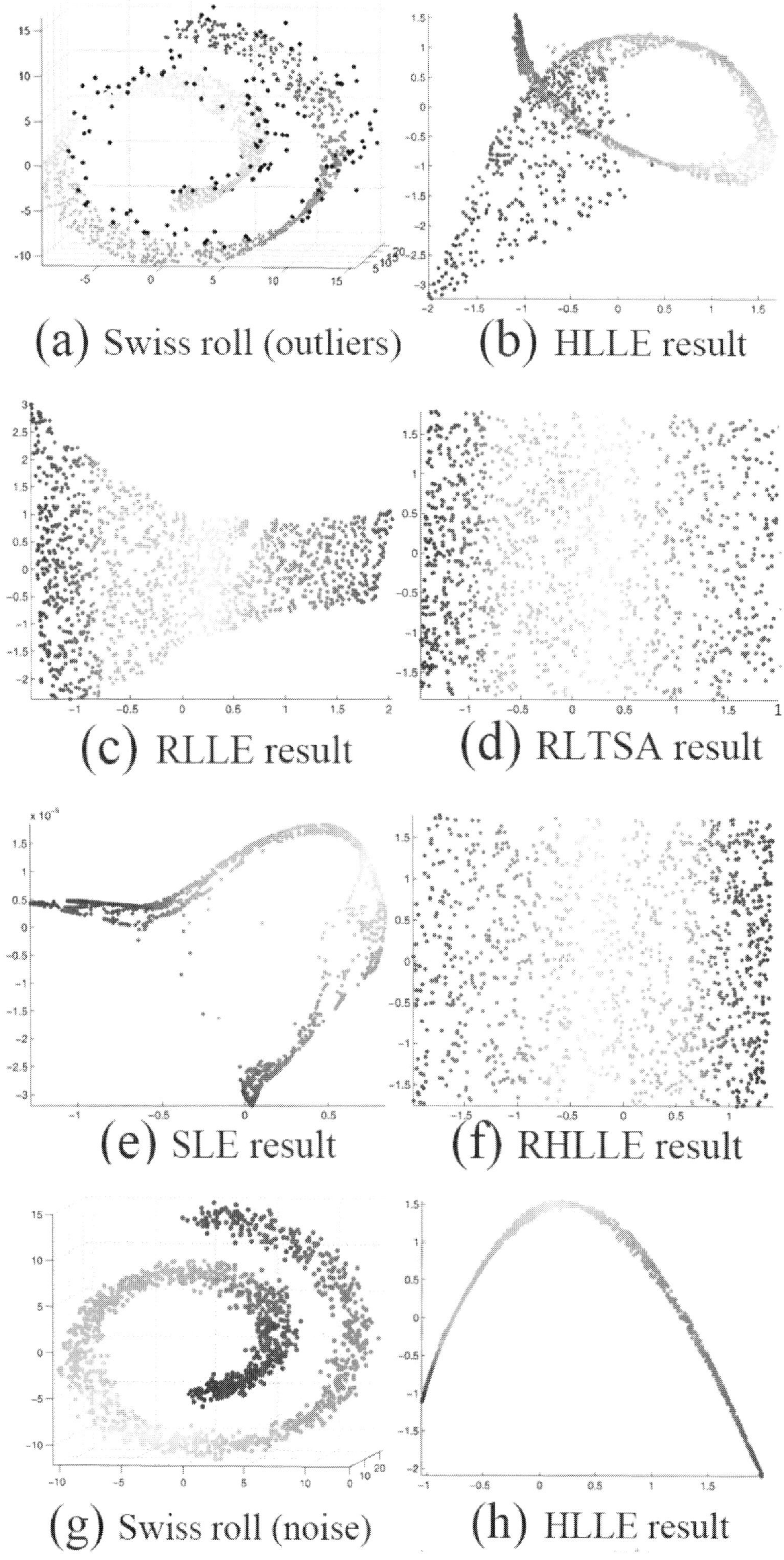

(a) Swiss roll (outliers) (b) HLLE result

(c) RLLE result (d) RLTSA result

(e) SLE result (f) RHLLE result

(g) Swiss roll (noise) (h) HLLE result

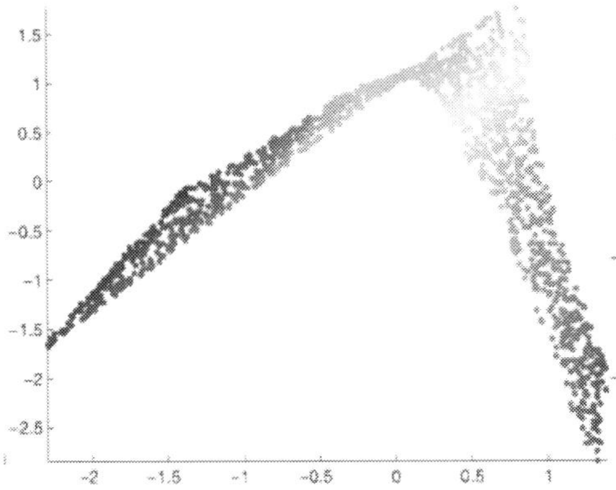

(i) RLLE result

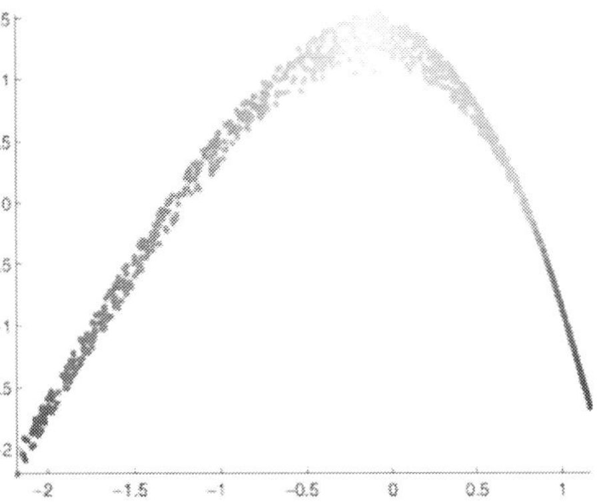

(j) RLTSA result

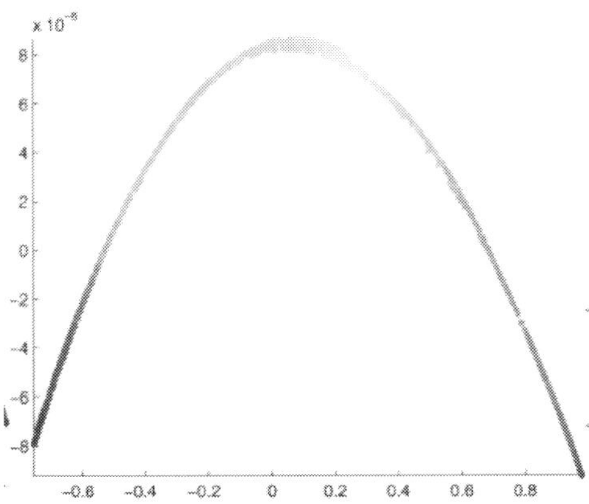

(k) SLE result

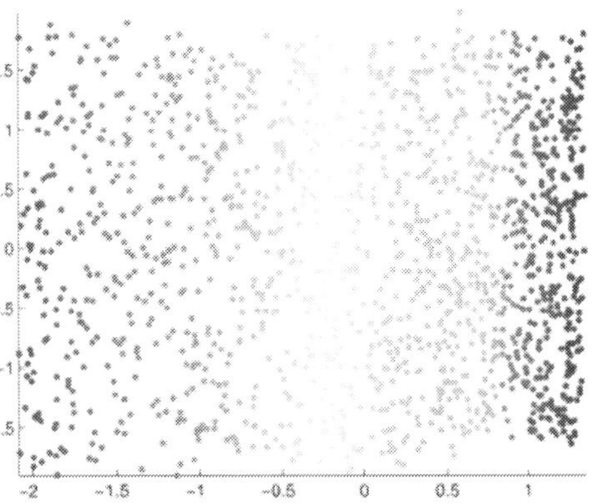

(l) RHLLE result

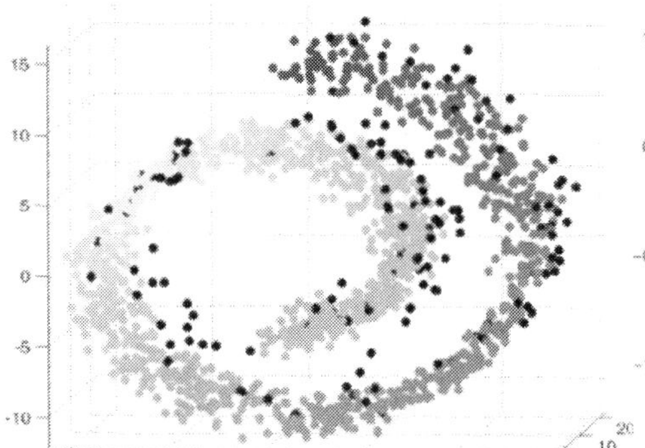

(m) Swiss roll (outliers+noise)

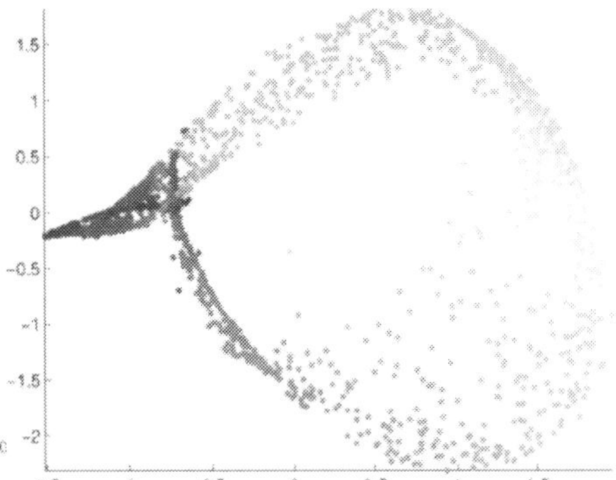

(n) HLLE result

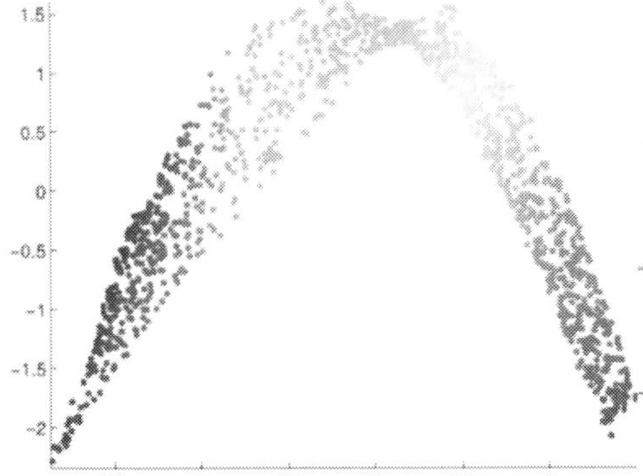

(o) RLLE result

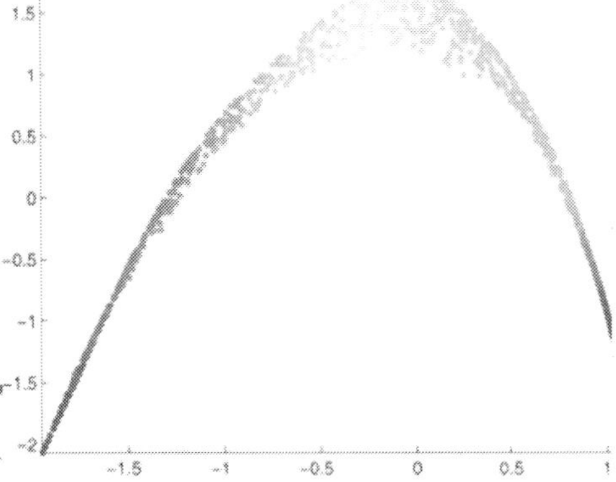

(p) RLTSA result

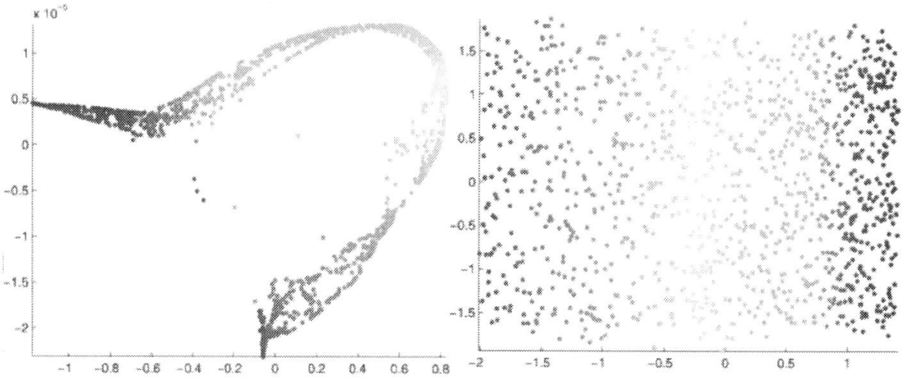

(q) SLE result (r) RHLLE result

Figure 3. The first row shows the Swiss roll dataset with outliers and the embedding results of different algorithms;The second row shows the Swiss roll dataset with noise and the embedding results of different algorithms; The third row shows the Swiss roll dataset with both outliers and noise and the embedding results of different algorithms.

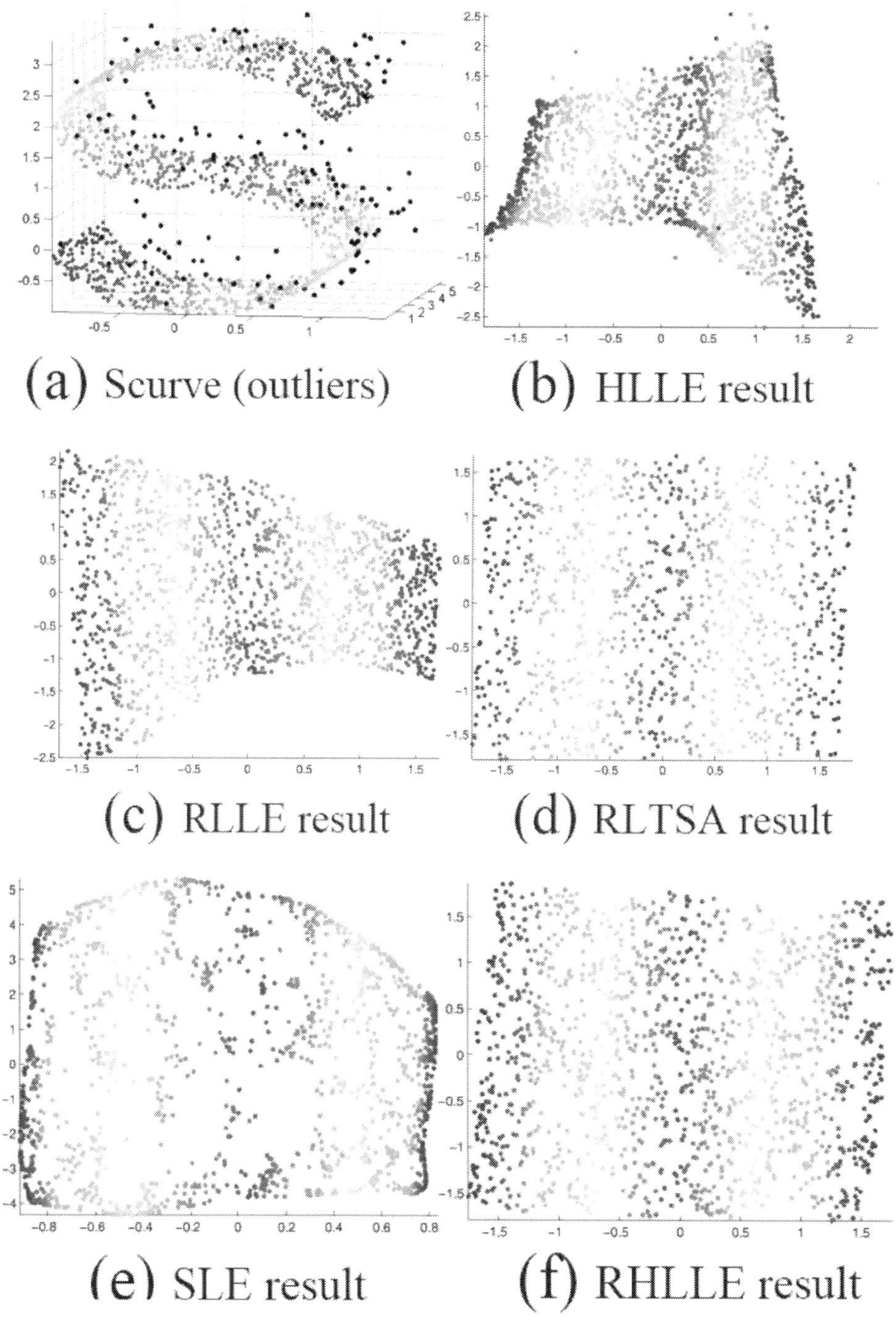

(a) Scurve (outliers) (b) HLLE result

(c) RLLE result (d) RLTSA result

(e) SLE result (f) RHLLE result

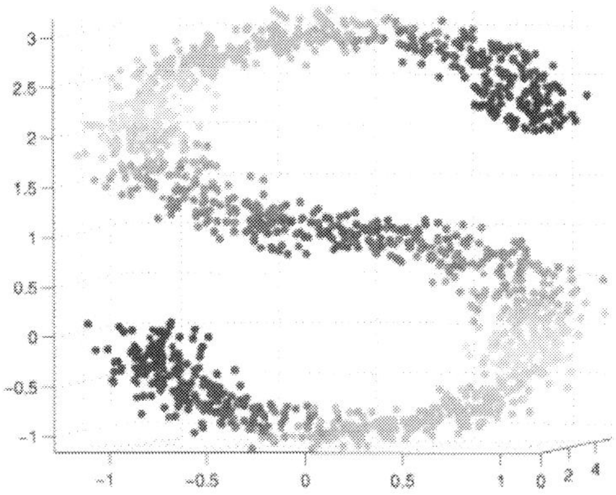

(g) Scurve (noise)

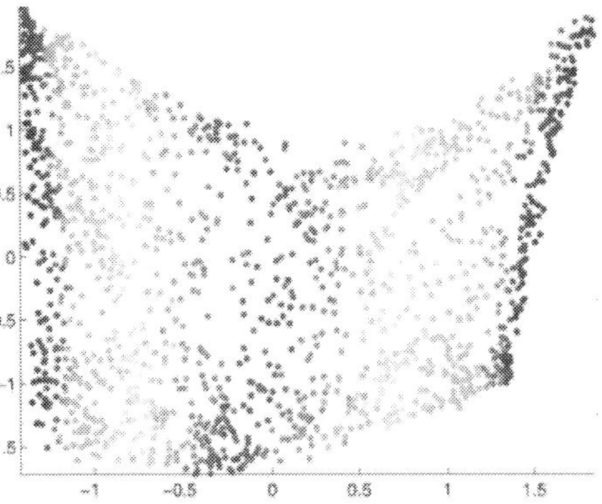

(h) HLLE result

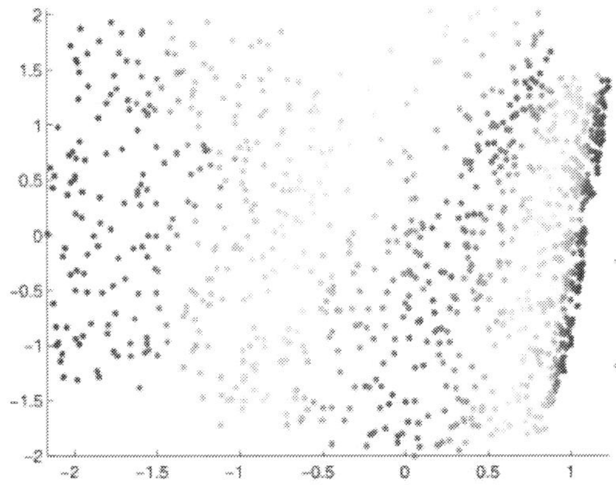

(i) RLLE result

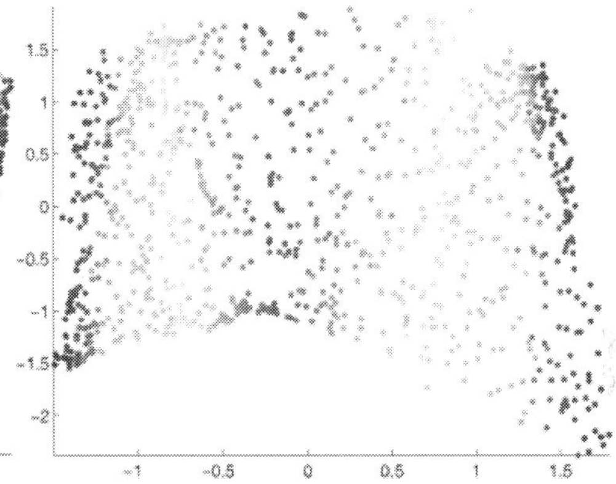

(j) RLTSA result

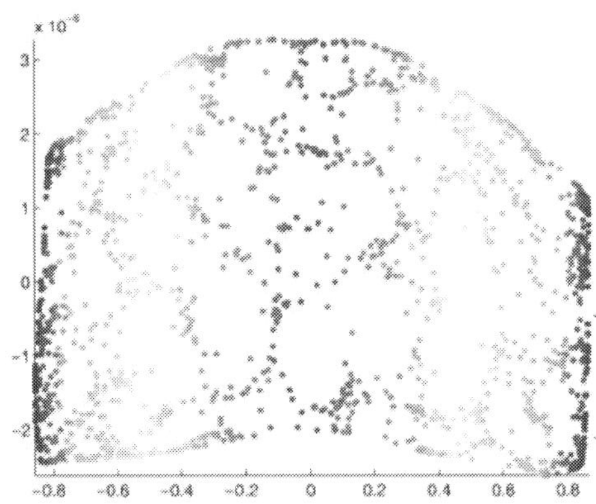

(k) SLE result

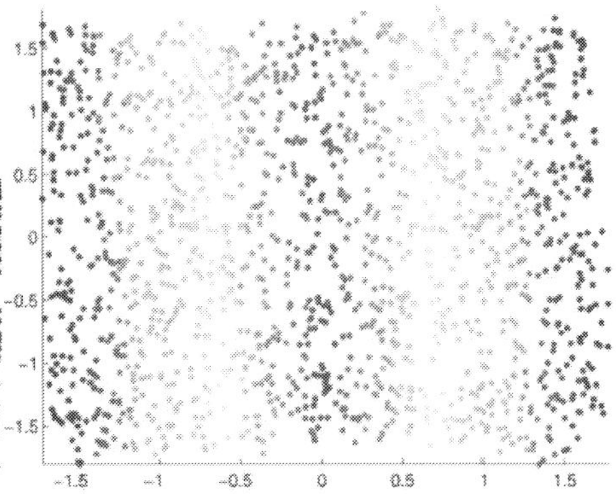

(l) RHLLE result

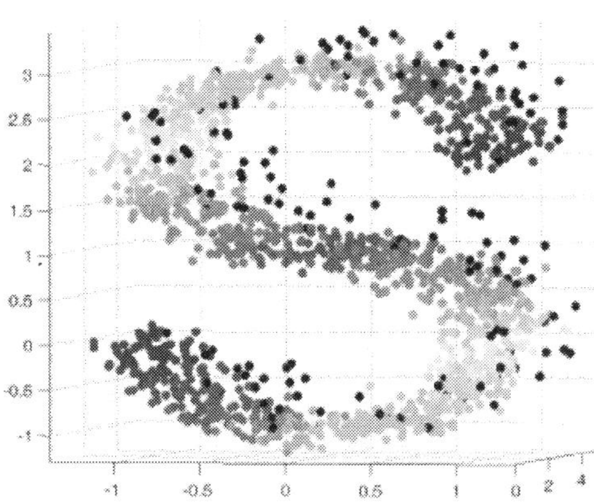

(m) Scurve (outliers+noise)

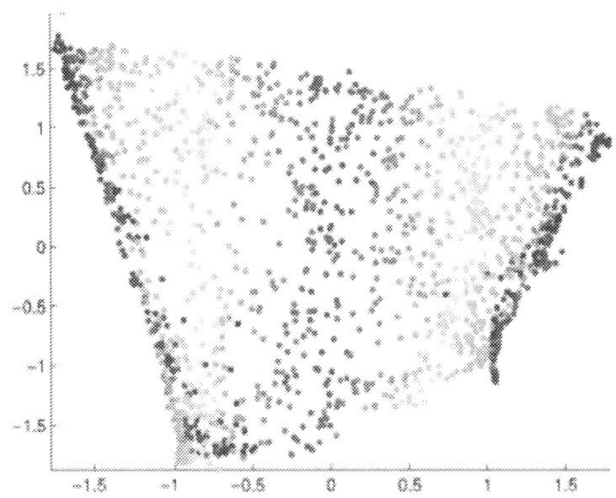

(n) HLLE result

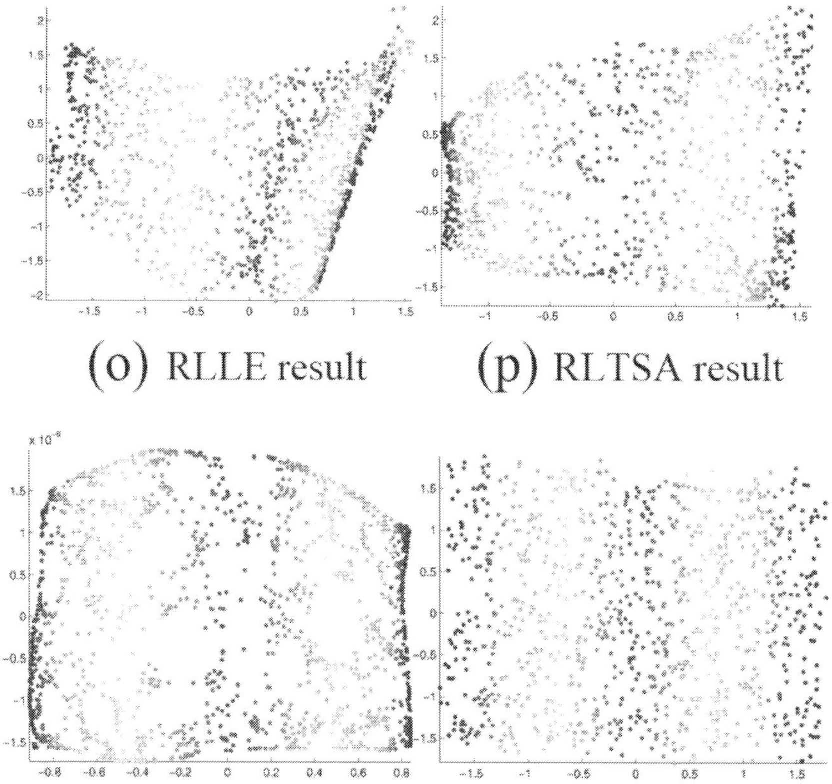

(o) RLLE result (p) RLTSA result

(q) SLE result (r) RHLLE result

Figure 4. The first row shows the S-curve dataset with outliers and the embedding results of different algorithms; The second row shows the S-curve dataset with noise and the embedding results of different algorithms; The third row shows the S-curve dataset with both outliers and noise and the embedding results of different algorithms.

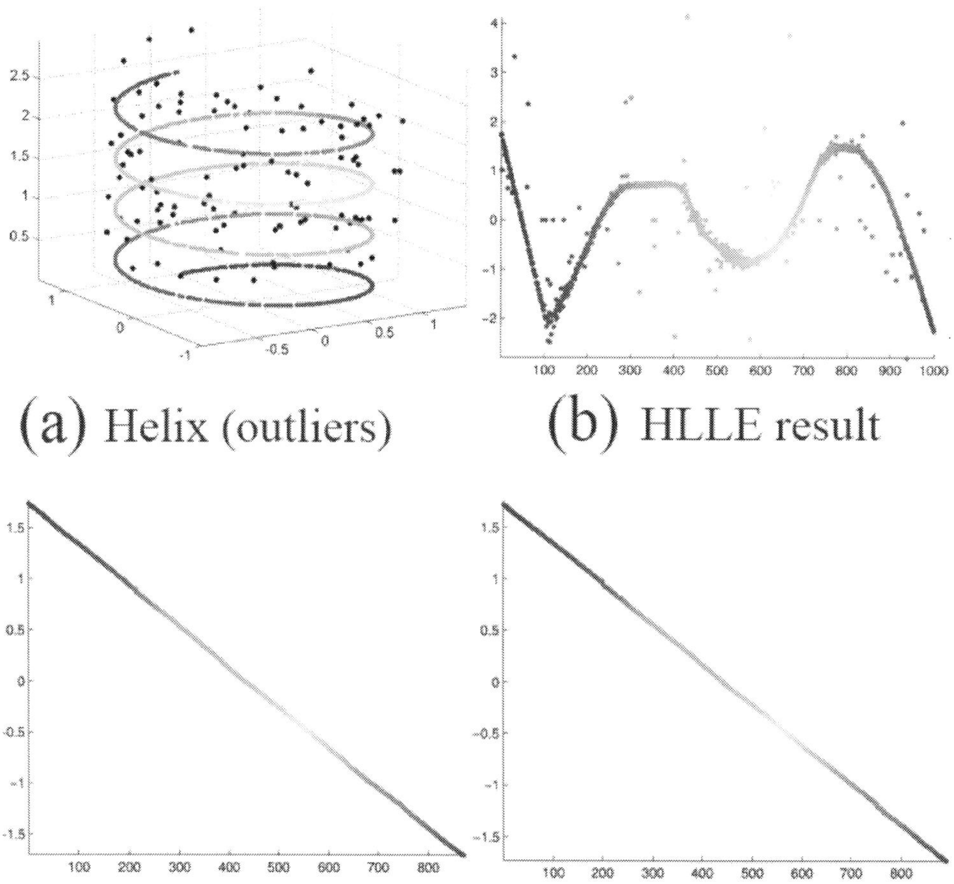

(a) Helix (outliers) (b) HLLE result

(c) RLLE result (d) RLTSA result

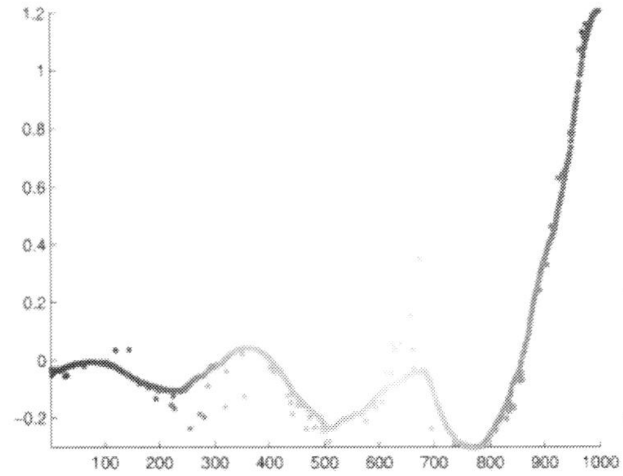

(e) SLE result

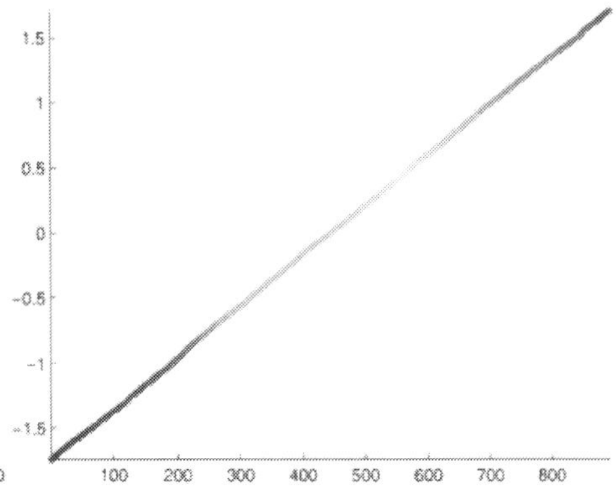

(f) RHLLE result

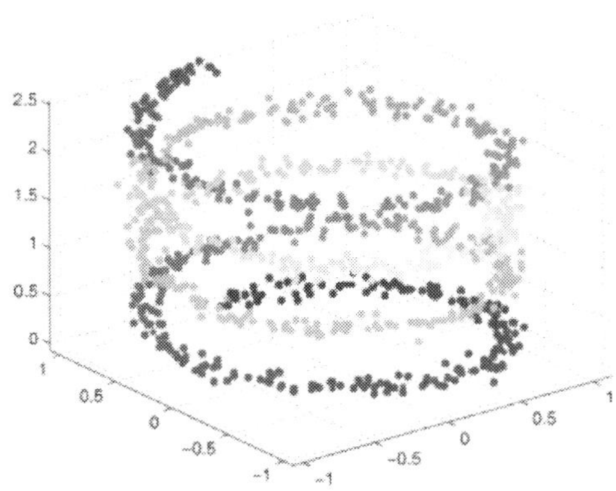

(g) Helix (noise)

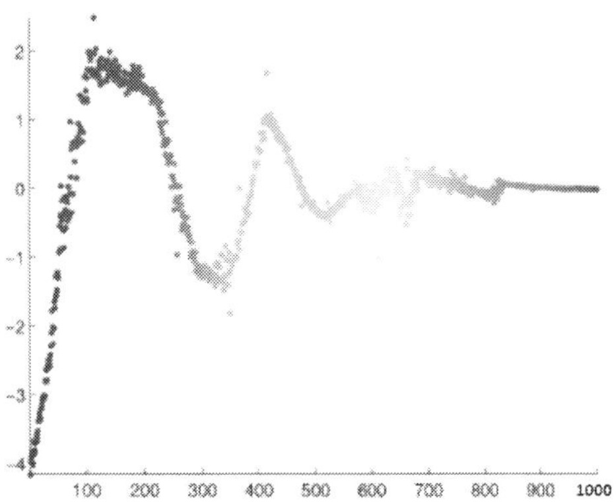

(h) HLLE result

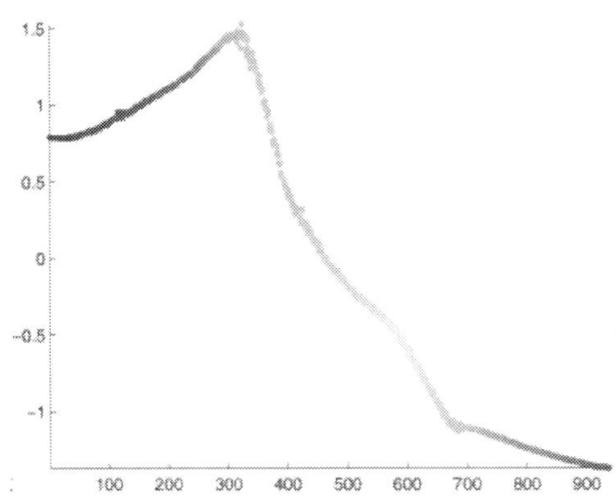

(i) RLLE result

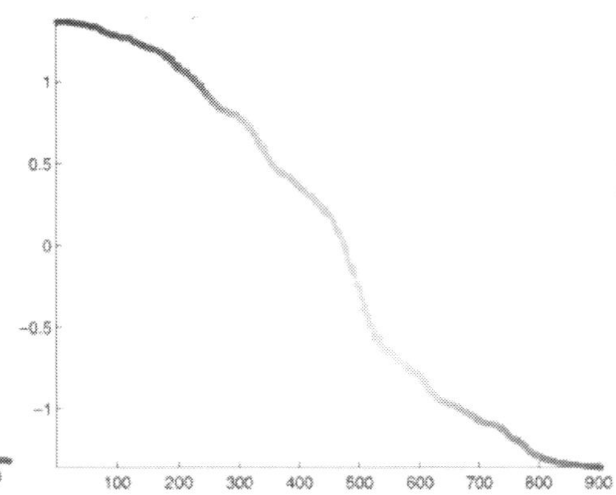

(j) RLTSA result

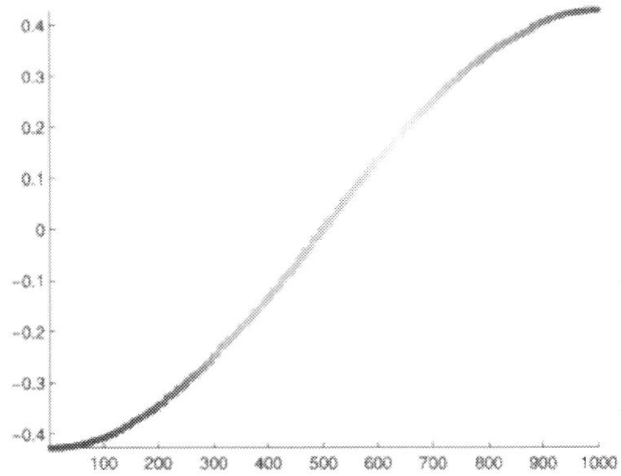

(k) SLE result

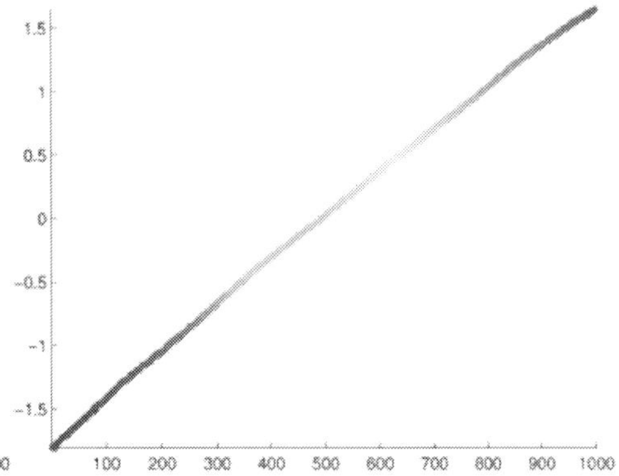

(l) RHLLE result

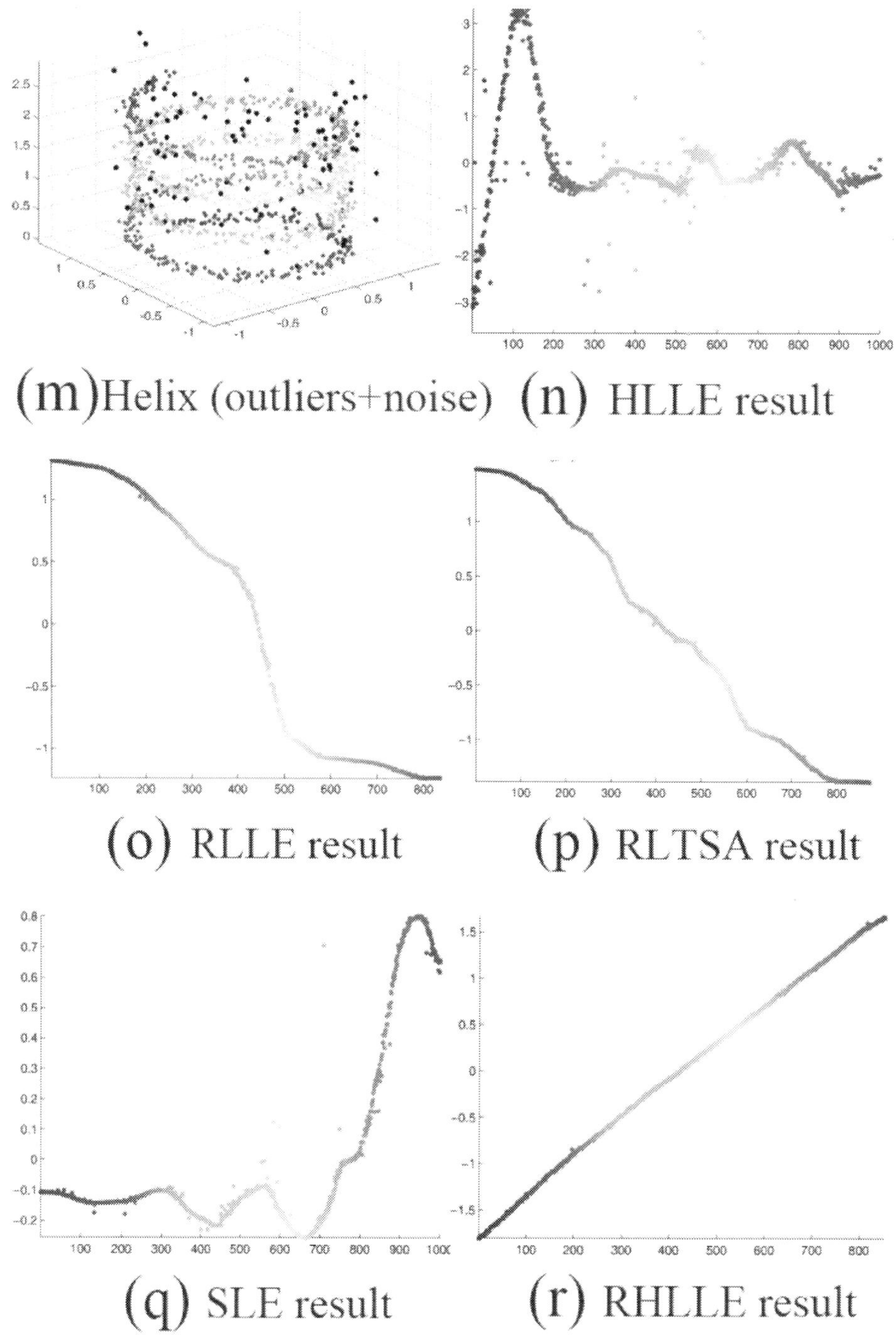

(m) Helix (outliers+noise) (n) HLLE result

(o) RLLE result (p) RLTSA result

(q) SLE result (r) RHLLE result

Figure 5. The first row shows the Helix curve dataset with outliers and the embedding results of different algorithms; The second row shows the Helix curve dataset with noise and the embedding results of different algorithms; The third row shows the Helix curve dataset with both outliers and noise and the embedding results of different algorithms.

Table 1. Parameter settings of the synthetic data experiments.

Parameters	Swiss Roll	S-Curve	Helix
Dimensionality of ambient space (D)	3	3	3
Dimensionality of embedding space (d)	2	2	1
Number of nearest neighbors (k)	15	15	10
Number of the data points	1500	1500	1000
Percentage of outlier points	10%	10%	10%
Amplitude of the outliers	3	0.5	0.5
Percentage of noise-corrupted points	90%	90%	90%
Standard deviation of the Gaussian noise	0.5	0.1	0.05

We compare our RHLLE with HLLE [5], RLLE [15], RLTSA [17] and SLE [35] on these datasets. The performance of these algorithms can be seen by comparing the coloring of the data points, the smoothness and the shape of the projection coordinates with their original manifolds. As we can see from Figure 3, Figure 4 and Figure 5, the traditional HLLE algorithm fails to recover the underlying manifold structure when there exist either or both outliers and noise-corrupted points (see Figure 3(b, h and n), Figure 4(b, h and n) and Figure 5(b, h and n). RLLE and RLTSA can recover the manifold structure when there are outliers (see Figure 3(c, d), Figure 4(c, d) and Figure 5(c, d)). However, RLLE and RLTSA cannot recover the manifold structure well when there exist large amounts of noise-corrupted points or both outliers and noise-corrupted points (see Figure 3(i, j, o and p), Figure 4(i, j, o and p) and Figure 5(i, j, o and p)). SLE can usually preserve the local geometry of the data manifolds in the embedding space when there exist large amounts of noise-corrupted points (see Figure 3k, Figure 4k and Figure 5k)). However, SLE cannot preserve the local geometry of the data manifolds well in the embedding space when there exist outliers or both outliers and noise-corrupted points (see Figure 3(e, q), Figure 4(e, q) and Figure 5(e, q)). The results in Figure 3, Figure 4 and Figure 5 show that only our RHLLE algorithm can accurately unfold and recover the original manifolds in the presence of either or both outliers and noise-corrupted points (see Figure 3(f, l and r), Figure 4(f, l and r) and Figure 5(f, l and r)). From the above experiments we can conclude that: (1) our RHLLE algorithm can significantly improve the performance of the Hessian LLE algorithm on the outliers and noise-corrupted data; (2) our RHLLE algorithm performs the best among the five methods on the synthetic datasets.

High-Dimensional Image Datasets

In the section, we present two experiments on high-dimensional real datasets to illustrate the effectiveness of our RHLLE algorithm. We compare our RHLLE with RLLE, RLTSA and SLE on these datasets.

The first experiment is performed on the teapot image [6] dataset. There are 400 color images of a teapot in this database. They are captured from different angles in a plane. In our experiment, we convert the color images to the 76×101 gray-level images, so the dimensionality of the vectorized image space is 7676.

In order to add some outliers to the original image dataset, we first randomly select 10% of the images and for each selected image we replace a rectangular block of the image (about 20% pixels) with independent and identically-distributed samples from a uniform distribution. The location of the corrupt rectangular block is unknown to the algorithm. In order to generate noise-corrupted images, we first randomly select 90% of the images and for each selected image we corrupt 10% of randomly-chosen pixels by replacing their values with independent and identically-distributed samples from a uniform distribution. The corrupted pixels are randomly-chosen for each image, and the locations are unknown to the algorithm. Figure 6 shows 10 original teapot images, their corresponding outlier images and noise-corrupted images.

Figure 6. Ten teapot images, their corresponding outlier images and noise-corrupted images.

The low-dimensional embeddings in $\mathbb{R}^2$ of RLLE, RLTSA, SLE and RHLLE are shown in Figure 7. For completeness and to provide a baseline, the results on the original data without being corrupted are shown in Figure 8. In the embeddings we uniformly mark about 2.5% of the points with red circles and attach their corresponding training images. In the experiment, we set the number of nearest neighbors k to 10. Figure 7 reveals the following points : (1) RLTSA and RHLLE perform better than RLLE and SLE when there are outliers in the image set (see Figure 7a – d); (2) SLE and RHLLE perform better than RLLE and RLTSA when there exist large amounts of noise-corrupted images (see Figure 7e – h); (3) RLLE and RLTSA perform even worse and fail to recover the underlying manifold structure when there exist both outliers and large amounts of noise-corrupted images in the teapot dataset (see Figure 7i, j); (4) The 2D embedding results obtained by our RHLLE are shown in Figure 7d, h and l. Along the circle we can see a clear and smooth change in the orientations of the teapot, which means that our RHLLE successfully uncovers the geometric structure of the image dataset. Therefore, our RHLLE is superior to RLLE, RLTSA and SLE in revealing the underlying manifold when there are either or both outliers and noise-corrupted images in the teapot dataset.

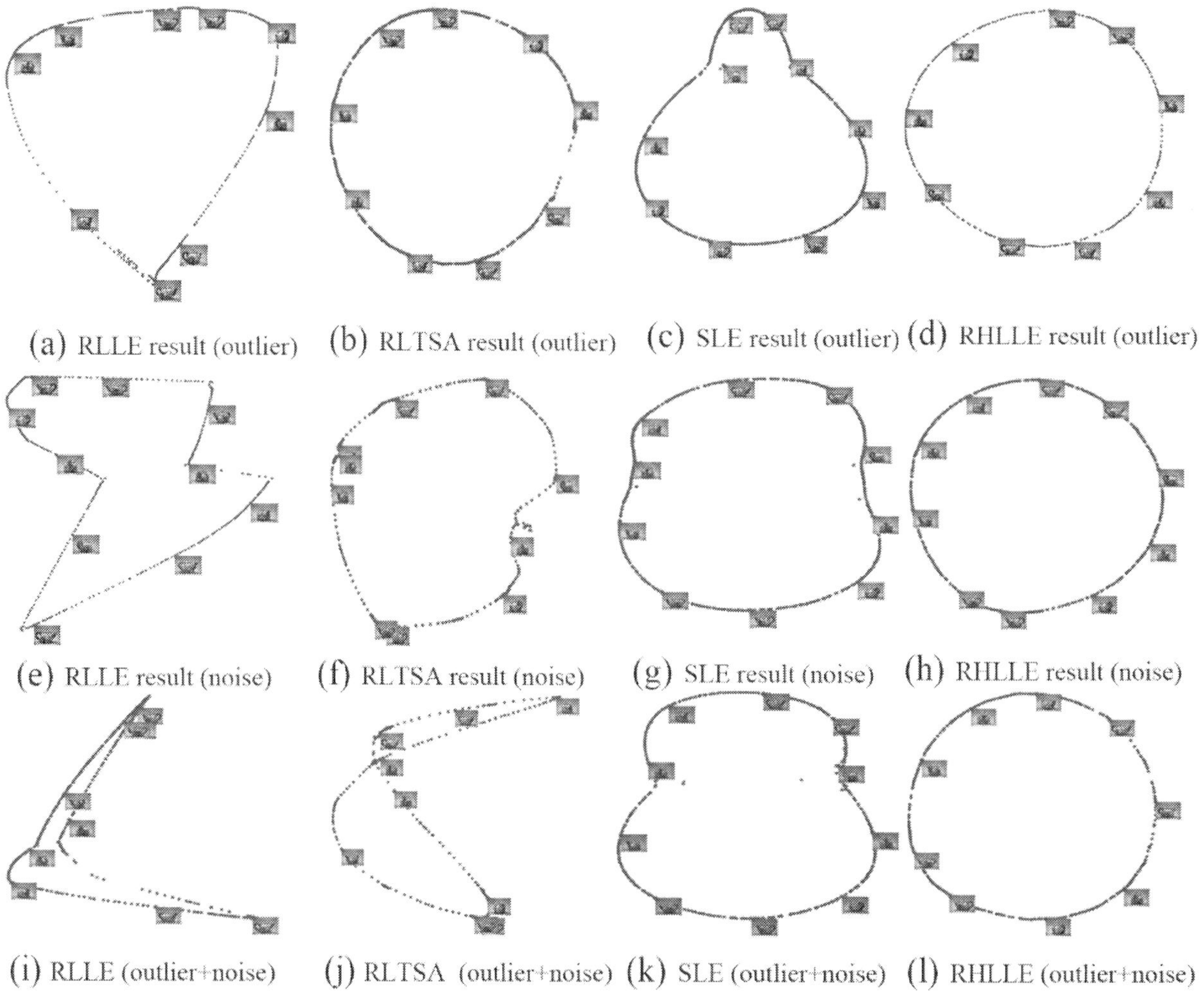

Figure 7. 2D embedding results of RLLE, RLTSA, SLE and RHLLE on the teapot image set with outliers, noise and both outliers and noise respectively.

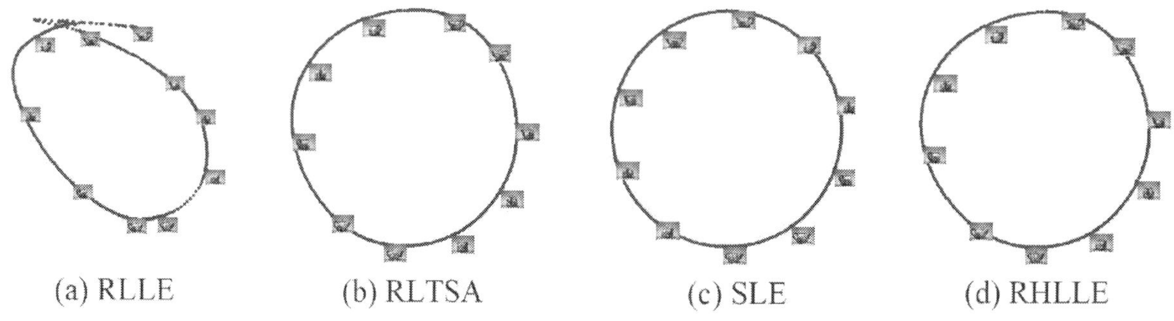

Figure 8. 2D embedding results of RLLE, RLTSA, SLE and RHLLE on the original teapot image set without being corrupted.

Besides the teapot image dataset, we also conduct experiments on the ISOFACE [1] dataset which is another benchmark dataset used by many manifold learning algorithms. This dataset contains 698 images of a 3D human head, which are collected under different poses and lighting directions. The resolution of each image is 64 × 64 and each image is represented as a 4096-dimensional vector. The intrinsic degrees of freedom are the horizontal rotation, vertical rotation and lighting direction. In order to add some outliers to the original face images, we first randomly select 10% of the images and for each selected face image we replace a square block of the image (about 20% pixels) with independent and identically-distributed samples from a uniform distribution. The location of the corrupt square block is unknown to the computer. In order to generate noise-corrupted face images, we first randomly select 30% of the face images and for each selected image we corrupt 10% of randomly-chosen pixels by replacing their values with independent and identically-distributed samples from a uniform distribution. The corrupted pixels are randomly-chosen for each face image, and the locations are unknown to the algorithm. Figure 9 shows 10 original face images, their corresponding outlier images and noise-corrupted images.

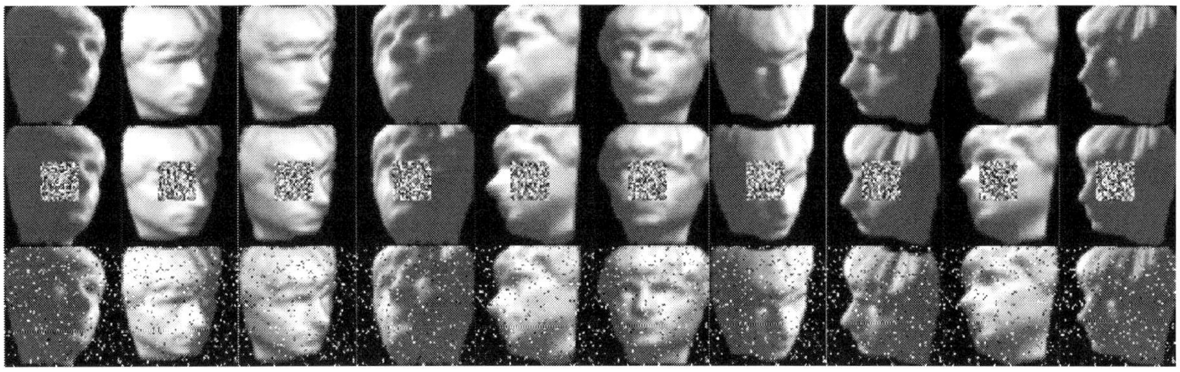

Figure 9. Ten ISOFACE images, their corresponding outlier images and noise-corrupt images.

The 2D embedding results of RLLE, RLTSA, SLE and RHLLE are shown in Figure 10. For completeness and to provide a baseline, the results on the original data without being corrupted are shown in Figure 11. In the embedding we randomly mark about 8% points with red circles and attach their corresponding training images. In the experiment, we set the number of nearest neighbors k to 15. Figure 10 reveals several interesting observations : (1) For the outliers situation, the embedding result of RLLE and SLE show that the orientations of the face change smoothly along the horizontal direction and the orientations of the face change from down to up along the vertical direction (see Figure 10a, c). The 2-D embedding results of RLTSA and RHLLE show that the poses and the light of the face images vary smoothly along the horizontal direction and the vertical direction respectively (see Figure 10b, d). Thus, all methods can approximately discover the intrinsic structures of this dataset with outliers; (2) For the noise-corrupted situation, the embedding results of RLLE and RLTSA are severely compressed and the changes in face rotation are not obvious (see Figure 10e and the right-hand side of Figure 10f). Therefore, RLLE and RLTSA cannot recover the underlying manifold structure well when there exist large amounts of noise-corrupted images; (3) For the outliers plus noise-corrupted situation, RLLE and RLTSA perform even worse (see Figure 10i, j), while SLE and our RHLLE successfully reveal the underlying manifold of the ISOFACE dataset with both outliers and noise-corrupted images (see Figure 10k, l).

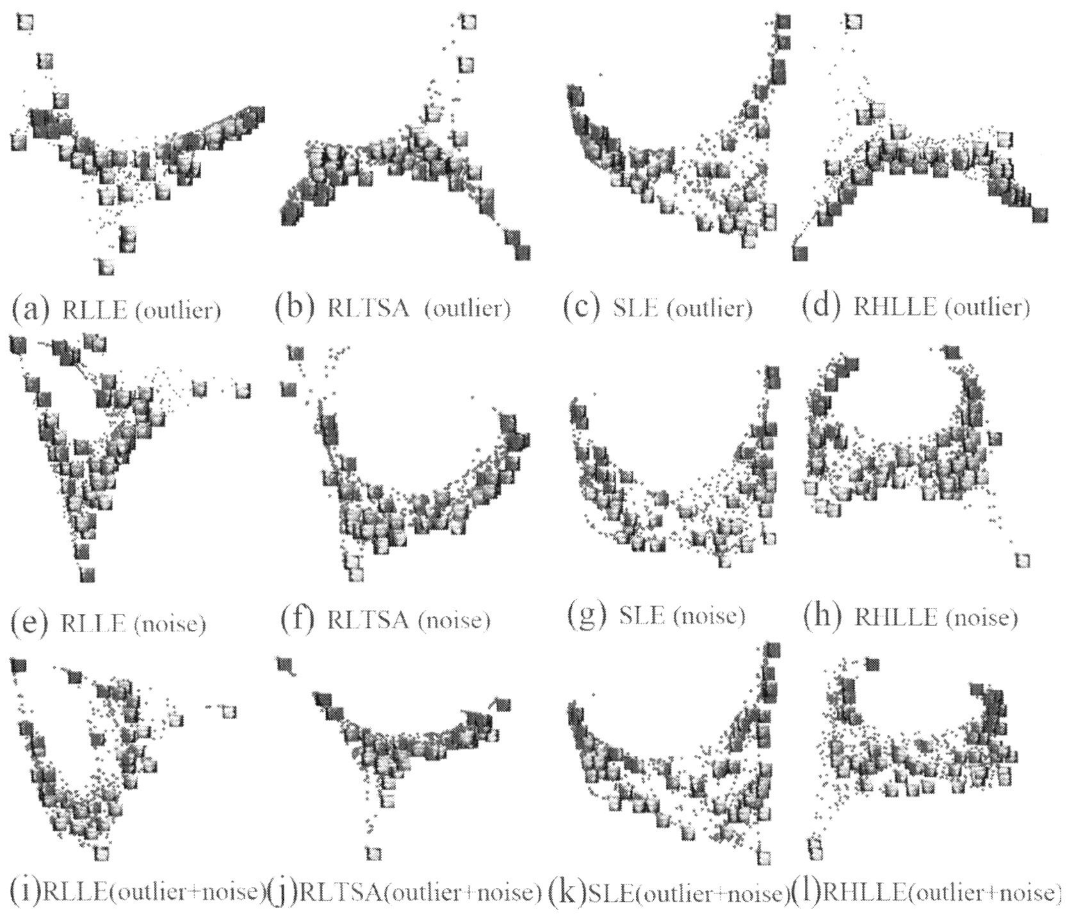

Figure 10. 2-D embedding results of RLLE, RLTSA, SLE and RHLLE on the ISOFACE image set with outliers, noise and both outliers and noise respectively.

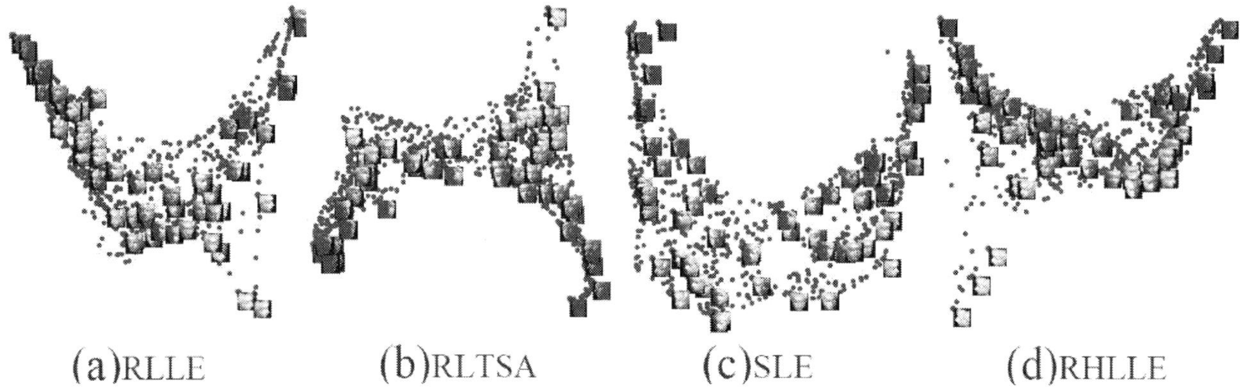

Figure 11. 2D embedding results of RLLE, RLTSA, SLE and RHLLE on the original ISOFACE image set without being corrupted.

To further quantitatively evaluate the embedding qualities obtained by RLLE, RLTSA, SLE and our RHLLE, we employ the global smoothness and co-directional consistence (GSCD) criteria introduced in [36]. Roughly speaking, the smaller the value of GSCD, the higher the global smoothness and the better co-directional consistence. For details about the GSCD criteria, please refer to [36]. Table 2 shows the GSCD values computed by different algorithms on the ISOFACE image set with outliers, noise and both outliers and noise respectively. As we can observe from Table 2, our RHLLE algorithm obtains the smallest GSCD value, this result reveals that our RHLLE performs the best in recovering the underlying manifold structure of the ISOFACE dataset with either or both outliers and noise-corrupted points. Moreover, these GSCD results further verify the visualization results (as shown in Figure 10) in a quantitative way.

Table 2. The GSCD results of RLLE, RLTSA, SLE and our RHLLE on the ISOFACE image set with outliers, noise and both outliers and noise respectively.

Method	**RLLE**	**RLTSA**	**SLE**	**Our RHLLE**
Outlier	0.2865	0.2411	0.2332	0.2294
Noise	0.3322	0.2771	0.1942	0.1843
Outlier+Noise	0.3747	0.3020	0.2148	0.2036

The average computation times over 10 independent runs of different methods are shown in Table 3. As we can observe from Table 3, our RHLLE takes significantly less time than RLLE and RLTSA for high-dimensional datasets. This result is because, for high-dimensional data, the computational complexity of RLLE and RLTSA are dominated by the iterative weighted PCA procedure which has the computational complexity of $O(kNLdD^2)$, where L is the number of iterations (usually less than 15); while our RHLLE designs a fast iterative algorithm with low computational complexity $O(kNLD)$ to approximate the original RPCA and the time-consuming reconstruction-errors procedure only need to be computed in one iteration, as we have discussed in Section 4.2. As we can observe from Table 3, SLE takes much more time than other algorithms when the number of data points N is relatively large. This is because that the computational complexity of SLE is dominated by the semi-definite program which scales as $O(N^3 + c^3)$, where c is the number of constraints. There are $O(Nk^2)$ constraints on $O(N^2)$ matrix elements, where k is the number of nearest neighbors [6, 35]. Therefore, SLE is more suited for small-scale problems compared to other methods.

Table 3. The average computation time (in seconds) for different methods on synthetic as well as real-world datasets. D denotes the dimensionality of the ambient space and N denotes the number of the data points in each dataset.

Method\Data	**Swiss Roll**	**S Curve**	**Helix**	**Teapot**	**Isoface**
	D = 3, N = 1500	**D = 3, N = 1500**	**D = 3, N = 1000**	**D = 7676, N = 400**	**D = 4096, N = 698**
RLLE	1.378	0.976	0.421	1999.3	1248.7
RLTSA	1.482	1.081	0.511	2006.1	1253.9
SLE	463.2	477.8	218.5	10.83	42.65
our RHLLE	1.572	1.256	0.792	514.8	263.3

CONCLUSIONS

In this paper, we propose the RHLLE (Robust Hessian LLE) method for robust manifold learning. We introduce a fast algorithm based on robust statistics to identify outliers in high-dimensional data. Moreover, RHLLE uses the local linear smoothing method to reduce the influence of noise. To further reduce the influence of outliers and noise, we propose to incorporate the total reliability scores of reliable local patches as weights into the global functional, then minimize the weighted global functional to obtain robust embedding results. The methods we developed can be used by other manifold learning algorithms to obtain a more accurate reconstruction of the underlying nonlinear manifolds. Extensive experiments on both artificial datasets and real datasets demonstrate the effectiveness of our RHLLE algorithm.

ACKNOWLEDGMENTS

This work was supported by the Postdoctoral Sustentation Fund, Natural Science Fund of Heilongjiang Province of China, Natural Science Foundation of China, and Fundamental Research Funds for the Central Universities of China under Grand No. LBH-Z14051, F2015033, 61573114, and HEUCF160415.

AUTHOR CONTRIBUTIONS

Xianglei Xing and Sidan Du conceived and designed the experiments; Xianglei Xing performed the experiments; Xianglei Xing and Kejun Wang analyzed the data; Xianglei Xing wrote the paper.

REFERENCES

1. Tenenbaum, J.B.; de Silva, V.; Langford, J.C. A global geometric framework for nonlinear dimensionality reduction. *Science* 2000, *290*, 2319 – 2323.
2. Roweis, S.T.; Saul, L.K. Nonlinear dimensionality reduction by locally linear embedding. *Science* 2000, *290*, 2323 – 2326.
3. Belkin, M.; Niyogi, P. Laplacian eigenmaps and spectral techniques for embedding and clustering. In *Advances in Neural Information Processing Systems 14 (NIPS)*; Dietterich, T.G., Becker, S., Ghahramani, Z., Eds.; Neural information processing systems foundation : Vancouver, BC, Canada, 2001; Volume 14, pp. 585 – 591.
4. Zhang, Z.Y.; Zha, H.Y. Principal manifolds and nonlinear dimensionality reduction via tangent space alignment. *J. Shanghai Univ. (Engl. Ed.)* 2004, *8*, 406 – 424.
5. Donoho, D.L.; Grimes, C. Hessian eigenmaps : Locally linear embedding techniques for high-dimensional data. *Proc. Natl. Acad. Sci.* 2003, *100*, 5591 – 5596.
6. Weinberger, K.Q.; Saul, L.K. Unsupervised learning of image manifolds by semidefinite programming. *Int. J. Comput. Vis.* 2006, *70*, 77 – 90.
7. Lin, T.; Zha, H. Riemannian manifold learning. *IEEE Trans. Pattern Anal. Mach. Intell.* 2008, *30*, 796 – 809.
8. Wang, R.; Shan, S.; Chen, X.; Chen, J.; Gao, W. Maximal linear embedding for dimensionality reduction. *IEEE Trans. Pattern Anal. Mach. Intell.* 2011, *33*, 1776 – 1792.
9. Xing, X.; Wang, K.; Lv, Z.; Zhou, Y.; Du, S. Fusion of Local Manifold Learning Methods. *IEEE Signal Process. Lett.* 2015, *22*, 395 – 399.
10. Seung, H.S.; Lee, D.D. The manifold ways of perception. *Science* 2000, *290*, 2268 – 2269.
11. Belkin, M.; Niyogi, P.; Sindhwani, V. Manifold regularization : A geometric framework for learning from labeled and unlabeled examples. *J. Mach. Learn. Res.* 2006, *7*, 2399 – 2434.
12. Xing, X.; Yu, Y.; Jiang, H.; Du, S. A multi-manifold semi-supervised Gaussian mixture model for pattern classification. *Pattern Recognit. Lett.* 2013, *34*, 2118 – 2125.
13. Souvenir, R.; Pless, R. Manifold clustering. In Proceeding of the Tenth IEEE International Conference on Computer Vision, ICCV 2005, Beijing, China, 17 – 21 October 2005; Volume 1, pp. 648 – 653.
14. Hawkins, D.M. *Identification of Outliers*; Springer : New York, NY, USA, 1980; Chapter 1.
15. Chang, H.; Yeung, D.Y. Robust locally linear embedding. *Pattern Recognit.* 2006, *39*, 1053 – 1065.
16. De La Torre, F.; Black, M.J. A framework for robust subspace learning. *Int. J. Comput. Vis.* 2003, *54*, 117 – 142.
17. Zhan, Y.; Yin, J. Robust local tangent space alignment via iterative weighted PCA. *Neurocomputing* 2011, *74*, 1985 – 1993.
18. Zhang, Z.; Zha, H. *Local Linear Smoothing for Nonlinear Manifold Learning*; Technical Report; CSE, Penn State University : Old Main, PA, USA, 2003.
19. Park, J.; Zhang, Z.; Zha, H.; Kasturi, R. Local smoothing for manifold learning. In Proceedings of the 2004 IEEE Computer Society Conference on Computer Vision and Pattern Recognition, Washington, DC, USA, 27 June – 2 July 2004; Volume 2, pp. 445 – 452.
20. Hein, M.; Maier, M. Manifold denoising. In *Advances in Neural Information Processing Systems 19 (NIPS)*; Schölkopf, B., Platt, J.C., Hoffman, T., Eds.; Neural Information Processing System Foundation : Vancouver, BC, Canada, 2006; Volume 19, pp. 561 – 568.
21. Zhou, D.; Bousquet, O.; Lal, T.N.; Weston, J.; Schölkopf, B. Learning with Local and Global Consistency. In*Advances in Neural Information Processing Systems 16 (NIPS)*; Thrun, S., Saul, L.K., Schölkopf, B., Eds.; Neural Information Processing Systems Foundation : Vancouver, BC, Canada, 2003; Volume 16, pp. 321 – 328.
22. Xing, X.; Du, S.; Jiang, H. Semi-Supervised Nonparametric Discriminant Analysis. *IEICE Trans. Inf. Syst.* 2013, *96*, 375 – 378.
23. Gashler, M.; Martinez, T. Robust manifold learning with CycleCut. *Connect. Sci.* 2012, *24*, 57 – 69.
24. Chern, S.S.; Chen, W.H.; Lam, K.S. *Lectures on Differential Geometry*; World Scientific Pub Co Inc. : Singapore, 1999; Volume 1.
25. Huber, P.J. *Robust Statistics*; Springer : Berlin, Germany, 2011.

26. Kim, K.I.; Steinke, F.; Hein, M. Semi-Supervised Regression Using Hessian Energy with an Application to Semi-Supervised Dimensionality Reduction. In *Advances in Neural Information Processing Systems 22 (NIPS)*; Bengio, Y., Schuurmans, D., Lafferty, J.D., Williams, C.K.I., Culotta, A., Eds.; Neural Information Processing Systems Foundation : Vancouver, BC, Canada, 2009; Volume 22, pp. 979 – 987.
27. Lin, B.; He, X.; Zhang, C.; Ji, M. Parallel vector field embedding. *J. Mach. Learn. Res.* 2013, *14*, 2945 – 2977.
28. Lin, B.; Zhang, C.; He, X. Semi-Supervised Regression via Parallel Field Regularization. In *Advances in Neural Information Processing Systems 24 (NIPS)*; Shawe-Taylor, J., Zemel, R.S., Bartlett, P.L., Pereira, F., Weinberger, K.Q., Eds.; Neural Information Processing Systems Foundation : Granada, Spain, 2011; Volume 24.
29. Turk, M.; Pentland, A. Eigenfaces for recognition. *J. Cognit. Neurosci.* 1991, *3*, 71 – 86.
30. Zhang, P.; Qiao, H.; Zhang, B. An improved local tangent space alignment method for manifold learning.*Pattern Recognit. Lett.* 2011, *32*, 181 – 189.
31. De la Torre, F.; Black, M.J. Robust principal component analysis for computer vision. In Proceeding of the Eighth IEEE International Conference on Computer Vision, 2001. ICCV 2001, Vancouver, BC, USA; 2001; Volume 1, pp. 362 – 369.
32. Holland, P.W.; Welsch, R.E. Robust regression using iteratively reweighted least-squares. *Commun. Stat. Theory Methods* 1977, *6*, 813 – 827.
33. Huber, P.J. Robust regression : Asymptotics, conjectures and Monte Carlo. *Ann. Stat.* 1973, *1*, 799 – 821.
34. Cleveland, W.S.; Loader, C. Smoothing by Local Regression : Principles and Methods. In *Statistical Theory and Computational Aspects of Smoothing*; Springer : Heidelberg, Germany, 1996; pp. 10 – 49.
35. Hou, C.; Zhang, C.; Wu, Y.; Jiao, Y. Stable local dimensionality reduction approaches. *Pattern Recognit.* 2009, *42*, 2054 – 2066.
36. Zhang, J.; Wang, Q.; He, L.; Zhou, Z.H. Quantitative analysis of nonlinear embedding. *IEEE Trans. Neural Netw.*2011, *22*, 1987 – 1998.

CHAPTER 6

ALGORITHMS FOR MANAGING, QUERYING AND PROCESSING BIG DATA IN CLOUD ENVIRONMENTS

Alfredo Cuzzocrea

DIA Department, University of Trieste and ICAR-CNR, Trieste 34127, Italy

Big data (e.g., [1,2,3]) has become one of the most challenging research topics in current years. Big data is everywhere, from social networks to web advertisements, from sensor and stream systems to bio-informatics, from graph management tools to smart cities, and so forth. Cloud computing environments (e.g., [4,5,6]) represent the "natural" context for such data, as they embed several emerging trends, both at the research level and the technological level, which comprise high-performance, high reliability, high availability, transparence, abstraction, virtualization, and so forth.

At the convergence of these emerging trends, managing, querying and processing big data in Cloud environments, which have received a great deal of attention from the research community recently (e.g., [7,8,9]), plays a leading role, and algorithmic approaches to these challenges are very promising now. These approaches come from a rich variety of multi-disciplinary areas, ranging from mathematical models to approximation models, from resource-constrained paradigms to memory-bounded methods, and so forth. Furthermore, algorithms for managing big data according to a "systematic" view of the problem are gaining momentum. For instance, algorithms for efficiently managing MapReduce tasks over Clouds are a clear instance of the latter scientific area.

Citation: Alfredo Cuzzocrea. Algorithms for managing, querying and processing big data in cloud environments, Algorithms 2016, 9(1), 13; DOI: 10.3390/a9010013

Inspired by these exciting research challenges, this special issue "Algorithms for Managing, Querying and Processing Big Data in Cloud Environments" of Algorithms focuses the attention on topics related to the theory and practice of algorithms for managing big data in Cloud environments, the design and analysis of algorithms for managing big data in Cloud environments, the tuning and experimental evaluation of algorithms for managing big data in Cloud environments, and so forth. The aim is that of providing a significant milestone on the road of the investigated topic, to be significant for both theory and practice, as well as applications and systems that are founded on such algorithms.

The special issue contains four papers which have been accepted after two rigorous review rounds. In the following, we provide an overview on these papers.

The first paper [10], entitled "Multiobjective Cloud Particle Optimization Algorithm Based on Decomposition", by Li *et al.*, investigates the relevant multi-objective evolutionary paradigm based on decomposition (MOEA/D) that, as the authors correctly state, has received attention from many researchers in recent years. The paper thus presents a novel multi-objective algorithm based on decomposition and the Cloud computing model called multi-objective decomposition evolutionary algorithm based on Cloud Particle Differential Evolution (MOEA/D-CPDE). In the proposed method, the best solution found so far acts as a seed in each generation and evolves two individuals by a cloud generator. A new individual is produced by updating the current individual with the position vector difference of these two individuals. The performance of the proposed algorithm is verified on 16 well-known multi-objective problems, and experimental results indicate that MOEA/D-CPDE is competitive.

The second paper [11], entitled "Implementation of a Parallel Algorithm Based on a Spark Cloud Computing Platform", by Wang *et al.*, proposes to parallelize the well-known MAX-MIN Ant System (MMAS) algorithm in order to solve the annoying Traveling Salesman Problem (TSP) based on a Spark Cloud computing platform. Indeed, as authors correctly highlight, parallel algorithms, such as the ant colony algorithm, take a long time when solving large-scale problems. In the solution proposed by authors, MMAS is combined with Spark MapReduce to execute the path building and the pheromone operation in a distributed computer Cluster. In addition to this, to improve the precision of the proposed solution, the local optimization strategy 2-opt is adapted in MMAS. Experimental results show that Spark has a very great accelerating effect on the ant colony algorithm when the city scale of TSP or the number of ants is relatively large.

The third paper [12], entitled "A Data Analytic Algorithm for Managing, Querying, and Processing Uncertain Big Data in Cloud Environments", by Jiang *et al.*, considers the problem of mining big data for supporting the discovery of useful information and knowledge. In this context, they propose a data analytic algorithm for managing, querying and processing transactions of uncertain big data in Cloud environments. The proposed framework, based on this algorithm, allows users to query these big data by specifying constraints expressing their interests, and processes the user-specified constraints to discover useful information and knowledge. Due to the fact that each item in every transaction in these uncertain big data is associated with an existential probability value expressing the likelihood of that item to be present in a particular transaction, computation could be intensive. In order to cope with this issue, the proposed algorithm makes use of the MapReduce model in a Cloud environment for effective data analytics on uncertain big data. Experimental results show the effectiveness of the overall solution.

Finally, the fourth paper [13], entitled "An Effective and Efficient MapReduce Algorithm for Computing BFS-based Traversals of Large-Scale RDF Graphs", by Cuzzocrea *et al.*, focuses its attention on Resource Description Framework (RDF) graphs in terms of a relevant case of Big Web Data occurring in the so-called Semantic Web, leading to the well-known large-scale RDF graphs. They study the problem of effectively and efficiently computing traversals of large-scale RDF graphs over MapReduce and propose a solution that is based on the Breadth First Search (BFS) strategy for visiting (RDF) graphs to be decomposed and processed according to the MapReduce framework. The authors demonstrate how such implementation speeds up the analysis of RDF graphs with respect to competitor approaches. Experimental results clearly support the reliability of the provided contributions.

The described contributions still open the door for future research challenges to be investigated in order to further improve the management of big data in Cloud environments, yet they are inspired by previous research experiences in related scientific areas. For instance, big data compression (e.g., [14,15,16,17]) seems a promising solution to this end, as compressing data improves data management efficiency, but it has yet to be provided under well-defined probabilistic guarantees on deriving accuracy (e.g., [18,19,20]). Similarly, data fragmentation/partition techniques (e.g., [21,22,23]) should be considered as well, in the area of further solutions for improving performance while taking advantage of the typical distributed nature of Cloud platforms that, in our opinion, still expose interesting features not yet completely exploited beyond those of previous (distributed) settings (e.g., Grids, Clusters, and so forth).

In conclusion, there is still a lot of work to do in the context of managing, querying and processing big data in Cloud environments. We firmly hope this special issue represents a reliable milestone towards this difficult, yet exciting, research direction.

ACKNOWLEDGMENTS

The Special Issue editor would like to express his gratitude to all contributors and reviewers whose efforts allowed making this special issue a success, as well as to the editorial staff of MDPI Algorithms Journal for their continuous and diligent assistance whenever needed.

REFERENCES

1. Agrawal, D.; Das, S.; El Abbadi, A. Big Data and Cloud Computing: Current State and Future Opportunities. Available online: http://citeseerx.ist.psu.edu/viewdoc/summary?doi=10.1.1.188.5819 (accessed on 29 January 2016).
2. Chen, C.L.P.; Zhang, C.-Y. Data-Intensive Applications, Challenges, Techniques and Technologies: A Survey on Big Data. *Inf. Sci.* 2014, *275*, 314–347.
3. Cuzzocrea, A.; Saccà, D.; Ullman, J.D. Big Data: A Research Agenda. In Proceedings of the 17th International Database Engineering & Applications Symposium (IDEAS'13), Barcelona, Spain, 9–11 October 2013; pp. 198–203.
4. Armbrust, M.; Fox, A.; Griffith, R.; Joseph, A.D.; Katz, R.; Konwinski, A.; Lee, G.; Patterson, D.; Rabkin, A.; Stoica, I.; *et al.* A View of Cloud Computing. *Commun. ACM* 2010, *53*, 50–58.
5. Buyya, R.; Yeo, C.S.; Venugopal, S.; Broberg, J.; Brandic, I. Cloud Computing and Emerging IT Platforms: Vision, Hype, and Reality for Delivering Computing as the 5th Utility. *Future Gener. Comput. Syst.* 2009, *25*, 599–616.
6. Cuzzocrea, A. Analytics over Big Data: Exploring the Convergence of Data Warehousing, OLAP and Data-Intensive Cloud Infrastructures. In Proceedings of the 2013 IEEE 37th Annual Computer Software and Applications Conference (COMPSAC'13), Kyoto, Japan, 22–26 July 2013; pp. 481–483.
7. Baker, T.; Al-Dawsari, B.; Tawfik, H.; Reid, D.; Ngoko, Y. GreeDi: An Energy Efficient Routing Algorithm for Big Data on Cloud. *Ad Hoc Netw.* 2015, *35*, 83–96.
8. Zhang, L.; Li, Z.; Wu, C.; Chen, M. Online Algorithms for Uploading Deferrable Big Data to the Cloud. In Proceedings of the IEEE 2014 International Conference on Computer Communications (INFOCOM'14),

Toronto, ON, Canada, 27 April 2014–2 May 2014; pp. 2022–2030.

9. Yu, B.; Cuzzocrea, A.; Jeong, D.H.; Maydebura, S. A Bigtable/MapReduce-Based Cloud Infrastructure for Effectively and Efficiently Managing Large-Scale Sensor Networks. In Proceedings of the 5th International Conference on Data Management in Cloud, Grid and P2P Systems (GLOBE'12), Vienna, Austria, 5–6 September 2012; pp. 25–36.
10. Li, W.; Wang, L.; Jiang, Q.; Hei, X.; Wang, B. Multiobjective Cloud Particle Optimization Algorithm Based on Decomposition. *Algorithms* 2015, *8*, 157–176.
11. Wang, L.; Wang, Y.; Xie, Y. Implementation of a Parallel Algorithm Based on a Spark Cloud Computing Platform. *Algorithms* 2015, *8*, 407–414.
12. Jiang, F.; Leung, C.K. A Data Analytic Algorithm for Managing, Querying, and Processing Uncertain Big Data in Cloud Environments. *Algorithms* 2015, *8*, 1175–1194.
13. Cuzzocrea, A.; Cosulschi, M.; De Virgilio, R. An Effective and Efficient MapReduce Algorithm for Computing BFS-Based Traversals of Large-Scale RDF Graphs. *Algorithms* 2016, *9*, 7.
14. Yang, C.; Zhang, X.; Zhong, C.; Liu, C.; Pei, J.; Ramamohanarao, K.; Chen, J. A Spatiotemporal Compression Based Approach for Efficient Big Data Processing on Cloud. *J. Comput. Syst. Sci.* 2014, *80*, 1563–1583.
15. Cuzzocrea, A.; Furfaro, F.; Masciari, E.; Saccà, D.; Sirangelo, C. Approximate Query Answering on Sensor Network Data Streams. In *GeoSensor Networks*; Stefanidis, A., Nittel, S., Eds.; CRC Press: Cleveland OH, 2004; pp. 53–72.
16. Cuzzocrea, A. Accuracy Control in Compressed Multidimensional Data Cubes for Quality of Answer-based OLAP Tools. In Proceedings of the 18th International Conference on Scientific and Statistical Database Management (SSDBM'06), Vienna, Austria, 3–5 July 2006; pp. 301–310.
17. Cuzzocrea, A. Improving Range-Sum Query Evaluation on Data Cubes via Polynomial Approximation. *Data Knowl. Eng.* 2006, *56*, 85–121.
18. Xi, R.; Lin, N.; Chen, Y. Compression and Aggregation for Logistic Regression Analysis in Data Cubes. *IEEE Trans. Knowl. Data Eng.* 2009, *21*, 479–492.
19. Cuzzocrea, A.; Furfaro, F.; Saccà, D. Hand-OLAP: A System for Delivering OLAP Services on Handheld Devices. In Proceedings of the 6th IEEE International Symposium on Autonomous Decentralized Systems (ISADS'03), Pisa, Italy, 9–11 April 2003; pp. 80–87.
20. Cuzzocrea, A.; Matrangolo, U. Analytical Synopses for Approximate Query Answering in OLAP Environments. In Proceedings of the 15th International Conference on Database and Expert Systems Applications (DEXA'04), Zaragoza, Spain, 30 August 2004–3 September 2004; pp. 359–370.
21. Daenen, J.; Neven, F.; Tan, T. Gumbo: Guarded Fragment Queries over Big Data. In Proceedings of the 18th International Conference on Extending Database Technology (EDBT'15), Brussels, Belgium, 23–27 March 2015; pp. 521–524.
22. Cuzzocrea, A.; Saccà, D.; Serafino, P. A Hierarchy-Driven Compression Technique for Advanced OLAP Visualization of Multidimensional Data Cubes. In Proceedings of the 8th International Conference on Data Warehousing and Knowledge Discovery (DaWaK'06), Krakow, Poland, 4–8 September 2006; pp. 106–119.
23. Cuzzocrea, A.; Darmont, J.; Mahboubi, H. Fragmenting Very Large XML Data Warehouses via K-Means Clustering Algorithm. *Int. J. Bus. Intell. Data Min.* 2009, *4*, 301–328.

CHAPTER 7 AN IMPROVED DYNAMIC JOINT RESOURCE ALLOCATION ALGORITHM BASED ON SFR

Yibing Li, Xueying Diao, Ge Dong, and Fang Ye

College of Information and Communication Engineering, Harbin Engineering University, Harbin 150001, China

ABSTRACT

Inter-cell interference (ICI) is the main factor affecting system capacity and spectral efficiency. Effective spectrum resource management is an important and challenging issue for the design of wireless communication systems. The soft frequency reuse (SFR) is regarded as an interesting approach to significantly eliminate ICI. However, the allocation of resource is fixed prior to system deployment in static SFR. To overcome this drawback, this paper adopts a distributed method and proposes an improved dynamic joint resource allocation algorithm (DJRA). The improved scheme adaptively adjusts resource allocation based on the real-time user distribution. DJRA first detects the edge-user distribution vector to determine the optimal scheme, which guarantees that all the users have available resources and the number of iterations is reduced. Then, the DJRA maximizes the throughput for each cell via optimizing resource and power allocation. Due to further eliminate interference, the sector partition method is used in the center region and in view of fairness among users, the novel approach adds the proportional fair algorithm at the end of DJRA. Simulation results show that the proposed algorithm outperforms previous approaches for improving the system capacity and cell edge user performance.

INTRODUCTION

With the rapid increasing data rate requirements of mobile users on multimedia applications, the design of spectrum resource allocation methods with high system throughput and spectral efficiency [1] has become one of the hot issues in LTE [2] and LTE-A [3]. In the multi-cell resource allocation environment, ICI is a major problem affecting system throughput, especially for the cell edge users. Fractional frequency reuse (FFR)Bv and soft frequency reuse (SFR) are two common deployments to improve spectral efficiency and reduce ICI. However, FFR eliminates frequency collisions at the cost of spectrum efficiency. The reason for this lies in interior users being forbidden to share the spectrum with cell-edge users in FFR. Soft frequency reuse (SFR) emerged as an alternative resource planning scheme to effectively mitigate ICI in cellular systems. SFR offers cell-center users access to spectrum with a frequency reuse factor equal to one, and cell-edge users with a frequency reuse factor which is greater than one. Reference [4] has proved that SFR outperforms FFR in spectrum efficiency. The original frequency reuse schemes are static frequency reuse. References [5] and [6] described static FFR and SFR, respectively. Although the so-called static frequency reuse scheme demands relatively lower complexity and overhead, it fixes the allocation of power and subcarriers in each cell beforehand, which greatly limits the communication performance. To overcome this drawback, dynamic resource

Citation: Yibing Li, Xueying Diao, Ge Dong, and Fang Ye. An improved dynamic joint resource allocation algorithm based on SFR, Algorithms 2016, 9(2), 29; DOI: 10.3390/a9020029

assignment has arisen. The authors of [7,8,9,10] introduced several dynamic FFR schemes. Dynamic SFR approaches were illustrated in [11,12,13,14]. However, there are no works about joint resource allocation for the SFR, except for the method proposed by Qian in [15,16], where [16] is the improvement of [15]. In this paper, we put forward an improved dynamic joint resource allocation algorithm based on SFR, referred to as DJRA. The new algorithm aims at solving several problems in [16]. Qian firstly utilizes joint resource allocation in SFR and proposes an adaptive soft frequency reuse scheme (ASFR). Nevertheless, ASFR can not guarantee that all the users have available resources. Accordingly, we propose two methods to solve this problem. Firstly, DJRA monitors edge-user distribution in the system before using an exhaustive search, which not only guarantees all the users have available resources but also reduces the number of iterations. Secondly, we take the multi-cell resource allocation fairness principle into account by utilizing the proportional fair algorithm (PF). To further mitigate interference, this paper presents the sector partition method in a cell-center.

DJRA obtains the optimal single cell resource allocation scheme by dynamically adjusting resource block (RB) and power allocation according to the real-time distribution of users per cell, and then uses an iteration method to acquire the optimum resource allocation scheme. Compared with previous schemes, it is worth pointing out that the improved dynamic joint resource allocation scheme reduces the influence of ICI, acquires a better cell edge user performance, and guarantees all the users have available resources.

The rest of this paper is structured as follows. Section 2 introduces the system model. The method of dynamic joint resource allocation algorithm based on SFR is described in detail in Section 3. Section 4 provides the results of simulation analysis. Finally, conclusing remarks are presented in Section 5.

SYSTEM MODEL AND PROBLEM FORMULATION

System Model

We consider an OFDM-based LTE downlink network where the number of multi-cells is C. Figure 1 illustrates the SFR deployment. Each cell has the same number of users and uniform user distribution is assumed in the whole coverage area. Each cell is divided into two regions, the colored areas are the edge region and the colorless area is the center region. We define a user with the worst channel gain as a virtual user. As seen from the Figure 1, virtual center user and virtual edge user are the users located in their corresponding border area.

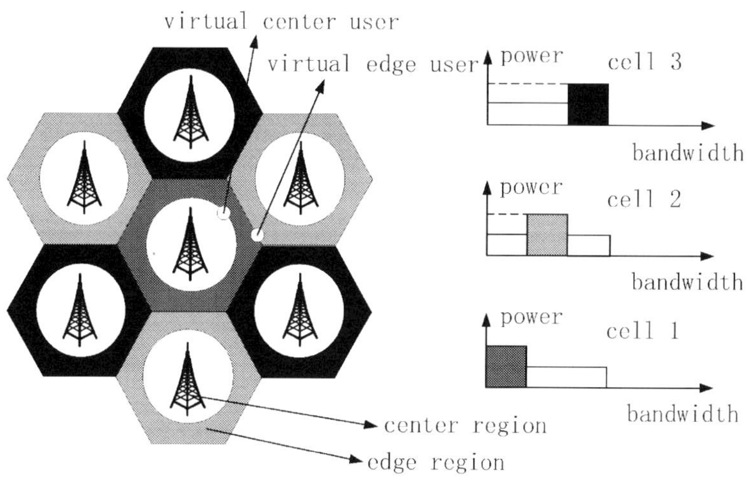

Figure 1. System networking.

In our system model, P_{max} denotes the maximum transmission power of the base station (BS). The cell-interior radius and the cell radius are r and R, respectively. The received noise power is N_0. B is the total system bandwidth, which is divided into N blocks, and each RB occupies a bandwidth of B_{sub}. In SFR, RBs are grouped to cell-edge blocks with a bandwidth of B^{major} and cell-center block with a bandwidth of B^{min} or, where $B^{major} \cup B^{min\,or} = B$. Other symbols are defined in Table 1.

Table 1. Symbols definition.

Definition	Symbol
Transmit power on edge RB in cell i	p_i^o
Transmit power on center RB in cell i	p_i^{in}
Channel gain for the edge-user located in cell i from its serving BS	$g_{i,i}^o$
Channel gain for the edge-user located in cell i from its adjacent BS m	$g_{i,m}^o$
Channel gain for the center-user located in cell i from its serving BS	$g_{i,i}^{in}$
Channel gain for the center-user located in cell i from its adjacent BS m	$g_{i,m}^{in}$
Number of cell-edge RBs in cell i	N_i^{major}
Number of cell-interior RBs in cell i	$N_i^{min\,or}$

In cellular networks, the signal power received gets weaker with the increasing of the propagation distance. For the convenience of discussion, we only consider the signals the come from three BSs in terms of 802.16e standard, including a serving BS and two interfering BSs. For a user in cell i, the signal-to-interference-noise ratio on RB j is given as

$$SINR_i^j = \frac{p_i^j g_{i,i}^j}{\sum_{m \in C_{adj}^i} p_m^j g_{i,m}^j + N_o} \quad (1)$$

where C_{adj}^i is the set of interfering cells which are adjacent to cell i. If j is the edge-block, j is equal to o. If j is the center-block, j is equal to in.

In the SFR system, the edge-user interference on RB j comes from the signals on RB j used by center-users in adjacent cells. Thus, we submit Equation (1) into the Shannon capacity formula [17]. The data rate of the edge-user situated in cell i is expressed as [16]

$$R_i^o = \sum_{j \in B_i^{major}} B_{sub} \log_2(1 + SINR_i^j)$$
$$= N_i^{major} B_{sub} \log_2\left(1 + \frac{p_i^o g_{i,i}^o}{\sum_{m \in C_{adj}^i} p_m^{in} g_{i,m}^o + N_o}\right) \quad (2)$$

The center-user interference on RB j has two sources: signals reusing the same resource by adjacent cell edge-user or adjacent cell center-user. For simplifying notation, the adjacent cell interference power is unified into the transmit power of cell-edge RBs, *i.e.*, p_m^o. Therefore, the date rate of center-user in cell i can be approximately given as:

$$R_i^{in} = \sum_{j \in B_i^{major}} B_{sub} \log_2(1 + SINR_i^j)$$
$$\approx N_i^{\min or} B_{sub} \log_2\left(1 + \frac{p_i^{in} g_{i,i}^{in}}{\sum_{m \in C_{adj}^i} p_m^o g_{i,m}^{in} + N_o}\right) \quad (3)$$

We already know if the data rate requirement of the virtual edge user in each cell is met; the data rate of all users in the same cell can therefore be satisfied. Thus, we take the minimum throughput demands for the virtual users as the minimum throughput requirements for the individual users situated in that cell zone. Thus, the minimum data rate for the edge and center zone in the target cell i is

$$R_i^{o\min} = \sum_{k \in K_i^o} \gamma_{i,k} \quad (4)$$

$$R_i^{in\min} = \sum_{k \in K_i^{in}} \gamma_{i,k} \quad (5)$$

Let k be the number of users in cell i, K_i^o and K_i^o be the set of cell edge users and inter users, respectively. $\gamma_{i,k}$ denotes the minimum throughput requirement for the user k.

Problem Formulation

The major contribution of the adaptive soft frequency reuse scheme is to allocate RBs and transmit powers dynamically, which can not only maximize the system capacity but also guarantee the minimum data rate requirement for each cell zone. Equation (6) is the objective function.

$$\max_{N_i^{major}, N_i^{\min or}, p_i^{in}, p_i^o} \sum_{i \in C} R_i^{in} + R_i^o \quad (6)$$

where

$$R_i^o \geq R_i^{o\min} \quad (7)$$

$$R_i^{in} \geq R_i^{in\min} \quad (8)$$

$$P_i \leq P_{max} \quad (9)$$

$$N_i^{major} + N_i^{\min or} = N \quad (10)$$

$$\sum_{i \in C_{adj}^3} N_i^{major} \leq N \quad (11)$$

In the above formulas, Constraints (7) and (8) denote the cell-interior and cell-edge users need to satisfy their lowest data rate requirements; Constraint (9) ensures that the total power used in each cell can not exceed the maximum power provided by each base station. Constraint (10) states that all RBs can be used in each cell. Constraint (11) indicates that the RBs in any three neighboring cells are non-overlapped, and C_{adj}^3 is the set of three adjacent cells. The total power for cell i is calculated as

$$P_i = N_i^{\min or} p_i^{in} + N_i^{major} p_i^o \quad (12)$$

PROPOSED ALGORITHM

An Improved Dynamic Joint Resource Allocation Algorithm Based on SFR

In this section, we put forward a novel scheme, referred to as the dynamic joint resource allocation algorithm. We aim to find a DJRA solution that maximizes the system data rate and meets the data rate requirements for cell center users and cell edge users at the same time. As objective function (6) is an

NP-hard problem and difficult to solve [18]. In this paper, we decompose the multi-cell resource allocation optimization into several single-cell optimization problems. The proposed method is first to find a single cell solution and then extend the solution to optimize multi-cell wireless network performance.

We first propose the single-cell resource allocation solution. For a single cell, we aim to find a RB-power allocation scheme which satisfies the condition that the required transmission power at each BS is lower than the maximum power. The single cell optimization problem is described as follows

$$\{P_i^{nplan} \mid P_i^{nplan} \leq P_{max}, i \in C, nplan \in W\} \tag{13}$$

where i is the target cell, W denotes the set of DJRA schemes and $nplan$ is one of the DJRA plan. P_i^{nplan} denotes the required transmission power at each BS in cell i when adopting the $nplan^{th}$ scheme. Equations (14) to (17) illustrates the constraint conditions.

$$R_i^o \geq R_o^{tar} \tag{14}$$

$$R_i^{in} \geq R_{in}^{tar} \tag{15}$$

$$N_i^{major} + N_i^{\min or} = N \tag{16}$$

$$N_i^{major} \leq N - \sum_{m \in C_{adj}^3, i \neq m} N_m^{major} \tag{17}$$

where R_o^{tar} and R_{in}^{tar} denotes the target data rate for edge user and center user respectively. The condition for equality is that the transmit power is the lowest power in Constraints (14) and (15). Once N_i^{major} is determined, we have $N_i^{\min or}$, P_i^{in}, P_i^o

$$N_i^{\min or} = N - N_i^{major} \tag{18}$$

$$p_i^o = (2^{\frac{R_o^{tar}}{N_i^{major} B_{sub}}} - 1) \cdot \frac{\sum_{m \in C_{adj}^i} p_m^{in} g_{1,m}^o + N_0}{g_{i,i}^o} \tag{19}$$

$$p_i^{in} = (2^{\frac{R_{in}^{tar}}{N_i^{\min or} B_{sub}}} - 1) \cdot \frac{\sum_{m \in C_{adj}^i} p_m^o g_{1,m}^{in} + N_0}{g_{i,i}^{in}} \tag{20}$$

where p_m^{in} and p_m^o denotes the power allocated to center RBs and edge RBs in cell m. As N_i^{major} and $N_i^{\min or}$ are both integers, there exist (N – 1) different combinations of RB-power in theory. Before applying the traversing method, DJRA detects edge-user distribution vector $K = \{k_1, k_2, \ldots k_i\}, i \in C$. For the sake of guaranteeing that each user has its frequency resource that can be used, there are only $N - k_i + 1$ combinations of FP (frequency block, power allocation) pairs. Then DJRA selects all the FP pairs that yield the throughput requirements as expressed in Constraints (14) and (15), and submits these FP pairs into Equation (12) to get the power set W.

Once the power set is set up by above steps, we obtain the total power for each allocation plan. Subsequently, we compute $P_{max} - P_i^{nplan}$ in the target cell. The residual power is equally allocated to each edge of RB to enhance the performance of edge users.

In the forth step, DJRA finds the maximum $R_i^o + R_i^{in}$ and set $R_i^o + R_i^{in}$ as the new target data rates to recalculate FP pairs, until the cell capacity does not change any more. The single-cell allocation (Algorithm 1) is shown below.

Algorithm 1. Single-cell Resource Allocation Solution of DJRA

(1) Monitor edge-user distribution;
(2) Find all the FP pairs that yield the throughput requirements and get the power set;
(3) Compute $P_{max} - P_i^{nplan}$ in the target cell and equally allocate the residual power to each edge RB;
(4) Find the maximum $R_i^o + R_i^{in}$ and set R_i^o and R_i^{in} as the new target data rates to recalculate Step 2 to Step 3, until the cell capacity does not change any more.

Next, we extend the single-cell solution to find the global joint resource allocation scheme for multi-cell scenarios by using the method illustrated in [16]. After resource allocation is achieved for each cell, DJRA takes the resource allocation in cell *i* as inputs to its adjacent cells and calculates the multi-cell data rate $\sum_{i \in C} R_i^{in} + R_i^o$. It repeats the above steps until the multi-cell data rate $\sum_{i \in C} R_i^{in} + R_i^o$ does not change any more. Then the algorithm stops iterating and we get the optimal solution. Finally, DJRA applies the sector partition method in the cell-center to further mitigate interference, and the proportional fair algorithm to guarantee that each user has available resources. Figure 2 shows the sector division in the center region. Each center zone is divided into three sub-regions: A, B and C. Different colors present different resource-using regions. As seen from the figure, increasing the pass loss of interfering signals can eliminate ICI, and thereby improve system performance.

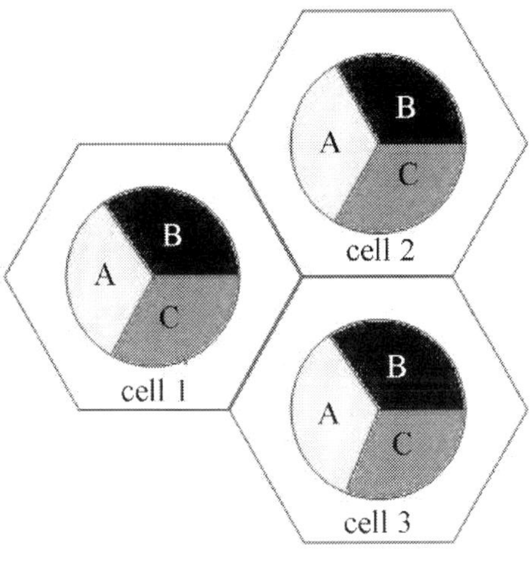

Figure 2. Interior sector partition.

Complexity Analysis

Firstly, we analyze the computational complexity of resource allocation for a single cell. Since there are $N - k_i + 1$ different combinations for $(N_i^{major}, N_i^{minor})$, DJRA needs traverse $N - k_i + 1$ to obtain the power set in Step 1. Similarly, Step 2 takes at most $N - k_i$ operations to assign the remaining powers to edge users. Therefore, the single cell resource allocation process will take $L' = L_1 + L_2$ operations in one cell per iteration. Step 3 only requires one process, so the complexity for Step 3 is of the order of $L_3 = O(1)$. So far, we completed the complexity analysis in a single cell.

We define τ as the number of iteration and the computational complexity of interior sector partition is of the order of $O(N)$. Based on the above analysis, the multi-cell computational complexity of DJRA is

$$L = \tau C L' + O(N) = O(\tau C N) + O(N) \tag{21}$$

In the traditional static resource allocation algorithms, the major/minor subcarrier and power allocations per cell are set prior to network deployment. Therefore, the computational cost for these algorithms is of the order of $O(1)$.

SIMULATION

In this section, we investigate the performance of proposed JPFA algorithm, static FFR, static FFR, and traditional dynamic joint resource allocation algorithm (ASFR) [16]. We consider a 19-cell downlink cellular network where service area consists of all 19 cells, the interior radius and the cell radius is equal to 600 and 750, respectively, each cell owns 50 RBs. There are 20 users in each cell and the lowest throughput requirement is 0.8 Mbps rate per user. A detailed description of simulation parameters is shown in Table 2.

Table 2. Main simulation parameters.

Parameter	Value
Number of cells C	19 wrap-around
Cell radius	750 m
Cell-interior radius	600 m
Physical resource blocks	50
Bandwidth	10 MHz
Users per cell	20
Pass loss	130.62 + 37.6 × log10(d)
Channel model	rayleigh multipath model
Fast fading	8 dBm
Total power	46 dBm
Thermal noise power	−174 dBm

In static FFR, we divided 50 physical RBs into two groups, Group 1 contains 30 which are shared by edge users with a cell-edge reuse factor of 3, and Group 2 is for the center region with a reuse factor of 1. The transmit power of each RBs is the same. In static SFR, 48 physical RBs are shared by edge users with a reuse factor of 3 and the power ratio factor is 0.5.

Figure 3 shows the user distribution in 19 cells under one simulation. Figure 4 compares the cell-edge RBs distribution of proposed DJRA with the aforementioned static SFR (SSFR) in one Monte Carlo simulation. As seen from Figure 4, a total of 16 sub-resources are available to edge users in SSFR. However, as the users are randomly distributed in each scenario, the resource allocation predetermined scheme can not obtain the best system performance. Compared with the static resource allocation, our dynamic joint resource allocation approach breaks the original fixed patterns via dynamically adjusting the resource allocation ratio of the central and edge regions as the user distribution changes. Each cell has its own resource configuration mode. Though the number of cell-edge RBs changes, the sum of RBs in the three adjacent cells is less than total RBs. In other words, variations in the cell-edge RBs will not influence the orthogonality of the edge zones in the three adjacent cells.

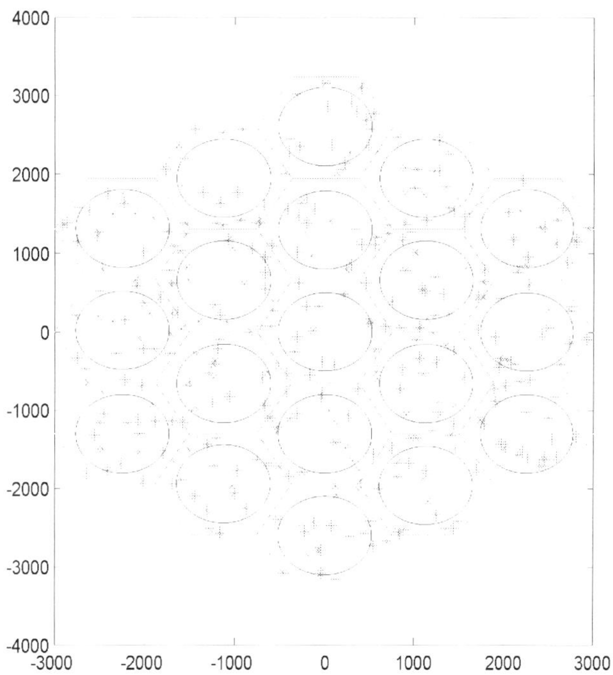

Figure 3. User distribution in 19 cells.

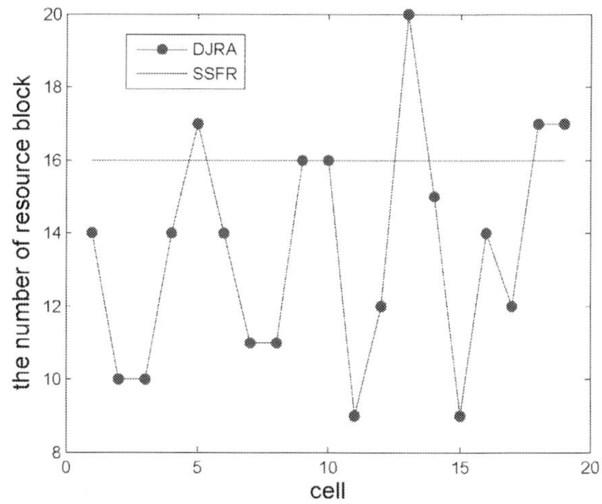

Figure 4. Cell-edge resource blocks (RBs) distribution of dynamic joint resource allocation algorithm (DJRA) and static soft frequency reuse (SFR).

In Figure 5, we plot the cumulative distribution function (CDF) to show data rate achieved by each user. As seen from the figure, the performance of SFFR is the worst. This is because SFFR sacrifices the spectrum efficiency to suppress ICI. Despite SSFR being superior to SFFR, the fixed resource allocation pattern still limits its performance improvement. ASFR and our scheme achieve a superior rate. As expected, the best results are provided by our scheme and there are significant improvement benefits from adopting the sector partition method in the center region.

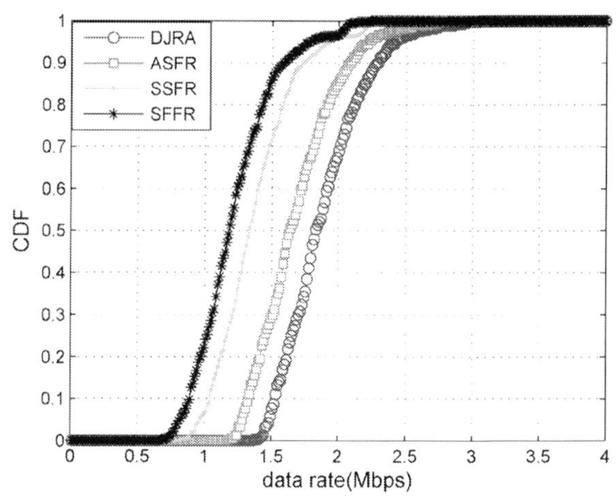

Figure 5. Data rate achieved by each user under different schemes.

Table 3 is the numerical analysis of Figure 5. It is obvious that our scheme gives a better solution to the cell-edge user interference and the data rate of DJRA is 0.2 Mbps higher than ASFR algorithm.

Table 3. Numerical analysis (Mbps).

DJRA	ASFR	SSFR	SFFR
1.369 – 3.245	1.169 – 3.044	0.805 – 2.844	0.622 – 2.385

We contrast the average throughput for a single cell and the average data rate achieved by each edge-user in Figure 6.Table 4 and Table 5 are the numerical analysis of Figure 6a,b. Comparing the DJRA algorithm with the ASFR algorithm, we can conclude that applying the sector partition method in the center region is an effective way to improve the system sum rate. This is because the center user interference mainly comes from the edge users in neighboring cells, and the edge user interference mainly comes from the center users in neighboring cells. Thus, eliminating cell-center users 'interference is equal to suppressing the edge users' interference in its adjacent cells. Thereby, our approach can also achieve a better behavior for cell-edge users.

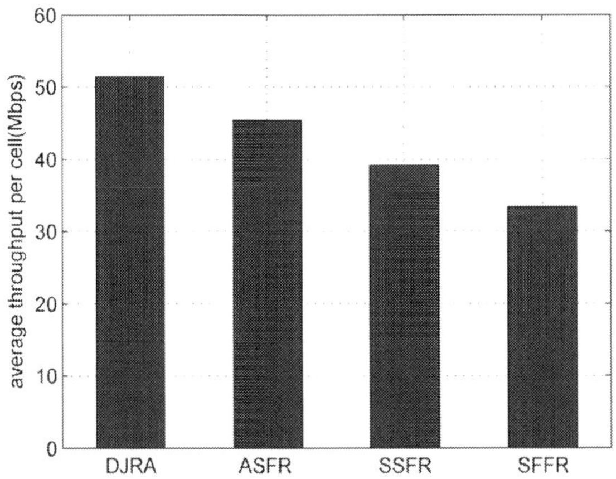

(a)

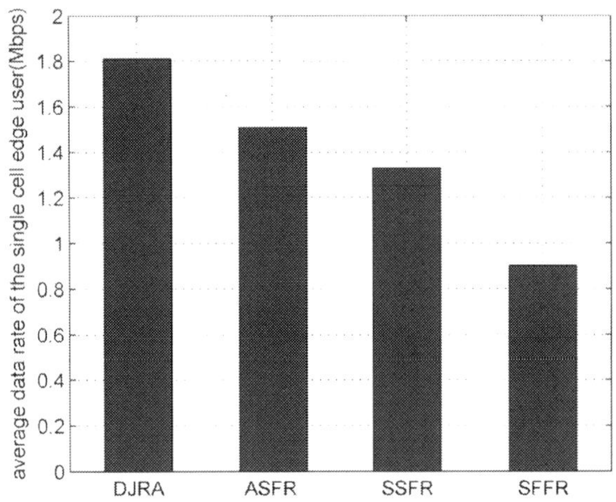

(b)

Figure 6. (a) Average throughput for a single cell (b) Average data rate for a edge-user.

Table 4. Single cell throughput numerical analysis (Mbps).

DJRA	ASFR	SSFR	SFFR
51.102	46.321	39.768	42.452

Table 5. Edge-user date rate numerical analysis (Mbps).

DJRA	ASFR	SSFR	SFFR
1.809	1.503	1.332	0.901

CONCLUSIONS

In this paper, the system model of soft frequency reuse is first analyzed. Then we put forward an improved dynamic joint resource allocation algorithm. The proposed scheme maximizes the system capacity and satisfies the minimum throughput requirements for each center zone and edge zone, simultaneously. DJRA obtains the optimal single cell resource allocation scheme by dynamically adjusting RB-power allocation according to the real-time distribution of users per cell, and then uses an iteration method to acquire the optimum resource allocation scheme. Finally, DJRA utilizes the interior sector partition method and proportional fair algorithm in each cell. Our scheme outperforms previous approaches for system capacity and cell edge user performance. Furthermore, DJRA guarantees that all the users have available resources. Despite the huge potential benefits of DJRA, several challenges must be overcome, for example, decreasing computational complexity. How to solve these problems is our next step along this research path.

ACKNOWLEDGMENTS

This paper is partially supported by National Natural Science Foundation of China (No. 61301095, No. 51509049), the Heilongjiang Province Natural Science Foundation(No. F201345) and the Fundamental Research Funds for the Central Universities of China (No. HEUCF160812/160810).

AUTHOR CONTRIBUTIONS

The idea of this work was proposed by Yibing Li and Xueying Diao. Yibing Li and Xueying Diao performed the experiments and analyzed the simulation results. Fang Ye and Ge Dong assisted in the research work and wrote the paper.

REFERENCES

1. Ohmori, S.; Yamao, Y.; Nakajima, N. The future generations of mobile communications based on broadband access technologies. *IEEE Commun. Mag.* 2000, *38*, 134 – 142.

2. E-UTRA and E-UTRAN Overall Description; Stage 2 (Release 8), 3GPP Technical Specification TS 36.300 V8.12.0. Available online: http://www.3gpp.org (accessed on 21 April 2016).
3. Dahlman, E.; Parkvall, S.; Skld, J. Chapter 1-Background of LTE. In *4G: LTE/LTE-Advanced for Mobile Broadband*, 2nd ed.; Elsevisr: Portland, OR, USA, 2014; pp. 1 – 15.
4. Novlan, T.; Andrews, J.G.; Sohn, I.; Ganti, R.K. Comparison of Fractional Frequency Reuse Approaches in the OFDMA Cellualar Downlink. In Procceings of the IEEE Global Telecommunications Conference (GLOBECOM), Miami, FL, USA, 6 – 10 December 2010; pp. 1 – 5.
5. Elayoubi, S.E.; BenHaddada, O.; Fourestie, B. Performance evaluation of frequency planning schemes in OFDMA-based networks. *IEEE Trans. Wirel. Commun.* 2008, *7*, 1623 – 1633.
6. R1-050507: Soft Frequency Reuse Scheme for UTRAN LTE. In Huawei 3GPP TSG RAN WG1 Meeting no.41, Athens, Greece, May 2005; Available online: http://www.ljemail.org/reference/ReferencesPapers.aspx?ReferenceID = 1192937(accessed on 22 April 2016).
7. Ali, S.H.; Leung, V.C.M. Dynamic Resource Allocation in Fractional Frequency Reused OFDMA Networks. *IEEE Trans. Wirel. Commun.* 2009, *8*, 4286 – 4295.
8. Stolyar, A.L.; Viswanathan, H. Self-organizing Dynamic Fractional Frequency Reuse for Best-Effort Traffic Through Distributed Inter-cell Coordination. In Proceedings of the IEEE INFOCOM 2009, Rio de Janeiro, Brazil, 19 – 25 April 2009; pp. 1287 – 1295.
9. Son, K.; Chong, S.; de Veciana, G. Dynamic Association for Load Balancing and Interference Avoidance in Multi-cell Networks. *IEEE Trans. Wirel. Commun.* 2009, *8*, 3566 – 3576.
10. Ksairi, N.; Bianchi, P.; Ciblat, P.; Hachem, W. Resource Allocation for Downlink Cellular OFDMA Systems-Part II: Practical Algorithms and Optimal Resue Factor. *IEEE Trans. Signal Process.* 2010, *58*, 735 – 749.
11. Zhang, X.; He, C.; Jiang, L.; Xu, J. Inter-cell Interference Coordination Based on Softer Frequency Reuse in OFDMA Cellular Systems. In Proceedings of the IEEE International Conference Neural Networks and Signal Processing, Nanjing, China, 7 – 11 June 2008; pp. 1 – 6.
12. Chen, L.; Yuan, D. Soft Frequency Reuse in large Networks with Irregular Cell Pattern: How Much Gains To Expect? In Proceedings of the IEEE PIMRC 09, Tokyo, Japan, 13 – 16 September 2009; pp. 1467 – 1471.
13. Mao, X.; Maaref, A.; Teo, K. Adaptive soft frequency reuse for inter-cell interference coordination in SC-FDMA based 3GPP LTE uplinks. In Proceedings of the IEEE GLOBECOM 2008, New Orleans, LO, USA, 30 November – 4 December 2008; pp. 1 – 6.
14. Yu, Y.; Dutkiewicz, E.; Huang, X. Adaptive power allocation for soft frequency reuse in multi-cell LTE networks. In Proceedings of the IEEE ISCIT 2012, Gold Coast, QLD, Australia, 2 – 5 October 2012; pp. 991 – 996.
15. Qian, M.; Hardjawana, W.; Li, Y.; Vucetic, B.; Shi, J.; Yang, X. Inter-cell Interference Coordination Through Adaptive Soft Frequency Reuse in LTE Networks. In Proceedings of the 2012 IEEE Wireless Communications and Networking Conference (WCNC), Shanghai, China, 1 – 4 April 2012; pp. 1618 – 1623.
16. Qian, M.; Hardjawana, W.; Li, Y.; Vucetic, B.; Yang, X.; Shi, J. Adaptive Soft Frequency Reuse Scheme for Wireless Cellular Networks. *IEEE Trans. Veh. Technol.* 2015, *64*, 118 – 131.
17. Andrea, G. *Wireless Communications*; Cambridge University Press: Cambridge, UK, 2005.
18. Tian, L.; Zhou, Y.; Zhang, Y.; Sun, G.; Shi, J. Resource allocation for multicast services in distributed antenna systems with QoS guarantees. *IET Commun.* 2012, *6*, 264 – 271.

CHAPTER 8

AN EFFECTIVE AND EFFICIENT MAPREDUCE ALGORITHM FOR COMPUTING BFS-BASED TRAVERSALS OF LARGE-SCALE RDF GRAPHS

Alfredo Cuzzocrea[1], Mirel Cosulschi[2], and Roberto de Virgilio[3]

[1]DIA Department, University of Trieste and ICAR-CNR, Trieste 34127, Italy

[2]Department of Computer Science, University of Craiova, Craiova 200585, Romania

[3]Dipartimento di Informatica e Automazione, Universitá Roma Tre, Rome 00146, Italy

ABSTRACT

Nowadays, a leading instance of big data is represented by Web data that lead to the definition of so-called big Web data. Indeed, extending beyond to a large number of critical applications (e.g., Web advertisement), these data expose several characteristics that clearly adhere to the well-known 3V properties (i.e., volume, velocity,variety). Resource Description Framework (RDF) is a significant formalism and language for the so-called Semantic Web, due to the fact that a very wide family of Web entities can be naturally modeled in a graph-shaped manner. In this context, RDF graphs play a first-class role, because they are widely used in the context of modern Web applications and systems, including the emerging context of social networks. When RDF graphs are defined on top of big (Web) data, they lead to the so-called large-scale RDF graphs, which reasonably populate the next-generation Semantic Web. In order to process such kind of big data, MapReduce, an open source computational framework specifically tailored to big data processing, has emerged during the last years as the reference implementation for this critical setting. In line with this trend, in this paper, we present an approach for efficiently implementing traversals of large-scale RDF graphs over MapReduce that is based on the Breadth First Search (BFS) strategy for visiting (RDF) graphs to be decomposed and processed according to the MapReduce framework. We demonstrate how such implementation speeds-up the analysis of RDF graphs with respect to competitor approaches. Experimental results clearly support our contributions.

INTRODUCTION

Big data describe data sets that grow so large that they become unpractical to be processed by traditional tools like database management systems, content management systems, advanced statistical analysis software, and so forth. The reason why they came into the attention of the research community is that the infrastructure to handle these data sets has become more affordable due to *Cloud Computing* and *MapReduce* [1] based open-source frameworks. The vision of everyday people inspecting large amounts of data, easily interacting with graphical interfaces of software applications that handle *data mining tasks*, has indeed enthused final users. On the other hand, those tools have to leverage people's ability to answer analytical processes by inference through large amounts of data.

The problem with this data is not the complexity of the processes involved, but rather the quantity of data and the rate of collecting new data. The following two examples are slightly illustrative of this phenomenon.

Citation: Alfredo Cuzzocrea, Mirel Cosulschi, and Roberto de Virgilio. An effective and efficient mapreduce algorithm for computing BFS-based traversals of large-scale RDF graphs, Algorithms 2016, 9(1), 7; DOI: 10.3390/a9010007

- In April 2009, *EBay* was using two Data Warehouses, namely *Teradata* and *Greenplum*, the former having 6.5 PB of data in form of 17 trillion records already stored, and collecting more than 150 billion new records/day, leading to an ingest rate well over 50 TB/day [2].
- In May 2009, *Facebook* estimates an amount of 2.5 PB of user data, with more than 15 TB of new data per day [3].

As another matter of question, the presence of *graph-based data structures* occurs almost everywhere starting with*social networks* like *Facebook* [4], *MySpace* [5] and *NetFlix* [6], and ending with *transportation routes* or *Internet infrastructure architectures*. These graphs keep growing in size and there are several new things that people would like to infer from the many facets of information stored in these data structures. Graphs can have billions of vertices and edges. Citation graphs, affiliation graphs, instant messenger graphs, phone call graphs and so forth, are part of the so-called *social network analysis and mining* initiative. Some recent works show that, despite the previously supposed sparse nature of those graphs, their density increases over time [7,8]. All considering, these trends tend towards the so-called *big Web data* (e.g., [9,10]), the transposition of big data on the Web.

On the other hand, *Semantic Web technologies* allow us to effectively support analysis of large-scale distributed data sets by means of the well-known *Resource Description Framework* (RDF) model [11], which, obviously represents data via a *graph-shaped approach*. As a consequence, in the Semantic Web initiative, the most prominent kind of graph data are represented by *RDF graphs*. This opens the door to a wide family of database-like applications, such as *keyword search over RDF data* (e.g., [12]).

While RDF graphs offer a meaningful data model for successfully representing, analyzing and mining large-scale graph data, the problem of *efficiently processing RDF graphs* is still an open issue in database research (e.g., [13,14,15]). Following this main consideration, in this paper, we focus on *the problem of computing traversals of RDF graphs*, being computing traversals of such graphs very relevant in this area, e.g., for RDF graph analysis and mining over large-scale data sets. Our approach adopts the *Breadth First Search* (BFS) strategy for visiting (RDF) graphs to be decomposed and processed according to the MapReduce framework. This with the goal of taking advantages from the powerful run-time support offered by MapReduce, hence reducing the computational overheads due to manage large RDF graphs efficiently. This approach is conceptually-sound, as similar initiatives have been adopted in the vest of viable solutions to *the problem of managing large-scale sensor-network data over distributed environments* (e.g., [16,17]), like for the case of Cloud infrastructures and their integration with sensor networks. We also provide experimental results that clearly confirm the benefits coming from the proposed approach.

The remaining part of this paper is organized as follows. In Section 2, we provide an overview of *Hadoop* [18], the software platform that incorporates MapReduce for supporting complex *e*-science applications over large-scale distributed repositories. Section 3 describes in more details principles and paradigms of MapReduce. In Section 4, we provide definitions, concepts and examples on RDF graphs. Section 5 contains an overview on state-of-the-art approaches that represent the knowledge basis of our research. In Section 6, we provide our efficient algorithms for implementing BFS-based traversals of RDF graphs over MapReduce. Section 7 contains the result of our experimental campaign according to which we assessed our proposed algorithm. Finally, in Section 8, we provide conclusions of our research and depict possible future work in this scientific field.

HADOOP: AN OVERVIEW

Hadoop is an open-source project from *Apache Software Foundation*. Its core consists of the MapReduce programming model implementation. This platform was created for solving the problem of processing very large amounts of data, a mixture of complex and structured data. It is used with predilection in the situation where data-analytics-based applications require a large number of computations have to be executed. Similar motivations can be found in related research efforts focused on the issue of effectively and efficiently managing large-scale data sets over*Grid environments* (e.g., [19,20,21]).

The key characteristic of Hadoop is represented by the property of enabling the execution of applications on thousands of nodes and peta-bytes of data. A typical enterprise configuration is composed by tens or thousands of physical or virtual machines interconnected through a fast network. The machines run a POSIX compliant operating system and a Java virtual machine.

Cutting was the creator of the Hadoop framework, and two papers published by Google's researchers had decisive influence on his work: *The Google File System* [22] and *MapReduce: Simplified Data Processing on Large Clusters* [1]. In 2005, he started to use an implementation of MapReduce in *Nutch* [23], an application software for web searching, and very soon the project becomes independent from *Nutch* under the codename *Hadoop*, with the aim of offering a framework for running many jobs within a cluster.

The language used for the development of the Hadoop framework was Java. The framework is providing the users with a Java API for developing MapReduce applications. In this way, Hadoop becomes very popular in the community of scientists whose name is linked to the big data processing. *Yahoo!* is an important player in this domain, this company having for a longer period a major role in the design and implementation of the framework. Another big player is Amazon [24], company currently offering a web service [25] based on Hadoop that is using the infrastructure provided by the *Elastic Compute Cloud—EC2* [26]. Meanwhile, Hadoop becomes very highly-popular, and, in order to sustain this allegation, it is sufficient just to mention the presence of other important players like *IBM,Facebook*, *The New York Times*, *Netflix* [27] and *Hulu* [28] in the list of companies deploying Hadoop-based applications.

The Hadoop framework hides the details of processing jobs, leaving the developers liberty to concentrate on the application logic. The framework has the following characteristic features:

- *Accessible*—it can be executed on large clusters or on Cloud computing services;
- *Robust*—it was designed to run on commodity hardware; a major aspect considered during its development was

the tolerance to frequent hardware failures and crash recovery;

- *Scalable*—it scales easily for processing increased amount of data by transparently adding more nodes to the cluster;
- *Simple*—it allows developers to write specific code in a short time.

There is quite a large application domain for Hadoop. Some examples include online *e*-commerce applications for providing better recommendations to clients looking after certain products, or finance applications for risk analysis and evaluation with sophisticated computational models whose results cannot be stored in a database.

Basically, Hadoop can be executed on each major OS: *Linux*, *Unix*, *Windows*, *Mac OS*. The platform officially supported for production is *Linux* only.

The framework is implementing a master-slave architecture used both for distributed data storage and for distributed computing. Hadoop framework running on a completely-configured cluster is composed of a set of *daemons* or *internal modules* executed on various machines of the cluster. These daemons have specific tasks, some of them running only on a single machine, others having instances running on several machines.

A sample Hadoop cluster architecture is depicted in Figure 1. For a small cluster, *Secondary NameNode* daemon can be hosted on a slave node, meanwhile, on a large cluster, it is customary to separate the *NameNode* and *JobTracker* daemons on different machines. In Figure 1, a master node is running *NameNode* and *JobTracker* daemons and an independent node is hosting the *Secondary NameNode* daemon, just in case of failure in the master node. Each slave machine hosts two daemons, *DataNode* and *TaskTracker*, in order to run computational tasks on the same node where input data are stored.

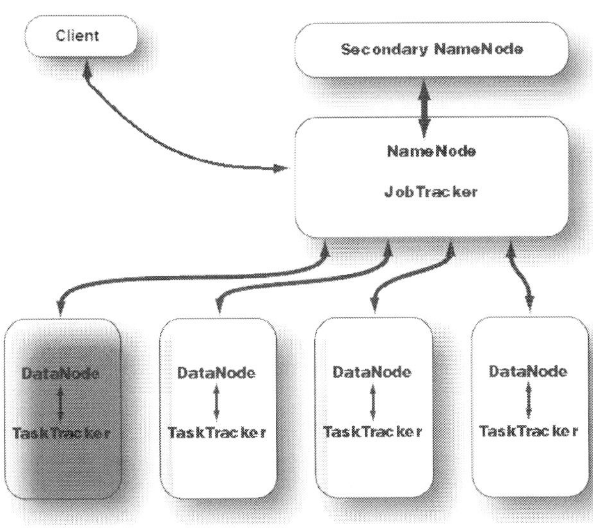

Figure 1. Hadoop cluster architecture.

As regards the proper data storage solution, Hadoop's ecosystem incorporates *HBase* [29]. HBase is a *distributed column-oriented database* (e.g., [30]), which also falls in the category of *NoSQL storage systems* (e.g., [31]), that founds on the underlying *Hadoop Distributed File System* (HDFS) (e.g., [32]) for common data processing routines. HBase has been proved to be highly scalable. HBase makes use of a specific model that is similar to *Google's BigTable* (e.g., [33]), and it is designed to provide fast random access to huge amounts of structured data. As regards the main software architecture organization, HBase performs read/write (fast) routines on HDFS while data consumer and data producer applications interact with (big) data through HBase directly. Recently, due to its relevance, several studies have focused on HBase.

MAPREDUCE: PRINCIPLES OF DISTRIBUTED PROGRAMMING OVER LARGE-SCALE DATA REPOSITORIES

MapReduce is both a programming model for expressing distributed computations on massive amounts of data and an execution framework for large-scale data processing on clusters of commodity servers [1,34]. MapReduce's programming model was released to the computer science community in 2004, being described in [1] after Google was already using this technology for a couple of years. MapReduce's processing scheme soon became very popular, including a broad adoption due to its open-source implementation. A job from MapReduce programming model splits the input data set into several independent blocks that are processed in parallel.

There are two seminal ideas that are encountered in MapReduce, which we report in the following.

- There is a previous well-known strategy in computer science for solving problems: *divide-et-impera*. According to this paradigm, when we have to solve a problem whose general solution is unknown, then the problem is decomposed in *smaller sub-problems*, the same strategy is applied for it, and the results/partial solutions corresponding to each sub-problem into a general solution are combined. The decomposing process continues until the size of the sub-problem is small enough to be handled individually.
- The basic data structures are *key-value pairs* and *lists*. The design of MapReduce algorithms involves usage of *key-value* pairs over arbitrary data sets.

Map and *Reduce* concepts were inspired from *functional programming*. *Lisp*, in particular, introduces two functions with similar meaning, *map* and *fold*. Functional operations have the property of preserving data structures such that the original data remains unmodified and new data structures are created. The *map* function takes as arguments a function *f* and a list, and it applies the function *f* to each element of the input list, resulting in a new output list. The*fold* function has an extra argument compared to the *map*: beyond the function *f* and the input list, there is an accumulator. The function *f* is applied to each element of the input list, the result is added to previous accumulator, thus obtaining the accumulator value for the next step.

Although the idea seems to be very simple, implementation details of a *divide-and-conquer* approach are not. There are several aspects with which practitioners must deal. Some are the following ones:

- Decomposition of the problem and allocation of sub-problems to workers;

- Synchronization among workers;
- Communication of the partial results and their merge for computing local solutions;
- Management of software/hardware failures;
- Management of workers' failures.

The MapReduce framework hides the peculiarities of these details, thus allowing developers to concentrate on the main aspects for implementation of target algorithms.

Technically-wise, for each job, the programmer has to work with the following functions: *mapper*, *reducer*, *partitioner*and *combiner*. The *mapper* and *reducer* have the following signatures:

$$Map : (k_1, v_1) \rightarrow [(k_2, v_2)]$$
$$Reduce : (k_2, [v_2]) \rightarrow [(k_3, v_3)]$$

where [...] denotes a list.

The input of a MapReduce's job is fetched from the data stored in the target distributed file system. For each task of type *map*, a *mapper* is created. This is a method which, applied to each input *key-value* pair, returns a number of intermediary *key-value* pairs. The *reducer* is another method applied to a list of values associated with the same intermediary key in order to obtain a list of *key-value* pairs. Transparently to the programmer, the framework implicitly groups the values associated with intermediary keys between the mapper and the reducer.

The intermediary data reach the *reducer* ordered by key, and there is no guarantee regarding the key order among different reducers. The *key-value* pairs from each *reducer* are stored in the distributed file system. The output values from each *reducer* are stored also in *m* files from the distributed file system, considered these latter as output files for each *reducer*. Finally, the map() and reduce() functions run in parallel, such that the first reduce() call cannot start before the last map() function ends. This is an important separation point among different phases. Simplifying, at least the MapReduce developer has to implement interfaces of the two following functions:

public void map (K_1 *key,* V_1 *value, OutputCollector* <K_2, V_2> *output, Reporter reporter) throws IOException*

public void reduce (K_2 *key, Iterator* <V_2> *values, OutputCollector* <K_3, V_3> *output, Reporter reporter) throws IOException*

hence allowing her/him to concentrate on the application logic while discarding the details of a high-performance, complex computational framework.

In the context of data processing and query optimization issues for MapReduce, *Bloom filters* [35] and *Snappy data compression* [36] play a leading role as they are very often used to further improve the efficiency of MapReduce. Indeed, they are not only conceptually-related to MapReduce but also very relevant for our research, as they are finally integrated in our implemented framework (see Section 6). Bloom filters are *space-efficient probabilistic data structures* initially thought to test whether an element is member of a set or not. Bloom filters have a 100% *recall rate*, since false positive matches are possible, whereas false negative matches are not possible. It has been demonstrated that Bloom filters are very useful tools within MapReduce tasks, since, given the fact that they avoid false negatives, they allow for getting rid of irrelevant records during *map* phases of MapReduce tasks, hence configuring themselves as a very reliable space-efficient solution for MapReduce. Snappy data compression is a *fast C++ data compression and decompression library* proposed by *Google*. It does not aim at maximizing compression, but, rather, it aims at achieving a very high compression speed at a reasonable compression ratio. Given its orthogonality, Snappy has been used not only with MapReduce but also in other Google projects like BigTable.

RDF GRAPHS: DEFINITIONS, CONCEPTS, EXAMPLES

Since RDF graphs play a central role in our research, in this Section, we focus in a greater detail on definitions, concepts and algorithms of such very important data structures of the popular Semantic Web. RDF is a Semantic Web data model oriented to represent *information on resources available on the Web*. To this end, a critical point is represented by the fact that RDF model *metadata* about such Web resources, which can be defined as data that describe other data. Thanks to metadata, RDF can easily implements some very important functionalities over the Semantic Web, such as: resource representation, querying resource on the Web, discovering resources on the Web, resource indexing, resource integration, interoperability among resources and applications, and so forth. RDF is primarily meant for managing resources on the Web for applications, not for end-users, as to support *querying the Semantic Web* (e.g., [37]), *Semantic Web interoperability* (e.g., [38]), *complex applications* (e.g., [39]), and so forth.

Looking into more details, RDF is founded on the main assertion that resources are identified on the Web via suitable *Web identifiers* like *Uniform Resource Identifiers* (URI) and they are described in terms of *property-value* pairs via *statements* that specify these properties and values. In an RDF statement, the *subject* identifies the resource (to be described), the *predicate* models the property of the subject, and the *object* reports the value of that property. Therefore, each RDF resource on the Web is modeled in terms of the triple (*subject*, *predicate*, *object*). This way, since Web resources are typically connected among them, the Semantic Web represented via RDF easily generates the so-called RDF graphs. In such graphs, RDF models statements describing Web resources via nodes and arcs. In particular, in this graph-ware model, a statement is represented by: (*i*) a node for the subject; (*ii*) a node for the object; (*iii*) an arc for the predicate, which is directed from the node modeling the subject to the node modeling the object. In terms of the popular *relational model*, an RDF statement can be represented like a tuple (*subject*, *predicate*, *object*) and, as a consequence, an RDF graph can be naturally represented via a *relational schema* storing information on subjects, predicated and objects of the corresponding Web resources described by the RDF statements modeled by that graph (e.g., [40]).

ID	Author	Title	Publisher	Year
ISBN 0-00-6511409-X	id_xyz	The Glass Palace	id_qpr	2000

ID	Name	Homepage
id_xyz	Ghosh, Amitav	http://www.amitavghosh.com

ID	Publisher's name	City
id_qpr	Harper Collins	London

	A	B	C	D
1	ID	Titre	Traducteur	Original
2	ISBN 2020286682	Le Palais des Miroirs	$A12$	ISBN 0-00-6511409-X
3				
4				
5				
6	ID	Auteur		
7	ISBN 0-00-6511409-X	$A11$		
8				
9				
10	Nom			
11	Ghosh, Amitav			
12	Besse, Christianne			

Figure 2. Different Web media for the same book (**left**); and their corresponding relational schemas (**right**) [41].

Figure 2, borrowed from [41], shows an example where information on the Web regarding the book "*The Glass Palace*", by A. Ghosh, occurs in two different sites in the vest of different media, one about the English version of the book, and the other one about the French version of the book. According to this, the two different Web resources are represented by two different relational schemas (see Figure 2). Figure 3, instead, shows the corresponding RDF graphs for the two different Web resources, respectively.

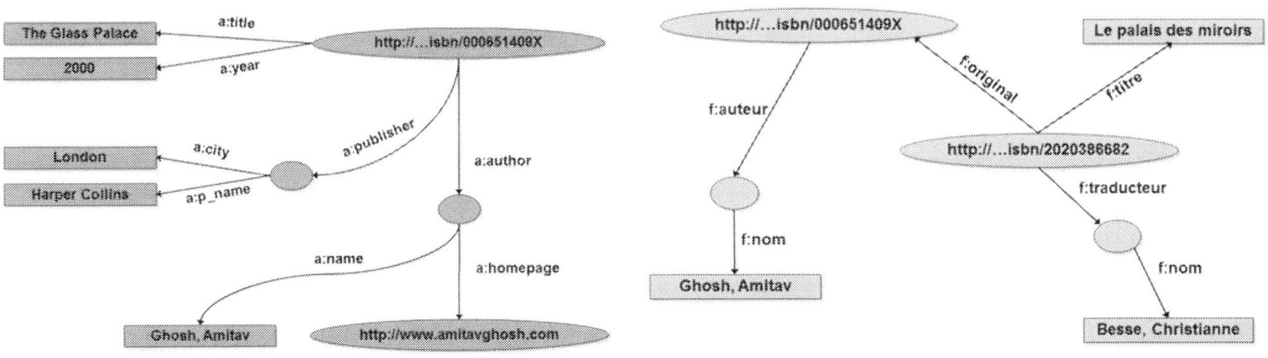

Figure 3. The two RDF graphs corresponding to the two different Web media for the same book reported in Figure 2 [41].

As highlighted before, one of the goals of RDF graphs is allowing the easy integration of correlated Web resources. This is, indeed, a typical case of Web resource integration because the two RDF graphs, even if different, describe two different media of the same resource. It is natural, as a consequence, to integrate the two RDF graphs in a unique (RDF) graph, even taking advantage from the "natural" topological nature of graphs, as shown in Figure 4. In particular, the integration process is driven by recognizing the same URI that identifies the book resource.

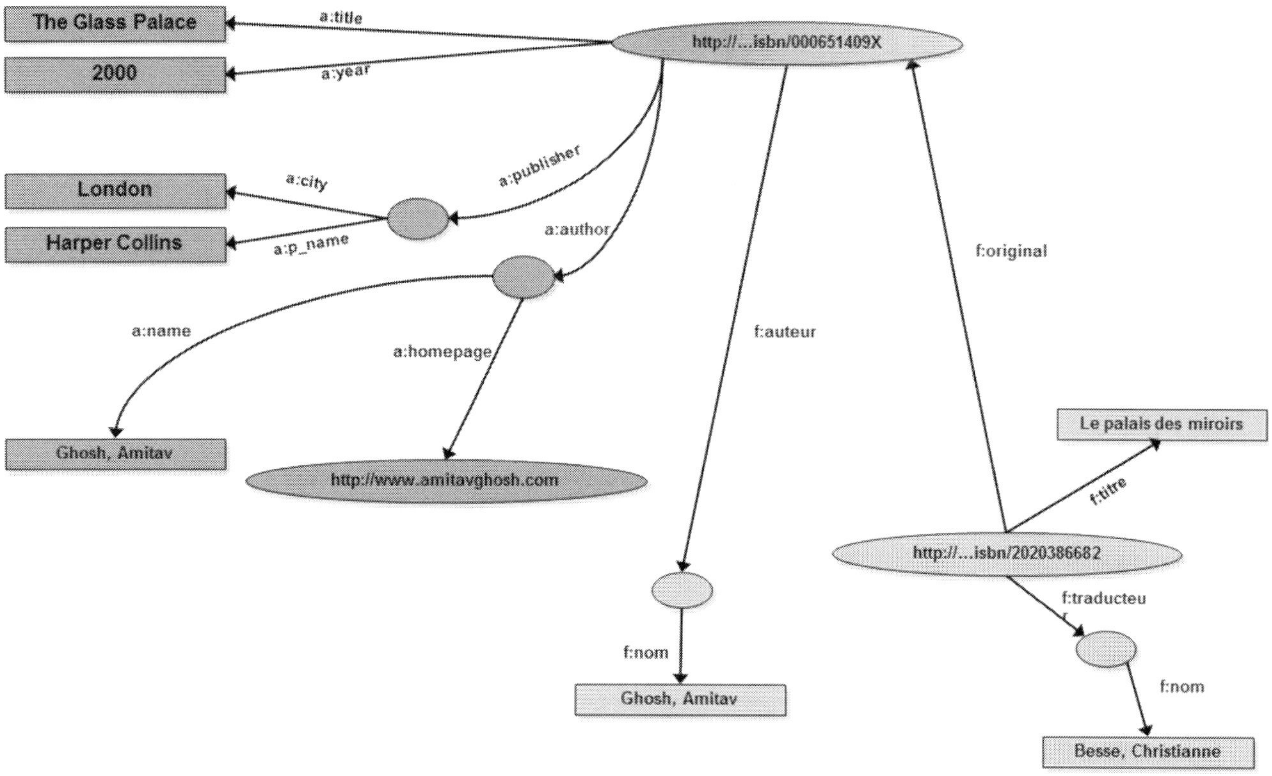

Figure 4. RDF graph obtained via integrating the two RDF graphs of Figure 3[41].

Another nice property of the RDF graph data model that makes it particularly suitable to Semantic Web is its "open" nature, meaning that any RDF graph can be easily integrated with *external knowledge* on the Web about resources identified by the URIs it models. For instance, a common practice is that of integrating RDF graph with Web knowledge represented by *Wikipedia* [42] via ad-hoc tools (e.g., *DBpedia* [43]). This contributes to move the actual Web towards the Web of data and knowledge. Figure 5 shows the RDF graph of Figure 4 integrated with knowledge extracted from Wikipedia via DBpedia.

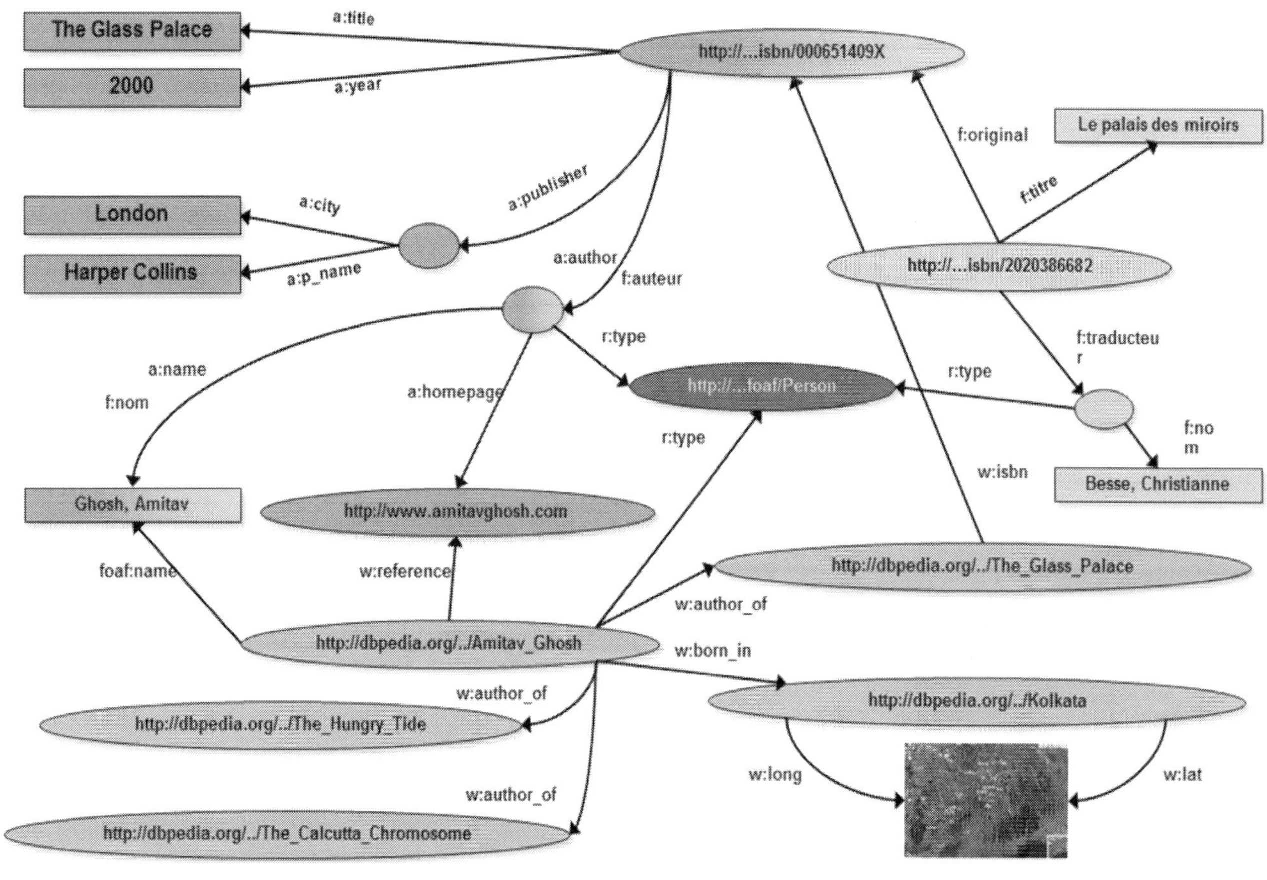

Figure 5. RDF graph obtained via integrating the RDF graph of Figure 4 with Wikipedia knowledge extracted via DBpedia [41].

It is worth noticing that, when RDF graphs are processed, applications can easily extract knowledge from them via so-called *RDF query language* [44] or other AI-inspired approaches (e.g., [45]). In addition to this, computing traversal paths over such graphs is critical for a wide range of Web applications. To give an example, traversal paths can be used as "basic" procedures of powerful *analytics over Web Big Data* (e.g., [46]). This further gives solid motivation to our research.

RELATED WORK

The conceptual and literature context of our research includes the following areas:

- Parallel BFS-based and DFS-based traversal strategies;
- MapReduce algorithms for big data processing;
- MapReduce algorithms over RDF databases;
- MapReduce algorithms over RDF graphs.

In the following, we provide a discussion of main approaches falling in the four distinct areas.

Parallel BFS-Based and DFS-Based Traversal Strategies

The basic problem we investigate in our research is strictly related to the issue of supporting parallel BFS-based and DFS-based traversal computing, as to gain into efficiency. Here, several proposals appear in literature, also based on the *Depth-First Search* (DFS) strategy, which is an alternative to BFS. In the following, we mention some noticeable ones. As regards BFS-based alternatives, [47] inspects the problem of supporting BFS-based traversals of *trees* in parallel. The proposed algorithm is *cost-optimal*, and it is based on the innovative vision of interpreting the BFS-based traversal problem into a *parentheses matching problem*. Performance analysis is promising as well. [48] instead introduces a *parallel external-memory algorithm* for supporting BFS-based traversal computing based on a *cluster of workstations*. The proposed algorithm has the merit of distributing the input workload according to intervals that are computed at runtime via a *sampling-based process*. An interesting experimental analysis focusing on how the operating system supports the caching of external memory into internal memory while running the algorithm is also proposed. Finally, as regards DFS-based alternatives, [49] proposes a modified version of [47], still focusing on trees, where the main algorithm is adapted as to work with the DFS's principle.

MapReduce Algorithms for Big Data Processing

Paper [50] puts light on main issues and challenges of big data processing over MapReduce, by highlighting actual data management solutions that found over this computational platform. Several aspects are touched, including *job optimization, physical data organization, data layouts, indexes*, and so forth. Finally, a comparative analysis between Hadoop-MapReduce and *Parallel DBMS* is provided, by highlighting their similarities and differences.

Contribution [51] *investigates interactive analytical processing in big data systems*, with particular emphasis over the case of MapReduce, even considering the industrial applicative setting. In more detail, authors capture and model typical *big data processing workloads*, which are characterized by several small, short and increasingly interactive jobs, which clearly contrast with the large, long-running batch jobs for which MapReduce was originally designed. In line with this trend, authors provide an empirical analysis of MapReduce traces from several business-critical deployments inside Facebook and Cloudera instances in a wide range of applications scenarios ranging from e-commerce to telecommunication systems, from social media to large-scale retail systems, and so forth. As a result of their empirical analysis, authors provide a new class of MapReduce workloads that are composed by *interactive analysis components* making heavy use of query-like programming frameworks on top of MapReduce.

Paper [52] introduces and experimentally assesses H_2RDF, an innovative, *fully-distributed RDF framework* that*combines MapReduce with NoSQL (distributed) data stores*. With respect to the state-of-the-art contributions, H_2RDFallows two distinctive characteristics to be achieved: (*i*) high efficiency in both *simple* and *multi-join SPARQL queries*[53] via joins that execute on the basis of query selectivity; (*ii*) alternatively-available centralized and MapReduce-based join execution that ensures higher speed-up during query evaluation. The system is targeted to billions of RDF triples even with small commodity Clouds, and its performance over that of comparative methods is experimentally proven.

Contribution [54] similarly focuses the attention on the problem of *efficiently supporting SPARQL join queries over big data in Cloud environments via MapReduce*. The novelty of this research effort relies on an implementation of the*distributed sort-merge join algorithm* on top of MapReduce where the join is computed during the map phase completely. The problem of *cascaded executions* that may derive from executing multiple joins is addressed during the reduce phase by ensuring that the "right-hand" side of the join is always pre-sorted on the required attributes. Experiments show an excellent performance over comparative approaches.

Finally, at the mere system-side, several works focus the attention on very interesting applicative settings, such as the case of supporting MapReduce-based big data processing on *multi-GPU systems* (e.g., [55]), and the case of efficiently supporting *GIS polygon overlay computation* with MapReduce for *spatial big data processing* (e.g., [56]).

MapReduce Algorithms for RDF Databases

The relevance of RDF query processing via MapReduce has been highlighted by several studies (e.g., [57,58,59]). Basically, these works focus the attention on RDF data management architectures and systems designed for Cloud environments, with a special focus to large-scale RDF processing. Approaches investigated here mainly consider several special tasks that can be performed on the Web via RDF, such as *Web data publishing* and *Web data exchanging*.

Paper [60] focuses the attention on *querying linked data based on MapReduce*. Linked data can easily be modeled via RDF databases. In particular, authors consider linked data that are arbitrarily partitioned and distributed over a set of Cloud nodes, such that input queries are decomposed into a set of suitable *sub-queries*, each one involving data stored in a specific node. The proposed method is two-step in nature. In the first step, sub-queries are executed on the respective node in an isolated manner. In the second step, intermediate results are combined in order to obtain the final answer to the input query. The innovation introduced by this research effort consists in the fact that the proposed query algorithm is independent of all the parameters of the model, *i.e.*, linked data partitioning, local data storage, query decomposition mechanism, local query algorithm.

SPARQL query processing over RDF data has attracted a lot of attention from the research community as well. In this context, several approaches have been proposed recently. [61] addresses the problem of *supporting SPARQL queries over very large RDF datasets* via mapping SPARQL statements over *PigLatin* [62] programs. These programs are finally executed in terms of a series of MapReduce jobs on top of a Hadoop cluster. The study also provides an interesting experimental trade-off analysis on top of a popular benchmark dataset. [63] also investigates *scalability issues of processing SPARQL queries over Web-scale RDF knowledge bases*. To this end, authors propose an innovative partitioning method particularly suitable to RDF data that introduces the nice amenity of providing *effective indexing schemes* for supporting efficient SPARQL query processing over MapReduce. Still in this area, [64,65] provide anatomy and main functionalities of *a semantic data analytical engine* and *a Cloud-enabled RDF triple store*, respectively. Both embed several points of research innovation over state-of-the-art proposals.

Contribution [66] studies how to apply *compression paradigms* to obtain *scalable RDF processing with MapReduce*. Authors point the specific case of Semantic Web, where *many billions of statements*, which are released using the RDF data model, exist. Therefore, they propose to apply a novel data compression technique in order to tame the severity of data size, and thus design *a set of distributed MapReduce algorithms* to efficiently compress and decompress a large amount of RDF data. In particular, they apply a *dictionary encoding technique* that maintains the structure of the (Web) data. The solution is implemented as a prototype using the Hadoop framework, and its performance is evaluated over a large amount of data and scales linearly on both input size and number of nodes.

Still in the context of optimization issues, [67] proposes *a novel nested data model for representing intermediate data* of RDF processing concisely using *nesting-aware dataflow operators* that allow for lazy and partial un-nesting strategies. Indeed, authors correctly recognize that, during RDF data processing, intermediate results of joins with multi-valued attributes or relationships contain redundant sub-tuples due to repetition of single-valued attributes. As a consequence, the amount of redundant content is high for real-world multi-valued relationships in typical data-intensive instances such as social networks or biological datasets. Unfortunately, in MapReduce-based platforms, redundancy in intermediate results contributes avoidable costs to the overall I/O, sorting, and network transfer overhead of join-intensive workloads due to longer workflows. Therefore, in order to deal with this challenge, the proposed approach reduces the overall I/O and network footprint of a workflow by concisely representing intermediate results during most of a workflow's execution, until complete un-nesting is absolutely necessary.

Finally, [68] focuses the attention on query optimization aspects of massive *data warehouses* over RDF data. In this context, a relevant problem is represented by the evaluation of join queries over RDF data *when triple patterns with unbound properties occur*. A clear example of this case is represented by edges with "don't" care labels. As a consequence, when evaluating such queries using relational joins, intermediate results contain *high redundancy* that is empathized by such unbound properties. In order to face-off this problem, authors propose *an algebraic optimization technique that interprets unbound-property queries on MapReduce via using a non-relational algebra based on a TripleGroup data model*. Novel logical and physical operators and query rewriting rules for interpreting unbound-property queries using the TripleGroup-based data model and algebra are formally introduced. The proposed framework is implemented on top of *Apache Pig* [69], and experiments on both synthetic and real-word benchmark datasets that show the benefits of the framework are provided and discussed in details.

MapReduce Algorithms for RDF Graphs

Paper [70] focuses the attention on the problem of effectively and efficiently supporting scalable storage and retrieval of large volumes of in-memory-representations of RDF graphs by exploiting a combination of MapReduce and HBase. The solution conveys the so-called RDFChain framework, whose storage schema reflects all the possible join query patterns, thus providing a reduced number of storage accesses on the basis of the joins embedded in the target queries. In addition to this, a cost-based map-side join of RDFChain is provided. This allows for reducing the number of map jobs significantly.

Contribution [71] considers the research challenge of *optimizing RDF graph pattern matching on MapReduce*. Authors correctly recognize that the MapReduce computation model provides limited *static optimization techniques* used in relational DBMS, such as indexing and cost-based optimizations, hence it is mandatory to investigate *dynamic optimization techniques* for join-intensive tasks on MapReduce. With this idea in mind, authors extend their previous*Nested Triple Group data model and Algebra* (NTGA) for efficient graph pattern query processing in the Cloud [72] and achieve the definition of a *scan-sharing technique* that is used to optimize the processing of graph patterns with repeated properties. Specifically, the proposed scan-sharing technique eliminates the need for repeated scanning of input relations when properties are used repeatedly in graph patterns.

Finally, [73] proposes *a cost-model-based RDF join processing solution using MapReduce* to minimize the query responding time as much as possible. In particular, authors focus the attention on *SPARQL queries in a shared-nothing environment on top of MapReduce*, and propose a technique based on which they (1) first transform a SPARQL query into a sequence of MapReduce jobs; and (2) then create a novel index structure, called *All Possible Join tree* (*APJ-tree*) for reducing the searching space inducted by the optimal execution plan of a set of MapReduce jobs. To speed up the join processing, they employ *hybrid join* and Bloom filters for performance optimization. Authors complete their analytical contributions by means of an extensive set of experiments on real data sets that prove the effectiveness of the proposed cost model.

BFS-BASED IMPLEMENTATION OF RDF GRAPH TRAVERSALS OVER MAPREDUCE

There exist in literature two well-known approaches for representing a graph: through an *adjacency matrix*, and through *adjacency lists*. The former has the advantage of $O(1)$ constant lookup over graph data, with the drawback of an increased usage of memory ($n \times n$, where n represents the number of vertices), also for sparse graphs. In practice, while the majority of graphs are not so dense, we end with a waste of space having a big matrix with few values (not all the cells of the matrix will be used to store a value). The latter stores, for every vertex, a list of vertices connected to it (called *adjacent nodes*), thus reducing the overall memory requirement. This representation has also the advantage of being suited to feed a MapReduce job. As regards the proper RDF graph implementation as *Abstract Data Type* (ADT), we exploited the well-known *Apache Jena RDF API* [74], which models the target RDF graph in terms of collection of *RDF nodes*, which are connected via a *direct graph* by means of *labelled relations*.

There are several algorithms for visiting a graph, but BFS (see Algorithm 1) has been proven to be more suited for parallel processing. BFS algorithm cannot be expressed into a single MapReduce job directly, because the whileconstruct at every step increments the *frontier* of exploration in the graph. Moreover, this frontier expansion permits the finding of the paths to *every* node explored from the source node. Since the BFS algorithm cannot be codified within a MapReduce job, we propose a novel approach to coordinate a series of MapReduce jobs that check when to stop the execution of these jobs. This is called *convergence criterion*. To this end, we propose feeding the output of a job as the input of the successive one, and to apply a way to count if further nodes must be explored via maintaining a*global counter* updated at each iteration that, in the standard BFS, is represented by the iterator's position in the queue itself. In our proposed implementation, the only convergence criterion that we make use of is thus represented by counting the jobs that terminate (to this end, MapReduce's *DistributedCache* is exploited), but of course other more complex criteria may be adopted in future research efforts (e.g., based on *load balancing issues*).

Algorithm 1: BFS(u, n, L)

```
Input: u -- source node from which the visit starts; n -- number of vertices;
L -- adjacency lists
Output: Q -- list of visited nodes

Begin
Q ← ∅;
visited ← ∅;
for (i = 0 to n -- 1) do
visited[i] = 0;
endfor;
visited[u] = 1;
Q ← u;
while (Q ≠ ∅) do
u ← Q;
for (each v ∈ L_u) do      // L_u is the adjacency list of u
  if (visited[v] == 0) then
    visited[v] = 1;
    Q ← v;
  endif;
endfor;
endwhile;
return Q;
End;
```

Basically, in order to control the algorithmic flow and safely achieve the convergence criterion, the proposed algorithm adopts the well-known *colorability programming metaphor*. According to this programming paradigm, graph processing algorithms can be implemented by assigning a color-code to each possible node's state (in the *proper*semantics of the target algorithm) and then superimposing certain actions for each specific node's state. This paradigm is, essentially, an enriched *visiting strategy* over graphs, and, in fact, BFS is only a possible instance of such strategy. To this end, the proposed approach makes use of suitable *metadata information* (stored into text files), which models, for each node of the graph stored in a certain Cloud node, its adjacent list plus additional information about the node's state. An example of these metadata is as follows:

- 1 3,2, | GREY | 1
- 10 12, | WHITE | ?
- 11 10, | WHITE | ?
- 12 NULL, | WHITE | ?
- 13 NULL, | WHITE | ?
- 14 6,12, | WHITE | ?

In more detail, for each row, stored metadata have the following semantics: (see the previous example—the description is field-based): (*i*) the first number is the node ID; (*ii*) the subsequent list of numbers represents the adjacent list for that node, and it is equal to NULL if empty; (*iii*) the subsequent color-code represents the state of the node; (*iv*) the last symbol states if the target node has been processed (*i.e.*, then, it is equal to "1") or not (*i.e.*, then, it is equal to "?"). The adoption of this metadata information exposes the clear advantage of supporting *portability* and*interoperability* within Cloud environments widely.

Looking into code-wise details, the proposed algorithm consists of a series of iterations where each iteration represents a MapReduce job using the output from the previous MapReduce job until the convergence criterion is met. The *Mapper* job (see Algorithm 2) allows us to expand the frontier of exploration by selecting the new nodes to explore (the ones that in the standard BFS algorithm are inserted into the queue) and the ones already explored (or still not explored), as to complete the output.

Algorithm 2: Map(*key, value*)

```
Input: key -- ID of the current node; value -- node information
Output: void -- a new node is emitted

Begin
u ← (Node)value;
if (u.color == GREY) then
for (each v ∈ L_u) do      // L_u is the adjacency list of u
  v ← new Node();
  v.color == GREY;      // mark v as unexplored
  for (each c ∈ P_u) do      // P_u is the path list of u
    c.ID = u.ID;
    c.tag = u.tag;
    v.add(c);
  endfor;
  emit(v.ID,v);
endfor;
u.color = BLACK;      // mark u as explored
endif;
emit(key,u);
return;
End;
```

The *Reducer* job (see Algorithm 3) allows us to (*i*) merge the data provided by the *Mapper* and re-create an adjacency list that will be used at the next step and (*ii*) update the counter for the convergence test. More in detail, in order to merge nodes with the same ID, a color priority method was devised so that, in the case of the generation of a node with the same ID with different color, the darkest one will be saved.

Algorithm 3: Reduce(*key, values*)

```
Input: key – ID of the current node; values – node information list

Output: void – updates for the current node are emitted


Begin
 newNode ← new Node();
 for (each u ∈ values) do
   merge(newNode.edgeList(),u.edgeList());   // merge the newNode's edge list with u's edge list
   merge(newNode.tagList(),u.tagList());   // merge the newNode's tag list with u's tag list
   newNode.setToDarkest(newNode.color,u.color);   // set color of newNode to the darkest color
 endfor;                      // between the newNode's color and the u's color
 update(WHITE,GREY,BLACK);  // update the number of processed nodes having color WHITE, GREY, BLACK
 emit(key.newNode);   // emit updates for the current node
 return;
End;
```

By inspecting our proposed algorithm, it clearly turns that new nodes are generated via a series of MapReduce steps. This may increase *communication costs*, but our experimental analysis proves that they are limited in impact. Indeed, in Section 7, we show that our throughput performance analysis, which includes the impact of communication costs, exposes a good behavior. This demonstrates that communication costs do not impact on the overall performance in a relevant percentage amount. Despite this, further optimizations of communication routines should be considered as future work.

Finally, it should be noted that, while our proposed approach is general enough for being applied to *any* kind of graph-like data (e.g., social networks, sensor networks, and so forth), it is specially focused on RDF graphs due to the prevalence of such graph-like data on the Web, as a major form of big Web data. Indeed, our main aim is that of taking advantage from the efficiency of MapReduce as to cope with the *volume* of big Web data, following the strict requirements dictated by recent applications dealing with this kind of data (e.g., [75,76]).

EXPERIMENTAL ANALYSIS AND RESULTS

In this Section, we illustrate our experimental assessment and analysis that we devised in order to demonstrate the feasibility of our approach, and the effectiveness and the efficiency of our algorithms. The experimental environment used for our experiments is depicted in Figure 6. In particular, the target cluster comprises five hosts having the hardware described in Table 1.

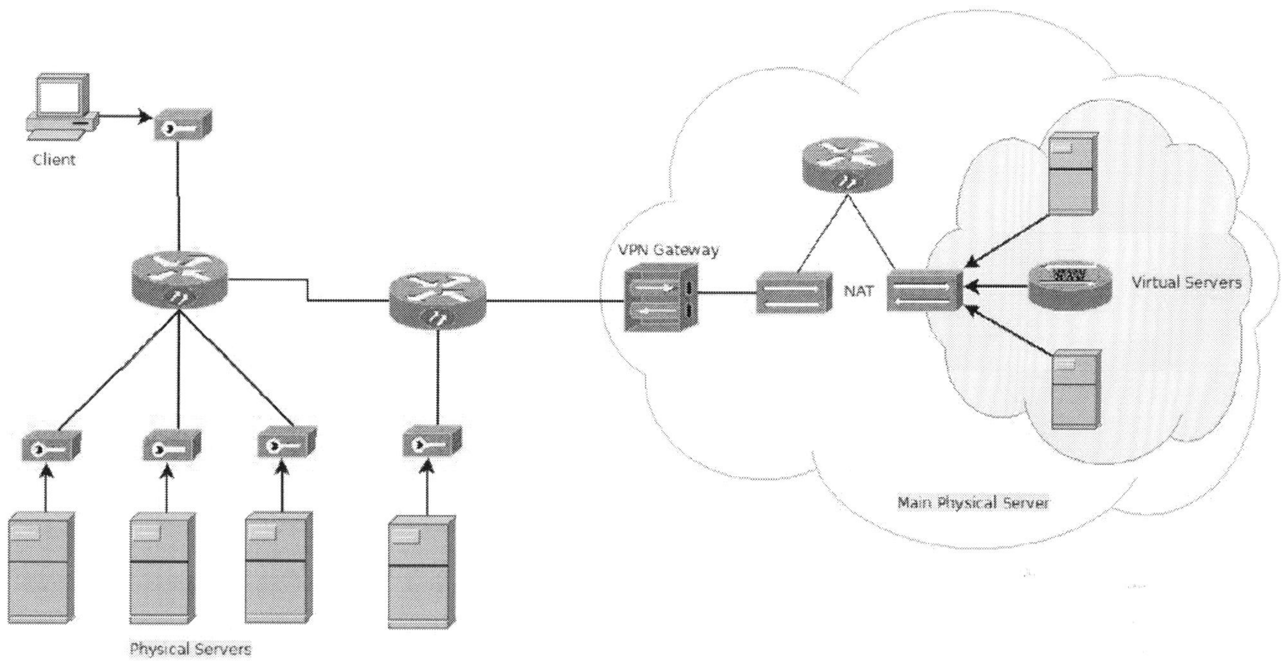

Figure 6. System environment.

Table 1. Hardware in the cluster of the experimental environment.

Core Num.	Core Speed (GHz)	HDD	RAM (GB)
6	2.4	1	6
8	2.4	1	2
4	2.7	1	4
4	2.7	1	4
4	2.7	1	4

In our experimental campaign, we ran tests on top of our cluster in order to verify its functionality and throughput first. These tests give us a baseline that was helpful to tune the cluster through the various configuration options and the schema of tables themselves. *The Yahoo! Cloud Serving Benchmark* (YCSB) [77] was used to run comparable workloads against different storage systems. While primarily built to compare various systems, YCSB is also a reasonable tool for performing an HBase cluster burn-in or performance-oriented tests (e.g., [78]). To this end, it is necessary to create some tables and load a bunch of test data (selected by the user or randomly generated) into these tables (generally, at least 10^8 rows of data should be loaded). In order to load data, we used the YCSB client tool [77] by generating a synthetic dataset that comprises 10^{12} rows. After loading the data, YCSB permits to run tests with the usage of the CRUD operations in a set of "workloads". In the YCSB's semantics, workloads are configuration files containing the percentage of operations to do, how many operations, how many threads should be used, and other useful experimental parameters.

We ran tests on both the default configuration and other tentative configurations by reaching a throughput of 1300 Op/s for reading-like operations and 3500 Op/s for writing-like operations, thus increasing by 50% the performance obtained with the default configurations. It is worth mentioning that, using both the Snappy compression scheme for reducing the size of data tables and Bloom filters for implementing the membership test in the adjacent lists (which may become very large in real-life RDF graphs) contributed in the performance gain heavily. Table 2 reports the experimental results provided by this experiment, which comprises the impact of communication costs.

Table 2. Throughput performance.

	Reading-Like Operations	Writing-Like Operations
Throughput (Op/s)	1300	3500

After the first series of experiments devoted to assess the throughput of the framework, we focused our attention on the data management capabilities of the framework by introducing an efficient schema and an efficient client capable of uploading and retrieving data efficiently, *i.e.*, based on the effective schema designed. The first solution contemplated an RDBMS(*Relational DataBase Management System*)-like approach to the schema design while the second one was more akin to NoSQL paradigms. As it will be mentioned later, the second approach is the one that exposes the best during the retrieval phase, lagging behind the first approach for data uploading. Due to the fact that the performance difference, however, was negligible, the second approach was the one to be implemented. To both solutions, all the optimizations about performance increasing discovered during the "load test" phase were applied (*i.e.*, table data Snappy-based compression and Bloom filters).

Therefore, we finally implemented three tables for HBase data storage (see Figure 7). As shown in Figure 7, the following tables have been devised: (i) table Path, shown in Figure 7a, is a repository of paths containing all the data modeling a path (*i.e.*, *Row key*, *Column family*, *etc.*); (*ii*) for each sink, table Sink-Path, shown in Figure 7b, contains the list of the path IDs (related to the first table) that ends with that node; (*iii*) for each node, table Node-Label, shown inFigure 7c, contains the labels of each node.

Row key	*Column family*	*Column family*	*Column family*	*Column family*	*Column family*
PathID (Long, auto increment)	Edges (List)	Nodes (List)	Final Node (Long)	Template (String)	Path Lenght (Int)

a)

Row key	*Column family*
Final Node (Long)	PathID (List of Long)

b)

Row key	*Column family*
Node id (Long)	Node name (String)

c)

Figure 7. HBase configuration for the running experiment: (**a**) table Path; (**b**) table Sink-PathID; (**c**) table Node-Label.

On top of this HBase data storage, we ran simple operations like Get, Batch and Scan, of course being the framework running our proposed algorithm. This allowed us to retrieve one million (1M) of rows within 5.5 ms through *cold-cache* experiments and within 1.3 ms through *warm-cache* experiments. Table 3 reports these results.

Table 3. Data management performance.

	Cold-Cache Mode	Warm-Cache Mode
Retrieval Time for 1 M Rows (ms)	5.5	1.3

Finally, by analyzing our experimental results, we conclude that our framework for computing BSF-based traversals of RDF graphs clearly exposes both effectiveness and efficiency. As future extension, in order to further improve performance, the proposed framework could be implemented on top of the well-known *Apache Spark analytical engine* [79], as Spark exposes an optimized in-memory computation scheme for large-scale data processing. This would allow us to improve response times.

CONCLUSIONS AND FUTURE WORK

In this paper, we propose an effective and efficient framework for computing BFS-based traversals of large-scale RDF graphs over MapReduce-aware platforms. Our approach embeds intelligent algorithms, and it turns out to be extremely useful in the emerging context of so-called big Web data. We have also provided experiments that clearly demonstrate the speed-up ensured by our solutions over comparative approaches. This offers exciting possibilities towards the support of *RDF graph analysis and mining methodologies* (e.g., [80,81]) over large-scale data sets, thanks to the powerful run-time support offered by MapReduce.

Future work is oriented towards the integration of our algorithms with Cloud-inspired frameworks devoted to the distributed management of large-scale data repositories via data compression metaphors (e.g., [82,83]).

REFERENCES

1. Dean, J.; Ghemawat, S. MapReduce: Simplified Data processing on Large Clusters. *Commun. ACM* 2008, *51*, 107–113.
2. Ebay Data Warehouses. Available online: http://www.dbms2.com/2009/04/30/ebays-two-enormous-data-warehouses/ (accessed on October 31 2015).
3. Facebook Hadoop and Hive. Available online: http://www.dbms2.com/2009/05/11/facebook-hadoop-and-hive/(accessed on October 31 2015).
4. Facebook. Available online: http://developers.facebook.com/ (accessed on October 31 2015).
5. MySpace. Available online: http://wiki.developer.myspace.com/index.php?title=Main_Page (accessed on October 31 2015).
6. NetFlix Documentation. Available online: http://developer.netflix.com/docs (accessed on October 31 2015).
7. Leskovec, J.; Kleinberg, J.M.; Faloutsos, C. Graphs over Time: Densification Laws, Shrinking Diameters and Possible Explanations. In Proceedings of the Eleventh ACM SIGKDD International Conference on Knowledge Discovery in Data Mining, Chicago, IL, USA, 21–24 August 2005; pp. 177–187.
8. Bahmani, B.; Kumar, R.; Vassilvitskii, S. Densest Subgraph in Streaming and MapReduce. *Proc. VLDB Endow.*2012, *5*, 454–465.
9. Zhong, N.; Yau, S.S.; Ma, J.; Shimojo, S.; Just, M.; Hu, B.; Wang, G.; Oiwa, K.; Anzai, Y. Brain Informatics-Based Big Data and the Wisdom Web of Things. *IEEE Intell. Syst.* 2015, *30*, 2–7.
10. Lane, J.; Kim, H.J. Big Data: Web-Crawling and Analysing Financial News Using RapidMiner. *Int. J. Bus. Inf. Syst.* 2015, *19*, 41–57.
11. W3C. RDF 1.1 Concepts and Abstract Syntax—W3C Recommendation 25 February 2014. Available online: http://www.w3.org/TR/rdf11-concepts/ (accessed on October 31 2015).
12. Cappellari, P.; Virgilio, R.D.; Roantree, M. Path-Oriented Keyword Search over Graph-Modeled Web Data.*World Wide Web* 2012, *15*, 631–661.
13. Bröcheler, M.; Pugliese, A.; Subrahmanian, V.S. Dogma: A Disk-Oriented Graph Matching Algorithm for RDF Databases. In *The Semantic Web—ISWC*; Springer: Berlin Heidelberg, Germany, 2009; pp. 97–113.
14. Fan, W.; Li, J.; Ma, S.; Tang, N.; Wu, Y.; Wu, Y. Graph Pattern Matching: From Intractable to Polynomial Time. *Proc. VLDB Endow.* 2010, *3*, 264–275.
15. Zhang, S.; Yang, J.; Jin, W. Sapper: Subgraph Indexing and Approximate Matching in Large Graphs. *Proc. VLDB Endow.* 2010, *3*, 1185–1194.
16. Yu, B.; Cuzzocrea, A.; Jeong, D.H.; Maydebura, S. On Managing Very Large Sensor-Network Data Using Bigtable. In Proceedings of the 12th IEEE/ACM International Symposium on Cluster, Cloud and Grid Computing (CCGrid), Ottawa, ON, Canada, 13–16 May 2012; pp. 918–922.
17. Yu, B.; Cuzzocrea, A.; Jeong, D.; Maybedura, S. A Bigtable/MapReduce-based Cloud Infrastructure for Effectively and Efficiently Managing Large-Scale Sensor Networks. In *Data Management in Cloud, Grid and P2P Systems*; Springer: Berlin Heidelberg, Germany, 2012; pp. 25–36.
18. Hadoop. Available online: http://wiki.apache.org/hadoop (accessed on October 31 2015).
19. Cuzzocrea, A.; Furfaro, F.; Mazzeo, G.M.; Saccà, D. A Grid Framework for Approximate Aggregate Query Answering on Summarized Sensor Network Readings. In Proceedings of the OTM Confederated International Workshops and Posters, GADA, JTRES, MIOS, WORM, WOSE, PhDS, and INTEROP 2004, Agia Napa, Cyprus, 25–29 October 2004; pp. 144–153.
20. Cuzzocrea, A.; Furfaro, F.; Greco, S.; Masciari, E.; Mazzeo, G.M.; Saccà, D. A Distributed System for Answering Range Queries on Sensor Network Data. In Proceedings of the Third IEEE International Conference on Pervasive Computing and Communications Workshops, 2005. PerCom 2005 Workshops, Kauai Island, HI, USA, 8–12 March 2005; pp. 369–373.
21. Cuzzocrea, A. Data Transformation Services over Grids With Real-Time Bound Constraints. In *On the Move to Meaningful Internet Systems: OTM 2008*; Springer: Berlin Heidelberg, Germany, 2008; pp. 852–869.
22. Ghemawat, S.; Gobioff, H.; Leung, S.T. The Google Fle System. In Proceedings of the Nineteenth ACM Symposium on Operating Systems Principles, Bolton Landing, NY, USA, 19–22 October 2003; pp. 29–43.
23. Apache Nutch. Available online: http://nutch.apache.org/ (accessed on October 31 2015).
24. Amazon. Available online: http://www.amazon.com (accessed on October 31 2015).
25. Elastic MapReduce Web Service. Available online: http://aws.amazon.com/elasticmapreduce/ (accessed on October 31 2015).
26. Amazon Elastic Compute Cloud—EC2. Available online: http://wiki.apache.org/hadoop/AmazonEC2 (accessed on October 31 2015).
27. NetFlix. Available online: https://www.netflix.com/ (accessed on October 31 2015).
28. Hulu. Available online: http://www.hulu.com/ (accessed on October 31 2015).
29. HBase—Apache Software Foundation Project Home Page. Available online: http://hadoop.apache.org/hbase/ (accessed on October 31 2015).
30. Abadi, D.J.; Boncz, P.A.; Harizopoulos, S. Column oriented Database Systems. *Proc. VLDB Endow.* 2009, *2*, 1664–1665.
31. Cattell, R. Scalable SQL and NoSQL Data Stores. *SIGMOD Rec.* 2010, *39*, 12–27.
32. Shvachko, K.; Kuang, H.; Radia, S.; Chansler, R. The Hadoop Distributed File System. In Proceedings of the IEEE 26th Symposium on Mass Storage Systems and Technologies (MSST), Incline Village, NV, USA, 3–7 May 2010; pp. 1–10.

33. Chang, F.; Dean, J.; Ghemawat, S.; Hsieh, W.C.; Wallach, D.A.; Burrows, M.; Chandra, T.; Fikes, A.; Gruber, R.E. Bigtable: A Distributed Storage System for Structured Data. *ACM Trans. Comput. Syst.* 2008, *26*.
34. Lin, J.; Dyer, C. Data-Intensive Text Processing with MapReduce. In *Synthesis Lectures on Human Language Technologies*; Morgan & Claypool Publishers: San Rafael, CA, USA, 2010.
35. Bloom, B.H. Space/Time Trade-Offs in Hash Coding with Allowable Errors. *Commun. ACM* 1970, *13*, 422–426.
36. Snappy: A Fast Compressor/Decompressor. Available online: https://google.github.io/snappy/ (accessed on October 31 2015).
37. Broekstra, J.; Kampman, A.; van Harmelen, F. Sesame: A Generic Architecture for Storing and Querying RDF and RDF Schema. In *The Semantic Web—ISWC*; Springer: Berlin Heidelberg, Germany, 2002; pp. 54–68.
38. Decker, S.; Melnik, S.; van Harmelen, F.; Fensel, D.; Klein, M.C.A.; Broekstra, J.; Erdmann, M.; Horrocks, I. The Semantic Web: The Roles of XML and RDF. *IEEE Intern. Comput.* 2000, *4*, 63–74.
39. Beckett, D.J. The Design and Implementation of the Redland RDF Application Framework. *Comput. Netw.* 2002,*39*, 577–588.
40. Huang, J.; Abadi, D.J.; Ren, K. Scalable SPARQL Querying of Large RDF Graphs. *Proc. VLDB Endow.* 2011, *4*, 1123–1134.
41. Herman, I. Introduction to Semantic Web Technologies. *SemTech*, 2010. Available online: http://www.w3.org/2010/Talks/0622-SemTech-IH/ (accessed on October 31 2015). – material redistributed under the Creative Common License (http://creativecommons.org/licenses/by-nd/3.0/ – accessed on October 31, 2015).
42. Wikipedia. Available online: https://www.wikipedia.org/ (accessed on October 31 2015).
43. DBpedia. Available online: http://wiki.dbpedia.org/ (accessed on October 31 2015).
44. W3C. RDQL—A Query Language for RDF—W3C Member Submission 9 January 2004. Available online: http://www.w3.org/Submission/RDQL/ (accessed on October 31 2015).
45. Gabrilovich, E.; Markovitch, S. Computing Semantic Relatedness Using Wikipedia-based Explicit Semantic Analysis. In Proceedings of the 20th International Joint Conference on Artifical Intelligence, Hyderabad, India, 6–12 January 2007; pp. 1606–1611.
46. Chandramouli, N.; Goldstein, J.; Duan, S. Temporal Analytics on Big Data for Web Advertising. In Proceedings of the 2012 IEEE 28th International Conference on Data Engineering (ICDE), Washington, DC, USA, 1–5 April 2012; pp. 90–101.
47. Chen, C.C.Y.; Das, S.K. Breadth-First Traversal of Trees and Integer Sorting in Parallel. *Inf. Process. Lett.* 1992,*41*, 39–49.
48. Niewiadomski, R.; Amaral, J.N.; Holte, R.C. A Parallel External-Memory Frontier Breadth-First Traversal Algorithm for Clusters of Workstations. In Proceedings of the International Conference on Parallel Processing, Columbus, OH, USA, 14–18 August 2006; pp. 531–538.
49. Chen, C.C.Y.; Das, S.K.; Akl, S.G. A Unified Approach to Parallel Depth-First Traversals of General Trees. *Inf. Process. Lett.* 1991, *38*, 49–55.
50. Dittrich, J.; Quiané-Ruiz, J.A. Efficient Big Data Processing in Hadoop MapReduce. *Proc. VLDB Endow.* 2012, *5*, 2014–2015.
51. Chen, Y.; Alspaugh, S.; Katz, R.H. Interactive Analytical Processing in Big Data Systems: A Cross-Industry Study of MapReduce Workloads. *Proc. VLDB Endow.* 2012, *5*, 1802–1813.
52. Papailiou, N.; Tsoumakos, D.; Konstantinou, I.; Karras, P.; Koziris, N. H2RDF: Adaptive Query Processing on RDF Data in the Cloud. In Proceedings of the 21st International Conference on World Wide Web, Lyon, France, 16–20 April 2012; pp. 397–400.
53. W3C. SPARQL 1.1 Overview—W3C Recommendation 21 March 2013. Available online: http://www.w3.org/TR/sparql11-overview/ (accessed on October 31 2015).
54. Przyjaciel-Zablocki, M.; Schätzle, A.; Skaley, E.; Hornung, T.; Lausen, G. Map-Side Merge Joins for Scalable SPARQL BGP Processing. In Proceedings of the 2013 IEEE 5th International Conference on Cloud Computing Technology and Science (CloudCom), Bristol, UK, 2–5 December 2013; pp. 631–638.
55. Jiang, H.; Chen, Y.; Qiao, Z.; Weng, T.H.; Li, K.C. Scaling Up MapReduce-based Big Data Processing on Multi-GPU Systems. *Clust. Comput.* 2015, *18*, 369–383.
56. Wang, Y.; Liu, Z.; Liao, H.; Li, C. Improving the Performance of GIS Polygon Overlay Computation with MapReduce for Spatial Big Data Processing. *Clust. Comput.* 2015, *18*, 507–516.
57. Kaoudi, Z.; Manolescu, I. RDF in the Clouds: A Survey. *VLDB J.* 2015, *24*, 67–91.
58. Rohloff, K.; Schantz, R.E. High-Performance, Massively Scalable Distributed Systems Using the MapReduce Software Framework: The SHARD Triple-Store. In Proceedings of the Programming Support Innovations for Emerging Distributed Applications, Reno, NV, USA, 17 October 2010.
59. Ladwig, G.; Harth, A. CumulusRDF: Linked Data Management on Nested Key-Value Stores. In Proceedings of the 7th International Workshop on Scalable Semantic Web Knowledge Base Systems (SSWS2011) at the 10th International Semantic Web Conference, Bonn, Germany, 23–27 October 2011; pp. 30–42.
60. Gergatsoulis, M.; Nomikos, C.; Kalogeros, E.; Damigos, M. An Algorithm for Querying Linked Data Using Map-Reduce. In Proceedings of the 6th International Conference, Globe 2013, Prague, Czech, 28–29 August 2013; pp. 51–62.
61. Schätzle, A.; Przyjaciel-Zablocki, M.; Lausen, G. PigSPARQL: Mapping SPARQL to Pig Latin. In Proceedings of the International Workshop on Semantic Web Information Management, Athens, Greece, 12–16 June 2011.

62. Olston, C.; Reed, B.; Srivastava, U.; Kumar, R.; Tomkins, A. Pig Latin: A Not-So-Foreign Language for Data Processing. In Proceedings of the 2008 ACM SIGMOD International Conference on Management of Data, Vancouver, BC, Canada, 2 March 2008; pp. 1099–1110.

63. Nie, Z.; Du, F.; Chen, Y.; Du, C.; Xu, L. Efficient SPARQL Query Processing in MapReduce through Data Partitioning and Indexing. In *Web Technologies and Applications*; Springer: Berlin Heidelberg, Germany, 2012; pp. 628–635.

64. Du, J.H.; Wang, H.; Ni, Y.; Yu, Y. HadoopRDF: A Scalable Semantic Data Analytical Engine. In *Intelligent Computing Theories and Applications*; Springer: Berlin Heidelberg, Germany, 2012; Volume 2, pp. 633–641.

65. Punnoose, R.; Crainiceanu, A.; Rapp, D. Rya: A Scalable RDF Triple Store for the Clouds. In Proceedings of the 1st International Workshop on Cloud Intelligence, Istanbul, Turkey, 31 August 2012.

66. Urbani, J.; Maassen, J.; Drost, N.; Seinstra, F.J.; Bal, H.E. Scalable RDF Data Compression with MapReduce. *Concurr. Comput. Pract. Exp.* 2013, *25*, 24–39.

67. Ravindra, P.; Anyanwu, K. Nesting Strategies for Enabling Nimble MapReduce Dataflows for Large RDF Data.*Int. J. Semant. Web Inf. Syst.* 2014, *10*, 1–26.

68. Ravindra, P.; Anyanwu, K. Scaling Unbound-Property Queries on Big RDF Data Warehouses Using MapReduce. In Proceedings of the 18th International Conference on Extending Database Technology (EDBT), Brussels, Belgium, 23–27 March 2015; pp. 169–180.

69. Apache Pig. Available online: https://pig.apache.org/ (accessed on October 31 2015).

70. Choi, P.; Jung, J.; Lee, K.H. RDFChain: Chain Centric Storage for Scalable Join Processing of RDF Graphs Using MapReduce and HBase. In Proceedings of the 12th International Semantic Web Conference and the 1st Australasian Semantic Web Conference, Sydney, Australia, 21–25 October 2013; pp. 249–252.

71. Kim, H.S.; Ravindra, P.; Anyanwu, K. Scan-Sharing for Optimizing RDF Graph Pattern Matching on MapReduce. In Proceedings of the 2012 IEEE 5th International Conference on Cloud Computing (CLOUD), Honolulu, HI, USA, 24–29 June 2012; pp. 139–146.

72. Ravindra, P.; Kim, H.S.; Anyanwu, K. An Intermediate Algebra for Optimizing RDF Graph Pattern Matching on MapReduce. In *The Semanic Web: Research and Applications*; Springer: Berlin Heidelberg, Germany, 2011; pp. 46–61.

73. Zhang, X.; Chen, L.; Wang, M. Towards Efficient Join Processing over Large RDF Graph Using MapReduce. In*Scientific and Statistical Database Management*; Springer: Berlin Heidelberg, Germany, 2012; pp. 250–259.

74. Apache Jena Core RDF API. Available online: http://jena.apache.org/documentation/rdf/index.html (accessed on October 31 2015).

75. Vitolo, C.; Elkhatib, Y.; Reusser, D.; Macleod, C.J.A.; Buytaert, W. Web Technologies for Environmental Big Data. *Environ. Model. Softw.* 2015, *63*, 185–198.

76. Jacob, F.; Johnson, A.; Javed, F.; Zhao, M.; McNair, M. WebScalding: A Framework for Big Data Web Services. In Proceedings of the IEEE First International Conference on Big Data Computing Service and Applications (BigDataService), Redwood City, CA, USA, 30 March–2 April 2015; pp. 493–498.

77. Cooper, B.F.; Silberstein, A.; Tam, E.; Ramakrishnan, R.; Sears, R. Benchmarking Cloud Serving Systems with YCSB. In Proceedings of the 1st ACM Symposium on Cloud Computing, SoCC 2010, Indianapolis, IN, USA, 10–11 June 2010; pp. 143–154.

78. Silberstein, A.; Sears, R.; Zhou, W.; Cooper, B.F. A Batch of PNUTS: Experiences Connecting Cloud Batch and Serving Systems. In Proceedings of the 2011 ACM SIGMOD International Conference on Management of Data, Athens, Greece, 12–16 June 2011; pp. 1101–1112.

79. Apache Spark. Available online: https://spark.apache.org/ (accessed on October 31 2015).

80. Abedjan, Z.; Grütze, T.; Jentzsch, A.; Naumann, F. Profiling and Mining RDF Data with ProLOD++. In Proceedings of the IEEE 30th International Conference on Data Engineering, Chicago, IL, USA, 30 March–4 April 2014; pp. 1198–1201.

81. Kushwaha, N.; Vyas, O.P. Leveragi0ng Bibliographic RDF Data for Keyword Prediction with Association Rule Mining (ARM). *Data Sci. J.* 2014, *13*, 119–126.

82. Cuzzocrea, A. A Framework for Modeling and Supporting Data Transformation Services over Data and Knowledge Grids with Real-Time Bound Constraints. *Concurr. Comput. Pract. Exp.* 2011, *23*, 436–457.

83. Cuzzocrea, A.; Saccà, D. Exploiting Compression and Approximation Paradigms for Effective And Efficient Online Analytical Processing over Sensor Network Readings in Data Grid Environments. *Concurr. Comput. Pract. Exp.* 2013, *25*, 2016–2035.

CHAPTER 9

A DATA ANALYTIC ALGORITHM FOR MANAGING, QUERYING, AND PROCESSING UNCERTAIN BIG DATA IN CLOUD ENVIRONMENTS

Fan Jiang and Carson K. Leung

Department of Computer Science, University of Manitoba, Winnipeg, MB, R3T 2N2, Canada

ABSTRACT

Big data are everywhere as high volumes of varieties of valuable precise and uncertain data can be easily collected or generated at high velocity in various real-life applications. Embedded in these big data are rich sets of useful information and knowledge. To mine these big data and to discover useful information and knowledge, we present a data analytic algorithm in this article. Our algorithm manages, queries, and processes uncertain big data in cloud environments. More specifically, it manages transactions of uncertain big data, allows users to query these big data by specifying constraints expressing their interests, and processes the user-specified constraints to discover useful information and knowledge from the uncertain big data. As each item in every transaction in these uncertain big data is associated with an existential probability value expressing the likelihood of that item to be present in a particular transaction, computation could be intensive. Our algorithm uses the MapReduce model on a cloud environment for effective data analytics on these uncertain big data. Experimental results show the effectiveness of our data analytic algorithm for managing, querying, and processing uncertain big data in cloud environments.

INTRODUCTION

Big data [1,2,3] are everywhere. They are high-veracity, high-velocity, high-value, and/or high-variety data with volumes beyond the ability of commonly-used software to manage, query, and process within a tolerable elapsed time. These high volumes of valuable data can be easily collected or generated at a high velocity from different data sources (which may lead to different data formats) in various real-life applications such as bioinformatics, graph management, sensor and stream systems, smart worlds, social networks, as well as the Web [4,5,6,7,8]. Characteristics of these big data can be described by the following "5 Vs":

1. Veracity, which focuses on the quality of data (e.g., uncertainty, messiness, or trustworthiness of data);
2. Velocity, which focuses on the speed at which data are collected or generated;
3. Value, which focuses on the usefulness of data;
4. Variety, which focuses on differences in types, contents or formats of data; and
5. Volume, which focuses on the quantity of data.

Embedded in the big data (e.g., biological data, medical images, streams of advertisements, surveillance videos, business transactions, financial charts, social media data, web logs, texts and documents) are rich sets of useful information

Citation: Fan Jiang and Carson K. Leung. A data analytic algorithm for managing, querying, and processing uncertain big data in cloud environments, Algorithms 2015, 8(4), 1175-1194; DOI: 10.3390/a8041175

and knowledge. Due to the "5 Vs" characteristics of big data, new forms of algorithm are needed for managing, querying, and processing these big data so as to enable enhanced decision making, insight, process optimization, data mining and knowledge discovery. This drives and motivates research and practices in data science, which aims to develop systematic or quantitative data analytic algorithm to analyze (e.g., inspect, clean, transform, and model) and mine big data.

Big data analytics [9,10,11,12] incorporates various techniques from a broad range of fields, which include cloud computing, data mining, machine learning, mathematics, and statistics. Data mining aims to extract implicit, previously unknown, and potentially useful information from data. With "5 Vs" characteristics of big data, it is natural to handle the data in a cloud computing environment as a cloud environment represents a "natural" context for big data by providing high performance, reliability, availability, transparency, abstraction, and/or virtualization. Various approaches—ranging from mathematical models to approximation models, from resource-constrained paradigms to memory-bounded methods—can be applied in cloud computing environments. Over the past few years, algorithms for handling big data according to a "systematic" view of the problem (e.g., MapReduce algorithms) are gaining momentum.

MapReduce [13] is a high-level programming model for handling high volumes of big data by using parallel and distributed computing [14,15,16] on clouds [17,18,19], which consist of a master node and multiple worker nodes. As implied by its name, MapReduce involves two key functions: "map" and "reduce" functions commonly used in functional programming languages such as LISP for list processing:

- The mapper applies a mapping function to each value in the list of values and returns the resulting list;
- The reducer applies a reducing function to combine all the values in the list of values and returns the combined result.

An advantage of using the MapReduce model is that users only need to focus on (and specify) these "map" and "reduce" functions—without worrying about implementation details for the following:

- handling machine failures,
- managing inter-machine communication,
- partitioning the input data, or
- scheduling and executing the program across multiple machines.

Several algorithms have been proposed over the past few years to use the MapReduce model—which mines the search space with parallel, distributed, or cloud computing—for big data analytics tasks like classification [20] and clustering [21]. In contrast, we focus on another big data analytics task—namely, association rule mining [22], which discovers interesting knowledge in the form of association rules $A \Rightarrow C$ revealing associative relationships between (i) shopper market baskets A and C of frequently purchased merchandise items or (ii) collections A and C of frequently co-located events.

By applying association rule mining to valuable big market basket data, data scientists can help shop owners/managers find interesting or popular patterns that reveal customer purchase behavior. The research problem of association rule mining usually consists of two key steps:

- Mining of frequent patterns [23], and
- Formation of association rules (by using the mined frequent patterns as antecedents and consequences of the rules).

Since the introduction of the frequent pattern mining problem [22], numerous studies [24,25,26] have been conducted (e.g., mining frequent patterns from traditional databases of shopper market basket transactions). With these traditional databases of precise data, users definitely know whether an item is present in (or is absent from) a transaction. In contrast, data in many real-life applications are riddled with uncertainty [27,28,29,30,31]. It is partially due to inherent measurement inaccuracies, sampling and duration errors, network latencies, or intentional blurring of data to preserve anonymity. As such, users are usually uncertain about the presence or absence of items. As a concrete example, a physician may highly suspect (but cannot guarantee) that a coughing patient suffers from the Middle East respiratory syndrome (MERS). The uncertainty of such suspicion can be expressed in terms of existential probability (e.g., a 60% likelihood of suffering from the MERS). With this notion, each item in a transaction t_j in databases containing precise data can be viewed as an item with a 100% likelihood of being present in t_j. To find frequent patterns from uncertain data, several uncertain data mining algorithms (e.g., UF-growth [32], tube-growth [33], and BLIMP-growth [34] algorithms) have been proposed.

For many real-life applications, users look for all frequent patterns. However, for some other real-life applications, users may have some particular phenomena in mind on which to focus the mining (e.g., a physician may want to find only those patients who are suffering from MERS). To avoid waiting for a long period of time for numerous patterns out of which only a tiny fraction may be interesting to the users, constrained pattern mining [35]—which aims to find those patterns that satisfy the user-specified constraints—is in demand. For example, we previously [36] exploited a special class of constraints called SAM constraints. Such exploitation helps reduce the search space when mining patterns satisfying user-specified SAM constraints. However, many commonly used constraints (e.g., sum(X.Expenses) < 300 CHF, which finds every combination X of items with a total cost less than 300 CHF) do not belong to the class of SAM constraints. In the current article, we explore another class of constraints, called anti-monotone (AM) constraints, to which commonly used constraints belong. We explore two sub-classes of anti-monotone constraints: (i) the frequency constraint; and (ii) non-frequency AM constraints.

In this article, our key contribution is our data analytic algorithm called MrCloud—which uses the MapReduce model in cloud environments for managing, querying, and processing uncertain big data. More specifically, MrCloud manages transactions of uncertain big data, allows users to query these big data by specifying anti-monotone constraints expressing their interests, and processes the user-specified constraints to discover useful information and knowledge in the form of frequent patterns from the uncertain big data. So, MrCloud can be considered as a non-trivial integration of (i) frequent pattern mining; (ii) big data mining; (iii) constrained mining; and (iv) uncertain data mining.

The remainder of this article is organized as follows. The next section presents background and related works. In Section 3, we propose our data analytic algorithm for mining patterns satisfying AM constraints from uncertain big data using MapReduce. Evaluation results and conclusions are given in Section 4 and Section 5, respectively.

BACKGROUND AND RELATED WORKS

In this section, we present some background information and related works on extensions of frequent pattern mining, namely (Section 2.1) big data mining with the MapReduce model, (Section 2.2) constrained mining, and (Section 2.3) uncertain data mining.

Big Data Mining with the MapReduce Model

MapReduce [13] is a high-level programming model for processing vast amounts of data. It usually uses parallel and distributed computing on clouds of nodes (i.e., computers). As implied by its name, MapReduce involves two key functions: "map" and "reduce".

First, the input data are read, divided into several partitions (sub-problems), and assigned to different processors. Each processor executes the map function on each partition (sub-problem). The map function takes a pair of ⟨key, value⟩ and returns a list of ⟨key, value⟩ pairs as an intermediate result:

$$\text{map: } \langle key_1, value_1 \rangle \mapsto \text{list of } \langle key_2, value_2 \rangle$$

where (i) key_1 & key_2 are keys in the same or different domains; and (ii) $value_1$ & $value_2$ are the corresponding values in some domains.

Afterwards, the pairs returned by the map function are shuffled and sorted. Each processor then executes the reduce function on (i) a single key from this intermediate result together with (ii) the list of all values that appear with this key in the intermediate result. The reduce function "reduces"—by combining, aggregating, summarizing, filtering, or transforming—the list of values associated with a given key (for all k keys) and returns a single (aggregated or summarized) value:

$$\text{reduce: } \langle key_2, \text{list of } value_2 \rangle \mapsto value_3$$

where (i) key_2 is a key in some domains; and (ii) $value_2$ & $value_3$ are the corresponding values in some domains. Examples of MapReduce applications include the construction of an inverted index as well as the word counting of a document for data processing [13].

To mine frequent patterns from precise data using the MapReduce model, three Apriori-based algorithms called SPC, FPC and DPC [37] were proposed. Among them, SPC uses single-pass counting to find frequent patterns of cardinality k at the k-th pass (i.e., the k-th database scan) for $k \geq 1$. FPC uses fixed-passes combined-counting to find all patterns of cardinalities k, (k + 1), ..., (k + m) in the same pass or database scan. On the one hand, this fixed-passes technique fixes the number of required passes from k_{max} (where k_{max} is the maximum cardinality of all frequent patterns that can be mined from the precise data) to a user-specified constant. On the other hand, due to combined-counting, the number of generated candidates is higher than that of SPC. In contrast, DPC uses dynamic-passes combined-counting, which takes the benefits of both SPC and FPC by taking into account the workloads of nodes when mining frequent patterns with MapReduce. In addition, a parallel randomized algorithm called PARMA [38] was proposed for mining approximations to the top-k frequent patterns and association rules from precise data by using MapReduce.

As a preview, our MrCloud algorithm also uses MapReduce. However, unlike SPC, FPC or DPC [37] (which use the Apriori-based approach to mine frequent patterns from precise data), our MrCloud uses a tree-based approach to mine frequent patterns from uncertain data—which deals with a much larger search space than that for mining precise data due to the presence of the existential probability values. Moreover, unlike PARMA (which mines all of the approximately frequent patterns from precise data), our data analytic algorithm mines some—specifically, those interesting patterns that satisfy the user-specified constraints—of the truly frequent patterns from uncertain data.

Constrained Mining

Allowing users to specify their interest via the use of constraints [35,39,40] helps guide the data mining process so that only those sets of frequently co-occurring items satisfying the user-specified constraints can be found, which in turn avoids unnecessary computation for mining those uninteresting frequent patterns. These user-specified constraints can be imposed on items, events or objects in various domains, including shopper market baskets, meteorological records, and event planning calendars. In general, these constraints can be categorized into several overlapping classes according to the properties that they possess. In this article, we examine one class of constraints called anti-monotone (AM) constraints, which possess the properties of anti-monotonicity. This class of constraints can be further subdivided into the following two sub-classes:

1. Frequency constraints include the following:
   - $C_1 \equiv \text{sup}(X) \geq \text{minsup}$ expresses the user interest in finding frequent patterns from precise data, i.e., every pattern X with actual support (or frequency) meeting or exceeding the user-specified minimum support threshold minsup; and $C_2 \equiv \text{expSup}(X) \geq \text{minsup}$ expresses the user interest in finding frequent patterns from uncertain data, i.e., every pattern X with expected support meeting or exceeding the user-specified minimum support threshold minsup.
2. Non-frequency AM constraints, with examples include the following:
   - $C_3 \equiv \min(X.\text{RewardPoints}) \geq 2000$ expresses the user interest in finding every pattern X such that the minimum reward points earned by travellers among all airports visited are at least 2000;
   - $C_4 \equiv \max(X.\text{Rainfall}) \leq 10$ mm says that the maximum rainfall among all meteorological records in X is at most 10 mm (i.e., "relatively dry");

- $C_5 \equiv$ X.Location = Europe expresses the user interest in finding every pattern X such that all places in X are located in Europe;
- $C_6 \equiv$ X.Weight $\leq$ 23 kg says that the weight of each object in X is at most 23 kg (e.g., no heavy checked baggage for a trip); and
- $C_7 \equiv$ sum(X.Expenses) < 300 CHF says that the total expenses on all items in X is less than 300 CHF.

Note that a constraint C is anti-monotone [40] if and only if all subsets of a pattern satisfying C also satisfy C. Equivalently, a constraint C is anti-monotone (AM) if and only if all supersets of a pattern violating C also violate C. A pattern X is valid in a database if such a pattern also satisfies the user-specified constraints. Given (i) a database; (ii) user-specified minsup; and (iii) user-specified AM constraints, the research problem of constrained pattern mining from uncertain data is to discover from the database a complete set of patterns satisfying the user-specified AM constraints (i.e., valid patterns).

Uncertain Data Mining

Let (i) Item be a set of m domain items and (ii) $X = \{x_1, x_2,\cdots,x_k\}$ be a k-itemset (i.e., a pattern consisting of k items), where $X \subseteq$ Item and $1 \leq k \leq m$. Then, a transactional database is the set of n transactions, where each transaction tj⊆tj⊆ Item (for 1≤j≤n1≤j≤n). The projected database of X is the set of all transactions containing X. Each item x_i in a transaction $t_j = \{x_1, x_2,\cdots,x_h\}$ in an uncertain database is associated with an existential probability $P(x_i, t_j)$, which represents the likelihood of the presence of x_i in t_j [41], with value

$0 < P(x_i, t_j) \leq 1$

The existential probability $P(x_i, t_j)$ of a pattern X in t_j is then the product of the corresponding existential probabilities of every item x_i within X when these items are independent [41,42]:

$$P(X, t_j) = \prod_{x_i \in X} P(x_i, t_j)$$

Finally, the expected support expSup(X) of X is the sum of $P(x_i, t_j)$ over all n transactions in the database:

$$expSup(X) = \sum_{j=1}^{n} P(X, t_j) = \sum_{j=1}^{n} \left(\prod_{x_i \in X} P(x_i, t_j) \right) \quad (1)$$

With this notion of expected support, existing tree-based algorithms—such as UF-growth [32], tube-growth [33] and BLIMP-growth [34]—mine frequent patterns from uncertain data by first scanning the uncertain database once to compute the expected support of all domain items (i.e., singleton patterns). Infrequent items are pruned as their extensions/supersets are guaranteed to be infrequent. The algorithms then scan the database a second time to insert all transactions (with only frequent items) into a tree (e.g., UF-tree [32], TPC-tree [33], or BLIMP-tree [34]). Each node in the tree captures (i) an item x; (ii) its existential probability $P(x_i, t_j)$; and (iii) its occurrence count. At each step during the mining process, the frequent patterns are expanded recursively.

A pattern X is frequent in an uncertain database if expSup(X) $\geq$ minsup. Given a database and minsup, the research problem of frequent pattern mining from uncertain data is to discover from the database a complete set of frequent patterns having expected support $\geq$ minsup.

MRCLOUD: OUR DATA ANALYTIC ALGORITHM

Given (i) uncertain big data; (ii) user-specified minsup; (iii) a user-specified constraint C (e.g., an AM constraint), the research problem of constrained frequent pattern mining from uncertain big data is to discover from big data a complete set of patterns having expected support $\geq$ minsup and satisfying C (i.e., valid frequent patterns). In this section, we present our data analytic algorithm—called MrCloud—that uses MapReduce for managing, querying, and processing uncertain big data in cloud environments. Specifically, our algorithm manages transactions of uncertain big data, allows users to query these big data by specifying constraints expressing their interests, and processes the user-specified constraints to discover useful information and knowledge from the uncertain big data.

Managing Uncertain Big Data

To manage uncertain big data, our MrCloud algorithm keeps track of both (i) the transactions of uncertain data; and (ii) an auxiliary file capturing information about domain items in uncertain data. Here, items in each transaction of uncertain data are associated with existential probability values expressing the likelihood of these items in the transaction in the form of a set of every item x_i with its existential probability value $P(x_i, t_j)$:

$$\{x_i\text{: } P(x_i, t_j)\}$$

See Table 1 for an illustrative sample capturing transactions of uncertain data collected about the airports visited by travelers. Also see Table 2 for the auxiliary information about reward points that can be earned by travelers visiting those airports. For instance, t_1 captures the uncertain data that a traveler may have visited six airports (namely, AMS, BCN, CPH, DEL, EDI and FRA). Among them, it is 100% sure that he has visited BCN and EDI (where he earned 3000 and 2000 points, respectively). There is a 90% chance that he has visited AMS or DEL (where he would earn 2400 and 3200 points, respectively), 50% chance that he has visited CPH (where he would earn 2600 points), and only 20% chance that he has visited FRA (where he would earn 2200 points).

Table 1. An illustrative sample set of uncertain big data.

TID	Content
t_1	{AMS: 0.9, BCN: 1.0, CPH: 0.5, DEL: 0.9, EDI: 1.0, FRA: 0.2}
t_2	{AMS: 0.8, BCN: 0.8, CPH: 1.0, EDI: 0.2, FRA: 0.2, IST: 0.6}
t_3	{AMS: 0.4, FRA: 0.2, GUM: 1.0, HEL: 0.5}

Table 2. Auxiliary information for the uncertain big data in Table 1.

IATA Code	Airport	Reward Points
AMS	Amsterdam	2400
BCN	Barcelona	3000
CPH	Copenhagen	2600
DEL	Delhi	3200
EDI	Edinburgh	2000
FRA	Frankfurt	2200
GUM	Guam	1800
HEL	Helsinki	2800
IST	Istanbul	1600

Querying Uncertain Big Data

Once our MrCloud algorithm managed uncertain big data, it allows users to query the data. Users can express their interests by selecting one of SQL-style constraints in the form of (i) "X.attribute θ constant"; (ii) "agg(X.attribute) θ constant"; and (iii) their logical combinations via the conjunction operator "AND" (∧) or the disjunction operator "OR" (∨), where (i) agg is an aggregate function including max, min, sum, and (ii) θ is a comparison operator including >, ≥, =, ≤, <. Examples are not confined to the aforementioned (i) frequency constraints C_1 & C_2 or (ii) non-frequency AM constraints $C_3 – C_7$, users can also specify AM constraints involving more than one aggregate function. The following is an example:

- $C_8 \equiv$ difference(X.Temperature) = max(X.Temperature) – min(X.Temperature) ≤ 10 °C says that the difference between the maximum and minimum temperatures in X is at most 10 °C (which involves the difference between two aggregate functions maximum and minimum).

Moreover, users can also specify constraints involving more than one AM constraint. Examples include the following:

- $C_9 \equiv$ [min(X.Temperature) ≥ 20 °C] ∧ [max(X. Temperature) ≤ 30 °C] expresses the user interest in finding every pattern X with temperature between 20 °C to 30 °C inclusive (which involves a logical conjunction "AND" of two AM constraints);
- $C_{10} \equiv$ [min(X.RewardPoints) ≥ 2000] ∧ [X.Location = Europe] expresses the user interest in finding every pattern Xsuch that the minimum reward points earned by travellers among all European airports visited are at least 2000 (which again involves a logical conjunction "AND" of two AM constraints); and
- $C_{11} \equiv$ [min(X.Temperature) ≥ 20 °C] ∨ [max(X.Rainfall) ≤ 10 mm] expresses the user interest in finding all meteorological records matching "warm" or "relatively dry" patterns (which involves a logical conjunction "OR" of two AM constraints).

Last but not least, users can also specify constraints that are not AM (e.g., $C_{12} \equiv$ avg(X.Temperature) ≥ 25 °C expressing the user interest in finding every pattern X with average temperature at least 25 °C). Since the users specify their constraints by selecting one of the SQL-style constraints, MrCloud can easily determine whether the user-specified constraints are AM or not. Table 3 shows examples of the classification.

Table 3. Classification of some AM and non-AM constraints.

Classification	Constraints
AM	X.attribute θ constant, where θ ∈{>, ≥=, ≤, <}
	max(X.attribute) θ constant, where θ ∈{=, ≤, <}
	min(X.attribute) θ constant, where θ ∈{>, ≥, =}
	sum(X.attribute) θ constant, where θ ∈{≤, <}
	$C_1 \wedge C_2$, where C_1 and C_2 are AM constraints
	$C_1 \vee C_2$, where C_1 and C_2 are AM constraints
non-AM	max(X.attribute) θ constant, where θ ∈{>, ≥}
	min(X.attribute) θ constant, where θ ∈{≤, <}
	sum(X.attribute) θ constant, where θ ∈{>, ≥}
	avg(X.attribute) θ constant, where θ ∈{>, ≥, =, ≤, <}

PROCESSING UNCERTAIN BIG DATA

Once the users queried uncertain big data by specifying their constraints that express their interest, our MrCloud algorithm processes these user-specified queries to find frequent patterns that satisfy these user-specified constraints. Given (i) an implicit frequency constraint $C_2 \equiv$ expSup(X) ≥ minsup; and (ii) an explicit user-specified constraints, MrCloud explores the anti-monotonicity of these constraints in pruning the search space. More specifically, the implicit frequency constraint satisfies the anti-monotonicity:

- If a pattern X is frequent (i.e., $expSup(X) \geq minsup$), then all subsets of X are guaranteed to satisfy the AM constraints because $expSup(X') \geq expSup(X) \geq minsup$ for every subset $X' \subseteq X$.
- If a pattern Y is infrequent (i.e., $expSup(Y) < minsup$), then all supersets of Y are guaranteed to be infrequent because $expSup(Y') < expSup(Y) < minsup$ for every superset $Y' \supseteq Y$. Thus, every superset Y′ of Y can be pruned.

However, if a pattern X is frequent, then some supersets of X may be frequent while some other may not be frequent. Thus, frequency checking is needed to be applied to every superset of X. Similarly, if the user-specified constraint satisfies the anti-monotonicity, then we can prune the search space due to the following:

- If a pattern X satisfies AM constraints, then all subsets of X are guaranteed to satisfy the AM constraints.
- If a pattern Y does not satisfy AM constraints, then all supersets of Y are guaranteed not to satisfy the AM constraints and thus can be pruned.

However, if a pattern X satisfies AM constraints, then some supersets of X may satisfy the AM constraints while some other may not satisfy the AM constraints. Thus, constraint checking is needed to be applied to every superset ofX. These observations about anti-monotone constraints hold not only for constraints involving one AM constraint but also constraints involving multiple AM constraints due to the following:

Theorem 1. If constraints C_a and C_b are anti-monotone, then the constraint $(C_a \wedge C_b)$ is also anti-monotone.

Proof. For anti-monotone constraints C_a and C_b, if a pattern X satisfies C_a and C_b, then all subsets of X are guaranteed to satisfy C_a and satisfy C_b. In other words, all subsets of X are guaranteed to satisfy $(C_a \wedge C_b)$. Conversely, if a pattern Y does not satisfy C_a and does not satisfy C_b, then all supersets of Y are guaranteed not to satisfy C_a and not to satisfy C_b. In other words, all supersets of Y are guaranteed not to satisfy $(C_a \wedge C_b)$. Thus, $(C_a \wedge C_b)$ is also anti-monotone.

Theorem 2. If constraints C_a or C_b are anti-monotone, then the constraint $(C_a \vee C_b)$ is also anti-monotone.

Proof. For anti-monotone constraints C_a or C_b, if a pattern X satisfies C_a and C_b, then all subsets of X are guaranteed to satisfy C_a or satisfy C_b. In other words, all subsets of X are guaranteed to satisfy $(C_a \vee C_b)$. Conversely, if a pattern Y does not satisfy C_a or does not satisfy C_b, then all supersets of Y are guaranteed not to satisfy C_a or not to satisfy C_b. In other words, all supersets of Y are guaranteed not to satisfy $(C_a \vee C_b)$. Thus, $(C_a \vee C_b)$ is also anti-monotone.

On the other hand, if the explicit user-specified constraints do not satisfy anti-monotonicity, our MrCloud first discovers all frequent patterns and then verifies the validity of each of these discovered patterns to see if it satisfies the user-specified constraints at a post-processing step.

To process uncertain big data, our MrCloud algorithm first reads and divides the uncertain big data into several partitions and assigns them to different processors. The map function (denoted as map_1) receives ⟨transaction ID, content of that transaction⟩ as input. To facilitate time-efficient and space-efficient constrained frequent pattern mining, MrCloud pushes the user-specified non-frequency AM constraints C_{AM} early in the mining process by pushing them into the map_1 function. So, for every transaction t_j, the map1map1 function performs constraint checking for C_{AM} and emits an $\langle x, P(x, t_j)\rangle$ pair for each occurrence of valid item $x \in t_j$ (i.e., those domain items satisfying the non-frequency AM constraints):

$$\text{map}_1\text{: } \langle \text{ID of transaction } t_j, \text{content of } t_j\rangle \mapsto \text{list of } \langle \text{valid } x, P(x, t_j)\rangle \tag{2}$$

In other words, by specifying the following, the map1map1 function produces a list of $\langle \text{valid } x, P(x, t_j)\rangle$ pairs with many different valid x and $P(x, t_j)$ for the keys and values:

for each $t_j \in$ partition of the uncertain big data **do**
  for each item $x \in t_j$ **and** $\{x\}$ satisfies C_{AM} **do**
    emit $\langle x, P(x, t_j)\rangle$.

Afterwards, these $\langle \text{valid } x, P(x, t_j)\rangle$ pairs are shuffled and sorted. Each processor then executes the reduce function (denoted as $reduce_1$) on the shuffled and sorted pairs to obtain the expected support of x. Recall that each item in the uncertain big data is associated with an existential probability value. The $reduce_1$ function computes the expected support of all domain items (i.e., singleton patterns) by using MapReduce with Equation (1), which can be simplified to become the following when computing singleton patterns:

$$expSup(\{x\}) = \sum_{j=1}^{n} P(x, t_j) \tag{3}$$

where $P(x, t_j)$ is an existential probability of item x in transaction t_j. In other words, the reduce1reduce1 function sums all existential probabilities of x for each valid x to compute its expected support:

$$\text{reduce}_1\text{: } \langle \text{valid } x, \text{list of } P(x, t_j)\rangle \mapsto \text{list of } \langle \text{valid frequent } \{x\}, expSup(\{x\})\rangle \tag{4}$$

More specifically, the reduce1reduce1 function finds those items satisfying the frequency constraints by specifying the following:

for each $x \in \langle \text{valid } x, \text{list of } P(x,t_j)\rangle$ **do**
  set $expSup(\{x\}) = 0$;
  for each $P(x,t_j) \in$ list of $P(x,t_j)$ **do**
    $expSup(\{x\}) = expSup(\{x\}) + P(x,t_j)$;
  if $expSup(\{x\}) \geq minsup$ **then**
    emit $\langle \{x\}, expSup(\{x\})\rangle$.

For the explicit user-specified non-frequency non-AM constraints C_{nonAM}, our MrCloud verifies the validity of each discovered frequent $\{x\}$ returned by the $reduce_1$ function to see if it satisfies the user-specified constraints. Consequently, we obtain all valid frequent singletons (i.e., domain items that satisfy the user-specified constraints) and their associated existential support values.

MrCloud then proceeds to the next step, which is computationally intensive, by rereading each transaction in the uncertain big data to form an $\{x\}$-projected database (i.e., a collection of all prefixes of transactions ending with x) for each valid frequent singleton {x} returned by the $reduce_1$ function. This second map function (denoted as map_2)

map_2: ⟨ID of transaction t_j, content of t_j⟩ ↦ list of ⟨valid frequent{x}, part of t_j with x⟩ (5)

can be specified as follows:

for each t_j ∈ partition of the uncertain big data **do**

for each {x} ∈ ⟨{x}, expSup({x})⟩ **do**

if prefix of t_j ending with x contains items besides x **then**

emit ⟨{x}, prefix of t_j ending with x⟩.

The worker node corresponding to each partition helps to form an {x}-projected database for every valid frequent item x in the transactions assigned to that partition. The {x}-projected database consists of prefixes of relevant transactions (from the uncertain big data) that end with x. More precisely, the worker node outputs ⟨{x}, portion of t_j for forming the {x}-projected database⟩ pairs.

Then, the reduce function

reduce2: ⟨valid frequent{x}, {x}−projected database⟩ ↦ list of ⟨valid frequent X, expSup(X)⟩ (6)

shuffles and sorts these pairs of {x}-projected databases, from which valid frequent non-singleton patterns can be found and their expected support values can be computed. As any non-singleton patterns containing valid singleton items are not guaranteed to be valid, additional constraint check on AM constraints C_{AM} is required when forming the projected database in mining valid frequent patterns. So, the worker node corresponding to each projected database then builds appropriate trees (e.g., UF-tree, TPC-tree, or BLIMP-tree)—based on the projected databases assigned to the worker node—to mine every valid frequent non-singleton pattern X (with cardinality k, where $k \geq 2$). The worker node also outputs ⟨X, expSup(X)⟩, i.e., every valid frequent non-singleton pattern with its expected support:

for each x ∈ {x}-projected database **do**

build a tree for {x}-projected database to find X;

if X satisfies C_{AM} **and** expSup(X) ≥ minsup **then**

emit ⟨X, expSup(X)⟩.

Again, for the explicit user-specified non-frequency non-AM constraints C_{nonAM}, our MrCloud verifies the validity of each discovered frequent X returned by the $reduce_2$ function to see if it satisfies the user-specified constraints.

Example 1. Let us consider an illustrative sample set of an uncertain big database (as shown in Table 1) and its auxiliary information (as shown in Table 2) with (i) the user-specified minsup=0.9; and (ii) a user-specified constraint C_{10} ≡ [min(X.RewardPoints) ≥ 2000] ∧ [X.Location = Europe] (which expresses the user interest in finding every pattern X such that the minimum reward points earned by travellers among all European airports visited are at least 2000). Based on the auxiliary information, we learn that airports AMS, BCN, CPH, EDI, FRA and HEL (but not DEL, GUM or IST) satisfy C_{10}. More specifically, (i) both DEL and GUM are not in Europe; and (ii) travellers visiting either GUM or IST would not be able to earn at least 2000 reward points.

Then, for the first transaction t_1, the map_1 function outputs only ⟨AMS, 0.9⟩, ⟨BCN, 1.0⟩, ⟨CPH, 0.5⟩, ⟨EDI, 1.0⟩ and ⟨FRA, 0.2⟩. Similarly, for the second transaction t_2, the map_1 function outputs ⟨AMS, 0.8⟩, ⟨BCN, 0.8⟩, ⟨CPH, 1.0⟩, ⟨EDI, 0.2⟩, and ⟨FRA, 0.2⟩. For the third transaction t_3, the map_1 function outputs only ⟨AMS, 0.4⟩, ⟨FRA, 0.2⟩ and ⟨HEL, 0.5⟩. These output pairs are then shuffled and sorted.

Note that the map_1 function does not output ⟨DEL, 0.9⟩ for t_1 because {DEL} does not satisfy C_{10}. Moreover, it also does not output ⟨IST, 0.6⟩ for t_2 or ⟨GUM, 1.0⟩ for t_3 because both {IST} and {GUM} also do not satisfy C_{10}.

Afterwards, the $reduce_1$ function first reads ⟨AMS, [0.9, 0.8, 0.4]⟩, ⟨BCN, [1.0, 0.8]⟩, ⟨CPH, [0.5, 1.0]⟩, ⟨EDI, [1.0, 0.2]⟩, ⟨FRA, [0.2, 0.2, 0.2]⟩ and ⟨HEL, [0.5]⟩; the function then outputs ⟨{AMS}, 2.1⟩, ⟨{BCN}, 1.8⟩, ⟨{CPH}, 1.5⟩ and ⟨{EDI}, 1.2⟩ (i.e., valid frequent singletons and their corresponding expected support).

Also note that, although the $reduce_1$ function reads ⟨FRA, [0.2, 0.2, 0.2]⟩ and ⟨HEL, [0.5]⟩, it does not output ⟨{FRA}, 0.6⟩ or ⟨{HEL}, 0.5⟩ because valid singletons {FRA} and {HEL} are infrequent.

After rereading the first transaction t_1, the map_2 function outputs ⟨{BCN}, {AMS: 0.9, BCN: 1.0}⟩ (where {AMS: 0.9, BCN: 1.0} is a prefix of t_1 ending with item BCN), ⟨{CPH}, {AMS: 0.9, BCN: 1.0, CPH: 0.5}⟩ and ⟨{EDI}, {AMS: 0.9, BCN: 1.0, CPH: 0.5, EDI: 1.0}⟩ (where {AMS: 0.9, BCN: 1.0, CPH: 0.5, EDI: 1.0} contains only valid frequent items—i.e., it does not contain invalid item DEL). Similarly, after rereading the second transaction t_2, the map $function_2$ outputs ⟨{BCN}, {AMS: 0.8, BCN: 0.8}⟩, ⟨{CPH}, {AMS: 0.8, BCN: 0.8, CPH: 1.0}⟩ and ⟨{EDI},{AMS: 0.8, BCN: 0.8, CPH: 1.0, EDI: 0.2}⟩. After rereading the third transaction t_3, the map_2 function does not output anything. All output pairs are then shuffled and sorted.

Note that the map_2 function does not output ⟨{AMS}, {AMS: 0.9}⟩ for t_1 because {AMS: 0.9} does not contain any valid frequent item other than AMS itself (i.e., singleton prefix of transactions does not contribute to the mining of non-singletons). The same comments apply to not outputting ⟨{AMS}, {AMS: 0.8}⟩ for t_2 or ⟨{AMS}, {AMS: 0.4}⟩ for t_3. Moreover, recall that the $reduce_1$ function outputs ⟨{AMS}, 2.1⟩, ⟨{BCN}, 1.8⟩, ⟨{CPH}, 1.5⟩ and ⟨{EDI}, 1.2⟩ (as FRA & HEL are infrequent and GUM is invalid). Hence, the map_2 function does not output anything for FRA, GUM, or HEL (i.e., not outputting ⟨{FRA}, {AMS: 0.9, BCN: 1.0, CPH: 0.5, EDI: 1.0, FRA: 0.2}⟩ for t_1; {AMS: 0.8, BCN: 0.8, CPH: 1.0, EDI: 0.2, FRA: 0.2}⟩ for t_2; ⟨{FRA}, {AMS: 0.4, FRA: 0.2}⟩ or ⟨{HEL}, {AMS: 0.4, FRA: 0.2, HEL: 0.5}⟩ for t_3).

Afterwards, the $reduce_2$ function reads ⟨{BCN}, {BCN}-projected database⟩. Based on this {BCN}-projected database (which consists of two sub-transactions {AMS: 0.9, BCN: 1.0} and {AMS: 0.8, BCN: 0.8}), a tree is built. Consequently, valid frequent pattern {AMS, BCN} with an expected support of 1.54 is found. Similarly, the $reduce_2$ function reads ⟨{CPH}, {CPH}-projected database⟩. It builds a tree based on this {CPH}-projected database (which consists of two sub-transactions {AMS: 0.9, BCN: 1.0, CPH: 0.5} and {AMS: 0.8, BCN: 0.8, CPH: 1.0}), and finds valid frequent patterns {AMS, CPH}, {AMS, BCN, CPH} and {BCN, CPH} with expected support values of 1.25, 1.09 and 1.3, respectively. The $reduce_2$ function then reads ⟨{EDI}, {EDI}-projected database⟩. It builds a tree based on this {EDI}-projected database (which consists of two sub-transactions {AMS: 0.9, BCN: 1.0, CPH: 0.5, EDI: 1.0} and {AMS: 0.8, BCN: 0.8, CPH: 1.0, EDI: 0.2}), and finds valid frequent patterns {AMS, EDI} and {BCN, EDI} with expected support values of 1.06 & 1.16, respectively.

Recall from Example 1 that the set of map_1 and $reduce_1$ functions discover four valid frequent singletons (with their corresponding expected support values): ⟨{AMS}, 2.1⟩, ⟨{BCN}, 1.8⟩, ⟨{CPH}, 1.5⟩ and ⟨{EDI}, 1.2⟩. Here, the set of map_2 and $reduce_2$ functions discover six additional valid frequent non-singleton patterns (with their corresponding expected support values): ⟨{AMS, BCN}, 1.54⟩, {AMS, BCN, CPH}, 1.09⟩, ⟨{AMS, CPH}, 1.25⟩, ⟨{AMS, HEL}, 1.06⟩, ⟨{BCN, CPH}, 1.3⟩ and ⟨{BCN, EDI}, 1.16⟩. Hence, MrCloud finds a total of 10 patterns satisfying both frequency constraint $C_2 \equiv \text{expSup}(X) \geq \text{minsup}$ and non-frequency AM constraint $C_{10} \equiv [\min(X.\text{RewardPoints}) \geq 2000] \wedge [X.\text{Location} = \text{Europe}]$ involving a logical conjunction of two non-frequency AM constraints.

EVALUATION RESULTS

We evaluated our proposed data analytic algorithm MrCloud in mining user-specified constraints from uncertain big data. We used various benchmark datasets, which include real-life datasets (e.g., accidents, connect4, and mushroom) from the UCI Machine Learning Repository (http://archive.ics.uci.edu/ml/) and the FIMI Repository (http://fimi.ua.ac.be/). We also used IBM synthetic datasets, which were generated using the IBM Quest Dataset Generator [22]. For our experiments, the generated data ranges from 2 M to 10 M transactions with an average transaction length of 10 items from a domain of 1 K items. As the above real-life and synthetic datasets originally contained only precise data, we assigned to each item contained in every transaction an existential probability from the range (0, 1.0]. All experiments were run using either (i) a single machine with an Intel Core i7 4-core processor (1.73 GHz) and 8 GB of main memory running a 64-bit Windows 7 operating system; or (ii) the Amazon Elastic Compute Cloud (EC2) cluster—specifically, 11 High-Memory Extra Large (m2.xlarge) computing nodes (http://aws.amazon.com/ec2/). We implemented existing mining framework [35,39,40], UF-growth [32], tube-growth [33], BLIMP-growth [34], and our data analytic algorithm MrCloud all in the Java programming language. The stock version of Apache Hadoop 0.20.0 was used.

First, we demonstrated the functionality and capability of MrCloud by using (i) a database consisting of items all with existential probability value of 1.0 (indicating that all items are definitely present in the database); and (ii) a user-specified AM constraint. Experimental results show that, in terms of accuracy, our data analytic algorithm returned the same collection of valid frequent patterns as those returned by the existing mining framework [35,39,40] for finding valid frequent patterns from precise data. Note that, in terms of flexibility, MrCloud is not confined to finding valid frequent patterns from a database in which existential probability values of all items are 1.0. MrCloud is capable of finding valid frequent patterns from any database, in which existential probability values of all items are ranging from 0 to 1.0.

Moreover, we also experimented with (i) an uncertain database; and (ii) a user-specified AM constraint with 100% selectivity (so that every item is selected). Experimental results show that, in terms of accuracy, MrCloud returned the same collection of frequent patterns as those returned by UF-growth [32], tube-growth [33] and BLIMP-growth [34]. Note that, in terms of flexibility, MrCloud is not confined to handling AM constraints with 100% selectivity. MrCloud is capable of handling AM constraints with any selectivity.

Afterwards, we demonstrated the efficiency of MrCloud. Figure 1 shows that MrCloud took much shorter runtimes than the runtimes required by the existing UF-growth algorithm [32] when handling AM constraints with 100% selectivity because UF-growth was not designed to handle different selectivity of constraints. Hence, for a fair comparison, we used 100% selectivity for this experiment. We will show in Figure 2 how the runtimes for MrCloud decreased when the selectivity increased (i.e., fewer patterns were selected). For the current experiment, MrCloud was run in the aforementioned EC2 cluster. As a MapReduce-based algorithm, MrCloud takes advantage of all 11 nodes in the EC2 cluster. In contrast, as a non-MapReduce-based algorithm, UF-growth was run on a single machine (i.e., does not take advantage of multiple nodes.) This explains why MrCloud is faster than UF-growth. Moreover, the figure shows the scalability of MrCloud. When the number of transactions in the IBM synthetic dataset increased, the runtimes required by both MrCloud and UF-growth also increased. However, MrCloud required significantly lower runtimes than UF-growth. The same comments apply to other tested datasets (e.g., real-life accidents, connect4, and mushroom datasets).

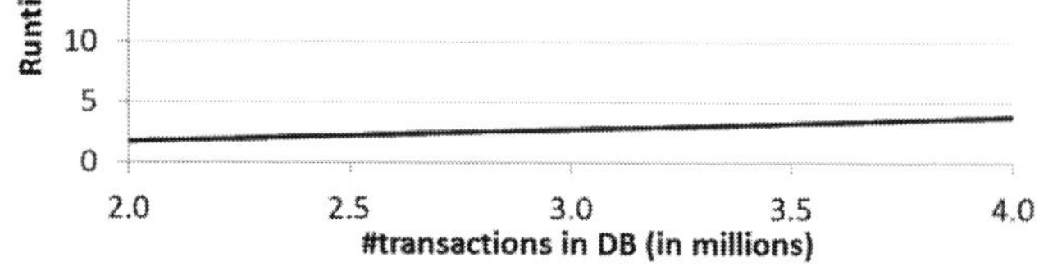

Figure 1. Runtime vs. #transactions.

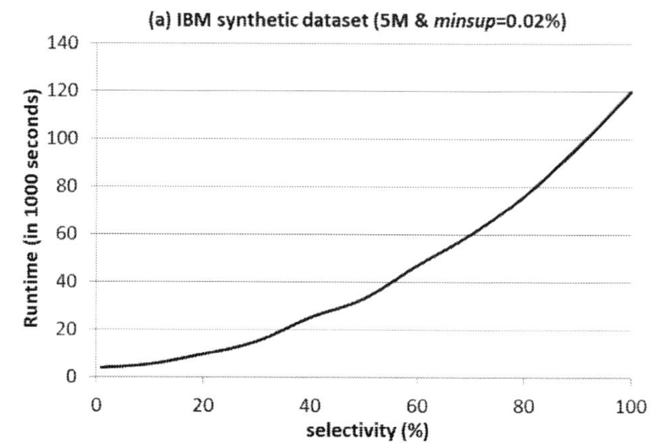

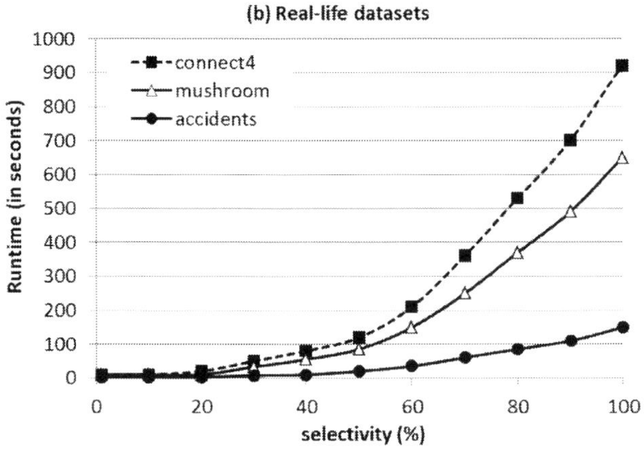

Figure 2. Runtime vs. selectivity on (a) synthetic dataset; and (b) real-life datasets.

Figure 2a shows the benefits of constraint pushing in the big data mining process than applying constraint pushing as a post-processing step in the IBM synthetic dataset, while Figure 2b shows those for the three real-life accidents, connect4, and mushroom datasets. Both figures show that, when selectivity decreased (i.e., fewer frequent patterns satisfy the constraints), runtimes also decreased, because (i) fewer pairs were returned by the map function; (ii) fewer pairs were shuffled and sorted by the reduce function; and/or (iii) fewer constraint checks were performed.

Figure 3 shows that MrCloud led to high speedup (e.g., more than 7 times for the IBM synthetic dataset) even with just 11 nodes when compared with UF-growth [32].

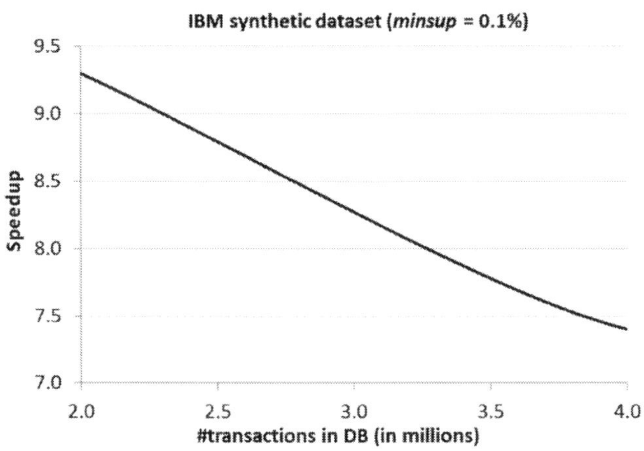

Figure 3. Speedup vs. #transactions.

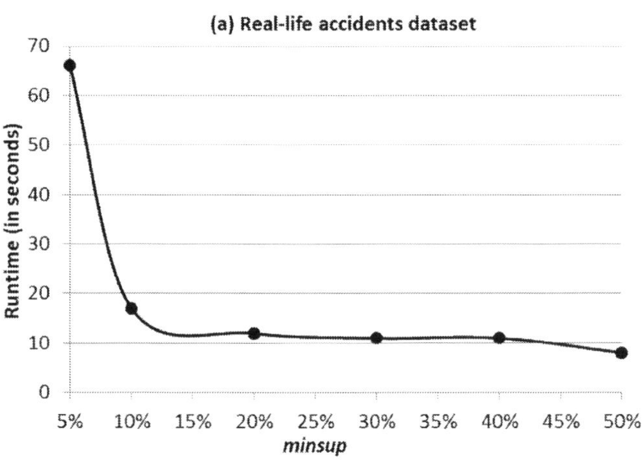

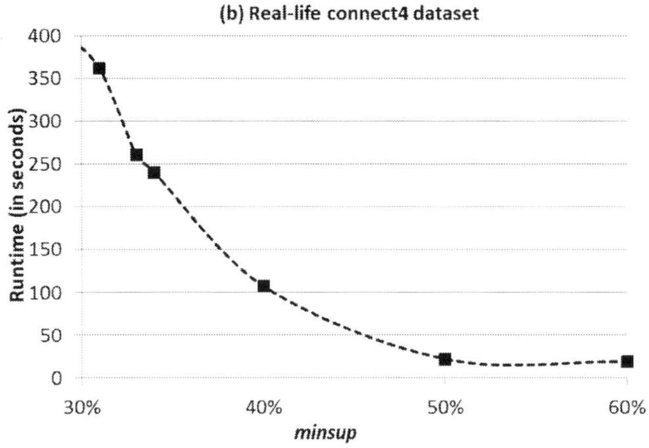

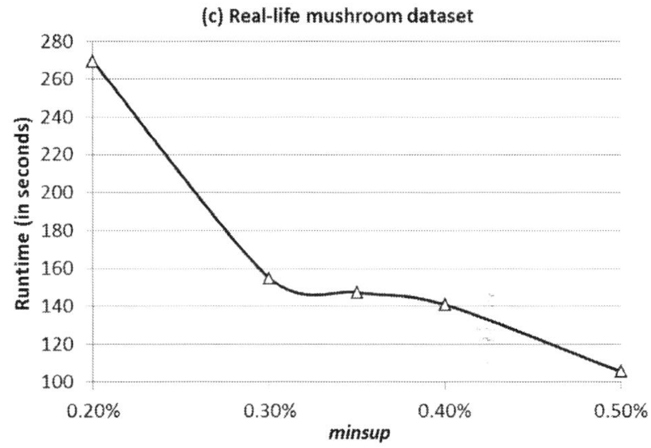

Figure 4. Runtime vs. minsup on (a) accidents; (b) connect4; and (c) mushroom datasets.

Figure 4a shows the efficiency of MrCloud for the real-life accidents dataset: The runtimes of MrCloud decreased when the user-specified minsup increased. Consistent results are shown on Figure 4b and Figure 4c for the real-life connect4 and mushroom datasets, respectively.

CONCLUSIONS

Big data are everywhere. Existing big data analytic algorithms discover frequent patterns from precise databases. However, there are situations in which data are uncertain. As items in each transaction of these uncertain data are usually associated with existential probabilities expressing the likelihood of these items to be present in the transaction, the corresponding search space for uncertain data is much larger than that for from precise data. This matter is worsened when we are dealing with uncertain big data. Furthermore, in many real-life applications, users may be interested in only a tiny portion of this large search space. To avoid wasting lots of time and space in first discovering all frequent patterns and then pruning uninteresting ones at a post-processing step, we presented in this article a data analytic algorithm called MrCloud that manages uncertain big data, allows users to query these uncertain big data by expressing their interest, and processes the user-specified query by using the MapReduce model in cloud environments. As an output, MrCloud discovers from uncertain big data all and only those patterns that are interesting to the users. Experimental results show the effectiveness of our data analytic algorithm for managing, querying, and processing uncertain big data in cloud environments.

ACKNOWLEDGMENTS

This project is partially supported by Natural Sciences and Engineering Research Council of Canada (NSERC) and the University of Manitoba.

AUTHOR CONTRIBUTIONS

Fan Jiang conducted this research project under the academic supervision of Carson K. Leung. Both of them contributed substantially to the work reported.

REFERENCES

1. Cuzzocrea, A.; Saccà, D.; Ullman, J.D. Big Data: A Research Agenda. In Proceedings of the 17th International Database Engineering & Applications Symposium (IDEAS), Barcelona, Spain, 9–11 October 2013; pp. 198–203.
2. Kejariwal, A. Big Data Challenges: A Program Optimization Perspective. In Proceedings of the Second International Conference on Cloud and Green Computing (CGC), Xiangtan, China, 1–3 November 2012; pp. 702–707.
3. Madden, S. From Databases to Big Data. IEEE Int. Comput. 2012, 16, 4–6.
4. Cuzzocrea, A.; Bellatreche, L.; Song, I.-Y. Data Warehousing and OLAP over Big Data: Current Challenges and Future Research Directions. In Proceedings of the 16th International Workshop on Data Warehousing and OLAP (DOLAP), San Francisco, CA, USA, 28 October 2013; pp. 67–70.
5. Jiang, F.; Kawagoe, K.; Leung, C.K. Big Social Network Mining for "Following" Patterns. In Proceedings of the Eighth International C* Conference on Computer Science & Software Engineering (C3S2E), Yokohama, Japan, 13–15 July 2015; pp. 28–37.
6. Kawagoe, K.; Leung, C.K. Similarities of Frequent Following Patterns and Social Entities. Proced. Comput. Sci.2015, 60, 642–651.
7. Leung, C.K.; Jiang, F. Big Data Analytics of Social Networks for the Discovery of "Following" Patterns. In Proceedings of the 17th International Conference on Big Data Analytics and Knowledge Discovery (DaWaK), Valencia, Spain, 1–4 September 2015; pp. 123–135.
8. Ting, H.-F.; Lee, L.-K.; Chan, H.-L.; Lam, T.W. Approximating Frequent Items in Asynchronous Data Stream over a Sliding Window. Algorithms 2011, 4, 200–222.
9. Kumar, A.; Niu, F.; Ré, C. Hazy: Making It Easier to Build and Maintain Big-Data Analytics. Commun. ACM2013, 56, 40–49.
10. Leung, C.K.; Hayduk, Y. Mining Frequent Patterns from Uncertain Data with MapReduce for Big Data Analytics. In Proceedings of the 18th International Conference on Database Systems for Advanced Applications (DASFAA), Part I, Wuhan, China, 22–25 April 2013; pp. 440–455.
11. Leung, C.K.; Jiang, F. A Data Science Solution for Mining Interesting Patterns from Uncertain Big Data. In Proceedings of the IEEE Fourth International Conference on Big Data and Cloud Computing (BDCloud), Sydney, NSW, Australia, 3–5 December 2014; pp. 235–242.
12. Leung, C.K.; MacKinnon, R.K. Reducing the Search Space for Big Data Mining for Interesting Patterns from Uncertain Data. In Proceedings of the 2014 IEEE International Congress on Big Data (BigData Congress), Anchorage, AK, USA, 27 June –2 July 2014; pp. 315–322.
13. Dean, J.; Ghemawat, S. MapReduce: Simplified Data Processing on Large Clusters. Commun. ACM 2008, 51, 107–113.
14. Cuzzocrea, A.; Leung, C.K.; MacKinnon, R.K. Mining Constrained Frequent Itemsets from Distributed Uncertain Data. Future Generation Comput. Syst. 2014, 37, 117–126.
15. Leung, C.K.; MacKinnon, R.K.; Jiang, F. Distributed Uncertain Data Mining for Frequent Patterns Satisfying Anti-Monotonic Constraints. In Proceedings of the IEEE 28th International Conference on Advanced Information Networking and Applications (AINA) Workshops, Victoria, BC, Canada, 13–16 May 2014; pp. 1–6.
16. Zaki, M.J. Parallel and Distributed Association Mining: A Survey. IEEE Concurr. 1999, 7, 14–25.
17. Ibrahim, A.; Jin, H.; Yassin, A.; Zou, D. Towards Privacy Preserving Mining over Distributed Cloud Databases. In Proceedings of the Second International Conference on Cloud and Green Computing (CGC), Xiangtan, China, 1–3 November 2012; pp. 130–136.
18. Ismail, L.; Zhang, L. Modeling and Performance Analysis to Predict the Behavior of a Divisible Load Application in a Cloud Computing Environment. Algorithms 2012, 5, 289–303.
19. Wang, L.; Wang, Y.; Xie, Y. Implementation of a Parallel Algorithm Based on a Spark Cloud Computing Platform. Algorithms 2015, 8, 407–414.
20. Alvi, A.K.; Zulkernine, M. A Natural Classification Scheme for Software Security Patterns. In Proceedings of the IEEE Ninth International Conference on Dependable, Autonomic and Secure Computing (DASC), Sydney, NSW, Australia, 12–14 December 2011; pp. 113–120.
21. Meng, Q.; Kennedy, P.J. Determining the Number of Clusters in Co-Authorship Networks Using Social Network Theory. In Proceedings of the Second International Conference on Cloud and Green Computing (CGC), Xiangtan, China, 1–3 November 2012; pp. 337–343.
22. Agrawal, R.; Srikant, R. Fast Algorithms for Mining Association Rules. In Proceedings of the 20th International Conference on Very Large Data Bases (VLDB), Santiago de Chile, Chile, 12–15 September 1994; pp. 487–499.
23. Fariha, A.; Ahmed, C.F.; Leung, C.K.; Samiullah, M.; Pervin, S.; Cao, L. A New Framework for Mining Frequent Interaction Patterns from Meeting Databases. Eng. Appl. Artif. Intell. 2015, 45, 103–118.
24. Cameron, J.J.; Cuzzocrea, A.; Jiang, F.; Leung, C.K. Frequent Pattern Mining from Dense Graph Streams. In

Proceedings of the Workshops of the EDBT/ICDT 2014 Joint Conference, Athens, Greece, 28 March 2014; pp. 240–247.

25. Chorley, M.J.; Colombo, G.B.; Allen, S.M.; Whitaker, R.M. Visiting Patterns and Personality of Foursquare Users. In Proceedings of the IEEE Third International Conference on Cloud and Green Computing (CGC), Karlsruhe, Germany, 30 September–2 October 2013; pp. 271–276.
26. Cuzzocrea, A.; Jiang, F.; Lee, W.; Leung, C.K. Efficient Frequent Itemset Mining from Dense Data Streams. In Proceedings of the 16th Asia-Pacific Web Conference (APWeb), Changsha, China, 5–7 September 2014; pp. 593–601.
27. Cameron, J.J.; Leung, C.K. Mining Frequent Patterns from Precise and Uncertain Data. Comput. Syst. J. 2011, 1, 3–22.
28. Cuzzocrea, A.; Furfaro, F.; Saccà, D. Hand-OLAP: A System for Delivering OLAP Services on Handheld Devices. In Proceedings of the Sixth International Symposium on Autonomous Decentralized Systems (ISADS), Pisa, Italy, 9–11 April 2003; pp. 80–87.
29. Leung, C.K.; MacKinnon, R.K. Balancing Tree Size and Accuracy in Fast Mining of Uncertain Frequent Patterns. In Proceedings of the 17th International Conference on Big Data Analytics and Knowledge Discovery (DaWaK), Valencia, Spain, 1–4 September 2015; pp. 57–69.
30. Tong, W.; Leung, C.K.; Liu, D.; Yu, J. Probabilistic Frequent Pattern Mining by PUH-Mine. In Proceedings of the 17th Asia-Pacific Web Conference (APWeb), Guangzhou, China, 18–20 September 2015; pp. 781–793.
31. Tong, Y.; Chen, L.; Cheng, Y.; Yu, P.S. Mining Frequent Itemsets over Uncertain Databases. PVLDB 2012, 5, 1650–1661.
32. Leung, C.K.; Mateo, M.A.F.; Brajczuk, D.A. A Tree-Based Approach for Frequent Pattern Mining from Uncertain Data. In Proceedings of the 12th Pacific-Asia Conference on Knowledge Discovery and Data Mining (PAKDD), Osaka, Japan, 20–23 May 2008; pp. 653–661.
33. Leung, C.K.; MacKinnon, R.K.; Tanbeer, S.K. Fast Algorithms for Frequent Itemset Mining from Uncertain Data. In Proceedings of the IEEE 14th International Conference on Data Mining (ICDM), Shenzhen, China, 14–17 December 2014; pp. 893–898.
34. Leung, C.K.; MacKinnon, R.K. BLIMP: A Compact Tree Structure for Uncertain Frequent Pattern Mining. In Proceedings of the 16th International Conference on Data Warehousing and Knowledge Discovery (DaWaK), Munich, Germany, 2–4 September 2014; pp. 115–123.
35. Ng, R.T.; Lakshmanan, L.V.S.; Han, J.; Pang, A. Exploratory Mining and Pruning Optimizations of Constrained Associations Rules. In Proceedings of the 1998 ACM SIGMOD International Conference on Management of Data, Seattle, WA, USA, 2–4 June 1998; pp. 13–24.
36. Jiang, F.; Leung, C.K.; MacKinnon, R.K. BigSAM: Mining Interesting Patterns from Probabilistic Databases of Uncertain Big Data. In Proceedings of the PAKDD 2014 International Workshops, Tainan, Taiwan, 13–16 May 2014; pp. 780–792.
37. Lin, M.-Y.; Lee, P.-Y.; Hsueh, S.-C. Apriori-Based Frequent Itemset Mining Algorithms on MapReduce. In Proceedings of the ACM Sixth International Conference on Ubiquitous Information Management and Communication (ICUIMC), Kuala Lumpur, Malaysia, 20–22 February 2012.
38. Riondato, M.; DeBrabant, J.; Fonseca, R.; Upfal, E. PARMA: A Parallel Randomized Algorithm for Approximate Association Rules Mining in MapReduce. In Proceedings of the ACM 21st International Conference on Information and Knowledge Management (CIKM), Maui, HI, USA, 29 October–2 November 2012; pp. 85–94.
39. Lakshmanan, L.V.S.; Leung, C.K.; Ng, R.T. Efficient Dynamic Mining of Constrained Frequent Sets. ACM Trans. Database Syst. 2003, 28, 337–389.
40. Leung, C.K. Frequent Itemset Mining with Constraints. In Encyclopedia of Database Systems; Springer: New York, NY, USA, 2009; pp. 1179–1183.
41. Leung, C.K. Uncertain Frequent Pattern Mining. In Frequent Pattern Mining; Springer International Publishing: Cham, Switzerland, 2014; pp. 417–453.
42. Leung, C.K. Mining Frequent Itemsets from Probabilistic Datasets. In Proceedings of the Fifth International Conference on Emerging Databases (EDB), Jeju Island, South Korea, 19–21 August 2013; pp. 137–148.

CHAPTER 10

GENERATING REALISTIC LABELLED, WEIGHTED RANDOM GRAPHS

Michael Charles Davis[1], Zhanyu Ma[2], Weiru Liu[3], Paul Miller[3], Ruth Hunter[4], and Frank Kee [4]

[1]Organisation Européene pour la Recherche Nucléaire (CERN), Route de Meyrin 385, 1217 Meyrin, Switzerland

[2]Pattern Recognition and Intelligent Systems (PRIS) Lab, Beijing University of Posts and Telecommunications (BUPT), 100876 Beijing, China

[3]School of Electrical and Electronic Engineering and Computer Science, Queen's University Belfast, University Road, Belfast BT7 1NN, UK

[4]Centre for Public Health, Queen's University Belfast, University Road, Belfast BT7 1NN, UK

ABSTRACT

Generative algorithms for random graphs have yielded insights into the structure and evolution of real - world networks. Most networks exhibit a well - known set of properties, such as heavy - tailed degree distributions, clustering and community formation. Usually, random graph models consider only structural information, but many real - world networks also have labelled vertices and weighted edges. In this paper, we present a generative model for random graphs with discrete vertex labels and numeric edge weights. The weights are represented as a set of Beta Mixture Models (BMMs) with an arbitrary number of mixtures, which are learned from real - world networks. We propose a Bayesian Variational Inference (VI) approach, which yields an accurate estimation while keeping computation times tractable. We compare our approach to state - of - the - art random labelled graph generators and an earlier approach based on Gaussian Mixture Models (GMMs). Our results allow us to draw conclusions about the contribution of vertex labels and edge weights to graph structure.

INTRODUCTION

Network analysis is concerned with finding patterns and anomalies in real - world graphs, such as social networks, computer and communication networks, or biological and ecological processes. Real graphs exhibit a number of interesting structural and evolutionary properties, such as the formation of a giant component, heavy - tailed degree distribution, small diameter, shrinking diameter, and the Densification Power Law (DPL) [1, 2, 3, 4, 5].

Besides discovering network properties, researchers are interested in the mechanisms of network formation. Generative graph models provide an abstraction of how graphs form: if the model is accurate, generated graphs will obey the same properties as real graphs. Generated graphs are also useful for simulation experiments, hypothesis testing and making predictions about graph evolution or missing graph elements. Most generative models are for unlabeled, unweighted graphs [1, 3, 4, 6, 7], although a few models take discrete vertex labels into account [8, 9, 10].

In this paper, we develop a generative model for labelled, weighted graphs. Weights are commonly used to represent the number of occurrences of each edge: e - mails sent between individuals in a social network [11]; calls to a subroutine in a software call graph [12]; or people walking between a pair of sensors in a building access control network [13]. In

Citation: Michael Charles Davis, Zhanyu Ma, Weiru Liu, Paul Miller, Ruth Hunter, and Frank Kee. Generating realistic labelled, weighted random graphs, Algorithms 2015, 8(4), 1143 - 1174; DOI: 10.3390/a8041143

other applications, the edge weight may represent continuous values: donation amounts in a bipartite graph of donors and political candidates [11]; distance or speed in a transportation network [12]; or elapsed time to walk between the sensors in the building network [13]. In some cases, the weight has more than one dimension [12, 13].

Our main motivation for this work is to create "realistic" random graphs for evaluating graph mining algorithms. Some interesting graph datasets are very small; our approach can generate large graphs with the same characteristics as a smaller input graph. Random graphs can also ameliorate concerns about privacy. A second motivation is to better understand the laws governing the relationship between graph structure and attributes. Our experiments show the extent to which various graph properties are related to labels and weights.

Our model, Agwan (Attribute Graph: Weighted and Numeric), represents the distribution of edge weights as Beta Mixture Models (BMMs) which are learned from weighted input graphs. Learning BMM parameters using Bayesian estimation is analytically intractable. Numerical solutions to simulate the posterior distribution are available, but these incur high computational cost. In Section 3, we introduce an approximation to the prior/posterior distribution of the parameters in the beta distribution and propose an analytically tractable (closed - form) Bayesian approach to parameter estimation, based on the Variational Inference (VI) framework. Following the principles of VI and utilizing the relative convexity bound, the extended factorized approximation method is applied to approximate the distribution of the BMM parameters. In a fully Bayesian model where all the parameters of the BMM are considered as variables and assigned proper distributions, our approach can asymptotically find the optimal estimate of the parameters of the posterior distribution. In addition, the model complexity depends on the empirical distribution of the data. A closed - form solution is proposed to avoid the need for numerical methods in each iteration. Our approach avoids the drawback of overfitting, as in the conventional Expectation Maximization (EM) algorithm.

This paper is arranged as follows: Section 2 is an overview of generative graph models and approaches to estimating mixture model parameters; Section 3 presents Agwan, our generative model for weighted and numeric labelled graphs, including our algorithm for fitting Agwan's parameters to real input graphs. Section 4 gives an overview of the datasets used in the experiments, and outlines the statistical measures and tests used to evaluate the generated graphs. The experiments in Section 5 demonstrate that the vertex labels and edge weights of a graph can predict the graph structure with high accuracy. Conclusions are in Section 6.

RELATED WORK

Our understanding of the mathematical properties of graph structure was pioneered by Paul Erdős and Alfréd Rényi [3]. Graph formation is modelled as a Bernoulli process, parameterized by the number of vertices and a wiring probability between each vertex pair. While it has been essential to our understanding of component sizes and expected diameter, the Erdős - Rényi model does not explain other important properties of real - world graphs such as degree distribution, transitivity and clustering [2, 5].

Barabási and Albert's Preferential Attachment model [1] uses the "rich get richer" principle to grow graphs from a few vertices up to the desired size. The probability of an edge is proportional to the number of edges already connected to a vertex. This generates graphs with power - law degree distributions. A number of variants of Preferential Attachment have been proposed [2, 5]. Still, Preferential Attachment models lack some desired properties, such as community structure.

The RMat algorithm [6] solves the community structure problem with its recursive matrix approach. RMat graphs consist of 2^n vertices and E edges, with four probabilities a, b, c, d to determine in which quadrant of the adjacency matrix each edge falls. These parameters allow the specification of power - law or log - normal degree distributions; if $a = b = c = d$, the result will be an Erdős - Rényi graph.

Kronecker Graphs [7] fulfil all the properties mentioned above, as well as the DPL (Densification Power Law) and shrinking diameter effect. The model starts with an initiator matrix. Kronecker multipication is recursively applied to yield the final adjacency matrix of the desired size. This work synthesises the previous work in random graphs in a very elegant way and proves that RMat graphs are a special case of Stochastic Kronecker graphs.

The models above tend to have a small number of parameters and are analytically tractable, with simple and elegant proofs of the desired properties. However, graph labels are not taken into consideration. Stochastic models are another class of generative algorithm which may not be amenable to analytical proofs but can be fit to real - world labelled graphs and used to learn the properties of those graphs. Models in this category include the Stochastic Block Model [10] and Latent Space approaches [8].

The Multiplicative Attribute Graph (MAG) model [9] draws on both of the above strands of research. MAG is parameterized by the number of vertices, a set of prior probabilities for vertex label values and a set of affinity matrices specifying the probability of an edge conditioned on the vertex labels. The affinity matrices can be learned from real graphs using Maximum Likelihood Estimation [14]. [9] proves that Kronecker Graphs are a special case of MAG graphs, and that suitably - parameterized MAG graphs fulfil all the desired properties: log - normal or power - law degree distribution, small diameter, the existence of a unique giant component and the DPL. However, the MAG model can only generate unweighted graphs. We believe that our method, described in the next section, is the first generative model for labelled, weighted graphs.

The Agwan model requires a suitable probability distribution to model the edge weights accurately and efficiently. The Gaussian distribution is popular as it has an analytically tractable Probability Density Function (PDF); a weighted mixture of Gaussian components provides a reasonable approximation to any general probability distribution [15]. The resulting Gaussian Mixture Model (GMM) is quite flexible and is used extensively in statistical pattern recognition [16]. If the number of mixture components is known in advance, the GMM parameters can be estimated using EM (Expectation Maximization) [17]. However, if the number of mixtures is unknown, EM can result in over fitting.

The problem of knowing the "correct" number of components can be avoided by using a non - parametric model: the approach in [18] assumes an infinite number of components and uses VI (Variational Inference) to determine the optimal number for a given dataset. The variational algorithm can be accelerated for higher - dimensional data using a kd - tree [19].

In [20], the edge weight parameters are specified as a GMM. However, the Gaussian distribution may not be the best choice where the weight is a countable quantity representing the number of occurrences of an edge. In this case, the weights are bounded by $(0, +\infty)$, while the Gaussian distribution is bounded by $(-\infty, +\infty)$. Although the weights can be modelled as a GMM, a large number of mixture components are required to describe the data close to the boundary [21]. Alternatives to the GMM include the truncated GMM [21] and the BMM [22]. We investigate these options in this paper.

The most central task in modeling the data with a BMM is parameter estimation. Since the normalization constant (the beta function) in the beta distribution is defined as a fraction of integrals, it is difficult to obtain a closed - form expression for estimating the parameters. For maximum likelihood estimation of the BMM parameters, [23, 24] proposed an EM algorithm [25], with iterative numerical calculations in the maximization step. As with GMMs, the EM algorithm for BMM has some disadvantages: it can lead to over fitting when the mixture models are excessively complex; and the iterative numerical calculation in the maximization step (e.g., with the Newton - Raphson method) has a high computational cost.

For Bayesian estimation, we can formally find the prior distribution and the conjugate posterior distribution of the parameters of the beta distribution. However, this posterior distribution is still defined with an integration expression in the denominator such that the closed - form of the posterior distribution is analytically intractable. [22] proposed a practical Bayesian estimation algorithm based on the Gibbs sampling method, which simulates the posterior distribution approximately rather than computing it. This method prevents the over fitting problem but still suffers from high computational cost because of the Gibbs sampling, especially when the data is in a high - dimensional space. To overcome this problem, [26, 27] proposed a full Bayesian estimation method for parameter estimation in a BMM, where the VI framework was employed and an analytically tractable solution can be obtained. The proposed method facilitates the parameter estimation.

AGWAN: A GENERATIVE MODEL FOR LABELLED, WEIGHTED GRAPHS

In this section, we present our generative model, Agwan (Attribute Graph: Weighted and Numeric). The model is illustrated in Figure 1.

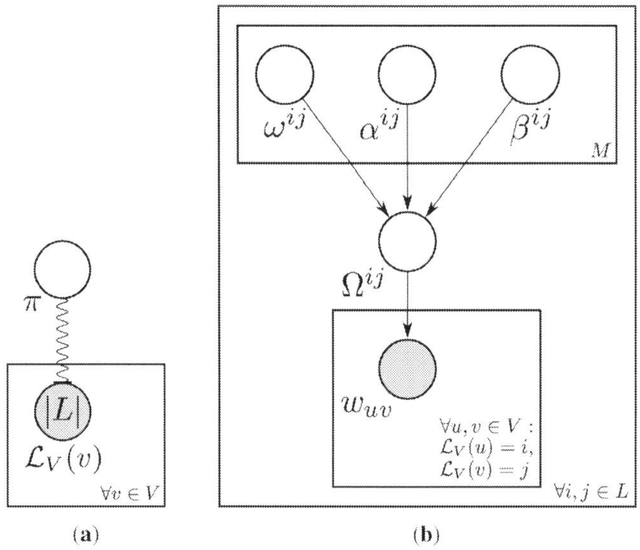

Figure 1. Agwan parameters. (**a**) Vertex Labels; (**b**) Edge Weights.

Consider a graph $G = (V, E)$ with discrete vertex label values drawn from a set L (Figure 1a). For each combination of vertex attributes $\langle i, j\rangle$, the corresponding mixture model Ω^{ij} parameterizes the distribution of edge weights, with an edge weight of 0 indicating no edge (Figure 1b). $u, v \in V$ are vertices and $w_{uv}, w_{vu} \in \mathbb{N}$ are edge weights. Edges $e \in E$ are specified as a 3 - tuple $\langle u, v, w_{uv}\rangle$. Thus, the Agwan model is parameterized by ϖ, the set of prior probabilities over L; and the set of edge weight mixture parameters $\Theta = \{\Omega^{ij} | i, j \in L\}$. For directed graphs, $|\Theta| = |L|^2|$ and we need to generate both w_{uv} and w_{vu}. For undirected graphs, $\Omega^{ij} = \Omega^{ji}$, so $|\Theta| = O(|L|^2/2)$ and $w_{vu} = w_{uv}$.

Ω^{ij} is specified as a BMM:

$$\Omega^{ij} = \sum_{m=1}^{M} \omega_m^{ij} \cdot \mathrm{Beta}(a_m^{ij}, b_m^{ij}) \tag{1}$$

where ω_m^{ij} is the weight of each component; and $\mathrm{Beta}(a_m^{ij}, b_m^{ij})$ is the beta distribution with shape parameters (a_m^{ij}, b_m^{ij}). The PDF of the beta distribution is:

$$\mathrm{Beta}(x; a, b) = \frac{1}{\mathrm{beta}(a, b)} x^{a-1}(1-x)^{b-1},\ a, b > 0 \tag{2}$$

where *beta*(*a*, *b*) is the beta function $\mathrm{beta}(a, b) = \frac{\Gamma(a)\Gamma(b)}{\Gamma(a+b)}$ and $\Gamma(\cdot)$ is the gamma function defined as $\Gamma(z) = \int_0^\infty t^{z-1}e^{-t}dt$. As the support of the BMM is (0, 1), we use a constant s^{ij} to scale the data into this range before fitting the BMM parameters. During graph generation, we draw values from the BMM and multiply by s^{ij}.

We specify Ω^{ij} such that the weight of the first component

($m = 0$) encodes the probability of no edge: $\omega_0^{ij} = 1 - P(e_{ij})$, where $P(e_{ij})$ is the probability of an edge between pairs of vertices with labels $\langle i, j\rangle$ and is learned from the input graph. The weights of the BMM components ($m \in [1, M]$) are normalized by $P(e_{ij})$, so the weights of all the components form a probability distribution: $\sum_{m=0}^{M} \omega_m^{ij} = 1$.

Graph Generation

Algorithm 1 describes how to generate a random graph using Agwan(N, L, π, Θ). The number of vertices in the generated graph is specified by N. After assigning discrete label values to each vertex (lines 2–3), the algorithm checks each vertex pair $\langle u, v\rangle$ for the occurrence of an edge (lines 4–7). If there is an edge, we assign its weight from mixture component m (lines 8, 9). The generated graph is returned as $G = (V, E)$.

Algorithm 1 AGWAN Graph Generation

Require: N (no. of vertices), L (set of discrete label values), π (prior distribution over L), $\Theta = \{\Omega^{ij}\}$ (set of mixture models)

1: Create vertex set V of cardinality N, edge set $E = \emptyset$
2: **for all** $u \in V$ **do**
3:     Randomly draw discrete label $l_u \in L$ according to prior π
4: **for all** $u, v \in V : u \neq v$ **do**
5:     $i = l_u, j = l_v$
6:     Randomly draw mixture component m according to mixture weights ω^{ij}
7:     **if** $m \neq 0$ **then**
8:         Randomly draw edge weight w_{uv} from $s^{ij} \cdot \mathrm{Beta}(a_m^{ij}, b_m^{ij})$
9:         Create edge $e = \langle u, v, w_{uv}\rangle$, $E = E \cup \{e\}$

return $G = (V, E)$

Parameter Fitting

To create realistic random graphs, we need to learn the parameters π, Θ from a real - world input graph G. For each $i, j \in V$, the edge weights $W^{ij} = \{w_{ij}\}$ follow an unknown, arbitrary probability distribution. For each set of edge weights W^{ij}, we choose the scaling parameter $s^{ij} \geq \max_{W^{ij}}$, then estimate the BMM parameters for the empirical distribution $1s^{ij}/\cdot W^{ij}$, which has support (0, 1].

In this section, we describe the Bayesian estimation of BMMs within a VI framework, followed by our algorithms for Agwan parameter fitting.

The beta distribtion has a conjugate prior in the exponential family. The conjugate prior density function can be written as [15, 28]:

$$f(a, b) = \frac{1}{C(\alpha_0, \beta_0, \nu_0)} \left[\frac{\Gamma(a+b)}{\Gamma(a)\Gamma(b)}\right]^{\nu_0} e^{-\alpha_0(a-1)} e^{-\beta_0(b-1} \tag{3}$$

where α_0, β_0, ν_0 are free positive parameters and $C(\alpha_0, \beta_0, \nu_0)$ is a normalization factor such that $\int_0^\infty \int_0^\infty f(a, b)\,da\,db = 1$. Then, we obtain the posterior distribution of a, b as (with N independent and identically distributed (i.i.d.) scalar observations $X = \{x_1, \ldots, x_N\}$)

$$\begin{aligned} f(a, b|X) &= \frac{f(X|a, b) f(a, b)}{\int_0^\infty \int_0^\infty f(X|a, b) f(a, b)\,da\,db} \\ &= \frac{1}{C(\alpha_N, \beta_N, \nu_N)} \left[\frac{\Gamma(a+b)}{\Gamma(a)\Gamma(b)}\right]^{\nu_N} e^{-\alpha_N(a-1)} e^{-\beta_N(b-1)}\,da\,db \end{aligned} \tag{4}$$

where

$\nu_N = \nu_0 + N$, $\alpha_N = \alpha_0 - \sum_{n=1}^{N} \ln x_n$ and $\beta_N = \beta_0 - \sum_{n=1}^{N} \ln(1 - x_n)$. To avoid infinity in the practical implementation, we assign ε_1 to x_n when $x_n = 0$ and $1 - \varepsilon_2$ to x_n when $x_n = 1$, where ε_1 and ε_2 are slightly positive real numbers.

We introduce an approximation to both the conjugate prior and the posterior distributions of the beta distribution and attempt to solve the Bayesian estimation problem via the factorized approximation method. A distribution can be used as the factorized distribution of the true posterior distribution if the optimal solution to this factorized distribution has exactly the same form as its initialization. This requirement guarantees that the estimation works iteratively. With the non - negative property of the parameters in the beta distribution and assuming that *a* and *b* are statistically independent, we could use some well - defined distribution with support $(0, +\infty)$ to approximate the conjugate prior. One possible way is to assign the gamma distribution to *a* and *b* as:

$$f(a;\mu,\alpha) = \frac{\alpha^{\mu}}{\Gamma(\mu)} a^{\mu-1} e^{-\alpha a};\ f(b;\nu,\beta) = \frac{\beta^{\nu}}{\Gamma(\nu)} b^{\nu-1} e^{-\beta b} \tag{5}$$

The conjugate prior is then approximated as:

$$f(a,b) \approx f(a)f(b) \tag{6}$$

The same form of approximation applies to the posterior distribution as:

$$f(a,b|\mathbf{X}) \approx f(a|\mathbf{X})f(b|\mathbf{X}) \tag{7}$$

For each observation x_n, the corresponding $\mathbf{z}_n = [z_{n1}, \ldots, z_{nM}]^T$ is the indication vector defined with respect to the *M* components in the mixture model. One element of z_n will be equal to 1 and the rest equal to 0, to indicate which mixture component z_n belongs to. Denoting $Z = \{z_1, \ldots, z_N\}$ and assuming the indication vectors are independent given the mixing coefficients, the conditional distribution of *Z* given *P* is:

$$f(Z|P) = \prod_{n=1}^{N} \prod_{m=1}^{M} p_m^{z_{nm}} \tag{8}$$

Introducing the Dirichlet distribution as the prior distribution of the mixing coefficients, the probability function of *P* can be written as:

$$f(P) = Dir(p|c) = C(\mathbf{c}) \prod_{m=1}^{M} p_m^{c_m - 1} \tag{9}$$

where $C(\mathbf{c}) = \frac{\Gamma(\widehat{c})}{\Gamma(c_1)\cdots\Gamma(c_M)}$ and $\widehat{c} = \sum_{m=1}^{M} c_m$. We consider the observation xnxn and the unobserved indication vector z_n as the *complete* data. The conditional distribution of $X = \{x_1, \ldots, x_N\}$ and $Z = \{z_1, \ldots, z_N\}$ given the latent variables $\{A, B, P\}$ is:

$$\begin{aligned} & f(\mathbf{X},\mathbf{Z}|\mathbf{A},\mathbf{B},\mathbf{P}) \\ &= f(\mathbf{X}|\mathbf{A},\mathbf{B},\mathbf{P},\mathbf{Z})f(\mathbf{Z}|\mathbf{P}) \\ &= f(\mathbf{X}|\mathbf{A},\mathbf{B},\mathbf{Z})f(\mathbf{Z}|\mathbf{P}) \\ &= \prod_{n=1}^{N}\prod_{m=1}^{M}[p_m \mathbf{Beta}(\mathbf{x}_n|\mathbf{a}_m,\mathbf{b}_m)]^{z_{nm}} \end{aligned} \tag{10}$$

The algorithm for Bayesian estimation of a BMM model is presented in Algorithm 2.

Algorithm 2 Bayesian estimation of a Beta Mixture Model (BMM)

Require: Number of components M, initial parameters for the Dirichlet distribution, initial parameters (element-wise) $\alpha_0 > 0$, $\beta_0 > 0$, $\mu_0 > 0.6156$, $\nu_0 > 0.6156$. Select initial parameters such that $\mu_0/\alpha_0 > 1$ and $\nu_0/\beta_0 > 1$.

1: Initialise r_{nm} with k-means
2: Calculate the initial guess of $\bar{a}$ and $\bar{v}$ from $\alpha_0, \beta_0, \mu_0, \nu_0$
3: **repeat**
4: Update the hyperparameters c_m^*, μ_{lm}^*, α_{lm}^*, ν_{lm}^* and β_{lm}^*
5: **until** convergence
return the current estimated hyperparameters

After initialization (lines 1, 2), Algorithm 2 iterates until the current estimated model and the previous estimated model are sufficiently close (lines 3–5). The order of updating (line 4) does not matter, but each hyperparameter should be updated exactly once during each iteration.) The algorithm returns the current estimated hyperparameters at the last iteration, which are used to get the approximating posterior distribution. The joint posterior distribution of a_{lm}, b_{lm} (Equation (4)) is approximated by the product of two gamma distributions with parameters $\mu_{lm}^*, \alpha_{lm}^*$ and ν_{lm}^*, β_{lm}^* (Equations (5) and (7)).

Agwan parameter fitting is performed by Algorithm 3. First, we estimate the vertex label priors (lines 1–3); Next, we sample the edge weights for each possible combination of vertex label values (lines 5–10); The proportion of non - edges is used to estimate the weight of mixture 0 (line 10). We estimate each scaled BMM Ω^{ij} from the appropriate set of samples W_{ij} using Algorithm 2 as described above (lines 12–13). Finally, the mixture weights ω_m^{ij} are normalized so that they sum to 1 (line 14).

Algorithm 3 AGWAN Parameter Fitting

Require: Input graph $G = (V, E)$

1: $L = \{\text{discrete vertex label values}\},\ d = |L|$
2: Calculate vertex label priors, apply Laplace smoothing $\forall l \in L : P(l) = \frac{count(l)+\alpha}{N+\alpha d}$
3: $\pi =$ the normalised probability distribution over L such that $\sum_{i=1}^{d} P(l_i) = 1$
4: $\forall i, j \in L : W^{ij} = \emptyset$
5: **for all** $u, v \in V : u \neq v$ **do**
6:     $i = l_u, j = l_v$
7:     **if** $\langle u, v \rangle \in E$ **then**
8:         $W^{ij} = W^{ij} \cup \{w_{uv}\}$
9:     **else**
10:         Increment ω_0^{ij}
11: **for all** $i, j \in L$ **do**
12:     $\omega_0^{ij} = 1 - P(e_{ij} \text{ exists})$
13:     $s^{ij} = \max_{W^{ij}}$
14:     estimate Ω^{ij} from $1/s^{ij} \cdot W^{ij}$ using Algorithm 2
15:     Normalise all ω_m^{ij}
        return $\pi, \Theta = \{\Omega^{ij}\}$

Extending Agwan to Multiple Attributes

Agwan can be extended to multiple numeric edge labels by generalizing the concept of edge weight to K dimensions. In this case, the weight is parameterized as the multivariate beta distribution. For any random vector x consisting of K elements, the dependencies among the elements $x_1, \ldots, x_K$ can be represented by a mixture model, even if each specific mixture component can only generate vectors with statistically independent elements. Therefore, we define the multivariate BMM as:

$$f(x; P, A, B) = \sum_{m=1}^{M} p_m \cdot \mathbf{Beta}(x; a_m, b_m) = \sum_{m=1}^{M} p_m \cdot \prod_{k=1}^{K} \mathrm{Beta}(x_k; a_{km}, b_{km}) \tag{11}$$

where $x = \{x_1, \ldots, x_K\}$, $P = \{p_1, \ldots, p_M\}$, $A = \{a_1, \ldots, a_M\}$ and $B = \{b_1, \ldots, b_M\}$. a_m, b_m denote the parameter vectors of the mth mixture component and a_{km}, b_{km} are the (scalar) parameters of the beta distribution for element x_k. Using this representation, we can apply Algorithm 2 to K - dimensional edge weights.

EXPERIMENTAL SECTION

We evaluate our approach by comparing Agwan with the state - of - the - art in labelled graph generation, represented by the MAG model [9, 14]. Agwan and MAG parameters are learned from real - world graphs. We generate random graphs from each model and calculate a series of statistics on each graph. As MAG does not generate weighted graphs, we fixed the weight of the edges in the generated graphs to the mean edge weight from the input graphs. This ensures that statistics such as average vertex strength are maintained.

We used two datasets for the experiments. The first is a graph of "who exercises with whom" from a behavioral health study (Figure 2a, $|V| = 279$, $|E| = 1308$) [29]. Vertices represent participants and are labelled with 28 attributes denoting demographic information and health markers obtained from questionnaire data. Participants were tracked during periods of physical activity; when two people frequently register at the same sensor at the same time, an undirected edge is created, weighted with the number of mutual coincidences. Our second dataset is the "who communicates with whom" graph of the Enron e - mail corpus (Figure 2b, $|V| = 159$, $|E| = 2667$) [11]. Vertices are labelled with the job role of the employee. Edges are weighted with the number of e - mails exchanged between sender and recipient. As e - mail communications are not symmetric, edges in the Enron graph are directed. Both graphs exhibit a core - periphery structure which is typical of many real - world networks [7].

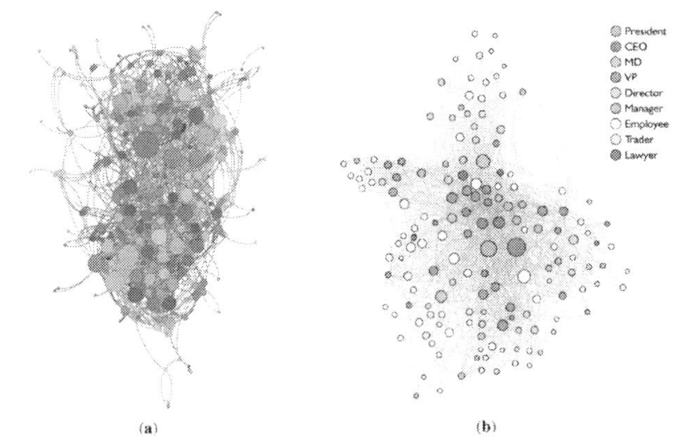

Figure 2. Input Graph Datasets, from (**a**) a health study and (**b**) the Enron e - mail corpus. (**a**) Undirected graph of who exercised with whom; (**b**) Directed graph of who e - mailed whom.

We evaluated Agwan against the following models:

Erdős - Rényi random graph (ER): The ER model $G(n, p)$ has two parameters. We set the number of vertices n and the edge probability p to match the input graphs as closely as possible. We do not expect a very close fit, but the ER model provides a useful baseline.

MAG model with real attributes (MAG - R1) The MAG model with a single real attribute has a set of binary edge probabilities, $\Theta = \{p^{ij}\}$ instead of a set of BMMs $\Theta = \{\Omega^{ij}\}$.

MAG model with latent attributes (MAG - L_x): The MAG model also allows for modelling the graph structure using latent attributes. The discrete labels provided in the input graph are ignored; instead MagFit [14] learns the values of a set of latent attributes to describe the graph structure. We vary the number of synthetic attributes x to investigate the relative contributions of vertex labels and edge weights to graph structure.

Agwan model with truncated GMMs: We compare our BMM model to an alternative approach using GMMs [20]. One drawback of using GMMs is that it is possible to draw edge weights $w_{uv} < 0$. To avoid negative edge weights, we implement a *tabula rasa* rule during graph generation, drawing new values from Ω^{ij} until $w_{uv} \geq 0$.

To evaluate the closeness of fit of each model, we use the following statistics:

Vertex Strength: For an unweighted graph, one of the most important measures is the degree distribution (the number of in - edges and out - edges of each vertex). Real - world graphs tend to have heavy - tailed power - law or log - normal degree distributions [2, 5]. For a weighted graph, we generalize the concept of vertex degree to vertex strength [30]:

$$s_u = \sum_{v \neq u} w_{uv} \quad (12)$$

We compare using the Complementary Cumulative Distribution Function (CCDF) of the strength of each vertex (both in - strength and out - strength in the case of the directed graph). For Cumulative Distribution Function (CDF) $F(x) = P(X \leq x)$, the CCDF is defined as $\bar{F} = P(X > x) = 1 - F(x)$. We show the unnormalized CCDFs in our plots; the normalized value can be obtained by integrating the area under the curve to 1. The CCDF of a power - law function will appear linear when plotted on a log - log scale, while the CCDF of a log - normal function will appear parabolic.

Spectral Properties: We use Singular Value Decomposition (SVD) to calculate the singular values and singular vectors of the graph's adjacency matrix, which act as a signature of the graph structure. In an unweighted graph, the adjacency matrix contains binary values, for "edge" or "no edge". In a weighted graph, the adjacency matrix contains the edge weights (with 0 indicating no edge). For SVD $U\Sigma V$, we plot the CCDFs of the singular values Σ and the components of the left singular vector U corresponding to the highest singular value.

Clustering Coefficients: the clustering coefficient C is an important measure of community structure. It measures the density of triangles in the graph, or the probability that two neighbors of a vertex are themselves neighbors [5]. We extend the notion of clustering coefficients to weighted, directed graphs by defining C_u, the weighted clustering coefficient for vertex u [30]:

$$C_u = \frac{[\mathbf{W}_u^{[\frac{1}{3}]} + (\mathbf{W}_u^T)^{[\frac{1}{3}]}]^3_{uu}}{2[d_u^{tot}(d_u^{tot} - 1) - 2d_u^{\leftrightarrow}]} \quad (13)$$

where W_u is the weighted adjacency matrix for u and its neighbors, W^T is the transpose of $\mathbf{W}$, d_u^{tot} is the total degree of a vertex (the sum of its in - and out - degrees) and $d_u^{\leftrightarrow}$ is the number of bilateral edges in u (the number of neighbors of u which have both an in - edge and an out - edge between themselves and u). The notation A_{uu} means the uth element of the main diagonal of A.

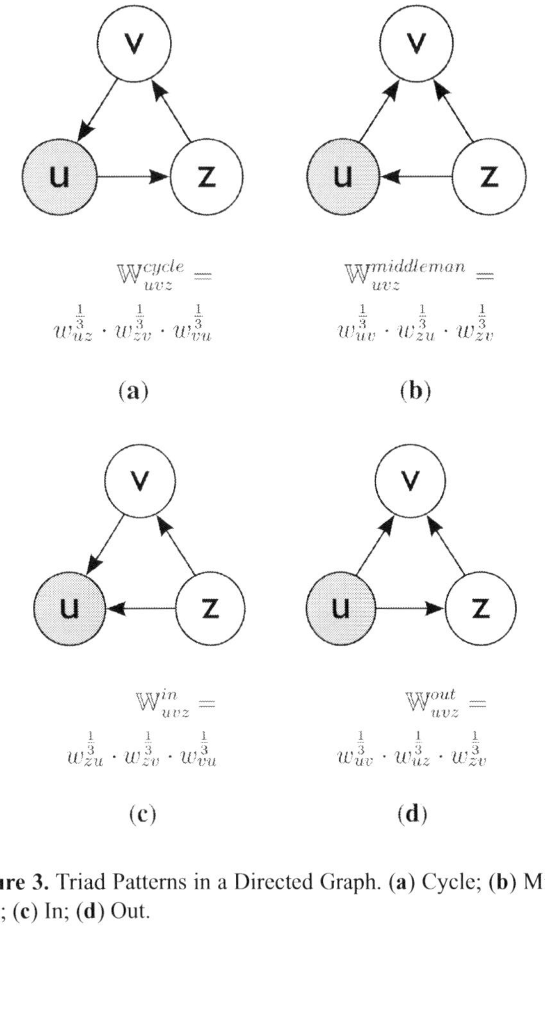

Figure 3. Triad Patterns in a Directed Graph. (**a**) Cycle; (**b**) Middleman; (**c**) In; (**d**) Out.

Triad Participation: Closely related to the clustering coefficient is the concept of triangle or triad participation. The number of triangles that a vertex is connected to is a measure of transitivity [5]. For the directed graphs, the triangles have a different interpretation depending on the edge directions. There are four types of triangle pattern [30], as shown in Figure 3. To generalize the concept of triad participation to weighted, directed graphs, we consider each of the four triangle types separately, and sum the total strength of the edges in each triad:

$$t_u^y = \sum_{v,z \in \mathbf{W}_u \setminus u} \mathbb{W}_{uvz}^y \qquad (14)$$

where $y = \{cycle, middleman, in, out\}$ is the triangle type and $\mathbb{W}_{uvz}^y$ is calculated as shown in Figure 3 for each triangle type y.

To give a more objective measure of the closeness of fit between the generated graphs and the input graph, we use a Kolmogorov - Smirnov (KS) test and the L2 (Euclidean) distance between the CCDFs for each statistic.

RESULTS AND DISCUSSION

In the experimental data, most of the edge weights follow a heavy - tailed distribution. The BMM achieves a very close fit with its primary mixture component (Figure 4a). The GMM would need several Gaussian components to achieve a similar fit. In practice the VI algorithm for GMMs [18] tries to fit to power law or log - normal distributions using a single Gaussian component, resulting in probability mass being assigned to the area x < 0, as shown inFigure 4a. This results in a fit that is not as close as the BMM (Figure 4b). To compensate for this effect, we used a truncated GMM for graph generation as discussed in Section 3.2.

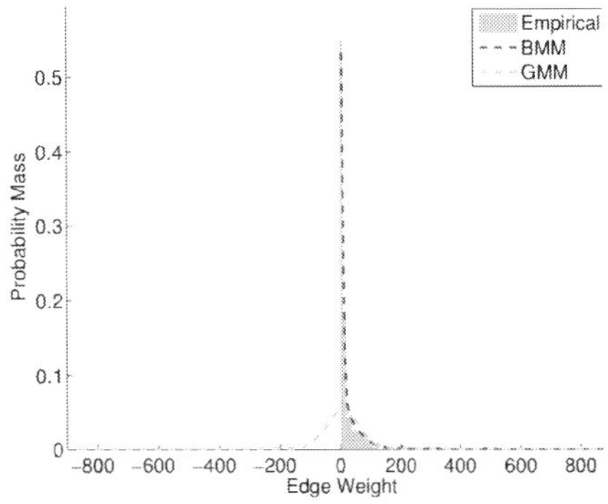

(a)

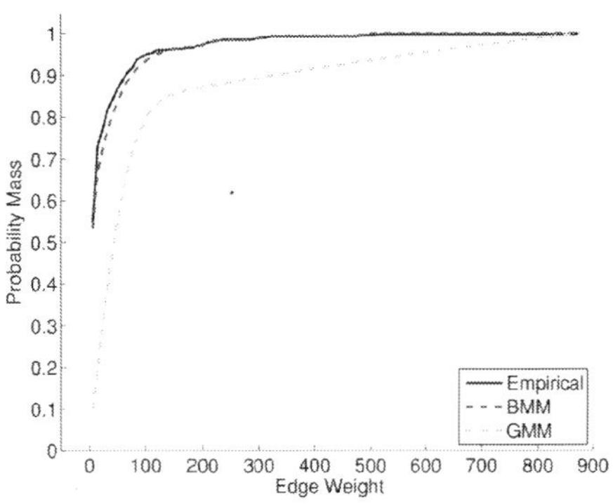

(b)

Figure 4. Fitting BMM and GMM models to edge weights. (**a**) Probability Mass Function; (**b**) Cumulative Distribution Function.

For our experiments, we generated 10 random graphs for each Agwan model. For each graph, we calculated the statistics for vertex strength, spectral properties, clustering and triad participation, as described in the previous section. We calculated the CCDFs for each set of statistics, and averaged the CCDF scores at each x - coordinate value across the 10 graphs, to smooth any random fluctuations. The plots of the averaged CCDFs for each model are shown in Figure 5, Figure 6, Figure 7, Figure 8, Figure 9, Figure 10, Figure 11, Figure 12.

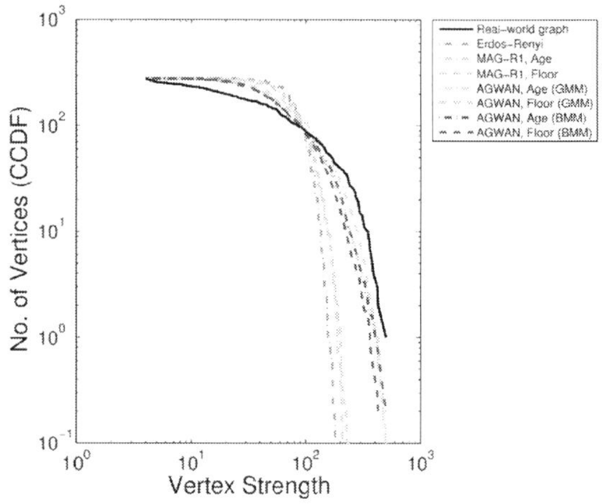

(a)

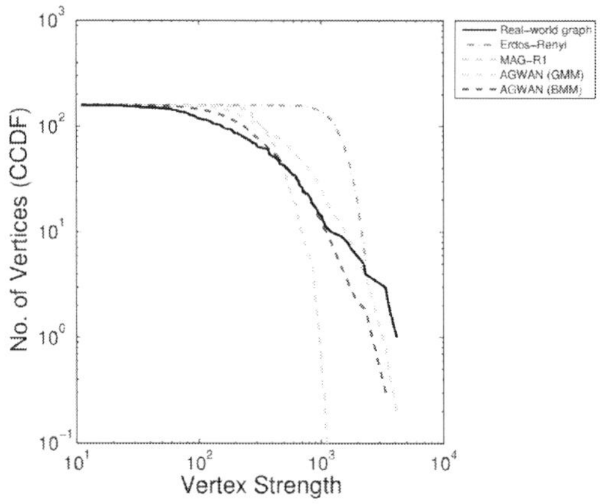

(b)

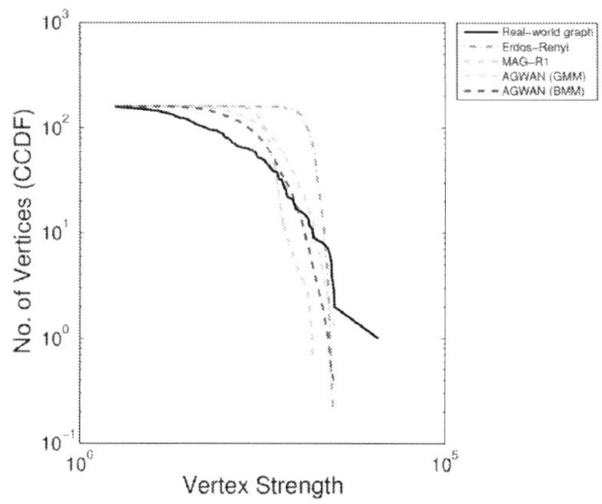

(c)

Figure 5. Vertex Strength Distribution—Real Attributes. (**a**) Undirected; (**b**) Directed (In - strength); (**c**) Directed (Out - strength).

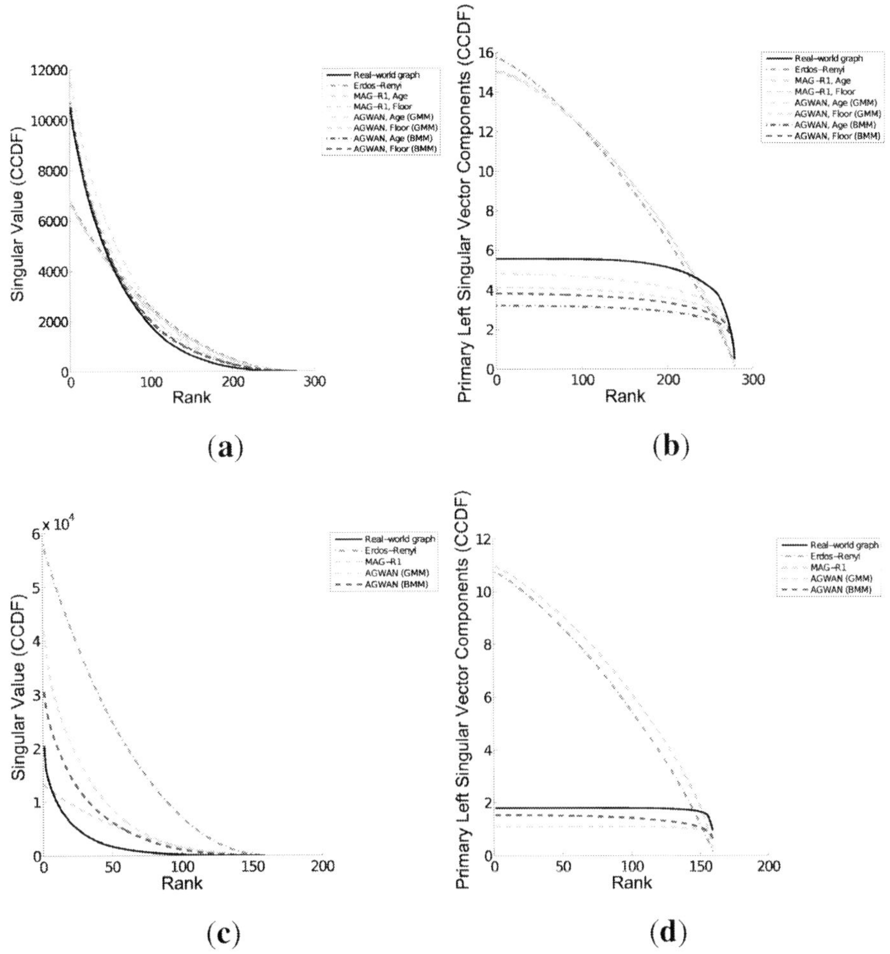

Figure 6. Spectral Properties—Real Attributes. (**a**) Undirected—Singular Values; (**b**) Undirected—Primary Left Singular Vector; (**c**) Directed—Singular Values; (**d**) Directed—Primary Left Singular Vector.

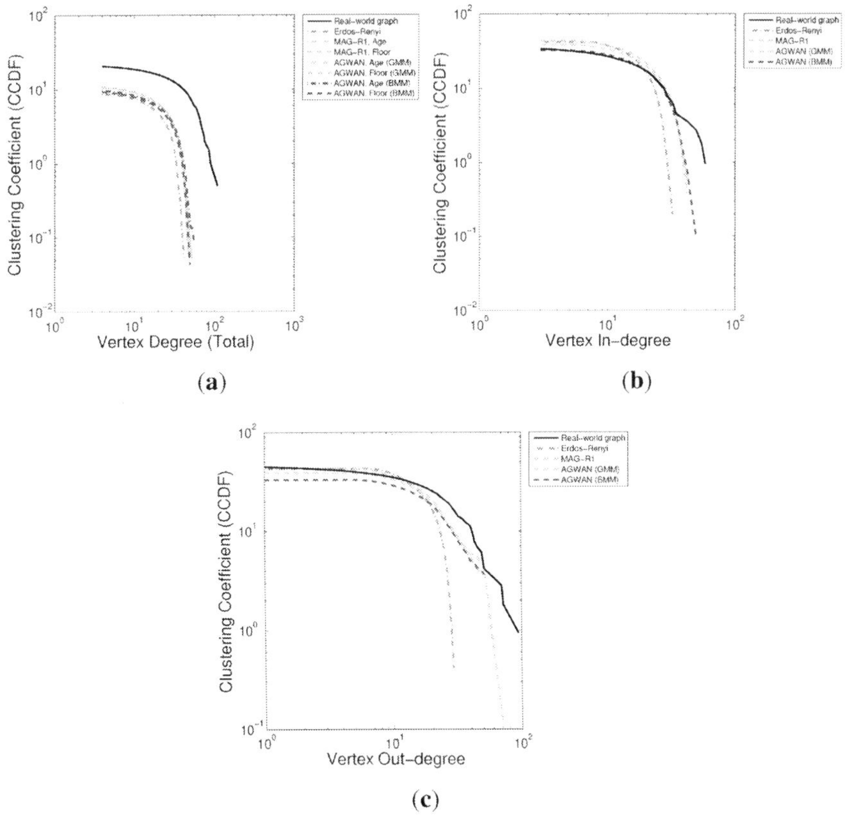

Figure 7. Clustering Coefficients—Real Attributes. (**a**) Undirected; (**b**) Directed (In - edges); (**c**) Directed (Out - edges).

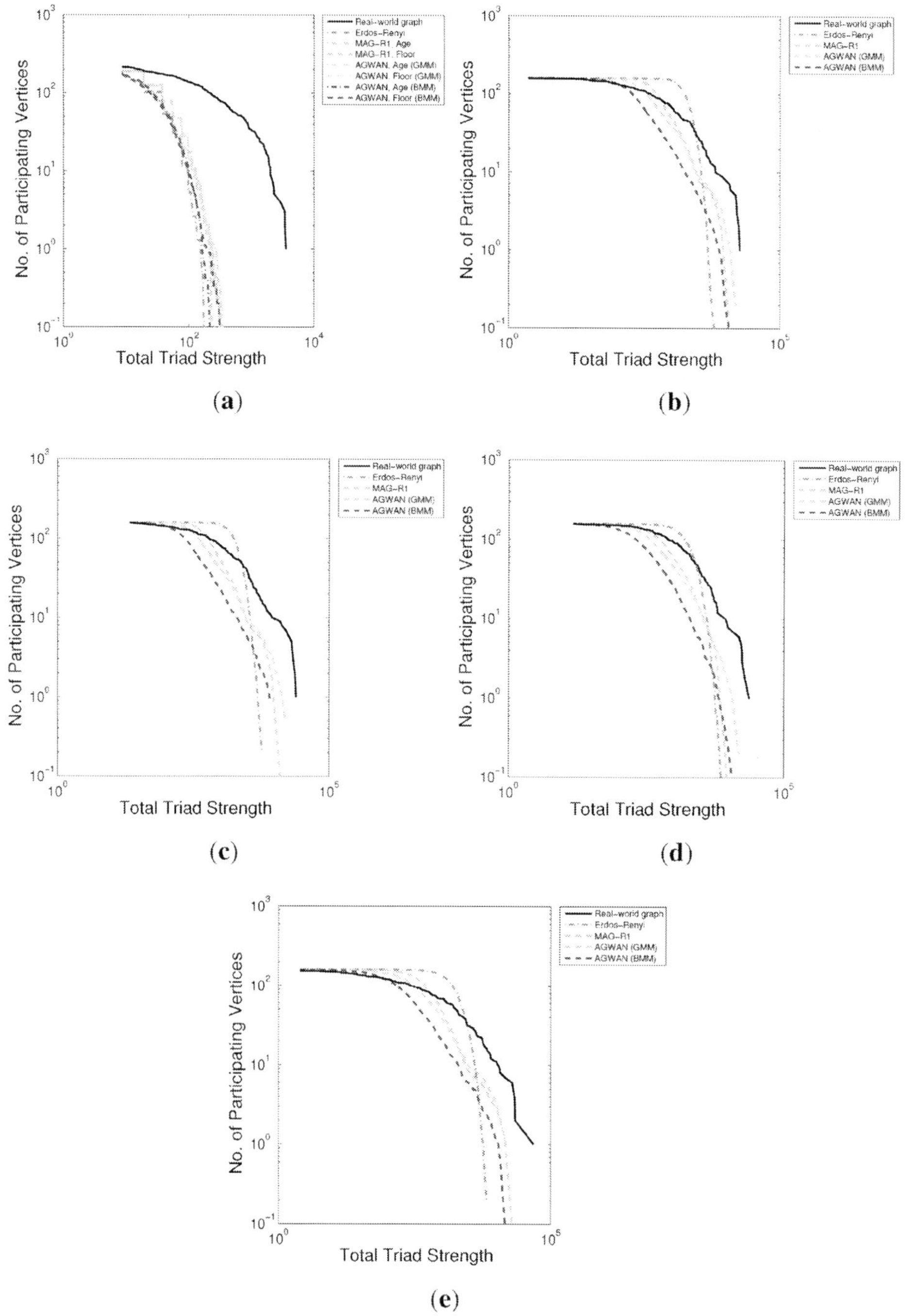

Figure 8. Triad Participation—Real Attributes. (**a**) Undirected; (**b**) Directed (Cycles); (**c**) Directed (Middlemen); (**d**) Directed (Ins); (**e**) Directed (Outs).

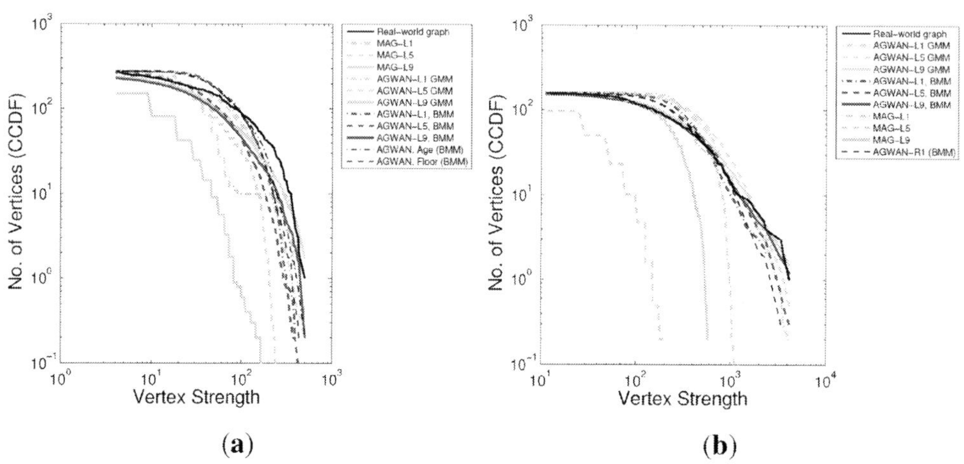

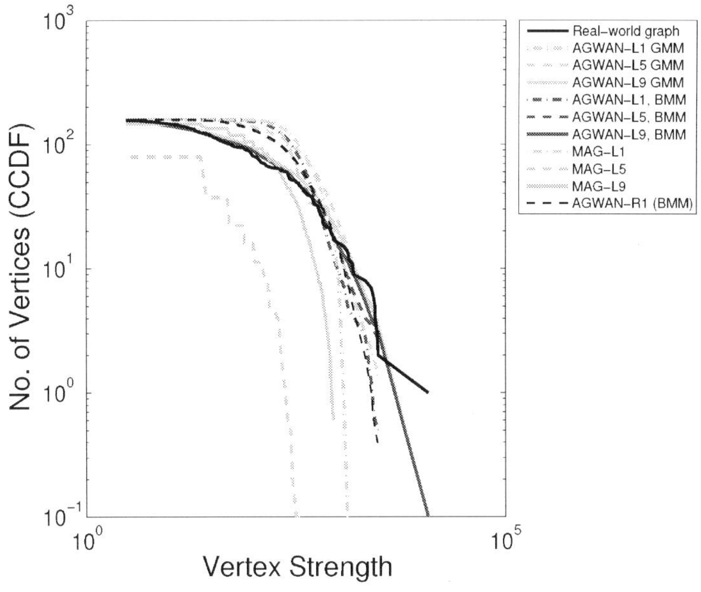

(c)

Figure 9. Vertex Strength Distribution—Synthetic Attributes. (**a**) Undirected; (**b**) Directed (In - strength); (**c**) Directed (Out - strength).

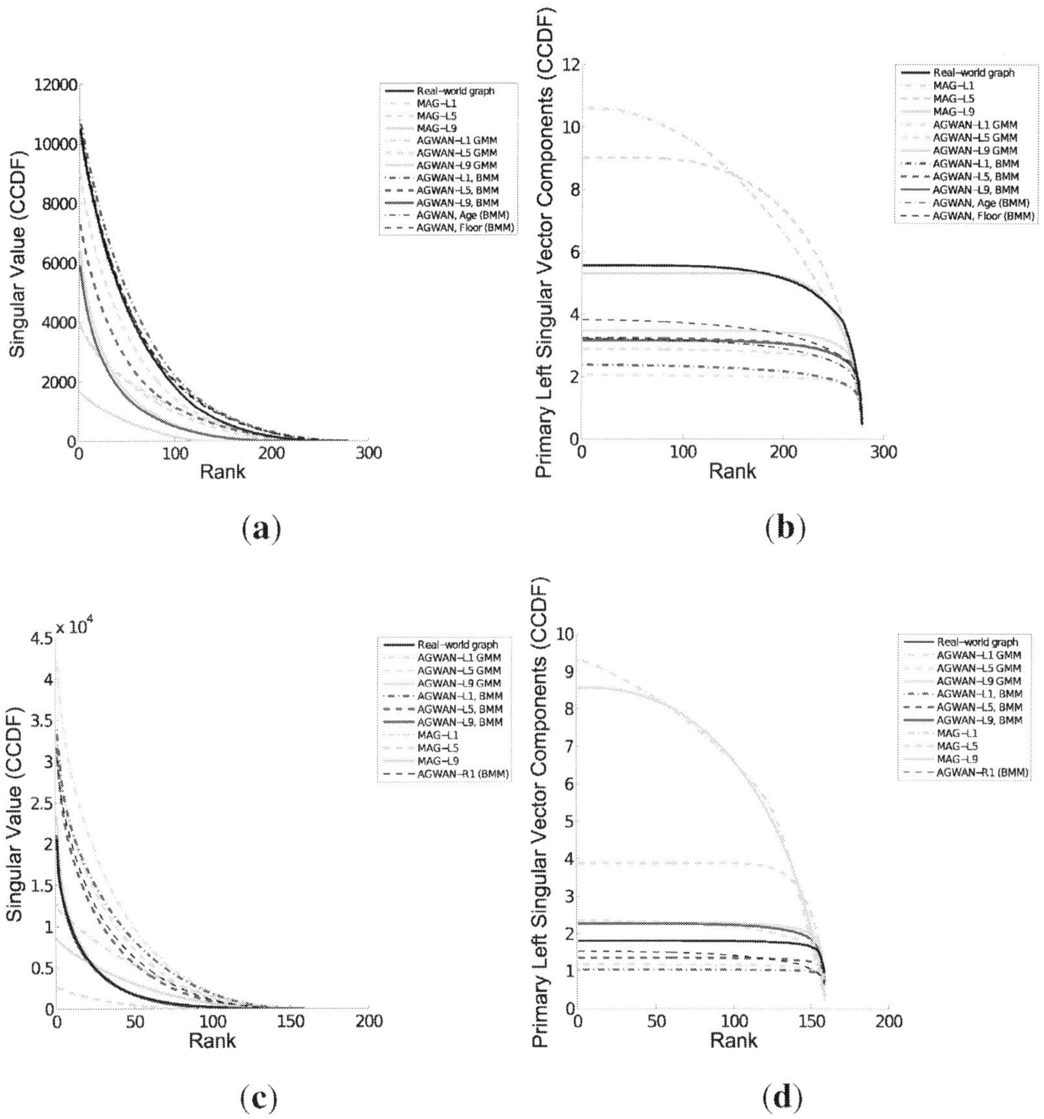

Figure 10. Spectral Properties—Synthetic Attributes. (**a**) Undirected—Singular Values; (**b**) Undirected—Primary Left Singular Vector; (**c**) Directed—Singular Values; (**d**) Directed—Primary Left Singular Vector.

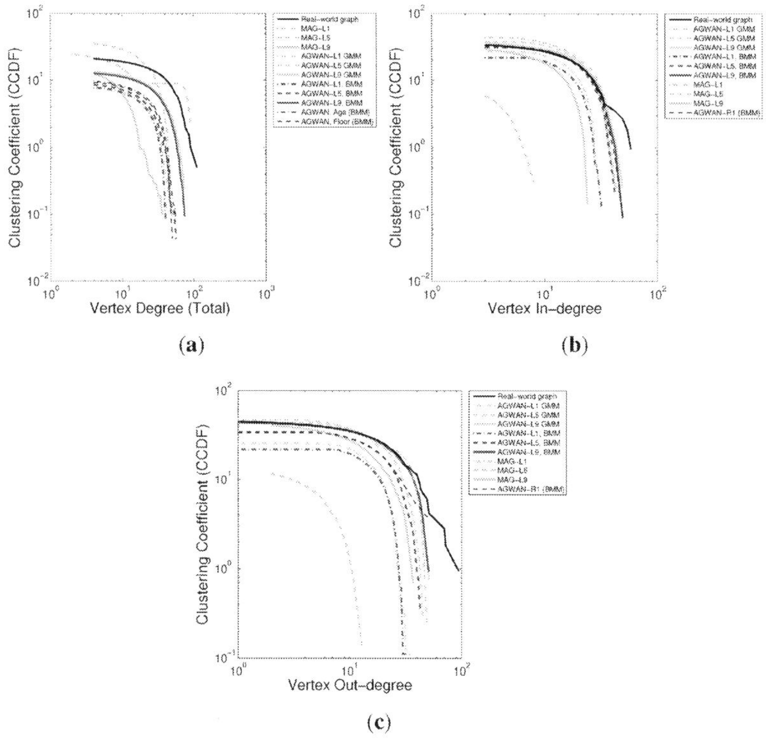

Figure 11. Clustering Coefficients—Synthetic Attributes. (**a**) Undirected; (**b**) Directed (In - edges); (**c**) Directed (Out - edges).

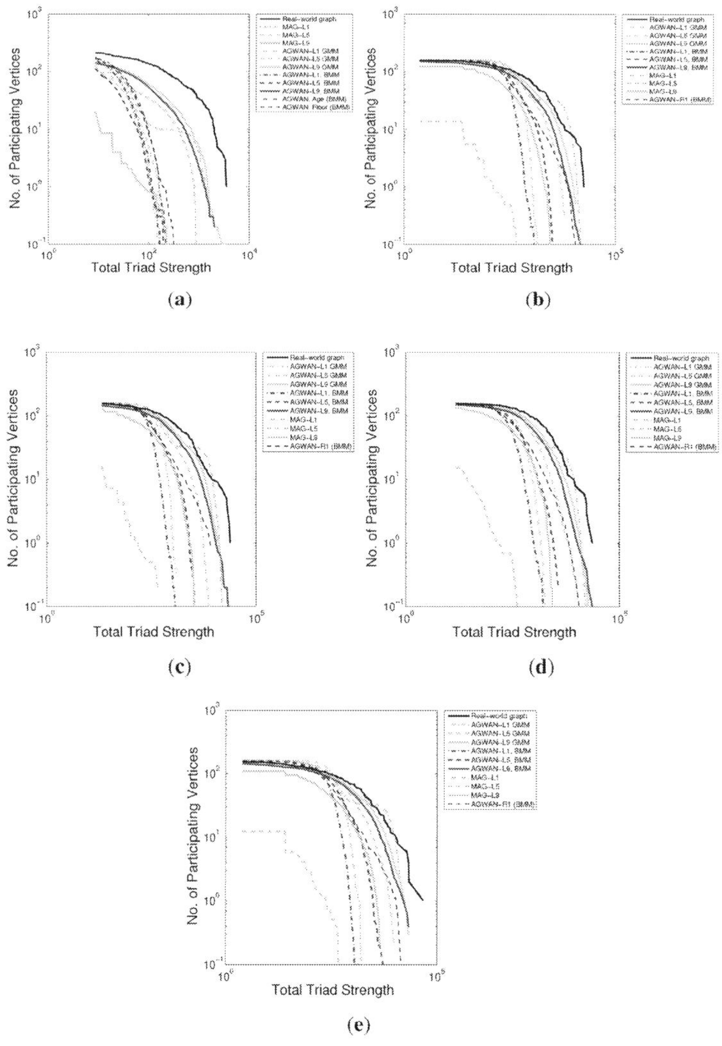

Figure 12. Triad Participation—Synthetic Attributes. (**a**) Undirected; (**b**) Directed (Cycles); (**c**) Directed (Middlemen); (**d**) Directed (Ins); (**e**) Directed (Outs).

Real Attributes

For the undirected graph (Health Study), we show results for two vertex attributes: Age and Floor (the building and floor number where the person works; people who work on the same floor were highly likely to exercise together). For the directed graph (Enron), there is one vertex attribute, the person's job role.

Vertex Strength (Figure 5): The graphs generated from Agwan have vertex strength distributions which map very closely to the input graphs. The graphs generated from MAG - R1 are better than random (ER), but the vertex strength distribution is compressed into the middle part of the range, with too few high - and low - strength vertices. This indicates that vertex strength depends on both the label distribution and the edge weight distribution; Agwan models both of these effectively.

Spectral Properties (Figure 6): The spectral properties of the Agwan graphs map very closely to the input graphs. The singular values follow the same curve as the input graphs. This is significant as it indicates that graphs generated with Agwan have similar connectivity to the input graph: the primary singular value has been shown to be the most significant measure of graph connectivity [2]. In contrast, MAG - R1 does not preserve the singular value curve, showing a linear relationship instead. MAG - R1 cannot model the singular vector components at all without taking the edge weights into account. These results show that the spectral properties of the graph are dependent on both the vertex label distribution and the edge weight distribution.

Clustering Coefficients (Figure 7): The accuracy of Agwan and MAG - R1 is similar. For the undirected graph, performance is little better than random. For the directed graph, Agwan gives reasonable performance for the low - degree vertices but drops away for the high - degree vertices. In all cases, the clustering is independent of the edge weight distribution. The accuracy of the results depends on which vertex attribute was chosen, implying that some attributes can predict community formation better than others. We hypothesize that cluster formation may in fact be (conditionally) independent of the vertex label values and may be better explained by triadic closure [5]: links are likely to form between two people who share a mutual friend, independently from their vertex attributes. The apparent dependency on vertex labels may be an artefact of the connection to the mutual friend, rather than the true explanation of why clustering asises. This aspect of network formation requires further investigation.

Triad Participation (Figure 8): Similar to clustering, triad participation appears to be dependent to some extent on vertex label values but independent of the edge weight distribution. We hypothesize that like clustering, the apparent dependency between vertex label and triad participation values may be due to triadic closure, which is not currently modelled by either MAG or Agwan.

Synthetic Attributes

The second set of experiments ignore the real attributes of the graph, replacing them with a set of randomly generated synthetic attributes. The purpose is to evaluate the relative contribution of the discrete vertex labels and numeric attributes to the graph structure. By reducing the number of numeric attributes to zero, we can evaluate the contribution of the numeric attributes in isolation.

We replaced the real labels in the input graph with a synthetic vertex attribute taking $2^0 \ldots 2^9$ values allocated uniformly at random, then learned the edge weight distributions using VI as normal. We compare our results with an alternate interpretation of the MAG model, which ignores the true attribute values from the input graph and represents attributes as latent variables, which are learned using a VI EM approach [14]. We also show Agwan with one real attribute for comparison.

Vertex Strength (Figure 9): Agwan with synthetic attributes significantly outperforms MAG for the accuracy of the vertex strength distribution, and has similar accuracy to Agwan - R1. Varying the number of synthetic attributes has a small effect on the accuracy. We conclude that vertex strength is dependent on both edge weight and vertex label distribution, but the edge weights play a more important role.

Spectral Properties (Figure 10): Agwan has a very close fit to the spectral properties of the input graphs. Varying the number of attributes has a moderate effect on the closeness of fit. On the undirected graph, MAG - L9 matches the singular vector very closely but performs poorly with the singular values; in general, MAG is a poor fit as the edge weight distribution is not taken into account. These results confirm that the spectral properties are dependent on both the vertex label distribution and the edge weight distribution, and the degrees of freedom of the vertex labels are important.

Clustering Coefficients (Figure 11): Agwan and MAG are both significantly more accurate using synthetic attributes than with real attributes. This (somewhat surprising) result implies that clustering is not closely related to the real attribute values. While real labels appear to be influenced by the (unobserved) process which gives rise to clustering, synthetic labels with more degrees of freedom can model it more accurately. We note that Agwan performs better where there are more degrees of freedom, while MAG performs better with few degrees of freedom (due to the independence assumption mentioned in Section 3.3). As before, clustering appears to be independent of the edge weight distribution.

Triad Participation (Figure 12): Similarly to clustering, Agwan and MAG are both more accurate using synthetic attributes than they were with real attributes. The effects of degrees of freedom of the synthetic attributes is even more pronounced than it was for clustering: Agwan - L9 has a good fit whereas Agwan - L1 is not so good. Edge weights appear to have little influence.

Graph Evolution

One of the goals of our model is to generate synthetic graphs which are larger than the input graph. We conducted experiments to measure how Agwan graph properties change as the number of vertices is increased. We generated sets of random graphs from the same model, with increasing numbers of vertices $N = \{10, 20, \ldots, 100, [1]200, \ldots, 3000\}$ vertices and measured the size of the giant component, the density and the diameter.

Giant Component: We measured the proportion of vertices in the largest component of the graph as the graph grows in size. Figure 13 shows that a giant component forms quickly, as in real graphs [5].

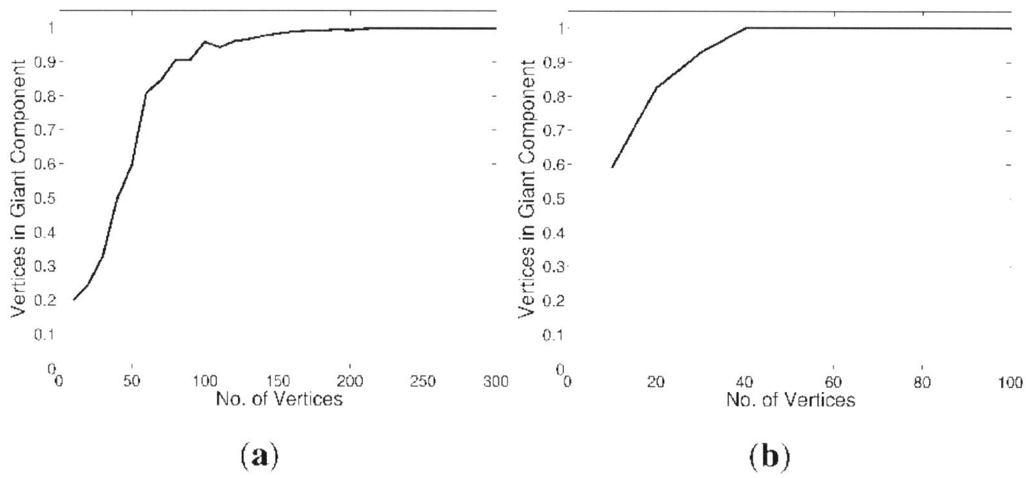

Figure 13. Giant Component. (**a**) Undirected; (**b**) Directed.

Densification Power Law: We measured graph densification as the ratio of the number of vertices to the number of edges as the graph grows in size. Figure 14 shows that Agwan graphs densify as they grow, as in real graphs. Real - world graphs have $e(t) \propto v(t)^{\gamma}$, with power - log exponent typically in the range (1, 2)(1, 2) [4]. When $\gamma = 1$, the rate of edge growth is linear in the number of vertices; $\gamma = 2$ means that on average, each vertex has edges to a constant fraction of all vertices. As Figure 14 shows, Agwan graphs have $\gamma \simeq 2$, because the model learns its edge probabilities independently from the size of the input graph. This means that Agwan overestimates density when generating graphs larger than the input graph.

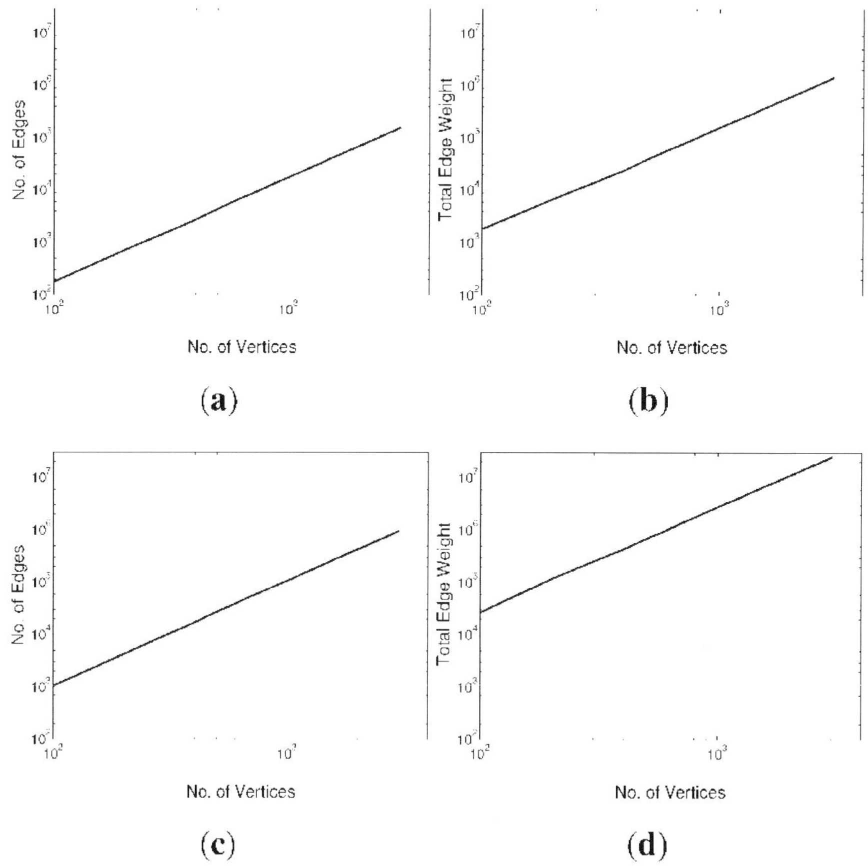

Figure 14. Densification Power Law. (**a**) Undirected, unweighted; (**b**) Undirected, weighted; (**c**) Directed, unweighted; (**d**) Directed, weighted.

Shrinking Diameter Effect (Figure 15): Agwan graphs exhibit the Small World Effect [5] and the unweighted diameter shrinks as the graphs grow, as in real graphs [4]. As the weighted diameter was calculated using Johnson's algorithm [31], which treats the edge weight as a cost function, we used the reciprocal of the edge weights. With this interpretation, the weighted diameter also shrinks as the graphs grow. It is interesting to note that the weighted diameters decay following a power law (with exponent $\gamma = -0.72$ for the undirected graph and $\gamma = -0.65$ for the directed graph).

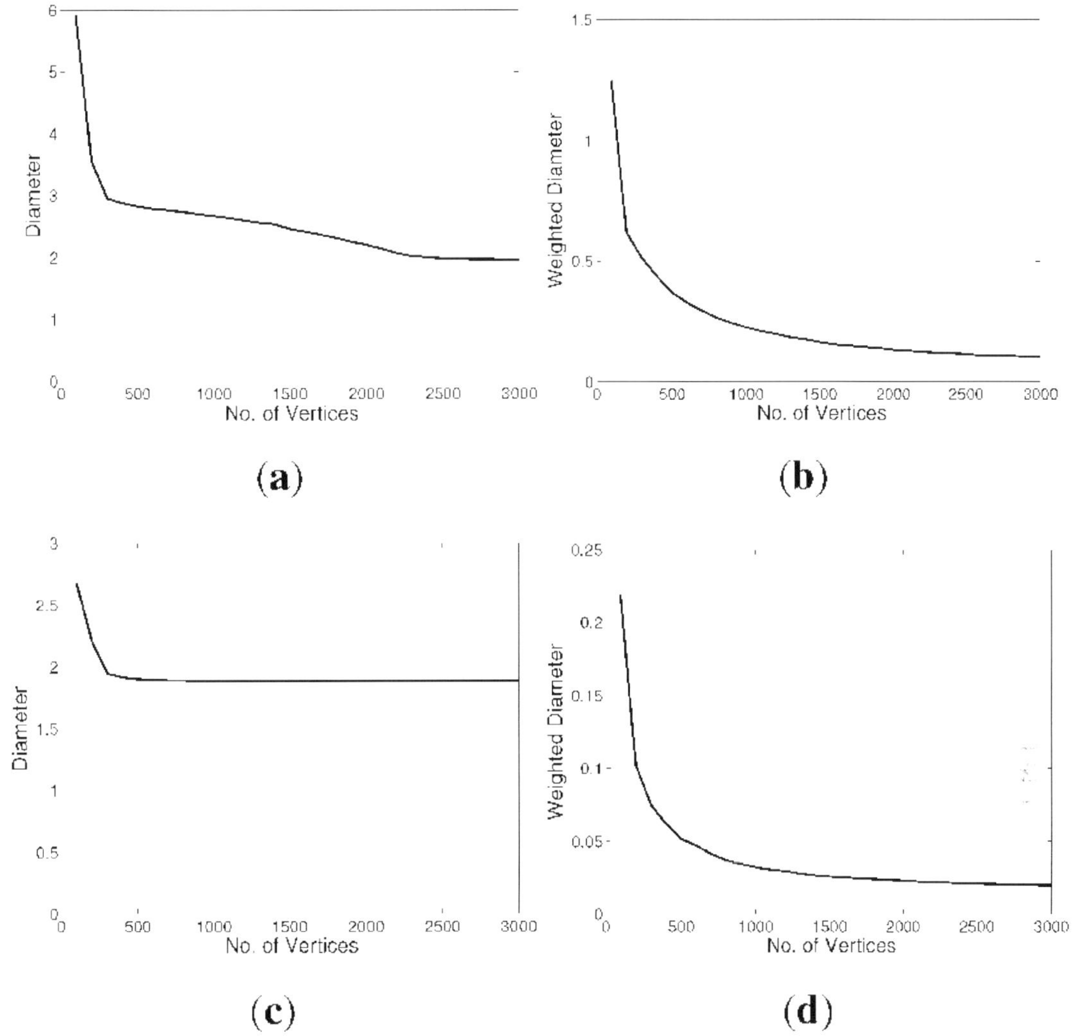

Figure 15. Shrinking Diameter Effect. (**a**) Undirected, unweighted; (**b**) Undirected, weighted; (**c**) Directed, unweighted; (**d**) Directed, weighted.

CONCLUSIONS AND FUTURE WORK

In this paper, we presented Agwan, a generative model for random graphs with discrete labels and weighted edges. We included a fitting algorithm to learn a model of edge weights from real - world graphs, and an algorithm to generate random labelled, weighted graphs with similar characteristics to the input graph.

We measured the closeness of fit of our generated graphs to the input graph over a range of graph statistics, and compared our approach to the state - of - the - art in random graph generative algorithms. Our results and findings are summarized in Table 1.

Table 1. Summary of results and findings: dependencies between graph labels and weights and structural properties (*hypothesised); relative accuracy of the properties of weighted graphs generated using Agwan and MAG models.

Statistic	Vertex Labels	Edge Weights	Agwan	MAG
Vertex Strength	Dependent	Dependent	Accurate	Less accurate
Singular Values	Dependent	Dependent	Accurate	Less accurate
Primary Singular Vector	Partially	Dependent	Accurate	Poor
	Dependent			
Clustering Coefficients	Conditionally	Independent	Less accurate when using real attributes	
	Independent*		More accurate with synthetic attributes	
Triad Participation	Conditionally	Independent	Less accurate when using real attributes	
	Independent*		More accurate with synthetic attributes	

Our results demonstrate that Agwan produces an accurate model of the weighted input graphs. The Agwan graphs reproduce many of the properties of the input graphs, including formation of a giant component, heavy - tailed degree distribution, Small World property, Densification Power Law and shrinking diameter effect. Vertex strength and spectral properties were modelled very closely, indicating that these properties are indeed dependent on vertex labels and edge weights. For clustering and triad participation, it appears that these properties are independent of the edge weight distribution. While there appears to be a relationship with the vertex label distribution, we suggest that this may be an artefact of the true process giving rise to these properties, triadic closure. Further research is required into the relationship between vertex attributes and triangle formation in graphs.

We investigated the accuracy of modelling edge weights using BMMs and compared to a previous approach which used GMMs. The edge weights often follow a power - law distribution, which the BMM approach fits more closely, particularly in the lower range of edge weight values. In general, BMMs are more suitable for bounded data; probability mass can only be assigned to the valid range of weight values. For the GMM model, we compensated for this by truncating the GMM during graph generation. We expected that Agwan (BMM) would consistently outperform Agwan (GMM), but the truncated GMM performed surprisingly well. We propose to conduct experiments on a wider range of datasets to investigate this further. It would also be interesting to compare with Poisson Mixture Models to model discrete edge weights.

ACKNOWLEDGMENTS

This research was supported by funding from the Engineering and Physical Sciences Research Council (grant No. EP/H049606/1), National Nature Science Foundation of China (NSFC) grant Nos. 61402047 and 61511130081, the National Prevention Research Initiative (grant No. G0802045) and their funding partners, and the Department for Employment and Learning (grant No. M6003CPH).

AUTHOR CONTRIBUTIONS

Michael Charles Davis is the principal author, responsible for the design of the study, conducting the experiments and analyzing the results. Zhanyu Ma contributed the variational inference approach used for Beta Mixture Modelling. Weiru Liu and Paul Miller supervised the study and provided substantial critique and guidance. Ruth Hunter and Frank Kee designed the social network study for the health intervention and provided data for the experiments.

REFERENCES

1. Barabási, A.L.; Albert, R. Emergence of Scaling in Random Networks. *Science* 1999, *286*, 509–512.
2. Chakrabarti, D.; Faloutsos, C. *Graph Mining: Laws, Tools, and Case Studies*; Morgan & Claypool Publishers: San Rafael, CA, USA, 2012.
3. Erdős, P.; Rényi, A. On the Evolution of Random Graphs. *Publ. Math. Inst. Hung. Acad. Sci.* 1960, *5*, 17–61.
4. Leskovec, J.; Kleinberg, J.; Faloutsos, C. Graph evolution: Densification and shrinking diameters. *ACM Trans. Knowl. Discov. Data* 2007.
5. Newman, M. *Networks: An Introduction*; OUP: New York, NY, USA, 2010.
6. Chakrabarti, D.; Zhan, Y.; Faloutsos, C. R - MAT: A Recursive Model for Graph Mining. In Proceedings of the 2004 SIAM International Conference on Data Mining, Lake Buena Vista, FL, USA; 2004; pp. 442–446.
7. Leskovec, J.; Chakrabarti, D.; Kleinberg, J.M.; Faloutsos, C.; Ghahramani, Z. Kronecker Graphs: An Approach to Modeling Networks. *J. Mach. Learn. Res.* 2010, *11*, 985–1042.
8. Hoff, P.D.; Raftery, A.E.; Handcock, M.S. Latent Space Approaches to Social Network Analysis. *J. Am. Stat. Assoc.* 2002, *97*, 1090–1098.
9. Kim, M.; Leskovec, J. Multiplicative Attribute Graph Model of Real - World Networks. *Internet Math.* 2012, *8*, 113–160.
10. Wang, Y.; Wong, G. Stochastic Block Models for Directed Graphs. *J. Am. Stat. Assoc.* 1987, *82*, 8–19.
11. Akoglu, L.; McGlohon, M.; Faloutsos, C. *OddBall: Spotting Anomalies in Weighted Graphs*; Zaki, M.J., Yu, J.X., Ravindran, B., Pudi, V., Eds.; Lecture Notes in Computer Science; Springer: Berlin, Germany, 2010; Volume 6119, pp. 410–421.
12. Eichinger, F.; Huber, M.; Böhm, K. *On the Usefulness of Weight - Based Constraints in Frequent Subgraph Mining*; Bramer, M., Petridis, M., Hopgood, A., Eds.; Springer: Berlin, Germany, 2010; pp. 65–78.
13. Davis, M.; Liu, W.; Miller, P. Finding the most descriptive substructures in graphs with discrete and numeric labels. *J. Intell. Inf. Syst.* 2014, *42*, 307–332.
14. Kim, M.; Leskovec, J. *Modeling Social Networks with Node Attributes Using the Multiplicative Attribute Graph Model*; Cozman, F.G., Pfeffer, A., Eds.; AUAI Press: Arlington, VA, USA, 2011; pp. 400–409.
15. Bishop, C.M. *Pattern Recognition and Machine Learning*, 3rd ed.; Springer: New York, NY, USA, 2011.
16. Jain, A.K.; Duin, R.P.W.; Mao, J. Statistical Pattern Recognition: A Review. *IEEE Trans. Pattern Anal. Mach. Intell.*2000, *22*, 4–37.
17. Figueiredo, M.A.T.; Jain, A.K. Unsupervised Learning of Finite Mixture Models. *IEEE Trans. Pattern Anal. Mach. Intell.* 2002, *24*, 381–396.
18. Blei, D.M.; Jordan, M.I. Variational inference for Dirichlet process mixtures. *Bayesian Anal.* 2005, *1*, 121–144.
19. Kurihara, K.; Welling, M.; Vlassis, N.A. *Accelerated Variational Dirichlet Process Mixtures*; Schölkopf, B., Platt, J.C., Hoffman, T., Eds.; MIT Press: Cambridge, MA, USA, 2006; pp. 761–768.
20. Davis, M.; Liu, W.; Miller, P. Agwan: A Generative Model for Labelled, Weighted Graphs. In *New Frontiers in Mining Complex Patterns*; 2014; pp. 181–200.
21. Lindblom, J.; Samuelsson, J. Bounded support Gaussian mixture modeling of speech spectra. *IEEE Transa. Speech Audio Process.* 2003, *11*, 88–99.

22. Bouguila, N.; Ziou, D.; Monga, E. Practical Bayesian estimation of a finite Beta mixture through Gibbs sampling and its applications. *Stat. Comput.* 2006, *16*, 215–225.
23. Ji, Y.; Wu, C.; Liu, P.; Wang, J.; Coombes, K.R. Applications of beta - mixture models in bioinformatics. *Bioinformatics* 2005, *21*, 2118–2122.
24. Ma, Z.; Leijon, A. Beta mixture models and the application to image classification. In Proceedings of 16th IEEE International Conference on Image Processing (ICIP), Cairo, Egypt, 7–10 November 2009; pp. 2045–2048.
25. McLachlan, G.J.; Krishnan, T. *The EM Algorithm and Extensions*, 1st ed.; Wiley: New York, NY, USA, 1997.
26. Ma, Z.; Leijon, A. Bayesian Estimation of Beta Mixture Models with Variational Inference. *IEEE Trans. Pattern Anal. Mach. Intell.* 2011, *33*, 2160–2173.
27. Ma, Z.; Rana, P.K.; Taghia, J.; Flierl, M.; Leijon, A. Bayesian Estimation of Dirichlet Mixture Model with Variational Inference. *Pattern Recognit.* 2014, *47*, 3143–3157.
28. Diaconis, P.; Ylvisaker, D. Conjugate Priors for Exponential Families. *Ann. Stat.* 1979, *7*, 269–281.
29. Hunter, R.F.; Davis, M.; Tully, M.A.; Kee, F. *The Physical Activity Loyalty Card Scheme: Development and Application of a Novel System for Incentivizing Behaviour Change*; Kostkova, P., Szomszor, M., Fowler, D., Eds.; Springer: Berlin, Germany, 2011; Volume 91, pp. 170–177.
30. Fagiolo, G. Clustering in complex directed networks. *Phys. Rev. E* 2007.
31. Johnson, D.B. Efficient Algorithms for Shortest Paths in Sparse Networks. *J. ACM* 1977, *24*, 1–13.
32. Attias, H. *A Variational Bayesian Framework for Graphical Models*; Solla, S.A., Leen, T.K., Müller, K.R., Eds.; MIT Press: Cambridge, MA, USA, 1999; pp. 209–215.
33. Jaakkola, T.S. Tutorial on Variational Approximation Methods. In *Advanced Mean Field Methods: Theory and Practice*; Opper, M., Saad, D., Eds.; MIT Press: Cambridge, MA, USA, 2001; pp. 129–159.
34. Jaakkola, T.S.; Jordan, M.I. Bayesian parameter estimation via variational methods. *Stat. Comput.* 2000, *10*, 25–37.
35. Ueda, N.; Ghahramani, Z. Bayesian model search for mixture models based on optimizing variational bounds. *Neural Netw.* 2002, *15*, 1223–1241.
36. Goldstein, M.; Morris, S.; Yen, G. Problems with fitting to the power - law distribution. *Eur. Phys. J. B Condens. Matter Complex Syst.* 2004, *41*, 255–258.

CHAPTER 11

SEMI-SUPERVISED CLASSIFICATION BASED ON MIXTURE GRAPH

Lei Feng[1] and Guoxian Yu[1, 2]

[1]College of Computer and Information Science, Southwest University, Chongqing 400715, China

[2]Key Laboratory of Symbolic Computation and Knowledge Engineering of Ministry of Education, Jilin University, Changchun 130012, China

ABSTRACT

Graph-based semi-supervised classification heavily depends on a well-structured graph. In this paper, we investigate a mixture graph and propose a method called semi-supervised classification based on mixture graph (SSCMG). SSCMG first constructs multiple k nearest neighborhood (kNN) graphs in different random subspaces of the samples. Then, it combines these graphs into a mixture graph and incorporates this graph into a graph-based semi-supervised classifier. SSCMG can preserve the local structure of samples in subspaces and is less affected by noisy and redundant features. Empirical study on facial images classification shows that SSCMG not only has better recognition performance, but also is more robust to input parameters than other related methods.

INTRODUCTION

Many real-world pattern classification and data mining applications are often confronted with a typical problem that is lacking of sufficient labeled data, since labeling samples usually requires domain-specific experts [1, 2]. Supervised classifiers, trained only on such scarcely labeled samples, often cannot have a good generalization ability. With the development of high-throughput techniques, a large number of unlabeled data can be easily accumulated. If we take these labeled samples as unlabeled ones and train unsupervised learners (i.e., clustering) on all the unlabeled samples, the valuable information in labeled samples is wasted. That is because the label information should be regarded as prior information, which can be used to boost the performance of a classifier [3]. Therefore, it is important to develop techniques that leverage both labeled and unlabeled samples.

Semi-supervised learning aims to leverage labeled and unlabeled samples to achieve a learner with good generalization ability [1]. In this paper, we focus on semi-supervised classification, and more specifically on graph-based semi-supervised classification (GSSC). In GSSC, labeled and unlabeled samples are taken as nodes (or vertices) of a weighted graph, and the edge weights reflect the similarity between samples [1]. Various effective GSSC methods have been proposed in the last decade. To name a few, Zhu et al. [4] utilized Gaussian fields and harmonic functions (GFHF) on a k nearest neighborhood (kNN) graph to predict the labels of unlabeled samples via label propagation on the graph. Zhou et al. [5] studied a learning with local and global consistence (LGC) approach on a completely connected graph based on the consistency assumption. These two methods can be regarded as label propagation on a graph under different assumptions or

Citation: Lei Feng and Guoxian Yu. Semi-supervised classification based on mixture graph, Algorithms 2015, 8(4), 1021-1034; DOI: 10.3390/a8041021

schemes [1]. Most GSSC methods focus on how to leverage labeled and unlabeled samples but pay little attention to construct a well-structure graph that faithfully reflects the distribution of samples. For low dimensional samples, these GSSC methods can achieve good performance by using a simple kNN graph. When dealing with high dimensional instances, their performance often drops sharply, since the noisy and redundant features of high dimensional samples destroy the underlying distance (or similarity) between samples [3, 6].

Recently, researchers recognized the importance of graph in GSSC and proposed various graph optimization based semi-supervised classification methods [1, 7, 8, 9, 10]. Zhu [1] gave a comprehensive literature review on semi-supervised learning. Here, we just name a few most related and representative methods, which will be used for experimental comparison. Wang et al. [11] used an l_2 graph [12], optimized by minimizing the l_2-norm regularized reconstruction error of locally linear embedding [13], and studied a linear neighborhood propagation (LNP) approach. Liu et al. [7] took advantage of iterative nonparametric matrix learning to construct a symmetric adjacent graph and proposed a robust multi-class graph transductive (RMGT) classification method. In addition, Fan et al. [9] constructed an l_1 graph by the coefficients of l_1-norm regularized sparse representation [14] to perform semi-supervised classification. Zhao et al. [10] suggested a compact graph based semi-supervised learning (CGSSL) method for image annotation. This method constructs a compact l_2 graph by utilizing not only the neighborhood samples of a sample, but also the neighborhood samples of its reciprocal neighbors. However, the effectiveness of these methods is not as good as expected when dealing with high dimensional data, since high dimensional data have a lot of noisy and redundant features, and it is difficult to optimize a graph distorted by these noisy features [2, 15].

More recently, some researchers studied how to synthesize multiple graphs, derived from multiple data sources or multiple modules data, for semi-supervised classification [16]. Wang et al. [17], Karasuyama and Mamitsuka [18], Shiga and Mamitsuka [19] and Yu et al. [20] explored different techniques (i.e., multiple kernel learning [21], kernel target alignment [22]) to assign different weights to the graphs and then weighted combined these graphs into a composite graph for semi-supervised classification. A number of researchers have applied the random subspace method (RSM) [23] to semi-supervised classification [2, 15] and dimensionality reduction [24]. Particularly, Yu et al. [2] proposed a GSSC method called semi-supervised ensemble classification in subspaces (SSEC in short). SSEC firstly constructs several kNN graphs in the random subspaces of samples; then, it trains several semi-supervised linear classifiers on these graphs, one classifier for each graph; next, it combines these classifiers into an ensemble classifier for prediction. The empirical study shows that the base classifiers trained on these simple kNN graphs outperform the classifier trained in the original space, and the ensemble classifier also works better than other graph optimization based semi-supervised classifiers (i.e., LNP and RMGT) and some representative ensemble classifiers (i.e., Random Forest [25] and Rotation Forest [26]).

In this paper, motivated by these observations, we investigate a mixture graph combined by multiple kNN graphs constructed in the subspaces, and study a semi-supervised classification method on this mixture graph ((semi-supervised classification based on mixture graph SSCMG)). Particularly, SSCMG first constructs multiple kNN graphs in different random subspaces (like the random subspace scheme in [23]) of samples, and then combines these graphs into a mixture graph. Finally, SSCMG incorporates this mixture graph into GFHF [4], a representative GSSC method, for semi-supervised classification. Since the distance metric is more reliable in the subspace than that in the original space and the mixture graph is constructed in subspaces, the mixture graph is less suffered from the noisy samples and features. Besides, it is able to hold complicated geometric distribution as the diversity of random subspaces. Experimental comparison with other related methods shows that SSCMG not only has higher classification accuracy, but also has wide ranges of effective input parameters. The main difference between SSCMG and aforementioned GFHF, LGC, LNP, RMGT and CGSSL is that SSCMG uses a mixture graph combined by multiple kNN graphs constructed in the subspaces, whereas the other methods just utilize (or optimize) a single graph alone. SSEC trains several semi-supervised linear classifiers based on kNN graphs constructed in randomly partitioned subspaces and incorporates these classifiers into an ensemble classifier for prediction. In contrast, SSCMG integrates multiple kNN graphs constructed in random subspaces into a mixture graph, and then trains one semi-supervised classifier based on the mixture graph.

In summary, the main contributions of this paper are summarized as follows: (1) A semi-supervised classification based on mixture graph (SSCMG) method is proposed for high-dimensional data classification; (2) Extensive experimental study and analysis demonstrate that SSCMG achieves higher accuracy and it can be more robust to input parameters than other related methods; (3) Mixture graph works better than the graph optimized by a singlekNN graph alone, and it can be used as a good alternative graph for GSSC methods on high dimensional data.

The rest of this paper is structured as follows: Section 2 describes the procedure of GFHF and introduces the construction of mixture graph. In Section 3, extensive experiments are conducted to study the performance and parameter sensitivity of SSCMG. Conclusions and future work are provided in Section 4.

METHODOLOGY

In this section, we introduce GFHF first and then provide the procedures of the mixture graph.

Gaussian Fields and Harmonic Functions

Suppose there are $n = l + u$ samples $\mathbf{x}_i \in \mathbb{R}^D$ $(1 \leq i \leq n)$, organized in a matrix $\mathbf{X} = [\mathbf{x}_1; \mathbf{x}_2; \cdots; \mathbf{x}_l; \mathbf{x}_{l+1}; \cdots; \mathbf{x}_{l+u}]$, where l is the number of labeled samples, u is the number of unlabeled samples. $\mathbf{y}_i \in \mathbb{R}^C$ is the label vector of the i-th samples, if x_i belongs to the c-th class then $y_{ic} = 1$; otherwise $y_{ic} = 0$. Obviously, $y_i = 0$ means the label of x_i is unknown (or unlabeled). The target is to predict the labels of u unlabeled samples.

Various semi-supervised classifiers can be used to infer the labels of these u unlabeled samples [1]. In this paper, we choose GFHF [4] for its simplicity and wide-application. To be self-consistent and to discuss the importance of graph for GSSC methods, the main procedures of GFHF are listed below and more details of GFHF can be found in reference [4].

$$w_{ij} = \begin{cases} e^{-\frac{\|\mathbf{x}_i - \mathbf{x}_j\|_2^2}{\sigma^2}}, & \text{if} \quad \mathbf{x}_j \in \mathcal{N}_k(\mathbf{x}_i) \text{ or } \mathbf{x}_i \in \mathcal{N}_k(\mathbf{x}_j) \\ 0, & \text{otherwise} \end{cases} \tag{1}$$

where σ is a scalar parameter to control the decaying rate of distance between x_i and x_j, and it is called Gaussian kernel width. $N_k(x_i)$ includes k nearest neighborhood samples of x_i. w_{ij} ensures two nearby samples have a large similarity and two faraway samples have a small or zero similarity.

GFHF assumes nearby samples having similar labels and propagates the labels of labeled samples in G to infer the labels of unlabeled samples in G. Particularly, it optimizes the predictive function $f(\mathbf{x}) \in \mathbb{R}^C$ on n samples as follows:

$$\min_f (\infty \sum_{i=1}^{l} (\|\mathbf{y}_i - f(\mathbf{x}_i)\|_2^2) + \frac{1}{2} \sum_{i,j=1}^{n} w_{ij} \|f(\mathbf{x}_i) - f(\mathbf{x}_j)\|_2^2) \tag{2}$$

where $f(\mathbf{x}_i) \in \mathbb{R}^C$ is the predicted likelihood of x_i with respect to C classes. To ensure the prediction on the first l samples be the same with their initial labels, an ∞ weight is assigned to the first term. The second term is to ensure nearby samples having similar predicted likelihoods. Equation (2) can be rewritten as:

$$\min_f (\infty \sum_{i=1}^{l} (\|\mathbf{y}_i - f(\mathbf{x}_i)\|_2^2) + \mathbf{f}^T \mathbf{L} \mathbf{f}) \tag{3}$$

where $\mathbf{f} = [f(\mathbf{x}_1); f(\mathbf{x}_2); \cdots ; f(\mathbf{x}_n)]$, L = D – W is the graph Laplacian matrix [27], DD is a diagonal matrix with $\mathbf{D}_{ii} = \sum_j \mathbf{W}_{ij}$. (3).

To get the harmonic solution of Equation (3), WW is divided into four blocks as follows:

$$\mathbf{W} = \begin{bmatrix} \mathbf{W}_{ll} & \mathbf{W}_{lu} \\ \mathbf{W}_{ul} & \mathbf{W}_{uu} \end{bmatrix} \tag{4}$$

where $\mathbf{W}_{ll} \in \mathbb{R}^{l \times l}$ describes the pairwise similarity between the first l samples, $\mathbf{W}_{lu} \in \mathbb{R}^{l \times u}$ (or W_{ul}) represents the similarity between the first l labeled samples and u unlabeled samples, and $\mathbf{W}_{uu} \in \mathbb{R}^{u \times u}$ captures the similarity between u unlabeled samples. Suppose $\mathbf{f}_u \in \mathbb{R}^{u \times C}$ be the predicted likelihoods on u unlabeled samples and $\mathbf{f}_l \in \mathbb{R}^{l \times C}$ be the predictions on the first l labeled samples. The explicit solution of Equation (3) is:

$$\mathbf{f}_u = (\mathbf{D}_{uu} - \mathbf{W}_{uu})^{-1} \mathbf{W}_{ul} \mathbf{f}_l \tag{5}$$

From Equation (5), it is easy to observe that W is the deciding factor of f_u, or in other words the graph constructed in Equation (1) determines the label of unlabeled samples.

Most GSSC methods can obtain good results on low dimensional data. However, when dealing with high-dimensional data, the effectiveness of these classifiers is often significantly reduced [2]. The reason is that there are many noisy and redundant features in high-dimensional data and these features distort the neighborhood relationship (or similarity) between samples [3, 6, 15]. Given that, the graph-based classifiers can not correctly and effectively use the labels associated with a sample's neighbors to predict its label. In fact, some researchers already claimed that graph determines the performance of graph-based semi-supervised learning [1, 7] and graph-based dimensionality reduction [28]. Maier et al. [29] found that a graph-based clustering approach has two optimal clustering solutions on two different graphs from the same dataset.

Mixture Graph Construction

Yu et al. [2] observed that a semi-supervised linear classifier based on a kNN graph in the subspace can achieve higher accuracy than the classifier based on a kNN graph in the original space. This observation indicates that a kNN graph in the high dimensional space is often suffered from noisy and redundant features. In contrast, a kNN graph in the low dimensional space is less suffered from the redundant and noisy features. In addition, Yu et al. [15] found that an l_1 graph constructed in the subspace is also less suffered from noise features than the l_1 graph in the original space. Inspired by these observations, we investigate a mixture graph, combined by kNN graphs constructed in several random subspaces of original space, for semi-supervised classification. The detailed procedure of mixture graph is listed as follows:

1) Randomly sampling d feature indices without replacement, and project X into $\mathbf{X}^t = [\mathbf{x}_1^t; \mathbf{x}_2^t; \cdots; \mathbf{x}_n^t] \in \mathbb{R}^{n \times d}$, $\mathbf{x}_i^t$ is consisted of the sampled d features of x_i.
2) Construct a kNN graph on X_t, and define the corresponding association matrix as:

$$\mathbf{W}_{ij}^t = \begin{cases} 1, & \text{if } \mathbf{x}_j^t \in \mathcal{N}_k(\mathbf{x}_i^t) \text{ or } \mathbf{x}_i^t \in \mathcal{N}_k(\mathbf{x}_j^t) \\ 0, & \text{otherwise} \end{cases} \tag{6}$$

where $\mathcal{N}_k(\mathbf{x}_i^t)$ includes k nearest neighborhood samples of $\mathbf{x}_i^t$, and the neighborhood relationship is determined by the Euclidean distance between samples. In this way, we can construct a kNN graph G^t and define its association matrix W^t in the t-th subspace.

3) Repeat the above two steps T times and thus T graphs can be constructed in T random subspaces, one graph for each subspace. Then, these kNN graphs can be integrated into a mixture graph and its association matrix is defined as follows:

$$\mathbf{W}_{ij}^{mg} = \frac{1}{T}\sum_{t=1}^{T} \mathbf{W}_{ij}^t \tag{7}$$

Since the mixture graph is combined with T graphs constructed in random subspaces, the impact of noisy and redundant features is reduced. The mixture graph can not only hold more complicated geometric distribution of samples than any of the T graphs as the diversity of random subspaces, but also be less sensitive to k than a singlekNN graph. From the viewpoint of ensemble learning [30] that the accuracy of an ensemble classifier is no smaller than the average accuracy of base classifiers; thus, the mixture graph avoids the risk of choosing a bad kNN graph. Some recent methods (i.e., diffuse interfaces [31], p-Laplacian [32]) were proposed to identify relevant features and to discard noisy features for semi-supervised learning. These methods are reported to perform well on samples with a large number of noisy features. In this case, our mixture graph may not work well as supposed. However, p-Laplacian can be borrowed by the mixture graph to discard these noisy features.

To investigate these potential advantages of mixture graph, we substitute W in Equation (1) with mixture graph W^{mg} and then perform semi-supervised classification on W^{mg} to predict the labels of unlabeled samples. In this way, we propose a method called Semi-Supervised Classification based on Mixture Graph (SSCMG). We study the characteristics of mixture graph by comparing it with several representative GSSC methods (i.e., RMGT [7], LNP [11], CGSSL[10]) and analyze its sensitivity under different values of input parameter.

EXPERIMENT

In this section, we conduct experiments on four publicly available face datasets to study the effectiveness of SSCMG. The face datasets used in the experiments are ORL [33], CMU PIE [34], AR [35], and extended YaleB [36]. ORL consists of 40 individuals with 10 images per person. We aligned and resized ORL images into 64 × 64 pixels in grey scale, thus each image can be viewed as a point in the 4096-dimensional space. CMU PIE face dataset contains 41, 368 face images from 68 individuals. The face images were captured under varying pose, illumination and expression conditions, and we chose a subset (Pose27) of CMU PIE as the second dataset. Pose27 includes 3329 face images from 68 individuals. Before the experiments, we resized the images to 64 × 64 pixels and each image is an 8 bit grayscale image. AR face dataset includes over 4000 color face images from 126 people (70 men and 56 women). In the experiments, 2600 images of 100 people (50 men and 50 women) were used. We aligned and resized these images into 42 × 30 pixels and then normalized them into 8 bit grayscale, thus each image is a point in the 1260-dimensional space. YaleB consists of 21, 888 single light source images of 38 individuals each captured under 576 viewing conditions (9 × 64 illumination conditions). We chose a subset that contains 2414 images and resized these images into 32 × 32 pixels, with 256 gray level per pixel, so each image is a 1024-dimensional vector. ORL and extended yaleB can be downloaded from the link in reference [37].

To comparatively study the performance of SSCMG, we take several representative methods as comparing methods, which include GFHF [4], LNP [11], RMGT [7], LGC [5], CGSSL [10]. We regard the classification accuracy on testing samples as the comparative index, and the higher the accuracy, the better the performance. Gaussian kernel used for graph construction can often be improved upon by using the 'local scaling' method [31, 38]. We utilize local scaling to adjust the graph defined in Equation (1) and name GFHF on the adjusted graph as LGFHF. The diffuse interfaces model in [31] is proposed for binary classification and it is not so straightforward for multi-class datasets. Since the target of this study is to investigate the effectiveness of mixture graph for semi-supervised classification and the proposed SSCMG is a special case of p-Laplacian with p = 2, we do not compare SSCMG with the diffuse interfaces model and p-Laplacian with different p values. In the following experiments, we firstly apply principal component analysis (PCA) [3] to project each facial image into a 100-dimensional vector, and then use different methods to predict the labels of unlabeled images. For convenience, notations used in the experiments are listed in Table 1.

Table 1. Notations used in the experiments.

Notation	Means
n	Number of labeled and unlabeled samples
l	Number of labeled samples
C	Number of classes
k	Neighborhood size
T	Number of subspaces
d	Dimensionality of random subspace
Ls	Number of labeled samples per class

In the experiments, if without extra specification, α in LGC [5] is set to 0.01, σ in Equation (1) is set to the average

Euclidean distance between n samples, and k is fixed as 3 for all the methods that based on a kNN graph. T and d are set to 70 and 40, respectively. Other parameters of these comparing methods are kept the same as reported in the original papers. The sensitivity of these input parameters will be studied later. To reduce random effect, all reported results are the average of 20 independent runs. In each run, the training set and testing set are randomly partitioned.

Performance on Different Datasets

In order to study the performance of SSCMG under different number of labeled images per people, we conduct experiments on ORL with Ls rising from 1 to 5, and on the other three datasets with Ls increasing from 1 to 10. The corresponding results are revealed in Figure 1. Each class in the four datasets has an equal (or nearly equal) number of samples as other classes, so the classes are balanced. Each dataset has more than 30 classes and the accuracy per class cannot be visualized in Figure 1. Given these reasons, we report the average accuracy for all the classes on each dataset.

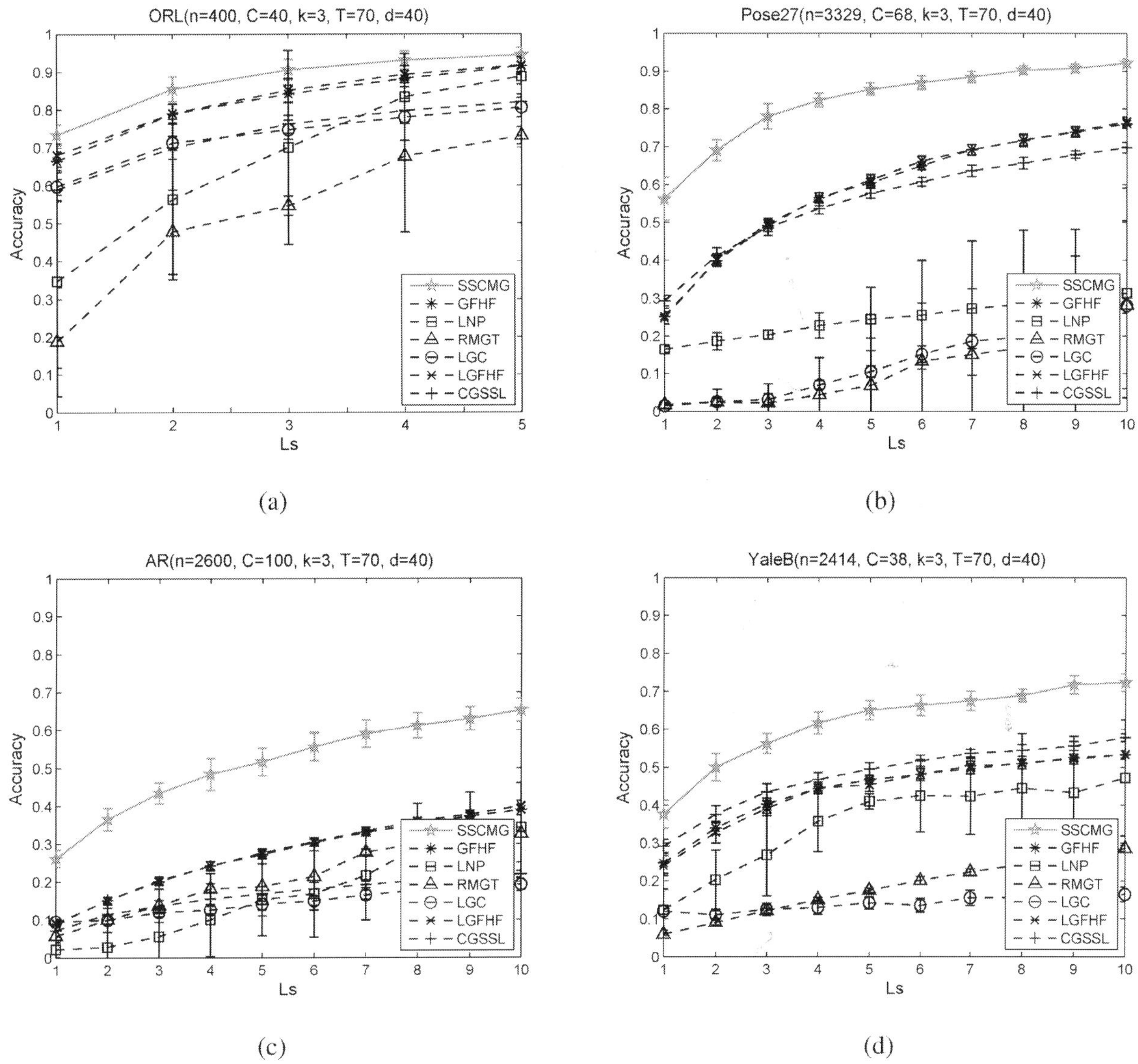

Figure 1. The performance of SSCMG on different Ls values. (**a**) Accuracy vs. Ls (ORL); (**b**) Accuracy vs. Ls (Pose27); (**c**) Accuracy vs. Ls (AR); (**d**) Accuracy vs. Ls (YaleB).

From these four sub-figures, it is easy to observe that SSCMG achieves better performance than these comparing methods on all facial datasets and GFHF almost ranks second among these comparing methods. Although SSCMG, LGFHF and GFHF are based on the same objective function, SSCMG always outperforms the latter two. That is because SSCMG utilizes a mixture graph combined by multiple kNN graphs defined in the subspaces, whereas the latter two depend on a single kNN graph constructed in the PCA reduced space. This observation not only justifies the statement that graph determines the performance of GSSC methods, but also supports our motivation to utilize mixture graph for semi-supervised classification. LGFHF is slightly superior to GFHF. This fact indicates local scaling technique can only improve the kNN graph in a small scale. LGC often loses to other methods. The reason is that LGC utilizes a fully connected graph rather than a kNN graph, and this fully connected graph is more heavily distorted by noisy features. RMGT and LNP apply different techniques to optimize a kNN graph, but their accuracies are almost always lower than that of SSCMG. The cause is that optimizing a kNN graph that distorted by noisy features is rather difficult. CGSSL uses a compact l_2 graph and it often outperforms LNP, which is based on a non-compact l_2 graph, but CGSSL is always outperformed by SSCMG. These facts suggest that optimizing an l_2 graph alone can only improve the performance in a small range, and it may not result in an optimal graph for semi-supervised classification.

As the number of labeled samples (Ls) increasing, the accuracy of SSCMG and other methods climbs steadily, for more labeled samples can often help to acquire a more accurate classifier. RMGT asks for a number of labeled samples to learn an optimized graph, but available labeled samples are not sufficient to optimize a good graph for RMGT. From these observations, we can conclude that mixture graphs can be used as a good alternative graph for GSSC methods on high dimensional data.

Sensitivity Analysis with Respect to Neighborhood Size

It is found that neighborhood size k of kNN graph can influence the results of GSSC. To investigate the sensitivity of SSCMG under different k values, we conduct experiments on ORL and Pose27. In the experiments, we fix Ls as 3 on ORL and as 5 on Pose27, we then vary k from 1 to 40. We also include the results of other comparing methods that utilize a kNN graph and report the results in Figure 2.

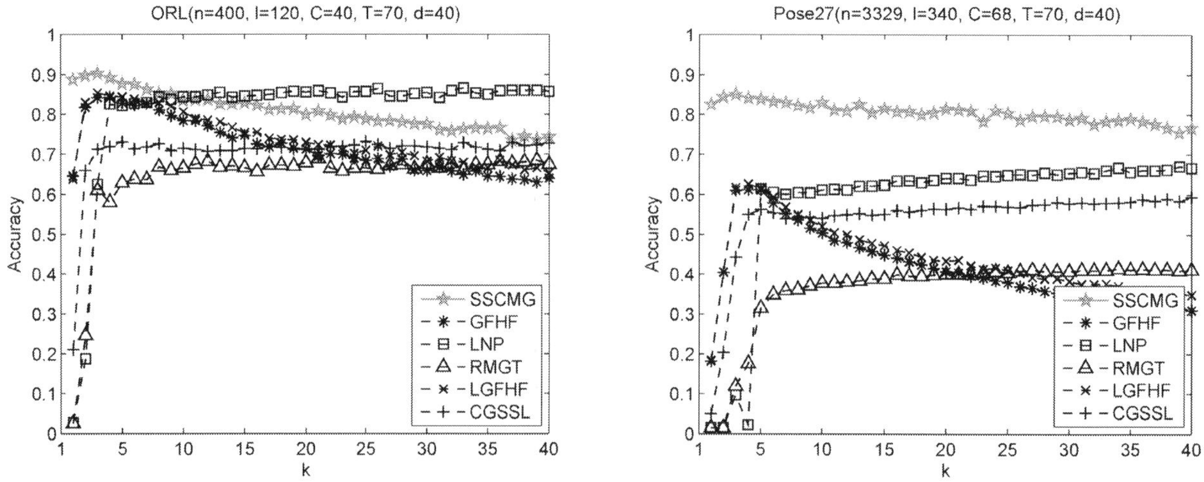

(a) (b)

Figure 2. Sensitivity under different values of k. (**a**) Accuracy vs. k (ORL); (**b**) Accuracy vs. k (Pose27).

From Figure 2, we can observe that SSCMG achieves better performance and it is less sensitive to k than other comparing methods when k ≤ 10. However, as k increasing, its accuracy downgrades gradually. This is because a large value of k means choosing more neighbors of a sample, so the constructed mixture graph is becoming denser and more noisy edges are included. On the other hand, the accuracy of GFHF and LGFHF first rise sharply as k increasing and then reduce gradually. The accuracy of LNP, RMGT and CGSSL increase as k rising and become relatively stable, and these methods sometimes get comparable (or better) results with SSCMG on ORL. The reason is that these three methods need a large number of neighbors to optimize a kNN graph for semi-supervised classification. CGSSL utilizes a compact l_2 graph by using the direct neighborhood samples of a sample and the neighborhood samples of its reciprocal neighbors. As k increasing, more neighborhood samples are included and thus the similarity between samples is more distorted by noisy neighbors. Given that, CGSSL loses to LNP, which is also based on an l_2 graph, but LNP only utilizes the direct neighborhood samples of a sample. As k increasing, the accuracy of GFHF and LGFHF on ORL and Pose27 downgrades much more than that of SSCMG, this observation suggests that mixture graph is less suffered from the choice of k than a single kNN graph. Figure 2 also shows that it is difficult to set a suitable k for GSSC methods. In contrast, there is a clear pattern and it is easy to select a suitable k for SSCMG. Although SSCMG, LGFHF and GFHF share the same classifier, the performance of SSCMG is always more stable than LGFHF and GFHF. This observation also justifies the advantage of mixture graph for GSSC.

Sensitivity Analysis with Respect to Dimensionality of Random Subspace

The dimensionality of random subspace is an influential parameter for the random subspace method [2, 23]. To study the sensitivity of mixture graph with respect to the dimensionality of random subspace, we conduct two experiments on ORL and Pose27 with d varying from 10 to 100. The corresponding experimental results are reported in Figure 3. For reference, we also include the results of GFHF, LGFHF, LNP, RMGT, LGC and CGSSL in Figure 3.

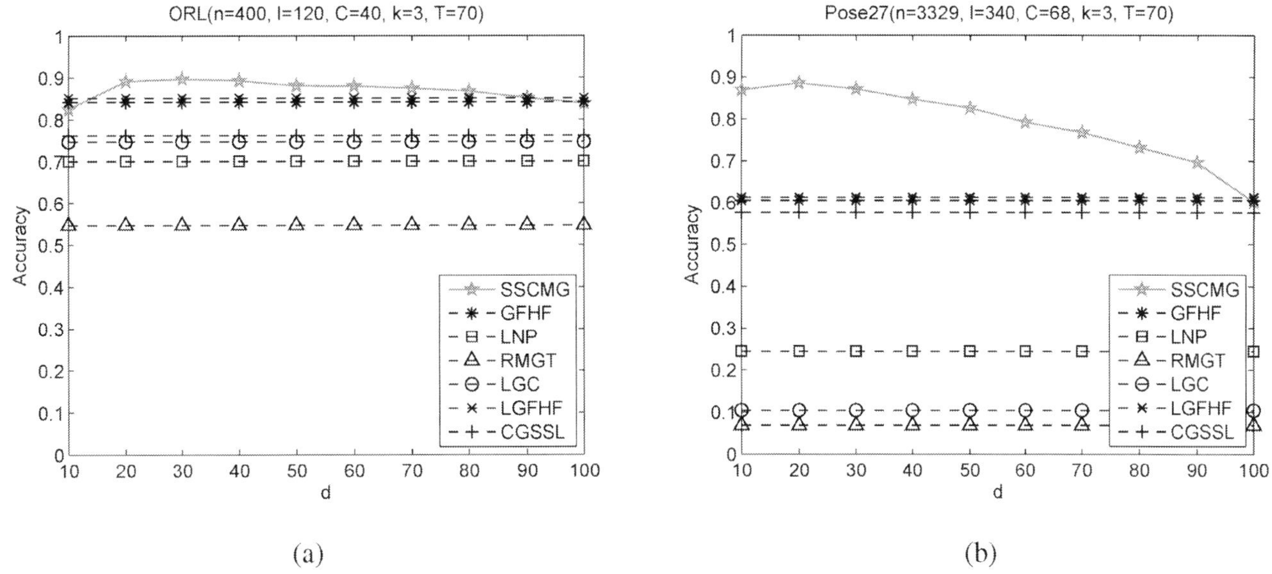

Figure 3. Sensitivity under different values of d. (**a**) Accuracy vs. d (ORL); (**b**) Accuracy vs. d (Pose27).

From Figure 3, we can observe that the accuracy of SSCMG increases slightly as d rising at first and then turns to downgrade, especially on Pose27. The reason is twofold: (i) when d is very small (i.e., d = 10), there are too few features to construct a graph that describes the distribution of samples projected in that subspace; (ii) as d is close to 100, more and more noisy features are included into the subspace and hence the graph is more and more distorted by noisy features. When d = 100 all the features are included, these T graphs are the same, and thus the performance of SSCMG is similar to that of GFHF. Overall, irrespective of the setting of d, the performance of SSCMG is always no worse than that of GFHF. However, how to choose an effective value of d (or design a graph less suffered from d) is still a future pursue.

Sensitivity Analysis with Respect to Number of Random Subspaces

The number of random subspaces is another influential parameter of random subspace method. To explore the performance of SSCMG under different number of random subspaces, additional experiments are conducted on ORL and Pose27 with T rising from 1 to 100, and the corresponding results are shown in Figure 4.

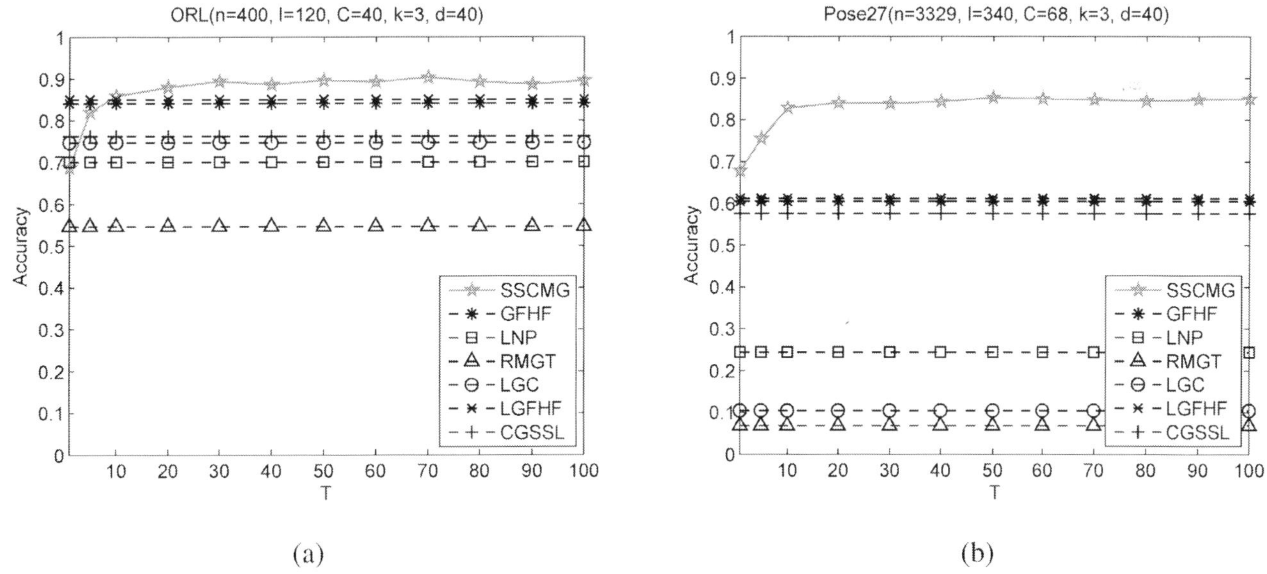

Figure 4. Sensitivity under different values of T. (**a**) Accuracy vs. T (ORL); (**b**) Accuracy vs. T (Pose27).

From Figure 4, we can clearly observe that when $T < 20$, the accuracy of SSCMG is relatively low, even lower than that of GFHF on ORL. The accuracy of SSCMG increases as T rising, and it reaches to relatively stable when $T \geq 20$. The cause is that too few kNN graphs in the subspaces cannot capture the distribution of samples. Overall, these experimental results suggest that SSCMG can easily choose a suitable value of T in a wide range.

CONCLUSIONS AND FUTURE WORK

In this paper, we studied a mixture graph, integrated by several kNN graphs constructed in the subspaces, and proposed a method called semi-supervised classification based on mixture graph (SSCMG). Experimental results on four publicly facial image datasets demonstrate that SSCMG not only achieves better results than other related methods, but also is less suffered from input parameters. In future work, we want to integrate graphs by setting different weights to these graphs and selectively integrate sub-graphs of each input graph for graph-based semi-supervised learning.

ACKNOWLEDGMENTS

This work is partially supported by Natural Science Foundation of China (No. 61402378), Natural Science Foundation of CQ CSTC (No. cstc2014jcyjA40031), Fundamental Research Funds for the Central Universities of China (No. 2362015XK07 and XDJK2016B009).

AUTHOR CONTRIBUTIONS

The idea for this research work is proposed by Guoxian Yu and Lei Feng. Lei Feng implemented the experiments and drafted the manuscript; Guoxian Yu conceived the whole process and revised the manuscript. All the authors read and approved the final manuscript.

REFERENCES

1. Zhu, X. Semi-Supervised Learning Literature Survey; Technical Report for Department of Computer Sciences; University of Wisconsin-Madision: Madision, WI, USA; 19; July; 2008.
2. Yu, G.; Zhang, G.; Yu, Z.; Domeniconi, C.; You, J.; Han, G. Semi-supervised Ensemble Classification in Subspaces. Appl. Soft Comput. 2012, 12, 1511–1522.
3. Duda, R.; Hart, P.; Stork, D. Pattern Classification; Wiley-Interscience: New York, NY, USA, 2001.
4. Zhu, X.; Ghahramani, Z.; Lafferty, J. Semi-Supervised Learning Using Gaussian Fields and Harmonic Functions. In Proceedings of the International Conference on Machine Learning, Washington, DC, USA, 21–24 August 2003; pp. 912–919.
5. Zhou, D.; Bousquet, O.; Lal, T.; Weston, J.; Schölkopf, B. Learning with Local and Global Consistency. In Proceedings of the Advances in Neural Information Processing Systems, Whistler, British Columbia, CA, 11–13 December, 2003; pp. 321–328.
6. Kriegel, H.; Kroger, P.; Zimek, A. Clustering High-Dimensional Data: A Survey on Subspace Clustering, Pattern-Based Clustering, and Correlation Clustering. ACM Trans. Knowl. Discov. Data 2009, 9, 1–58.
7. Liu, W.; Chang, S.F. Robust Multi-Class Transductive Learning with Graphs. In Proceedings of the IEEE Conference on Computer Vision and Pattern Recognition, Miami, FL, USA, 20–25 June 2009; pp. 381–388.
8. Jebara, T.; Wang, J.; Chang, S.-F. Graph Construction and b-Matching for Semi-Supervised Learning. In Proceedings of the International Conference on Machine Learning, Montreal, QC, Canada, 14–18 June 2009; pp. 81–88.
9. Fan, M.; Gu, N.; Qiao, H.; Zhang, B. Sparse Regularization for Semi-supervised Classification. Pattern Recognit.2011, 44, 1777–1784.
10. Zhao, M.; Chow, T.W.S.; Zhang, Z.; Li, B. Automatic Image Annotation via Compact Graph based Semi-Supervised Learning. Knowl. Based Syst. 2014, 76, 148–165.
11. Wang, J.; Wang, F.; Zhang, C.; Shen, H.; Quan, L. Linear Neighborhood Propagation and Its Applications. IEEE Trans. Pattern Anal. Mach. Intell. 2009, 31, 1600–1615.
12. Yan, S.; Wang, H. Semi-Supervised Learning by Sparse Representation. In Proceedings of the SIAM International Conference on Data Mining, Sparks, NV, USA, 30 April–2 May 2009; pp. 792–801.
13. Roweis, S.T.; Saul, L.K. Nonlinear Dimensionality Reduction by Locally Linear Embedding. Science 2000, 290, 2323–2326.
14. Wright, J.; Yang, A.Y.; Ganesh, A.; Sastry, S.S.; Ma, Y. Robust Face Recognition via Sparse Representation. IEEE Trans. Pattern Anal. Mach. Intell. 2009, 2, 210–217.
15. Yu, G.; Zhang, G.; Zhang, Z.; Yu, Z.; Deng, L. Semi-Supervised Classification Based on Subspace Sparse Representation. Knowl. Inf. Syst. 2015, 43, 81–101.
16. Foggia, P.; Percannella, G.; Vento, M. Graph Matching and Learning in Pattern Recognition in the Last 10 Years. Int. J. Pattern Recognit. Artif. Intell. 2014, 28.
17. Wang, M.; Hua, X.; Hong, R.; Tang, J.; Qi, G.; Song, Y. Unified Video Annotation via Multigraph Learning. IEEE Trans. Circuits Syst. Video Technol. 2009, 19, 733–746.
18. Karasuyama, M.; Mamitsuka, H. Multiple Graph Label Propagation by Sparse Integration. IEEE Trans. Neural Netw. Learning Syst. 2013, 24, 1999–2012.
19. Shiga, M.; Mamitsuka, H. Efficient Semi-Supervised Learning on Locally Informative Multiple Graphs. Pattern Recognit. 2012, 45, 1035–1049.
20. Yu, G.; Zhu, H.; Domeniconi, C.; Guo, M. Integrating Multiple Networks for Protein Function Prediction. BMC Syst. Biol. 2015, 9, 1–14.
21. Gönen, M.; Alpaydin, E. Multiple Kernel Learning Algorithms. J. Mach. Learning Res. 2011, 12, 2211–2268.
22. Cortes, C.; Mohri, M.; Rostamizadeh, A. Algorithms for Learning Kernels based on Centered Alignment. J. Mach. Learning Res. 2012, 13, 795–828.
23. Ho, T.K. The Random Subspace Method for Constructing Decision Forests. IEEE Trans. Pattern Anal. Mach. Intell. 1998, 20, 832–844.
24. Yu, G.; Peng, H.; Wei, J.; Ma, Q. Mixture Graph based Semi-Supervised Dimensionality Reduction. Pattern Recognit. Image Anal. 2010, 20, 536–541.
25. Breiman, L. Random Forest. Mach. Learning 2001, 45, 5–32.
26. Rodriguez, J.; Kuncheva, L.; Alonso, C. Rotation forest: A New Classifier Ensemble Method. IEEE Trans. Pattern Anal. Mach. Intell. 2006, 28, 1619–1630.
27. Chung, F.R.K. Spectral Graph Theory; American Mathematical Soc.: Ann Arbor, MI, USA, 1997; pp. 1–212.
28. Yan, S.; Xu, D.; Zhang, B.; Zhang, H.J.; Yang, Q.; Lin, S. Graph Embedding and Extensions: A General

Framework for Dimensionality Reduction. IEEE Trans. Pattern Anal. Mach. Intell. 2007, 29, 40–51.

29. Maier, M.; Luxburg, U.V.; Hein, M. Influence of Graph Construction on Graph-based Clustering Measures. In Proceedings of the Advances in Neural Information Processing Systems, Vancouver, BC, Canada, 8–10 December 2008; pp. 1025–1032.

30. Zhou, Z. Ensemble Methods: Foundations and Algorithms; CRC Press: Boca Raton, FL, USA, 2012.

31. Bertozzi, A.L.; Flenner, A. Diffuse Interface Models on Graphs for Classification of High Dimensional Data. Multiscale Modeling Simul. 2012, 10, 1090–1118.

32. Buhler, T.; Hein, M. Spectral Clustering Based on the Graph p-Laplacian. In Proceedings of the International Conference on Machine Learning, Montreal, QC, Canada, 14–18 June 2009; pp. 81–88.

33. Samaria, F.S.; Harter, A.C. Parameterisation of a Stochastic Model for Human Face Identification. In Proceedings of the 2nd IEEE Workshop on Applications of Computer Vision, Sarasota, FL, USA, 5–7 December 1994; pp. 138–142.

34. Bsat, M.; Baker, S.; Sim, T. The CMU Pose, Illumination, and Expression Database. IEEE Trans. Pattern Anal. Mach. Intell. 2003, 25, 1615–1618.

35. Martmhnez, A.M. The AR-Face Database; CVC Technical Report 24; Computer Vision Center: Barcelona, Spain; 1; June; 1998.

36. Georghiades, A.S.; Belhumeur, P.N.; Kriegman, D.J. From Few to Many: Illumination Cone Models for Face Recognition under Bariable Lighting and Pose. IEEE Trans. Pattern Anal. Mach. Intell. 2001, 23, 643–660.

37. Four Face Databases in Matlab Format. Available online: http://www.cad.zju.edu.cn/home/dengcai/Data/FaceData.html (accessed on 8 November 2015).

38. Zelnik-Manor, L.; Perona, P. Self-Tuning Spectral Clustering. In Proceedings of the Advances in Neural Information Processing Systems, Vancouver, BC, Canada, 17–19 December 2004; pp. 1601–1608.

CHAPTER 12

MODIFIED CLASSICAL GRAPH ALGORITHMS FOR THE DNA FRAGMENT ASSEMBLY PROBLEM

Guillermo M. Mallén-Fullerton[1], J. Emilio Quiroz-Ibarra[2], Antonio Miranda[3], and Guillermo Fernández-Anaya[3]

[1]Engineering Department, Universidad Iberoamericana Ciudad de México, Prolongación Paseo de la Reforma 880, Lomas de Santa Fe, Distrito Federal 01219, Mexico

[2]Universidad Iberoamericana Ciudad de México, DCI, Prolongación Paseo de la Reforma 880, Lomas de Santa Fe, Distrito Federal 01219, Mexico

[3]Physics and Mathematics Department, Universidad Iberoamericana Ciudad de México, Prolongación Paseo de la Reforma 880, Lomas de Santa Fe, Distrito Federal 01219, Mexico

ABSTRACT

DNA fragment assembly represents an important challenge to the development of efficient and practical algorithms due to the large number of elements to be assembled. In this study, we present some graph theoretical linear time algorithms to solve the problem. To achieve linear time complexity, a heap with constant time operations was developed, for the special case where the edge weights are integers and do not depend on the problem size. The experiments presented show that modified classical graph theoretical algorithms can solve the DNA fragment assembly problem efficiently.

INTRODUCTION

Since its discovery by Watson and Crick [1], the importance of DNA to biology, medicine and human kind has been evident. However, we had to wait some time until it was possible to sequence the DNA bases, which was accomplished by Sanger in the mid-1970s [2], by detecting small dark bands on a thin gel layer. This method severely constrains the length of the DNA to be sequenced due to the limited resolution of the dark bands. In order to solve this problem, the DNA is first cut in known places by using restriction enzymes, which will divide the DNA at the point where a specific base sequence is found. The resulting sub-sequences, are divided again, this time using a different restriction enzyme, and this process is repeated until the resulting fragments can be divided in random places yielding sub-fragments that are small enough as to provide the complete sequence of bases using Sanger's method. This process was slow and expensive because every time that a sequence was divided, each resulting subsequence had to be cloned in order to have enough material for the next division. This problem prompted scientists to start dividing sequences in random positions from the beginning, instead of doing it after several divisions, saving time and money [3]. This method, in turn, created a severe computational problem since there is no information about the order of the fragments. If one starts with many copies of the original problem and the derived fragments are sequenced, then each base of the original problem could appear in several fragments. The sum of the lengths of the fragments divided by the length of the original problem is known as its *coverage*. We hope that if we have a large enough coverage, the fragments will overlap in such a way that the sequence at the end of a fragment overlaps with the sequence at the beginning of another one. Hence, in theory, we should be able to use this information to sort the fragments and reconstruct the original DNA sequence.

What really happens is not very simple since, by chance, there are a huge number of false overlaps amongst the

Citation: Guillermo M. Mallén-Fullerton, J. Emilio Quiroz-Ibarra, Antonio Miranda, and Guillermo Fernández-Anaya. Modified classical graph algorithms for the DNA fragment assembly problem, Algorithms 2015, 8(3), 754-773; DOI: 10.3390/a8030754

fragments. There is also the problem that fragment sequencing is not perfect. Two percent error is common, as well as having fragments that do not belong to the original problem, some due to contamination with DNA foreign to the problem, and others because of the appearance of chimeras from the process of DNA cloning, in which bacteria DNA is used, so that we could get fragments with portions of bacteria DNA. On top of what was said, we have repeats, which are DNA sections that appear tens or hundreds of times one after another (tandem repeats) or in far away parts of the original DNA (interspersed repeats) [4].

As far as we know, at this point there is no good probabilistic model of DNA. Simple, or relatively simple ones do not explain the repeats. For instance, in the real life problem that we will present later in this paper, there are sequences of A bases that are extremely long. Figure 1 show some examples of fragments that come from the sample problem that we will use in Section 4 of this paper and Table 1 shows the probability that it happens considering that among the total number of fragments, the A bases occurs with probability 0.3249. As can be seen from the figure, the number of times that the A chain occurs in the real data is much larger than the expected value according to a simple probabilistic model. Despite these anomalies and some others, some of the parameters that are used in the assembly of fragments, such as the minimum number of bases that an overlap must have to be considered important, have an empirical basis [5].

There is also the problem that in real situations, sections of the original DNA problem have no coverage since fragments are obtained by a random process and it is not possible guarantee that there are fragments from every part of the genome under study. This is the reason why the resulting assembly of all fragments is a set of *contigs* or subsequences and almost never the entire sequence of the problem. It is the job of specialized biologists to fill in the gaps and correct assembly errors made during the automated process.

AAAAAAAAAAAAAAAAAAAAAAAAAAAAAAAAAAAAAAAAA

AAACAAAAAAAAAAAAAAAAAAAAAAAAAAAAAAAAAAAAA

AAAAACAAAAACAAAAAAAAAAAAAAAAAAAAAAAAAAAAA

AAAAAAAAAAAAAAAAAAAAAAAAAAAACAAATAAAAAAAC

AAAAAAAAAAAAAAAAAACAAAAAAAAAAAATAAAAAAAAA

ACAAAAAAAAAAAAAAAAAAAAACAAAAAAAAAAAAAAAAA

Figure 1. Some fragments from the *S. aureus* strain MW2 problem.

Table 1. Observed frequency on *n* bases A *vs.* expected value for p = 0.3249 and 5,324,340 fragments.

n	Observed	Probability	Expected Value
15	101	0.000000475	2.528889873
16	74	0.000000147	0.784225487
17	65	0.000000046	0.242640081
18	51	0.000000014	0.074884674
19	40	4.32861E−09	0.023046972
20	39	1.32807E−09	0.007071095
21	18	4.06052E−10	0.002161959
22	28	1.23662E−10	0.000658416
23	14	3.74924E−11	0.000199622
24	15	1.13089E−11	0.000060212
25	22	3.3908E−12	0.000018054
26	15	1.00958E−12	0.000005375
27	22	2.9809E−13	0.000001587
28	11	8.71281E−14	0.000000464
29	15	2.51495E−14	0.000000134
30	10	7.14487E−15	3.80417E−08
31	9	1.98796E−15	1.05846E−08
32	6	5.37563E−16	2.86217E−09
33	4	1.3946E−16	7.42531E−10
34	4	3.38757E−17	1.80366E−10
35	1	7.29107E−18	3.88201E−11

DNA fragment sequencing technology has continued to advance while costs continue to go down. The original *shotgun* technology has been called "long reads" because the fragments would normally have more than 500 bases. Using new technologies, commonly known as Next Generation Sequencing, the cost to sequence a million bases is about $1 [6]. Unfortunately, the length of the fragments is shorter using this newer technology. Today, 150 bases reads are common with the Illumina sequencers. To compensate for the problems derived from the short size of each fragment, coverage of about 40 is needed instead of a coverage of about 10 in the case of long reads. If we consider the number of fragments to be sequenced with newer technologies, we need to assemble three to four million fragments to sequence a bacterium, while using long reads, only 50,000 fragments were enough. These are really bad news due to the combinatorial nature of the solutions to the problem.

Since the very beginning of DNA fragment sequencing, greedy algorithms have been used; for instance, we pick a random fragment and connect to it the one that has the longest overlap. This process is repeated until no overlapping fragments are available. Nowadays, this technique would be difficult to use, since fragments are too short, which often produces several different fragments with the same overlap size. Another popular technique is the use of De Bruijn graphs [7]. In order to build these graphs, all possible *k-mers* (subsequence of *k* consecutive bases) of each fragment are used to find all possible overlaps among them. Using these graphs, several problems can be solved by using heuristics; for instance, given a *k-mer*, there might be two parallel paths to other *k-mer*, creating what is called a bubble. The bubble is then popped by removing the shortest side or projecting one side onto the other when they have the same length. Short sequences that originate from long ones are eliminated. It is common to use a value of *k*close to 20 in order to obtain the *k-mers*.

An approach based on genetic algorithm optimization was suggested by Parsons in 1993 [8]. Later, other scientists applied similar metaheuristics [9,10,11,12], but their results were based on very small benchmarks, the largest had about 1000 fragments, and even though results were improving slowly, they were still far from real problems, including the long reading ones, with tens of thousands of fragments. In 2013, a reduction from fragment DNA sequencing to the Traveling Salesman Problem (TSP) was used [13]. Taking advantage of formal heuristics and algorithms for the TSP, optimal values were found for the most commonly used benchmarks, and, for the first time, a real life problem was solved using optimization.

The remainder of this paper is organized as follows: Section 2 provides the basic ideas on the use of graph theory for the solution of DNA sequencing problems; Section 3 explains those algorithms that are necessary to tackle the problem; Section 4 illustrates the use of our algorithms on real life problem benchmarks; and, in Section 5, we give our conclusions and future work.

USE OF GRAPH THEORY

Generalities

In reference [13], a graph theory approach was used by means of the TSP, where the solution obtained from the assembly of fragments is a series of *contigs* rather than a Hamiltonian Path. In TSP, all possible edges of the graph are considered, but when there is no possible connection between two nodes, it is usually represented using a very large weight to prevent it from showing up in the final solution. Applying TSP to DNA fragment assembly might be considered excessive, even though the expected results are obtained, since the fraction of real connections is very small. A graph theoretical approach using other algorithms might give better results.

The size of real life DNA fragment assembly problems is huge, with 35 base fragments and a coverage of 40, we get about 700 million fragments for human chromosome number 1, which has 245 million base pairs. It is known that the DNA fragment assembly problem is NP-hard (Non-deterministic Polynomial time hard), since it can be reduced from the shortest common superstring problem [14]; in practice, we must only use linear time algorithms, even if by doing so we sacrifice correctness and obtain only an approximate solution.

DNA Fragment Assembly as a Graph

The DNA fragment assembly problem can be transformed into a directed graph: we need to find a sequence of fragments where each one is always the prefix of the next one. We know that DNA comes in pairs of strands (double helix) that run in opposite directions, where in front of each base of one strand, there is a base of the reverse-complement on the other; for instance, an A in front of a T and a C in front of a G, which clearly means that the information contained in each one of the strands is the same. When DNA fragment overlaps are obtained, it is not known what strand they come from, *i.e.*, every time that an overlap is computed, the strand and its reverse-complement must be considered. This means that a prefix of a normal overlap becomes a suffix of the reverse-complement. At first, it might seem that this case could be represented by a simple non-directed edge between the two fragments. However, this is not so if we consider that each node or fragment that is a reverse-complement must also be a reverse-complement for every edge that connects to it.

As a small example, we present a set of 13 fragments, Table 2, the associated overlap matrix, Table 3 and the resulting graph, Figure 2.

Table 2. Graph example: fragments.

Fragment number	Sequence
1	GTGTACCACGTACTGATGTACTATTTGAAGCTTAT
2	CCCAATTCCTAATGTACTATTTGAAGCTTATTCGG
3	CATAAGCTTCATGATGAAGCTTATTCGGCCAATCG
4	TTTGATTCCTGCTGATGTACTATTTGATGAAGCTT
5	ATGTACTATTTGAAGCTTATTCGGCCAATCGTACT
6	GAAGCTTATTCGGCCAATCGTACTGATGTACTATT
7	CTTATTCGGCCAATCGTACTATTTACTGATGTACA
8	TGATGAAGCTTATTCGGCCAATCGTACTGATGTAC
9	GGCCAATCGTACTGATGTACTATTTGATGAAGCTT
10	CTGATGTACTATTTGATGAAGCTTATTCGGCCAAT
11	TGTACTATTTGATGAAGCTTATCAGTACGTGGAAC
12	AATCGTACTGATGTACTATTTACTGATGTACAATA
13	CTATTTACTGATGTACAATAGTACATCAGTAAAAA

Table 3. Graph example: overlaps matrix.

	1	2	3	4	5	6	7	8	9	10	11	12	13
1					20								
2					24								
3						20		24					
4										24			
5						20	20						
6									24			20	
7													17
8									20				
9										24	20		
10								22					
11													
12													20
13													

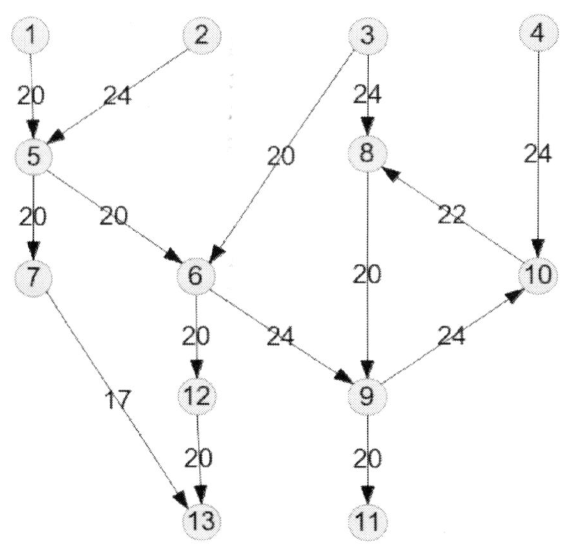

Figure 2. Graph example: graph.

Objective Function

In the literature, using nature inspired algorithms to solve the DNA fragment assembly problem published after Parsons [8], the associated graph has been considered to be an undirected graph. Other literature considered bi-directed graphs, especially when De Bruijn graphs were proposed. It is common to use a Hamiltonian path, even though sometimes Eulerian paths have been used too [7]. In any case, it is not entirely clear how many times each one of the fragments should be used, since, from the physical point of view, it is feasible for a sequence to repeat in different sections of the DNA, and for identical fragments to come from different places. Thinking that a fragment and it reverse-complement are the same, creates too much complexity from the algorithmic point of view as well as from the programming one, and would only be justified as long as it was strictly required to consider Hamiltonian paths. Hence, we consider each reverse-complement fragment as an independent fragment. Another possibility might be to trust the huge cover that is customary in Next Generation Sequencing (NGS) and not use reverse-complements.

With respect to the objective function for the optimization, in many papers, the sum of the overlaps of each fragment with the next one is used, which has probably been inherited from the use of some greedy algorithms. In addition to this objective function, we propose to maximize the sum of the lengths of the *contigs*. This can be achieved by considering that each time that a new fragment is added at the end of a *contig*, its length is incremented by an amount equal to the length of the fragment minus the overlap length. So we would have the following objective functions:

$$\max F_1 = \sum_{i=1}^{n-1} w(i,i+1) \tag{1}$$

$$\max F_2 = \sum_{i=1}^{n-1} (L - w(i,i+1)) \tag{2}$$

where $w(i, i+1)$ is the number of overlapped bases between fragment i and the next one in the sequence, n is the number of fragments, and L is the length of the fragment. Notice that Equation (2) can easily be transformed into a minimization:

$$\min F_2^{'} = \sum_{i=1}^{n-1} w(i,i+1) \tag{3}$$

Because

$$F_2 = (n-1)L - F_2^{'} \tag{4}$$

The boundary between *contigs* appears because there are values of $w(i, i+1)$ that are equal to 0. Since there is usually some contamination with foreign DNA and there might be chimeras, some of the obtained *contigs* do not belong to the original DNA, and, at some point, which is not within the scope of this paper, useful *contigs* must be separated from the useless ones.

In order to obtain each *contig*, an agreement must be reached (computed) for each base, *i.e.*, since we know that there might be redundancy for each base (due to the original cover) and that there might be sequencing errors in the fragments, it is possible for each base in each *contig* to have several versions, from which the most frequent value must be accepted, even if it is the minimum acceptable value. Since most of the errors in the *contigs* are at the ends, due to chemical problems in the sequencing equipment or because of the lack of enough redundancy, it might be necessary to cut them off.

ALGORITHMS

Basic Algorithm for F_1 and F_2

For the objective function F_1, we propose an algorithm similar to topological sorting. Let $G = (V, E)$ be a directed acyclic graph (DAG) where V is the set of vertices, E is the set of edges and $w(u, v)$ is the weight of edge u v. In this graph, the longest path will go from a node that has no edge going in (initial vertex) and those nodes that are connected to it. Notice that there might be several "initial vertices", and that there is no single privileged node. Let $S \subseteq V$ be the set of vertices with in-degree $d_{in}(v) = 0$ and let Q be a stack. The algorithm to determine the longest distance from a given vertex to each of the other vertices is the following (Algorithm 1):

Algorithm 1. Longest distance from initial vertices	
1.	For each vertex v∈S with $d_{in}(v) = 0$
1.1.	*push(Q,v)*
1.2.	*d(v):=0*
1.3.	*origin(v):=v*
2.	While Q is not empty
2.1.	*u:=pop(Q)*
2.2.	for each vertex v (u,v)∈E
2.2.1.	$d_{in}(v):=d_{in}(v)-1$
2.2.2.	if $d_{in}(v)=0$
2.2.2.1.	*push(Q,v)*
2.2.2.2.	d(v):=max(x,v)∈E(d(x)+w(x,v))
2.2.2.3.	*father(v):=x*

This algorithm only works if the graph is acyclic. In real life DNA fragment assembly problems, there are cycles. When this algorithm is applied to a graph with cycles, neither the cycles nor the nodes that are further from the cycles are detected. Later we will discuss how to take care of cycles.

Constant Time Heap

Aside from a modified version of the algorithm of Section 3.1, there are other ways to tackle the cycle problem. One way, not necessarily the best way, would be to build a minimum spanning tree, even if it ignores the direction of the edges. It is clear that if there are no undirected cycles in the equivalent undirected graph, there should be no directed cycles in its directed version. So we could use one of several algorithms like Prim [15] and Kruskal [16], both with time complexity in $O(|E| \log|V|)$ when using a Fibonacci Heap.

In order to achieve the linear time complexity that we require, we notice that in the case of the DNA fragment sequencing problem, we should use a heap that can insert and extract-min in constant time, thus improving the time complexity of other data structures where the extract-min operation is in $O(\log n)$.

Our heap requires that the ordering values are integers independent from the number of nodes in the graph. In the DNA fragment sequencing problem, the edges of the graph are the fragment overlaps, hence it is an integer value representing the number of bases, and its value is also bounded by $0 < w(u, v) < L$, where L does not depend of the number of fragments, and has a value of at most a few hundred bases. The heap that we propose is based on a *Stack* P_i for each possible value to be introduced. The heap operations are:

Algorithm 2. Stack heap insert and extract min
insert x
1. $push(P_x,x)$
2. if $x<xmin$
2.1. $xmin:=x$
3. *if* $x > xmax$
3.1. $xmax:=x$
extract-min
1. $x:=pop(P_{xmin})$
2. While the stack P_{xmin} is empty and $xmin \le xmax$
2.1. $xmin: = xmin + 1$

In the extract-min operations shown, the value that is in the stack corresponding to x_{min} is extracted. If the stack is empty, the next non-empty stack smaller than the maximum value is used. When the number of stacks is large enough, it is useful to use some other kind of heap, such as a binary or a Fibonacci heap instead of sequential search. In the example that we provide in Section 4, we use no more than 34 stacks ($0 \le x \le 34$), hence sequential search turns out to be faster. The time complexity of the insert operation is constant because Steps 1 through 3.1 always require the same amount of time. In the extract-min operation, Step 1 is of constant time and Step 2, which is only executed when the stack with the minimum values is empty, in the worst case depends on the value x_{max}, and could be linear, in the case of sequential search, or logarithmic if a heap is used. In the case of DNA fragment assembly, millions of edges or nodes will be inserted into the heap, hence the value of x_{max} should be close to a few hundred, which makes the probability of Step 2 executing more than once negligible. In any case, since the time complexity of our heap is independent from the number of nodes or vertices inserted into it, then Prim's algorithm [15] as well as Kruskal's [16] algorithm become linear. Even though our technique is designed to work in the particular case of DNA fragment assembly, it is possible that it could also be used in other problems.

MST in Linear Time

As mentioned before, when using our heap, Algorithm 2, Prim's algorithm as well as Kruskal's algorithm become linear, and even though it is possible to implement operations such as delete-key and decrease-key in our heap, it is more convenient to allow the edge values to create a cycle and discard them when leaving the heap, since this is more efficient and is also of constant time. Let $M(F, V)$ be the MST of graph $G(E, V)$ and let S be the set of vertices that have been added to the MST at some point during the execution of Prim's algorithm. Here is our version of Prim's algorithm:

Algorithm 3. Prim's algorithm
1. For some vertex u
1.1. Put u in S
1.2. For each (u,v)∈E
1.2.1. insert $w(u,v)$ in the heap
2. While the heap is not empty
2.1. Extract the edge (u, v) from the heap
2.1.1. if u∉S
2.1.1.1. Put u in S and (u,v) in F
2.1.1.1.1. For each (u,v)∈E insert $w(u,x)$ in the heap
2.1.2. if v∉S
2.1.2.1. Put v in S and (v,u) in F
2.1.2.1.1. For each (v,x)∈E insert $w(v,x)$ in the heap

Since at most $|E|$ edges will be inserted and extracted in constant time, Algorithm 3 will have a time complexity in $O(|E|)$.

Now, our version of Kruskal's algorithm (Algorithm 4):

Algorithm 4. Kruskal's algorithm
1. Insert E in a *heap* in increasing order of $w(u,v)$
2. Create a forest F where each vertex is an independent tree
3. While the heap is not empty
3.1. Extract (u,v) from heap
3.1.1. If u and v belong to different trees, merge both trees

In order to merge the trees, we use union by rank with path compression [17]. The time complexity of Step 1 is $O(|E|)$, Step 2 is $O(|V|)$. Step 3 is repeated $|E|$ times and every time the following operations are performed: extraction of the minimum value from the heap, a find of two nodes, and in the worst case, the union of two trees. Find is in $O(1)$ and the union is $O(\log^*|E|)$ [17], which for problems with 65,535 edges up to the maximum physical size of DNA fragment assembly problems is 5; therefore, in practice the algorithm is in $O(1)$. The total running time of Kruskal's algorithm using our heap, Algorithm 2, with union by rank and path compression, applied to the DNA fragment assembly problem is in $O(|E| + |V|)$. Once the MST has been computed, its maximum distances are computed using Algorithm 1. In this case, there are no cycles (directed or undirected), so Algorithm 1 works correctly.

Modification of the Basic Algorithm

There are two kinds of cycles that cause trouble: cycles that are connected to a start node, and disconnected cycles. In both cases, there might be sets of nodes that are created like attachments to nodes of the cycle, but do not belong to them, and are not detected by Algorithm 1. In the case of disconnected cycles, we would need to take any node as a start node, which can require some trial and error since a randomly selected node could be attached to the cycle but not necessarily in the cycle itself. However, disconnected cycles in real life DNA fragment sequencing problems are rare, and when they appear, they are usually very small, two or three nodes, that lead to *contigs* that are too small and that would have been discarded anyway.

A cycle connected to a start node of the graph appears when there are nodes for which, even when paths that go from a start node to another node *u* in the cycle, the value of $d_{in}(u)$ never goes to zero because at least one edge comes from the cycle. When Algorithm 1 is done, we can take one of the nodes that went through Step 2.2.1, but that remained with a final value of $d_{in}(u) > 0$, and insert it into the stack to continue with Step 2 of the algorithm. It is necessary, however, to mark those nodes so that they will not be considered again and to avoid the cycle being traversed more than once. The total distance from a start node to the last processed node in the cycle is the sum of the distance from a start point to the cycle entry point plus the length of the cycle, minus the edge that would close the cycle on the start node in the cycle. So we have that if the selected node is *s*, the previous node in the cycle is *t*, and the total length of the cycle is *C* then:

$$d(t) = d(s) + C - w(t,s) \tag{5}$$

Among the distinct entry nodes to the cycle, we could select one with the longest distance to a start node. However, it does not guarantee that we will always find the longest distance to node *t* since the value of *w(t, s)* changes with the selection of *s* and there could be another cycle entry node with a smaller value of *d(s)* but with a small enough value of *w(t, s)* to give a longest distance. In the case of the DNA fragment assembly problem the values of *w( )* are in a very narrow range, most of the distances to the start node are big and it is uncommon for them to be similar, so that if our heuristic consists of selecting an s with the longest distance to the start point, we will have a high probability of finding the maximum distance. The modified algorithm (Algorithm 5) is as follows:

Algorithm 5. Modified maximum distance algorithm
1. For each v∈S vertex with $d_{in}(v) = 0$
1.1. *push(Q,v)*
1.2. *d(v):=0*
1.3. *origin(v):=v*
2. While there are vertices *v* with $d_{in}(v) > 0$
2.1. While *Q* is not empty
2.1.1. *u:=pop(Q)*
2.1.2. For every vertex *v* where (u,v)∈E and *v* is not marked
2.1.2.1. $d_{in}(v):=d_{in}(v)-1$
2.1.2.2. If $d_{in}(v)=0$
2.1.2.2.1. *push(Q,v)*
2.1.2.2.2. d(v):=max(x,v)∈E(d(x)+w(x,v)
2.1.2.2.3. insert *d(v)* in a *heap*
2.1.2.2.4. *father(v):=x*
2.1.2.2.5. *origin(v):=origin(x)*
2.2. If the *heap* is not empty
2.2.1. extract the node *v* from *heap*
2.2.1.1. If $d_{in}(v)>0$
2.2.1.1.1. Make $d_{in}(v)=0$
2.2.1.1.2. Insert *v* in the stack
2.2.1.1.3. Mark the node *v*
2.2.1.1.4. Go to step 2.1

Notice that Step 2.2.1.1 is required since node *v* could have gone through Step 2.1.1 and already be in a path. In this case, we can use the heap to keep the time complexity of the algorithm linear.

Assembly Algorithm

The output from Algorithms 1 and 4 is a sequence of directed edges and nodes that allow us to directly build the*contigs*. Considering reverse-complement fragments as independent of the original ones makes the job easier. The reconstruction of the sequence of DNA in the *contig* consists of placing the first fragment, and then adding the overlap-free portion of the next fragment. In our method, we do not need to reach a computed agreement as in other methods [18] since we do not differentiate among overlapped bases from one or other fragment. However, the ends of the *contig* might have sequencing errors and there is nothing to verify that there are no such errors. The solution is to cut off the ends in such a way that a minimum agreement is reached, *i.e.*, that the bases must appear in at least a given number of fragments.

EXPERIMENTS

In order to test our algorithms, we used several benchmarks that are available for use by researchers [19]. We selected the benchmarks of *S. aureus* MW2 with short reads. The benchmarks that we used have the following number of fragments: 2,278,504, 730,201, 298,194, 89,718 and 22,447. From now on, we will refer to each one of these problems by its number of fragments. In order to have something to compare our results to, we ran the Edena assembler using the same data, Table 4. This comparison has some limitations due to the fact that Edena uses a series of heuristics in order to refine its solution, by eliminating *contigs* that have no real meaning, while our results are those directly generated by our algorithms with no refinement. Refining the raw results from our algorithms might be part of our future research.

Table 4. Edena benchmark results.

		Problem				
Fragments		22,448	89,718	298,194	730,201	2,278,504
Contigs Obtained		186	258	575	837	2046
Total Number of Bases		26,284	102,684	314,120	788,198	2,526,278
Contigs Found	Contigs Found	184	256	565	823	1920
	%	98.9	99.2	98.3	98.3	93.8
	Bases Found	26,024	102,249	310,965	777,583	2,463,563
	%	99	99.6	99	98.7	97.5
	N50	188	1247	2911	4132	5250
	Average Length	141.4	399.4	550.4	944.8	1283.10
	Minimum Length	52	52	52	52	52
	Maximum Length	880	7295	10,985	20,521	20,579
Contigs not Found	Contigs not Found	2	2	10	14	126
	%	1.1	0.8	1.7	1.7	6.2
	Bases not Found	260	435	3155	10,615	62,715
	%	1	0.4	1	1.3	2.5
	N50	NA	NA	NA	NA	5599
	Average Length	130	217.5	315.5	758.2	497.7
	Minimum Length	99	99	56	56	52
	Maximum Length	161	336	2521	5941	18,158

From each benchmark, we took only the fragment file in FASTA format, and from it we computed the overlaps among all fragments considering that reverse-complement fragments are also independent fragments (In the original benchmarks, there is a file of overlaps where reverse-complements are not considered as independent fragments). To compute overlaps, we used a *trie* (prefix tree). The computed overlaps are all larger than 20 bases. From these overlaps other sets of test data were obtained: one discarding redundant overlaps because of transitivity, and the other one, computing the MST. In all of the cases, the minimum agreement in Algorithm 5 was 4. The *contigs* obtained in each experiment were searched in the complete genome [20].

In Experiment 1, we used all of the overlaps larger than 20 bases and executed Algorithm 1 for the two objective functions. The results are presented in Table 5, Table 6 and Table 7.

Table 5. Experiments summary.

			Problem				
Algorithm		Fragments	22,448	89,718	298,194	730,201	2,278,504
Edena	Edena	Contigs Found	184	256	565	823	1920
		%	98.9	99.2	98.3	98.3	93.8
		Bases Found	26,024	102,249	310,965	777,583	2,463,563
		%	99	99.6	99	98.7	97.5
Algorithm 1	F1 Objective Function, all Overlaps.	Contigs Found	74	101	149	204	480
		%	90.2	88.6	91.4	91.1	94.1
		Bases Found	15,822	70,250	206,826	463,582	1,102,152
		%	81.8	83	86.1	83.9	83.4
Algorithm 1	F2 Objective Function, all Overlaps	Contigs found	74	102	146	189	450
		%	90.2	89.5	89.6	84.4	88.2
		Bases found	15,515	70,843	189,927	369,001	931,343
		%	81.5	83.8	79	66.8	69.9
Algorithm 1	F1 Objective Function, no Transitive overlaps	Contigs found	74	102	149	204	481
		%	90.2	89.5	91.4	91.1	93.9
		Bases found	15,806	71,652	206,826	462,774	1,103,587
		%	83.7	84.6	86.1	83.9	82.7

Algorithm 1	**F2 Objective Function, no Transitive Overlaps**	**Contigs found**	75	103	142	181	417
		%	91.5	90.4	87.1	80.8	81.4
		Bases found	15,599	72,245	174,244	320,502	791,376
		%	84	85.4	72.5	58.1	58.9
Algorithm 1	**F1 Objective Function, MST**	**Contigs found**	304	1827	5980	15,443	46,187
		%	91	97	98.4	98.9	95.7
		Bases found	35,980	256,641	815,994	2,081,306	6,208,258
		%	89.8	96.6	98.1	98.7	93.9
Algorithm 5	**F1 Objective function, no Transitive Edges**	**Contigs found**	74	102	150	205	480
		%	90.2	88.7	91.5	91.1	94.1
		Bases found	15,822	70,318	206,927	463,684	1,102,152
		%	81.8	83	86.1	83.9	83.4

Table 6. Algorithm 1, F_1 objective function, all overlaps.

		Problem				
Fragments		22,448	89,718	298,194	730,201	2,278,504
Contigs Obtained		82	114	163	224	510
Total Number of Bases		19,343	84,659	240,314	552,408	1,321,969
Contigs Found	**Contigs Found**	74	101	149	204	480
	%	90.2	88.6	91.4	91.1	94.1
	Bases Found	15,822	70,250	206,826	463,582	1,102,152
	%	81.8	83	86.1	83.9	83.4
	N50	360	1614	3326	4937	4499
	Average Length	213.8	695.5	1388.10	2272.50	2296.20
	Minimum Length	54	58	54	62	53
	Maximum Length	882	7261	10,943	22,745	24,396
Contigs not Found	**Contigs not Found**	8	13	14	20	30
	%	9.8	11.4	8.6	8.9	5.9
	Bases not Found	3521	14,409	33,488	88,826	219,817
	%	18.2	17	13.9	16.1	16.6
	N50	758	2308	3954	7258	11,798
	Average Length	440.1	1108.40	2392.00	4441.30	7327.20
	Minimum Length	95	95	95	181	255
	Maximum Length	826	3703	6809	9542	23,614

Table 7. Algorithm 1, F_2 objective function, all overlaps.

		Problem				
Fragments		22,448	89,718	298,194	730,201	2,278,504
Contigs Obtained		82	114	163	224	510
Total Number of Bases		19,028	84,584	240,280	552,509	1,331,757
Contigs Found	**Contigs Found**	74	102	146	189	450
	%	90.2	89.5	89.6	84.4	88.2
	Bases Found	15,515	70,843	189,927	369,001	931,343
	%	81.5	83.8	79	66.8	69.9
	N50	356	1527	3184	4298	4201
	Average Length	209.7	694.5	1300.90	1952.40	2069.70
	Minimum Length	54	58	54	59	53
	Maximum Length	882	7261	10,943	21,185	16,135

Contigs not Found	Contigs not Found	8	12	17	35	60
	%	9.8	10.5	10.4	15.6	11.8
	Bases not Found	3513	13,741	50,353	183,508	400,414
	%	18.5	16.2	21	33.2	30.1
	N50	758	2308	6336	7620	9472
	Average Length	439.1	1145.10	2961.90	5243.10	6673.60
	Minimum Length	95	96	103	181	251
	Maximum Length	826	3703	7626	22,745	24,396

From the DNA fragment assembly point of view, we are interested in large *contigs* with no errors. The most important elements to be computed are the number of bases and the *contigs* that were found in the complete genome, as well as the mean length of each *contig*. When we compare the results obtained by Algorithm 1 for F_1 and F_2 using all overlaps, we find that F_1 is a little bit better than F_2, except in the number of bases found for problem 89,718. In terms of multi objective function optimization, the solution obtained for F_1 is not enough to dominate the solution obtained by F_2, but since it is better in most of the test, we can say that it is almost dominant. In the other experiments, we find a similar situation, where F_1 is almost dominant with respect to F_2.

For Experiment 2, we excluded transitive overlaps and used Algorithm 1 for F_1 and F_2. The results are given inTable 5, Table 8 and Table 9.

Table 8. Algorithm 1, F_1 objective function, no transitive overlaps.

		Problem				
Fragments		22,448	89,718	298,194	730,201	2,278,504
Contigs Obtained		82	114	163	224	512
Total Number of Bases		18,879	84,646	240,314	551,600	1,333,881
Contigs Found	Contigs Found	74	102	149	204	481
	%	90.2	89.5	91.4	91.1	93.9
	Bases Found	15,806	71,652	206,826	462,774	1,103,587
	%	83.7	84.6	86.1	83.9	82.7
	N50	360	1527	3326	4937	4499
	Average Length	213.6	702.5	1388.10	2268.50	2294.40
	Minimum Length	54	58	54	62	53
	Maximum Length	882	7261	10,943	22,745	24,396
Contigs not Found	Contigs not Found	8	12	14	20	31
	%	9.8	10.5	8.6	8.9	6.1
	Bases not Found	3073	12,994	33,488	88,826	230,294
	%	16.3	15.4	13.9	16.1	17.3
	N50	539	2308	3954	7258	11,657
	Average Length	384.1	1082.80	2392.00	4441.30	7428.80
	Minimum Length	95	95	95	181	255
	Maximum Length	826	3703	6809	9542	23,614

In general, we found that F_1 is better than F_2 without dominating it. Comparing the results where transitive overlaps are excluded (Table 8 and Table 9 or Table 5) to those where they are not (Table 6 and Table 7 or Table 5), we can see that the results are similar for F_1, hence it is not clear whether it is better to exclude or not to exclude transitive overlaps. There is, however, an obvious advantage of excluding transitive overlaps, which is that the problem size is reduced and requires less computational resources. So, our recommendation is to exclude transitive overlaps.

Comparing our results so far to Edena, we find out that we obtained fewer correct bases and more *contigs* that are not in the genome, but the length of our *contigs* is better.

Table 9. Algorithm 1, F_2 objective function, no transitive overlaps.

		Problem				
Fragments		22,448	89,718	298,194	730,201	2,278,504
Contigs Obtained		82	114	163	224	512
Total Number of Bases		18,579	84,571	240,265	551,701	1,343,637
Contigs Found	**Contigs Found**	75	103	142	181	417
	%	91.5	90.4	87.1	80.8	81.4
	Bases Found	15,599	72,245	174,244	320,502	791,376
	%	84	85.4	72.5	58.1	58.9
	N50	356	1527	2984	3910	4135
	Average Length	208	701.4	1227.10	1770.70	1897.80
	Minimum Length	54	58	54	59	53
	Maximum Length	882	7,261	10,943	10,648	16,135
Contigs not Found	**Contigs not Found**	7	11	21	43	95
	%	8.5	9.6	12.9	19.2	18.6
	Bases not Found	2980	12,326	66,021	231,199	552,261
	%	16	14.6	27.5	41.9	41.1
	N50	539	2308	6336	8135	7554
	Average Length	425.7	1120.50	3143.90	5376.70	5813.30
	Minimum Length	95	96	103	181	251
	Maximum Length	826	3703	10,648	22,745	24,396

Table 10. Algorithm 1, F_1 objective function, Minimum Spanning Tree (MST).

		Problem				
Fragments		22,448	89,718	298,194	730,201	2,278,504
Contigs Obtained		334	1883	6080	15,618	48,263
Total Number of Bases		40,076	265,584	831,449	2,109,070	6,613,747
Contigs Found	**Contigs Found**	304	1827	5980	15,443	46,187
	%	91	97	98.4	98.9	95.7
	Bases Found	35,980	256,641	815,994	2,081,306	6,208,258
	%	89.8	96.6	98.1	98.7	93.9
	N50	135	165	154	153	153
	Average Length	118.4	140.5	136.5	134.8	134.4
	Minimum Length	62	62	61	57	57
	Maximum Length	446	660	747	894	1152
Contigs not Fund	**Contigs not Found**	30	56	100	175	2076
	%	9	3	1.6	1.1	4.3
	Bases not Found	4096	8943	15,455	27,764	405,489
	%	10.2	3.4	1.9	1.3	6.1
	N50	154	199	198	194	245
	Average Length	136.5	159.7	154.6	158.7	195.3
	Minimum Length	64	65	65	64	63
	Maximum Length	362	481	481	493	1130

In Experiment 3, we obtained the Minimum Spanning Tree (MST) from all overlaps using our version of Kruskal's algorithm. We only show the results for F_1 (Table 5 and Table 10). In this case, we were able to find much more bases in the genome than in previous experiments, including Edena, but the size of our *contigs* is small. There appears to be a tradeoff between the number of bases that can be found and *contig* length.

In other experiments, we used Algorithm 4 without transitive overlaps, obtaining similar results to those of Algorithm 1 for F_1 (F_1 was again better than F_2). Analyzing the *contigs* obtained by the algorithm, we found that if the*contig* is split at the edge that joins the cycle with the path, we have a better chance of finding both *contigs*. Therefore, we modified Algorithm 4 making d(v) = 0 in Step 2.2.1.1 and repeated Experiment 4 without transitive overlaps. In this case, the objective function F_1 was better than F_2 without being dominant. These results are given in Table 5 andTable 11.

Table 11. Algorithm 5, F_1 objective function, no transitive edges.

		Problem				
Fragments		22,448	89,718	298,194	730,201	2,278,504
Contigs Obtained		82	115	164	225	510
Total Number of Bases		19,343	84,727	240,415	552,510	1,321,969
Contigs Found	**Contigs Found**	74	102	150	205	480
	%	90.2	88.7	91.5	91.1	94.1
	Bases Found	15,822	70,318	206,927	463,684	1,102,152
	%	81.8	83	86.1	83.9	83.4
	N50	360	1614	3326	4937	4499
	Average Length	213.8	689.4	1379.50	2261.90	2296.20
	Minimum Length	54	58	54	62	53
	Maximum Length	882	7261	10,943	22,745	24,369
Contigs not Found	**Contigs not Fund**	8	13	14	20	30
	%	9.8	11.3	8.5	8.9	5.9
	Bases not Found	3521	14,409	33,488	88,826	219,817
	%	18.2	17	13.9	16.1	
	N50	758	2308	3954	7258	11,798
	Average Length	440.1	1108.40	2392.00	4441.30	7327.20
	Minimum Length	95	95	95	181	255
	Maximum Length	826	3703	6809	9542	23,614

In an analysis of those *contigs* that were not found in the genome, we considered the possibility of splitting them in two or more pieces hoping that all of them could be found. There are few cases in which *contigs* should be divided; in problem 730,201, using the modified Algorithm 4 with F_I, there were 513 *contigs* from which 414 were found directly, 76 were split in two to be found, 14 in three, 10 in four or more pieces, and two produced pieces that were too small to be considered. With appropriate rules, it should be possible to find the correct split points in most of the cases, as other assemblers do. We also analyzed residual paths, after removing paths of maximum length, from which we considered the possibility of recovering several long *contings*, which we will do in the future.

CONCLUSIONS AND FUTURE WORK

In order to assemble DNA, it is possible to use traditional graph theory concepts being careful to use only linear algorithms due to the large amount of data that is handled. With this idea, we developed a constant time heap, appropriate for this particular case (and maybe to other cases as well), which allowed us to reduce the time complexity of other algorithms, such as Prim's and Kruskal's, making them linear.

If we compare the results of the objective functions F_1 and F_2, even though one does not dominate over the other, better results are obtained using F_1, hence we recommend its use. We also recommend the removal of transitive overlaps because of resource reduction considerations, even though the results of the assembly are almost the same for function F_1. The use of the MST considerably improves the number of correct bases, but the *contigs* obtained in this way are too small. It can be seen from the experiments that there is a tradeoff between *contig* length and the number of bases detected. Comparing our results to those of Edena is not completely objective since we do not apply heuristics after the algorithms are executed in order to refine the solutions, but Edena (as well as the Velvet assembler) do so intensively. In any case, compared to Edena, our method produced, in some cases, less bases but longer *contigs*, while, in other cases, we found more bases, but shorter *contigs*, especially when using MST. Therefore, the problem must be considered as a multi objective optimization, with an objective function that is able to maximize the number of mean *contig* length, giving the user a Pareto Front from which he can obtain the most convenient solution according to his particular criteria.

Our future work includes:

- Developing rules to split *contigs* in such a way that most of the pieces can be found.
- Attempting to recover other *contigs* after extracting the longest ones.
- Implementing a solution to DNA fragment assembly as a multi objective optimization problem.

ACKNOWLEDGMENTS

This work has been developed with the support of Universidad Iberoamericana.

AUTHOR CONTRIBUTIONS

Guillermo Mallén-Fullerton started the idea and developed the algorithms. Emilio Quiroz-Ibarra developed test programs and provided helpful observations about the implementation problems associated with some of the algorithms. Antonio Miranda and Guillermo Fernández-Anaya provided algorithms complexity analysis and observations to improve it. Guillermo Fernández-Anaya collaborated in the experiments design and interpretation and Antonio Miranda wrote the English version of the article. All authors approved the manuscript.

REFERENCES

1. Watson, J.D.; Crick, F.H. Molecular structure of nucleic acids. *Nature* 1953, *171*, 737–738.
2. Sanger, F.; Nicklen, S.; Coulson, A.R. DNA sequencing with chain-terminating inhibitors. *Proc. Natl. Acad. Sci.*1977, *74*, 5463–5467.
3. Staden, R. A strategy of DNA sequencing employing computer programs. *Nucl. Acid. Res.* 1979, *6*, 2601–2610.
4. Van Belkum, A.; Scherer, S.; van Alphen, L.; Verbrugh, H. Short-sequence DNA repeats in prokaryotic genomes. *Microbiol. Mol. Biol. Rev.* 1998, *62*, 275–293.
5. Salzberg, S.L.; Phillippy, A.M.; Zimin, A.; Puiu, D.; Magoc, T.; Koren, S.; Yorke, J.A. GAGE: A critical evaluation of genome assemblies and assembly algorithms. *Gen. Res.* 2012, *22*, 557–567.
6. Shendure, J.; Ji, H. Next-generation DNA sequencing. *Nat. Biotechnol.* 2008, *26*, 1135–1145.
7. Pevzner, P.A.; Tang, H.; Waterman, M.S. An Eulerian path approach to DNA fragment assembly. *Proc. Natl. Acad. Sci.* 2001, *98*, 9748–9753.
8. Parsons, R.J.; Forrest, S.; Burks, C. Genetic algorithms for DNA sequence assembly. In Proceedings of the First International Conference on Intelligent Systems for Molecular Biology (ISMB), Bethesda, MD, USA, 6–9 July 1993; pp. 310–318.
9. Krause, J.; Cordeiro, J.; Parpinelli, R.S.; Lopes, H.S. A Survey of Swarm Algorithms Applied to Discrete Optimization Problems. In *Swarm Intelligence and Bio-inspired Computation: Theory and Applications*; Elsevier Science Publishers: Amsterdam, The Netherlands, 2013.
10. Alba, E.; Luque, G. A new local search algorithm for the DNA fragment assembly problem. In *Evolutionary Computation in Combinatorial Optimization*; Springer: Berlin/Heidelberg, Germany, 2007; pp. 1–12.
11. Luque, G.; Alba, E. Metaheuristics for the DNA fragment assembly problem. *Int. J. Comput. Intel. Res.* 2005, *1*, 98–108.
12. Firoz, J.S.; Rahman, M.S.; Saha, T.K. Bee algorithms for solving DNA fragment assembly problem with noisy and noiseless data. In Proceedings of the 14th ACM Annual Conference on Genetic and Evolutionary Computation, Philadelphia, PA, USA, 7–11 July 2012; pp. 201–208.
13. Mallen-Fullerton, G.M.; Fernandez-Anaya, G. DNA fragment assembly using optimization. In Proceedings of the 2013 IEEE Congress on Evolutionary Computation (CEC), Cancun, Mexico, 20–23 June 2013; pp. 1570–1577.
14. Gallant, J.; Maier, D.; Astorer, J. On finding minimal length superstrings. *J. Comput. Syst. Sci.* 1980, *20*, 50–58.
15. Prim, R.C. Shortest connection networks and some generalizations. *Bell Syst. Tech. J.* 1957, *36*, 1389–1401.
16. Kruskal, J.B. On the shortest spanning subtree of a graph and the traveling salesman problem. *Proc. Am. Math. Soc.* 1956, *7*, 48–50.
17. Hopcroft, J.E.; Ullman, J.D. Set merging algorithms. *SIAM J. Comput.* 1973, *2*, 294–303.
18. Bonfield, J.K.; Smith, K.; Staden, R. A new DNA sequence assembly program. *Nucl. Acid. Res.* 1995, *23*, 4992–4999.
19. Mallén-Fullerton, G.M.; Hughes, J.A.; Houghten, S.; Fernández-Anaya, G. Benchmark datasets for the DNA fragment assembly problem. *Int. J. Bio-Inspir. Comput.* 2013, *5*, 384–394.
20. Staphylococcus *aureus* subsp. aureus MW2 DNA, complete genome, GenBank: BA000033.2. Available online: http://www.ncbi.nlm.nih.gov/nuccore/47118312?report=fasta (accessed on 3 June 2015).

CHAPTER 13

A BENCHMARKING ALGORITHM TO DETERMINE MINIMUM AGGREGATION DELAY FOR DATA GATHERING TREES AND AN ANALYSIS OF THE DIAMETER-AGGREGATION DELAY TRADEOFF

Natarajan Meghanathan

Computer Science, Jackson State University, Jackson, MS 39217, USA; Tel.: +1-601-979-3661

ABSTRACT

Aggregation delay is the minimum number of time slots required to aggregate data along the edges of a data gathering tree (DG tree) spanning all the nodes in a wireless sensor network (WSN). We propose a benchmarking algorithm to determine the minimum possible aggregation delay for DG trees in a WSN. We assume the availability of a sufficient number of unique CDMA (Code Division Multiple Access) codes for the intermediate nodes to simultaneously aggregate data from their child nodes if the latter are ready with the data. An intermediate node has to still schedule non-overlapping time slots to sequentially aggregate data from its own child nodes (one time slot per child node). We show that the minimum aggregation delay for a DG tree depends on the underlying design choices (bottleneck node-weight based or bottleneck link-weight based) behind its construction. We observe the bottleneck node-weight based DG trees incur a smaller diameter and a larger number of child nodes per intermediate node; whereas, the bottleneck link-weight based DG trees incur a larger diameter and a much lower number of child nodes per intermediate node. As a result, we observe a complex diameter-aggregation delay tradeoff for data gathering trees in WSNs.

INTRODUCTION

Wireless Sensor Networks (WSNs) are typically deployed for monitoring environmental data such as temperature, pressure, humidity, *etc*. Sensor nodes operate under limited battery charge and transmission range. Hence, the data sensed at one or more sensor nodes cannot be directly propagated to the control center (a.k.a. sink); multi-hop data propagation is the norm. Various algorithms for determining communication topologies (like cluster [1], grid [2], chain [3], connected dominating set [4], tree [5], *etc.*) that support the many-to-one reporting style have been proposed in the literature. Among these, the data gathering trees (DG trees) have been considered energy-efficient due to the use of the minimum number of links for data transmission and reception [5,6,7].

In this research, we focus on the delay incurred for data aggregation along the edges of a DG tree. We define the aggregation delay as the minimum number of time slots it takes for the data to be aggregated in a data gathering tree (DG tree) spanning all the nodes of the network. Various algorithms (e.g., [8,9,10,11,12,13]) have been proposed to determine the aggregation delay for DG trees and all of these assume limited availability of the communication channels and focus on scheduling the channels for the different nodes to minimize the aggregation delay. In this paper, we consider a channel availability model such that the intermediate nodes at the same level or different levels could simultaneously aggregate data from their respective child nodes using different CDMA (Code

Citation: Natarajan Meghanathan. A benchmarking algorithm to determine minimum aggregation delay for data gathering trees and an analysis of the diameter-aggregation delay tradeoff, Algorithms 2015, 8(3), 435-458; DOI: 10.3390/a8030435

Division Multiple Access) codes [14]. An intermediate node has to schedule non-overlapping time slots (one for each of its child nodes: Time Division Multiple Access, TDMA) to aggregate data from its child nodes. Given a DG tree with sufficient availability of communication channels with unique CDMA codes, we propose a benchmarking algorithm to determine the minimum aggregation delay at every intermediate node (including the root node) of the DG tree.

We run the proposed algorithm on four broad categories of DG trees typically used for data aggregation in WSNs [5,15,16,17,18,19,20]: The Maximum Bottleneck Node Weight-based Data Gathering trees (MaxBNW-DG trees) are the ones for which the bottleneck node weight (minimum node weight) of the path from any node to the root node is the maximum; the Minimum Bottleneck Node Weight-based Data Gathering trees (MinBNW-DG trees) are the ones for which the bottleneck node weight (maximum node weight) of the path from any node to the root node is the minimum. The Maximum Bottleneck Link Weight-based Data Gathering trees (MaxBLW-DG trees) are the ones for which the bottleneck link weight (minimum link weight) of the constituent links of a path from any node to the root node is the maximum; the Minimum Bottleneck Link Weight-based Data Gathering trees (MinBLW-DG trees) are the ones for which the bottleneck link weight (maximum link weight) of the constituent links of a path from any node to the root node is the minimum. MaxBNW-DG trees could be used to determine DG trees with a larger residual energy per intermediate node such that the minimum node energy of the path from any node to the root node is the maximum (e.g., [15,16]). The MinBNW-DG trees could be used to determine DG trees in mobile sensor networks with lower velocity for the intermediate nodes such that the maximum node velocity of the path from any node to the root node is the minimum (e.g., [17]). MaxBLW-DG trees could be used to determine DG trees with a larger trust score for each link on the tree such that the minimum trust score for any of the constituent links of a path from any node to the root node is the maximum (e.g., [18]); the MinBLW-DG trees could be used to determine DG trees with maximum of the square of the link distance (measure of the transmission energy loss) for any of the constituent links for a path from any node to the root node is the minimum (e.g., [19]).

Most of the work conducted in the literature focus on deriving bounds for the aggregation delay for the data gathering trees as a function of various networking parameters (like density, diameter, node degree, *etc.*). To the best of our knowledge, we have not come across any work that has analyzed the aggregation delay for data gathering trees as a function of the structure of the data gathering tree itself. We hypothesize that there could be two distinct types of data gathering trees depending on the way they are constructed (bottleneck node-weight based and bottleneck link-weight based). Our hypothesis is confirmed through the simulations. We observe the bottleneck node-weight based data gathering trees to incur a smaller diameter and a larger number of child nodes per intermediate node, thereby incurring a larger aggregation delay compared to that of the bottleneck link-weight based data gathering trees that incur a relatively larger diameter and a fewer number of child nodes per intermediate node. We thus see a diameter-aggregation delay tradeoff for data gathering trees in sensor networks and this has been hitherto not reported in the literature.

The rest of the paper is organized as follows: Section 2 discusses related work on the lower and upper bounds for aggregation delay in sensor networks and highlights our contributions. Section 3 presents the system model and presents in detail the Maximum Bottleneck Node Weight-based data gathering (MaxBNW-DG) algorithm. The section also presents the modifications to the MaxBNW-DG algorithm to determine the MinBNW-DG, MaxBLW-DG and MinBLW-DG trees, as defined above. Section 4 presents in detail the algorithms to determine the diameter of the DG tree and the minimum aggregation delay for a DG tree. Section 5 presents results of simulation studies conducted on the four categories of DG trees and discusses the results obtained for the diameter, aggregation delay, hop count per path and the distribution of the child nodes per intermediate node and the leaf nodes as well analyzes the tradeoffs.Section 6 concludes the paper and discusses plans for future work.

RELATED WORK AND OUR CONTRIBUTIONS

In this section, we first present the existing work in the literature on algorithms related to aggregation delay for data gathering trees in sensor networks. We then motivate the need for analyzing the aggregation delay as a function of the type of the data gathering trees and thereby also exploring the diameter-aggregation delay tradeoff. Most of the work conducted in the literature focus on deriving theoretical bounds for the minimum and maximum aggregation delay as a function of the network parameters such as the number of nodes, maximum node degree, diameter of the network, transmission range of the nodes, *etc.*, without considering the type of data gathering trees that are determined. For example, the paper [8] proposes $O(\Delta + D/2)$ as the upper bound for aggregation delay where Δ is the maximum node degree and D is the diameter of the network (in terms of the number of hops), and in [10], the authors showed that the upper bound for aggregation latency in a multi-sink scenario is $O(\Delta + k*D/2)$, where k is the number of sinks. In [21], the authors show that the lower bound for the aggregation delay is $\max\{D/2, \log_2^n\}$, where n is the number of nodes in the network. However, the aforementioned works do not analyze the possible differences in the minimum or maximum aggregation delays due to the type of the underlying data gathering trees involved.

To the best of our knowledge, ours is the first such work to show that for a given network, the minimum aggregation delay principally depends on the type of the data gathering tree (bottleneck node weight-based or bottleneck link weight-based) and could be significantly different for the two categories of data gathering trees. Likewise, the focus of tradeoff analysis has been on the aggregation delay—energy consumption tradeoff (e.g., [22,23,24]) as a function of the underlying interference models, availability of the channels and the channel scheduling schemes used. To the best of our knowledge, ours is the first such work to analyze the diameter-aggregation delay tradeoff as a function of the type of the underlying data gathering tree (bottleneck node weight-based or bottleneck link weight-based) involved.

Some of the works in the literature (e.g., [25]) focus on developing distributed algorithms to minimize the aggregation delay as much as possible (given a set of available channels). A common trend among these distributed algorithms is to first construct a spanning tree of the network based on a link or node criterion, determine a connected dominating set (CDS) [26] of the nodes (a CDS is a set of nodes such that every node in the network is either in this set or is a neighbor of the nodes in this set) in the spanning tree, form a data gathering tree of the nodes that are part of the CDS and construct a TDMA-schedule of the nodes that are part of the CDS to aggregate data according to the availability of the channels. Our approach in the paper is different. Given a graph with node weights or link weights, we directly construct a bottleneck node weight or bottleneck link weight-based data gathering tree of the network. We make use of the observation made in [27] that the intermediate nodes of a bottleneck node weight or bottleneck link weight based DG tree are also the nodes constituting a CDS constructed with the objective of optimizing the bottleneck node weight or bottleneck link weight.

Our contributions in this paper are twofold: First, we propose a benchmarking algorithm that, given a DG tree, (with sufficient number of communication channels with unique CDMA codes) determines the minimum aggregation delay at every intermediate node (including that of the root node) of the DG tree. To the best of our knowledge, we have not come across a benchmarking algorithm that gives the minimum aggregation delay for any intermediate node *vis-à-vis* its position in the DG tree. The aggregation delays obtained with our centralized benchmarking algorithm will serve as a lower bound for the aggregation delays determined with the distributed algorithms proposed in the literature. Second, for a given WSN graph, we observe the bottleneck link-weight based data gathering trees to incur a lower aggregation delay, but a larger diameter; on the other hand, the bottleneck node-weight based data gathering trees incur a larger aggregation delay but a smaller diameter. Ours is the first work to comprehensively analyze the diameter-aggregation delay tradeoff for sensor networks and show that the tradeoff depends on the type of the underlying data gathering trees used (bottleneck node-weight based or bottleneck link-weight based).

GENERIC ALGORITHM TO DETERMINE MAXIMUM BOTTLENECK NODE WEIGHT-BASED DATA GATHERING TREES

In this section, we present an algorithm to determine maximum bottleneck node weight-based data gathering trees (MaxBNW-DG trees) that could work with any notion of node weights. We then illustrate the generic nature of the algorithm by explaining how it could be easily adapted and be used for determining minimum bottleneck node weight-based data gathering trees as well as the maximum and minimum bottleneck link-weight based data gathering trees.

System Model

In this subsection, we present the graph model considered for the sensor networks, the channel availability model for the nodes and an overview of the data aggregation process. We assume a wireless sensor network (WSN) to be modeled as a weighted undirected graph $G = (V, E, W_V, W_E)$ of a set of vertices (V) and edges (E); the link weights (W_E) may or may not be related to node weights (W_V). The link weights and node weights are positive real numbers. We assume each node in the graph has a weight; if two or more nodes have the same weight during the execution of the algorithms (described in Section 3.2, Section 3.3, Section 3.4 and Section 3.5), ties are broken arbitrarily. We do not anticipate frequently encountering ties, as the node weights (as well as link weights) are real numbers (and not integers). We use higher precisions for the real numbers (of length allowed by the programming environment) in the simulations. In addition, in the simulations, since we run multiple iterations of the algorithms for the same operating condition and average the results, our conjecture is that the arbitrary breaking of the ties is the best way to avoid any bias towards excessive usage of any particular node. For example, if the ties are broken in favor of the node with a smaller ID or larger ID, then such nodes get overused all the time in situations of a tie and the results could be biased.

Each vertex in the graph corresponds to a node in the WSN. There exists an undirected edge between two vertices if the Euclidean distance between the corresponding nodes in the network is within the transmission range of the nodes. We assume the transmission range of the nodes to be identical. A data-gathering tree (DG tree) of a WSN graph is rooted at a particular node (referred to as the leader node) and spans all the vertices of the graph and aggregation of data proceeds from the leaf nodes towards the leader node. An intermediate node waits for aggregated data or individual data (depending on the case) coming from its immediate child nodes, aggregates its own data with it and forwards the aggregated data to its own upstream node in the tree. We assume the energy level at the sensor nodes to be sufficient enough throughout the network session and that there would be no failure of nodes due to energy exhaustion (this way, we could extract the best possible and/or expected performance from the benchmarking algorithms with respect to the metrics that they are designed to optimize). We assume the sensor nodes to be both TDMA (Time Division Multiple Access) and CDMA (Code Division Multiple Access) enabled [14]. An intermediate node assigns TDMA time slots to its immediate child nodes so that they can send the aggregated data to their parent node, one at a time, without any collision. However, two intermediate nodes at the same level or different levels of the DG tree could simultaneously gather data from their respective child nodes by using different CDMA codes.

Description of the MaxBNW-DG Algorithm

The underlying theme behind the MaxBNW-DG algorithm is to give preference for nodes with larger weights to serve as intermediate nodes. The bottleneck weight of a path between two nodes is the minimum of the weights of the nodes on the path (including those of the end nodes). Each node prefers to join the DG tree through a neighbor that has the largest bottleneck weight path to the root node. The bottleneck weight of the path that connects a node to the root node of the DG tree is referred to as the *Tree-join-weight*. We maintain three lists during the execution of the algorithm: *Candidate-Nodes-List*, *Optimized-Nodes-List* and *Parent-Node-List*. The bottleneck path weights of the vertices in the *Candidate-Nodes-List* are referred to as the *Estimated-join-weights* (an estimate of the optimal bottleneck weight of the path to the root node) and when a vertex is removed from the *Candidate-Nodes-List* and included in the *Optimized-Nodes-List*, we set its *Tree-join-weight* to the value of the *Estimated-join-weight* of the vertex at the time of its removal from the *Candidate-Nodes-List*. The *Candidate-Nodes-List* is implemented as a priority queue (maximum heap) [26]. The*Parent-Node-List* keeps track of the predecessor node for every node in the DG tree. Algorithm 1 presents the pseudo code for the MaxBNW-DG algorithm.

Algorithm 1. Pseudo Code for the Algorithm to Determine Maximum Bottleneck Node Weight-DG Trees.

Input: Graph $G = (V, E, W_V, W_E)$

Output: $T_{Max}^{BNW}(V, E_T)$ where E_T is the set of edges in the MaxBNW-DG tree

Auxiliary Variables: *Optimized-Nodes-List, Candidate-Nodes-List, Parent-Node-List*
Estimated-join-weight, Tree-join-weight, Leader Node

Initialization: *Optimized-Nodes-List* = ϕ; *Candidate-Nodes-List* = ϕ, *Parent-Node-List* = ϕ, $E_T = \phi$
$\forall u \in V$: *Estimated-join-weight*(u) = -1, *Tree-join-weight*(u) = -1

```
Begin MaxBNW-DG Algorithm
    Leader Node s = {u | Maximum_{u∈V}(W_V(u)) }
    Parent-Node-List(s) = NULL
    Candidate-Nodes-List = Candidate-Nodes-List ∪ {s}
    Estimated-join-weight(s) = W_V(s)
    while (Candidate-Nodes-List ≠ ϕ) do
        Node u = {i | Maximum_{i∈Candidate-Nodes-List} (Estimated-join-weights(i)}
        Candidate-Nodes-List = Candidate-Nodes-List - {u}
        Optimized-Nodes-List = Optimized-Nodes-List ∪ {u}
        Tree-join-weight(u) = Estimated-join-weight(u)
        for ( Node v ∈ Neighbors(u) AND v ∉ Optimized-Nodes-List) do
            if (Estimated-join-weight(v) < Minimum( W_V(v), Tree-join-weight(u) ) ) then
                Estimated-join-weight(v) = Minimum( W_V(v), Tree-join-weight(u) )
                Parent-Node-List(v) = u
            end if
        end for
    end while
    if (Candidate-Nodes-List = ϕ AND | Optimized-Nodes-List | < | V | ) then
        return NULL; // the graph is not connected
    end if
    if (Candidate-Nodes-List = ϕ AND | Optimized-Nodes-List | = | V | ) then
        for (Node u ∈ V AND u ≠ Leader Node ) do
            E_T = E_T ∪ {(u, Parent-Node-List(u))}
        end for
    end if
    return T_Max^BNW (V, E_T)
End MaxBNW-DG Algorithm
```

The algorithm proceeds in iterations; in each iteration, we explore the neighborhood (*i.e.*, visit the neighbor nodes) of a vertex that currently has the largest *Estimated-join-weight* among the vertices in the *Candidate-Nodes-List*. As part of this procedure, the vertex is also removed from the *Candidate-Nodes-List* and added to the *Optimized-Nodes-List*; we say the vertex has been optimized (*i.e.*, its *Estimated-join-weight* cannot be further increased) and set its *Tree-join-weight* to be its *Estimated-join-weight* value at the time of exploring its neighbors and removal from the *Candidate-Nodes-List*. Thus, the *Optimized-Nodes-List* includes vertices whose neighborhood has been already explored and the *Tree-join-weight* of a vertex at the time of its inclusion in the *Optimized-Nodes-List* is the best possible bottleneck path weight with which the node can be part of the DG tree.

The root node of the DG tree (also called the leader node) is the vertex with the largest weight among the vertices in the graph. The leader node is on the largest bottleneck weight path to itself. Initially, the leader node has an *Estimated-join-weight* corresponding to its individual weight and the *Estimated-join-weight* of the other vertices in the graph is set to −1. We start the algorithm by including the leader node as the only vertex in the *Candidate-Nodes-List* and explore its neighbors. In each iteration, as we explore the neighborhood of a vertex u with the largest *Estimated-join-weight* (that is also the *Tree-join-weight* for node u, pending u's removal from the *Candidate-Nodes-List*) among the vertices in the *Candidate-Nodes-List*, we examine whether the *Estimated-join-weight* values for each of the neighbors (say, v) of u could be improved further by making u as the parent node of v. We do this by first checking whether the currently *Estimated-join-weight* of node v is still less than both the individual weight of node v and the *Tree-join-weight*of node u, and if found so, we set the *Estimated-join-weight* of node v to the minimum of the individual weight of node$v$ and the *Tree-join-weight* of node u as well as set node u to be the parent (predecessor) for node v in the DG tree. We continue the iterations until the *Candidate-Nodes-List* gets empty (by this time, all the vertices in the graph are in the*Optimized-Nodes-List* if the graph is connected) and every node other than the leader node would have a parent node in the tree. If the graph is not connected, the *Candidate-Nodes-List* gets empty when there is still at least one vertex that is not yet in the *Optimized-Nodes-List*; the vertices not included in the *Optimized-Nodes-List* are not in the same connected component of the leader node.

Modifications to the MaxBNW-DG Algorithm to Determine MinBNW-DG Tree

A MinBNW-DG tree is the one for which the bottleneck node weight on a path is defined as the maximum of the node weights (instead of the minimum of the node weights as in a MaxBNW-DG tree) and the objective would be to determine a DG tree for which the bottleneck node weight for a path from any node to the root node is the minimum. Accordingly, we start with the node having the minimum node weight and accommodate nodes in the increasing order of the *Tree-join-weight*; we modify the pseudo code of the MaxBNW-DG algorithm as shown in Algorithm 2: the lines that are not explicitly shown are the same as in the MaxBNW-DG algorithm.

Algorithm 2. Pseudo Code for the Algorithm to Determine Minimum Bottleneck Node Weight-DG Trees.

Input: Graph $G = (V, E, W_V, W_E)$

Output: $T_{Min}^{BNW}(V, E_T)$ where E_T is the set of edges in the MinBNW-DG tree

Auxiliary Variables: *Optimized-Nodes-List, Candidate-Nodes-List, Parent-Node-List*
Estimated-join-weight, Tree-join-weight, Leader Node

Initialization: *Optimized-Nodes-List* = ϕ; *Candidate-Nodes-List* = ϕ, *Parent-Node-List* = ϕ, $E_T = \phi$
$\forall u \in V$: *Estimated-join-weight*(u) = ∞, *Tree-join-weight*(u) = ∞

Begin *MinBNW-DG Algorithm*

1 *Leader Node* $s = \{u \mid Minimum(W_V(u))\}$

2...4 (as in the pseudo code for the MaxBNW-DG algorithm, refer Algorithm 1)

5 ***while*** (*Candidate-Nodes-List* $\neq \phi$) ***do***

6 Node $u = \{i \mid \underset{i \in Candidate-Nodes-List}{Minimum} (Estimated\text{-}join\text{-}weights(i)\}$

7...8 (as in the pseudo code for the MaxBNW-DG algorithm, refer Algorithm 1)

10 ***for*** (Node $v \in Neighbors(u)$ AND $v \notin$ *Optimized-Nodes-List*) ***do***

11 ***if*** (*Estimated-join-weight*(v) > ***Maximum***($W_V(v)$, *Tree-join-weight*(u))) ***then***

12 *Estimated-join-weight*(v) = ***Maximum***($W_V(v)$, *Tree-join-weight*(u))

13 *Parent-Node-List*(v) = u

14 ***end if***

15 ***end for***

16...24 (as in the pseudo code for the MaxBNW-DG algorithm, refer Algorithm 1)

25 ***return*** $T_{Min}^{BNW}(V, E_T)$

End *MinBNW-DG Algorithm*

Modifications to the MaxBNW-DG Algorithm to Determine the MaxBLW-DG Tree

A MaxBLW-DG tree is the one for which the bottleneck link weight (minimum of the weights of the constituent links) for a path from any node to the root node is the maximum. In this section, we illustrate the modification of the MaxBNW-DG algorithm to determine a MaxBLW-DG tree. Instead of starting with a node having the largest or smallest weight, we could start with an arbitrarily chosen node and set its *Tree-join-weight* to ∞ and initialize the *Estimated-join-weights* of the other vertices to -1. Assuming the graph has positive edge weights, the objective would be then to increase the *Estimated-join-weights* of the other vertices as much as possible and eventually join a vertex to the DG tree through an incident edge that has the largest weight (that is also the *Tree-join-weight* of the vertex). We modify the pseudo code of the MaxBNW-DG algorithm as in Algorithm 3 to obtain the MaxBLW-DG tree.

Algorithm 3. Pseudo Code for the Algorithm to Determine Maximum Bottleneck Link Weight-DG Trees.

Input: Graph $G = (V, E, W_V, W_E)$

Output: $T_{Max}^{BLW}(V, E_T)$ where E_T is the set of edges in the MaxBLW-DG tree

Auxiliary Variables: *Optimized-Nodes-List, Candidate-Nodes-List, Parent-Node-List*
Estimated-join-weight, Tree-join-weight, Leader Node

Initialization: *Optimized-Nodes-List* = ϕ; *Candidate-Nodes-List* = ϕ, *Parent-Node-List* = ϕ, $E_T = \phi$
$\forall u \in V$: *Estimated-join-weight*(u) = -1, *Tree-join-weight*(u) = -1

Begin ***MaxBLW-DG Algorithm***

1 *Leader Node s* is arbitrarily chosen among the vertices in V
2...3 (as in the pseudo code for the MaxBNW-DG algorithm, refer Algorithm 1)
4 *Estimated-join-weight*(s) = ∞
5 ***while*** (*Candidate-Nodes-List* $\neq \phi$) ***do***
6 Node $u = \{i \mid \underset{i \in Candidate-Nodes-List}{Maximum}$ (*Estimated-join-weights*(i))$\}$
7...9 (as in the pseudo code for the MaxBNW-DG algorithm, refer Algorithm 1)
10 ***for*** (Node $v \in$ *Neighbors*(u) AND $v \notin$ *Optimized-Nodes-List*) ***do***
11 ***if*** (*Estimated-join-weight*(v) < $W_E(u\text{-}v)$) ***then***
12 *Estimated-join-weight*(v) = $W_E(u\text{-}v)$
13 *Parent-Node-List*(v) = u
14 ***end if***
15 ***end for***
16...24 (as in the pseudo code for the MaxBNW-DG algorithm, refer Algorithm 1)
25 ***return*** $T_{Max}^{BLW}(V, E_T)$

End ***MaxBLW-DG Algorithm***

Modifications to the MaxBNW-DG Algorithm to Determine the MinBLW-DG Tree

For a MinBLW-DG tree, we define the bottleneck link weight for a path as the maximum of the weights of the constituent links of the path. The objective would be then to determine a DG tree for which the bottleneck link weight for a path from any node to the root node of the MinBLW-DG tree is the minimum. Accordingly, we start with an arbitrarily chosen node as the root node of the MinBLW-DG tree and set its *Tree-join-weight* to $-\infty$ and initialize the *Estimated-join-weight* for every other vertex to ∞. In each iteration of the algorithm, we attempt to decrease the *Estimated-join-weight* of the vertices as much as possible and eventually join a vertex to the MinBLW-DG tree through an incident edge that has the smallest weight (that also becomes the *Tree-join-weight* of the vertex). Algorithm 4 illustrates modifications to the pseudo code of the MaxBNW-DG algorithm to determine the MinBLW-DG trees.

Algorithm 4. Pseudo Code for the Algorithm to Determine Minimum Bottleneck Link Weight-DG Trees.

Input: Graph $G = (V, E, W_V, W_E)$

Output: $T_{Min}^{BLW}(V, E_T)$ where E_T is the set of edges in the MinBLW-DG tree

Auxiliary Variables: *Optimized-Nodes-List, Candidate-Nodes-List, Parent-Node-List*
Estimated-join-weight, Tree-join-weight, Leader Node

```
Initialization: Optimized-Nodes-List = ϕ; Candidate-Nodes-List = ϕ, Parent-Node-List = ϕ, E_T = ϕ
    ∀u ∈ V : Estimated-join-weight(u) = ∞, Tree-join-weight(u) = ∞

Begin MinBLW-DG Algorithm
1       Leader Node s is arbitrarily chosen among the vertices in V
2...3   (as in the pseudo code for the MaxBNW-DG algorithm, refer Algorithm 1)
4       Estimated-join-weight(s) = -∞
5       while (Candidate-Nodes-List ≠ ϕ) do
6           Node u = {i | Minimum_{i∈Candidate-Nodes-List} (Estimated-join-weights(i)}
7...9   (as in the pseudo code for the MaxBNW-DG algorithm, refer Algorithm 1)
10          for ( Node v ∈ Neighbors(u) AND v ∉ Optimized-Nodes-List) do
11              if (Estimated-join-weight(v) > W_E(u-v)) then
12                  Estimated-join-weight(v) = W_E(u-v)
13                  Parent-Node-List(v) = u
14              end if
15          end for
16...24 (as in the pseudo code for the MaxBNW-DG algorithm, refer Algorithm 1)
25      return T_Min^BLW (V, E_T)
End MinBLW-DG Algorithm
```

ALGORITHMS TO DETERMINE THE DIAMETER OF THE DG TREE AND MINIMUM DELAY FOR DATA AGGREGATION

In this section, we describe algorithms to determine the diameter of a data gathering (DG) tree and the minimum delay for data aggregation spanning across all the nodes of the DG tree. We also discuss the time complexity of the benchmarking algorithm to determine minimum aggregation delay as well as present its proof of correctness. Finally, we illustrate examples to compute the minimum aggregation delay and illustrate the relationship between aggregation delay and metrics such as the tree diameter and the number of child nodes per intermediate node (further analyzed through simulations, Section 5).

The diameter of a DG tree (also referred to as the height of the tree) is the maximum distance from any leaf node to the root of the tree [26]. We first identify the level of each node in the DG tree, with the root node (leader node) set to be at level 0, its immediate child nodes at level 1 and so on. Two intermediate nodes at a particular level or different levels can simultaneously communicate with their respective child nodes at the same time using different CDMA (Code Division Multiple Access) codes [14] to avoid any interference. An intermediate node could only communicate sequentially with its immediate downstream nodes using TDMA (Time Division Multiple Access) time slots (one data aggregation per time unit).

Algorithm to Determine Diameter of a Data Gathering Tree

In this subsection; we present an algorithm (see Algorithm 5 for the pseudo code) to compute the diameter of a data gathering tree; using the MaxBNW-DG tree as reference. The algorithm can be used to determine the diameter of any DG tree rooted at a particular node. We perform Breadth First Search (BFS) [26] on the edges of the DG tree to determine the diameter of the tree as well as the level (distance) of the vertices from the root node of the tree. As part of this procedure; we use the auxiliary variables; *Neighbor-List* storing the neighbors of each of the vertices in the DG tree; *Nodes-Explored* storing the list of nodes whose neighborhood is already explored as part of BFS; *Candidate-Nodes-List* containing the list of nodes (maintained in a First-in First-out basis; the front vertex in the list is extracted using a dequeue operation) that are visited while exploring the neighborhood of some other vertices; but their own neighborhood is not yet explored; and *Node-Level* that stores the level (distance) of a node from the root node of the DG tree. In addition to the *Diameter* of the DG tree; the algorithm outputs the *Child-Nodes-List* that contains the list of child nodes (if any) for each node in the DG tree and a two-dimensional data structure referred to as *Nodes-At-Levels* that stores a list of nodes at each level of the DG tree. The *Node-Level* for the root node/leader node is 0. In each iteration of the BFS algorithm, we remove (dequeue) the vertex in the front of the *Candidate-Nodes-List* and add it to the *Nodes-Explored* list as well as explore its neighbors. If a neighbor node v that has not been visited (explored) so far is visited for the first time as part of the exploration of the neighborhood of a node u; we add node v to the *Candidate-Nodes-List* and *Nodes-Explored* list as well as set *Node-Level*[v] = *Node-Level*[u] + 1 and set node u to be the parent node for node v in the DG tree. We also add node v to the list of nodes at level *Node-Level*[v]. If the value for *Node-Level*[v] is greater than the currently known diameter of the DG tree; we set the diameter of the tree to *Node-Level*[v]; implying we have found a node that is farther away from the leader node of the DG tree. The complexity of the algorithm to determine the diameter of a DG tree is the complexity incurred with running the BFS algorithm on the $|V| - 1$ edges of the DG tree spanning over all the $|V|$ vertices of the graph. Hence; the time complexity of the algorithm to determine the diameter of a DG tree is $\Theta(|V|)$.

Algorithm to Determine the Minimum Aggregation Delay of a Data Gathering Tree

In this subsection, we present the benchmarking algorithm to determine the minimum aggregation delay for a data gathering tree. Algorithm 6 presents the pseudo code that makes use of the diameter of the DG tree and the list of nodes at various levels of the tree to determine the delay for data aggregation. An intermediate node cannot forward an aggregated data to its upstream node unless it gets the aggregated data from all its immediate downstream child nodes. We assume it takes one time unit for a child node to send aggregated data to its parent node. We assume the leaf nodes of the DG tree (at all the levels) to have data readily available at time unit 0 (hence, the delay at any leaf node is 0). The delay at an intermediate node u, *Delay*[u], is iteratively computed over all its child nodes as shown in lines 6–8 of Algorithm 6 and explained here: We first sort the delays of the child nodes of u and maintain *Sorted-Delay-Child-Nodes*[u]. We maintain a temporary estimate of the delay (initialized to zero) at the intermediate node u using a running variable *Temp-Delay*[u] that is incremented as follows for each child node of u considered in the increasing order of their delays: For a child node $v \in$ *Child-Nodes-List*[u], *Temp-Delay*[u] = Maximum(*Temp-Delay*[u] + 1, *Delay*[v] + 1), as we assume it takes one time unit for data to reach from a child node to the immediate parent node. The increment of the *Temp-Delay*[u] by 1 within the Maximum function takes into consideration scenarios when the delay at the child node v would be smaller than the *Temp-Delay* already computed at the parent node u due to data aggregation delays involving the siblings of node v (*i.e.*, the other child nodes of node u). The delay associated with an intermediate node u, *Delay*[u], is the final value of *Temp-Delay*[u] after going through the delay-based sorted list of the child nodes of u. The above procedure is repeated at all the intermediate nodes, including the leader node. The aggregation delay at the leader node is considered to be the aggregation delay of the entire DG tree. The overall time complexity of the algorithm to compute the aggregation delay of a DG tree is dominated by the time incurred to sort the delays of the child nodes of the intermediate nodes at the different levels.

Algorithm 5. Pseudo Code for an Algorithm to Determine the Diameter of a Data Gathering Tree.

Input: DG Tree $T_{Max}^{BNW}(V, E_T)$, Leader Node s

Output: *Diameter*, *Nodes-At-Levels*, *Child-Nodes-List*

Auxiliary Variables: *Nodes-Explored*; *Candidate-Nodes-List*, *Child-Nodes-List*; *Neighbor-List*; *Node-Level*

Initialization: $\forall i \in V$: *Neighbor-List*[i] = ϕ, *Node-Level*[i] = 0; *Child-Nodes-List*[i] = ϕ
Nodes-At-Levels = ϕ; *Diameter* = 0; *Nodes-Explored* = ϕ; *Candidate-Nodes-List* = ϕ

```
Begin Algorithm Diameter-DG Tree
    for (edge (u, v) ∈ E_T) do
        Neighbor-List[u] = Neighbor-List[u] ∪ {v}
        Neighbor-List[v] = Neighbor-List[v] ∪ {u}
    end for
    Candidate-Nodes-List = {s}
    Node-Level[s] = 0
    Nodes-At-Levels[0].add({s})    // adds the leader node s to the list of nodes at level 0
    Nodes-Explored = Nodes-Explored ∪ {s}
    while (Candidate-Nodes-List ≠ ϕ) do
        Node u = Dequeue(Candidate-Nodes-List) // removes u from Candidate-Nodes-List
        for ( Node v ∈ Neighbor-List(u) AND v ∉ Nodes-Explored) do
                Node-Level[v] = Node-Level[u] + 1
                Nodes-At-Levels[Node-Level[v]].add({v})
                Child-Nodes-List(u) = Child-Nodes-List(u) ∪ {v}
                Nodes-Explored = Nodes-Explored ∪ {v}
                Candidate-Nodes-List = Candidate-Nodes-List ∪ {v}
                if (Diameter < Node-Level[v]) then
                    Diameter = Node-Level[v]
                end if
        end for
    end while
    return Diameter, Nodes-At-Levels, Child-Nodes-List
End Algorithm Diameter-DG Tree
```

Time Complexity and Proof of Correctness

In this subsection, we discuss the time complexity and proof of correctness for the benchmarking algorithm to determine minimum aggregation delay of a data gathering tree. In the worst case, an intermediate node could have the rest of the nodes as its child nodes and it would take $\Theta(|V|*\log|V|)$ time to sort the delays of the $|V|-1$ child nodes. To calculate the *Temp-Delay* values and the delay at each of the nodes, we spend one time unit for each edge at its upstream node. Hence, the overall time complexity of the algorithm to compute the aggregation delay of the DG tree is $\Theta(|V|*\log|V|)$.

The proof of correctness of the algorithm to determine the minimum aggregation delay for a DG tree simply follows from line 7 of the pseudo code (see Algorithm 6): For every intermediate node u, the estimate of the delay in each iteration of the loop (lines 6–8) while aggregating data received from a child node v is the maximum of the two values: one more than the current estimate of the delay at node u and one more than the aggregation delay at node v. The increment by one for both the parameters of the maximum function is the minimum possible increment that can be assigned to transmit data on a link. An intermediate node has to merely wait for data if none of its child nodes are ready with the data. However, if all the child nodes are ready with the data, the intermediate node aggregates data at a rate of just spending one additional time unit per child node.

Algorithm 6. Pseudo Code for an Algorithm to Determine the Minimum Aggregation Delay of a Data Gathering Tree.

Input: *Diameter*, *Nodes-At-Levels*, *Child-Nodes-List*, Leader Node *s*
Output: *Delay*[*s*]
Auxiliary Variables: *Temp-Delay*, *Sorted-Delay-Child-Nodes*
Initialization: $\forall i \in V$: *Delay*[*i*] = 0, *Temp-Delay*[*i*] = 0, *Sorted-Delay-Child-Nodes*[*i*] = ϕ

```
Begin Algorithm Aggregation-Delay-DG Tree
1     for (Node-level = Diameter to 0) do
2         for (Node u ∈ Nodes-At-Levels.get(Node-level) ) do
3             for (Node v ∈ Child-Nodes-List[u]) do
4                 Insert (v, Delay[v]) at appropriate entry in Sorted-Delay-Child-Nodes[u]
5             end for
6             for (tuple (v, Delay[v]) in Sorted-Delay-Child-Nodes[u]) do
7                 Temp-Delay[u] = Maximum(Temp-Delay[u] + 1, Delay[v] + 1)
8             end for
9             Delay[u] = Temp-Delay[u]
10        end for
11    end for
12    return Delay[s]
End Algorithm Aggregation-Delay-DG Tree
```

Examples to Compute the Minimum Aggregation Delay of Data Gathering Trees

Figure 1 illustrates examples to compute the minimum aggregation delay of two different data gathering trees that have the same diameter. In both the examples, the number inside the circle indicates the node ID and the number outside the circle indicates the minimum aggregation delay for the node. DG trees that have a larger fraction of leaf nodes (and hence fewer intermediate nodes) are more likely to have a larger number of child nodes per intermediate node. For such DG trees, it would take relatively more time slots for an intermediate node to sequentially aggregate data from its child nodes (especially for intermediate nodes at higher levels), resulting in a larger aggregation delay at the leader node. Hence, even if two DG trees have the same diameter (as shown in Figure 1), it could take a relatively longer time to aggregate data from the DG tree that has a larger number of child nodes per intermediate node. This is the trend of performance that is also observed with the DG trees in the simulations, especially for networks of high–very high node density.

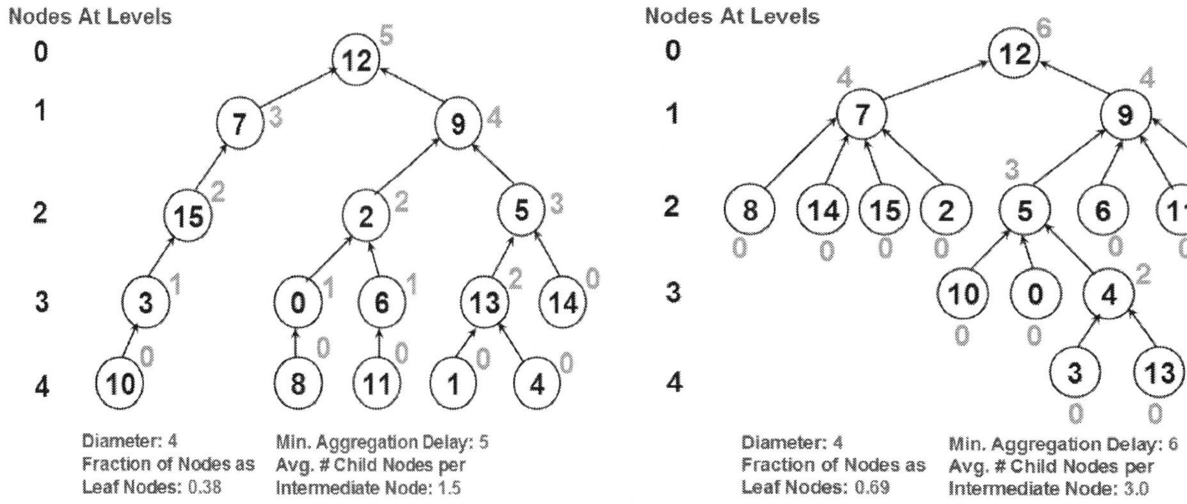

Figure 1. Examples to Determine the Minimum Aggregation Delay for a Data Gathering Tree.

SIMULATIONS

In this section, we present the simulation environment and examine the results of the simulation study conducted on the four categories of data gathering trees with respect to five performance metrics (see Section 5.1 for the list of metrics), including the aggregation delay-the primary metric of interest in this paper. We evaluate results of statistical tests conducted on the values obtained for the performance metrics and arrive at significant conclusions. We explore the contributions of the other four performance metrics for minimizing the aggregation delay as well as analyze the performance tradeoffs. We also calculate the margin of error values for the minimum aggregation delay (confidence interval: 95%). Finally, we discuss the impact of the algorithm design choices on the structure of the two categories of data gathering trees (bottleneck node-weight based and bottleneck link-weight based trees) and their performance.

We conduct simulations in a discrete-event simulator implemented in Java. We implemented the algorithms to determine the four types of data gathering trees (MaxBNW-DG, MinBNW-DG, MaxBLW-DG and MinBLW-DG trees) described in Section 3 and the algorithms to determine the diameter and minimum aggregation delay for data gathering trees described in Section 4. We conducted the simulations with networks of 50 nodes and 100 nodes, with the transmission ranges of the nodes varied from 25 m to 50 m, in increments of 5 m. The network dimensions are 100 m × 100 m. These are the usual parameters considered for simulation in sensor networks (e.g., refer [1,3,5,6,8]). The average number of neighbors per node is given by $\pi R^2/A$, where R is the transmission range and A is the network area. We consider the 50-node network to be of moderate to high node density (20 to 40 neighbors per node on average) and the 100-node network to be of high to very high node density (40 to 80 neighbors per node on average).

We assume an ideal medium access control (MAC) channel protocol [28] for the underlying wireless channel (*i.e.*, there are no collisions during channel access). We also assume the number of unique CDMA codes to be sufficient enough for the intermediate nodes at the same level or different levels to simultaneously aggregate data from their respective child nodes, if the latter are ready with the data. Such idealistic assumptions have been successfully applied in the literature for wireless ad hoc networks and sensor networks (e.g., [29,30,31,32,33]) to extract optimal performance from the benchmarking algorithms run in the higher layers and to delineate the effects of the design choices.

The weights for the edges are uniform-randomly assigned in the range [0...1] and the weights for the nodes are also uniform-randomly assigned in the range [0...1]; the node weights are independent of the link weights. We generate 200 snapshots of the network graphs for each combination of the number of nodes and the transmission range per node and run the algorithms to determine the four DG trees on each of these graph snapshots and average the results (shown in Figure 2). Section 5.4 discusses about the margin of error values for the minimum aggregation delay (confidence interval is 95%).

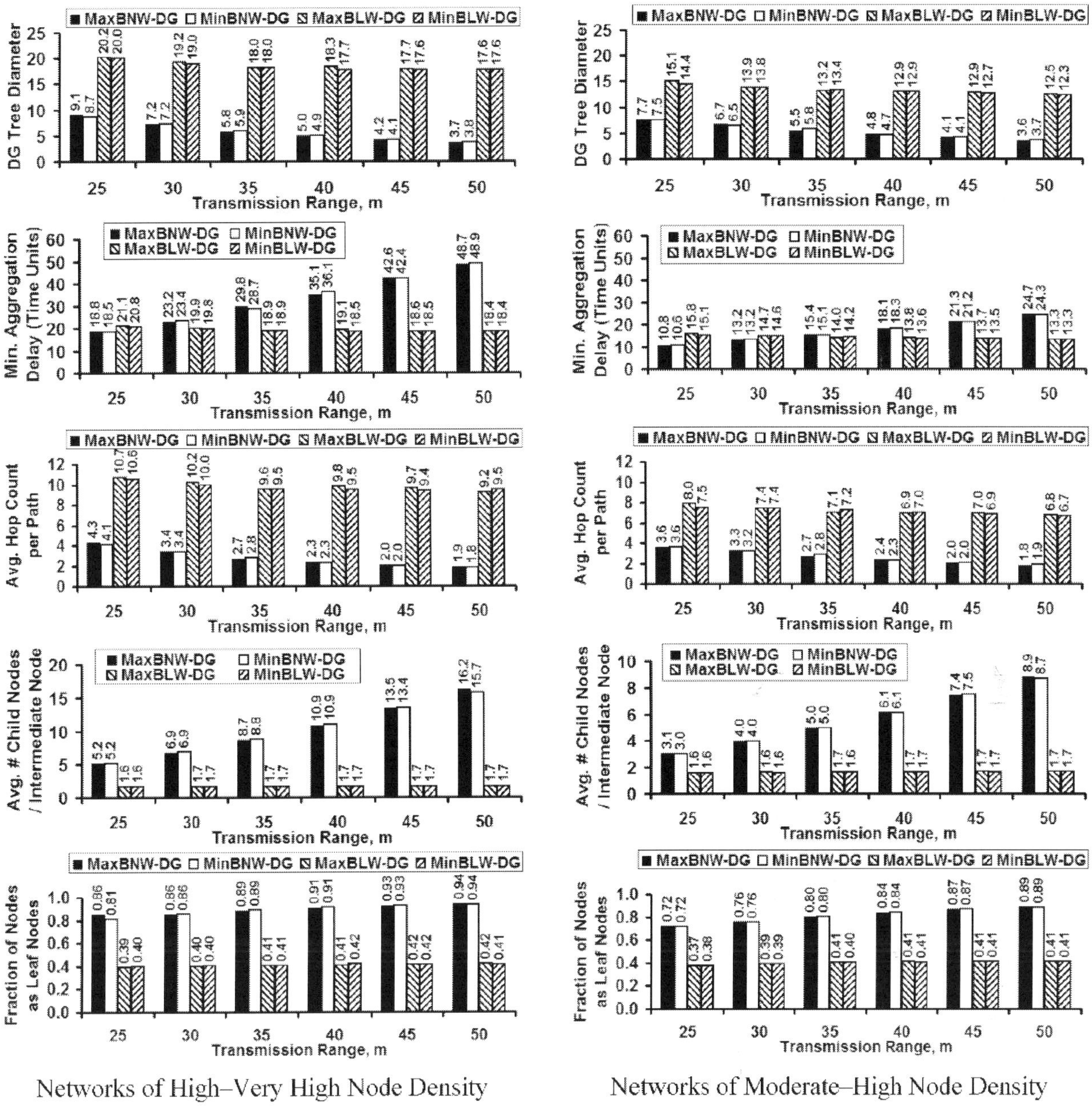

Figure 2. Performance of the Max/Min Bottleneck Node Weight and Link Weight-based DG Trees.

Performance Metrics

In this subsection, we introduce the performance metrics that are measured in the simulations. The performance metrics measured are as follows:

- *Diameter of the DG Tree*—The maximum distance (number of hops) from any leaf node to the root node of the DG tree.
- *Minimum Aggregation Delay*—The minimum number of time slots it takes for the data to get aggregated, starting from the leaf nodes and propagating to the root node of the DG tree
- *Hop Count per Path*—The average of the number of hops per path from every node (other than the root node) to the root node of the DG tree.
- *Number of Child Nodes per Intermediate Node*—The average of the number of immediate child nodes per intermediate node, considered across all the intermediate nodes (including the root node) of the DG tree.
- *Fraction of Nodes as Leaf Nodes*—The ratio of the total number of leaf nodes (nodes without any child nodes) at all levels divided by the total number of nodes in the network.

MaxBNW-DG Trees vs. MinBNW-DG Trees and MaxBLW-DG Trees vs. MinBLW-DG Trees

A significant result from the simulations is that the performance of the MaxBNW-DG trees is almost the same as that of the MinBNW-DG trees with respect to all the metrics; and likewise, the performance of the MaxBLW-DG trees is the same as that of the MinBLW-DG trees with respect to all the metrics. This could be observed from the results displayed in Figure 2 for all the metrics. The vertical bars for the MaxBNW-DG trees (■)

and MinBNW-DG trees (□) are almost the same height for each of the performance metrics with respect to any operating condition, and this could be also confirmed on the basis of the magnitude of the average values for the performance metrics listed on the top of the bars. Likewise, the vertical bars for the MaxBLW-DG trees (▧) and MinBLW-DG trees (▨) are almost the same height for each performance metric with respect to any operating condition, and this is further confirmed on the basis of the magnitude of the average values for the performance metrics listed on the top of the bars. We also further confirm our assertion through statistical tests. For any performance metric under a particular operating condition, the ratios for the median and maximum absolute difference in the average values incurred for the MaxBNW-DG trees and MinBNW-DG trees (as well as for the MaxBLW-DG trees and MinBLW-DG trees) to that of the average values incurred for each of these trees is not more than 0.008 and 0.06 respectively. Hence, we hereafter discuss simply on the basis of bottleneck node-weight based DG trees *vs.* bottleneck link-weight based DG trees.

Discussion of the Results

In this subsection, we discuss the results for the two categories of data gathering trees with respect to each of the performance metrics and explore the dependence of the aggregation delay on metrics such as the diameter, number of child nodes per intermediate node and the fraction of nodes as leaf nodes. We also discuss the impact of node density on the performance of the two data gathering trees. To begin with, we observe the diameter of the bottleneck node-weight based DG trees to be significantly smaller than the diameter of the bottleneck link-weight based DG trees. The diameter of the bottleneck link-weight based DG trees is about 100–270% larger (for networks of moderate-high node density) and 120%–370% larger (for networks of high–very high node density) compared to that of the bottleneck node-weight based DG trees. With increase in node density, the diameter of the bottleneck link-weight based DG trees increases by about 30–50%, whereas the diameter of the bottleneck node-weight based DG trees increases only by at most 20% with increase in node density. To vindicate the diameters observed for the bottleneck node *vs.* bottleneck link-weight based DG trees, the average hop count per path for both the categories of DG trees is about half the diameter values observed for the DG trees (for a given node density and transmission range). The smaller diameter and the correspondingly smaller average hop count per path incurred with the bottleneck node weight-based DG trees augurs well for real-time reporting of data by any sensor node to the root node of the DG tree (*i.e.*, one-to-one communication between a sensor node and the root node).

As a consequence of incurring a smaller diameter, the average number of child nodes per intermediate node for the bottleneck node-weight based DG trees is significantly larger (by factors of two to five in networks of moderate-high node density and by factors of 3 to 10 in networks of high–very high node density) than the average number of child nodes per intermediate node incurred with the bottleneck link-weight based DG trees. On the other hand, the fraction of nodes as leaf nodes is more than 0.7 (and could be as large as 0.94 in networks of very high node density) for the bottleneck node-weight based DG trees, whereas the fraction of nodes as leaf nodes is at most 0.42 for the bottleneck link-weight based DG trees.

We observe the minimum aggregation delay for the bottleneck node weight-based DG trees to be lower than that of the bottleneck link weight-based DG trees when the network is operated under moderate transmission range values (of 25 m and 30 m) in networks of moderate-high node density and at 25m transmission range in networks of high–very high node density. As the diameter values are moderate (and not too low) and the average number of child nodes per intermediate node is not too high for the above said conditions, we observe the minimum aggregation delay to be relatively lower for the bottleneck node weight-based DG trees compared to that incurred with the bottleneck link weight-based DG trees (for which the impact of a larger diameter could be felt at these operating conditions). However, as the node density increases with increase in the transmission range and the number of nodes in the network, the minimum aggregation delay for the bottleneck node weight-based DG trees starts increasing significantly and becomes much larger than the minimum aggregation delay incurred with the bottleneck link weight-based DG trees.

With increase in node density, the reduction in the tree diameter and a concave-up pattern of increase (*i.e.*, the rate of increase increases with increase in node density) in the number of child nodes per intermediate node significantly impact the aggregation delay of the bottleneck node weight-based DG trees. The number of time slots required at an intermediate node to sequentially aggregate data from each of its child nodes would get high, especially at intermediate nodes that are closer to the leader node, thereby increasing the aggregation delay at the leader node. On the other hand, the average number of child nodes per intermediate node for the bottleneck link weight-based DG trees remains the same with increase in node density and the tree diameter only marginally reduces; as a result, the aggregation delay for the bottleneck link weight-based DG trees remains about the same with increase in node density (and even marginally reduces with increase in node density). The minimum aggregation delay incurred with the bottleneck node weight-based DG trees could be at most 85% and 160% larger than the aggregation delay incurred with the bottleneck link weight-based DG trees in networks of moderate–high and high–very high node density respectively.

Margin of Error for Minimum Aggregation Delay

We calculate and display (see Figure 3) the margin of error values (confidence interval: 95%) for the minimum aggregation delay, the primary performance metric of interest in this paper. Since the aggregation delay is directly dependent on the other three key performance metrics (diameter, fraction of leaf nodes and the number of child nodes per intermediate node), the margin of error values for the minimum aggregation delay could be considered as a measure of the statistical accuracy of the simulations. The procedure followed to calculate the margin of error values (using a z-score of 1.96 for a 95% confidence interval) for the minimum aggregation delay is briefly explained below.

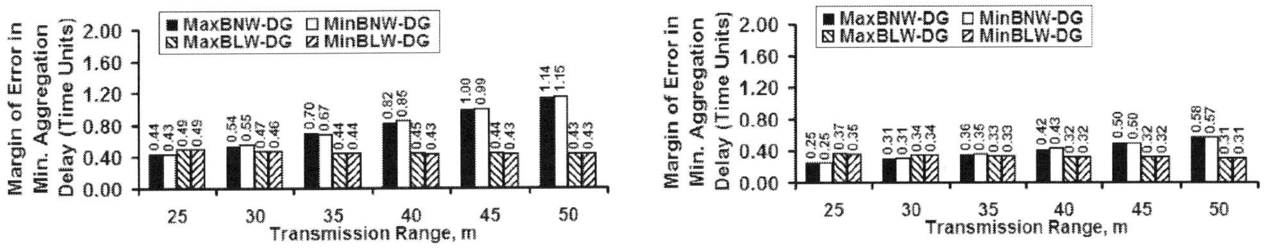

Networks of High–Very High Node Density

Networks of Moderate–High Node Density

Figure 3. Margin of Error Values for Minimum Aggregation Delay.

The margin of error for the minimum aggregation delay under a particular operating condition (number of nodes and transmission range per node) is calculated as $z*\sigma/\sqrt{n_s}$, where z is the z-score 1.96, σ is the standard deviation of the samples collected for the minimum aggregation delay under the particular operating condition and n_s is the number of samples collected (200 graph snapshots). If $\bar{x}$ is the average value of the n_s samples collected for the minimum aggregation delay under a particular operating condition, then one could say that the range of values for the minimum aggregation delay is $\left(\bar{x}-z*\sigma/\sqrt{n_s},...,\bar{x}+z*\sigma/\sqrt{n_s}\right)$ with a probability of 0.95 (95% confidence interval; z-score is 1.96).

As the magnitude of the average value for the minimum aggregation delay increases, we observe the margin of error to also increase, especially in the case of the bottleneck node-weight based DG trees. For networks of high to very high density, we observe the margin of error values for the minimum aggregation delay to be relatively low for the bottleneck link weight-based DG trees, partly attributed to the lower values for the average minimum aggregation delay. Only for networks of moderate density, the margin of error values for the bottleneck node-weight base DG trees are slightly lower than that of the bottleneck link-weight based DG trees. We also observe negligible difference in the margin of error values incurred for the MaxBNW-DG trees and MinBNW-DG trees; likewise, there is negligible difference in the margin of error values incurred for the MaxBLW-DG and MinBLW-DG trees. This further vindicates our reason to just base our discussion of the results as bottleneck node-weight based DG trees *vs.* bottleneck link-weight based DG trees.

Performance Tradeoffs

In this subsection, we look at each of the performance metrics (listed in Section 5.1) in isolation, independent of the trend of values expected of them to minimize the aggregation delay. This way, we are able to identify the desirable trend of values (low, moderate or high) that would be typically expected of these metrics to optimize network measures other than aggregation delay (such as node lifetime and network lifetime) and thereby also identify any tradeoffs. We define node lifetime [34] as the time of first node failure due to energy exhaustion; whereas, network lifetime [34] is the time the network gets disconnected due to the failure of one or more nodes due to energy exhaustion.

As noticed in Section 5.3 and Figure 2, to obtain a lower aggregation delay (especially with increase in node density), it would be preferable for the data gathering trees to have a moderate-larger diameter, a smaller fraction of nodes as leaf nodes and a low-moderate number of child nodes per intermediate node. However, one or more of these trend in the values for the above metrics may not be desirable for real-time reporting of events from any node to the leader node and/or for optimizing energy consumption-related performance measures such as the node lifetime and network lifetime. To begin with, we typically desire to have lower values for the tree diameter and hop count per path to facilitate faster real-time reporting of events from an individual node to the leader node of the data gathering tree [12]. However, if we were to incur a smaller hop count per path, then the diameter of the data gathering tree would have to be also smaller [23], thereby increasing the aggregation delay (*diameter-aggregation delay tradeoff*).

With respect to the fraction of nodes as leaf nodes, from a network lifetime standpoint, we would typically desire to have a larger number of leaf nodes. This is because the leaf nodes tend to lose relatively less energy compared to the intermediate nodes [16]. For every data aggregation cycle, the leaf nodes lose energy for transmitting the data only once to their upstream intermediate node and there is no energy lost due to reception. On the other hand, the intermediate nodes lose energy for both transmitting (to an upstream node) as well as for receiving and aggregating data (from the downstream child nodes) [22]. Thus, a larger number of leaf nodes in a data gathering tree is desirable to prolong the lifetime of a majority of the nodes in the network so that the time of network disconnection due to node failures (typically referred to as the network lifetime) could be prolonged as much as possible [16,34]. However, a larger fraction of nodes as leaf nodes would more likely increase the number of child nodes per intermediate node (also confirmed through the simulation results in Figure 2) and thereby increase the aggregation delay (*network lifetime-aggregation delay tradeoff*).

With respect to the number of child nodes per intermediate node, we notice that a larger value for this metric could increase the aggregation delay as well as trigger premature node failures. As intermediate nodes have to spend energy to aggregate data from their child nodes, a larger number of child nodes per intermediate node could overuse certain nodes (the intermediate nodes) at the cost of the other nodes (the leaf nodes) [24]. A very low value for the number of child nodes per intermediate node would not be desirable either as it would lead to a significantly larger number of nodes functioning as intermediate nodes and aggregating the data (such a scenario could only lower the node lifetime) [6]. Hence, if we are interested in prolonging the lifetime of every node in the network (*i.e.*, maximizing the time of first node failure, typically referred to as the node lifetime [34]), it would be desirable to have a moderate number of child nodes per intermediate node. An open question is how to define the range of moderate values for the number of child nodes per intermediate node. From Figure 2, we also see that a moderate number of child nodes per intermediate node could also lower the aggregation delay, especially if the diameter of the tree is not very high (as observed in the case of bottleneck node-weight based data gathering trees in networks of moderate node density). However, we notice that if each intermediate node can accommodate only moderate number of child nodes, we would need more nodes to serve as intermediate nodes and the fraction of nodes as leaf nodes would only decrease, thereby increasing the energy consumption at several nodes (*node lifetime-network lifetime tradeoff*).

Impact of the Algorithm Design Choices on the Structure of the DG Trees and their Performance

The simulation results vindicate the impact of the design choices behind the algorithms for the construction of the two categories of data gathering trees (bottleneck node-weight *vs.* bottleneck link-weight based trees) on their structure as well as the performance. The smaller diameter of the bottleneck node-weight based data gathering trees is primarily attributed to limiting the *Tree-join-weight* of a downstream node from not becoming more than the *Tree-join-weight* of an upstream node (in the case of MaxBNW-DG trees) or from not becoming less than the *Tree-join-weight* of an upstream node (in the case of MinBNW-DG trees). As a result, a node that is not yet included in a bottleneck node-weight based DG tree simply prefers to join the tree through an upstream node that has the largest *Tree-join-weight* (for MaxBNW-DG trees) or the smallest *Tree-join-weight* (for MinBNW-DG trees). Such upstream nodes are more likely to be closer to the root/leader node of the data gathering tree, as the *Tree-join-weight* for any node cannot be larger than that of the leader node (for MaxBNW-DG trees) or smaller than that of the leader node (for MinBNW-DG trees). In the case of bottleneck link-weight based DG trees, there is no such restriction as seen in the case of bottleneck node-weight based DG trees. A node that is not yet included in a bottleneck link-weight based DG tree could simply join the tree via any upstream node through a link of the largest weight (in case of MaxBLW-DG trees) or the smallest weight (in case of MinBLW-DG trees). Such upstream nodes need not be always closer to the leader node, and this contributes to a relatively larger diameter (and a lower number of child nodes per intermediate node) for the bottleneck link-weight based DG trees vis-a-vis the bottleneck node-weight based DG trees. Thus, the simulation results observed here are only influenced by the structure of the data gathering trees and their construction procedure, and are not influenced by the configuration of the simulation. In other words, the simulation results merely confirm the performance expected of the two categories of DG trees owing to their design choices.

CONCLUSIONS AND FUTURE WORK

The high-level contributions of our paper are as follows: We have proposed a benchmarking algorithm to determine the minimum aggregation delay for data gathering trees in wireless sensor networks. We have shown that the performance of the maximum and minimum bottleneck node weight-based DG trees (and likewise for the maximum and minimum bottleneck link weight-based DG trees) to be almost the same with respect to the performance metrics (aggregation delay, diameter/hop count and distribution of child nodes/leaf nodes in the DG tree) evaluated in this paper, indicating that it would be sufficient to compare the performance with respect to just two categories of DG trees (bottleneck node weight *vs.* bottleneck link weight based; using either the maximum or minimum bottleneck weight-based DG tree from each category would just be sufficient).

The simulation results confirm the diameter-aggregation delay tradeoff that was expected between the bottleneck node and bottleneck link weight-based data gathering trees owing to their design. The bottleneck node weight-based DG trees incur a smaller diameter and a larger number of child nodes per intermediate node (both contributing to the larger aggregation delay, especially in networks of high–very high node density), whereas the bottleneck link weight-based DG trees incur a larger diameter and a much smaller number of child nodes per intermediate node. The larger diameter makes the bottleneck link weight-based DG trees incur a data aggregation delay that is at most 40% larger than that incurred with the bottleneck node weight-based DG trees in networks of moderate node density operated under moderate transmission range values (25m). However, with increase in the node density, the aggregation delay incurred with the bottleneck node weight-based DG trees starts becoming significantly larger than the aggregation delay incurred with the bottleneck link weight-based DG trees (that do not show any significant impact of the increase in node density). We also anticipate observing a similar diameter-aggregation delay tradeoff even for any other complex network of high node density.

The contributions and observations made throughout this paper could be used to focus future research on exploring strategies for maintaining the diameter of the bottleneck node weight-based DG trees at moderate values (and not allowing the number of child nodes per intermediate node to become significantly high) with increase in node density and thereby reducing the network-wide aggregation delay for data gathering. Note that the simulations assume the availability of a sufficient number of unique CDMA codes for the intermediate nodes at the same level or different levels to simultaneously aggregate data from their respective child nodes, if the latter are ready with the data. We will extend our simulation study by running the benchmarking algorithm on a wireless medium with a limited number of CDMA codes and evaluate the impact on the diameter-aggregation delay tradeoff. Likewise, we will also run the benchmarking algorithm under various medium access control protocols for wireless sensor networks [28] and evaluate the impact of collisions (expected to be significant in networks of high–very high node density) on the diameter-aggregation delay tradeoff.

ACKNOWLEDGMENTS

This work is supported through the NASA EPSCoR sub award (#: NNX14AN38A) from the University of Mississippi.

REFERENCES

1. Heinzelman, W.R.; Chandrakasan, A.; Balakarishnan, H. Energy-Efficient Communication Protocols for Wireless Microsensor Networks. In Proceedings of the Hawaiian International Conference on Systems Science, Maui, HI, USA, 4–7 January 2000; p. 8020.
2. Meghanathan, N. Grid Block Energy based Data Gathering Algorithms for Wireless Sensor Networks. *Int. J. Commun. Netw. Inf. Secur.* 2010, *2*, 151–161.
3. Lindsey, S.; Raghavendra, C.; Sivalingam, K.M. Data Gathering Algorithms in Sensor Networks using Energy Metrics. *IEEE Trans. Parallel Distrib. Syst.* 2002, *13*, 924–935.
4. Meghanathan, N. A Data Gathering Algorithm based on Energy-aware Connected Dominating Sets to Minimize Energy Consumption and Maximize Node Lifetime in Wireless Sensor Networks. *Int. J. Interdiscip. Telecommun. Netw.* 2010, *2*, 1–17.
5. Meghanathan, N. A Comprehensive Review and Performance Analysis of Data Gathering Algorithms for Wireless Sensor Networks. *Int. J. Interdiscip. Telecommun. Netw.* 2012, *4*, 1–29.
6. Lindsey, S.; Raghavendra, C.; Sivalingam, K.M. Data Gathering in Sensor Networks using the Energy*Delay Metric. In Proceedings of the 15th International Parallel and Distributed Processing Symposium, San Francisco, CA, USA, 23–27 April 2001; pp. 2001–2008.
7. Liang, J.; Wang, J.; Cao, J.; Chen, J.; Lu, M. An Efficient Algorithm for Constructing Maximum Lifetime Tree for Data Gathering without Aggregation in Wireless Sensor Networks. In Proceedings of the 29th IEEE Conference on Computer Communications, San Diego, CA, USA, 15–19 March 2010; pp. 1–5.
8. Huang, S.C.; Wan, P.-J.; Vu, C.T.; Li, Y.; Yao, F. Nearly Constant Approximation for Data Aggregation Scheduling in Wireless Sensor Networks. In Proceedings of the 26th IEEE International Conference on Computer Communications, Anchorage, AK, USA, 6–12 May 2007; pp. 366–372.
9. Wan, P.-J.; Huang, S.C.-H.; Wang, L.; Wan, Z.; Jia, X. Minimum-Latency Aggregation Scheduling in Multi-hop Wireless Networks. In Proceedings of the 10th ACM International Symposium on Mobile Ad hoc Networking and Computing, New Orleans, LA, USA, 18–21 May 2009; pp. 185–194.
10. Yu, B.; Li, J. Minimum-Time Aggregation Scheduling in Multi-Sink Sensor Networks. In Proceedings of the 8th IEEE Conference on Sensor, Mesh and Ad hoc Communications and Networks, Salt Lake City, UT, USA, 27–30 June 2011; pp. 422–430.
11. Li, Y.; Guo, L.; Prasad, S.K. An Energy-Efficient Distributed Algorithm for Minimum-Latency Aggregation Scheduling in Wireless Sensor Networks. In Proceedings of the 30th IEEE International Conference on Distributed Computing Systems, Genova, Italy, 21–25 June 2010; pp. 827–836.
12. Xu, X.; Li, X.-Y.; Mao, X.; Tang, S.; Wang, S. A Delay-Efficient Algorithm for Data Aggregation in Multi-hop Wireless Sensor Networks. *IEEE Trans. Parallel Distrib. Syst.* 2011, *22*, 163–175.
13. Yu, B.; Li, J.; Li, Y. Distributed Data Aggregation Scheduling in Wireless Sensor Networks. In Proceedings of the 28th IEEE International Conference on Computer Communications, Rio de Janeiro, Brazil, 19–25 April 2009; pp. 2159–2167.
14. Viterbi, A.J. *CDMA: Principles of Spread Spectrum Communication*, 1st ed.; Prentice Hall: Upper Saddle River, NJ, USA, 1995.
15. Wu, Y.; Fahmy, S.; Shroff, N.B. On the Construction of a Maximum Lifetime Data Gathering Tree in Sensor Networks: NP-Completeness and Approximation Algorithm. In Proceedings of the 27th IEEE Conference on Computer Communications, Phoenix, AZ, USA, 13–18 April 2008; pp. 1013–1021.
16. Meghanathan, N. An Algorithm to Determine Energy-aware Maximal Leaf Nodes Data Gathering Tree for Wireless Sensor Networks. *J. Theor. Appl. Inform. Technol.* 2010, *15*, 96–107.
17. Meghanathan, N.; Mumford, P. Centralized and Distributed Algorithms for Stability-based Data Gathering in Mobile Sensor Networks. *Macrothink Netw. Protoc. Algorithms* 2013, *5*, 84–116.
18. Meghanathan, N. A Pair-wise Key Distribution Mechanism and Distributed Trust Evaluation Model for Secure Data Aggregation in Mobile Sensor Networks. *Int. J. Comb. Optim. Probl. Inform.* 2014, *5*, 29–46.
19. Xie, R.; Jia, X. Minimum Transmission Data Gathering Trees for Compressive sensing in Wireless Sensor Networks. In Proceedings of the IEEE Global Telecommunications Conference, Houston, TX, USA, 5–9 December 2011; pp. 1–5.
20. Ramanan, K.; Baburaj, E. Data Gathering Algorithms for Wireless Sensor Networks: A Survey. *Int. J. Ad hoc Sens. Ubiquitous Comput.* 2010, *1*, 102–114.
21. Li, H.; Hua, Q.S.; Wu, C.; Lau, F.C.M. Minimum-Latency Aggregation Scheduling in Wireless Sensor Networks under Physical Interference Model. In Proceedings of the 13th ACM International Conference on Modeling, Analysis, and Simulation of Wireless and Mobile Systems, Bodrum, Turkey, 17–21 October 2010; pp. 360–367.
22. Yu, Y.; Krishnamachari, B.; Prasanna, V.K. Energy-Latency Tradeoffs for Data Gathering in Wireless Sensor Networks. In Proceedings of the 23rd IEEE Conference on Computer Communications, Hong Kong, China, 7–11 March 2004; pp. 244–255.
23. Ammari, H.M.; Das, S.K. Trade-off between Energy Savings and Source-to-Sink Delay in Data Dissemination for Wireless Sensor Networks. In Proceedings of the 8th ACM International Symposium on Modeling, Analysis and Simulation of Wireless and Mobile Systems, Montreal, QC, Canada, 10–13 October 2005; pp. 126–133.
24. Ballister, P.; Bollobas, B.; Anandkumar, A.; Willsky, A. Energy-Latency Tradeoff for In-Network Function Computation in Random Networks. In Proceedings of the

23rd IEEE Conference on Computer Communications, Shanghai, China, 10–15 April 2011; pp. 1575–1583.

25. Li, H.; Wu, C.; Yu, D.; Hua, Q.-S.; Lau, F.C.M. Aggregation Latency-Energy Tradeoff in Wireless Sensor Networks with Successive Interference Cancellation. *IEEE Trans. Parallel Distrib. Syst.* 2013, *24*, 2160–2170.

26. Cormen, T.H.; Leiserson, C.E.; Rivest, R.L.; Stein, C. *Introduction to Algorithms*, 3rd edition; MIT Press: Cambridge, MA, USA, 2009.

27. Meghanathan, N. Graph Theory Algorithms for Mobile Ad hoc Networks. *Inform. Int. J. Comput. Inform.* 2012,*36*, 185–200.

28. Demirkol, I.; Ersoy, C.; Alagoz, F. MAC Protocols for Wireless Sensor Networks: A Survey. *IEEE Commun. Magazine* 2006, *44*, 115–121.

29. Stojmenovic, I. Simulations in Wireless Sensor and Ad hoc Networks: Matching and Advancing Models, Metrics, and Solutions. *IEEE Commun. Magazine* 2008, *46*, 102–107.

30. Cagalj, M.; Phubaux, J.; Enz, C. Minimum-Energy Broadcast in All-Wireless Networks: NP-Completeness and Distribution Issues. In Proceedings of the 8th annual international conference on Mobile computing and networking, Atlanta, GA, USA, 23–28 September 2002; pp. 172–182.

31. Wieselthier, E.; Nguyen, G.D.; Ephremides, A. Energy-Efficient Broadcast and Multicast Trees in Wireless Networks. *Mob. Netw. Appl.* 2002, *7*, 481–492.

32. Williams, B.; Camp, T. Comparison of Broadcasting Techniques for Mobile Ad hoc Networks. In Proceedings of the 3rd ACM International Symposium on Mobile Ad hoc Networking and Computing, Lausanne, Switzerland, 9–11 June 2002; pp. 194–205.

33. Keshavarz, A.H.; Ribeiro, V.; Riedi, R. Color-Based Broadcasting for Ad Hoc Networks. In Proceedings of the 4th International Symposium on Modeling and Optimization in Mobile, Boston, MA, USA, 3–6 April 2006; pp. 1–10.

34. Meghanathan, N. Stability-based and Energy-Efficient Distributed Data Gathering Algorithms for Mobile Sensor Networks. *Ad hoc Netw.* 2014, *19*, 111–131.

CHAPTER 14

A LINEAR TIME ALGORITHM FOR SHORTEST CYCLIC COVER OF STRINGS

Bastien Cazaux[a, b] and Eric Rivals[a, b]

[a]LIRMM, CNRS and Université de Montpellier, 161 rue Ada, 34095 Montpellier Cedex 5, France

[b]Institut de Biologie Computationnelle, CNRS and Université de Montpellier, 860 rue Saint Priest, 34095 Montpellier Cedex 5, France

ABSTRACT

Merging words according to their overlap yields a superstring. This basic operation allows to infer long strings from a collection of short pieces, as in genome assembly. To capture a maximum of overlaps, the goal is to infer the shortest superstring of a set of input words. The Shortest Cyclic Cover of Strings (SCCS) problem asks, instead of a single linear superstring, for a set of cyclic strings that contain the words as substrings and whose sum of lengths is minimal. SCCS is used as a crucial step in polynomial time approximation algorithms for the notably hard Shortest Superstring problem, but it is solved in cubic time. The cyclic strings are then cut and merged to build a linear superstring. SCCS can also be solved by a greedy algorithm. Here, we propose a linear time algorithm for solving SCCS based on a Eulerian graph that captures all greedy solutions in linear space. Because the graph is Eulerian, this algorithm can also find a greedy solution of SCCS with the least number of cyclic strings. This has implications for solving certain instances of the Shortest linear or cyclic Superstring problems.

INTRODUCTION

The possibility of merging two words into a longer one according to their overlap – for instance merging abcde with cdeba into abcdeba – allows to infer the sequence of a target molecule from the short reads produced by sequencing machines. In computer science, merging results in a superstring of the input words. The action of merging is heavily used in any genome assembler (although not necessarily on the complete reads, sometimes only on substrings of the reads) and given the redundancy of the sequencing, which yields a high density of reads, the objective is to compute a shortest superstring of a set of input words [10]. In bioinformatics, the task of genome assembly is worsened by the inaccuracy of the sequencing and by the structure of the genome which contains repeated sequences [10]. However, progresses on the model question, called Shortest (linear) Superstring Problem (SLiS) – or often Shortest Common Superstring – still shed light on the difficulty of assembly. Moreover, the target molecule can be a linear or a circular structure. It is also interesting to address the question of the Shortest Cyclic Superstring (SCyS). Finding superstrings also has application in data compression. Indeed, as a superstring represents a condensed representation of the initial language, it can serve as a compressed version of the input set.

Let P: = $\{s_1, \ldots, s_{|P|}\}$ be a set of input words and denote the sum of their lengths by $||P||$, i.e. the norm of P. Without loss of generality, we always assume that P is factor free, i.e.

Citation: Bastien Cazaux, Eric Rivals, A linear time algorithm for Shortest Cyclic Cover of Strings, Journal of Discrete Algorithms, Volume 37, March 2016, Pages 56-67, ISSN 1570-8667, http://dx.doi.org/10.1016/j.jda.2016.05.001.

for any two strings of P, none is a substring of the other. From the computational viewpoint, finding a shortest superstring is known to be hard to solve (NP-hard even on a binary alphabet) and to approximate (Max-SNP hard) [7] and [1]. The research in the last 25 years has mainly focused on polynomial time approximation algorithms for SLiS (see[8] for a recent list). Despite these efforts, the algorithm greedy (Algorithm 1), an algorithm that iteratively updates the input set by merging two maximally overlapping strings until one string is left, was conjectured to approximate the length of the shortest superstring with ratio 2 [17] and [1]. This is better than most known algorithms, and the conjecture is still valid. For linear superstrings on the constant size alphabets, Ukkonen proposed a linear time implementation of the algorithm greedy based on the Aho–Corasick automaton[19]; later, another implementation using the suffix tree was given in [12] and [13].

Algorithm 1: The algorithm `greedy` for Shortest Cyclic Cover of Strings.

```
Input: P a set of linear words;
Output: S a set of cyclic strings that cover P;
S := ∅
while P is not empty do
    u and v two elements of P having the longest overlap (u can be equal to v)
    w is the merge of u and v
    P := P \ {u, v}
    if u = v (i.e. w is a cyclic string) then S := S ∪ {w} else P := P ∪ {w}
return S
```

The question of approximating the superstring can be reformulated on a complete weighted digraph, the so-called distance graph: each input word is a vertex and an arc encodes the directional merging of the two words. The weight of an arc from u to v equals the length of the prefix of u that is not covered by the overlap of v (e.g. , the corresponding prefix of abcde to cdeba is ab, and the weight would be 2). Then a shortest linear superstring is associated with a Hamiltonian path on this graph, and a shortest cyclic superstring with a Hamiltonian cycle [1]. Yet those problems are also hard to approximate and most approximation algorithms for SLiS resort to a relaxed question, namely Shortest Cyclic Cover of Strings (SCCS). These algorithms solve SCCS by computing a minimum assignment on the distance graph in $O(||P|| + |P|^3)$ [16], and then transform the cycles into cyclic strings. Our work focuses on SCCS. We propose an algorithm that uses only linear time in ||P||, and for this sake introduce the superstring graph, which captures all solutions of greedy for SCCS (see Sections 4 and 3). These greedy solutions are called greedy superstrings. Exploring the graph properties, we show that it gives, for a subset of instances of the shortest linear and cyclic superstring problems, interesting approximations or even exact solutions (Section 4).

Notation and Problem Definition

For any rooted tree T, V_T is the set of nodes of T. For a node v of V_T, $\text{Children}_T(v)$is the set of children of v in T . We denote by [i, j] the set of integers between i and j.

We consider two kinds of strings: linear and cyclic strings (see Figs. 1a and 1b). For a string s, the length of s is |s|. For a linear string s and $i \leq j$ in [1, |s|], s[i, j] is the linear substring of s beginning at the position i and ending at the position j, s[i] is the substrings[i, i], s[1, j] is a prefix of s and s[i, |s|] is a suffix of s . A prefix (or suffix) s′ of s is proper if s′ is different of s. For another linear string t, the overlap from s to t, denoted by ov(s, t), is the longest substring which is a proper suffix of s and a proper prefix of t. The prefix from s to t, denoted by pr(s, t), is such that s = pr(s, t)ov(s, t). The merge of s with t is the linear word pr(s, t)t if $s \neq t$, and the cyclic word pr(s, t) otherwise. A linear superstring of a set P of linear strings is a linear string w such that each string of P is a substring of w. We say that a linear string w is a substring of a cyclic string c if there exists w_c a linear permutation of c such that w is a substring of w_c^∞ (where $w_c^\infty = w_c w_c \ldots$) – see Fig. 1c. A cyclic cover of P is a set C of cyclic strings such that each linear string of P is a substring of a cyclic string of C.

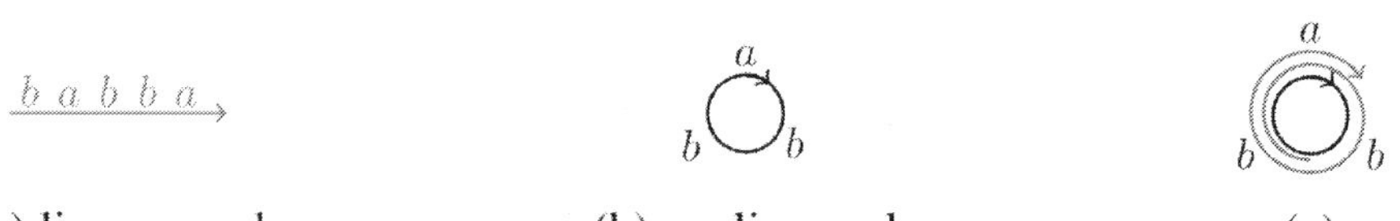

(a) linear word (b) cyclic word (c)

Figure 1. (c) Shows how the linear word (a) is included in the cyclic word (b).

We define the following problem:

Problem 1 Shortest cyclic cover of strings.

Input:

A set of linear strings P.

Output:

A cyclic cover C of P that minimizes ||C||.

Let σ be a permutation of {1, …, |P|}, we can split up σ in cyclic permutations: $\sigma = \sigma_1 \circ \ldots \circ \sigma_m$. For each cyclic permutation σ_i of length n_i, we denote the cyclic string by:

$$P(\sigma_i) := pr(s_{\sigma_i(1)}, s_{\sigma_i(2)}) \ldots pr(s_{\sigma_i(n_i-1)}, s_{\sigma_i(n_i)})\ pr(s_{\sigma_i(n_i)}, s_{\sigma_i(1)}),$$

and

$P(\sigma) := \{P(\sigma_1), \ldots, P(\sigma_m)\}$ (See Fig. 2).

It is easy to see, that for each permutation σ of $\{1, \ldots, |P|\}$, $P(\sigma)$ is a cyclic cover of P and for each optimal solution w of Problem 1 (SCCS), there exists σ a permutation of $\{1, \ldots, |P|\}$ such that $w = P(\sigma)$.

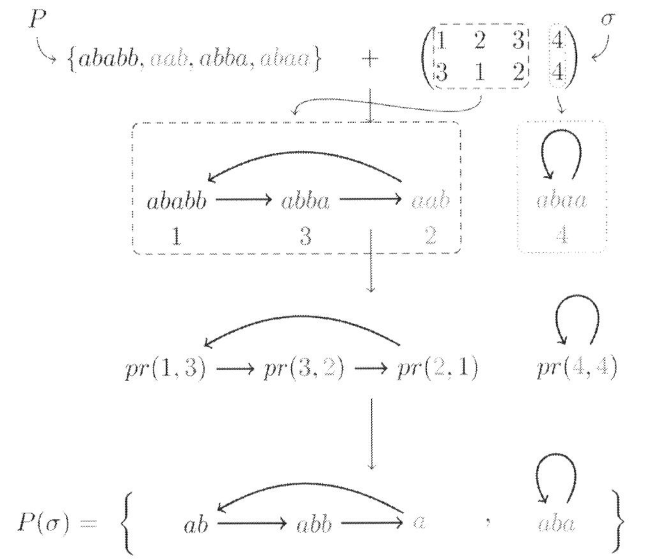

Figure 2. Running example with the input set $P := \{ababb, aab, abba, abaa\}$. Instance of a cyclic cover of P obtained with a permutation σ. We obtain the cyclic cover $P(\sigma) = \{ababba, aba\}$ (ababba and aba are cyclic words).

Related Works

Let us briefly recall some crucial works in the study of shortest superstrings and of Shortest Cyclic Cover of Strings.

Since SLiS does not admit a PTAS, numerous works on SLiS have reported polynomial time approximation algorithms with a constant ratio ranging from 4 to > 2 (see [8, Table 1]). A majority of these model SLiS as a minimum weight Hamiltonian path problem on the distance graph G of P (where an arc (s_i, s_j) is weighted by $|pr(s_i, s_j)|$ for any valid i, j). Note that if instead it is weighted by $|ov(s_i, s_j)|$, we obtain the Overlap Graph, and SLiS becomes equivalent to finding a maximum weight Hamiltonian path [1]. Clearly, the weight of a cyclic cover of G (i.e., the sum of the weight of all cycles) is lower than that of a Hamiltonian cycle, which itself gives a lower bound of the weight of a Hamiltonian path on G. Hence, most approximation algorithms for SLiS rely on solving SCCS, which is polynomial. Blum et al. [1] were the first to exhibit such an algorithm and to prove that it achieves a constant ratio of 3 for SLiS. This algorithm first solves SCCS and in a second step combines the cyclic strings by running a greedy algorithm on them. Teng and Yao improved this ratio by an algorithm that recursively solves SCCS [18]. After that, many authors have investigated the combinatorial properties of words and of some specific cycles, which enabled them to further improve the approximation (e.g. [3], [14] and [15]), but all need to solve SCCS. To do so, they compute a Minimum Assignment on the distance graph. An assignment (or cyclic cover) of a digraph G is a set of cycles such that every vertex of G belongs to exactly one cycle. To solve SCCS on an instance P, approximation algorithms for SLiS first 1/ build the distance graph of P, with $|P|$ nodes and $|P|(|P|-1)$ arcs, which requires $O(||P|| + |P|^2)$ time and space using the Generalized Suffix Tree (GST) of P [11], then 2/ compute a minimum cyclic cover using the Hungarian algorithm in $O(|P|^3)$ time [16]. Once the cyclic cover is known, the algorithm in [18] also requires to compute a particular assignment called a canonical assignment, which takes an additional $O(||P||)$ using the suffix tree based algorithm of[9]. However, the complexity bottleneck of algorithms using a cyclic cover remains the $O(||P|| + |P|^3)$ time to build the graph and compute the cover. It was also shown that greedy (Algorithm 1) solves SCCS exactly [4]. To the best of our knowledge, there is currently no linear time algorithm for solving SCCS.

Theorem 1 [6]. For Shortest Cyclic Cover of Strings, Algorithm greedy yields an optimal solution.

Explanations about Algorithm Greedy

An overlap is said to be greedy-feasible if a greedy solution takes it. Let u_1, u_2, v_1 and v_2 be four strings. We say that the overlaps $ov(u_1, u_2)$ and $ov(v_1, v_2)$ are dependent if and only if $u_1 = v_1$ or $u_2 = v_2$. When Algorithm greedy merges u with v, it chooses the overlap between u and v and forbids any overlap beginning by u or ending by v, i.e. it forbids all overlaps that are dependent of ov(u, v). We say that a set of overlaps is independent if each overlap is not dependent of another.

Thus, Algorithm greedy makes a series of choices to select a sequence of greedy-feasible and independent overlaps:

- In the first step of the Algorithm greedy chooses an overlap among the longest overlaps.
- In the second step, it chooses an overlap among the longest overlaps which are independent of the first overlap.
- At each further step, it takes a maximum overlap that is independent of the previously selected overlaps.
- In the end, it outputs a set of overlaps that are maximal (for the inclusion as a base in a matroid). This set of overlaps is independent.

As the set of overlaps at the end of greedy is maximal, there exists a permutation σ of $\{1, \ldots, |P|\}$, such that for all i in $\{1, \ldots, |P|\}$, $ov(s_i, s_{\sigma(i)})$ is an overlap of our set of overlaps. Thus, we obtain the following property which is similar to a well-known property on the solution of the greedy algorithm for SLiS [20, Def. of Induced (π, S) and Def. 2]:

Proposition 2. Let w a greedy solution of SCCS. There exists a permutation σ of $\{1, \ldots, |P|\}$such that $w = P(\sigma)$.

GENERALISED SUFFIX TREE, OVERLAP, MERGE, AND RED–BLUE PATHS

The suffix tree of a word w is a data structure that indexes all substrings of w. Each arc is labelled with a substring of w such that the concatenation of the labels along a branch from the root to a leaf spells out a suffix of w. A constraint requires that the labels of arcs from a node to its offspring start with different symbols. Thus, each node represents a prefix of a suffix, i.e. a substring of w. In fact, each internal node is the longest common prefix of all leaves in its subtree. Traversing an arc extends the represented string on its right. The word depth of a node is the length of the string it represents. An example of (generalized) suffix tree is shown in Fig. 3: the sole suffix tree structure is displayed in Fig. 3a. For instance, the node 3 represents the string aa. Going from node 3 to node 1 extends the string represented by a b to yield the string aab.

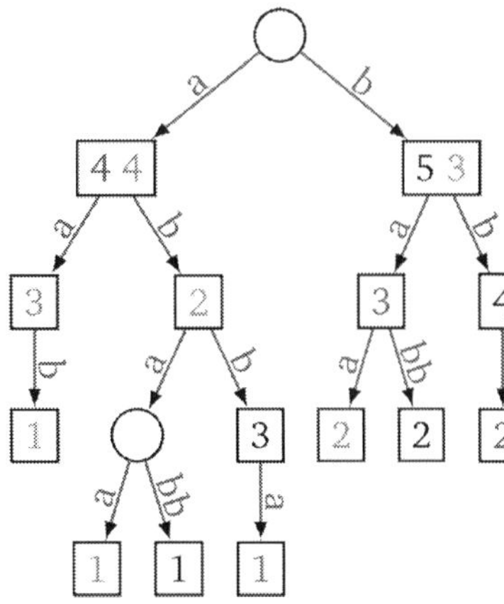

(a) T: tree structure of the suffix tree of P

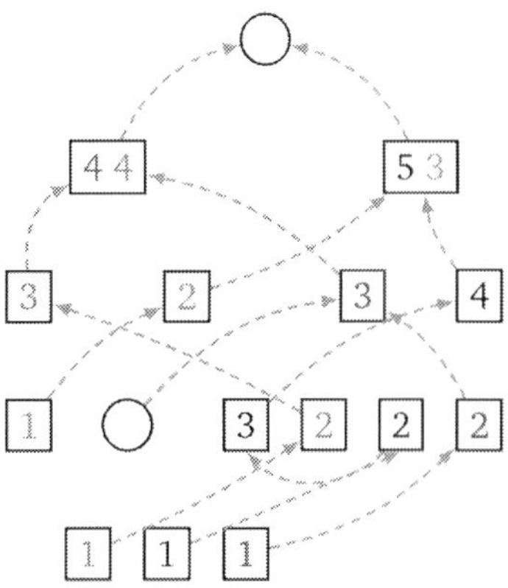

(b) L: the tree made by the suffix links of T

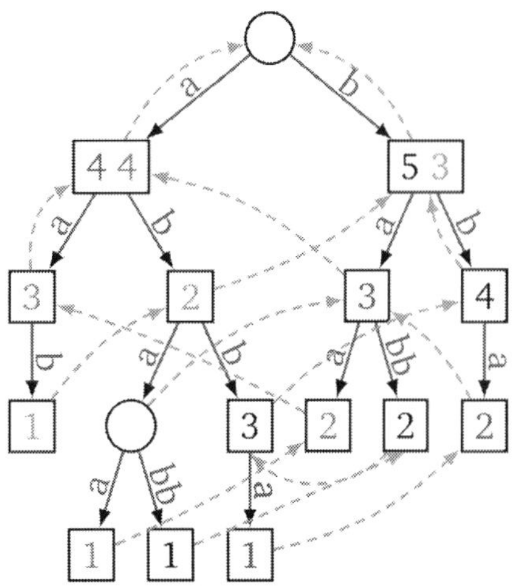

(c) The GST of P is made of T and L

Figure 3. (c) The Generalised Suffix Tree (GST) of $P := \{ababb, aab, abba, abaa\}$. The GST of P is in fact composed of two trees: (a) the tree T, which is the basic structure of the suffix tree – in blue arcs, and (b) L, the tree made by the suffix links of T – in red arcs. Square nodes represent words that occur as a suffix of some input word, circle nodes are the other nodes of T. Each square node stores its positions of occurrences in S; for simplicity, we display the starting position as a number and the word of S in which it occurs as its color, instead of showing the list of pairs (i, j). The square node labelled by a red 2, which represents the string ab, means that this string occurs as the suffix starting at position 2 in the red word aab. A square node labelled with a 1 represents an input word. (For interpretation of the references to color in this figure legend, the reader is referred to the web version of this article.)

ST are equipped with additional arcs called Suffix Links (SL): a SL links a node representing au (with a a letter and u a string) to the node representing u. Let us label the SL by the letter a. The notion of SL is usually restricted to internal nodes, but it extends naturally to leaves. We consider that each node has its SL. Traversing a SL removes the first letter of the word: it shortens the represented word at the front. To each SL, we associate a label, which is the letter it removes. For instance, in Fig. 3, traversing the SL of node 1 shortens the word aab to ab, which is the string represented by node 2. The label of that SL is a (labels of SL are not represented in this figure). It is known that, if SLs are reversed (considered in the other direction), they form a tree rooted in the root of the ST, and all leaves are on the same branch of this tree [5]. Note that the chain of SL starting from any node goes up to the root of T (For simplicity, assume the root has a SL to itself). The tree composed by the suffix links is displayed on Fig. 3b. Moreover, in the figures, the SL are drawn as an arc from a child to its parent in L (see Fig. 3).

For simplicity, we say that a suffix tree arc is blue, while SL are red. So, we have the blue tree, denoted T, and the red tree, denoted L, on the same nodes.

The GST generalizes this principle to several words. From now on, the generalized suffix tree of P is the pair (T, L). An extensive introduction to GST and their applications can be found in [10]. The distinction between explicit and implicit nodes is skipped here, but explained in [10] and [2].

Overlaps

Basically, all suffixes and all substrings of words of P are represented in the GST. If a word u overlaps a word v, then a suffix of u equals to a prefix of v. Hence, one expects the overlap to be represented somewhere in the GST. Indeed, if an internal node representing the suffix of u appears on the branch spelling v, then u overlaps v. This internal node exists since this substring occurs at least twice (in u and in v), and represents the overlap. Let us call such node an overlap node from u to v. In our representation, the internal node is labelled with the starting position of that suffix in u on the branch leading to the leaf of v. For example, in Fig. 3 the node 2 is located on the branch of 1. It is also on the branches of 1 and 1. It represents the string ab. So we know that aab overlaps abba, abaa and ababb, with the overlap ab.

Clearly, all overlap nodes from u to v are ancestors of another. Moreover, the word depth of an overlap node gives the length of the corresponding overlap. Hence, the maximum overlap between two words is the deepest overlap node of those words. For instance, both nodes 4 and 3 are ancestors of 1 meaning that abaa overlaps aab with two possible overlaps: a and aa, of length 1 and 2 respectively.

All these notions are known. Indeed, it is known that one can compute efficiently all overlaps for each pair of words in P using the GST of P. In fact, one usually computes pairwise the maximum overlaps for P [11], to build the prefix or the overlap graph of P (as mentioned in introduction).

Merge and Red–Blue Paths

Above the overlap node was defined only using T; the SL (hence L) were not involved. Let us now give an alternative definition using T and L.

If u overlaps v, then a suffix of u equals a prefix of v. We have seen that the overlaps is a node on the branch spelling v. We can also find this precise suffix of u starting at the node representing u by following enough suffix links. This means going up in the red tree from the node u. Hence, one sees that an overlap node from u to v is an ancestor of u in L (the red tree), and an ancestor of v in T (the blue tree). We obtain an alternative definition: an overlap node from u to v is a red ancestor of u and a blue ancestor of v. For simplicity, let us say it is a red–blue ancestor of the ordered pair (u, v).

Now, we see that the maximum overlap of (u, v) is the lowest red–blue ancestor of(u, v). Also, if the red path reaches the root, then the overlap is the empty word (and their merge is simply their concatenation).

In other words, any overlap for a pair (u, v) corresponds to a Red–Blue path from u to v in (T, L).

The merge of u and v using their maximum overlap ov(u, v) is the wordw: = pr(u, v)ov(u, v)su(u, v), where u: = pr(u, v)ov(u, v) andv: = ov(u, v)su(u, v). We state this definition with the maximum overlap, but it is valid with any overlap; the larger the overlap, the shorter the merge. We denote by RB-path(u, v) the Red–Blue path which corresponds to the maximum overlap between uand v.

Assume we want to spell out the (linear) merge of u and v using the overlap node w in(T, L). It can be done in three steps:

- traverse T from the root to u: this spells out u with the labels of blue arcs;
- go up L from u to w following the red arcs: it is possible since w is a red ancestor of u (here we skip one by one all letters of pr(u, v));
- go down T from w to v using blue arcs, which is possible since v is a descendant of w ; this spells out su(u, v).

A merge of (u, v) is a linear superstring of {u, v}. The process above can be generalised to spell out any cyclic superstring of a cyclic permutation of words (w_1, w_2, …, w_n)using some given pairwise overlaps: one starts from the node representing w_1, then performs steps 2 and 3 using the appropriate Red–Blue path from w_1 to w_2 to merge them, then iterates only steps 2 and 3 for each following word until one reaches $w_1$again. This circuit on the GST is called a Red–Blue circuit.

Example 1. For instance in Fig. 3, the Red–Blue circuit corresponding to the cyclic merge of the words ababb, abba, and then aab in this order, contains three Red–Blue paths: for the pairs (ababb, abba), (abba, aab) and then for (aab, ababb). This circuit starts at node $\boxed{1}$ goes up with SL to node $\boxed{2}$ and then $\boxed{3}$ which is a red–blue ancestor of (ababb, abba), then goes down with blue arcs to $\boxed{1}$. This is the Red–Blue path for (ababb, abba), which spells out ab with the SL labels. Then the circuit goes up with SL to $\boxed{2}$, $\boxed{3}$, and $\boxed{4}$, which is an ancestor of$\boxed{1}$. This spells out abb with SL labels. Then, it goes down to $\boxed{1}$. This makes up the Red–Blue path for (abba, aab). Then, the circuit goes up to $\boxed{2}$, which is an ancestor of $\boxed{1}$; this spells out a with one red label. Then, it goes down and back to $\boxed{1}$, which was the starting node. Altogether the sequence of red labels spells out ababba, while the sequence of blue labels yields aababb: both write the same cyclic word.

Now, let us state a more subtle property. For a Red–Blue circuit, writing all blue labels in order or writing all red labels in order spell out the same superstring (a red label is a label of a SL). Hence, the number of blue arcs is smaller than the number of red arcs, which is the superstring length. A proof of a slightly different version of this property can be found in [5, Section 4.3 on p. 18].

THE SUPERSTRING GRAPH

Here, we are going to show that the choices made by Algorithm greedy for SCCS are not really choices. In fact, we will show that each greedy solution can be represented by a unique graph embedded in the Generalised Suffix Tree. As this graph turns out to be computable in linear time, one can derive a greedy solution for SCCS in linear time.

Equivalence of Greedy Solutions

Let w be a greedy solution of SCCS. By Proposition 2, there exists a permutation σ such that w = P(σ). For each cyclic permutation σ_i of σ , we denote by c(σ_i) the Red–Blue circuit obtained from σ_i in the GST.

We denote by $G_P(\sigma)$ = (V, R, B) the directed multigraph built with the arcs of the Red–Blue circuits of all the c(σ_i), where R denotes the set of Red arcs, and B denotes the set of Blue arcs of all the c(σ_i).

A graph is said to be Eulerian, if there exists a Eulerian path on this graph, i.e. a path that visits each arc of the graph exactly once. As $G_P(\sigma)$ is a collection of Red–Blue circuits, which are made of Red–Blue paths, each connected component of $G_P(\sigma)$ is Eulerian. (With each additional circuit, the graph remains Eulerian.)

For each permutation of {1, …, |P|}, we can build the corresponding multigraph $G_P()$. We have the following proposition.

Proposition 3. Let $w_1$and $w_2$be two greedy solutions of SCCS and let $\sigma_1$and $\sigma_2$be their respective permutations of {1, …, |P|}. Then $G_P(\sigma_1) = G_P(\sigma_2)$.

Proposition 3 states a key property of greedy solutions for SCCS. Below, we give two lines of proof: the first one explains why the property is valid (and better conveys the intuition to the reader), while the second gives a more formal, but less explanatory, demonstration.

Proof. Let $w = P(\sigma)$ be a greedy solution of SCCS. Let us show that the choices made by Algorithm greedy for SCCS do not influence $G_p(\sigma)$. greedy faces a choice when several overlaps of the same length are dependent (Clearly, independent overlaps can be swapped in a permutation and thus do not influence the graph).

Let $ov(u_1, v_1)$ and $ov(u_1, v_2)$ be two dependent and greedy-feasible overlaps. Assume that $ov(u_1, v_1)$ is the overlap choosen by greedy to obtain w , and let u_2 in P be the successor of v_2 in σ . It implies that $ov(u_2, v_2)$ is the overlap that merges u_2 andv_2 in w. By the definition of greedy, we have that $|ov(u_1, v_1)| \geq |ov(u_2, v_2)|$. Let us show that there exits a Red–Blue path from u_2 to v_1 in $G_p(\sigma)$.

As $|ov(u_1, v_1)| \geq |ov(u_2, v_2)|$, we have that $ov(u_2, v_2)$ is a prefix of $ov(u_1, v_2)$, and thus a prefix of $ov(u_1, v_1)$. Hence in the GST, the node $ov(u_2, v_2)$ is an ancestor of $ov(u_1, v_1)$, and $ov(u_1, v_1)$ is a node in the Red–Blue paths from u_1 to v_1 and fromu_2 to v_2. Thus, we have both Red–Blue paths from u_1 to v_2 and from u_2 to v_1 are in$G_p(\sigma)$ (see Fig. 4). □

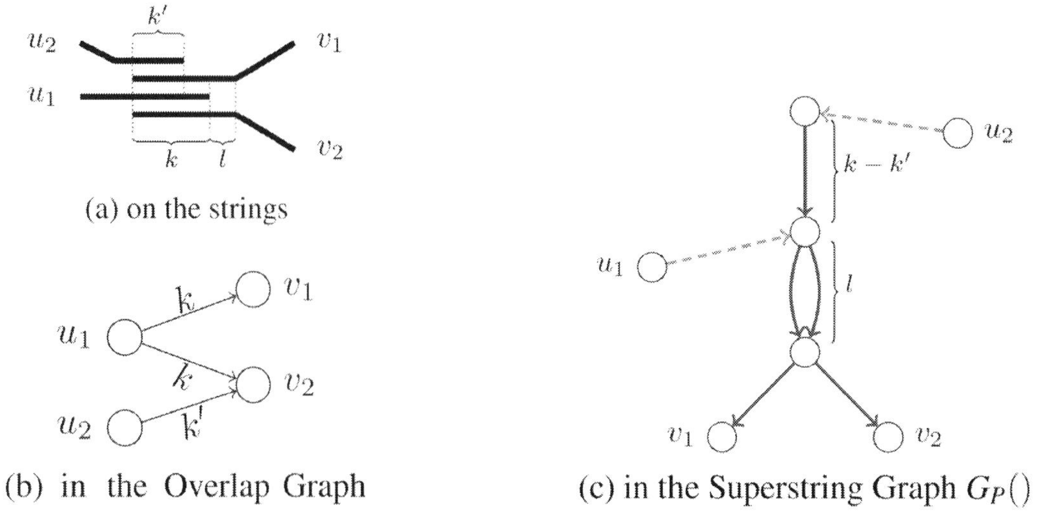

Figure 4. Example with three overlaps: two dependent ones, between u_1 and v_1 and between u_1 and v_2, and another overlap between u_2 and v_2: shown on the strings (a), in the overlap graph (b), and in the Superstring Graph (c).

An alternative proof. Let σ_1 and σ_2 be two permutations of P corresponding to two distinct greedy solutions for SCCS. We set $G_p(\sigma_1) := (V_1, R_1, B_1)$ and $G_p(\sigma_2) := (V_2, R_2, B_2)$.

We proceed by contraposition and assume that $G_p(\sigma_1) \neq G_p(\sigma_2)$; then$((R_1 \cup B_1) \setminus (R_2 \cup B_2)) \cup ((R_2 \cup B_2) \setminus (R_1 \cup B_1)) \neq \emptyset$. As the role of both permutations is symmetrical, we assume that $(R_1 \cup B_1) \setminus (R_2 \cup B_2) \neq \emptyset$. Let $e := (u, v)$ be an arc of $(R_1 \cup B_1) \setminus (R_2 \cup B_2)$ such that $\max(|u|, |v|)$ is maximal among all possible arcs of $(R_1 \cup B_1) \setminus (R_2 \cup B_2)$. According to the definition of $G_p(\sigma_1)$, there exist i and j such that $\sigma_1(i) = j$ and e is an arc on the Red–Blue path linking s_i to s_j(formally $e \in \text{RB-path}(s_i, s_j)$). Two cases arise.

Case $e \in B_1$: Let i_2 denote the predecessor of j in σ_2, in other words, the element of $\sigma_2$satisfying $j = \sigma_2(i_2)$. But, one gets that $ov(s_{i2}, s_j)$ is a prefix of $ov(s_i, s_j)$, since otherwise there would exist $j_1 := \sigma_1(i_2)$, such that $|ov(s_i, s_j)| < |ov(s_{i2}, s_{j1})|$, which would imply that e is not maximal. It follows that e belongs to RB-path(s_{i2}, s_j), and thus to B_2, which contradicts our hypothesis.

Case $e \in R_1$:Let j_2 denote the successor of i in σ_2, that is $j_2 := \sigma_2(i)$. Clearly, $ov(s_i, s_{j2})$ must be a suffix of $ov(s_i, s_j)$, since otherwise there would exist i_1 such that $j_2 = \sigma_1(i_1)$and $|ov(s_i, s_j)| < |ov(s_{i1}, s_{j2})|$, which would mean that e is not maximal. One obtains that $e \in \text{RB-path}(s_i, s_{j2})$, and thus e belongs to R_2, which is a contradiction.

This ends the proof. By Proposition 3, the graph $G_p()$ represents all the solutions of the greedy algorithm for SCCS. We called this graph, the Superstring Graph of P , and denote it by G_p. An example of Superstring Graph for $P := \{abb, bbb, bbc\}$ is shown in Fig. 7.

To sum up, we know that for each greedy solution w , there exists a permutation of $\{1, \ldots, |P|\}$ that can be translated into a set of Red–Blue circuits, $c(w) = \{c_1(w), \ldots, c_m(w)\}$. Remember that each Red–Blue circuit is made by chaining Red–Blue paths. Let c be a multi-cycle of G. We say that c covers G_P if each arc of G_P is included in a single cycle of c. By Proposition 3, for each greedy solution w we have that c(w) covers G_P.

By the following proposition, we have that each multi-cycle that covers G comes from a greedy solution.

Proposition 4. {multi-cycle p|p covers G_P} = {c(w)|w is a greedy solution}.

To prove Proposition 4, we first need a lemma. A crossing in G_P is a node that has red in- and out-going arcs and blue in- and out-going arcs.

Lemma 5 Absence of crossing. $G_P$does not contain any crossing.

Proof of Lemma 5. It is enough to see that the only nodes that can have a red out-going arc and a blue in-going arc correspond to the words of P . But if $v \in P$, v is a leaf in T and in L by definition of the GST, and thus v has neither a blue arc going out, nor a red arc going in.

Proof of Proposition 4. To understand this equality, it is sufficient to note that there is a relation between choosing the longest overlap in greedy and the absence of crossing in G_P.

Proof of ⊆.

Let us show {multi-cycle p|p covers G_P}⊆{c(w)|w is a greedy solution} by contraposition. Assume that there exists a multi-cycle p covering G_P and there does not exist a greedy solution w of P such that p = c(w). By hypothesis, there exist four nodes v_1, v_2, v_3 and v_4 in P that do not satisfy the greedy property. In other words, although $|ov(v_1, v_2)| < |ov(v_3, v_4)|$, both Path($v_1$, v_4) andPath(v_3, v_2) are in p . Hence, the node ov(v_3, v_4) is a crossing in G_P (see Fig. 5). As there does not exist any crossing in G_P (Lemma 5), we obtain a contradiction, and get $\{$multi-cycle p|p covers $G_P\} \subseteq \{c(w)|$w is a greedy solution$\}$.

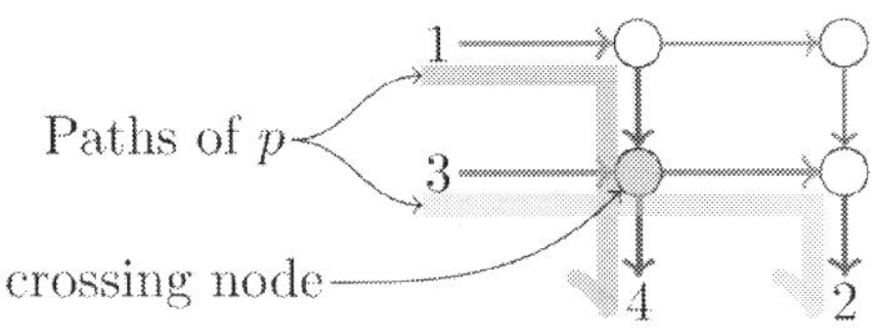

Figure 5. Illustration for the proof of Proposition 4. In the proof of ⊆, the argument is the existence of a crossing node in a non-greedy solution. This figure displays the four nodes v_1, …, v_4 and the nodes (circles) representing their overlaps. Then, the node representing ov(v_3, v_4) (grey node) is a crossing, i.e. it has blue and red in-going and out-going arcs. (For interpretation of the references to colour in this figure legend, the reader is referred to the web version of this article.)

Proof of ⊇.

Reciprocally, assume that there exists a greedy solution w of P and there does not exist a multi-cycle p that covers G_P such that p = c(w). Thus, there exists an arc of c(w)which is not an arc of G_P. Among those arcs, let e = (u, v) be the one with the deepest node (i.e. longest word) v in T . By the definition of G_P, e belongs to R (i.e. is a red arc), because it is the deepest of its kind. Let v_1 and v_2 be the nodes of P such that e belongs to Path(v_1, v_2). As e is not in G_P, for each u in P such that Path(v_1, u) is in G_P, $u \neq v_2$. Thus, there exists v_4 in P such that Path(v_1, v_4) is in G_P and $|ov(v_1, v_2)| < |ov(v_1, v_4)|$. As w is a greedy solution of P , there exists v_3 in P and not in G_P such that Path(v_3, v_4) is in c(w) and $|ov(v_1, v_4)| \leq |ov(v_3, v_4)|$. Thus, there exists an arc in c(w) that is not in G_P with a deeper extremity than e . This contradicts our hypothesis and we get $\{c(w)|$w is a greedy solution$\} \subseteq \{$multi-cycle p|p covers $G_P\}$. □

Characterization of the Superstring Graph and a Construction Algorithm

Now, we are going to characterize the Superstring Graph and give a linear time algorithm to build it from a set of words. For this algorithm, we define and compute weights (respectively n(.) and d(.)) for the red and for the blue arcs of the GST. Finally, the SG will be composed of those arcs having a strictly positive weight (and of the nodes visited by them).

As greedy selects overlaps in order of decreasing length, one can see it as a recursive algorithm that progresses along the branches of the GST of P. On the GST, greedyprogresses from the leaves toward the root, i.e. in order of decreasing word depth of the nodes. Let us use this recursive side of greedy to explain the Superstring Graph.

Let v be a node of the GST; when greedy sees the overlaps of length |v|, it has already considered overlaps of larger lengths. We define two weights n() and d() such that:

- n(v) is the number of strings of P which have v as suffix and are not merged on their right with another string of P with a larger overlap.
- d(v) is the number of strings of P which have v as prefix and are not merged on their left with another string of P with a larger overlap.

In other words, n(v) is the number of leaves of the subtree of v in L that have not yet been merged on their right, and d(v) is the number of leaves of the subtree of v in T that have not yet been merged on their left.

First, it can be seen easily seen that a node v which has no other leaf both in its subtrees in L and in T, is a string of P. Thus, for these nodes we set, n(v) = d(v): = 1.

For the other nodes, we use the recursion of greedy. In fact, we can determine how many strings of P have not yet been merged with another string by looking the weights n(.) and d(.) of the children of v in L and of its children in T (see Fig. 6).

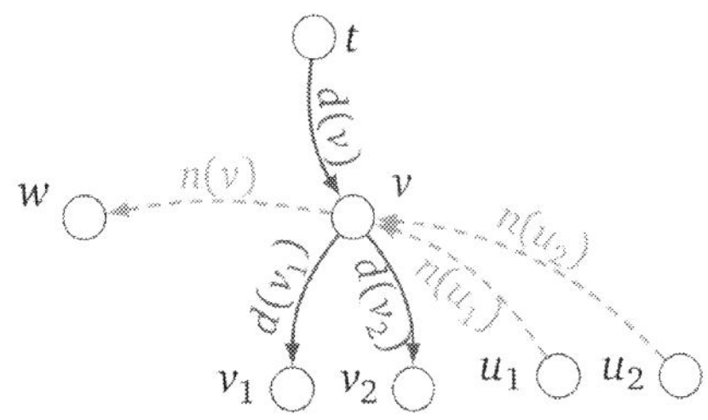

Figure 6. General scheme of the in- and out-going arcs of a node v in GST. The red arcs belong to R and the blue arcs to B. If a weight is zero, the arc is not included in the Superstring Graph. (For interpretation of the references to color in this figure legend, the reader is referred to the web version of this article.)

Let a(v) be the difference between the sum of the n(u′) of the children u′ of v in L and the sum of the d(u) of the children u of v in T:

$$a(v) := \sum_{u' \in Children_L(v)} n(u') - \sum_{u \in Children_T(v)} d(u).$$

Hence, the absolute value of a(v) is the largest number of strings of P that greedy can merge with other strings of P using the overlap v . With a(v), we can calculate n(v)and d(v):

$$\text{If } a(v) \geq 0, \text{ we have } \begin{cases} n(v) := a \\ d(v) := 0, \end{cases}$$

$$\text{if } a(v) < 0, \text{ we have } \begin{cases} n(v) := 0 \\ d(v) := -a. \end{cases}$$

With this recursive definition of the weights n() and d(), we can construct the Superstring Graph from the GST of P. Whenever the weight of an arc of the GST is equal to 0, this arc does not belong to the Superstring Graph. Similarly, if for a node, say v, all of its in-going and out-going arcs have a zero weight, v is isolated and is not included in the Superstring Graph – this corresponds to the subset U in Definition 1 (which states another definition of the Superstring Graph).

Definition 1. The Superstring Graph G_P = (V, R, B) where

$$V = V_T \setminus U$$

$$R = \{(u, w)^{n(u)} \mid u \in V_T,\ w \text{ the parent of } u \text{ in } L\}$$

$$B = \{(t, v)^{d(v)} \mid v \in V_T,\ t \text{ the parent of } v \text{ in } T\}$$

and $U = \{v \in V_T \mid v \text{ is not an extremity of an arc of } R \cup B\}$ where n() and d() are the weights on arcs as defined above.

Now that we can build the Superstring Graph for an input P by traversing the generalized suffix tree of P, we provide an algorithm (Algorithm 2) that uses this graph to solve SCCS for P.

Algorithm 2: The Superstring Graph algorithm for SCCS.

1 **Input**: P a set of linear words. **Output**: w a greedy solution for SCCS;
2 build G_P the Superstring Graph of P;
3 compute a cyclic cover $c := (c_1, \ldots, c_n)$ of G_P;
4 **for** $i \in [1, n]$ **do**
5 traverse c_i: list the words of P whose node are in c_i and create w_i by concatenating cyclically $pr(s_j, s_k)$ whenever s_k is the successor of s_j;
6 insert the cyclic string w_i in w;
7 **return** w

Theorem 6. Algorithm 2solves SCCS in linear time and space.

Proof. Correctness. By Proposition 4, the set w of cyclic words computed by Algorithm 2 is a solution of greedy for SCCS. Hence, each word of P appears as a substring of a cyclic word in w, and by Theorem 1, the norm of w is minimal.

Complexity. The Superstring Graph of P is embedded in the generalised suffix tree of P , and thus built in a time linear in ||P||.

First the cyclic concatenation of the words in P is longer than the SCCS obtained through any cyclic permutation of P. By Proposition 2, the length of a solution of greedy is bounded by ||P||; thus, the length of a multi-cycle of G_P is bounded by 2 × ||P||. Consequently, one can find a multi-cycle also in O(||P||) time and space. Finally, traversing all its cycles takes a time proportional in the size of the Superstring Graph. □

Note that with Algorithm 2, one obtains a cyclic cover.

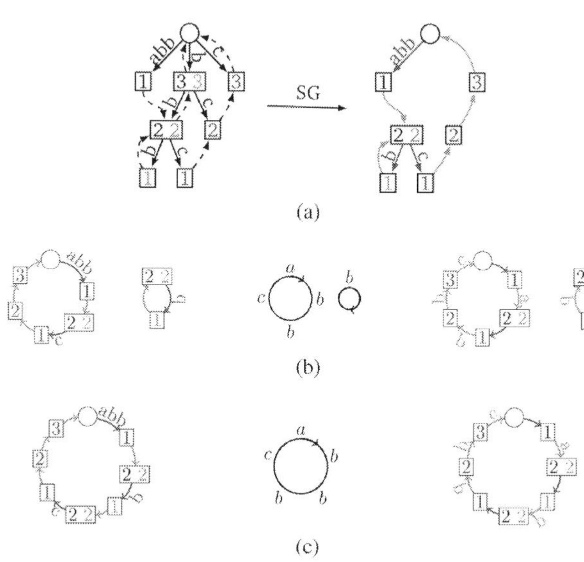

Figure 7. A Superstring Graph and SCCS solutions. (a) The generalized suffix tree and the Superstring Graph (SG) for $P := \{abb, bbb, bbc\}$. Square nodes of T represent strings that are suffixes of some word of P: the integer in the square node is a starting position of its suffix. A word of P is identified by its color. Figure (b) and (c) show the two multi-cycles that cover the SG and their respective sets of cyclic strings. This example is well known for showing the lower bound of the approximation ratio of the greedy algorithm for SLiS. The SG for this instance is connected and thus it also gives an optimal cyclic superstring (a solution of SCyS). As the Eulerian circuit visits the root of the GST, this optimal cyclic superstring can be cut at the root to obtain an optimal linear superstring.

IMPLICATIONS OF THE SUPERSTRING GRAPH

SCCS with a Cardinality Constraint on Greedy Solutions

We can split up G_P into connected components: $G_P = \{C_1, \ldots, C_g\}$. By Proposition 4, each multi-cycle c of G_P can be partitioned in a subset of cycles $c = S_1 \cup \ldots \cup S_g$, where each set of cycles S_i covers a connected component C_i of G_P.

Algorithm 2, on its third line (in blue), [1] computes a cyclic cover of G_P. This requires to perform a random choice when facing two alternative out-going arcs. Clearly, the combination of all possible successive choices allows to produce all possible cyclic covers of G_P. Certain choices will generate a solution containing several cycles to cover one connected component (see Fig. 7b), although it is always possible to cover one connected component with a single cycle (see Fig. 7c). Thus, any two cyclic covers may differ in their number of cycles, i.e. in their cardinality. This gives rise naturally to a new question, to a new variant of SCCS, which we define below.

Problem 2 SCCS with a cardinality constraint on greedy solutions.

Input: A set of linear strings P.

Output: A set of cyclic strings c, with the least number of elements, that is a solution of the greedy algorithm on Shortest Cyclic Cover of Strings.

Algorithm 3 differs from Algorithm 2 only on the third line: instead of computing any cyclic cover of G_P, it computes a Eulerian multi-cycle of G_P. This is possible since each connected component of the Superstring Graph is Eulerian and it can be done in linear time in the norm of P . A Eulerian multi-cycle of G_p covers each connected component with a single cycle, hence it minimises the cardinality of the cyclic cover, and as it is a greedy solution it solves Problem 2. We obtain Theorem 7. The minimisation of the number of cyclic strings by Algorithm 3 is illustrated in Fig. 7.

Algorithm 3: The Superstring Graph algorithm for SCCS with a cardinality constraint.

```
Input: P a set of linear words. Output: w a greedy solution for SCCS;
build G_P the Superstring Graph of P;
compute a Eulerian multi-cycle c = (c_1, ..., c_n) of G_P;
for i ∈ [1, n] do
    traverse c_i: list the words of P whose node are in c_i and create w_i by concatenating cyclically pr(s_j, s_k) whenever s_k is the successor of s_j;
    insert the cyclic string w_i in w;
return w
```

Theorem 7. Algorithm 3solves Problem 2in linear time.

Proof. As the connected components of the Superstring Graph are Eulerian, this is done in linear time and space in the size of G_p. By Proposition 4, a label of a Eulerian multi-cycle of G_p is an optimal solution for the Problem 2.

Remark. Although for SCCS, all solutions of greedy are optimal, some optimal solutions are not output by greedy. Thus, the question of finding a shortest cyclic cover with a minimum number of elements is not solved by the Algorithm 3 (see a counter example in Fig. 8).

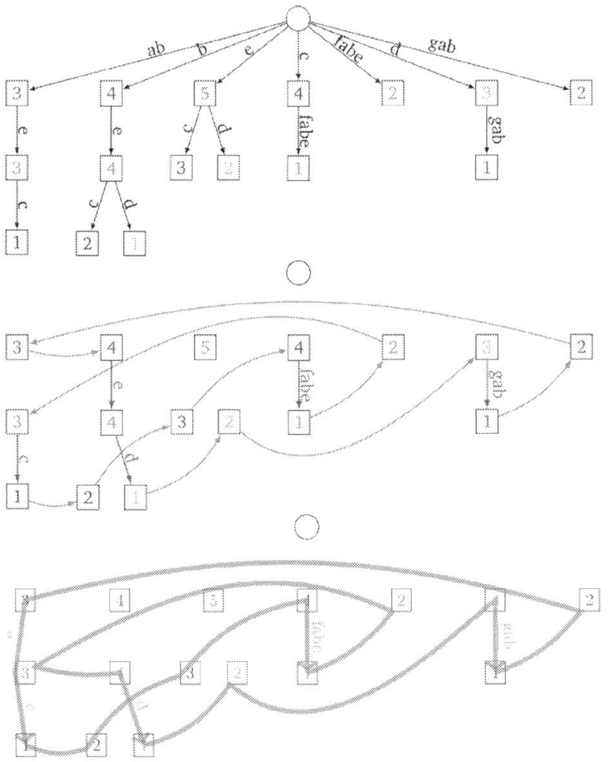

Figure 8. An instance with an optimal solution that is not a solution of greedy for SCCS (however, the solution of the SG is also optimal). Let $P = \{abec, bed, cfabe, dgab\}$. (Top) the generalized suffix tree, (middle) the SG, and (bottom) an optimal solution of SCCS that consists in single cycle, while the SG has two components.

Consequences of the Topology of the Superstring Graph

The characterization of the SG can also be applied to solve or approximate the "classical" shortest superstring problem (SLiS – for Shortest Linear Superstring), in which the solution is a linear superstring, as well as its variant where the solution is a single cyclic word (SCyS - = for Shortest Cyclic Superstring). Let $w_{OPT(SLiS)}$, respectively$w_{OPT(SCyS)}$, denote an optimal solution for SLiS, resp. for SCyS. Let w a greedy solution for SCCS, we have: $|w| \leq |w_{OPT(SCyS)}| \leq |w_{OPT(SLiS)}|$. If the SG is connected, then w is a cyclic superstring of P, i.e. a solution of SCyS. By the above relation, it is an optimal solution for SCyS.

Now, from this cyclic superstring, we can easily derive a linear superstring of P. Basically, we cut the cyclic string at the start of a suffix of a word of P and pre-catenate the corresponding prefix. Let v a node of the SG such that n(v) = d(v) = 0, then v is a prefix of some word of P. Then vw makes up a linear superstring of P . We obtain $|w| \leq |w_{OPT(SLiS)}| \leq |v| + |w|$. As $|v| \leq |w_{OPT(SLiS)}|$, we get $|v| + |w| \leq 2|w_{OPT(SLiS)}|$. In other words, for instances P that have a connected SG, we obtain a 2-approximation for the shortest linear superstring. Furthermore, if the Eulerian cycle visits the root of the suffix tree, then v is the empty word and then $|w| \leq |w_{OPT(SLiS)}| \leq |w|$, meaning that wis an optimal linear superstring.

Note that there exist non-trivial instances, with an arbitrary large norm, whose SG is connected: any instance in which all words are cyclic shifts of another belong to this class. As the SG can be built and explored in linear time in ||P||, one can use this procedure as a predicate to check whether SCyS or SLiS are solvable in linear time. If not, one can launch a more complex approximation algorithm [15].

CONCLUSION

We consider the problem Shortest Cyclic Cover of Strings, which is solved by Algorithmgreedy. The set of solutions of greedy can be exponential. Nevertheless, with the SG, we exhibit a characterisation of this set in a graph that is Eulerian and linear in the input size. This enables us to solve SCCS in linear time, but also to find a greedy solution with the least number of cyclic strings. Moreover, this approach can solve or approximate some non-trivial instances of the shortest superstring problems. Our approach can be adapted to a variant of SCCS where the multiplicity of each input word is given as input.

Currently, approximation algorithms for shortest superstring problems use a procedure for solving SCCS that takes cubic time (i.e. $O(||P|| + |P|^3)$ time) and quadratic space in the number of strings. This step represents their time complexity bottleneck since other steps can be done in O(||P||) time. Using our algorithm makes the overall time complexity linear in the input size.

ACKNOWLEDGMENTS

This work is supported by ANR Colib'read (ANR-12-BS02-0008), by ANR Institut de Biologie Computationnelle (ANR-11-BINF-0002), and by CNRS (Défi MASTODONS).

REFERENCES

1. A. Blum, T. Jiang, M. Li, J. Tromp, M. Yannakakis, Linear approximation of shortest superstrings, in: ACM Symposium on the Theory of Computing, 1991, pp. 328–336.
2. D. Breslauer, G.F. Italiano, On suffix extensions in suffix trees, Theor. Comput. Sci. 457 (2012) 27–34.
3. D. Breslauer, T. Jiang, Z. Jiang, Rotations of periodic strings and short superstrings, J. Algorithms 24 (2) (1997) 340–353.
4. B. Cazaux, E. Rivals, Approximation of greedy algorithms for Max-ATSP, Maximal Compression, Maximal Cycle Cover, and Shortest Cyclic Cover of Strings, in: Proc. of Prague Stringology Conference, PSC, Czech Technical Univ. Prague, 2014, pp. 148–161, http://www.stringology. org/event/2014/p14.html.
5. B. Cazaux, E. Rivals, Reverse engineering of compact suffix trees and links: a novel algorithm, J. Discret. Algorithms 28 (2014) 9–22, http:// dx.doi.org/10.1016/j.jda.2014.07.002.
6. B. Cazaux, E. Rivals, The power of greedy algorithms for approximating Max-ATSP, Cyclic Cover, and superstrings, Discrete Appl. Math. (2015), http://dx.doi.org/10.1016/j.dam.2015.06.003.
7. J. Gallant, D. Maier, J.A. Storer, On finding minimal length superstrings, J. Comput. Syst. Sci. 20 (1980) 50–58.
8. A. Golovnev, A. Kulikov, I. Mihajlin, Approximating shortest superstring problem using de Bruijn Graphs, in: Combinatorial Pattern Matching, in: Lect. Notes Comput. Sci., vol. 7922, Springer Verlag, 2013, pp. 120–129.
9. D. Gusfield, Faster implementation of a shortest superstring approximation, Inf. Process. Lett. 51 (5) (1994) 271–274.
10. D. Gusfield, Algorithms on Strings, Trees and Sequences, Cambridge Univ. Press, 1997.
11. D. Gusfield, G.M. Landau, B. Schieber, An efficient algorithm for the all pairs suffix–prefix problem, Inf. Process. Lett. 41 (4) (1992) 181–185.
12. S.R. Kosaraju, A.L. Delcher, Large-scale assembly of DNA strings and space-efficient construction of suffix trees, in: Proceedings of the Twenty-Seventh Annual ACM Symposium on Theory of Computing, STOC '95, 1995, pp. 169–177.
13. S.R. Kosaraju, A.L. Delcher, Large-scale assembly of DNA strings and space-efficient construction of suffix trees, in: Proceedings of the Twenty-Eighth Annual ACM Symposium on Theory of Computing, STOC '96, ACM, New York, NY, USA, 1996, p. 659.
14. M. Mucha, Lyndon words and short superstrings, in: Proceedings of the Twenty-Fourth Annual ACM–SIAM Symposium on Discrete Algorithms, SODA, 2013, pp. 958–972.
15. K.E. Paluch, Better approximation algorithms for maximum asymmetric traveling salesman and shortest superstring, CoRR arXiv:1401.3670 [abs], 2014.
16. C.H. Papadimitriou, K. Steiglitz, Combinatorial Optimization: Algorithms and Complexity, 2nd edition, Dover Publications, Inc., 1998, 496 pp.
17. J. Tarhio, E. Ukkonen, A greedy approximation algorithm for constructing shortest common superstrings, Theor. Comp. Sci. 57 (1988) 131–145.
18. S. Teng, F.F. Yao, Approximating shortest superstrings, in: 34th Annual Symposium on Foundations of Computer Science, 1993, pp. 158–165.
19. E. Ukkonen, A linear-time algorithm for finding approximate shortest common superstrings, Algorithmica 5 (1–4) (June 1990) 313–323.
20. V. Vassilevska, Explicit inapproximability bounds for the shortest superstring problem, in: Mathematical Foundations of Computer Science 2005, 30th International Symposium, Proceedings, MFCS 2005, Gdansk, Poland, August 29–September 2, 2005, in: Lect. Notes Comput. Sci., vol. 3618, Springer, 2005, pp. 793–800.

CHAPTER 15 AN ELEGANT ALGORITHM FOR THE CONSTRUCTION OF SUFFIX ARRAYS

Sanguthevar Rajasekaran and Marius Nicolae

Dept. of Computer Science and Engineering, Univ. of Connecticut, Storrs, CT, USA

ABSTRACT

The suffix array is a data structure that finds numerous applications in string processing problems for both linguistic texts and biological data. It has been introduced as a memory efficient alternative for suffix trees. The suffix array consists of the sorted suffixes of a string. There are several linear time suffix array construction algorithms (SACAs) known in the literature. However, one of the fastest algorithms in practice has a worst case run time of $O(n^2)$. The problem of designing practically and theoretically efficient techniques remains open.

In this paper we present an elegant algorithm for suffix array construction which takes linear time with high probability; the probability is on the space of all possible inputs. Our algorithm is one of the simplest of the known SACAs and it opens up a new dimension of suffix array construction that has not been explored until now. Our algorithm is easily parallelizable. We offer parallel implementations on various parallel models of computing. We prove a lemma on the ℓ-mers of a random string which might find independent applications. We also present another algorithm that utilizes the above algorithm. This algorithm is called RadixSA and has a worst case run time of $O(n \log n)$. RadixSA introduces an idea that may find independent applications as a speedup technique for other SACAs. An empirical comparison of RadixSA with other algorithms on various datasets reveals that our algorithm is one of the fastest algorithms to date. The C++ source code is freely available at http://www.engr.uconn.edu/~man09004/radixSA.zip.

INTRODUCTION

The suffix array is a data structure that finds numerous applications in string processing problems for both linguistic texts and biological data. It has been introduced in [17] as a memory efficient alternative to suffix trees. The suffix array of a string T is an array A, (|T| = |A| = n) which gives the lexicographic order of all the suffixes of T. Thus, A[i] is the starting position of the lexicographically i-th smallest suffix of T.

The original suffix array construction algorithm [17] runs in $O(n \log n)$ time. It is based on a technique called prefix doubling: assume that the suffixes are grouped into buckets such that suffixes in the same bucket share the same prefix of length k. Let b_i be the bucket number for suffix i. Let $q_i = (b_i, b_{i+k})$. Sort the suffixes with respect to q_i using radix sort. As a result, the suffixes become sorted by their first 2k characters.

Citation: Sanguthevar Rajasekaran, Marius Nicolae, An elegant algorithm for the construction of suffix arrays, Journal of Discrete Algorithms, Volume 27, July 2014, Pages 21-28, ISSN 1570-8667, http://dx.doi.org/10.1016/j.jda.2014.03.001.

Update the bucket numbers and repeat the process until all the suffixes are in buckets of size 1. This process takes no more than log n rounds. The idea of sorting suffixes in one bucket based on the bucket information of nearby suffixes is called induced copying. It appears in some form or another in many of the algorithms for suffix array construction.

Numerous papers have been written on suffix arrays. A survey on some of these algorithms can be found in [22]. The authors of [22] categorize suffix array construction algorithms (SACA) into five based on the main techniques employed: 1) Prefix Doubling (examples include [17] – run time $O(n\log n)$; [15] – run time $O(n\log n)$); 2) Recursive (examples include [11] – run time = $O(n\log\log n)$); 3) Induced Copying (examples include[1] – run time); 4) Hybrid (examples include [7] and [12] – run time =$O(n^2\log n)$); and 5) Suffix Tree (examples include [13] – run time = $O(n\log\sigma)$ where σ is the size of the alphabet).

In 2003, three independent groups [12], [9] and [10] found the first linear time suffix array construction algorithms which do not require building a suffix tree beforehand. For example, in [12] the suffixes are classified as either L or S. Suffix i is an L suffix if it is lexicographically larger than suffix i + 1, otherwise it is an S suffix. Assume that the number of L suffixes is less than n/2, if not, do this for S suffixes. Create a new string where the segments of text in between L suffixes are renamed to single characters. The new text has length no more than n/2 and we recursively find its suffix array. This suffix array gives the order of the L suffixes in the original string. This order is used to induce the order of the remaining suffixes.

Another linear time algorithm, called skew, is given in [9]. It first sorts those suffixes i with $i \bmod 3 \neq 0$ using a recursive procedure. The order of these suffixes is then used to infer the order of the suffixes with $i \bmod 3 = 0$. Once these two groups are determined we can compare one suffix from the first group with one from the second group in constant time. The last step is to merge the two sorted groups, in linear time.

Several other SACAs have been proposed in the literature in recent years (e.g., [20] and [25]). Some of the algorithms with superlinear worst case run times perform better in practice than the linear ones. One of the currently best performing algorithms in practice is the BPR algorithm of [25] which has an asymptotic worst-case run time of $O(n^2)$. BPR first sorts all the suffixes up to a certain depth, then focuses on one bucket at a time and repeatedly refines it into sub-buckets.

In this paper we present an elegant algorithm for suffix array construction. This algorithm takes linear time with high probability. Here the probability is on the space of all possible inputs. Our algorithm is one of the simplest algorithms known for constructing suffix arrays. It opens up a new dimension in suffix array construction, i.e., the development of algorithms with provable expected run times. This dimension has not been explored before. We prove a lemma on the ℓ-mers of a random string which might find independent applications. Our algorithm is also nicely parallelizable. We offer parallel implementations of our algorithm on various parallel models of computing.

We also present another algorithm for suffix array construction that utilizes the above algorithm. This algorithm, called RadixSA, is based on bucket sorting and has a worst case run time of $O(n\log n)$. It employs an idea which, to the best of our knowledge, has not been directly exploited until now. RadixSA selects the order in which buckets are processed based on a heuristic such that, downstream, they impact as many other buckets as possible. This idea may find independent application as a standalone speedup technique for other SACAs based on bucket sorting. RadixSA also employs a generalization of Seward's copy method [26] (initially described in [4]) to detect and handle repeats of any length. We compare RadixSA with other algorithms on various datasets.

A USEFUL LEMMA

Let Σ be an alphabet of interest and let $S = s_1s_2\ldots s_n \in \Sigma^*$. Consider the case when S is generated randomly, i.e., each s_i is picked uniformly randomly from Σ ($1 \leq i \leq n$). Let L be the set of all ℓ-mers of S. Note that $|L| = n - \ell + 1$. What can we say about the independence of these ℓ-mers? In several papers analyses have been done assuming that these ℓ-mers are independent (see e.g., [2]). These authors point out that this assumption may not be true but these analyses have proven to be useful in practice. In this section we prove the following lemma on these ℓ-mers.

Lemma 1. Let L be the set of all ℓ-mers of a random string generated from an alphabet Σ. Then, the ℓ-mers in L are pairwise independent. These ℓ-mers need not be k-way independent for $k \geq 3$.

Proof. Let A and B be any two ℓ-mers in L. If x and y are non-overlapping, clearly, $\text{Prob}[A = B] = (1/\sigma)^\ell$, where $\sigma = |\Sigma|$. Thus, consider the case when x and y are overlapping.

Let $P_i = s_is_{i+1}\ldots s_{i+\ell-1}$, for $1 \leq i \leq (n - \ell + 1)$. Let $A = P_i$ and $B = P_j$ with $i < j$ and $j \leq (i + \ell - 1)$. Also let $j = i + k$ where $1 \leq k \leq (\ell - 1)$.

Consider the special case when k divides ℓ. If A = B, then it should be the case that $s_i = s_{i+k} = s_{i+2k} = \cdots = s_{i+\ell}$; $s_{i+1} = s_{i+k+1} = s_{i+2k+1} = \cdots = s_{i+\ell+1}$; ⋯; and $s_{i+k-1} = s_{i+2k-1} = s_{i+3k-1} = \cdots = s_{i+\ell+k-1}$. In other words, we have k series of equalities. Each series is of length $(\ell/k) + 1$. The probability of all of these equalities is $(\frac{1}{\sigma})^{\ell/k}(\frac{1}{\sigma})^{\ell/k}\cdots(\frac{1}{\sigma})^{\ell/k} = (\frac{1}{\sigma})^{\ell}$.

As an example, let S = abcdefghi, ℓ = 4, k = 2, $A = P_1$, and $B = P_3$. In this case, the following equalities should hold: a = c = e and b = d = f. The probability of all of these equalities is $(1/\sigma)^2(1/\sigma)^2 = (1/\sigma)^4 = (1/\sigma)^\ell$.

Now consider the general case (where k may not divide ℓ). Let $\ell = qk + r$ for some integers q and r where $r < k$. If A = B, the following equalities will hold: $s_i = s_{i+k} = s_{i+2k} = \cdots = s_{i+\lfloor(\ell+k-1)/k\rfloor k}$; $s_{i+1} = s_{i+1+k} = s_{i+1+2k} = \cdots = s_{i+1+\lfloor(\ell+k-2)/k\rfloor k}$; ⋯; and $s_{i+k-1} = s_{i+k-1+k} = s_{i+k-1+2k} = \cdots = s_{i+k-1+\lfloor(\ell/k)\rfloor k}$.

Here again we have k series of equalities. The number of elements in the q -th series is $1 + \lfloor\frac{\ell+k-q}{k}\rfloor$, for $1 \leq q \leq k$. The probability of all of these equalities is $(1/\sigma)^x$ where $x = \sum_{q=1}^{k}\lfloor\frac{\ell+k-q}{k}\rfloor$.

$$x = \left\lfloor \frac{(q+1)k+r-1}{k} \right\rfloor + \left\lfloor \frac{(q+1)k+r-2}{k} \right\rfloor + \cdots + \left\lfloor \frac{(q+1)k}{k} \right\rfloor$$
$$+ \left\lfloor \frac{(q+1)k-1}{k} \right\rfloor + \left\lfloor \frac{(q+1)k-2}{k} \right\rfloor + \cdots + \left\lfloor \frac{(q+1)k-(k-r)}{k} \right\rfloor$$
$$= (q+1)r + (k-r)q = kq + r = \ell.$$

The fact that the ℓ-mers of L may not be k-way independent for $k \geq 3$ is easy to see. For example, let S = abcdefgh, $\ell = 3$, A = P_1, B = P_3, and C = P_4. What is Prob.[A = B = C]? If A = B = C, then it should be the case that a = c, b = d = a, b = c = e, and c = f. In other words, a = b = c = d = e = f. The probability of this happening is $(1/\sigma)^5 \neq (1/\sigma)^6$.

Note

To the best of our knowledge, the above lemma cannot be found in the existing literature. In [27] a lemma is proven on the expected depth of insertion of a suffix tree. If anything, this only very remotely resembles our lemma but is not directly related. In addition the lemma in [27] is proven only in the limit (when n tends to ∞).

Our Basic Algorithm

Let $S = s_1 s_2 \cdots s_n$ be the given input string. Assume that S is a string randomly generated from an alphabet Σ. In particular, each s_i is assumed to have been picked uniformly randomly from Σ (for $1 \leq i \leq n$). For all the algorithms presented in this paper, no assumption is made on the size of Σ. In particular, it could be anything. For example, it could be O(1), $O(n^c)$ (for any constant c), or larger.

The problem is to produce an array A[1:n] where A[i] is the starting position of the i-th smallest suffix of S, for $1 \leq i \leq n$. The basic idea behind our algorithm is to sort the suffixes only with respect to their prefixes of length $O(\log n)$ (bits). The claim is that this amount of sorting is enough to order the suffixes with high probability. By high probability we mean a probability of $\geq (1 - n^{-\alpha})$ where α is the probability parameter (typically assumed to be a constant ≥ 1). The probability space under concern is the space of all possible inputs.

Let S_i stand for the suffix that starts at position i, for $1 \leq i \leq n$. In other words, $S_i = s_i s_{i+1} \cdots s_n$. Let $P_i = s_i s_{i+1} \cdots s_{i+\ell-1}$, for $i \leq (n - \ell)$. When $i > (n - \ell)$, let $P_i = S_i$. The value of ℓ will be decided in the analysis. A pseudocode of our basic algorithm follows.

Algorithm SA1

Sort $P_1, P_2, \ldots, P_n$ using radix sort;
The above sorting partitions the P_i's into buckets where equal ℓ-mers are in the same bucket;
Let these buckets be $B_1, B_2, \ldots, B_m$ where $m \leq n$;
for $i := 1$ **to** m **do**
    if $|B_i| > 1$ **then** sort the suffixes corresponding to the ℓ-mers in B_i using any relevant algorithm;

Lemma 2. Algorithm SA1 has a run time of O(n) with high probability.

Proof. Consider a specific P_i and let B be the bucket that P_i belongs to after the radix sorting step in Algorithm SA1. How many other P_j's will there be in B? Using Lemma 1, Prob.[$P_i = P_j$] = $(1/\sigma)^\ell$. This means that Prob.[$\exists j$: $i \neq j$ & $P_i = P_j$] $\leq n(1/\sigma)^\ell$. As a result, Prob.[$\exists j$:$|B_j| > 1$] $\leq n^2(1/\sigma)^\ell$. If $\ell \geq ((\alpha + 2)\log_\sigma n)$, then, $n^2(1/\sigma)^\ell \leq n^{-\alpha}$.

In other words, if $\ell \geq ((\alpha + 2)\log_\sigma n)$, then each bucket will be of size 1 with high probability. Also, the radix sort will take O(n) time. Note that we only need to sort $O(\log n)$ bits of each P_i $(1 \leq i \leq n)$ and this sorting can be done in O(n) time (see e.g., [6]).

Observation 1. We could have a variant of the algorithm where if any of the buckets is of size greater than 1, we abort this algorithm and use another algorithm. A pseudocode follows.

Algorithm SA2

1 Sort $P_1, P_2, \ldots, P_n$ using radix sort;
The above sorting partitions the P_i's into buckets where equal ℓ-mers are in the same bucket;
Let these buckets be $B_1, B_2, \ldots, B_m$ where $m \leq n$;
2 **if** $|B_i| = 1$ for each i, $1 \leq i \leq m$
3 **then** output the suffix array and quit;
4 **else** use another algorithm (let it be **Algorithm SA**) to find and output the suffix array;

Observation 2. Algorithm SA1 as well as Algorithm SA2 run in O(n) time on at least $(1 - n^{-\alpha})$ fraction of all possible inputs. Also, if the run time of Algorithm SA is t(n), then the expected run time of Algorithm SA2 is $(1 - n^{-\alpha})O(n) + n^{-\alpha}(O(n) + t(n))$. For example, if Algorithm SA is the skew algorithm [9], then the expected run time of Algorithm SA2 is O(n) (the underlying constant will be smaller than the constant in the run time of skew).

Observation 3. In general, if T(n) is the run time of Algorithm SA2 lines 1 through 3 and if t(n) is the run time of Algorithm SA, then the expected run time of Algorithm SA2 is $(1 - n^{-\alpha})T(n) + n^{-\alpha}(T(n) + t(n))$.

The case of non-uniform probabilities. In the above algorithm and analysis we have assumed that each character in S is picked uniformly randomly from Σ. Let $\Sigma = \{a_1, a_2, \ldots, a_\sigma\}$. Now we consider the possibility that for any $s_i \in S$, $Prob.[s_i = a_j] = p_j$, $1 \le i \le n; 1 \le j \le \sigma$. For any two ℓ-mers A and B of S we can show that $Prob.[A = B] = (\sum_{j=1}^{\sigma} p_j^2)^\ell$. In this case, we can employ Algorithms SA1 and SA2 with $\ell \ge (\alpha + 2)\log_{1/P} n$, where $P = \sum_{j=1}^{\sigma} p_j^2$.

Observation 4. Both SA1 and SA2 can work with any alphabet size. If the size of the alphabet is O(1), then each P_i will consist of $O(\log n)$ characters from Σ. If $|\Sigma| = \Theta(n^c)$ for some constant c, then P_i will consist of O(1) characters from Σ. If $|\Sigma| = \omega(n^c)$ for any constant c, then each P_i will consist of a prefix (of length $O(\log n)$ bits) of a character in Σ.

PARALLEL VERSIONS

In this section we explore the possibility of implementing SA1 and SA2 on various models of parallel computing.

Parallel Disks Model

In a Parallel Disks Model (PDM), there is a (sequential or parallel) computer whose core memory is of size M. The computer has D parallel disks. In one parallel I/O, a block of size B from each of the D disks can be fetched into the core memory. The challenge is to devise algorithms for this model that perform the least number of I/O operations. This model has been proposed to alleviate the I/O bottleneck that is common for single disk machines especially when the dataset is large. In the analysis of PDM algorithms the focus is on the number of parallel I/Os and typically the local computation times are not considered. A lower bound on the number of parallel I/Os needed to sort N elements on a PDM is $\frac{N}{DB}\frac{\log(N/B)}{\log(M/B)}$. Numerous asymptotically optimal parallel algorithms have been devised for sorting on the PDM. For practical values of N, M, D, and B, the lower bound basically means a constant number of passes through the data. Therefore, it is imperative to design algorithms wherein the underlying constants in the number of I/Os is small. A number of algorithms for different values of N, M, D, and B that take a small number of passes have been proposed in [23].

One of the algorithms given in [23] is for sorting integers. In particular it is shown that we can sort N random integers in the range [1, R] (for any R) in $(1+\nu)\frac{\log(N/M)}{\log(M/B)} + 1$ passes through the data, where ν is a constant < 1. This bound holds with probability $\ge (1 - N^{-\alpha})$, this probability being computed in the space of all possible inputs.

We can adapt the algorithm of [23] for constructing suffix arrays as follows. We assume that the word length of the machine is $O(\log n)$. This is a standard assumption made in the algorithms literature. Note that if the length of the input string is n, then we need a word length of at least log n to address the suffixes. To begin with, the input is stored in the D disks striped uniformly. We generate all the ℓ-mers of S in one pass through the input. Note that each ℓ-mer occupies one word of the machine. The generated ℓ-mers are stored back into the disks. Followed by this, these ℓ-mers are sorted using the algorithm of [23]. At the end of this sorting, we have m buckets where each bucket has equal ℓ-mers. As was shown before, each bucket is of size 1 with high probability.

We get the following:

Theorem 1. We can construct the suffix array for a random string of length n in $(1+\nu)\frac{\log(n/M)}{\log(M/B)} + 2$ passes through the data, where ν is a constant < 1. This bound holds for $\ge (1 - n^{-\alpha})$ fraction of all possible inputs.

The Mesh and the Hypercube

Optimal algorithms exist for sorting on interconnection networks such as the mesh (see e.g., [28] and [8]), the hypercube (see e.g., [24]), etc. We can use these in conjunction with Algorithms SA1 and SA2 to develop suffix array construction algorithms for these models. Here again we can construct all the ℓ-mers of the input string. Assume that we have an interconnection network with n nodes and each node stores one of the characters in the input string. In particular node i stores s_i, for $1 \le i \le n$. Depending on the network, a relevant indexing scheme has to be used. For instance, on the mesh we can use a snake-like row-major indexing. Node i communicates with nodes i + 1, i + 2, …, i + ℓ − 1 to get $s_{i+1}, s_{i+2}, \ldots, s_{i+\ell-1}$. The communication time needed is $O(\log n)$. Once the node i has these characters it forms P_i. Once the nodes have generated the ℓ-mers, the rest of the algorithm is similar to the Algorithm SA1 or SA2. As a result, we get the following:

Theorem 2. There exists a randomized algorithm for constructing the suffix array for a random string of length n in $O(\log n)$ time on a n-node hypercube with high probability. The run time of[24]'s algorithm is $O(\log n)$ with high probability, the probability being computed in the space of all possible outcomes for the coin flips made. Also, the same can be done in $O(\sqrt{n})$ time on a $\sqrt{n} \times \sqrt{n}$ mesh with high probability.

Observation

Please note that on a n-node hypercube, sorting n elements will need $\Omega(\log n)$ time even if these elements are bits, since the diameter of the hypercube is $\Omega(\log n)$. For the same reason, sorting n elements on a $\sqrt{n} \times \sqrt{n}$ mesh will need $\Omega\left(\sqrt{n}\right)$ time since $2\left(\sqrt{n}-1\right)$ is the diameter.

PRAM Algorithms

In [9] several PRAM algorithms are given. One such algorithm is for the EREW PRAM that has a run time of $O\left(log^2 n\right)$, the work done being $O\left(n log n\right)$. We can implement Algorithm SA2 on the EREW PRAM so that it has an expected run time of $O\left(log n\right)$, the expected work done being $O\left(n log n\right)$. Details follow. Assume that we have n processors. 1) Form all possible ℓ-mers. Each ℓ-mer occupies one word; 2) Sort these ℓ-mers using the parallel merge sort algorithm of [5]; 3) Using a prefix computation check if there is at least one bucket of size > 1; 4) Broadcast the result to all the processors using a prefix computation; 5) If there is at least one bucket of size more than one, use the parallel algorithm of [9].

Steps 1 through 4 of the above algorithm take $O\left(log n\right)$ time each. Step 5 takes $O\left(log^2 n\right)$ time. From Observation 3, the expected run time of this algorithm is $(1 - n^{\alpha})$ O(log n) + n^{α} (O(log n) + O($\log^2$ n) = O(log n). Also, the expected work done by the algorithm is $(1 - n^{\alpha})$ O(n log n) + n^{α} (O(n log n) + O(n $\log^2$ n) = O(n log n).

PRACTICAL IMPLEMENTATION

In this section we discuss the design and implementation of the RadixSA algorithm. The following is the pseudocode of the RadixSA algorithm:

Algorithm RadixSA

1. **radixSort** all suffixes by d characters
2. **let** $b[i]$ = bucket of suffix i
3. **for** $i := n$ **down to** 1 **do**
4.   **if** ($b[i].size > 1$) **then**
5.   **if detectPeriods**($b[i]$) **then**
6.   **handlePeriods**($b[i]$);
7.   **else radixSort** all suffixes $j \in b[i]$ with respect to $b[j+d]$

A bucket is called singleton if it contains only one suffix, otherwise it is called non-singleton. A singleton suffix is the only suffix in a singleton bucket. A singleton suffix has its final position in the suffix array already determined.

We number the buckets such that two suffixes in different buckets can be compared by comparing their bucket numbers. The **for** loop traverses the suffixes from the last to the first position in the text and sorts the bucket in which the current suffix resides. This order ensures that after each step, suffix i will be found in a singleton bucket. This is easy to prove by induction. Thus, at the end of the loop, all the buckets will be singletons. If each bucket is of size O(1) before the **for** loop is entered, then it is easy to see that the algorithm runs in O(n) time. In lines 5 and 6 we detect periodic regions of the input. This is discussed in the next section.

Even if the buckets are not of constant size (before the **for** loop is entered) the algorithm is still linear if every suffix takes part in no more than a constant number of radix sort operations. The order in the **for** loop is deceptively simple but it sorts the buckets in an order which favors quick breakdown of non-singleton buckets. Intuitively, say a pattern $P = a_1a_2a_3\ldots a_k$ appears multiple times in the input. After the initial radix sort, we will have the suffixes which start with a_1 in a bucket b_1, the suffixes which start with a_2 in a bucket b_2 and so on. Assume that the initial sorting depth D is much smaller than k. If we sort these buckets in the order $b_1, b_2, \ldots, b_k$ most of them remain the same, except that now we know we have them sorted by at least 2D characters. On the other hand, our algorithm will sort these buckets in the order $b_k, b_{k-1}, \ldots, b_1$. If bucket b_k separates into singleton buckets after sorting, then all the other buckets will subsequently separate into singletons. This way, every suffix in these buckets is placed in a singleton bucket at a constant cost per suffix. Due to this traversal order, in practice, our algorithm performs a small number of accesses to each suffix, as we show in the results section.

Table 1 shows an example of how the algorithm works. Each column illustrates the state of the suffix array after sorting one of the buckets. The order in which buckets are chosen to be sorted follows the pseudocode of RadixSA. The initial radix sort has depth 1 for illustration purpose. The last column contains the fully sorted suffix array.

Table 1. Example of suffix array construction steps for string 'cdaxcdayca'. b[suffix] stands for the bucket of suffix. Underlines show the depth of sorting in a bucket at a given time. The initial radix sort has depth 1 for illustration purpose.

Initial buckets	Sort b[a]	Sort b[ca]	Sort b[dayca]	Sort b[cdayca]
a	a	a	a	a
ayca	axcdayca	axcdayca	axcdayca	axcdayca
axcdayca	ayca	ayca	ayca	ayca
ca	ca	ca	ca	ca
cdayca	cdayca	cdayca	cdayca	cdaxcdayca
cdaxcdayca	cdaxcdayca	cdaxcdayca	cdaxcdayca	cdayca
dayca	dayca	dayca	daxcdayca	daxcdayca
daxcdayca	daxcdayca	daxcdayca	dayca	dayca
xcdayca	xcdayca	xcdayca	xcdayca	xcdayca
yca	yca	yca	yca	yca

However, the algorithm as is described above has a worst case runtime of $O(n\sqrt{n})$ (proof omitted). We can improve the runtime to $O(n \log n)$ as follows. If, during the **for** loop, a bucket contains suffixes which have been accessed more than a constant C number of times, we skip that bucket. This ensures that the for loop takes linear time. If at the end of the loop there have been any buckets skipped, we do another pass of the for loop. After each pass, every remaining non-singleton bucket has a sorting depth at least C + 1 times greater than in the previous round (easy to prove by induction). Thus, no more than a logarithmic number of passes will be needed and so the algorithm has worst case runtime $O(n \log n)$.

Periods

In lines 5 and 6 of the RadixSA pseudocode we detect periodic regions of the input as follows: if the suffixes starting at positions i, i − p, i − 2p, ... appear in the same bucket b, and bucket b is currently sorted by d ≥ p characters, it is easy to see that we have found a periodic region of the input, where the period P is of length p. In other words, suffix i is of the form $PS_{i+p+1...n}$, suffix i − p is of the form $PPS_{i+p+1...n}$, suffix i − 2p is of the form $PPPS_{i+p+1...n}$ and so on. We can easily see that these suffixes can be placed in separate buckets based on the relationship between suffixes i and i + p by the following rule. If suffix i is less than suffix i + p, then suffix i − p is less than suffix i, suffix i − 2p is less than i − p, and so on. The case where i is greater than i + p is analogous.

The depth of each bucket increases after each sorting, therefore periods of any length are eventually detected. This method can be viewed as a generalization of Seward's copy method [26] where a portion of text of size p is treated as a single character.

Implementation Details

Radix sorting is a central operation in RadixSA. We tried several implementations, both with Least Significant Digit (LSD) and Most Significant Digit (MSD) first order. The best of our implementations was a cache-optimized LSD radix sort. The cache optimization is the following. In a regular LSD radix sort, for every digit we do two passes through the data: one to compute bucket sizes, one to assign items to buckets. We can save one pass through the data per digit if in the bucket assignment pass we also compute bucket sizes for the next round [14]. We took this idea one step forward and we computed bucket counts for all rounds before doing any assignment. Since in our program we only sort numbers of at most 64 bits, we have a constant number of bucket size arrays to store in memory. To sort small buckets we employ an iterative merge sort.

To further improve cache performance, in the bucket array we store not only the bucket start position but also a few bits indicating the length of the bucket. Since the bucket start requires $\lfloor \log n \rfloor$ bits, we use the remaining bits, up to the machine word size, to store the bucket length. This prevents a lot of cache misses when small buckets are the majority. For longer buckets, we store the lengths in a separate array which also stores bucket depths.

The total additional memory used by the algorithm, besides input and output, is 5n + o(n) bytes: 4n for the bucket array, n bytes for bucket depths and lengths, and a temporary buffer for radix sort.

EXPERIMENTAL RESULTS

One of the fastest SACAs, in practice, is the Bucket Pointer Refinement (BPR) algorithm[25]. Version 0.9 of BPR has been compared [25] with several other algorithms: deep shallow [18], cache and copy by Seward [26], qsufsort [16], difference-cover [3], divide and conquer by Kim et al. [11], and skew [9]. BPR 0.9 has been shown to outperform these algorithms on most inputs [25]. Version 2.0 of BPR further improves over version 0.9. We compare RadixSA with both versions of BPR.

Furthermore, a large set of SACAs are collected in the jSuffixArrays library [21] under a unified interface. This library contains Java implementations of: DivSufSort [19], QsufSort [16], SAIS [20], skew [9] and DeepShallow [18]. We include them in the comparison with the note that these Java algorithms may incur a performance penalty compared to their C counterparts.

We tested all algorithms on an Intel core i 3 machine with 4 GB of RAM, Ubuntu 11.10 Operating System, Sun Java 1.6.0_26 virtual machine and gcc 4.6.1. The Java Virtual Machine was allowed to use up to 3.5 GB of memory. As inputs, we used the datasets of [25] which include DNA data, protein data, English alphabet data, general ASCII alphabet data and artificially created strings such as periodic and Fibonacci strings.[1]

For every dataset, we executed each algorithm 10 times. The average run times are reported in Table 2 where the best run times are shown in bold. Furthermore, we counted the number of times RadixSA accesses each suffix. The access counts are shown in Fig. 1. For almost all datasets, the number of times each suffix is accessed is a small constant. For the Fibonacci string the number of accesses is roughly logarithmic in the length of the input.

Table 2. Comparison of run times on datasets from [25] on a 64-bit Intel CORE i3 machine with 4 GB of RAM, Ubuntu 11.10 Operating System, Sun Java 1.6.0_26 and gcc 4.6.1. Run times are in seconds, averaged over 10 runs. Bold font indicates the best time. ML means out of memory, TL means more than 1 hour.

Dataset			Run time							
Name	**Length**	**|Σ|**	**RadixSA**	**BPR2**	**BPR.9**	**DivSuf Sort**	**QSuf Sort**	**SAIS**	**skew**	**Deep Shallow**
Fibonacci	20 000 000	2	7.88	12.48	14.05	6.81	26.44	**5.50**	14.53	369.48
period_1000	20 000 000	26	**2.12**	3.52	5.71	3.15	20.42	6.59	23.27	TL
period_20	20 000 000	17	**1.44**	1.95	43.39	1.83	11.05	2.83	7.15	TL
period_500000	20 000 000	26	**2.78**	4.60	6.31	4.74	23.32	8.56	25.68	2844.37
random	20 000 000	26	**2.25**	3.34	4.87	6.35	5.02	11.75	22.05	5.69
3Ecoli.dna	14 776 363	5	**2.23**	2.67	3.43	4.00	13.85	6.14	19.62	433.54
4Chlamydophila.dna	4 856 123	6	**0.61**	0.67	0.90	1.71	3.24	1.93	5.24	4.80
6Streptococci.dna	11 635 882	5	**1.63**	1.79	2.38	2.88	7.08	4.98	14.88	4.26
A_thaliana_Chr4.dna	12 061 490	7	**1.27**	1.74	2.40	3.02	5.13	5.37	15.71	3.52
C_elegans_Chr1.dna	14 188 020	5	**1.61**	1.95	2.65	3.21	6.91	5.69	17.18	6.92
E_coli.dna	4 638 690	4	**0.41**	0.51	0.58	1.36	1.72	1.96	5.04	1.37
H_sapiens_Chr22.dna	34 553 758	5	**4.40**	5.66	8.21	7.76	15.31	15.59	49.70	10.98
bible	4 047 391	63	0.51	**0.48**	0.80	1.24	1.38	1.56	4.64	1.08
etext	105 277 339	146	**19.40**	23.09	43.46	26.56	62.63	54.70	ML	119.96
etext_50M	50 000 000	120	**8.13**	9.74	17.26	11.94	26.40	24.46	88.57	79.07
gcc	86 630 400	150	**13.84**	15.58	24.50	15.84	46.20	33.62	135.12	80.78
gcc_50M	50 000 000	121	**7.21**	9.56	13.26	8.31	28.43	17.73	68.65	264.90
howto	39 422 104	197	**5.96**	6.35	10.26	8.41	17.64	16.67	64.73	16.33
jdk	69 728 898	113	**12.07**	12.54	26.86	12.74	39.92	24.66	102.76	58.22
jdk_50M	50 000 000	110	**8.32**	**8.30**	17.05	8.91	26.30	17.58	71.31	36.98
linux	116 254 720	256	**19.27**	**19.34**	29.67	21.17	61.99	44.47	ML	58.71
linux_50M	50 000 000	256	**7.62**	**7.60**	10.50	8.84	27.54	18.18	76.10	31.92
reuters	114 711 150	93	**19.76**	25.08	60.72	25.07	74.78	49.17	ML	87.57
reuters_50M	50 000 000	91	**7.84**	9.53	20.41	10.24	26.94	20.29	77.25	33.68
rfc	116 421 900	120	**21.18**	22.08	42.75	22.55	66.28	47.99	ML	42.14

rfc_50M	50 000 000	110	**8.23**	8.39	14.85	9.24	24.80	19.61	76.64	16.63
sprot	109 617 186	66	**18.48**	22.79	47.07	25.52	69.58	50.40	ML	48.69
sprot_50M	50 000 000	66	**7.57**	9.10	16.81	10.88	28.07	21.69	78.47	20.03
w3c	104 201 578	256	**18.82**	**18.78**	35.94	20.01	74.09	38.29	ML	1964.80
w3c_50M	50 000 000	255	**7.93**	8.33	17.67	8.73	25.95	17.26	71.42	36.59
world	2 473 399	94	0.30	**0.27**	0.42	0.91	0.86	0.91	2.35	0.78

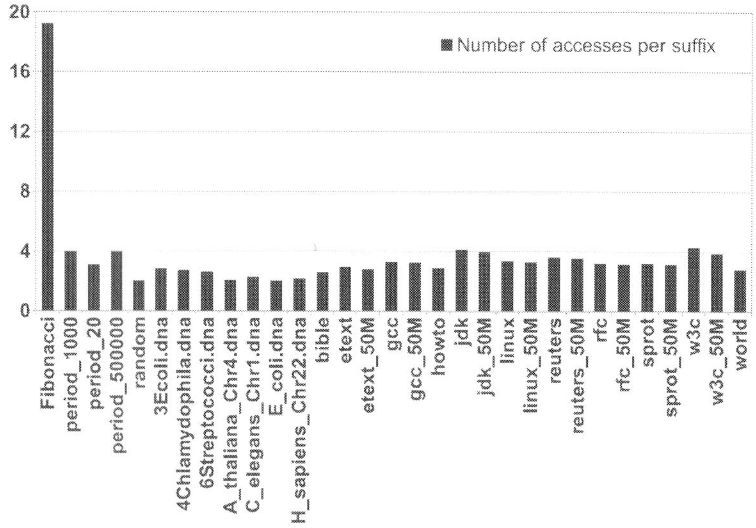

Figure 1. Average number of times RadixSA accesses each suffix, for datasets from [25].

DISCUSSION AND CONCLUSIONS

In this paper we have presented an elegant algorithm for the construction of suffix arrays. This algorithm is one of the simplest algorithms known for suffix arrays construction and runs in O(n) time on a large fraction of all possible inputs. It is also nicely parallelizable. We have shown how our algorithm can be implemented on various parallel models of computing.

We have also given an extension of this algorithm, called RadixSA, which has a worst case runtime of $O(n \log n)$. RadixSA uses a deceptively simple heuristic to select the order in which buckets are processed so as to reduce the number of operations performed. As a result, RadixSA performed a small number of accesses per suffix on all but one of the inputs tested (the Fibonacci string). This heuristic, together with a careful implementation designed to increase cache performance, makes RadixSA very efficient in practice.

The RadixSA heuristic could find application as an independent speedup technique for other algorithms which use bucket sorting and induced copying. For example, BPR could use it to determine the order in which it chooses buckets to be refined. A possible research direction is to improve RadixSA's heuristic. Buckets can be processed based on a topological sorting of their dependency graph. Such a graph has at most n/2 nodes, one for each non-singleton bucket, and at most n/2 edges. Thus, it has the potential for a lightweight implementation.

An interesting open problem is to devise a randomized algorithm that has a similar performance.

AUTHORS CONTRIBUTIONS

SR and MN designed and analyzed the algorithms. MN implemented RadixSA and carried out the empirical experiments. SR and MN analyzed the empirical results and drafted the manuscript.

ACKNOWLEDGMENTS

This work has been supported in part by the following grants: NSF0829916 and NIHR01LM010101.

REFERENCES

1. D. Baron, Y. Bresler, Antisequential suffix sorting for bwt-based data compression, IEEE Trans. Comput. 54 (4) (2005) 385–397.
2. J. Buhler, M. Tompa, Finding motifs using random projections, in: RECOMB, 2001, pp. 69–76.
3. S. Burkhardt, J. Kärkkäinen, Fast lightweight suffix array construction and checking, in: R. Baeza-Yates, E. Chávez, M. Crochemore (Eds.), Combinatorial Pattern Matching, in: Lecture Notes in Computer Science, vol. 2676, Springer, Berlin/Heidelberg, 2003, pp. 55–69.
4. M. Burrows, D. Wheeler, A block-sorting lossless data compression algorithm, Tech. Rep. 124, 1994.

5. R. Cole, Parallel merge sort, SIAM J. Comput. 17 (4) (1988) 770–785.

6. E. Horowitz, S. Sahni, S. Rajasekaran, Computer Algorithms, Silicon Press, 2008.

7. H. Itoh, H. Tanaka, An efficient method for in memory construction of suffix arrays, in: Proceedings of the Sixth Symposium on String Processing and Information Retrieval, IEEE Computer Society, 1999, pp. 81–88.

8. C. Kaklamanis, D. Krizanc, L. Narayanan, T. Tsantilas, Randomized sorting and selection on mesh-connected processor arrays (preliminary version), in: Proceedings of the Third Annual ACM Symposium on Parallel Algorithms and Architectures, SPAA '91, ACM, New York, NY, USA, 1991, pp. 17–28.

9. J. Kärkkäinen, P. Sanders, Simple linear work suffix array construction, in: ICALP, 2003, pp. 943–955.

10. D. Kim, J. Sim, H. Park, K. Park, Linear-time construction of suffix arrays, in: CPM, 2003, pp. 186–199.

11. D. Kim, J. Jo, H. Park, A fast algorithm for constructing suffix arrays for fixed size alphabets, in: C.C. Ribeiro, S.L. Martins (Eds.), Proceedings of the 3rd Workshop on Experimental and Efficient Algorithms (WEA 2004), Springer-Verlag, Berlin, 2004, pp. 301–314.

12. P. Ko, S. Aluru, Space efficient linear time construction of suffix arrays, in: CPM, 2003, pp. 200–210.

13. S. Kurtz, Reducing the space requirement of suffix trees, Softw. Pract. Exp. 29 (13) (1999) 1149–1171.

14. A. LaMarca, R.E. Ladner, The influence of caches on the performance of sorting, in: Proceedings of the Eighth Annual ACM–SIAM Symposium on Discrete Algorithms, SODA '97, Society for Industrial and Applied Mathematics, Philadelphia, PA, USA, 1997, pp. 370–379.

15. J. Larsson, K. Sadakane, Faster suffix sorting, Tech. Rep. LU-CS-TR:99-214 [LUNFD6/(NFCS-3140)/1-20/(1999)], Department of Computer Science, Lund University, Sweden, 1999.

16. N. Larsson, K. Sadakane, Faster suffix sorting, Theor. Comput. Sci. 387 (3) (2007) 258–272.

17. U. Manber, G. Myers, Suffix arrays: a new method for on-line string searches, in: Proceedings of the First Annual ACM–SIAM Symposium on Discrete Algorithms, SODA '90, Society for Industrial and Applied Mathematics, Philadelphia, PA, USA, 1990, pp. 319–327.

18. G. Manzini, P. Ferragina, Engineering a lightweight suffix array construction algorithm, Algorithmica 40 (2004) 33–50.

19. Y. Mori, Short description of improved two-stage suffix sorting algorithm, http://homepage3.nifty.com/wpage/software/itssort.txt, 2005.

20. G. Nong, S. Zhang, W. Chan, Linear suffix array construction by almost pure induced-sorting, in: Data Compression Conference, 2009, pp. 193–202.

21. S. Osinski, ´ D. Weiss, jsuffixarrays: suffix arrays for java, http://labs.carrotsearch.com/jsuffixarrays.html, 2002–2011.

22. S. Puglisi, W. Smyth, A. Turpin, A taxonomy of suffix array construction algorithms, ACM Comput. Surv. 39 (2) (2007), http://dx.doi.org/10.1145/ 1242471.1242472.

23. S. Rajasekaran, S. Sen, Optimal and practical algorithms for sorting on the pdm, IEEE Trans. Comput. 57 (4) (2008) 547–561.

24. J. Reif, L. Valiant, A logarithmic time sort for linear size networks, J. ACM 34 (1) (1987) 60–76.

25. K.-B. Schürmann, J. Stoye, An incomplex algorithm for fast suffix array construction, Softw. Pract. Exp. 37 (3) (2007) 309–329.

26. J. Seward, On the performance of bwt sorting algorithms, in: Proceedings of the Conference on Data Compression, DCC '00, IEEE Computer Society, Washington, DC, USA, 2000, pp. 173–182.

27. W. Szpankowski, Average Case Analysis of Algorithms on Sequences, John Wiley & Sons, Inc., 2001.

28. C. Thompson, H.T. Kung, Sorting on a mesh-connected parallel computer, Commun. ACM 20 (4) (1977) 263–271.

CHAPTER 16

DICYCLE COVER OF HAMILTONIAN ORIENTED GRAPHS

Khalid A. Alsatami[1], Hong-Jian Lai[2], and Xindong Zhang[3]

[1]Department of Mathematics, College of Science, Qassim University, Buraydah 51452, Saudi Arabia

[2]Department of Mathematics, West Virginia University, Morgantown, WV 26506, USA

[3]College of Mathematics Sciences, Xinjiang Normal University, Urumqi 830054, China

ABSTRACT

A dicycle cover of a digraph D is a family $\mathscr{F}$ of dicycles of D such that each arc of D lies in at least one dicycle in $\mathscr{F}$. We investigate the problem of determining the upper bounds for the minimum number of dicycles which cover all arcs in a strong digraph. Best possible upper bounds of dicycle covers are obtained in a number of classes of digraphs including strong tournaments, Hamiltonian oriented graphs, Hamiltonian oriented complete bipartite graphs, and families of possibly non-Hamiltonian digraphs obtained from these digraphs via a sequence of 2-sum operations.

THE PROBLEM

We consider finite loopless graphs and digraphs, and undefined notations and terms will follow [1] for graphs and [2] for digraphs. In particular, a cycle is a 2-regular connected nontrivial graph. A cycle cover of a graph G is a collection $\mathscr{C}$ of cycles of G such that $E(G) = \bigcup_{C \in \mathscr{C}} E(C)$. Bondy [3] conjectured that if G is a 2-connected simple graph with $n \geq 3$ vertices, then G has a cycle cover C with $|\mathscr{C}| \leq (2n - 3)/3$. Bondy [3] showed that this conjecture, if proved, would be best possible. Luo and Chen [4] proved that this conjecture holds for 2-connected simple cubic graphs. It has been shown that, for plane triangulations, serial-parallel graphs, or planar graphs in general, one can have a better bound for the number of cycles used in a cover [5–8]. Barnette [9] proved that if G is a 3-connected simple planar graph of order n, then the edges of G can be covered by at most $(n + 1)/2$ cycles. Fan [10] settled this conjecture by showing that it holds for all simple 2-connected graphs. The best possible number of cycles needed to cover cubic graphs has been obtained in [11, 12]

A directed path in a digraph D from a vertex u to a vertex V is called a (u, v)-dipath. To emphasize the distinction between graphs and digraphs, a directed cycle or path in a digraph is often referred to as a dicycle or dipath. It is natural to consider the number of dicycles needed to cover a digraph. Following [2], for a digraph D, (D) and $A(D)$ denote the vertex set and arc set of D, respectively. If $A' \subseteq A(D)$, then $D[A']$ is the subdigraph induced by A'. Let K_n^* denote the complete digraph on n vertices. Any simple digraph D on n vertices can be viewed as a subdigraph of K_n^*. If W is an arc subset of $A(K_n^*)$, then $D + W$ denotes the digraph $K_n^*[A(D) \cup W]$.

A digraph D is strong if, for any distinct u, V $\in (D)$, D has a (u, v)-dipath. As in [2], (D) denotes the arc-strong connectivity of D. Thus a digraph D is strong if and only if $(D) \geq 1$. We use (u, v) denoting an arc with tail u and head v. For $X, Y \subseteq (D)$, we define

Citation: Khalid A. Alsatami, Hong-Jian Lai, and Xindong Zhang, "Dicycle Cover of Hamiltonian Oriented Graphs,"Journal of Discrete Mathematics, vol. 2016, Article ID 7942192, 5 pages, 2016. doi:10.1155/2016/7942192

$$(X,Y)_D = \{(x,y) \in A(D) : x \in X,\ y \in Y\};$$

$$\partial_D^+(X) = (X, V(D) - X)_D. \quad (1)$$

Let

$$d_D^+(X) = |\partial_D^+(X)|,$$

$$d_D^-(X) = |\partial_D^-(X)|. \quad (2)$$

When $X=\{v\}$, we write $d_D^+(v) = |\partial_D^+\{v\}|$ and $d_D^-(v) = |\partial_D^-\{v\}|$. Let $N_D^+(v) = \{u \in V(D) - v : (v,u) \in A(D)\}$ and $N_D^-(v) = \{u \in V(D) - v : (u,v) \in A(D)\}$ denote the out-neighborhood and in-neighborhood of v in D, respectively. We call the vertices in $N_D^+(v)$ and $N_D^-(v)$ the out-neighbors and the in-neighbors of v. Thus, for a digraph D, $(D) \geq 1$ if and only if, for any proper nonempty subset $\emptyset \neq X \subset V(D)$, $|\partial_D^+(X)| \geq 1$.

A dicycle cover of a digraph D is a collection $\mathscr{C}$ of dicycles of D such that $\bigcup_{C \in \mathscr{C}} A(C) = A(D)$. If D is obtained from a simple undirected graph G by assigning an orientation to the edges of G, then D is an oriented graph. The main purpose is to investigate the number of dicycles needed to cover a Hamiltonian oriented graph. We prove the following.

Theorem 1*. Let D be an oriented graph on n vertices and m arcs. If D has a Hamiltonian dicycle, then D has a dicycle cover $\mathscr{C}$ with $|\mathscr{C}| \leq m - n + 1$. This bound is best possible.*

In the next section, we will first show that every Hamiltonian oriented graph with n vertices and m arcs can be covered by at most $m - n + 1$ dicycles. Then we show that, for every Hamiltonian graph$G$with n vertices and m edges, there exists an orientation $D = D(G)$ of G such that any dicycle cover of D must have at least $m - n + 1$ dicycles.

PROOF OF THE MAIN RESULT

In this section, all graphs are assumed to be simple. We start with an observation, stated as lemma below. A digraph D is weakly connected if the underlying graph of D is connected.

Lemma 2*. A weakly connected digraph D has a dicycle cover if and only if (D) ≥ 1.*

Proof. Suppose that D has a dicycle cover $\mathscr{C}$. If D is not strong, then there exists a proper nonempty subset $\emptyset \neq X \subset$ □(D) such that $|\partial_D^+(X)| = 0$. Since D is weakly connected, D contains an arc $(u, v) \in ((D) - X), X)_D$. Since $\mathscr{C}$ is a dicycle cover of D, there exists a dicycle $C \in \mathscr{C}$ with $(u, v) \in (C)$. Since $(u, v) \in ((D) - X), X)_n$, we conclude that $\emptyset \neq A(C) \cap (X, V(D) - X))_D \subseteq \partial_D^+(X)$, contrary to the assumption that $|\partial_D^+(X)| = 0$. This proves that D must be strong.

Conversely, assume that D is strong. For any arc $a = (u, v) \in (D)$, since D is strong, there must be a directed (v, u)-path P in D. It follows that $C_a = P+a$ is a dicycle of D containing a, and so $\{C : a \in A(D)\}$ is a dicycle cover of D.

Let C be a dicycle and let $a = (u, v)$ be an arc not in (C) but with u, V $\in V(C)$. Then $C+a$ contains a unique dicycle C_a containing a. In the following, we call C_a the fundamental dicycle of a with respect to C.

Lemma 3*. Let D be an oriented graph on n vertices and m arcs. If D has a Hamiltonian dicycle, then D has a dicycle cover $\mathscr{C}$ with $|\mathscr{C}| \leq m - n + 1$.*

Proof. Let C_0 denote the directed Hamiltonian cycle of D. For each $a \in A(D) - A(C)$, let C_a denote the fundamental dicycle of $a$with respect to C.Then $\mathscr{C} = \{C_0\} \cup \{C_a : a \in A(D) - A(C)\}$ is a dicycle cover of D with $|\mathscr{C}| \leq m - n + 1$.

To prove that Theorem 1 is best possible, we need to construct, for each integer $n \geq 4$, a Hamiltonian oriented graph on n vertices and m arcs D such that any dicycle cover $\mathscr{C}$ of D must have at least $m - n + 1$ dicycles in $\mathscr{C}$.

Let G be a Hamiltonian simple graph. We present a construction of such an orientation $D = (G)$. Since G is Hamiltonian, we may assume that $(G) = \{v_1, v_2, \ldots, v_n\}$ and $C = v_1 v_2, \ldots, v_n v_1$ is a Hamiltonian cycle of G.

Definition 4*. One defines an orientation D = (G) as follows.*

1. Orient the edges in the Hamiltonian cycle $C = v_1 v_2, \ldots, v_n v_1$ as follows:

$$(v_{i+1}, v_i) \in A(D), \quad i = 1, 2, \ldots, n-1, \ (v_1, v_n) \in A(D). \quad (3)$$

2. For each $i = 2, 3, \ldots, n-2$, and for each $j = i+2, i+3, \ldots, n$, assign directions to edges of G not in $E(C)$ as follows:

$$(v_i, v_j) \in A(D), \quad \text{if } v_i v_j \in E(G) - E(C),\ i+1 < j \leq n,$$

$$(v_1, v_j) \in A(D), \quad \text{if } v_1 v_j \in E(G) - E(C),\ i+1 < j \leq n-1. \quad (4)$$

We make the following observations stated in the lemma below.

Lemma 5*. Each of the following holds for the digraph D:*

3. The dicycle $C_0 = v_1 v_n v_{n-1}, \ldots, v_3 v_2 v_1$ is a Hamiltonian dicycle of D.
4. The digraph $D - (C_0)$ is acyclic.
5. $N_D^+(v_n) = \{v_{n-1}\};\ N_D^-(v_1) = \{v_2\};\ N_D^-(v_2) = \{v_3\}$.
6. The dicycle C_0 is the only dicycle of D containing the arc (v_1, v_n).
7. The dicycle C_0 is the unique Hamiltonian dicycle of D.
8. If C'' is a dicycle of D, then C'' contains at most one arc in $(D) - A(C_0)$.

Proof

1. follows immediately from Definition 4(i).
2. By Definition 4, the labels of the vertices $(D) = \{v_1, v_2,..., v_n\}$ satisfy $(v_i, v_j) \in A(D) - A(C_0)$ only if $i < j$. It follows (e.g., Section 2.1 of [2]) that $D - (C_0)$ is acyclic, and so (ii) holds.
3. This follows immediately from Definition 4.
4. Let C' be a dicycle of D with $(v_1, v_n) \in (C')$. Since $(v_1, v_n) \in (C') \cap A(C_0)$, we choose the largest label $i \leq n$, such that $(v_1, v_n), (v_n, v_{n-1}), \ldots, (v_{i+1}, v_i) \in A(C') \cap A(C_0)$. Since $C' \neq C_0$, we have $i \geq 3$. Since C' is a dicycle, there must be a vertex $v_j \in (D)$ such that $(v_i, v_j) \in A(C')$. By the choice of i, we must have $(v_i, v_j) \notin (C_0)$, and so $(v_i, v_j) \in A(D) - A(C_0)$. By Definition 4(ii), we have $i + 2 \leq j \leq n$, contrary to the fact that C' is a dicycle of D containing (v_1, v_n). This proves (iv).
5. Let C' be a Hamiltonian dicycle of D. Since $(C') = V(D)$, we have $v_n \in V(C')$. We claim that $(v_1, v_n) \in (C')$. If $(v_1, v_n) \notin (C')$, then there exists $v_i \in V(C)$ $(i \in \{v_2, v_3,..., v_{n-1}\})$ such that $(v_i, v_n) \in A(C')$. Hence, $(v_i, v_n), (v_n, v_{n-1}), \ldots, (v_{i+2}, v_{i+1}) \in A(C')$. By Definition 4(i) and (ii), $N+(v_{i+1}) \subset \{v_{i+2}, v_{i+3},..., v_n\}$, contrary to the fact that C' is a Hamiltonian dicycle of D. Thus, $(v_1, v_n) \in (C')$. It follows from Lemma 5(iv) that we must have $C' = C_0$.
6. By contradiction, we assume that D has a dicycle C'' which contains two arcs: $a_1, a_2 \in (D) - A(C_0)$. Since $(D) = \{v_1, v_2,..., v_n\}$, we assume that $a_1 = (V_i, V_{i'})$ and $a_2 = (v_j, v_{j'})$. Without loss of generality and by Lemma 2, we further assume that $1 \leq i < j < n$.

Let $i \geq t \geq 1$ be the smallest integer such that $v_t \in (C'')$. Since C'' is a dicycle of D, there must be $v_s \in (C'')$ such that $(v_s, v_t) \in A(C'')$. By Definition 4, either $(v_s, v_t) \in A(C_0)$ and $s = t+1 < j$ or $(v_s, v_t) \in A(D) - A(C_0)$ and $1 < s + 1 < j$ such that $(v_{t+1}, v_t), (v_{t+2}, v_{t+1}), \ldots, (v_h, v_{h-1}) \in A(C'') \cap A(C_0)$. Since C'' is a dicycle, there must be v_k with $1 \leq k \leq n$ such that $(v_k, v_h) \in (C'')$. By the maximality of h and by Definition 4(i), we conclude that $(v_k, v_h) \notin (C_0)$. By Definition 4(ii), $1 \leq k \leq h - 2$. By the minimality of t, we must have $t \leq k \leq h - 2$. It follows by $j > h$ that C'' cannot contain $a_2 = (v_j, v_{j'})$, contrary to the assumption. This contradiction justifies (vi).

To complete the proof of Theorem 1, we present the next lemma.

Lemma 6. *Let G be a Hamiltonian simple graph. There exists an orientation D = (G) such that every dicycle cover of D must have at least* $m - n + 1$ *dicycles.*

Proof. Let G be a Hamiltonian graph and let $D = (G)$ be the orientation of G given in Definition 4. For notational convenience, we adopt the notations in Definition 4 and denote $(D) = \{v_1, v_2,..., v_n\}$. Thus, by Lemma 5(v), $C_0 = v_1 v_n v_{n-1},..., v_2 v_1$ is the unique Hamiltonian dicycle of D.

Let $\mathscr{C}$ be a dicycle cover of D. By Lemma 5(iv), we must have $C_0 \in \mathscr{C}$. For each arc $a \in (D) - A(C_0)$, since $\mathscr{C}$ is a dicycle cover of D, there must be a dicycle $C(a) \in \mathscr{C}$ such that $a \in A(C(a))$. By Lemma 5(vi), $(C(a)) \cap A(D) - A(C_0) = \{a\}$. It follows that if $a, a' \in (D) - A(C_0)$, then $a \neq a'$ implies $C(a) \neq C(a')$ in $\mathscr{C}$. Thus we have $\{(a) \mid a \in A(D) - A(C_0)\} \subseteq \mathscr{C}$. Hence

$$|\mathscr{C}| \geq \left|\{C(a) : a \in A(D) - A(C_0)\} \cup \{C_0\}\right|$$

$$= m - n + 1. \tag{5}$$

This proves the lemma.

By Lemmas 3 and 6, Theorem 1 follows. We are about to show that Theorem 1 can be applied to obtain dicycle cover bounds for certain families of oriented graphs. Let T_n denote a tournament of order n. Then T_n is an oriented graph. Camion [13, 14] proved that every strong tournament is Hamiltonian. Hence the corollary below follows from Theorem 1.

Corollary 7. *Every strong tournament on n vertices has a dicycle cover* $\mathscr{C}$ *with* $|\mathscr{C}| \leq (n - 1)/2 - n + 1$. *This bound is best possible.*

A bipartite graph (A, B) with vertex bipartition (A, B) is balanced if $|A| = |B|$. If bipartite graph (A, B) has a Hamiltonian cycle, then$G$ is balanced. Let K_m be a complete bipartite graph with vertex bipartition (A, B) and $|A| = m$, $|B| = n$; then $K_{m,n}$ has Hamiltonian cycle if and only if $m = n \geq 2$; that is, $K_{m,n}$ is balanced. Let K_n denote a balanced complete bipartite graph.

Corollary 8. *Every Hamiltonian orientation of balanced complete bipartite graph* K_n *has a dicycle cover* $\mathscr{C}$ *with* $|\mathscr{C}| \leq (n - 1)^2$. *This bound is best possible.*

Proof. Since an oriented balanced complete bipartite graph K_n has n^2 arcs, so, by Theorem 1, we have $|\mathscr{C}| \leq n^2 - 2n + 1 = (n - 1)^2$.

To prove the bound is best possible, we need to construct, for each integer $n \geq 2$, a Hamiltonian oriented balanced complete bipartite graph on $2n$ vertices such that any dicycle cover $\mathscr{C}$ of Kn,n must have at least $(n - 1)2$ dicycles in $\mathscr{C}$. We may assume that $(K_{n,n}) = \{u_1, u_2,...,u_n, v_1, v_2,..., v_n\}$ and $C=u_1 v_1 u_2 v_2,...,u_n v_n u_1$ is a Hamiltonian cycle of Kn,n. We construct an orientation $D_n = D(K_{n,n})$ as the orientation of Definition 4; thus, by Lemmas 5 and 6, every dicycle cover $\mathscr{C}$ of $D_{n,n}$ must have at least $(n - 1)^2$ dicycles. This proves the corollary.

DICYCLE COVERS OF 2 SUMS OF DIGRAPHS

In this section, we will show that Theorem 1 can also be applied to certain non-Hamiltonian digraphs which can be built via 2 sums. We start with 2 sums of digraphs.

Definition 9. *Let* $D_{n_1} = (V(D_{n_1}), A(D_{n_1}))$ and $D_{n_2} = (V(D_{n_2}), A(D_{n_2}))$ *be two disjoint digraphs;* $a_1 = (v_{12}, v_{11}) \in A(D_{n_1})$ *and* $a_2 = (v_{22}, v_{21}) \in A(D_{n_2})$.*The 2-sum* $D_{n_1} \oplus_2 D_{n_2}$ *of* D_{n_1} *and* D_{n_2} *is obtained from the union of* D_{n_1} *and* D_{n_2} *by identifying the arcs* a_1 *and* a_2*; that is,* $v_{11} = v_{21}$ *and* $v_{12} = v_{22}$.

Definition 10. *Let* $D_{n_1}, D_{n_2},..., D_{n_s}$ *be s disjoint digraphs with* $n_1, n_2,...,n_s$ *vertices, respectively. Let* $D_{n_1} \oplus_2 D_{n_2} \oplus_2 \cdots \oplus_2 D_{n_s}$ *denote a sequence of 2 sums of* $D_{n_1}, D_{n_2}, ..., D_{n_s}$, *that is,* $(((D_{n_1} \oplus_2 D_{n_2}) \oplus_2 D_{n_3}) \oplus 2 \cdots) \oplus_2 D_{n_s}$.

Theorem 11. *Let* $D_{n_1}, D_{n_2},..., D_{n_s}$ *be s disjoint*

Hamiltonian oriented graphs on $n_1, n_2,...,n_s$ vertices and $m_1, m_2,...,m_s$ arcs, respectively, and let $D = D_{n_1} \oplus_2 D_{n_2} \oplus_2 \cdots \oplus_2 D_{n_s}$. Then D has a dicycle cover with $|\mathscr{C}| \le |(D)| - |V(D)| + 1$. This bound is best possible.

Proof. By Theorem 1, D_{n_i} $(i = 1, 2, \ldots, s)$ has a dicycle cover $\mathscr{C}_i$ with $|\mathscr{C}_i| \le m_i - n_i + 1$. Let $\mathscr{C} = \bigcup_{i=1}^{s} \mathscr{C}_i$. Then $|\mathscr{C}| \le (m_1 - n_1 + 1) + (m_2 - n_2 + 1) + \cdots + (m_s - n_s + 1) = (m_1 + m_2 + \cdots + m_s) - (n_1 + n_2 + \cdots + n_s) + s = (m_1 + m_2 + \cdots + m_s - (s - 1)) - (n_1 + n_2 + \cdots + n_s - 2(s - 1)) + 1 = |A(D)| - |V(D)| + 1$. By Definition 10, $\mathscr{C}$ is a dicycle cover of D. Thus, D has a dicycle cover $\mathscr{C}$ with $|\mathscr{C}| \le |(D)| - |V(D)| + 1$.

Let G_{n_i} be s disjoint Hamiltonian simple graphs for $i \in \{1, 2, \ldots, s\}$. We may assume that $V(G_{n_i}) = \{v_{i1}, v_{i2}, \ldots, v_{in_i}\}$ and $C_i = v_{i1}v_{i2}, \ldots, v_{in_i}v_{i1}$ is a Hamiltonian cycle of G_{n_i}, and let

$$D_{n_i} = D\left(G_{n_i}\right) \text{ be the orientation of } G_{n_i} \text{ given in Definition 4.} \tag{6}$$

For notational convenience, we adopt the notations in Definition 4 and denote $V(D_{n_i}) = \{v_{i1}, v_{i2}, \ldots, v_{in_i}\}$. Thus, by Lemma 5(v), $C_{i_0} = v_{i1}v_{in_i}, \ldots, v_{i2}v_{i1}$ is the unique Hamiltonian dicycle of D_{n_i}. Let $a_i = (v_{i2}, v_{i1})$ be an arc of D_{n_i}. We construct the 2-sum digraph $D_{n_1} \oplus_2 D_{n_2} \oplus_2 \cdots \oplus_2 D_{n_s}$ from the union of $D_{n_1}, D_{n_2}, \ldots, D_{n_s}$ by identifying the arcs $a_1, a_2, \ldots, a_s$ such that $v_{11} = v_{21} = \cdots = v_{s1}$ and $v_{12} = v_{22} = \cdots = v_{s2}$. We assume that $v_1 := v_{11} = v_{21} = \cdots = v_{s1}$ and $v_2 := v_{12} = v_{22} = \cdots = v_{s2}$ (the case when $s = 2$ is depicted in Figure 1).

Claim 1. There does not exist a dicycle whose arcs intersect arcs in two or more D_{n_i}'s $(i = 1, 2, \ldots, s)$.

By Definition 9, we have $(D_{n_i}) \cap V(D_{n_j}) = \{v_1, v_2\}$ $(i \neq j)$. Without loss of generality, we consider oriented graphs D_{n_1} and D_{n_2}; suppose that there exists a dicycle C_0 such that

$$\{A(C_0) - (v_2, v_1)\} \cap A\left(D_{n_1}\right) \neq \emptyset,$$

$$\{A(C_0) - (v_2, v_1)\} \cap A\left(D_{n_2}\right) \neq \emptyset. \tag{7}$$

Thus, there must exist four different arcs

$$\left\{\left(v_{1i'}, v_1\right), \left(v_1, v_{2i''}\right), \left(v_{2j''}, v_2\right), \left(v_2, v_{1j'}\right)\right\} \in A\left(C_0\right) \tag{8}$$

with $(v_{1i'}, v_1), (v_2, v_{1j'}) \in A(D_{n_1})$ and $(v_1, v_{2i''}), (v_{2j''}, v_2) \in A(D_{n_2})$, as shown in Figure 2, or four different arcs

$$\left\{\left(v_{1s'}, v_2\right), \left(v_2, v_{2s''}\right), \left(v_{2k''}, v_1\right), \left(v_1, v_{1k'}\right)\right\} \in A\left(C_0\right) \tag{9}$$

with $(v_{1s'}, v_2), (v_1, v_{1k'}) \in A(D_{n_1})$ and $(v_2, v_{2s''}), (v_{2k''}, v_1) \in A(D_{n_2})$, as shown in Figure 3.

By Definition 9, Lemma 5(iii), and (6), we have $N_D^-(v_1) = \{v_2\}$, and so $v_{1i'} = v_2$ or $v_{2k''} = v_2$, contrary to the assumption that C_0 is a dicycle. This proves Claim 1.

By Claim 1, for every dicycle C in D, all arcs in C (except for the arc (v_2, v_1)) belong to exactly one of oriented graphs D_{n_i} $(i = 1, 2, \ldots, n)$. By Definition 4 and Lemma 6, every dicycle cover of oriented graph D_{n_i} $(i = 1, 2, \ldots, n)$ must have at least $m_i - n_i + 1$ dicycles. This completes the proof.

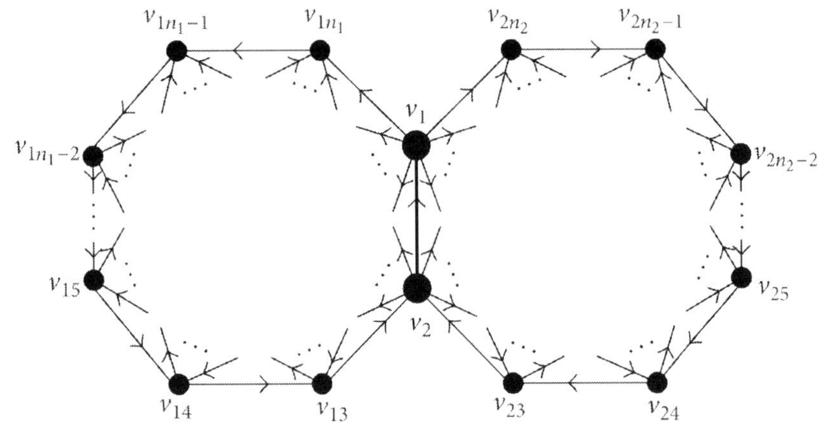

Figure 1: The 2-sum digraph for D_{n_1} and D_{n_2}.

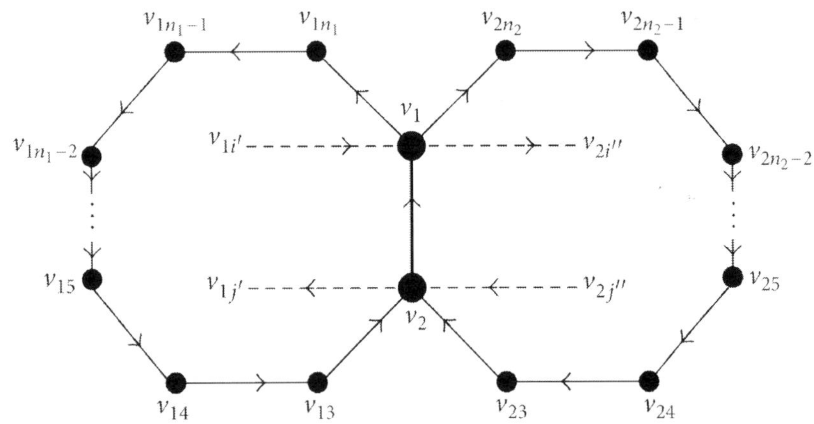

Figure 2

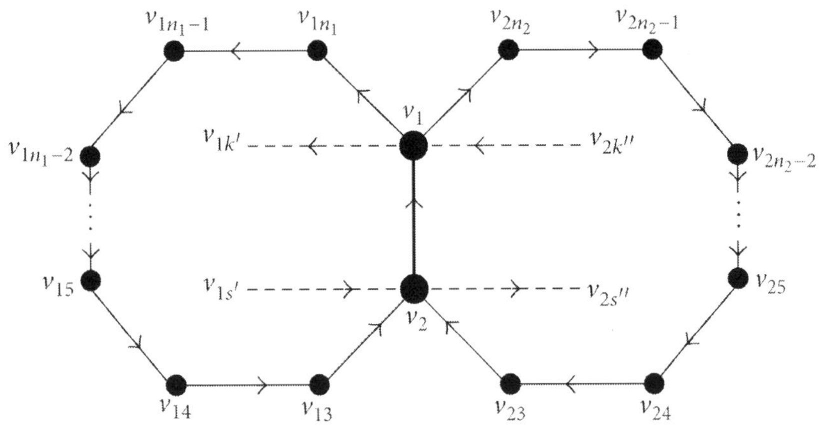

Figure 3:

By Corollary 7 and Theorem 11, we have the following corollary.

Corollary 12. *Let* $D_{n_1}, D_{n_2}, \ldots, D_{n_s}$ *be s disjoint strong tournaments with* n_1, n_2,…,$_s$ *vertices, respectively. Then* $D_{n_1} \oplus_2 D_{n_2} \oplus_2 \cdots \oplus_2 D_{n_s}$ *has a dicycle cover* $\mathscr{C}$ *with* $|\mathscr{C}| \leq (n_1(n_1 - 1)/2 + n_2(n_2 - 1)/2 + \cdots + n_s(n_s - 1)/2) - (n_1 + n_2 + \cdots + n_s) + s$*. This bound is best possible.*

Let G_n be a Hamiltonian graph with n vertices and m arcs; let D_n^i (i is an integer) denote a Hamiltonian orientation of G_n. For a positive integer s, let (G_n, s) denote the family of all 2-sum generated digraphs $D_n^1 \oplus_2 D_n^2 \oplus_2 \cdots \oplus_2 D_n^s$, as well as a member in the family (for notational convenience). By the definition of (G_n, s), we have $H(G_n, 1) = D_n^1$ and $H(G_n, s) = H(G_n,$

$s-1) \oplus_2 D_n^s$. The conclusions of the next corollaries follow from Theorem 1. The sharpness of these corollaries can be demonstrated using similar constructions displayed in Lemma 6 and Corollary 8.

Corollary 13. *Let m, $n \geq 3$ be integer, let G_n be a Hamiltonian graph with n vertices and m edges, and let K_n be a complete graph on $n \geq 3$ vertices:*

1. Any member in (G_n, s) has a dicycle cover $\mathscr{C}$ with $|\mathscr{C}| \leq s(m-n+1)$. This bound is best possible.
2. In particular, any (K_n, s) has a dicycle cover $\mathscr{C}$ with $|\mathscr{C}| \leq s(n(n-1)/2 - n + 1)$. This bound is best possible.

Corollary 14. Let m, $n \geq 3$ be integer, let B_n be a Hamiltonian bipartite graph with $2n$ vertices and m edges, and let $K_{n,}$ be a complete bipartite graph:

1. Any (B_n, s) has a dicycle cover $\mathscr{C}$ with $|\mathscr{C}| \leq s(m-2n+1)$. This bound is best possible.
2. In particular, any $(K_{n,n}, s)$ has a dicycle cover $\mathscr{C}$ with $|\mathscr{C}| \leq s(n-1)^2$. This bound is best possible.

REFERENCES

1. J. A. Bondy and U. S. R. Murty, Graph Theory, vol. 244 of Graduate Texts in Mathematics, Springer, New York, NY, USA, 2008.
2. J. Bang-Jensen and G. Gutin, Digraphs: Theory, Algorithms and Applications, Springer, 2nd edition, 2010.
3. J. A. Bondy, "Small cycle double covers of graphs," in Cycles and Rays, pp. 21–40, Kluwer Academic Publishers, Dordrecht, The Netherlands, 1990.
4. Y. X. Luo and R. S. Chen, "Cycle covers of 2-connected 3-regular graphs," Mathematics and Applications, vol. 9, supplement, pp. 23–25, 1996 (Chinese).
5. H.-J. Lai, "Cycle covers of planar graphs," Congressus Numerantium, vol. 122, pp. 33–46, 1996.
6. H.-J. Lai and H. Y. Lai, "Cycle covering of plane triangulations," Journal of Combinatorial Mathematics and Combinatorial Computing, vol. 10, pp. 3–21, 1991.
7. H.-J. Lai and H. Y. Lai, "Cycle covers in graphs without subdivisions of K4," Journal of Combinatorial Mathematics and Combinatorial Computing, vol. 9, pp. 201–207, 1991.
8. H.-J. Lai and H. Y. Lai, "Small cycle covers of planar graphs," Congressus Numerantium, vol. 85, pp. 203–209, 1991.
9. D. W. Barnette, "Cycle covers of planar 3-connected graphs," Journal of Combinatorial Mathematics and Combinatorial Computing, vol. 20, pp. 245–253, 1996.
10. G. Fan, "Subgraph coverings and edge switchings," Journal of Combinatorial Theory Series B, vol. 84, no. 1, pp. 54–83, 2002.
11. H.-J. Lai and X. Li, "Small cycle cover of 2-connected cubic graphs," Discrete Mathematics, vol. 269, no. 1–3, pp. 295–302, 2003.
12. F. Yang and X. Li, "Small cycle covers of 3-connected cubic graphs," Discrete Mathematics, vol. 311, no. 2-3, pp. 186–196, 2011.
13. P. Camion, "Chemins et circuits hamiltoniens des graphes complets," Comptes Rendus de l'Académie des Sciences, vol. 249, pp. 2151–2152, 1959.
14. J. W. Moon, "On subtournaments of a tournament," Canadian Mathematical Bulletin, vol. 9, pp. 297–301, 1966.

CHAPTER 17

ON REDUCED ZERO-DIVISOR GRAPHS OF POSETS

Ashish Kumar Das and Deiborlang Nongsiang

Department of Mathematics, North-Eastern Hill University, Permanent Campus, Shillong, Meghalaya 793022, India

ABSTRACT

We study some properties of a graph which is constructed from the equivalence classes of nonzero zero-divisors determined by the annihilator ideals of a poset. In particular, we demonstrate how this graph helps in identifying the annihilator prime ideals of a poset that satisfies the ascending chain condition for its proper annihilator ideals.

INTRODUCTION

The study of the interrelationship between algebra and graph theory by associating a graph to an algebraic object was initiated, in 1988, by Beck [1] who developed the notion of a zero-divisor graph of a commutative ring with identity. Since then, a number of authors have studied various forms of zero-divisor graphs associated to rings and other algebraic structures (see, e.g., [2–5]).

In 2009, Halaš and Jukl [6] introduced the notion of a zero-divisor graph of a partially ordered set (in short, a poset). The study of various types of zero-divisor graphs of posets was then carried out by many others in [7–9]. However, the zero-divisor graph of a poset considered in this paper was actually introduced by Lu and Wu [10], which is slightly different from the one introduced in [6].

In this paper, inspired by the ideas of Mulay [11] and Spiroff and Wickham [12], we study some properties of a graph which is constructed from the equivalence classes of nonzero zero-divisors determined by the annihilator ideals of a poset. This graph is the same as the reduced graph of the zero-divisor graph of a poset (see [10, page 798]). In particular, we demonstrate how this graph helps in identifying the annihilator prime ideals of a poset that satisfies the ascending chain condition for its proper annihilator ideals.

PREREQUISITES

In this section, we put together some well-known concepts, most of which can be found in [13–16].

We begin by recalling some of the basic terminologies from the theory of graphs. Needless to mention that all graphs considered here are simple graphs, that is, without loops or multiple edges. Let G be a graph and $x, y \in (G)$ the vertex set of G. Then, x and y are said to be *adjacent* if $x \neq y$ and there is an edge x–y between x and y. A walk between x and y is a sequence of adjacent vertices, often written as $x - x_1 - x_2 - \cdots - x_n - y$. A walk between x and y is called *path* if the vertices in it are all distinct (except, possibly, x and y). A path between x and y is called a *cycle* if $x=y$. The number of edges in a path or a cycle is called its *length*. If $x = y$, then the minimum of the lengths of all paths between x and y in G is called the *distance*

Citation: Ashish Kumar Das and Deiborlang Nongsiang, "On Reduced Zero-Divisor Graphs of Posets," Journal of Discrete Mathematics, vol. 2015, Article ID 736326, 7 pages, 2015. doi:10.1155/2015/736326

between x and y in G and is denoted by dist(x, y). If there is no path between x and y, then we define dist(x, y) = ∞. The maximum of all possible distances in G is called the *diameter* of G and is denoted by diam(G). The girth of a graph G is the minimum of the lengths of all cycles in G and is denoted by girth(G). If G is *acyclic*, that is, if G has no cycles, then we write girth(G) = ∞. A cycle graph is a graph that consists of a single cycle (an n-gon).

A subset of the vertex set of a graph G is called a *clique* of G if it consists entirely of pairwise adjacent vertices. The least upper bound of the sizes of all the cliques of G is called the *clique number* of G and is denoted by (G).

The neighborhood of a vertex x in a graph G, denoted by nbd(x), is defined to be the set of all vertices adjacent to x while the degree of x in G, denoted by deg(x), is defined to be the number of vertices adjacent to x, and so deg(x) = |nbd(x)|. If deg(x) = 1, then x is said to be an end vertex in G. If deg(x) = deg(y) for all x, $y \in V(G)$, then the graph G is said to be a regular graph.

A graph G is said to be connected if there is a path between every pair of distinct vertices in G. A graph G is said to be complete if there is an edge between every pair of distinct vertices in G. We denote the complete graph with n vertices by K_n. An r-partite graph, $r \geq 2$, is a graph whose vertex set can be partitioned into r disjoint parts in such a way that no two adjacent vertices lie in the same part. Among the r-partite graphs, the complete r-partite graph is the one in which two vertices are adjacent if and only if they lie in different parts. The complete r-partite graph with parts of size n_1, n_2,..., $_r$ is denoted by $K_{n_1,n_2,\ldots,n_r}$. The 2-partite and complete 2-partite graphs are popularly known as bipartite and complete bipartite graphs, respectively. A bipartite graph of the form $K_{1,}$ is also known as a star graph.

Next we turn to partially ordered sets and their zero-divisor graphs. A nonempty set is said to be a partially ordered set (in short, a poset) if it is equipped with a partial order, that is, a reflexive, antisymmetric, and transitive binary relation. It is customary to denote a partial order by "$\leq$."

Let Q be a nonempty subset of a poset P. If there exists $y \in Q$ such that $y \leq x$ for every $x \in Q$, then y is called the least element of Q. The least element of P, if exists, is usually denoted by 0. An element $x \in Q$ is called a *minimal element* of Q if $y \in Q$ and $y \leq x$ imply that $y = x$. We denote the set of minimal elements of Q by Min(Q)

Let P be a poset with least element 0. An element $x \in P$ is called a zero-divisor of P if there exists $y \in P^{\times} := P \setminus \{0\}$ such that the set $L(x, y) := \{z \in P \mid z \leq x \text{ and } z \leq y\} = \{0\}$. We denote the set of zero-divisors of P by (P) and write $Z(P)^{\times} := Z(P) \setminus \{0\}$. By an ideal of P we mean a nonempty subset I of P such that $y \in I$ whenever $y \leq x$ for some $x \in I$. We say that the ideal I is proper if $I \neq P$. For each $x \in P$, it is easy to see that the set $(x] := \{y \in P \mid y \leq x\}$ is an ideal of P, called the principal ideal of P generated by x. Given $x \in P$, the annihilator of x in P is defined to be the set ann(x) := $\{y \in P \mid L(x, y) = \{0\}\}$, which is also an ideal of P. Note that $x \notin$ ann(x) for all $x \in P^{\times}$. A proper ideal $\mathfrak{p}$ of P is called a *prime ideal* of P if, for every x, $y \in P$, $(x, y) \subseteq \mathfrak{p}$ implies that either $x \in \mathfrak{p}$ or $y \in \mathfrak{p}$. A prime ideal $\mathfrak{p}$ of P is said to be an annihilator prime ideal (or, an associated prime) if there exists $x \in P$ such that p = ann(x). Two annihilator prime ideals ann(x) and ann(y) are distinct if and only if $L(x, y) = \{0\}$ (see [6, Lemma 2.3]). We write Ann(P) to denote the set of all annihilator prime ideals of P.

Let P be a poset with least element 0 and with $(P)^{\times} \neq \emptyset$. As in [10], the zero-divisor graph of$P$ is defined to be the graph $\Gamma(P)$ in which the vertex set is $Z(P)^{\times}$, and two vertices x and y are adjacent if and only if $L(x, y) = \{0\}$. Clearly, $\Gamma(P)$ is a simple graph; in fact, nbd(x) = ann(x) \ $\{0\}$ for all $x \in V(\Gamma(P))$. It is well known that $\Gamma(P)$ is a connected graph with diam($\Gamma(P)$) $\in \{1, 2, 3\}$ and girth($\Gamma(P)$) $\in \{3, 4, \infty\}$ (see, e.g., [9]). The clique number ($\Gamma(P)$) of $\Gamma(P)$ is usually denoted, in short, by $\omega(P)$. Clearly, $(P) \geq 2$. It may be noted here that (P) = clique(P) − 1, where clique(P) is the clique number of the zero-divisor graph considered in [6] whose vertex set is the whole of P.

Finally, we would like to mention that all posets considered in this paper are with least element 0 and have nonzero zero-divisors, unless explicitly written otherwise.

REDUCED GRAPH OF F $\Gamma(P)$: BASIC PROPERTIES

In this section, we study some of the basic properties of the reduced graph of the zero-divisor graph of a poset.

Let P be a poset with least element 0 and with $(P)^{\times} \neq \emptyset$. Given x, $y \in P$, set $x \sim y$ if ann(x) = ann(y). Clearly, $\sim$ is an equivalence relation in P. Let $[x]$ denote the equivalence class of $x \in P$. Note that if $x \in (P)^{\times}$, then $[x] \subseteq Z(P)^{\times}$. Also, note that $[0] = \{0\}$ and $[x] = P \setminus (P)$ for all $x \in P \setminus Z(P)$. In analogy with [11, 12], the graph of equivalence classes of zero divisors of P may be defined to be the graph $\Gamma_E(P)$in which the vertex set is the set of all equivalence classes of the elements of $Z(P)^{\times}$, and two vertices$[x]$ and $[y]$ are adjacent if and only if $L(x, y) = \{0\}$, that is, if and only if x and y are adjacent in $\Gamma(P)$. Note that two adjacent vertices in $\Gamma(P)$ represent two distinct equivalence classes and, hence, two distinct vertices in $\Gamma_E(P)$. Thus $\Gamma(P)$ is also a simple graph. It may be recalled (see [12]) that, in case of a commutative ring R with unity, two adjacent vertices in $\Gamma(R)$ do not necessarily represent two distinct vertices in $\Gamma_E(R)$. Since nbd(x) = ann(x)$\setminus\{0\}$ for all $x \in V(\Gamma(P))$, one obtains the same graph $\Gamma_E(P)$ if the equivalence relation $\sim$ is defined on $V(\Gamma(P)) = Z(P)^{\times}$ by setting $x \sim y$, where x, $y \in V(\Gamma(P)) = Z(P)^{\times}$, if and only if nbd($x$) = nbd($y$) in $\Gamma(P)$. Thus, the graph $\Gamma(P)$ is the same as the reduced graph of $\Gamma(P)$ considered by Lu and Wu in [10]. In particular, $\Gamma(P)$ is also a zero-divisor graph of some poset, and, hence, there are lots of structural similarities between $\Gamma(P)$ and $\Gamma_E(P)$. There are however some more features of $\Gamma(P)$ which are worth looking into.

The graph $\Gamma(P)$ has some advantages over the zero divisor graph $\Gamma(P)$. In many cases $\Gamma(P)$ is finite when $\Gamma(P)$ is infinite. For example, consider the poset $P_0 = \{\emptyset, \{1\}, \{2\}, \{2, 3\}, \{2, 4\}, \ldots\}$ under the set inclusion with least element $\emptyset$. Then $\Gamma(P_0)$ is infinite, whereas $\Gamma_E(P_0)$ is finite and has only two vertices. In fact, the zero-divisors $\{2\}$, $\{2, 3\}$, $\{2, 4\}$, . . ., have the same annihilator and so they represent a single vertex in $\Gamma_E(P_0)$; the other vertex in $\Gamma_E(P_0)$ is represented by $\{1\}$. Another important aspect of $\Gamma(P)$ is its connection to the annihilator prime ideals of the poset P, which we discuss in detail in the next section. Let us now rewrite a fact, just noted above, in a more explicit manner for the ease of its extensive use (often without a mention) in this paper.

Fact 1. Given a poset P, two vertices in $\Gamma(P)$ are adjacent if and only if they represent two adjacent vertices in $\Gamma_E(P)$.

In view of Fact 1, it is easy to see that, given a poset P, we have $(P) = \omega(\Gamma_E(P))$; that is, the clique numbers of $\Gamma(P)$ and $\Gamma_E(P)$ are the same.

By [10, Corollary 3.3 (2)], we know that $\Gamma(P)$ is also a zero-divisor graph of some poset. Therefore, in view of [9, Theorem 3.3], $\Gamma(P)$ is a connected graph with diam $\Gamma_E(P) \leq 3$. Our first result of this section not only generalizes Fact 1 but also shows some similarity between $\Gamma(P)$ and $\Gamma_E(P)$ as far as their diameter is concerned.

Proposition 1. *Let P be a poset. If* $[x]$ *and* $[y]$ *are two distinct vertices in* $\Gamma(P)$, *then* $\text{dist}([x], [y]) = \text{dist}(x, y)$. *Moreover, the following assertions hold*:

- $\text{diam}(\Gamma_E(P)) = 3$ *if and only if* $\text{diam}(\Gamma(P)) = 3$,
- $\text{diam}(\Gamma_E(P)) = 2$ *if and only if* $\text{diam}(\Gamma(P)) = 2$ *and* $\text{ann}(x) \neq \text{ann}(y)$ *for some* $x, y \in Z(P)^{\times}$ *with* $L(x, y) \neq \{0\}$,
- $\text{diam}(\Gamma_E(P)) = 1$ if *and only if* $\text{ann}(x) = \text{ann}(y)$ *for all* $x, y \in Z(P)^{\times}$ *with* $L(x, y) \neq \{0\}$.

Proof. Let$[x]$ and $[y]$ be two distinct vertices in $\Gamma_E(P)$. If$[x]-[x_1]-\cdots-[x_n]-[y]$ is a path in $\Gamma_E(P)$, then, by Fact 1, $x-x_1-\cdots-x_n-y$ is a path in $\Gamma(P)$. Therefore, $\text{dist}([x], [y]) \geq \text{dist}(x, y)$. On the other hand, if $x-x_1-\cdots-x_n-y$ is a path in $\Gamma(P)$, then, once again using Fact 1, $[x]-[x_1]-\cdots-[x_n]-[y]$ is a walk in $\Gamma_E(P)$. It follows that $\text{dist}([x], [y]) \leq \text{dist}(x, y)$, and, hence, the equality holds.

For proving the given assertions, we first note that there exist two distinct vertices $[x]$ and $[y]$ of $\Gamma(P)$ such that $\text{dist}([x], [y]) = \text{diam}(\Gamma_E(P))$. Therefore, it follows from the first half of this proposition that we always have $\text{diam}(\Gamma_E(P)) \leq \text{diam}(\Gamma(P))$. However, for the reverse inequality it is not enough to have two distinct vertices $x, y \in (\Gamma(P))$ such that $\text{dist}(x, y) = \text{diam}(\Gamma(P))$; we must also have an additional requirement; namely, $\text{ann}(x) \neq \text{ann}(y)$. If $\text{dist}(x, y) = 3$, then this additional requirement is guaranteed by the existence of a path of the form $x-a-b-y$ in $\Gamma(P)$. Hence, the assertion (a) follows. This in turn also proves the assertion (b), because the extra condition included in (b) fulfills the additional requirement mentioned above. The last assertion, namely, (c), now follows from the assertions (a) and (b).

From [9, 10], we know that $\text{girth}(\Gamma_E(P)) \in \{3, 4, \infty\}$. In this context, we have the following result.

Proposition 2. *Let P be a poset. Then,*

$$\text{girth}\left(\Gamma_E(P)\right) = 3$$

$$\Longleftrightarrow \text{girth}\left(\Gamma(P)\right) = 3 \Longleftrightarrow \left|V\left(\Gamma_E(P)\right)\right| \geq 3. \quad (1)$$

Consequently, $\text{girth}(\Gamma_E(P)) = \infty$ *if and only if* $|V(\Gamma_E(P))| = 2$.

Proof. Assume that $|(\Gamma_E(P))| \geq 3$. Then we also have $|(\Gamma(P))| \geq 3$. Moreover, $\Gamma(P)$ is not a star graph; otherwise we would have $|V(\Gamma_E(P))| = 2$. By [9, Theorem 4.2], we have $\text{girth}(\Gamma(P)) \in \{3, 4, \infty\}$. If girth $(\Gamma(P)) = 4$ or ∞, then it follows from [9, Remark 4.12] that $\Gamma(P)$is a complete bipartite graph, which in turn implies that $|V(\Gamma_E(P))| = 2$. Therefore, we have girth $(\Gamma(P)) = 3$. Hence, in view of Fact 1, we have girth $(\Gamma(P)) = 3$. On the other hand, if $\text{girth}(\Gamma_E(P)) = 3$ then we obviously have $|V(\Gamma_E(P))| \geq 3$.

The consequential statement is clear as, by the choice of P, we always have $|(\Gamma_E(P))| \geq 2$.

As an immediate consequence, we have the following corollary which may be compared with [12, Proposition 1.8].

Corollary 3. *There is no poset P for which* $\Gamma(P)$ *is a cycle graph with at least four vertices.*

Our next result is a small observation, which has some interesting consequences in contrast to some results of a similar nature in [12].

Proposition 4. *Let P be a poset. Then no two distinct vertices of* $\Gamma(P)$ *have the same neighborhood. Equivalently, given* $[x], [y] \in (\Gamma_E(P))$, *one has* $\text{nbd}([x]) = \text{nbd}([y])$ *if and only if* $\text{ann}(x) = \text{ann}(y)$.

Proof. Let $[x]$ and $[y]$ be two distinct vertices in $\Gamma(P)$ such that $\text{nbd}([x]) = \text{nbd}([y])$. Let $z \in \text{ann}(x)$, $z \neq 0$. Then, by Fact 1, we have $[z] \in \text{nbd}([x]) = \text{nbd}([y])$, whence $z \in \text{ann}(y)$. Thus, it follows that $\text{ann}(x) \subseteq \text{ann}(y)$. Similarly, we have $\text{ann}(y) \subseteq \text{ann}(x)$, and so $\text{ann}(x) = \text{ann}(y)$. This contradiction proves the proposition.

The above proposition says, in other words, that the reduced zero-divisor graph of a poset cannot be further reduced (symbolically, $\Gamma(P) \cong (\Gamma_E)_E(P)$).

Corollary 5. *Let P be a poset and* $r \geq 2$. *Then,* $\Gamma(P)$ *is a complete r-partite graph if and only if it is a complete graph with r-vertices.*

Proof. Let $\Gamma(P)$ be a complete r-partite graph with $V(\Gamma_E(P)) = V_1 \sqcup V_2 \sqcup \cdots \sqcup V_r$. Let $[x], [y] \in V_j$, where $1 \leq j \leq r$. Then, $\text{nbd}([x]) = \text{nbd}([y]) = V(\Gamma_E(P)) \setminus V_j$, and so, by Proposition 4,$[x] = [y]$.Thus, $|V_j|=1$ for all $j \in \{1, 2, \ldots, r\}$, which means that $\Gamma_E(P)$ is a complete graph with r vertices. The converse is trivial.

Corollary 6. *Let P be a poset such that* $|(\Gamma_E(P))| \geq 3$. *Then* $\Gamma(P)$ *is not a star graph.*

Proof. It is enough to note that in a star graph with at least three vertices all the end vertices have the same neighborhood. Alternatively, one may also note that star graphs are complete bipartite graphs.

Corollary 7. *There is only one graph with exactly three vertices that can be realized as the graph* $\Gamma(P)$ *for some poset P, and it is the cycle/complete graph* K_3.

Proof. Since, given a poset P, the graph $\Gamma(P)$ is a connected but not a star graph, we need only to note that the graph of equivalence classes of zero-divisors of the poset $\{\emptyset, \{1\}, \{2\}, \{3\}\}$ is precisely K_3.

One of the obvious consequences of Fact 1 is that if for some poset P the graph $\Gamma(P)$ is complete, then the corresponding graph $\Gamma E(P)$ is also complete; in fact, $\Gamma_E(P) \cong \Gamma(P)$. Also, it follows from the definition of $\Gamma(P)$ that if $\Gamma(P)$ is a complete r-partite graph, $r \geq 2$, then $\Gamma_E(P)$ is a complete graph with r vertices. Thus, for every $n \geq 2$, the complete graph K_n can be realized as $\Gamma(P)$ for some poset P; for example, we may consider the poset $\{\emptyset, \{1\}, \{2\}, \ldots, \{n\}\}$. This is not the case for rings (see [12, Proposition 1.5]).

POSETS WITH AN ASCENDING CHAIN CONDITION

In this section, imposing certain restrictions on a given poset, we study some properties of its reduced zero-divisor graph in terms of the annihilator prime ideals.

Let P be a poset. We say that P is a poset with ACC for annihilators if the ascending chain condition holds for its annihilator ideals, that is, if there is no infinite strictly ascending chain in the set $\mathfrak{A} := \{\text{ann}(x) \mid x \in P^{\times}\}$ under set inclusion. Equivalently, P is a poset with ACC for annihilators if and only if every nonempty subset of $\mathfrak{A}$ has a maximal element. Thus, if P is a poset with ACC for annihilators, then $\mathfrak{A}$ has a maximal element and every element of $\mathfrak{A}$ is contained in a maximal element of $\mathfrak{A}$. We denote the set of all maximal elements of $\mathfrak{A}$ by $\text{Max}(\mathfrak{A})$.

If P is a poset such that $(P) < \infty$, then from [6, Lemma 2.4] it follows that P is a poset with ACC for annihilators. In particular, if P is a poset such that $\deg(x) < \infty$ for all $x \in V(\Gamma(P))$, then P is a poset with ACC for annihilators; noting that $\Gamma(P)$ has no infinite clique and so, by [6, Lemma 2.10], we have $\omega(P) < \infty$. On the other hand, consider the poset

$$P = \{\emptyset\} \cup \{\{n\} \mid n \in \mathbb{N}\} \cup \{\{m, m+1, \ldots\} \mid m \in \mathbb{N},\ m \neq 1\} \quad (2)$$

under set inclusion, where $\mathbb{N}$ denotes the set of all positive integers. It is easy to see that there is an infinite strictly ascending chain of annihilator ideals of P given by

$$\text{ann}(\{2,3,\ldots\}) \subsetneq \text{ann}(\{3,4,\ldots\}) \subsetneq \ldots, \quad (3)$$

which means that P is a poset without ACC for annihilators.

Remark 8. If P is a poset with ACC for annihilators, then the clique number of $\Gamma(P)$ need not be finite; that is, $\Gamma(P)$ may contain an infinite clique; for example, consider the poset $P = \{\emptyset\} \cup \{\{n\} \mid n \in \mathbb{N}\}$ under set inclusion. This is contrary to what has been asserted in Proposition 2.6 of [10]. In fact, a careful look at the proof of [10, Proposition 2.6] reveals that while proving "(2) ⇒ (3)" the authors mistakenly assumed the validity of the first statement of the said proposition.

Our first result concerning the set of all annihilator prime ideals of a poset is given as follows.

Proposition 9. *Let P be a poset. Then,*

$$\text{Ann}(P) = \text{Max}(\mathfrak{A}). \quad (4)$$

In particular, if P is a poset with ACC *for annihilators, then* $\text{Ann}(P) \neq \emptyset$.

Proof. By [6, Lemma 2.2], we have $\text{Max}(\mathfrak{A}) \subseteq \text{Ann}(P)$. Conversely, suppose that $\text{ann}(x) \in \text{Ann}(P) \setminus \text{Max}(\mathfrak{A})$. Then there exists $\text{ann}(y) \in \mathfrak{A}$ such that $\text{ann}(x) \subsetneq \text{ann}(y)$. Choose $z \in \text{ann}(y)\setminus\text{ann}(x)$. Since $(z, y) = \{0\} \subseteq \text{ann}(x)$ and $\text{ann}(x)$ is a prime ideal, it follows that $y \in \text{ann}(x) \subset \text{ann}(y)$ which is absurd. Hence, we have $\text{Ann}(P) = \text{Max}(\mathfrak{A})$. The particular case follows from the fact that if P is a poset with ACC for annihilators, then $\text{Max}(\mathfrak{A}) \neq \emptyset$.

Given a poset P, consider the set $\mathfrak{B} := \{\text{ann}(x) \mid x \in Z(P)^{\times}\}$. Clearly, $\emptyset \neq \mathfrak{B} \subseteq \mathfrak{A}$; in fact, $\mathfrak{B} = \mathfrak{A} \setminus \{0\}$. Since $(P)^{\times} \neq \emptyset$, $\{0\}$ is not a prime ideal of P, and so, it follows that $\text{Ann}(P) \subseteq \mathfrak{B}$. Note that there is a natural bijective map from $\mathfrak{B}$ to the vertex set of $\Gamma(P)$ given by $\text{ann}(x) \mapsto [x]$. As such, we may treat $\mathfrak{B}$ as the vertex set of $\Gamma(P)$. In view of this, with a slight abuse of terminology, we sometimes refer to $[x] \in (\Gamma_E(P))$ as an annihilator ideal (resp., an annihilator prime ideal) if we have $\text{ann}(x) \in \mathfrak{B}$ (resp., $\text{ann}(x) \in \text{Ann}(P)$). All the forthcoming results of this section are under this identification.

The following lemma plays a crucial role in this section.

Lemma 10. *Let P be a poset. Then the following assertions hold.*

- Given $\text{ann}(x), \text{ann}(y) \in \mathfrak{B}$, one has $\text{ann}(x) \subsetneq \text{ann}(y)$ if and only if $\text{nbd}([x]) \subsetneq \text{nbd}([y])$ in $\Gamma_E(P)$.
- Given $\text{ann}(x) \in \mathfrak{B}$ and $\text{ann}(z) \in \text{Ann}(P)$, one has $\text{ann}(x) \not\subseteq \text{ann}(z)$ if and only if $L(x, z) = \{0\}$; equivalently, one has $\text{nbd}([x]) \subseteq \text{nbd}([z])$ if and only if the vertices $[x]$ and $[z]$ are not adjacent in $\Gamma_E(P)$.
- Given $\text{ann}(x), \text{ann}(y) \in \mathfrak{B}$, if $\text{ann}(x) \cup \text{ann}(y) \subseteq \text{ann}(z)$ for some $\text{ann}(z) \in \text{Ann}(P)$, then the vertices$[x]$ and $[y]$ are not adjacent in $\Gamma_E(P)$; that is, $L(x, y) \neq \{0\}$. The converse is also true if P is a poset with ACC for annihilators.
- If P is a poset with ACC for annihilators, then for each $\text{ann}(x) \in \mathfrak{B}$ there exists $\text{ann}(z) \in \text{Ann}(P)$ such that $\text{ann}(x) \not\subseteq \text{ann}(z)$.
- If $\text{ann}(x) \in \mathfrak{B} \setminus\text{Ann}(P)$, then there exist $u, V \notin \text{ann}(x)$ such that $L(u, V) = \{0\}$.

Proof.

- In view of Proposition 4 and the definition of $\Gamma(P)$, it is enough to note that, given $u, x \in Z(P)^{\times}$, one has $u \in \text{ann}(x)$ if and only if $[u] \in \text{nbd}([x])$ in $\Gamma_E(P)$.
- If $\text{ann}(x) \not\subseteq \text{ann}(z)$, then, choosing $y \in \text{ann}(x) \setminus \text{ann}(z)$, we have $L(x, y) = \{0\} \subseteq \text{ann}(z)$, and so $x \in \text{ann}(z)$, since $\text{ann}(z)$is a prime ideal. Conversely, if $(x, z) = \{0\}$, then $z \in \text{ann}(x)$, and so $\text{ann}(x) \not\subseteq \text{ann}(z)$, since $z \notin \text{ann}(z)$. The equivalent assertion follows from part (a).
- If $\text{ann}(x) \cup \text{ann}(y) \subseteq \text{ann}(z)$ for some $\text{ann}(z) \in \text{Ann}(P)$, then, by part (b), we have $x, y \notin \text{ann}(z)$, which implies that $L(x, y) \neq \{0\}$, since $\text{ann}(z)$ is a prime ideal. Conversely, if $L(x, y) \neq \{0\}$, then, choosing $w \in L(x, y) \setminus \{0\}$, we have $\text{ann}(x) \cup \text{ann}(y) \subseteq \text{ann}(w) \subseteq \text{ann}(z)$ for some $\text{ann}(z) \in \text{Ann}(P)$.
- Let $y \in \text{ann}(x) \setminus \{0\}$. Choose $\text{ann}(z) \in \text{Ann}(P)$ such that $\text{ann}(y) \subseteq \text{ann}(z)$. Since $x \in \text{ann}(y)$, we have $x \in \text{ann}(z)$, or, equivalently, $z \in \text{ann}(x)$. Thus $\text{ann}(x) \not\subseteq \text{ann}(z)$, since $z \notin \text{ann}(z)$.
- If $\text{ann}(x) \in \mathfrak{B} \setminus \text{Ann}(P)$, then, by Proposition 9, there exists $\text{ann}(u) \in \mathfrak{A}$ such that $\text{ann}(x) \subsetneq \text{ann}(u)$, and so we may choose $V \in \text{ann}(u) \setminus \text{ann}(x)$ to complete the proof.

Proposition 11. *Let P be a poset. Then, the following assertions hold.*

- $\text{Ann}(P)$ *is a clique of* $\Gamma_E(P)$.

- *Given* $[z] \in \mathfrak{B}$, *one has* $[z] \in \text{Ann}(P)$ *if and only if no two vertices in the set* $V(\Gamma_E(P))\backslash\text{nbd}([z])$ *are adjacent.*
- *If P is a poset with ACC for annihilators, then every vertex in* $\Gamma(P)$ *is adjacent to an annihilator prime ideal; consequently,* $|\text{Ann}(P)| \geq 2$.

Proof. In view of Fact 1, the results follow from Lemma 10. More precisely, the first part follows from part (b) using maximality of the annihilator prime ideals, the second part from parts (b), (c), and (e), and the third part from parts (b) and (d) of Lemma 10. The first part also follows directly from [6, Lemma 2.3].

If P is a poset with $(P) < \infty$, then, in view of [6, Lemmas 2.6], it follows from Proposition 9 that $|\text{Ann}(P)| < \infty$. In this context, we have a stronger result in the following form.

Proposition 12. *Let P be a poset with ACC for annihilators. Then,*

$$|\text{Ann}\,(P)| = \omega\,(P). \tag{5}$$

In particular, $|\text{Ann}(P)| \geq 3$ *if and only if* $|V(\Gamma_E(P))| \geq 3$.

Proof. By Proposition 11(a), we have $|\text{Ann}(P)| \leq \omega(\Gamma_E(P)) = \omega(P)$. Conversely, suppose that $\{x_1, x_2, \ldots, _k\}$ is a clique of $\Gamma(P)$. For each $i \in \{1, 2, \ldots, k\}$, choose $\text{ann}(z_i) \in \text{Max}(\mathfrak{A}) = \text{Ann}(P)$ such that $\text{ann}(x_i) \subseteq \text{ann}(z_i)$. By Lemma 10(c), the annihilator prime ideals $\text{ann}(z_1), \text{ann}(z_2), \ldots, \text{ann}(z_k)$ are all pairwise distinct. It follows that $|\text{Ann}(P)|$ is an upper bound for the sizes of all the cliques of $\Gamma(P)$, and hence, $|\text{Ann}(P)| \geq \omega(P)$. This proves the first part. The particular case follows from Proposition 2.

It follows immediately from Proposition 11(a) and Proposition 12 that, given a poset P with ACC for annihilators, $\text{Ann}(P)$ is a clique of maximal size in $\Gamma_E(P)$.

Remark 13. *Let P be a poset with ACC for annihilators. Then, as a trivial consequence of Proposition* 12, *we have* $|V(\Gamma_E(P))| \geq 3$ *if and only if no annihilator prime ideal in* $\Gamma_E(P)$ *is an end vertex, and so, by Proposition* 11(c), *every vertex in* $\Gamma_E(P)$ *that is adjacent to an end vertex is an annihilator prime ideal (compare with* [12, *Proposition* 3.2 *and Corollary* 3.3]).

Given a poset P, if the degree of some annihilator prime ideal in $\Gamma(P)$ is infinity, then obviously $|V(\Gamma_E(P))| = \infty$. We have, however, a stronger converse given by the following result which may be compared and contrasted with [12, Proposition 2.2].

Proposition 14. *Let P be a poset. If the vertex set of* $\Gamma(P)$ *is infinite, then the degree of each annihilator prime ideal in* $\Gamma_E(P)$ *is infinity.*

Proof. Suppose that $|(\Gamma_E(P))| = \infty$. In view of Proposition 11(a), we may assume that $|\text{Ann}(P)| < \infty$. In that case the set $\mathfrak{B} \setminus \text{Ann}(P)$ is infinite; that is, there are infinitely many vertices in $\Gamma_E(P)$ which are not annihilator prime ideals. Let $\text{ann}(z) \in \text{Ann}(P)$ such that $\deg([z]) < \infty$. Then there exists an infinite set $S \subseteq \mathfrak{B} \setminus \text{Ann}(P)$ such that no member of S is adjacent to $[z]$ in $\Gamma_E(P)$. Therefore, by Lemma 10(b), we have $\text{nbd}([x]) \subseteq \text{nbd}([z])$ for all $[x] \in S$. Hence, using Proposition 4, it follows that the neighborhood $\text{nbd}([z])$ is an infinite set. This contradiction completes the proof.

Given a poset P, if there is a vertex $[z] \in V(\Gamma_E(P))$ such that $\deg([z]) > \deg([x])$ for all $[x] \in V(\Gamma_E(P)) \setminus \{[z]\}$, then it follows from Lemma 10(a) that $[z]$ is a maximal element of $\mathfrak{A}$, that is, an annihilator prime ideal of P (compare with [12, Proposition 3.1]). In this context we have a more general result given as follows (compare with [12, Proposition 3.6]).

Proposition 15. *Let P be a poset such that* $|(\Gamma_E(P))| < \infty$. *Then every vertex of maximal degree in* $\Gamma(P)$ *is a maximal element of* $\mathfrak{A}$, *that is, an annihilator prime ideal of P.*

Proof. If a vertex of maximal degree in $\Gamma(P)$ is not a maximal element of $\mathfrak{A}$, then, using Lemma 10(a) and the condition that $|V(\Gamma_E(P))| < \infty$, we have a contradiction to the maximality of its degree. Hence the result follows.

Note that the converse of the above proposition is false; that is, an annihilator prime ideal need not always be of maximal degree. For example, consider the poset $\{\emptyset, \{1\}, \{2\}, \{3\}, \{4\}, \{5\}, \{6\}, \{1, 2\}, \{3, 4\}, \{3, 5\}, \{3, 6\}\}$ under set inclusion, in which $\text{ann}(\{3\})$is a prime ideal but $\text{ann}(\{1, 2\})$is not; however, in the corresponding reduced zero-divisor graph, the degree of $\text{ann}(\{3\})$ is 6 and that of $\text{ann}(\{1, 2\})$ is 7.

As an immediate consequence of Proposition 15, we have the following result.

Corollary 16. *Let P be a poset such that* $V|(\Gamma_E(P))| < \infty$.*Then* $\Gamma_E(P)$ *is a regular graph if and only if it is a complete graph.*

Proof. In a regular graph, every vertex is of maximal degree. Therefore, if $\Gamma(P)$ is a regular graph, then, by Proposition 15, $V(\Gamma_E(P))$ coincides with $\text{Ann}(P)$. Thus, by Proposition 11(a), $\Gamma(P)$ is a complete graph. The converse is trivial.

In the same context, it may be worthwhile to mention the following result.

Proposition 17. *Let P be a poset. If* $\Gamma(P)$ *is an r-regular graph, then* $\Gamma_E(P)$ *is a complete graph.*

Proof. In view of Proposition 11(a), it is sufficient to show that $\text{Ann}(P) = V(\Gamma_E(P))$. On the contrary, suppose that there exists a vertex $\text{ann}(x) \in V(\Gamma_E(P)) \setminus \text{Ann}(P)$. Since the degree of each vertex in $\Gamma(P)$ is finite, P is a poset with ACC for annihilators. Therefore, there exists $\text{ann}(z) \in \text{Ann}(P)$ such that $\text{ann}(x) \subsetneq \text{ann}(z)$, whence $\deg(x) + 1 \leq \deg(z)$. This contradicts the fact that $\Gamma(P)$ is an r-regular graph, and the proposition is proved.

Proposition 18. *Let P be a poset with ACC for annihilators. If* $|\text{Ann}(P)| < \infty$, *then* $|V(\Gamma_E(P))| < \infty$; *in fact,* $|V(\Gamma_E(P))| \leq 2^{|\text{Ann}(P)|} - 2$.

Proof. Consider the set $\mathfrak{S}$ of all subsets of $\text{Ann}(P)$. Then $|\mathfrak{S}| = 2^{|\text{Ann}(P)|} < \infty$. Given $\text{ann}(x) \in \mathfrak{B} = V(\Gamma_E(P))$, let S_x denote the largest subset of $\text{Ann}(P)$ such that $\text{ann}(x) \subseteq \text{ann}(z)$ for all $\text{ann}(z) \in S_x$; in other words, $S_x = \{\text{ann}(z) \in \text{Ann}(P) \mid \text{ann}(x) \subseteq \text{ann}(z)\}$. Note that each member of $\mathfrak{B}$ is contained in some member of $\text{Ann}(P)$ but no member of $\mathfrak{B}$ is contained in every member of $\text{Ann}(P)$. Therefore, we have a well-defined map : $V(\Gamma_E(P)) \to \mathfrak{S}$ given by $\text{ann}(x) \mapsto S_x$ such that $\emptyset, \text{Ann}(P) \notin \text{Im}(\psi)$. It is now enough to show that ψ is a one-one map. So, let $\text{ann}(x), \text{ann}(y) \in \mathfrak{B}$ such that $S_x = S_y$. Let $w \in \text{ann}(x) \setminus \{0\}$. Then, by Lemma 10(c) and the definition of S_x, we have $\text{ann}(w) \not\subseteq \text{ann}(z)$ for each $\text{ann}(z) \in S_x$. It follows that $\text{ann}(w) \cup \text{ann}(y) \not\subseteq \text{ann}(z)$for each $\text{ann}(z) \in S_x = S_y$. Also, by the maximality of S_y, we have $\text{ann}(w) \cup \text{ann}(y) \not\subseteq \text{ann}(z)$ for each $\text{ann}(z) \in \text{Ann}(P) \setminus S_y$. Therefore, using Lemma 10(c) once again, we have $w \in \text{ann}(y)$. Thus, $\text{ann}(x) \subseteq \text{ann}(y)$. Similarly, we have $\text{ann}(y) \subseteq$

ann(x), and hence, $[x] = [y]$. This completes the proof.

It may noted here that the bound mentioned in the above proposition is the best possible. For example, consider a finite set $X = \{1, 2, \ldots, n\}$ and define P to be the set of all subsets of X partially ordered under set inclusion with least element ϕ. It is then easy to see that the vertex set of $\Gamma(P)$ consists precisely of nontrivial proper subsets of X, $\mathrm{Ann}(P) = \{\{1\}, \{2\}, \ldots, \{n\}\}$, and $\Gamma_E(P) \cong \Gamma(P)$.

As an immediate consequence of Proposition 18, we have the following result.

Corollary 19. *Let P be a poset. Then* $|(\Gamma_E(P))| < \infty$ *if and only if* $\omega(P) < \infty$.

Proof. If $(P) < \infty$, then, by [6, Lemma 2.4], P is a poset with ACC for annihilators, and so it follows from Propositions 12 and 18 that $V|(\Gamma_E(P))| < \infty$. The converse is trivial, since $(P) = \omega(\Gamma_E(P))$.

Note that if P is a poset such that $(x] \cap \mathrm{Min}(P^{\times}) = \emptyset$ for all $x \in Z(P)^{\times}$, then P is not necessarily a poset with ACC for annihilators. For example, one may look at the same poset that has been considered in the para preceding Proposition 9. However, we have the following small result concerning such posets.

Proposition 20. *Let P be a poset such that* $(x] \cap \mathrm{Min}(P^{\times}) \neq \emptyset$ *for all* $x \in Z(P)^{\times}$. *Then* $\mathrm{Ann}(P) = \{\mathrm{ann}(z) \mid z \in \mathrm{Min}(P^{\times})\}$.

Proof. Let $z \in \mathrm{Min}(P^{\times})$. Suppose that $\mathrm{ann}(z) \subseteq \mathrm{ann}(x)$, where $\mathrm{ann}(x) \in \mathfrak{A}$. Clearly, $x \notin \mathrm{ann}(z)$, which means that $z \leq x$. But then $\mathrm{ann}(x) \subseteq \mathrm{ann}(z)$, and so it follows that $\mathrm{ann}(z) \in \mathrm{Max}(\mathfrak{A}) = \mathrm{Ann}(P)$. Conversely, suppose that $\mathrm{ann}(x) \in \mathrm{Ann}(P)$. Choose $z \in (x] \cap \mathrm{Min}(P^{\times})$. Then, $\mathrm{ann}(x) \subseteq \mathrm{ann}(z)$, and so it follows from the maximality of $\mathrm{ann}(x)$ in $\mathfrak{A}$ that $\mathrm{ann}(x) = \mathrm{ann}(z)$. This completes the proof

We conclude our discussion with the following example.

Example 21. Consider a partially ordered set

$$P = \{0\} \cup A \cup \left(\bigcup_{k \in \mathbb{N}} B_k \right),$$

where A is any set (finite or infinite), $B_k = \{(1/n_1, 1/n_2, \ldots, 1/n_k) | n_i \in \mathbb{N}$ for $1 \leq i \leq k\}$, and the partial order is defined as follows:

$$a, \left(\frac{1}{n_1}, \frac{1}{n_2}, \ldots, \frac{1}{n_k}\right) > 0,$$

$$\left(\frac{1}{n_1}, \frac{1}{n_2}, \ldots, \frac{1}{n_k}\right) > \left(\frac{1}{n_1}, \frac{1}{n_2}, \ldots, \frac{1}{n_k}, \frac{1}{n_{k+1}}, \ldots, \frac{1}{n_{k+t}}\right),$$

$$\left(\frac{1}{n_1}, \frac{1}{n_2}, \ldots, \frac{1}{n_{k-1}}, \frac{1}{n_k}\right) > \left(\frac{1}{n_1}, \frac{1}{n_2}, \ldots, \frac{1}{n_{k-1}}, \frac{1}{n_k + 1}\right)$$

for all $a \in A$ and for all $k, t, n_i \in \mathbb{N}$ with $1 \leq i \leq k$. It is not difficult to see that $\mathrm{Ann}(P) = \{\mathrm{ann}(a) \mid a \in A\}$, the set $\{(1/n, 1/n) \mid n \in \mathbb{N}\}$ is an infinite clique, and $\mathrm{ann}((1)) \subsetneq \mathrm{ann}((1/2)) \subsetneq \mathrm{ann}((1/3)) \subsetneq \cdots$ is an infinite strictly ascending chain of annihilator ideals in P. Thus, a poset may have finitely many annihilator prime ideals but fail to be a poset with ACC for annihilators. In this example we also have $A = \mathrm{Min}(P^{\times})$ but $(x] \cap \mathrm{Min}(P^{\times}) = \emptyset$ for all $x \in Z(P)^{\times} \setminus \mathrm{Min}(P^{\times})$, showing that the converse of Proposition 20 is far from being true.

ACKNOWLEDGMENTS

The first author wishes to express his thanks to M. R. Pournaki of Sharif University of Technology and M. Alizadeh of University of Tehran, both from Iran, for their encouragement and useful suggestions. The second author is grateful to Council of Scientific and Industrial Research (India) for its financial assistance (File no. 09/347(0209)/2012-EMR-I).

REFERENCES

1. I. Beck, "Coloring of commutative rings," Journal of Algebra, vol. 116, no. 1, pp. 208–226, 1988.
2. D. D. Anderson and M. Naseer, "Beck's coloring of a commutative ring," Journal of Algebra, vol. 159, no. 2, pp. 500–514, 1993.
3. D. F. Anderson and P. S. Livingston, "The zero-divisor graph of a commutative ring," Journal of Algebra, vol. 217, no. 2, pp. 434–447, 1999.
4. S. K. Nimbhokar, M. P. Wasadikar, and L. DeMeyer, "Coloring of meet-semilattices," Ars Combinatoria, vol. 84, pp. 97–104, 2007.
5. R. Halaš and H. Langer, "The zerodivisor graph of a qoset," Order, vol. 27, no. 3, pp. 343–351, 2010.
6. R. Halaš and M. Jukl, "On Beck's coloring of posets," Discrete Mathematics, vol. 309, no. 13, pp. 4584–4589, 2009.
7. Z. Xue and S. Liu, "Zero-divisor graphs of partially ordered sets," Applied Mathematics Letters, vol. 23, no. 4, pp. 449–452, 2010.
8. V. Joshi, "Zero divisor graph of a poset with respect to an ideal," Order, vol. 29, no. 3, pp. 499–506, 2012.
9. M. Alizadeh, A. K. Das, H. R. Maimani, M. R. Pournaki, and S. Yassemi, "On the diameter and girth of zero-divisor graphs of posets," Discrete Applied Mathematics, vol. 160, no. 9, pp. 1319–1324, 2012.
10. D. Lu and T. Wu, "The zero-divisor graphs of posets and an application to semigroups," Graphs and Combinatorics, vol. 26, no. 6, pp. 793–804, 2010.
11. S. B. Mulay, "Cycles and symmetries of zero-divisors," Communications in Algebra, vol. 30, no. 7, pp. 3533–3558, 2002. of zero divisors,"Communications in Algebra, vol. 39, no. 7, pp. 2338–2348, 2011.
12. G. Chartrand and O. R. Oellermann, Applied and Algorithmic Graph Theory, International Series in Pure and Applied Mathematics, McGraw-Hill, New York, NY, USA, 1993.
13. B. A. Davey and H. A. Priestley, Introduction to Lattices and Order, Cambridge University Press, New York, NY, USA, 2nd edition, 2002.
14. R. Halaš, "Annihilators and ideals in ordered sets," Czechoslovak Mathematical Journal, vol. 45(120), no. 1, pp. 127–134, 1995.
15. R. Halaš, "Relative polars in ordered sets," Czechoslovak Mathematical Journal, vol. 50, no. 2, pp. 415–429, 2000.

CHAPTER 18 RADIO NUMBERS OF CERTAIN m-DISTANT TREES

Srinivasa Rao Kola[1] and Pratima Panigrahi[2]

[1]Department of Mathematical and Computational Sciences, National Institute of Technology Karnataka, Karnataka 575025, India

[2]Department of Mathematics, Indian Institute of Technology Kharagpur, Kharagpur 721302, India

ABSTRACT

Radio coloring of a graph G with diameter d is an assignment f of positive integers to the vertices of G such that $|(u) - f(V)| \geq 1 + d - d(u, V)$, where u and V are any two distinct vertices of G and $d(u, V)$ is the distance between u and V. The number max $\{(u) : u \in V(G)\}$ is called the span of f. The minimum of spans over all radio colorings of G is called radio number of G, denoted by (G). An m-distant tree T is a tree in which there is a path P of maximum length such that every vertex in $(T) \setminus (P)$ is at the most distance m from P. This path P is called a central path. For every tree T, there is an integer m such that T is a m-distant tree. In this paper, we determine the radio number of some m-distant trees for any positive integer $m \geq 2$, and as a consequence of it, we find the radio number of a class of 1-distant trees (or caterpillars).

INTRODUCTION

The channel assignment problem is the problem of assigning frequencies to transmitters in some optimal manner and with no interferences; see Hale [1]. Chartrand et al. [2] introduced radio k-colorings of graphs which is a variation of Hale's channel assignment problem, in which one seeks to assign positive integers to the vertices of a graph G subject to certain constraints involving the distance between the vertices. For any simple connected graph G with diameter d and a positive integer k, $1 \leq k \leq d$, specifically, a radio k-coloring of G is an assignment f of positive integers to the vertices of G such that $|f(u) - f(V)| \geq 1 + k - d(u, V)$, where u and V are any two distinct vertices of G and $d(u, V)$ is the distance between u and V. The maximum color (positive integer) assigned by f to some vertex of G is called the span of f, denoted by $r(f)$. The minimum of spans of all possible radio k-colorings of$G$is called the radio k-chromatic number of G, denoted by $r(G)$. A radio k-coloring with span $r(G)$ is called minimal radio k-coloring of G. Radio k-colorings have been studied by many authors; see [3–9].

Although the positive integer k can have value in-between 1 and d, the case k=d has become a special interest for many authors. Radio d-coloring is simply called radio coloring and radio d-chromatic number is radio number. Here we concentrate on radio number of trees. Kchikech et al. [4] have found the exact value of the radio k-chromatic number of stars $K_{1,n}$ as $n(k - 1) + 2$ and have also given an upper bound for radio k-chromatic number, $rc_k(T)$, $k \geq 2$, of an arbitrary non-star-tree T on n vertices as$(n - 1)(k - 1)$. Liu [5] has given a lower bound for the radio number $rn(T)$ of an n-vertex tree with diameter d as $(n - 1)(d + 1) + 1 - 2w(T)$, where $w(T)$ is the weight of T defined as $w(T) = \min_{u \in V(T)}\{\sum_{V \in V(T)} d(u, V)\}$. She also has characterized the trees achieving this bound. In

Citation: Srinivasa Rao Kola and Pratima Panigrahi, "Radio Numbers of Certain m-Distant Trees," Journal of Discrete Mathematics, vol. 2014, Article ID 486354, 6 pages, 2014. doi:10.1155/2014/486354

the same paper, Liu considered spiders denoted by $Sl1,l2,l3,\ldots,lm$, which are trees having a vertex V of degree $m \geq 3$, and m number of paths of length $l1$, $l2,\ldots,lm$ whose one end vertex is V and other ends are pendant vertices. She has given a lower bound for the radio number of $S_{l_1,l_2,l_3,\ldots,l_m}$ as $\sum_{i=1}^{m} l_i(l_1 + l_2 - l_i) + \lceil (l_1 - l_2)/2 \rceil \lfloor (l_1 - l_2)/2 \rfloor + 1$, where $l_1 \geq l_2 \geq \cdots \geq l_m$, and has also characterized the spiders achieving this bound. Li et al. [10] have determined the radio number of complete m-ary trees ($m \geq 3$) with height k (≥ 2), denoted by T_k, as $(m^{k+2} + m^{k+1} - 2km^2 + (2k-3)m + 1)/(m-1)^2$.

In this paper, we determine the radio number of some m-distant trees for any positive integer $m \geq 2$, and as a consequence of it, we find the radio number of a class of 1- distant trees (or caterpillars)..

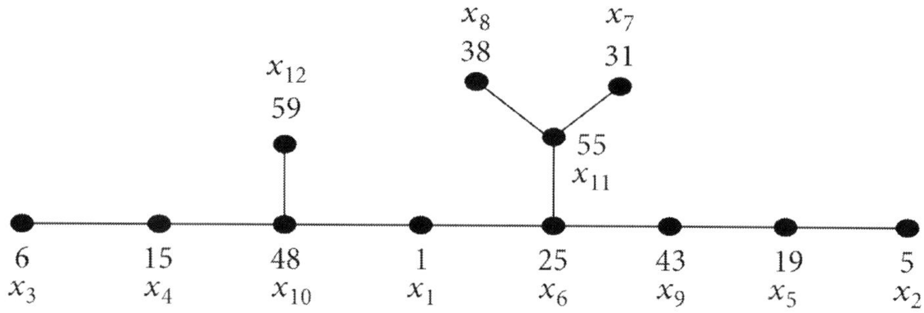

Figure 1: A radio coloring of a tree of order 12 and diameter 7

RADIO NUMBERS OF SOME m-DISTANT TREES

Recall that an m-distant tree T is a tree in which there is a path P of maximum length such that every vertex in $(T)\backslash(P)$ is at the most distance m from P. This path P is called a central path. Since we consider the path P as a path of maximum length, the end vertices of P are of degree one vertices in the m-distant tree; that is, if P: $a_1a_2 \cdots a_k$ is a central path of T, then $deg_T(a_1) = deg_T(a_k)=1$. For every tree T, there is an integer m such that T is a m-distant tree. Usually 1-distant trees are known as caterpillars

Before we present the main result of the paper, we give a definition and a lemma below which will be used in the sequel. From the definition of a radio coloring$f$, one observes that for any two vertices u and V, the quantity $|(u) - f(\mathrm{V})| - \{1 + d - d(u, \mathrm{V})\}$ is an excess for f to achieve the minimum span. In the definition, we give notation for these excesses corresponding to pair of vertices. In the lemma, we show that to get an optimal radio k-coloring, one has to minimize this sum of excesses.

Definition 1*. For any radio coloring f of a simple connected graph G on n vertices and an ordering $x_1, x_2,\ldots,x_n$ of vertices of G with $f(x_i) \leq f(x_{i+1})$, $1 \leq i \leq n-1$, we define ϵ_i (or ϵ_i^f to specify the coloring f) = $\{f(x_i) - f(x_{i-1})\} - \{1 + d - d(x_i, x_{i-1})\}$, $2 \leq i \leq n$. It is clear from the definition of radio coloring that $\epsilon_i \geq 0$, for all i. With respect to the ordering of vertices of G induced by f, we denote $d(f) = \sum_{i=2}^{n} d(x_i, x_{i-1})$. In other words, every radio coloring f is associated with a unique positive integer (f) called distance sum of f.*

Example 2*. In this example, we explain Definition 1.*

In Figure 1, a radio coloring f of a tree T is given. The labels $x_1, x_2, x_3,\ldots,_{12}$ are an ordering of vertices of T with $f(x_i) \leq f(x_{i+1})$, $1 \leq i \leq 11$. Here $\epsilon_2 = \{f(x_2) - f(x_1)\} - \{1 + 7 - d(x_1, x_2)\} = (5-1) - (1+7-4) = 0$, $\epsilon_3 = 0$, $\epsilon_4 = 2$, $\epsilon_5 = 1$, $\epsilon_6 = 0$, $\epsilon_7 = 0$, $\epsilon_8 = 1$, $\epsilon_9 = 0$, $\epsilon_{10} = 0$, $\epsilon_{11} = 2$, $\epsilon_{12} = 0$, and $d(f) = \sum_{i=2}^{12} d(x_i, x_{i-1}) = d(x_2, x_1) + d(x_3, x_2) + d(x_4, x_3) + d(x_5, x_4) + d(x_6, x_5) + d(x_7, x_6) + d(x_8, x_7) + d(x_9, x_8) + d(x_{10}, x_9) + d(x_{11}, x_{10}) + d(x_{12}, x_{11}) = 4+7+1+5+2+2+2+3+3+3+4 = 36.$

The following lemma gives the span of a radio coloring of a graph of order n in terms of n, d, distance sum, and ϵ's sum.

Lemma 3*. For any radio coloring f of G, the span of f* $r(f) = f(x_n) = (n-1)(1+d\ \sum_{i=2}^{n} d(x_i, x_{i-1}) + \sum_{i=2}^{n} \epsilon_i^f + 1$, *where x_i's are arranged as in Definition 1.*

Proof. Consider $f(x_n) - f(x_1) = \sum_{i=2}^{n}[f(x_i) - f(x_{i-1})] = \sum_{i=2}^{n}[1+d-d(x_i, x_{i-1})+\epsilon_i^f] = (n-1)(1+d) - \sum_{i=2}^{n} d(x_i, x_{i-1}) + \sum_{i=2}^{n} \epsilon_i^f$.

Since $(x_1)=1$, we get $f(x_n) = (n-1)(1+d) - \sum_{i=2}^{n} d(x_i, x_{i-1}) + \sum_{i=2}^{n} \epsilon_i^f + 1$.

Lemma 3 says that to obtain a minimal radio coloring of a graph, one should maximize (f) and minimize $\sum_{i=2}^{n} \epsilon_i^f$ over all possible radio colorings of the graph. Since this fact is the basic concept to construct a minimal radio coloring, we express it as the theorem below.

Theorem 4*. If g is a radio coloring of G such that* $\sum_{i=2}^{n} \epsilon_i^g = 0$ *and* $(g) = \max\{d(f)$: *f is a radio coloring* of G$\}$, *then g is a minimal radio coloring of G.*

Proof. For any radio coloring f of G, Lemma 3 gives that $r(f) = (n-1)(1+d) - d(f) + \sum_{i=2}^{n} \epsilon_i^f$. Then

$rc_d(G)$

$$= \min\{rc_d(f) : f \text{ is a radio coloring of } G\}$$

$$= \min\left\{(n-1)(1+d) - d(f) + \sum_{i=2}^{n} \epsilon_i^f : f \text{ is a radio coloring of } G\right\}$$

$$= (n-1)(1+d) - \max_f d(f) + \min_f \sum_{i=2}^{n} \epsilon_i^f$$

$$= (n-1)(1+d) - d(g)$$

$$\left(\text{since } \epsilon_i,\ i = 2,3,\ldots,n \text{ is nonnegative, } \sum_{i=2}^{n} \epsilon_i^g = 0\right)$$

$$= rc_d(g). \tag{1}$$

Now, we determine the radio number of an m-distant tree T with $di(T) = 2p - 1$, $p \geq 2$, $m \leq p - \sqrt{p-1}$, and the degrees of the vertices on the central path satisfy certain conditions (given in the theorem below).

Theorem 5*. Let T be an m-distant tree of order n with a central path P:* $a_1 a_2 \cdots a_{2p-1} a_{2p}$, *and satisfy*

- $m \leq p - \sqrt{p-1}$;
- $deg(a_i)=2$, for $i = 2, 3, \ldots, m, 2p - m + 1, 2p - m + 2, \ldots, 2p$;
- $deg(a_j) = deg(a_{j+p-m}) = s_j + 2$, $s_j \geq 0$, $j = m + 1, m + 2, \ldots, p$;
- *for every* a_l, $l = m + 1, m + 2, \ldots, 2p - m$, *the number of vertices at distance i and lying on a branch incident on* a_l, $2 \leq i \leq m$, *is a constant say* t_i ($t_i \geq 0$).

Then

$$rn(T) = 2(p-m)\left[(p+m)\sum_{i=2}^{m} t_i - \sum_{i=2}^{m} 2it_i\right] + \left[2(p+m) - 4\right]\sum_{i=m+1}^{p} s_i + 2p(p-1) + 3.$$

Proof. The idea is to define a radio coloring f of T and show that f is minimal by Theorem 4. We first give an algorithm to order the vertices of T.

Algorithm 6

Step I. Step I. We make an ordering $x_1, x_2, \ldots, x_{2p}$ of the vertices on the central path as $a_p, a_{2p}, a_{p-1}, a_{2p-1}, a_{p-2}, a_{2p-2}, \ldots, a_1, a_{p+1}$, that is, $x_1 = a_p$, $x_2 = a_{2p}, \ldots, x_{2p} = a_{p+1}$.

Step II. Let $x_{l_1}, x_{l_2}, \ldots, x_{l_{2p-2m}}$ be equal to the vertices $a_p, a_{2p-m}, a_{p-1}, a_{2p-(m+1)}, \ldots, a_{m+1}, a_{p+1}$, respectively. Let $B = \left(b_1^{(i)}, b_2^{(i)}, \ldots, b_{2p-2m}^{(i)}\right)$ be an ordered tuple of vertices in $T \backslash P$ such that $b_j^{(i)}$ is at distance i from P and lies on a branch incident on x_{l_j}, $i = 2, 3, \ldots, m$, and $j = 1, 2, \ldots, 2p - 2m$. So for any i, there are ti disjoint such tuples, $i = 2, 3, \ldots, m$. Consider the sequence S: $x_{2p+1}, x_{2p+2}, \ldots$, where $r = 2p + 2(p-m)\sum_{i=2}^{m} t_i$.

Step III. We take $i = m$. In this case, there are t_m disjoint tuples B. Select an arbitrary such tuple B and use the first $2p - 2m$ terms of the sequence S to name the vertices in B in order. For the next tuple Bwe use the next $2p - 2m$ terms of the sequence S to name the vertices in B in order. We proceed like this until we cover all the t_m disjoint tuples.

Step IV. We name the vertices in $T \backslash P$ which are at distance $m-1$ from P, in the similar manner. We proceed like this until we name all the vertices in $T \backslash P$ and are of distance 2 from P.

Step V. Consider the sequence $S_1 : x_{r+1}, x_{r+2}, \ldots, x_n$. The terms in the beginning of $S1$ are assigned (or named) to the distance one vertices in $T \backslash P$ adjacent to x_{l_1} and x_{l_2} alternately (the number of distance one vertices in $T \backslash P$ adjacent to x_{l_i} and $x_{l_{i+1}}$, $1 \leq i \leq 2p - 2m - 1$ are equal). The next terms of S_1 are assigned to the distance one vertices in $T \backslash P$ adjacent to x_{l_3} and x_{l_4} alternately, and so on, till we name all the vertices of T. Observe that $n = 2p + (2p - 2m)\sum_{i=2}^{m} t_i + 2\sum_{i=2}^{m} t_i + 2 \times \sum_{i=m+1}^{p} s_i$.

Now $x_1, x_2, \ldots$, is an ordering of all the vertices of T.

Let f be a coloring to the vertices of T defined by

$$f(x_1) = 1$$

$$f(x_i) = f(x_{i-1}) + 2p - d(x_i, x_{i-1}), \quad 2 \leq i \leq n. \tag{2}$$

Before we prove that f is a minimal radio coloring of T, we give an illustration of f.

***Example** 7. In this example, we illustrate the above coloring f by considering the* 3-*distant tree T given in Figure* 2

Here $p = 6$, the central path P: $a_1 a_2 \cdots a_{12}$, $m = 3$, $t_2 = 1$, $t_3 = 2$, $s_4 = 3$, $s_5 = 1$, $s_6 = 2$, $x_1 = a_6$, $x_2 = a_{12}$, $x_3 = a_5$, $x_4 = a_{11}$, $x_5 = a_4$, $x_6 = a_{10}$, $x_7 = a_3$, $x_8 = a_9$, $x_9 = a_2$, $x_{10} = a_8$, $x_{11} = a_1$, $x_{12} = a_7$, $x_{l_1} = a_6, x_{l_2} = a_9, x_{l_3} = a_5, x_{l_4} = a_8, x_{l_5} = a_4, x_{l_6} = a_7$, S: $x_{13}, x_{14}, \ldots, x_{30}$, and S_1: $x_{31}, x_{32}, \ldots, x_{42}$. So the ordering of the vertices of this 3-distant tree is in Figure 3.

The assignment f is given in Figure 4.

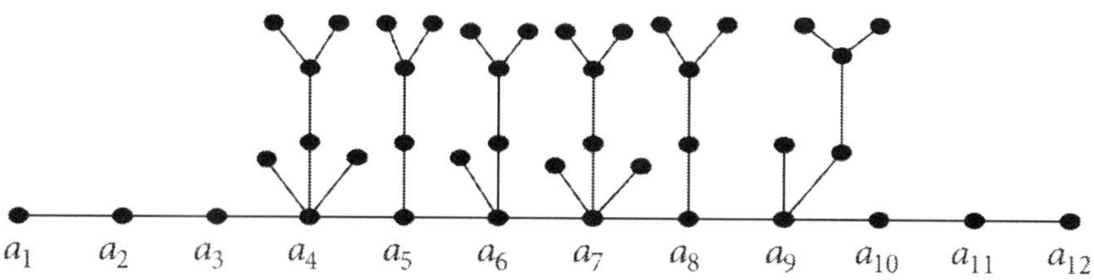

Figure 2: Tree T to illustrate Theorem 5.

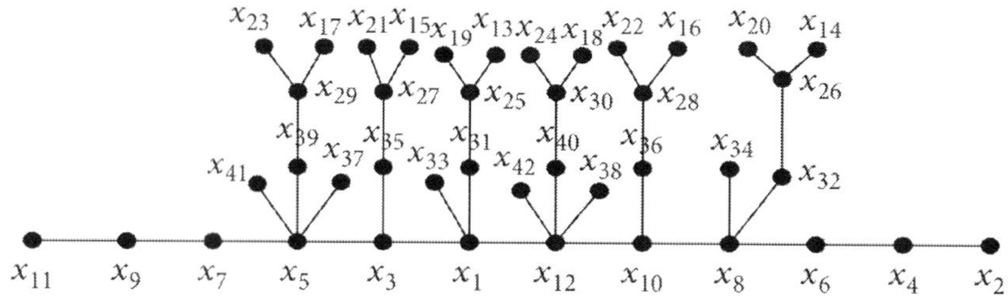

Figure 3: Ordering of vertices of T obtained from Theorem 5.

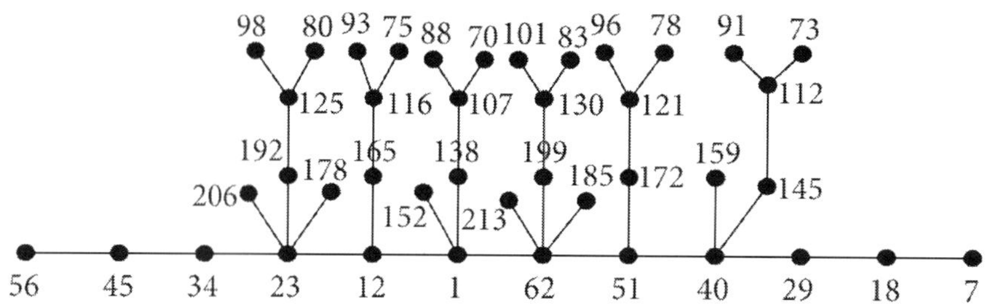

Figure 4: Radio coloring of T obtained from Theorem 5.

Continuation of the Proof of Theorem. We first show that f is a radio coloring. We need to check that $|(x_i) - f(_{xj})| \geq 1 + (2p - 1) - d(x_i, x_j)$, $1 \leq i \neq j \leq n$ (we call this as radio condition). From the definition of f, radio condition holds true for pair of vertices x_i and x_{i-1}, $2 \leq i \leq n$. For $1 \leq i \leq 2p$,

$$\begin{aligned} f(x_{i+2}) - f(x_i) &= f(x_{i+2}) - f(x_{i+1}) + f(x_{i+1}) - f(x_i) \\ &= 2p - d(x_{i+2}, x_{i+1}) + 2p - d(x_{i+1}, x_i) \\ &= 4p - \{d(x_{i+2}, x_{i+1}) + d(x_{i+1}, x_i)\} \\ &= 4p - \{2p + 1\} \\ &= 2p - 1 \\ &\geq 1 + 2p - d(x_i, x_{i+2}). \end{aligned} \quad (3)$$

Since

$$\begin{aligned} f\left(x_{2p+1}\right)-f\left(x_{2p-1}\right) &= f\left(x_{2p+1}\right)-f\left(x_{2p}\right) \\ &\quad + f\left(x_{2p}\right)-f\left(x_{2p-1}\right) \\ &= 2p-(m+1)+2p-(p) \\ &= 3p-(m+1) \\ &\geq 2p-1, \end{aligned} \tag{4}$$

radio condition holds true for all the pair of vertices x_i and x_j, where one of them is on the central path P and the other in $T\backslash P$.

Now,

$$\begin{aligned} f\left(x_{2p+3}\right)-f\left(x_{2p+1}\right) &= f\left(x_{2p+3}\right)-f\left(x_{2p+2}\right) \\ &\quad + f\left(x_{2p+2}\right)-f\left(x_{2p+1}\right) \\ &= 2p-d\left(x_{2p+2},x_{2p+3}\right)+2p \\ &\quad -d\left(x_{2p+1},x_{2p+2}\right) \\ &= 2p-\{p-m+1+2m\}+2p \\ &\quad -\{p-m+2m\} \\ &= 4p-\{(p-m+2m) \\ &\qquad +(p-m+1+2m)\} \\ &= 2p-(2m+1) \\ &= 2p-d\left(x_{2p+1},x_{2p+3}\right). \end{aligned} \tag{5}$$

Since $x_{2p+4}, x_{2p+5},\ldots,x_{2p+2p-2m}$ are at least $2m+1$ distance apart from x_{2p+1} and have colors greater than $f(x_{2p+3})$, radio condition automatically holds true, and

$$\begin{aligned} & f\left(x_{2p+2(p-m)}\right)-f\left(x_{2p+1}\right) \\ &= \sum_{i=2}^{2(p-m)} f\left(x_{2p+i}\right)-f\left(x_{2p+i-1}\right) \\ &= 2p\left(2\left(p-m\right)-1\right) \\ &\quad -\sum_{i=2}^{2(p-m)} d\left(x_{2p+i},x_{2p+i-1}\right) \\ &= 4p^2-4pm-2p \\ &\quad -\left[\left(\frac{2\left(p-m\right)-2}{2}\right)\left(p+m+p+m+1\right)+p+m\right] \\ &= 2p^2-(4m+2)\,p+2m\left(m+1\right)+1. \end{aligned} \tag{6}$$

If $x_{2p+2(p-m)+1}$ is at a distance m from P, then

$$\begin{aligned} & f\left(x_{2p+2(p-m)+1}\right)-f\left(x_{2p+1}\right) \\ &= f\left(x_{2p+2(p-m)+1}\right)-f\left(x_{2p+2(p-m)}\right) \\ &\quad +2p^2-(4m+2)\,p+2m\left(m+1\right)+1 \\ &= 2p-(2m+1)+2p^2-(4m+2)\,p \\ &\quad +2m\left(m+1\right)+1 \\ &= 2\left(p-m\right)^2 \\ &\geq 2\left(p-\left(p-\sqrt{p-1}\right)\right)^2 \\ &= 2p-2 \\ &= 2p-d\left(x_{2p+1},x_{2p+2(p-m)+1}\right). \end{aligned} \tag{7}$$

Since $(x_{2p+2(p-m)+1})-f(x_{2p+1})\geq 2p-2$, radio condition holds true between x_{2p+1} and all other vertices.

Let $i=2p+(2p-2m)_m$. Then x_i is the last vertex at distance m from P. Since, from the definition of f, radio condition holds true for x_i and x_{i+1}, and $d(x_i, x_{i+1})=m+1+m-1=2m\leq d(x_i, x_{i+j})$, $2\leq j\leq 2p-2m-1$, radio condition automatically holds true between x_i and x_{i+j}, $2\leq j\leq 2p-2m-1$.

Since $f(x_{i+1})-f(x_i)=2p-\{m+(m-1)+1\}=2(p-m)$, $f(x_{i+2})-f(x_{i+1})=2p-\{2(m-1)+p-m\}=p-m+2$, and $f(x_{i+3})-f(x_{i+2})=2p-\{2(m-1)+p-m+1\}=p-m+1$, we have

$$\begin{aligned} & f\left(x_{i+2p-2m}\right)-f\left(x_i\right) \\ &= \sum_{l=2}^{2p-2m}\left[f\left(x_{i+l}\right)-f\left(x_{i+l-1}\right)\right]+f\left(x_{i+1}\right)-f\left(x_i\right) \\ &= \frac{2p-2m}{2}\left(p-m+2\right)+\frac{2p-2m-2}{2}\left(p-m+1\right) \\ &\quad +2\left(p-m\right) \\ &= 2\left(p-m\right)^2+4\left(p-m\right)-1 \\ &\geq 2p-1 \\ &= 2p-d\left(x_i,x_{i+2p-2m}\right). \end{aligned} \tag{8}$$

In a similar manner, one can check the radio condition for the remaining pair of vertices. Therefore, f is a radio coloring. Next, we show that f is minimal. Let x and y be any two vertices of T. Then we get vertices a_i and a_j on the central path P such that $x=a_i$ or x is on a branch incident on a_i, and $y=a_j$ or y is on a branch incident on a_j. Then

$$d(x, y) = \begin{cases} |j-i|, \\ \quad \text{if } x = a_i \text{ and } y = a_j \\ |j-i| + j_1, \\ \quad \text{if } x = a_i \text{ and } y \text{ lies on a branch} \\ \quad \text{and is } j_1 \text{ distance from } a_j \\ |j-i| + j_2, \\ \quad \text{if } y = a_j \text{ and } x \text{ lies on a branch} \\ \quad \text{and is } j_2 \text{ distance from } a_i \\ |j-i| + j_1 + j_2, \\ \quad \text{if } x \text{ and } y \text{ lie on branches and are} \\ \quad j_2 \text{ and } j_1 \text{ distances from } a_i \text{ and } a_j \text{ respectively.} \end{cases} \tag{9}$$

So, each term in the distance sum of a radio coloring contains two indices from $\{1, 2, \ldots, 2p\}$ with different signs because from (9), distance between every pair of vertices contains $|j-i|$, $i, j \in \{1, 2, \ldots, 2p\}$. Since there are $n-1$ terms in the distance sum, it contains $2(n-1)$ elements from the set $\{1, 2, \ldots, 2p\}$ with half positive and half negative sign. Also, the indices $1, 2, 3, \ldots, m$ and $2p-(m-1), 2p-(m-2), \ldots, 2p-1, 2p$ occur at most twice, and the index $j \in \{m+1, m+2, \ldots, 2p-m\}$ occur at most $2\left(\sum_{i=2}^{m} t_i + s_i + 2\right)$ times, where $deg(a_j) = deg(a_{j+p-m}) = sj + 2$. So, the possible maximum distance sum is $2\left(\sum_{i=2}^{m} t_i + s_{m+2} + 1\right)[(p+2)-(m+2)] + 2\left(\sum_{i=2}^{m} t_i + s_{m+3} + 1\right)[(p+3)-(m+3)] + \cdots + 2\left(\sum_{i=2}^{m} t_i + s_{p-1} + 1\right)[(2p-(m+1))-(p-1)] + 2\left(\sum_{i=2}^{m} t_i + s_p + 1\right)(2p-m) - 2\left(\sum_{i=2}^{m} t_i + s_p + (1/2)\right)(p) + 2\left(\sum_{i=2}^{m} t_i + s_{m+1} + (1/2)\right)(p+1) - 2\left(\sum_{i=2}^{m} t_i + s_{m+1} + 1\right)(m+1) + 2(2p + 2p-1 + 2p-2 + \cdots + 2p-(m-1)) - 2(1+2+3+\cdots+m) + \sum_{i=2}^{m} 2it_i + 2\sum_{i=m+1}^{p} 2s_i - 1.$

Now, the distance sum

$$\begin{aligned} d(f) &= \sum_{i=2}^{n} d(x_i, x_{i-1}) \\ &= \sum_{i=2}^{2p} d(x_i, x_{i-1}) + \sum_{i=2p+1}^{2p+(2p-2m)t_m} d(x_i, x_{i-1}) \\ &+ \sum_{i=2p+(2p-2m)t_m+1}^{2p+(2p-2m)t_m+(2p-2m)t_{m-1}} d(x_i, x_{i-1}) + \cdots \\ &+ \sum_{i=2p+(2p-2m)t_m+(2p-2m)t_{m-1}+\cdots+(2p-2m)t_3+1}^{2p+(2p-2m)t_m+(2p-2m)t_{m-1}+\cdots+(2p-2m)t_3+(2p-2m)t_2} d(x_i, x_{i-1}) \\ &+ \sum_{i=2p+(2p-2m)t_m+(2p-2m)t_{m-1}+\cdots+(2p-2m)t_3+(2p-2m)t_2+1}^{n} d(x_i, x_{i-1}), \end{aligned} \tag{10}$$

where $n = 2p + \sum_{i=2}^{m}(2p-2m)t_i + 2\sum_{i=m+1}^{p} s_i$ coincides with the possible maximum distance sum above and is equal to $2(p-m)[(p-m)\sum_{i=2}^{m} t_i + \sum_{i=2}^{m} 2it_i] + [2(p-m)+4]\sum_{i=m+1}^{p} 2s_i + 2p^2 - 2$.

One observes that $\sum_{i=2}^{n} \epsilon_i^f = 0$. Therefore, from Theorem 4, the radio coloring f is minimal and

$$
\begin{aligned}
(T) &= rc_{2p-1}(f) \\
&= (n-1)(1+2p-1) - \sum_{i=2}^{n} d(x_i, x_{i-1}) + 1 \\
&= \left[2p + 2(p-m)\left(\sum_{i=2}^{m} t_i\right) + 2\sum_{i=m+1}^{p} s_i - 1\right](2p) \\
&\quad - \sum_{i=2}^{n} d(x_i, x_{i-1}) + 1 \\
&= 2(p-m)\left[(p+m)\sum_{i=2}^{m} t_i - \sum_{i=2}^{m} 2it_i\right] \\
&\quad + [2(p+m)-4]\sum_{i=m+1}^{p} s_i + 2p(p-1) + 3.
\end{aligned} \tag{11}
$$

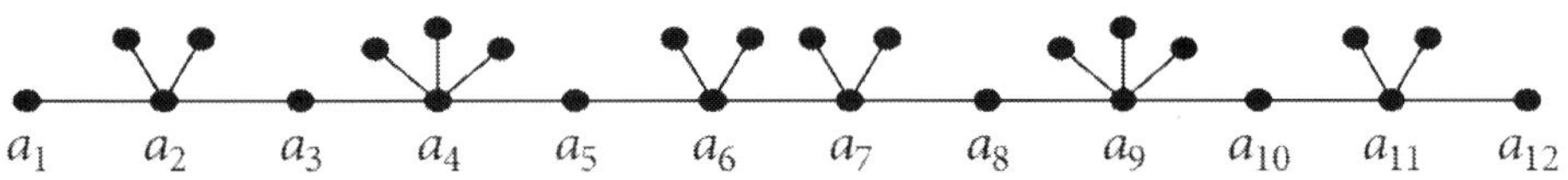

Figure 5: A caterpillar to illustrate Corollary 8.

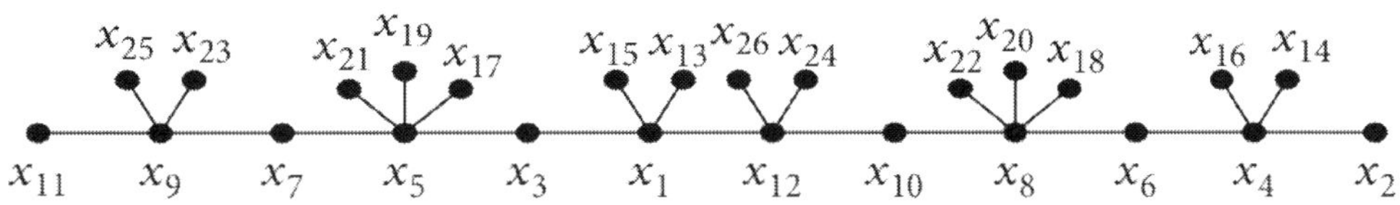

Figure 6: Ordering of vertices of the caterpillar given in Figure 5.

As a consequence of the above theorem, we determine the radio number of a class of caterpillars (1-distant trees). In the corollary below, we find radio number of caterpillars of odd diameter in which the degrees of every pair of nonpendant vertices on the central path lying at distance $p-1$ apart have the same degree (where $2p$ is the total number of vertices on the central path).

Corollary 8. Let C be a caterpillar of order n and with a central path $P{:}a_1a_2a_3\cdots a_{2p}$. If $de(a_i) = deg(a_{p+i-1}) = s_i + 2$, $s_i \geq 0$, $i = 2, 3, \ldots, p$, then

$$
rn(C) = 2\left[(p-1)\sum_{i=2}^{p} s_i + p(p-1)\right] + 3. \tag{12}
$$

Proof. This is $m = 1$ case of Theorem 5. The ordering of vertices in this case includes Step I and Step V of algorithm in the proof of Theorem 5 with only variation that if a vertex on the central path is not adjacent to any pendant vertex, then we move to the next possible vertex.

Example 9. In this example, we illustrate Corollary 8 by considering the caterpillar given in Figure 5.

Here $p = 6$, the central path P: $a_1a_2\cdots a_{12}$ and $s_2 = 2$, $s_3 = 0$, $s_4 = 3$, $s_5 = 2$. So the ordering of vertices of the caterpillar is illustrated in Figure 6 and the coloring f is given in Figure 7.

The corollary below is also a consequence of Theorem 5 in which we find the radio number of caterpillars of odd diameter in which all nonpendant vertices on the central path are of the same degree.

Corollary 10. Let C be a caterpillar of order n with a central path P: $a_1a_2a_3\cdots a_{2p}$. If $deg(a_i) = s + 2$, $i = 2, 3, \ldots, 2p-1$, $s \geq 0$, then $rn(C) = 2[s(p-1)^2 + p(p-1)] + 3$.

Proof. One can prove this result by substituting $s_i = s$, $i = 2, 3, \ldots, p$ in Corollary 8.

Example 11. In this example we illustrate Corollary 10 by considering the caterpillar given in Figure 8.

Here $p = 6$, the central path P: $a_1a_2\cdots a_{12}$ and $t = 2$. So the ordering of vertices of the caterpillar is illustrated in Figure 9 and the coloring f is given in Figure 10.

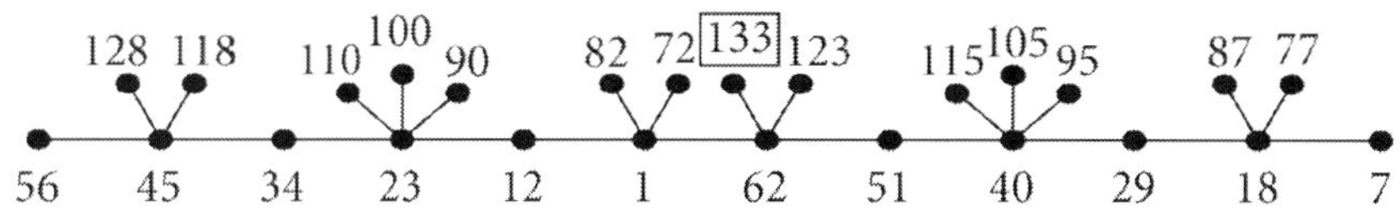

Figure 7: Radio coloring f of the caterpillar given in Figure 5.

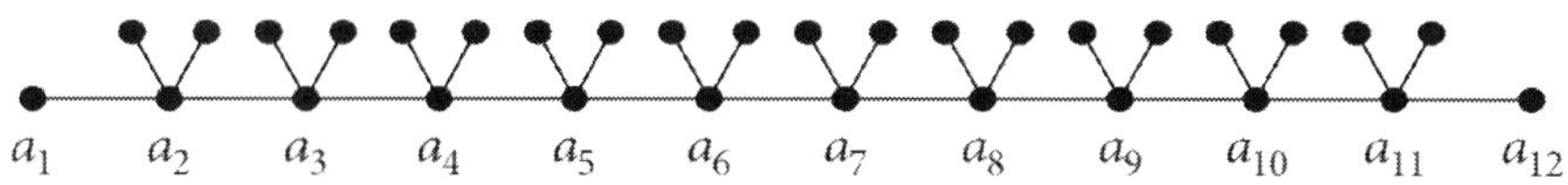

Figure 8: A caterpillar for illustration of Corollary 10.

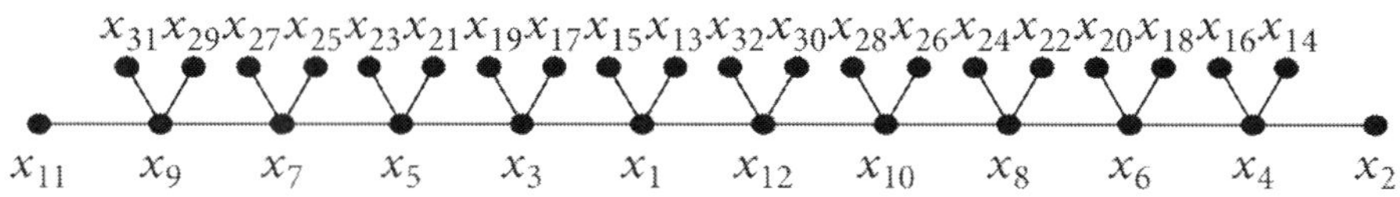

Figure 9: Ordering of vertices of the caterpillar given in Figure 8.

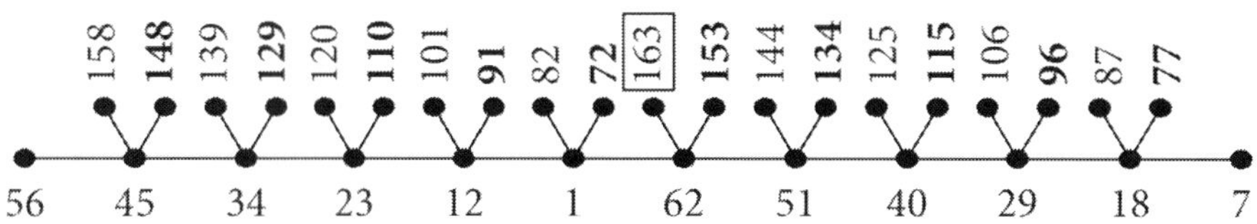

Figure 10: Minimal radio coloring of the caterpillar given in Figure 8.

ACKNOWLEDGMENT

The authors are thankful to the referee for his/her valuable comments and suggestions which improved the presentation of the paper.

REFERENCES

1. W. K. Hale, "Frequency assignment: theory and applications," Proceedings of the IEEE, vol. 68, no. 12, pp. 1497–1514, 1980.
2. G. Chartrand, D. Erwin, P. Zhang, and F. Harary, "Radio labelings of graphs," Bulletin of the Institute of Combinatorics and its Applications, vol. 33, pp. 77–85, 2001.
3. G. Chartrand, D. Erwin, and P. Zhang, "A graph labeling problem suggested by FM channel restrictions,"Bulletin of the Institute of Combinatorics and Its Applications, vol. 43, pp. 43–57, 2005.
4. M. Kchikech, R. Khennoufa, and O. Togni, "Linear and cyclic radio k-labelings of trees," Discussiones Mathematicae. Graph Theory, vol. 27, no. 1, pp. 105–123, 2007.
5. D. D. Liu, "Radio number for trees," Discrete Mathematics, vol. 308, no. 7, pp. 1153–1164, 2008.
6. D. D. Liu and X. Zhu, "Multilevel distance labelings for paths and cycles," SIAM Journal on Discrete Mathematics, vol. 19, no. 3, pp. 610–621, 2005.
7. P. Panigrahi, "A survey on radio k-colorings of graphs," AKCE International Journal of Graphs and Combinatorics, vol. 6, no. 1, pp. 161–169, 2009.
8. S. R. Kola and P. Panigrahi, "Improved lower bound for radio k-chromatic number of hypercube Qn,"Computers and Mathematics with Applications, vol. 60, pp. 2131–2140, 2010.
9. P. Zhang, "Radio labelings of cycles," Ars Combinatoria, vol. 65, pp. 21–32, 2002.
10. X. Li, V. Mak, and S. Zhou, "Optimal radio labellings of complete m-ary trees," Discrete Applied Mathematics, vol. 158, no. 5, pp. 507–515, 2010.

CHAPTER 19

DISTANCE DEGREE REGULAR GRAPHS AND DISTANCE DEGREE INJECTIVE GRAPHS: AN OVERVIEW

Medha Itagi Huilgol

Department of Mathematics, Bangalore University, Central College Campus, Bangalore 560001, India

ABSTRACT

The distance (v, u) from a vertex v of G to a vertex u is the length of shortest v to u path. The eccentricity (v) of v is the distance to a farthest vertex from v. If (v, u) = e(v), ($u \neq$ v), we say that u is an eccentric vertex of v. The radius rad(G) is the minimum eccentricity of the vertices, whereas the diameter diam(G) is the maximum eccentricity. A vertex v is a central vertex if (v) = rad(G), and a vertex is a peripheral vertex if e(v) = diam(G). A graph is self-centered if every vertex has the same eccentricity; that is, rad(G) = diam(G). The distance degree sequence (dds) of a vertex v in a graph G = (V, E) is a list of the number of vertices at distance 1, 2, ..., e(v) in that order, where e(v) denotes the eccentricity of v in G. Thus, the sequence $(d_{i_0}, d_{i_1}, d_{i_2}, \ldots, d_{i_j}, \ldots)$ is the distance degree sequence of the vertex v_i in G where d_{i_j} denotes the number of vertices at distance j from v_i. The concept of distance degree regular (DDR) graphs was introduced by Bloom et al., as the graphs for which all vertices have the same distance degree sequence. By definition, a DDR graph must be a regular graph, but a regular graph may not be DDR. A graph is distance degree injective (DDI) graph if no two vertices have the same distance degree sequence. DDI graphs are highly irregular, in comparison with the DDR graphs. In this paper we present an exhaustive review of the two concepts of DDR and DDI graphs. The paper starts with an insight into all distance related sequences and their applications. All the related open problems are listed.

INTRODUCTION

The study of sequences in Graph Theory is not new. A sequence for a graph acts as an invariant that contains a list of numbers rather than a single number. A sequence can be handled and studied as easily as a single numerical invariant, but a sequence carries more information about the graph it represents. There are many sequences representing a graph in literature, namely, the degree sequence, the eccentric sequence, the distance degree sequence, the status sequence, the path degree sequence, and so forth. A sequence S is said to begraphical if there is a graph which realizes S. Degree sequences of graphs were the first ones to be studied, as the question of realizability of any sequence for a graph was a fundamental one. An existential characterization was given by Erdos and Gallai [1]. Then the constructive characterization was found independently by Havel [2] and later by Hakimi [3] that is now referred to as the Havel and Hakimi algorithm. The eccentric sequences were the next and the first in the class of distance related sequences to be studied for undirected graphs. Some fundamental results in this direction are due to Lesniak-Foster [4], Ostrand [5], Behzad,

Citation: Medha Itagi Huilgol, "Distance Degree Regular Graphs and Distance Degree Injective Graphs: An Overview,"Journal of Discrete Mathematics, vol. 2014, Article ID 358792, 12 pages, 2014. doi:10.1155/2014/358792

and Simpson [6], which primarily deal with the conditions for graphical eccentric sequences. The minimal eccentric sequences were mainly studied by Nandakumar [7]. But, for digraphs, the eccentric sequences were studied quite late. We can find some papers in 2008 due to Gimbert and Lopez [8].

Next distance based sequences were the path degree sequences and distance degree sequences. These were studied by Randic [9] for the purpose of distinguishing chemical isomers by their graph structure. Path degree sequence of a graph has its application in describing atomic environments and in various classification schemes for molecules.

We will now define all the terms that give graph theoretic expressions for the above discussed cases.

For all undefined terms we refer to [10].

Let $G = (V, E)$ denote a graph with the set of vertices V, whose cardinality is the order p and two element subsets of V, known as edges forming E, whose cardinality is size q. Unless mentioned otherwise, in this article, by a graph we mean an undirected, finite graph without multiple edges and self-loops.

The distance (v, u) from a vertex v of G to a vertex u is the length of shortest v to u path. The degree of a vertex v is the number of vertices at distance one.

The sequence of numbers of vertices having degree 0, 1, 2, 3, . . . is called the degree sequence, which is the list of the degrees of vertices of G in non-decreasing order.

The eccentricity (v) of v is the distance to a farthest vertex from v.

A graph G is said to be self-centered if all vertices have the same eccentricity

If $(v, u) = e(v)$, $(u \neq v)$, we say that u is an eccentric vertex of v.

The eccentric sequence of a connected graph G is a list of the eccentricities of its vertices in non-decreasing order.

The distance and path degree sequences of a vertex are generalizations of the degree of a vertex. The distance degree sequence (DDS) of a vertex v in a graph G is a list of the number of vertices at distance 1, 2, . . . , $e(v)$ in that order, where $e(v)$ denotes the eccentricity of v in G. Thus, the sequence $(d_{i_0}, d_{i_1}, d_{i_2}, \ldots, d_{i_j}, \ldots)$ is the distance degree sequence of the vertex v_i in G where d_{i_j} denotes the number of vertices at distance j from v_i. The p-tuple of distance degree sequences of the vertices of G with entries arranged in lexicographic order is the distance degree sequence (DDS) of G. Similarly, we define the path degree sequence (PDS) of v_i as the sequence $(p_{i_0}, p_{i_1}, p_{i_2}, \ldots, p_{i_j}, \ldots)$ where p_{i_j} denotes the number of paths in G of length j having v_i as the initial vertex. The ordered set of all such sequences arranged in lexicographic order is called the path degree sequence (PDS) of G. Clearly, for any graph $d_{i_j} \le p_{i_j}$.

The distance distribution of G is the sequence $(d_1, d_2, \ldots, d_j, \ldots)$, where d_j is the number of pairs of vertices in G that are at distance j apart.

The status(v) of a vertex v in $G$is the sum of the distances from v to all other vertices in G. This concept was introduced by Harary [11]. Thus, using the distance degree sequence of v_i, we have $s(v_i) = \sum_{j=1}^{\text{diam}(G)} j d_{ij}$.

The median (G) of$G$is the set of vertices with minimum status. A graph is called a self-median graph if all of its vertices have the same status.

The status of a vertex is also called the distance at that vertex. The mean distance at the vertex v_i, denoted by $\mathrm{MD}(v_i)$, is defined as $\mathrm{MD}(v_i) = s(v_i)/(p-1)$.

The mean distance for the graph, denoted by $\mathrm{MD}(G)$, is defined as the mean of the distances between all pairs of vertices of G; that is, $MDG = \sum_{\{u,v\}} d(u,v) \Big/ \binom{p}{2}$, where u and v are vertices of G. In terms of status, we get $MDG = \sum_{i=1}^{p} \left(MD(v_i)/p \right)$.

As an illustration consider the graph G as shown in Figure 1.

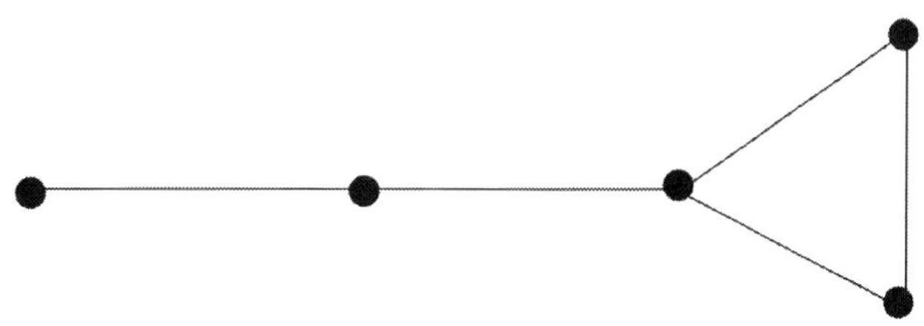

Figure 1

$\mathrm{DDS}(G) = ((1, 1, 1, 2), (1, 2, 2), (1, 3, 1), (1, 2, 1, 1)^2)$ and $\mathrm{PDS}(G) = ((1, 1, 1, 2, 2), (1, 2, 2, 2), (1, 2, 3, 2, 1)^2, (1, 3, 3))$.

If we consider the 3-dimensional cube Q_3 as an example, we will get $\mathrm{DDS}(Q_3) = ((1, 3, 3, 1)^8)$ and $\mathrm{PDS}(Q_3) = ((1, 3, 6, 12, 12, 12)^6)$.

In [12], Kennedy and Quintas have examined how the distance degree sequences relate to embedding trees in lattice-graphs and other spaces as well as the consequential relations to physical theories. Chemists have also proposed and discussed other sequences for this purpose. Their objective and hope are to develop a "chemical indicator" which would be useful both for the graph isomorphism problem and to predict various properties of the molecule at hand. In this connection, Randic [9] proposed the structural similarity depending on the graph property as follows.

Conjecture 1 (see [9]). *Between pairs of atoms in acyclic structures there is a unique path so that the number of paths of a given length corresponds to the number of neighbors at a given distance.*

This can be rephrased in graph theoretic terms as follows.

Conjecture 2 (see [9]). *For a connected graph G, DD(G) = PDS(G) if and only if G is a tree.*

A nonassertive proof was given by Quintas and Slater [13].

Hence, this kind of study leads to the problem of finding the smallest order for which there exists a pair of nonisomorphic graphs which are equivalent relative to some set of graphical invariants. So the following conjecture was made in line with the above conjecture by Randic [9] that sought for graph isomorphism by comparing their sequences.

Conjecture 3 (see [9]). *Two graphs G_1 and G_2 are isomorphic if and only if $PD(G_1) = PDS(G_2)$.*

This conjuncture was also shown to be invalid, by citing infinite class of pairs of nonisomorphic trees having the property that the two members of each pair have the same path degree sequence by Quintas and Slater [13]. To extend this notion to nontree graphs, the same examples were considered to construct pairs of nonisomorphic graphs having a variety of properties and invalidate the conjecture.

As noted above, a tree is not, in general, characterized by its path (or distance) degree sequence. The least order for which there exists a pair of nonisomorphic trees with the same path degree sequence has been shown to be more than 14 for acyclic alkanes, that is, trees with no vertex of degree more than 4 and less than or equal to 18 for trees without vertex degree restrictions.

On similar lines one can search for pairs of nonisomorphic graphs having the same distance degree sequence. Slater [14] constructed a pair of nonisomorphic 18 vertex trees having the same distance degree sequence as shown in Figure 2. He had subsequently conjectured that no such smaller order pair exists. Later, Gargano and Quintas [15] considered the problem with respect to the number of independent cycles in a graph having the same distance degree sequence. We can recall that $\beta=q-p+k$, where β is the number of independent cycles, k is the number of components in the graph, and p, q are the order and size, respectively. For $\beta=0$, Slater's constructions hold good. For $\beta=1$, Gargano and Quintas [15] constructed two pairs of graphs on 14 vertices. For $\beta=2$, the smallest order pair of nonisomorphic graphs with the same distance degree sequence is given as in Figure 3.

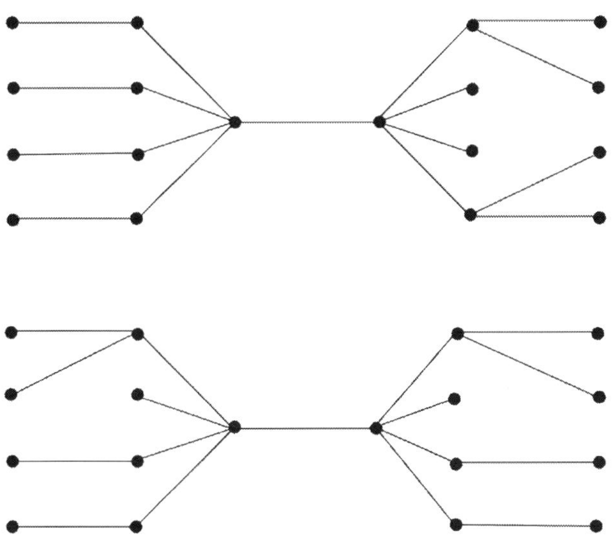

Figure 2: A pair of nonisomorphic trees with the same path degree sequence.

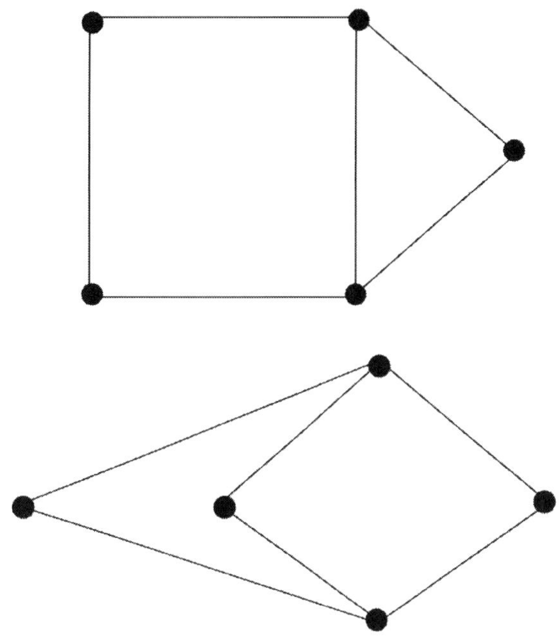

Figure 3: Smallest order graphs with the same distance degree sequence.

And this is the only such pair as noted by Quintas and Slater in [13]. This class of graphs was generalized by Gargano and Quintas [15] for $\beta \geq 2$ as follows.

Theorem 4 (see [15]). *If $\beta \geq 2$, then there exists a pair of nonisomorphic connected graphs having the same distance degree sequence and β independent cycles. The smallest order p for such a pair is given by $p = \left\lceil \left(3+\sqrt{33+8\beta}\right)/2 \right\rceil$, where $\lceil s \rceil$ denotes the least integer greater than or equal to s.*

Two problems were asked in the same paper.

Problem 5 (see [15]). What is the smallest order p for which there exists a pair of nonisomorphic connected graphs having the same distance degree sequence and β = 0, 1 independent cycles?

Problem 6 (see [15]). What is the smallest order p for which there exists a pair of nonisomorphic connected graphs having the same distance degree sequence and $\beta \geq 0$ ($\beta \neq 2$, 3, 4, 5 and 7) independent cycles and such that the graphs have no vertex with degree greater than four?

With reference to Problem 6, consider the following.

If $\beta = 0$, then p is at least 15 (see Slater [14]; p.17).

If $\beta = 1$, Gargano and Quintas [15] conjectured $p = 14$.

If $\beta = 2$, the solution is $p = 5$ (see Figure 3).

For several values of $\beta \geq 3$, the solution is the same as that for Problem 5. Specifically for β = 3, 4, 5 and 7 each of the graphs constructed in the proof of the theorem in [15] has no vertex of degree greater than four. Thus the open cases are β = 0, 1, 6 and $\beta \geq 8$.

If one asks for the smallest order for which the distance degree sequence fails to distinguish between k-regular graphs, there exists the following result due to Quintas and Slater [13].

Proposition 7 (see [13]). *Let (k) denote the smallest order for which there exist at least two nonisomorphic connected k-regular graphs on $R(k)$ vertices such that each has the same* *distance degree sequence. Then* $(k) = k + 3$, if $k = 3, 4, 5, \ldots$ *and* $R(k)$ *does not exist if* $k = 0, 1, 2$.

As noted above, there does not exist a pair of nonisomorphic graphs with the same path degree sequence on less than 12 vertices. It also follows from the above result that the least order for which such a k-regular pair of graphs can exist is at least $k + 3$ for $k \geq 3$ and that none exist if $k = 0, 1, 2$. Thus the investigation to produce at least one pair of nonisomorphic k-regular graphs having the same path degree sequence has resulted in an open problem.

Problem 8 (see [13]). *For* $k \geq 3$*, does there exist a pair of nonisomorphic connected k-regular graphs having the same path degree sequence? If the answer is yes, what is the smallest order* (k) *realizable by such a pair?*

In fact, a paper by Slater [14] discusses the counterexamples to Randic's conjectures on distance degree sequences on trees.

In [16] Bussemaker et al. have investigated all connected cubic graphs on $p \leq 14$ vertices and for each such graph the following properties were determined and tabulated:

- Its description by means of its edges and for $p \leq 12$, by a drawing;
- The coefficients of its characteristic polynomial;
- The eigenvalues of its (0, 1)-adjacency matrix;
- The number of its cycles of length $3, 4, \ldots, p$;
- Its diameter, connectivity, and planarity;
- The order of its automorphism group.

From their table the girth, the circumference, and the chromatic number are easily determined. The graphs were classified according to their order and within each such class the graphs were ordered lexicographically according to their eigenvalues, which for each graph were listed in nonincreasing order. In addition, a number of observations concerning the spectral properties of these graphs were made. The study was motivated by the importance of cubic graphs and by the search for cospectral cubic graphs. The cubic graph generation is looked into by Brinkmann [17]. In [18] Halberstam and Quintas have extended the results of Bussemaker et al. [16] mainly considering the sequences associated with the graphs. In this report they have determined the following information for each cubic graph on less than or equal to 14 vertices:

- Its distance degree sequence;
- Its distance distribution;
- The mean distance at each vertex;
- The mean distance for the graph;
- Its path degree sequence;
- The number of paths of specified length;
- The total number of paths for the graph.

For each graph a number of other parameters can be determined from these tables. The radius, the diameter, and the eccentricity of every vertex can be read directly by noting the length of the appropriate distance degree sequence. By inspection one can determine the order of the center and of the median of the graph. In addition, the computation of other parameters is facilitated by making use of the given data.

DISTANCE DEGREE REGULAR (DDR) GRAPHS

Now we have the stage set for the discussion on the highly regular class of graphs involving the distance degree sequences, namely, the distance degree regular graphs. The concept of distance degree regular (DDR) graphs was introduced by Bloom et al. [19], as the graphs for which all vertices have the same distance degree sequence; that is, for all vertices V of a graph G, the distance degree sequence is $(d_{i_0}, d_{i_1}, d_{i_2}, \ldots, d_{i_j}, \ldots)$.

For example, the three-dimensional cube $Q_3 = K_2 \times K_2 \times K_2$ is a DDR graph having (1, 3, 3, 1) as the distance degree sequence of each of its vertex. Likewise, cycles, complete graphs are all DDR graphs. Lattice-graphs and infinite order regular trees are examples of infinite order DDR graphs. However, in this paper, we consider finite order graphs only. DDR graphs have peculiar relations to many parameters of graphs. On one extreme complete graphs are DDR and at the other end, there are DDR graphs having identity automorphism group. If a graph has a vertex-transitive automorphism group, then the graph is DDR, but not conversely. And the properties of DDR graphs being self-centered and selfmedian find applications even in operations research. Thus the study of DDR graphs is interesting.

In [19], Bloom et al. have discussed many properties of DDR graphs. It is clear that the set of DDR graphs of degree ≤ 2 consists of the following types: (i) a collection of k isolated vertices, (ii) a collection of k disjoint edges; and (iii) k copies of n-cycles. Hence, the next result is a fundamental one.

Proposition 9 (see [19]). *Each regular graph of diameter* ≤ 2 *is DDR and the complement of each regular graph of diameter* ≥ 3 *is DDR.*

This result ensures that "every regular graph with diameter at most two is DDR." We know that every DDR graph is regular, but the distribution of DDR graphs in regular graphs is not clear. So, the following question is relevant.

Problem 10 (see [19]). What proportion of k-regular graphs are DDR?

Following constructions help in getting DDR graphs of arbitrarily chosen diameter and degree. For these methods we require the following terms.

Definition 11 (see [19]). Let G denote a vertex-labeled graph with vertex set $V = \{1, 2, \ldots, p\}$. For any permutation α of V the k-cycle-α-permutation graph of G, denoted by $kCP(G)$, consists k copies of G joined by the additional edges $\{(i, j), (\alpha(i), j + 1)\}$, where (i, j) is the ith vertex of the jth copy of G and $j + 1 = 1$ when $j = k$.

Note that the special case $2CP(G)$ is the α-permutation graph of G, $P\alpha(G)$, introduced by Chartrand and Harary [20], if and only if α is a permutation of order less than or equal to 2. Furthermore, $kCP_i(G)$ is the cartesian product $C_k \times G$ of the k-cycle C_k and the graph G. Thus, if G is a n-cycle, it follows that $kCP_i(C_n) = nC\,P_{id}(C_k)$.

So the next result gives a family of DDR graphs.

Proposition 12 (see [19]). If G is any DDR graph of diameter m and degree D_1, then (i) $P_{id}(G)$ is a DDR graph of diameter $m + 1$ and degree $D_1 + 1$ and (ii), for $k \geq 3$, $kCP_{id}(G)$

$= C_k \times G$ is a DDR graph of diameter $m + \lfloor k/2 \rfloor$ and degree $D_1 + 2$.

This result can be extended to N iterated cartesian products as shown by the following corollary.

Corollary 13 (see [19]). *$P_{id}^{N}(G) = K_2^N \times G$ has diameter $m+N$ and degree $D_1 + N$ and $C_k^N \times G \equiv C_k^{N-1} \times G$ has diameter $m + N\lfloor k/2 \rfloor$ and degree $D_1 + 2N$, where $P_{id}^{N}(G) = P_{id}(P_{id}^{N-1}(G)) = K_2^N \times G$, as $P_{id}(G) = K_2^N \times G$, that is, the N iterated cartesian products.*

The existence of a DDR graph having diameter$m$is shown as follows.

Proposition 14 (see [19]). *There exist DDR graphs having diameter m and degree D_1 for all positive integers m and D_1, except for $m>D_1 = 1$.*

Observe that the only connected 1-regular graph is K_2.

But, characterizing DDR graphs of higher diameter is challenging. In [19] the following problem was cited.

Problem 15 (see [19]). Characterize DDR graphs having diameter ≥ 3.

Since then there is no answer to this question. A step forward was taken by Huilgol et al. [21], where they have characterized DDR graphs of diameter three with extremal degree regularity. They have shown that there are exactly 7 DDR graphs of diameter three of extreme regularity. The following result gives a clear picture about diameter three DDR graphs.

Theorem 16 (see [21]). Let$G$be a DDR graph of diameter three of regularity d_1. Then

- $d_1 = p - 4$, if and only if $G = C_6$;
- $d_1 = p - 5$, if and only if $G = C_7$; or $G = Q_3 = K_2 \times K_2 \times K_2$;
- $d_1 = p - 6$, if and only if G is one of the graphs given in Figure 4;
- $d_1 = 2$, if and only if $G = C_6$ or $G = C_7$.

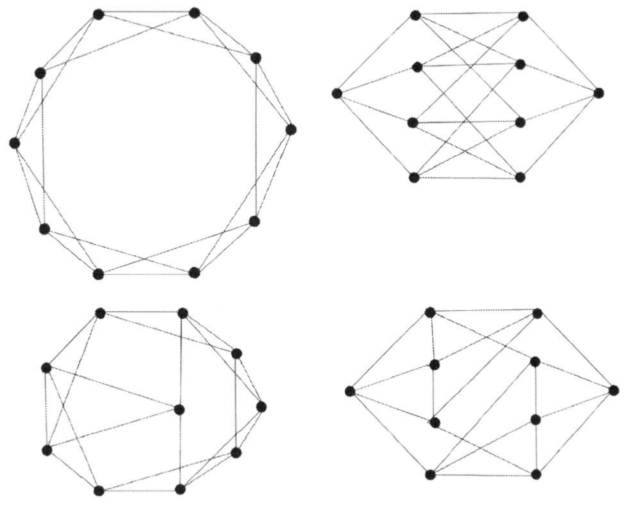

Figure 4

The proof of the above theorem is primarily based on the following two results.

Proposition 17 (see [3]). Every connected self-centered graph of order p satisfies the inequality $\Delta \leq p - 2r + 2$, where $\Delta = \Delta(G)$ and $r = \text{rad}(G)$ denote, respectively, the maximum degree and the radius of the graph G.

Proposition 18 (see [10]). In a connected graph G of order p and radius r, for any two arbitrarily chosen vertices u and v, the following inequality holds: $\deg(u) + \deg(v) \leq p - 2r + 4$.

As the diameter three DDR graphs are considered, which are self-centered graphs, satisfying the inequality, $2 \leq \Delta(G) \leq p-4$. In the above theorem, the DDR graphs of regularity 2 are characterized at one extreme and of regularities $p-4$, $p-5$, and $p-6$ at the other extreme of the above mentioned inequality. Using these results, we can find a bound on the order of the graph as $p \leq 2i - 4$, with degree regularity $d_1 = p-i$. Hence, for the degree regularity $d_1 = p-i$, $i \in \{4, 5, 6\}$, of a DDR graph of order p, we get $p = 6, 8, 10$, respectively. But, in general, the question of characterizing DDR graphs of diameter greater than two still remains open. At least the existence is answered by Huilgol et al. in [21], by proving the following result.

Theorem 19 (see [21]). For any integer k, there exists a DDR graph of diameter three and regularity k.

So, the construction of new families of DDR graphs is very interesting. In [22] Huilgol et al. have constructed some more DDR graphs of higher diameter and considered the behavior of DDR graphs under other graph binary operations. In this paper, the authors have given several DDR graphs of arbitrary diameter. Few of them depend on the generalized lexicographic product of graphs.

The lexicographic product is defined as follows.

Given graphs G and H, the lexicographic product $[H]$ has the vertex set $\{(g, h) : g \in V(G), h \in V(H)\}$ and two vertices (g, h), (g', h') are adjacent if and only if either gg' is an edge of G or $g = g'$ and hh' is an edge of H.

Proposition 20 (see [22]). Let G be a DDR graph and let G_i, $1 \leq i \leq p$, be undirected graphs such that $|V(G_i)| = p$, for all i, $1 \leq i \leq p$, and then $G[G_1, G_2, G_3, \ldots, G_p]$, the generalized lexicographic product, is a DDR graph if and only if all G_i, $1 \leq i \leq p$, are regular graphs with the same regularity.

This characterizes the generalized lexicographic products. Next result uses the generalized lexicographic product to show the existence of a DDR graph of arbitrary diameter.

Proposition 21 (see [23]). There exists a DDR graph of diameter $d \geq 3$ of order $p = (2d + 1)$ and $p = 2dn$, where $n=1, 2, 3, \ldots$.

Proposition 22 (see [22]). There exists a DDR graph G of diameter d such that G^2 is also DDR with diameter $d/2$, if d is even and $(d + 1)/2$, if d is odd.

Proposition 23 (see [22]). If G is a DDR graph with diameter d and regularity d_1, then the prism of G is also a DDR graph on $2p$ number of vertices with diameter $d + 1$ and regularity $d_1 + 1$.

In [23], Huilgol et al. have constructed higher order DDR graphs by considering the simplest of the products, namely, the cartesian and normal product. The cartesian product of two graphs G and H, denoted by $G \square H$, is a graph with vertex set $V(G \square H) = V(G) \times V(H)$; that is, the set $\{(g, h)/g \in V(G), h \in V(H)\}$. The edge set of $G \square H$ consists of all pairs $[(g_1, h_1), (g_2,$

$h_2)]$ of vertices with $[g_1, g_2] \in (G)$ and $h_1 = h_2$ or $g_1 = g_2$ and $[h_1, h_2] \in E(H)$.

And the normal product of two graphs G and H, denoted by $G \oplus H$, is a graph with vertex set $V(G \oplus H) = V(G) \times V(H)$; that is, the set $\{(g, h)/g \in V(G), h \in V(H)\}$, and an edge $[(g_1, h_1), (g_2, {}_{h2})]$ exists whenever any of the following conditions hold good: (i) $[g_1, g_2] \in E(G)$ and $h_1 = h_2$, (ii) $g_1 = g_2$ and $[h_1, h_2] \in E(H)$, and (iii) $[g_1, g_2] \in E(G)$ and $[h_1, h_2] \in E(H)$.

Theorem 24 (see [23]). Cartesian product of two graphs G_1 and G_2 is a DDR graph if and only if both G_1 and G_2 are DDR graphs.

Lemma 25 (see [23]). Let $S = \{G_i/i \geq 2\}$. If there exists k such that G_k is self-centered and $\text{diam}(G_k) \geq \text{diam}(G_i)$ for all $i \geq 2$ then normal product of all the graphs in S is a self-centered graph with diameter equal to $\text{diam}(G_k)$.

The next result characterizes the normal product of two DDR graphs.

Theorem 26 (see [23]). Normal product$G_1 \oplus G_2$ of two graphs G_1 and G_2 is DDR if and only if bothG_1 and G_2 are DDR graphs.

RELATIONSHIP WITH OTHER PROPERTIES

As mentioned earlier, the relation of DDR graphs with other graph properties is relatively an unexplored area. In this section we try to relate DDR graphs with some symmetry properties.

Let G denote a connected graph with automorphism group Aut(G). Then, G is distance-transitive, if for each quartet of vertices x, y, u and v in G such that $(x, y) = d(u, v)$, there is some γ in Aut(G) satisfying $\gamma(x) = u$ and $\gamma(y) = v$.

G is symmetric (1-transitive), if for each quartet of vertices x, y, u, and v in G such that x is adjacent to y and u is adjacent to v, there is some γ in Aut(G) satisfying $\gamma(x) = u$ and $\gamma(y) = v$.

G is vertex-transitive, if, for each pair of vertices x and y in G, there is some γ in Aut(G) satisfying $\gamma(x) = u$.

G is edge-transitive, if for each pair of edges $\{x, y\}$ and $\{u, v\}$ in G, there is some γ in Aut(G) satisfying $\gamma\{x, y\} \equiv \{\gamma(x), \gamma(y)\} = \{u, v\}$.

G is distance-regular with diameter m, if it is a k-regular connected graph with the following property

There are natural numbers $b_0 = k, b_1, \ldots, {}_{m-1}, c_1 = 1, c_2, \ldots, c_m$ such that for each pair of vertices x and y in G satisfying $d(x, y) = j$, it follows that

- The number of vertices at distance $j - 1$ from y and adjacent to x is c_j $(1 \leq j \leq m)$;
- The number of vertices at distance $j + 1$ from y and adjacent to x is b_j $(0 \leq j \leq m - 1)$.

In [24] Biggs has listed the results to show that a symmetric graph is both vertex-transitive and edge-transitive and that a distance-transitive graph is edge-transitive, symmetric, and distance regular. Based on these two results, Bloom et al. [19] proved the following.

Proposition 27 (see [19]). A graph that is vertex-transitive or distance-regular must be DDR.

In the next result Bloom et al. [19] have shown that distance degree regularity is weaker than other symmetry conditions and it is also indicated that other well-studied symmetry conditions do not imply DDR.

Proposition 28 (see [19]). Distance degree regularity does not imply edge-transitivity, vertex-transitivity, nor distance-regularity. Also, an edge-transitive graph is not necessarily DDR (and hence neither vertex-transitive, symmetric, nor distance transitive).

Vertex-transitivity does not imply edge-transitivity, symmetry, nor distance-regularity. Using the following Bloom et al. [19] have shown that a DDR graph is vertex-transitive, but not distance-regular.

The graph shown in Figure 5 is $C_5 \times C_3$, which is a DDR graph. This graph is not distance-regular, as there are two vertices adjacent to both x and y, whereas only one vertex is adjacent to both x and v, given that $(x, y) = d(x, v)$=2. Also, since the edge $\{u, v\}$ lies on a triangle and $\{u, z\}$ does not, and these two edges are not equivalent, it shows that the graph is not edge-transitive. Hence, it is not symmetric.

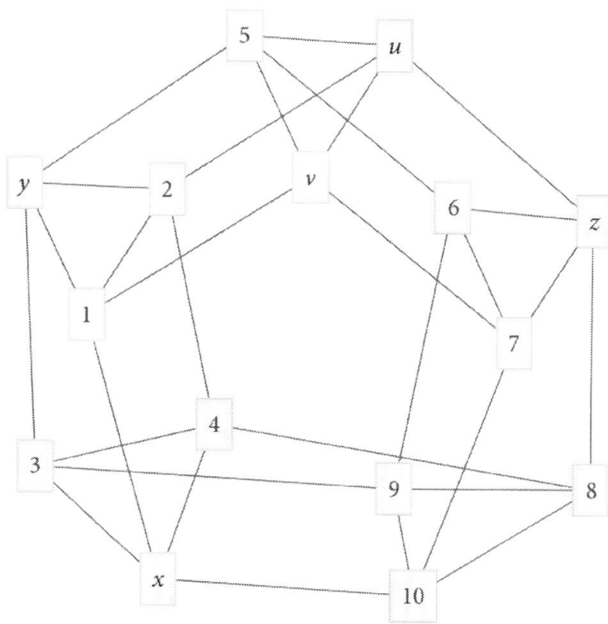

Figure 5

Distance-regularity does not imply vertex-transitivity. This is shown by an example, noted by Biggs, in [24, p. 139] and attributed to Adel'son-Velskii [25], of a distance-regular graph, hence DDR, with 26 vertices which is not vertex-transitive and, therefore, is neither symmetric nor distance-transitive.

Symmetry implies neither distance-transitivity nor distanceregularity. The former observation is demonstrated by a DDR example due to Frucht et al. [26]. They showed the implication did not hold for the permutation graph P(8-*cycle*), where α is the permutation (2, 4)(3, 7)(6, 8). This is the symmetric generalized Petersen graph (8, 3). Bloom et al. [19] demonstrated the second implication by the DDR example $P_{id}^2(6\text{-}cycle) = K_2^2 \times C_6 = C_4 \times C_6$ as shown in Figure 6. This graph can be shown to be symmetric by viewing it on a torus. But we can show that it is not a distance-regular graph on similar lines as done for the graph of Figure 5, by considering the vertex x with the vertices y and u.

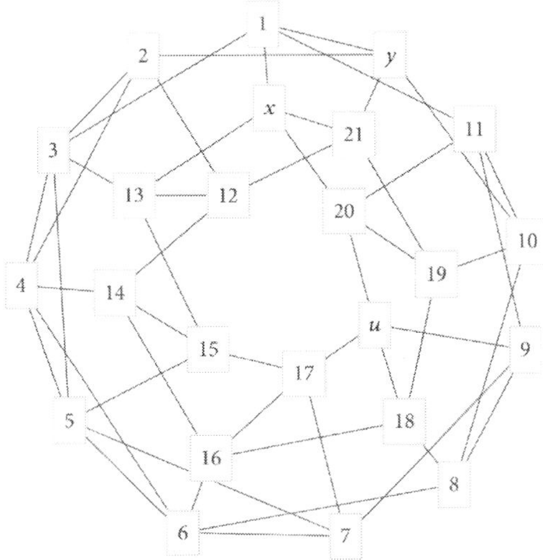

Figure 6

Bloom et al. [19] have shown that most of the well-studied symmetry conditions imply the DDR property. For example, among the four permutation graphs of the 5-cycle, only the most symmetric pair, that is, the P_i(*5-cycle*) and the Petersen graph, are DDR. So, they posed the following question, to check the effect of symmetry on permutation graphs.

Problem 29 (see [19]). Which k-cycle-α-permutation graphs of a given graph are DDR?

It is interesting to know that although most symmetry conditions suffice to make a graph DDR, there are DDR examples among the least symmetric graphs. One such class is DDR graphs having identity automorphism group. If $k < 3$, the only k-regular graph having identity automorphism group is the singleton graph K_1, which is trivially DDR. For $k \geq 3$, there exist k-regular graphs having identity automorphism group. For these the least order realizable has been determined by [27–30]. Bloom et al. [19] got the least ordered DDR graphs of identity graphs as the complements of the graphs given in [30]. Hence, they proved the following result.

Proposition 30 (see [19]). If (k) is the least order realizable by a k-regular DDR graph having identity automorphism group, then $V(5) = 10$, $V(6) = 11$, and for $k \geq 7$, $V(k) = k + 4$, if k is even and $V(k) = k + 5$, if k is odd.

For graphs with regularities 3 and 4 the situation is not clear. Although a least-order 3-regular identity graph has 12 vertices, none of the five graphs (see [30]) satisfying this condition is DDR. Thus, (3) ≥ 14. It has also been shown by Haigh (in a private communication to Bloom et al. [19]) that there are no DDR graphs among the 103 cubic identity graphs on 14 vertices which are contained in the complete tabulation of cubic graphs on graphs up to 14 vertices given in [16]. Thus, (3) ≥ 16. But the existence of a order 10 DDR identity graph is shown by Bloom et al. [19]. Also, they posed the following problem.

Problem 31 (see [19]). If k=3 or 4, do there exist any k-regular DDR graphs having identity automorphism group? If the answer is yes, what is the least order realizable by such graphs?

Next we will consider the relation of DDR graphs with a binary relation defined on the graph, namely, the eccentric digraph. The eccentric digraph of a graph or digraph is a distance based mapping, defined on a relation induced by distances in a graph or digraph, that is also represented by a graph. Many distance based relations can be found in literature in the study of antipodal graphs [31], antipodal digraphs [31], eccentric graphs [32, 33], and so forth. The eccentric digraph ED(G) of a graph (or digraph) G is the digraph that has the same vertex as G and an arc from u to V exists in ED(G) if and only if v is an eccentric vertex of u in G. Eccentric digraphs were defined by Buckley in [34]. In [22], Huilgol et al. have considered the relations between the distance degree regular (DDR) graphs and eccentric digraphs. The DDR graphs being self-centered yield symmetric eccentric digraphs. The study of eccentric digraphs involves the behavior of sequences of iterated eccentric digraphs and they are studied by Gimbert et al. [35]. Given a positive integer $k \geq 2$, the kth iterated eccentric digraph of G is written as $\mathrm{ED}^k(G) = \mathrm{ED}(\mathrm{ED}^{k-1}(G))$ where $\mathrm{ED}^0(G) = G$ and $\mathrm{ED}^1(G) = \mathrm{ED}(G)$. For every digraph G there exist smallest integerss $s > 0$ and $t \geq 0$ such that $\mathrm{ED}^t(G) = \mathrm{ED}^{s+}(G)$. In case of labeled graphs s is called the period of G and t the tail of G whereas for unlabeled graphs these quantities are referred to as isoperiod, denoted by s' (G) and iso-tail, t' (G), respectively.

In [22] Huilgol et al. have showed that the unique eccentric vertex DDR graphs have all their iterated eccentric digraphs as DDR graphs. In the same paper many results are proved showing the relation between DDR graphs and eccentric digraphs.

Proposition 32 (see [22]). There exists a DDR graph G such that $\mathrm{ED}(G) \cong G$.

Proposition 33 (see [22]). There exists a DDR graph G such that ED(G) is a disconnected graph each of whose components is complete bipartite graph.

Proposition 34 (see [22]). For a unique eccentric vertex DDR graph, if p>4 then tail = 1, period = 2, and if p=4, tail = 0, period = 2.

Proposition 35 (see [22]). For a given diameter (≥ 3), there exist $2d - 6$ DDR graphs with tail = 1 and period = 1.

Remark 36. The unique eccentric vertex DDR graphs have all their iterated eccentric digraphs as DDR graphs.

For nonunique eccentric vertex DDR graphs the problem remains still open.

Problem 37 (see [22]). When do nonunique eccentric vertex DDR graphs have all their iterated digraphs as DDR graphs?

DISTANCE DEGREE INJECTIVE (DDI) GRAPHS

In contrast to distance degree regular (DDR) graphs the Distance Degree Injective (DDI) graphs are the graphs with no two vertices of G having the same distance degree sequence (dds). These were also defined by Bloom et al. [36]. So these graphs are highly irregular, compared to the DDR graphs. But, the other extreme of the DDR graphs as we noted above, to have identity automorphism group, becomes an inherent property of DDI graphs, which is evident by the next result.

Theorem 38 (see [36]). If G is a DDI graph, then G has an identity automorphism group, but not conversely.

The converse is obvious as there are DDR graphs with identity automorphism group.

As DDR graphs, the characterizations elude DDI graphs. But there are many existential results and examples of DDI graphs.

Theorem 39 (see [36]). A smallest order nontrivial DDI graph has order 7 and there exist DDI graphs having order p for all $p \geq 7$.

The smallest order nontrivial identity graph has 6 vertices and there are exactly eight identity graphs on 6 vertices and these are not DDI. So the least order is 7. Actually, the identity tree as shown in Figure 7 is the smallest DDI graph.

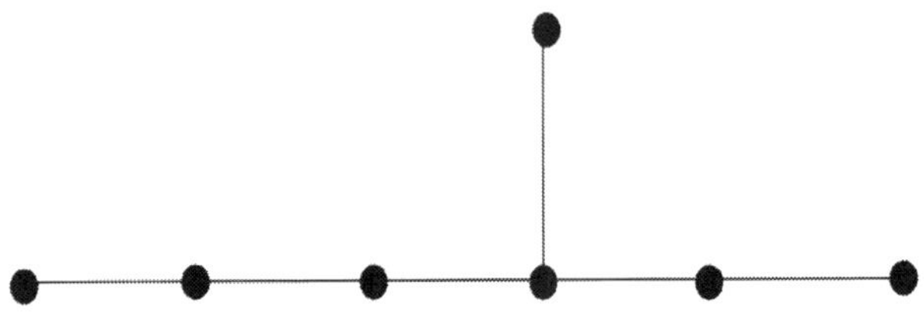

Figure 7

The following result shows the existence of a DDI graph of arbitrary diameter.

Theorem 40 (see [36]). A smallest diameter nontrivial DDI graph has diameter 3 and there exist DDI graphs having diameter m for all $m \geq 3$.

The graphs shown in Figure 8 are DDI and have diameter 3 and 4, respectively. The graph of Figure 7 is a DDI graph with diameter 5. For DDI graphs of diameter 6, 7, . . . we can consider the same graph as shown in Figure 7 and go on adding vertices on the left of the path P_6.

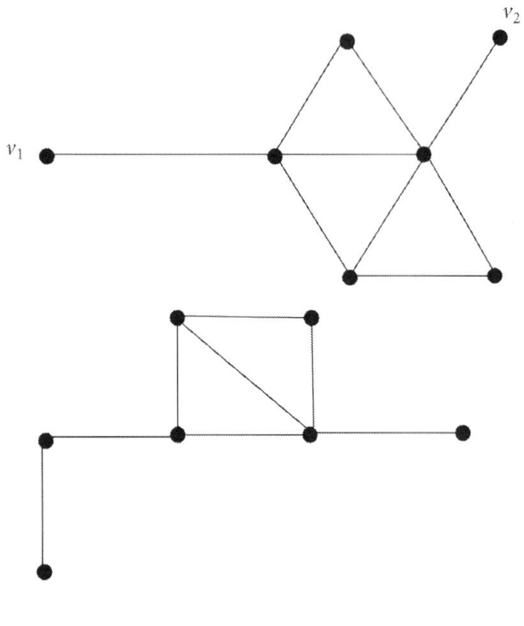

Figure 8

Theorem 41 (see [36]). If G is a connected DDI graph and $G \neq K_1$, then the diameter of G is bounded by 3 and sharply bounded by $|G| - 2$.

The following theorem is useful in showing that a graph is not DDI.

Theorem 42 (see [36]). If G contains two vertices v_1, v_2 with the same degree and such that no vertex of G is further than distance 2 from both v_1 and v_2, then G is not DDI.

Note that the complement of the diameter three graph shown in Figure 8 is the diameter three identity graph shown in Figure 9. We can see that the above theorem is applicable for this graph and hence it is not DDI.

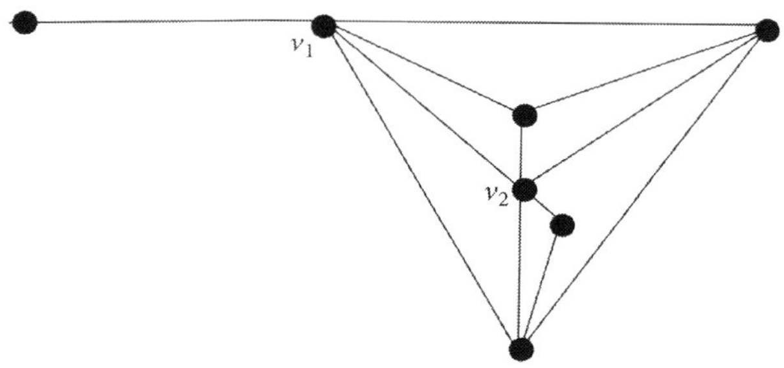

Figure 9

But the picture is not clear when we wish to have a graph and its complement to be DDI.

Problem 43 (see [36]). Does there exist a graph $G \neq K_1$ such that G and its complement are both DDI?

So the next question was on k-regular DDI graphs as posed by Bloom et al. [36].

Problem 44 (see [36]). Does there exist a nontrivial k-regular DDI graph?

This problem got resolved by the existence of a cubic DDI graph on 24 vertices and having diameter 10 as found in [37]. The general existence problem was resolved by Bollobas in [38] where he showed the following.

Theorem 45 (see [38]). Let $k \geq 3$ and $\epsilon > 0$ be fixed. Set $k = \lfloor (1/2 + \epsilon)(\log p)/\log(k-1) \rfloor$. Then, as p goes to infinity, the probability tends to one that every vertex v_i in a k-regular labeled graph of order p is uniquely determined by the initial segments $d_{i_0}, d_{i_1}, d_{i_2}, \ldots, d_{i_j}$ of its distance degree sequence.

Since the distance degree sequence of a graph is independent of a labeling, this result shows that almost all k-regular graphs of order p are DDI provided that p is large enough. The problem that remains unresolved is that of finding minimal DDI regular graphs.

In this direction there was one more problem defined by Halberstam and Quintas [37] as follows.

Problem 46 (see [37]). For $k \geq 3$ what is the smallest order and/or diameter for which there exists a k-regular DDI graph?

Martinez and Quintas [39] found a cubic DDI graph having diameter 8 and order 22, as in Figure 10. They also showed that if in the graph of Figure 10 the edges ab and cd are replaced by the graph shown in Figure 11, one can obtain a cubic DDI graph with 22 + $2m$ vertices and diameter 8+m. This was further reduced to order 18 and diameter 7 cubic graph by Volf [40] by constructing the graph of Figure 12. From [18, 36, 37, 39, 40], it follows that

If there is a cubic DDI graph having less than 18 vertices, then its order must be 16;

If there is a cubic DDI graph having diameter less than 7, then its diameter must be 4, 5, or 6.

So all these cases were considered by Huilgol and Rajeshwari [41] and proved the nonexistence of such a cubic DDI graph.

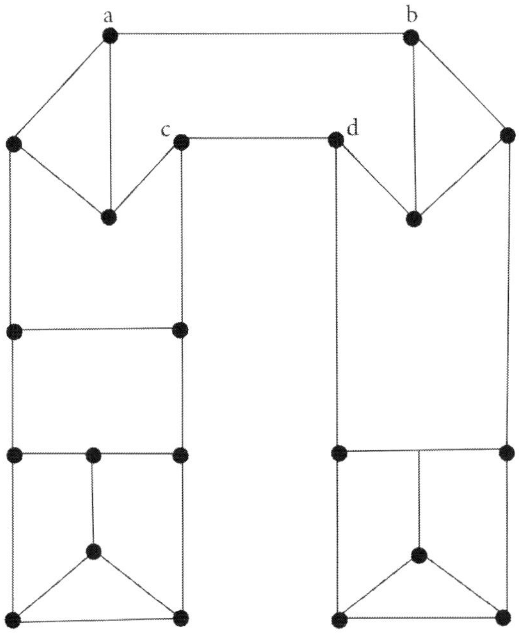

Figure 10

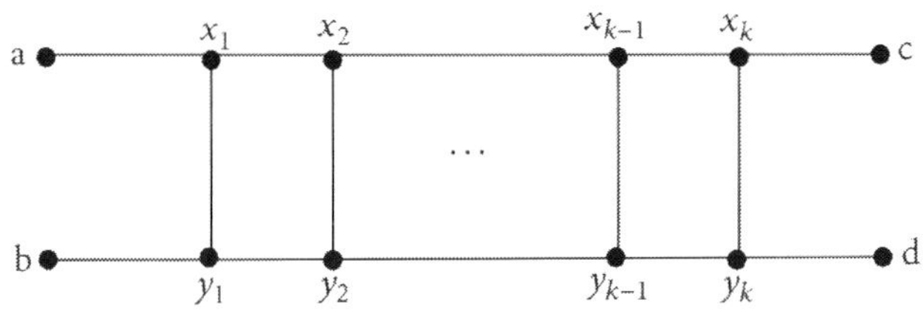

Figure 11

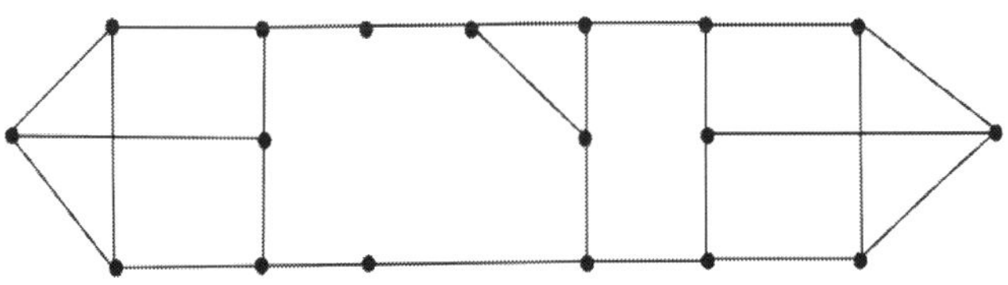

Figure 12

Theorem 47 (see [41]). There does not exist a cubic DDI graph of order 16 with diameters 4, 5, and 6.

So the graph of order 18 as in [40] shown in Figure 12 is the smallest order cubic DDI graph.

On the other extreme, construction of new DDI graphs from the smaller order/diameter is also interesting and is looked into by Huilgol et al. [23]. In this paper many results are discussed for different products and the behavior of DDI graphs with respect to these products.

Theorem 48 (see [23]). If the cartesian product of two graphs G_1 and G_2 is DDI then both G_1 and G_2 are DDI graphs.

But the converse is not true, as the cartesian product of the DDI graph represented by Figure 7 and diameter 4 DDI graph of Figure 8 is not a DDI graph.

Lemma 49 (see [23]). Let G_1 and G_2 be two DDI graphs. Let $A = \{dd(u_i)/u_i \in V(G_1)\}$ and $B = \{dds(v_i)/v_i \in V(G_2)\}$. If $|A \cap B| \geq 2$ then $G_1 \square G_2$ is not DDI.

Theorem 50 (see [23]). Let G_1 and G_2 be any two graphs. Let u be a vertex in G_1 and let S be a subset of $V(G_2)$ such that no two vertices of S have the same distance degree sequence; then, no two vertices of$\{u\} \times S$ have the same distance degree sequence in $G_1 \square G_2$.

Let S_1 and S_2 be two subsets of (G_1). For each pair(x, y), with $x \in S_1$ and $y \in S_2$ we can see that $dds(x) \neq dds(y)$, by applying the Theorem 50. Let $z \in (G_2)$ be any vertex in G_2, and then in $G_1 \square G_2$, the subsets $\{(x, z)/x \in S_1\}$ and $\{(y, z)/y \in S_2\}$ are such that every pair $((x, z), (y, z))/x \in S_1, y \in S_2$ satisfies $dds(x, z) \neq dds(y, z)$.

Similar results are proved for normal product of DDI graphs.

Proposition 51 (see [23]). If the normal product $G_1 \oplus G_2$ of two graphs is DDI then both G_1 and G_2 are DDI.

As in the case of cartesian product, the normal product of two DDI graphs need not be DDI and the same example serves the purpose.

Lemma 52 (see [23]). Let G_1 and G_2 be two DDI graphs. Let $A = \{dd(u_i)/u_i \in V(G_1)\}$ and $B = \{dds(v_i)/v_i \in V(G_2)\}$. If $|A \cap B| \geq 2$ then $G_1 \oplus G_2$ is not DDI.

Proposition 53 (see [23]). Let G_1 and G_2 be any two graphs. Let u be a vertex in G_1 and let S be a subset of $V(G_2)$ such that no two vertices of S have the same distance degree sequence; then, no two vertices of $\{u\} \times S$ have the same distance degree sequence in $G_1 \oplus G_2$.

Remark 54. Let there be two sets S_1 and S_2, subsets of (G_1) such that every pair (x, y), with $x \in S_1$ and $y \in S_2$, satisfies $dds(x) \neq dds(y)$. Let $z \in (G_2)$ be any vertex in G_2, and then in $G_1 \oplus G_2$, the subsets $\{(x, z)/x \in S_1\}$ and $\{(y, z)/y \in S_2\}$ are such that every pair $((x, z), (y, z))/x \in S_1, y \in S_2$ satisfies $dds(x, z) \neq dds(y, z)$.

EMBEDDINGS

Kennedy and Quintas [12] considered the extremality of f-trees when they are constrained by embedding either in lattice-graphs or in Euclidean spaces. In chemistry, such constraints appear in the form of postulates concerning the minimal energy which can be attained by certain connectivity patterns of atoms in space. This approach offers a framework ensuring a physical theory to remain self-consistent with respect to its embedding space requirements. So given the distance degree sequence of a graph, it is interesting to see whether we can get some information about the embedding properties of the graph. Hence the next natural question will be on embedding a graph in DDR/DDI graph; if not possible, then try to find the forbidden class of subgraphs. In this context two problems were posed by Bloom et al. [36] which are listed below.

Problem 55 (see [36]). Does there exist a pair of nonisomorphic graphs having the same distance degree sequence and such that one of them is nonplanar with a subgraph homeomorphic to K_5 and the other graph is planar?

Problem 56 (see [36]). Does there exist a pair of nonisomorphic graphs having the same path degree sequence and such that only one of the graphs is planar?

At the other extreme Huilgol et al. [42] have considered the embedding of DDR and DDI graphs. The following result rules out the forbidden class of subgraphs for DDR graphs by embedding any graph into a DDR graph.

Theorem 57 (see [42]). Any graph can be embedded in a DDR graph.

DDR graphs exhibit high regularity in terms of the vertices and their distance distribution. If we relax one vertex to have different distance degree sequence, then we call such a graph an almost distance degree regular graph, or in short, an ADDR graph. Similarly, we define ADDI graphs.

Definition 58 (see [42]). A graph G of order p is said to be almost DDR if $p-1$ vertices have the same distance degree sequence and one vertex with different distance degree sequence.

Definition 59 (see [42]). A graph G of order p is said to be almost DDI if $p-2$ vertices have different distance degree sequences and two vertices with the same distance degree sequence.

Embedding in DDI graphs seems not so easy. But Huilgol et al. [42] could embed only cycles, paths in DDI graphs as follows.

Theorem 60 (see [42]). Any path can be embedded in an almost DDI graph.

Proposition 61 (see [42]). Every cycle can be embedded in a DDI graph.

So the following problems were posed in [42].

Problem 62 (see [42]). Can any graph be embedded in a DDI graph?

Problem 63 (see [42]). Does there exist a k-regular DDI graph for $k \geq 4$?

One more problem can be posed at this juncture as follows.

Problem 64. Does there exist a self-centered, k-regular DDI graph?

We conclude this article with a comment that even though there are numerous examples and results on DDR and DDI graphs available in literature, the characterizations elude. Hence, many open problems in these areas still persist and keep researchers working.

REFERENCES

1. P. Erdos and T. Gallai, "Graphs with prescribed degrees of vertices," Matematikai Lapok, vol. 11, pp. 264–274, 1960 (Hungarian).
2. V. Havel, "A remark on the existence of finite graphs," Časopis Pro Pěstování Matematiky, vol. 80, pp. 477–480, 1955 (Czech).
3. S. L. Hakimi, "On realizability of a set of integers as degrees of the vertices of a linear graph. I," Journal of the Society for Industrial and Applied Mathematics, vol. 10, pp. 496–506, 1962.
4. L. M. Lesniak-Foster, "Eccentric sequences in graphs," Periodica Mathematica Hungarica, vol. 6, no. 4, pp. 287–293, 1975.
5. P. A. Ostrand, "Graphs with specified radius and diameter," Discrete Mathematics, vol. 4, pp. 71–75, 1973.
6. M. Behzad and J. E. Simpson, "Eccentric sequences and eccentric sets in graphs," Discrete Mathematics, vol. 16, no. 3, pp. 187–193, 1976.
7. R. Nandakumar, On some eccentric properties of graphs [PhD Thesis], Indian Institute of Technology, New Delhi, India, 1986.
8. J. Gimbert and N. Lopez, "Eccentric sequences and eccentricity sets in digraphs," Ars Combinatoria, vol. 86, pp. 225–238, 2008.
9. M. Randic, "Characterizations of atoms, molecules, and classes of molecules based on paths enumerations," MATCH, vol. 7, pp. 5–64, 1979.
10. F. Buckley and F. Harary, Distance in Graphs, Addison-Wesley, 1990.
11. F. Harary, "Status and contrastatus," Sociometry, vol. 22, pp. 23–43, 1959.
12. J. W. Kennedy and L. V. Quintas, "Extremal f-trees and embedding spaces for molecular graphs," Discrete Applied Mathematics, vol. 5, no. 2, pp. 191–209, 1983.
13. L. V. Quintas and P. J. Slater, "Pairs of nonisomorphic graphs having the same path degree sequence,"Match, no. 12, pp. 75–86, 1981.
14. P. J. Slater, "Counterexamples to Randić's conjecture on distance degree sequences for trees," Journal of Graph Theory, vol. 6, no. 1, pp. 89–91, 1982.
15. M. Gargano and L. V. Quintas, "Smallest order pairs of non-isomorphic graphs having the same distance degree sequence and specified number of cycles," in Notes from New York Graph Theory Day VI, pp. 13–16, New York Academy of Sciences, 1983.
16. F. C. Bussemaker, S. Cobeljic, D. B. Cvetkovic, and J. J. Seidel, "Computer investigation of cube Graphs,"T. H. Report 76-WSK-01, Technological University Eindhoven, Eindhoven, The Netherlands, 1976.
17. G. Brinkmann, "Fast generation of cubic graphs," Journal of Graph Theory, vol. 23, no. 2, pp. 139–149, 1996.
18. F. Y. Halberstam and L. V. Quintas, A Note on Tables of Distance and Path Degree Sequences for Cubic Graphs, Mathematics Department, Pace University, New York, NY, USA, 1982.
19. G. S. Bloom, L. V. Quintas, and J. W. Kennedy, "Distance degree regular graphs," in The Theory and Applications of Graphs, 4th International Conference, Western Michigan University, Kalamazoo, MI, May, 1980, pp. 95–108, John Wiley & Sons, New York, NY, USA, 1981.
20. G. Chartrand and F. Harary, "Planar permutation graphs," Annales de l›Institut Henri Poincaré B, vol. 3, pp. 433–438, 1967.
21. M. I. Huilgol, H. B. Walikar, and B. D. Acharya, "On diameter three distance degree regular graphs,"Advances and Applications in Discrete Mathematics, vol. 7, no. 1, pp. 39–61, 2011.
22. M. I. Huilgol, M. Rajeshwari, and S. Syed Asif Ulla, "Distance degree regular graphs and their eccentric digraphs," International Journal of Mathematical Sciences and Engineering Applications, vol. 5, no. 6, pp. 405–416, 2011.
23. M. I. Huilgol, M. Rajeshwari, and S. S. A. Ulla, "Products of distance degree regular and distance degree injective graphs," Journal of Discrete Mathematical Sciences &

Cryptography, vol. 15, no. 4-5, pp. 303–314, 2012.
24. N. L. Biggs, Algebraic Graph Theory, Cambridge Tracts in Mathematics 67, Cambridge University Press, London, UK, 1974.
25. G. M. Adelьson-Velskii, "Example of a graph without a transitive automorphism group," Soviet Mathematics-Doklady, vol. 10, pp. 440–441, 1969.
26. R. Frucht, J. E. Graver, and M. E. Watkins, "The groups of the generalized Petersen graphs," Proceedings of the Cambridge Philosophical Society, vol. 70, pp. 211–218, 1971.
27. A. T. Balaban, R. O. Davies, F. Harary, A. Hill, and R. Westwick, "Cubic identity graphs and planar graphs derived from trees," Journal of the Australian Mathematical Society, vol. 11, pp. 207–215, 1970.
28. G. Baron and W. Imrich, "Asymmetrische reguläre Graphen," Acta Mathematica Academiae Scientiarum Hungaricae, vol. 20, pp. 135–142, 1969.
29. A. Gewirtz, A. Hill, and L. V. Quintas, "El numero minimo de puntos para grafos regulares y asimetricos," Scientia, vol. 138, pp. 103–111, 1969.
30. V. A. Kokhov, "All cubic graphs of least order with identity automorphism group," Programmirovanie, vol. 4, pp. 106–107, 1976.
31. G. Johns and K. Sleno, "Antipodal graphs and digraphs," International Journal of Mathematics and Mathematical Sciences, vol. 16, no. 3, pp. 579–586, 1993.
32. J. Akiyama, K. Ando, and D. Avis, "Eccentric graphs," Discrete Mathematics, vol. 56, no. 1, pp. 1–6, 1985.
33. G. Chartrand, W. Gu, M. Schultz, and S. J. Winters, "Eccentric graphs," Networks, vol. 34, no. 2, pp. 115–121, 1999.
34. F. Buckley, "The Eccentric digraph of a graph," Congressus Numerantium, vol. 149, pp. 65–76, 2001.
35. J. Gimbert, M. Miller, F. Ruskey, and J. Ryan, "Iterations of eccentric digraphs," Bulletin of the Institute of Combinatorics and Its Applications, vol. 45, pp. 41–50, 2005.
36. G. S. Bloom, J. W. Kennedy, and L. V. Quintas, "Some problems concerning distance and path degree sequences," in Graph Theory, vol. 1018 of Lecture Notes in Mathematics, pp. 179–190, Springer, Berlin, Germany, 1983.
37. F. Y. Halberstam and L. V. Quintas, "A note on tables of distance and path degree sequences for cubic graphs," in Proceedings of the Silver Jubilee Conference on Combinatorics, University of Waterloo, Ontario, Canada, June–July 1982.
38. B. Bollobas, "Distinguishing vertices of random graphs," Annals of Discrete Mathematics, vol. 13, pp. 33–50, 1982.
39. P. Martinez and L. V. Quintas, "Distance degree injective regular graphs," in Notes from New York Graph Theory Day VIII, pp. 19–21, New York Academy of Sciences, New York, NY, USA, 1984.
40. J. Volf, "A small distance degree injective cubic graphs," in Notes from New York Graph Theory Day XIII, pp. 31–32, New York Academy of Sciences, 1987.
41. M. I. Huilgol and M. Rajeshwari, "Non-Existence of cubic DDI graphs of order 16 with diameter 4, 5, 6," (Communicated).
42. M. I. Huilgol, M. Rajeshwari, and S. Syed Asif Ulla, "Embedding in distance degree regular and distance degree injective graphs," Malaya Journal of Mathematik, vol. 4, no. 1, pp. 134–141, 2013.

CHAPTER 20 NEW CLASSES OF GRACEFUL TREES

Md. Forhad Hossain, Md. Momin Al Aziz, and M. Kaykobad

Department of Computer Science and Engineering, Bangladesh University of Engineering and Technology, Dhaka 1000, Bangladesh

ABSTRACT

Graceful labeling is one of the most researched problems. One of the earliest results is that caterpillars are graceful. We show that caterpillars connected to a vertex recursively satisfying certain conditions are also graceful.

INTRODUCTION

Let T be any arbitrary tree on m edges. If its vertices can be distinctly labeled using integers $0, 1, \ldots, m$ so that all the induced edge labels (vertices labeled i and j induce label $|i - j|$ on edge (i, j)) are also distinct, then the labeling is called graceful. It was conjectured that all trees are graceful. This has connection with Ringel's conjecture and some related results can be found in [1, 2]; Kotzig later conjectured that such a decomposition could be achieved cyclically. Rosa [2] established that these conjectures could be solved by showing that every tree is graceful.

The conjecture has been very widely studied and new classes of trees have been proved to be graceful (see [3–5]). However, it has not been possible to devise a single algorithm to stand out against the conjecture for any arbitrary tree. The research has continued in two directions: newer and more generalized classes of graceful trees are discovered [6–8] or graceful labeling has been computed for all larger trees up to a fixed order. Computationally, it has been shown so far that all trees with up to 35 vertices are graceful [9]. Graceful labeling has found useful applications in coding theory, X-ray crystallography, radar, astronomy, circuit design, communication network addressing, and database management (see [10, 11]).

In Section 2, we define the classes of trees that have already been proved graceful and critical to our work. Section 3 defines our work of two new classes of trees that have been proved graceful.

GRACEFULLY LABELED TREES

Let us introduce the classes of trees for which graceful labeling has been found.

A path is a tree with only two leaves. A caterpillar is a tree such that if all leaves are removed, the remaining graph is a path. This path can be termed as backbone of the caterpillar. Rosa [12] proved that all caterpillars are graceful. In Figure 1, a gracefully labeled caterpillar has been shown. A caterpillar is labeled from one end of its backbone with 0. Its adjacent vertices are labeled using so far unused largest labels in such a way that vertices on the path get alternately the largest and smallest labels. In this way, while we label vertices the largest

Citation: Md. Forhad Hossain, Md. Momin Al Aziz, and M. Kaykobad, "New Classes of Graceful Trees," Journal of Discrete Mathematics, vol. 2014, Article ID 194759, 6 pages, 2014. doi:10.1155/2014/194759

unused edge labels are generated. It may be noted that for an m-edge tree if (i) is a graceful labeling, then so is $m - f(i)$. So we can label any end of a caterpillar by 0 or by m.

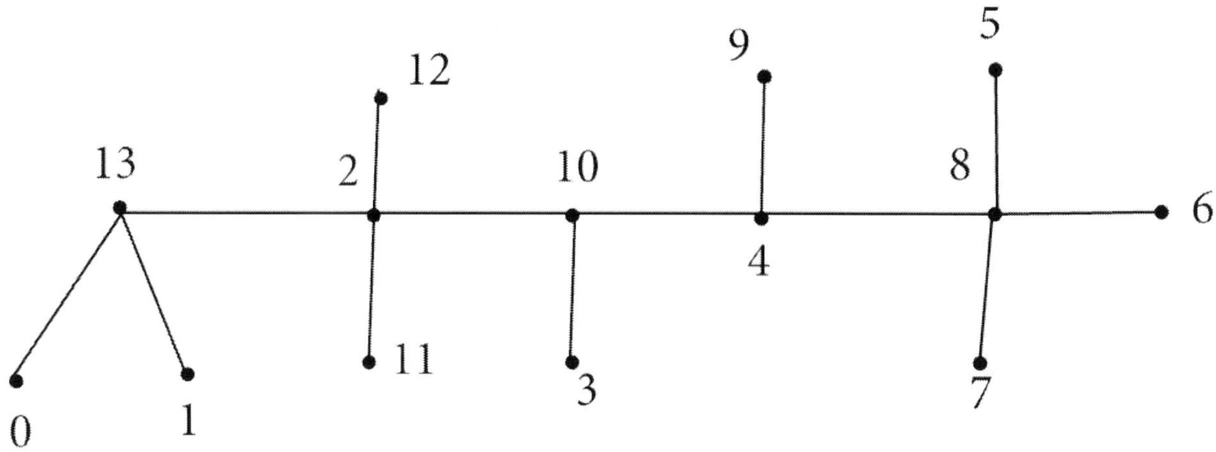

Figure 1: An example of gracefully labeled 14-vertex caterpillar.

A rooted tree in which every level contains vertices of the same degree is called symmetrical trees. Bermond and Schönheim [13] proved that all symmetrical trees are graceful as in Figure 2.

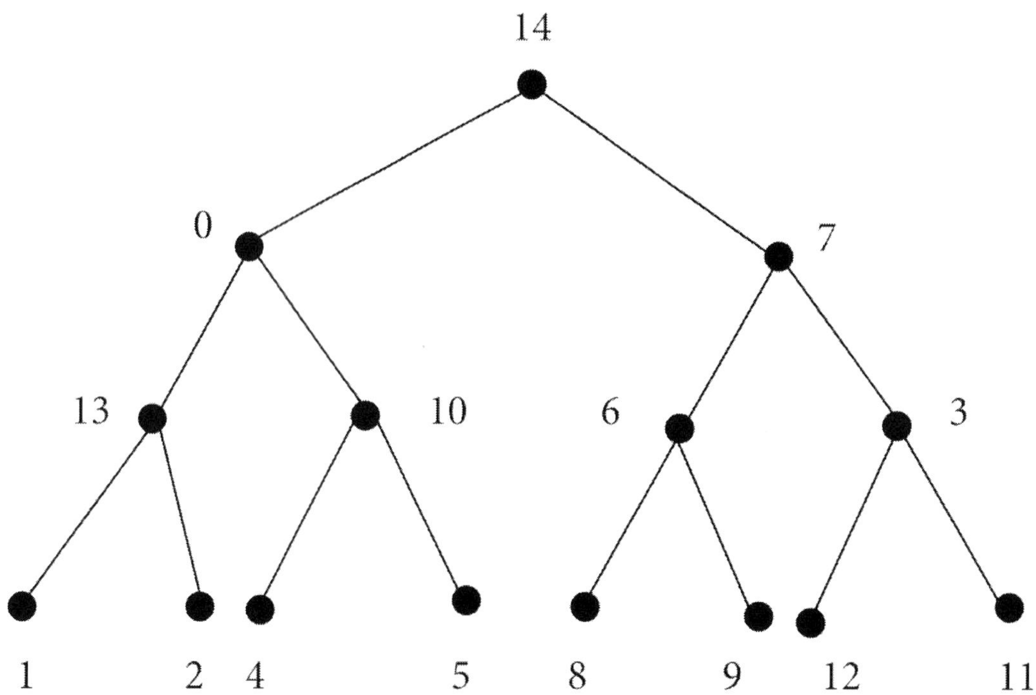

Figure 2: An example of gracefully labeled 15-vertex symmetrical tree.

In this paper, we prove that super-caterpillars obtained by joining a set of caterpillars of a special type to a vertex are also graceful (Figures 4 and 5).

NEW CLASSES OF GRACEFUL TREES

Let us introduce the following classes of trees.

Definition 1. Let T_0 be any arbitrary caterpillar and let T_i, $i = 1, \ldots, k$, be caterpillars with $|T_i|=m$ number of vertices and the sum of vertex numbers is the same in odd levels of all pairs T_{2i+1} and T_{2i+2}. In case of k being an odd number, one caterpillar will be without a pair. Let a leaf attached to backbone of each T_i be joined to a vertex v by an edge. Then the resulting tree is called a super-caterpillar.

Two super-caterpillars are illustrated in Figure 3 with odd and even k. Now we have the following result.

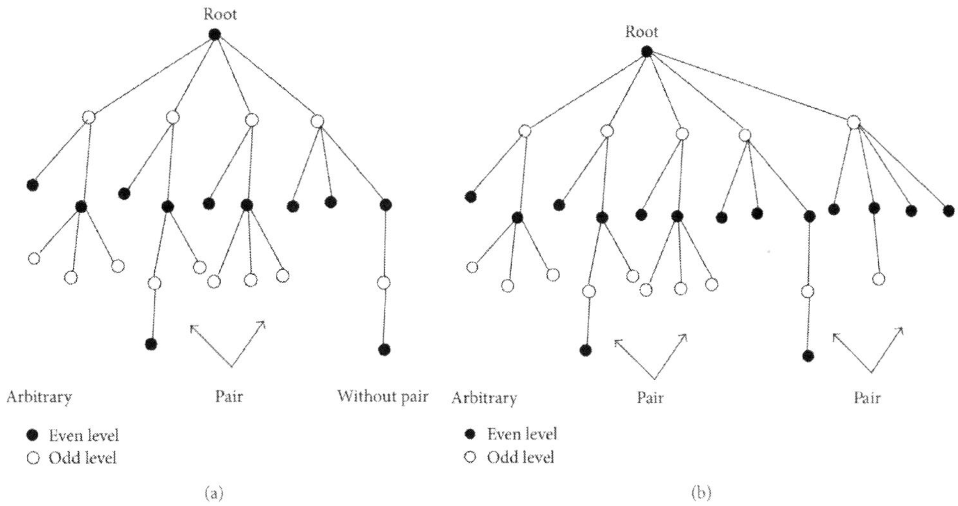

Figure 3: Example of a super-caterpillar with (a) odd k and (b) even k, with an arbitrary caterpillar joined with a root.

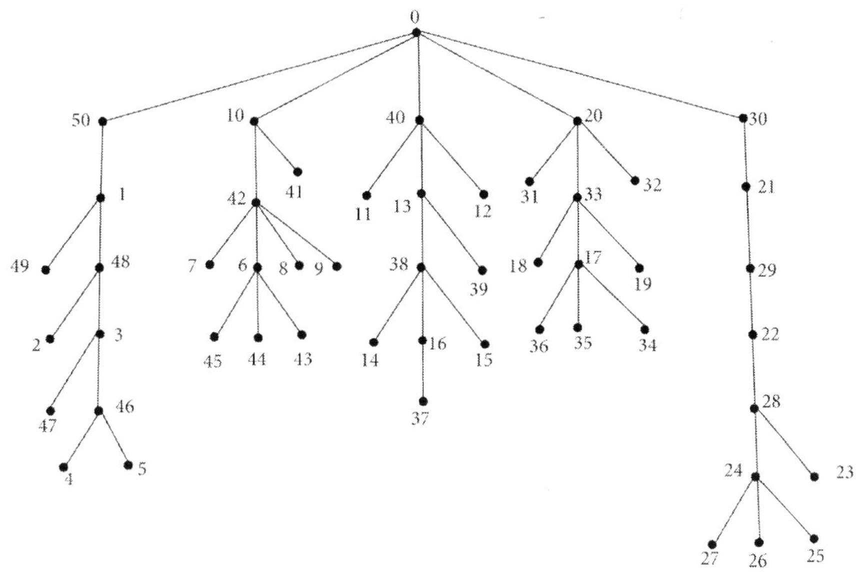

Figure 4: Example of a super-caterpillar gracefully labeled.

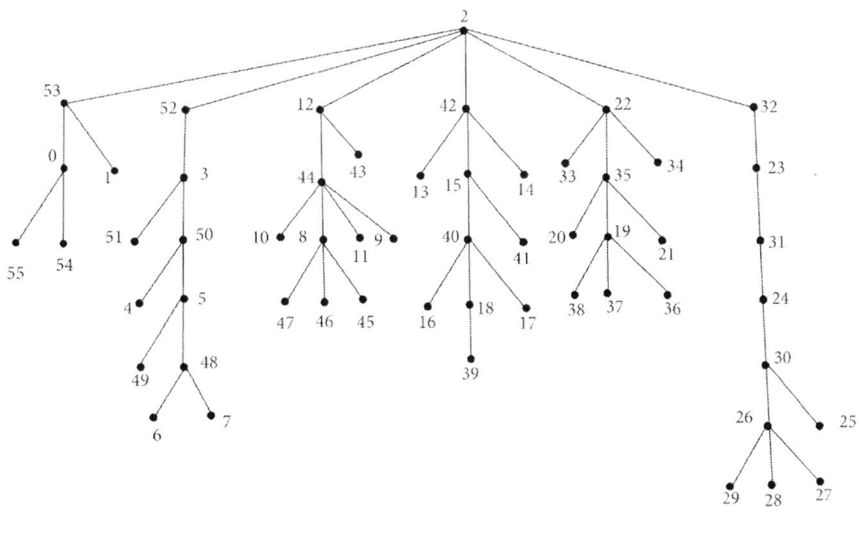

Figure 5: Example of super-caterpillar gracefully labeled with an arbitrary caterpillar where $s_0 = 2$.

Theorem 2. All super-caterpillars are graceful.

Proof of Theorem 2 Let us assume for simplicity that we have k caterpillars joined to v and that each caterpillar has the same number m of vertices, also a total of si vertices in odd levels, si being equal for each pair of caterpillars T_{2i+1} and T_{2i+2}. We also denote the vertex of T_j connected to v by v_j. Let us label v by 0. Now vertices of caterpillars will be in turn labeled using the smallest and largest labels following caterpillar-labeling schemes so that edge numbers are generated in descending order. The endpoint of T_1 connected to v is labeled km, and we will use up m labels in T_1 of which s_1 large, namely, km, $km - 1, \ldots, km - s_1 + 1$, and $m - s_1$ small labels, namely, $1, \ldots, m - s_1$. Thus the last edge label created is $km - s_1 + 1 - (m - s_1) = (k - 1) + 1$. In the next caterpillar, both the smallest and largest labels will differ by 1 from the labels used in the previous tree. In particular, one vertex will get label $km - s_1 - 1$ and the other one $m - s_1$ resulting in edge label $km - s_1 - (m - s_1 + 1) = (k - 1) - 1$ missing the label $(k - 1)m$. We are going to use up $m - s_2$ large and s_2 small labels in T_2 in bottom up fashion. Note that $s_2 = s_1$. T_2 will be labeled in such a way that v_2 ends getting the smallest unused label, that is, label m. In this way in tandem vertices of odd levels will be numbered by big and small numbers, respectively, for odd and even indexed caterpillars. This will result in label $(v_i) = (k - \lfloor(i - 1)/2\rfloor)m$ for odd i, whereas label $(v_i) = im/2$ is for even ones. For each pair of caterpillars, labels $(k - \lfloor(i - 1)/2\rfloor)m$ and $im/2$ will be missing which will be generated on edges incident to vertex v.

Now assume that we have one arbitrary caterpillar T_0 and any k caterpillars having the same number of vertices m and that the last caterpillar has m vertices but not necessarily having equal number of vertices in odd levels as all previous pairs have. One end of backbone of each caterpillar is connected to v. So total number of edges in the tree will be $km + m_0$. Now start labeling T_0 in such a way that we end up labeling v by s_0 shifting label of v by s_0. Large labels have also been shifted by $0 - (m_0 - s_0) = s_0$, thus producing $(k - \lfloor(i - 1)/2\rfloor)m$ labels on the edge incident to v, which we have missed in moving from one caterpillar to the next. Now for T_1 we are left with numbers from $s_0 + 1$ to $km + m_0 - m + s_0 = (k - 1)m + m_0 + s$. This way all v_is, adjacent to root v, will be labeled by multiples of m. After we have completed labeling all pairs of caterpillars, we will be left with consecutive integers to label the vertices of the unpaired caterpillar and generate the remaining smallest possible edge labels.

Definition 3. Let there be any numbers of kp caterpillars each having m vertices and total number of vertices in odd (or even) levels of these caterpillars are the same. These caterpillars are grouped in k groups each having p caterpillars. Let backbones of each group i of caterpillars be connected to vertex v_i that is connected to vertex v. Then the resulting tree is called an extended super-caterpillar.

An extended super-caterpillar is illustrated in Figure 6 with six caterpillars grouped in two ($k = 2$), where each group has three caterpillars ($p = 3$) joined with a vertex v_i. Each caterpillar contains nine vertices ($s = 9$). Now we have the following result.

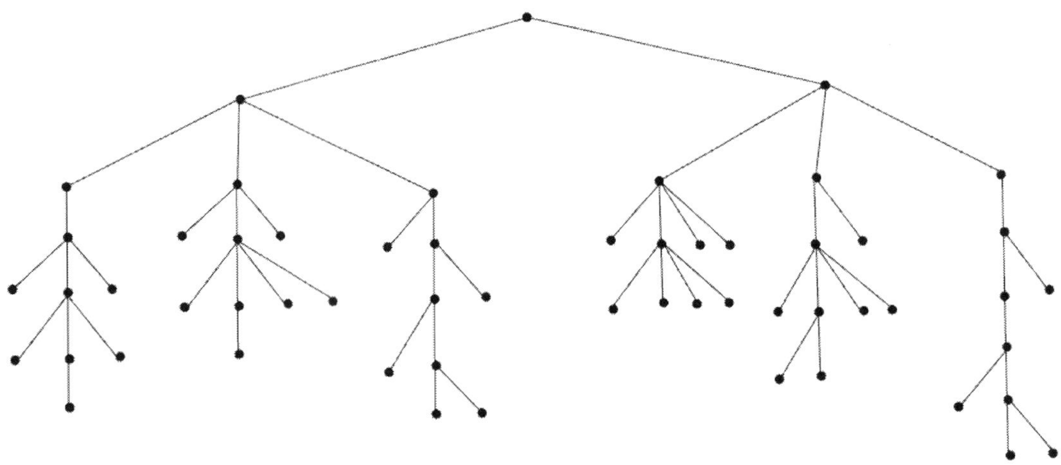

Figure 6: Example of an extended super-caterpillar with two groups ($k = 2$) consisting of three caterpillars.

Theorem 4. All extended super-caterpillars are graceful.

Proof of Theorem 4. Theorem 2 asserts that we can label each group i of caterpillars with root v_i, $\forall i = 1, \ldots, k$, gracefully. Root v, connected to all v_i, is labeled 0 and labels of the remaining vertices in the tree are incremented by one. Lets be the total number of vertices in each group (where $s = pm + 1$). For group i, we will be labeling all odd level vertices by adding an offset $(k - i)$ and for even level vertices $(i - 1)s$ where $i = 1, 2, 3, \ldots, k$. So v_i gets label $(k - i)$, and therefore edge (v, v_i) gets label $(k - i)s$.

We will get the consecutive edge labels having the largest differences $(k - 0) - 1$ to $(k - 2)s + 1$ in groups T_i and $T_{(k-i+1)}$ for $i = 1$ except $(k - 1)s$ and ks (Figure 9). Similarly, next consecutive differences $(k - 2) - 1$ to $(k - 4)s + 1$ are found in T_i and $T_{(k-i+1)}$ for $i = 2$ again missing $(k - 3)s$ and $(k - 2)s$. So in general we can say that differences $(k - 2(d - 1))s - 1$ to $(k - 2d)s + 1$ are generated while missing $(k - 2d + 1)s$ and $(k - 2(d - 1))s$ where $d = 1, 2, \ldots, \lceil k/2\rceil$. These numbers are multiples of s which have already been generated in edges (v, v_i), $i = 1, \ldots, k$.

The following examples show how this labeling is done in an extended super-caterpillar consisting of six caterpillars as in Figure 7 grouped in three (Figure 8) or two (Figure 10) ($k = 2$ or $k = 3$). Here each caterpillar has 9 vertices ($m = 9$). Then both of these groups are connected with v and gracefully labeled as in Figures 9 and 11.

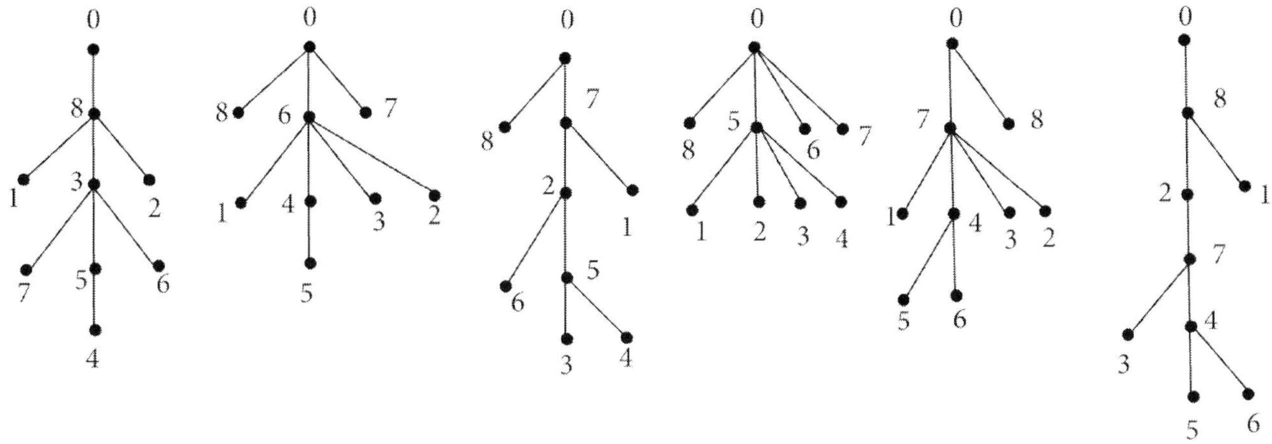

Figure 7: Six graceful caterpillars.

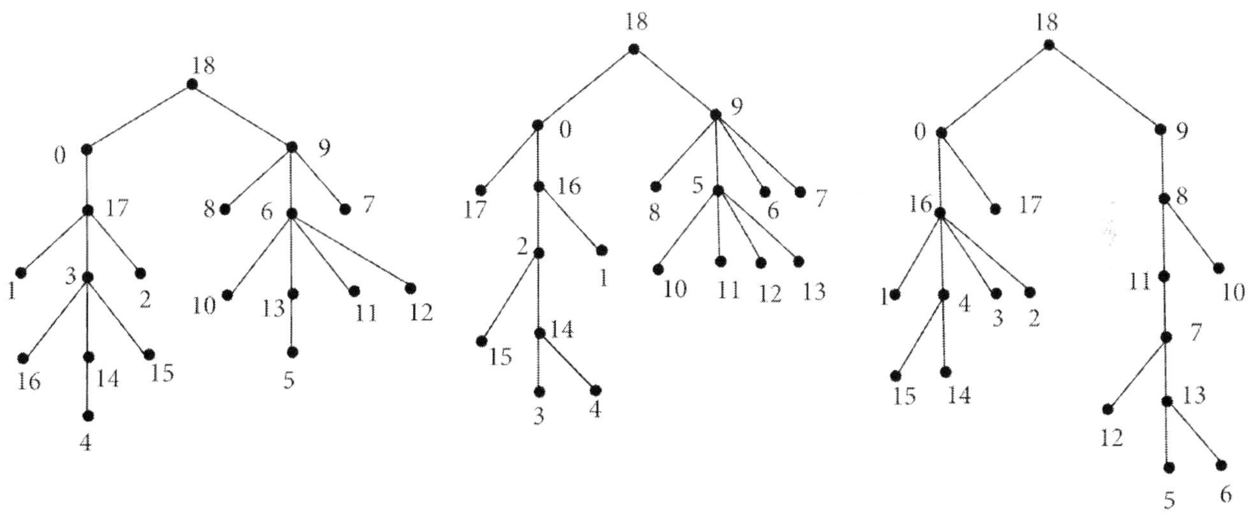

Figure 8: Graceful labeling of three grouped caterpillars which are joined to a single vertex v_i.

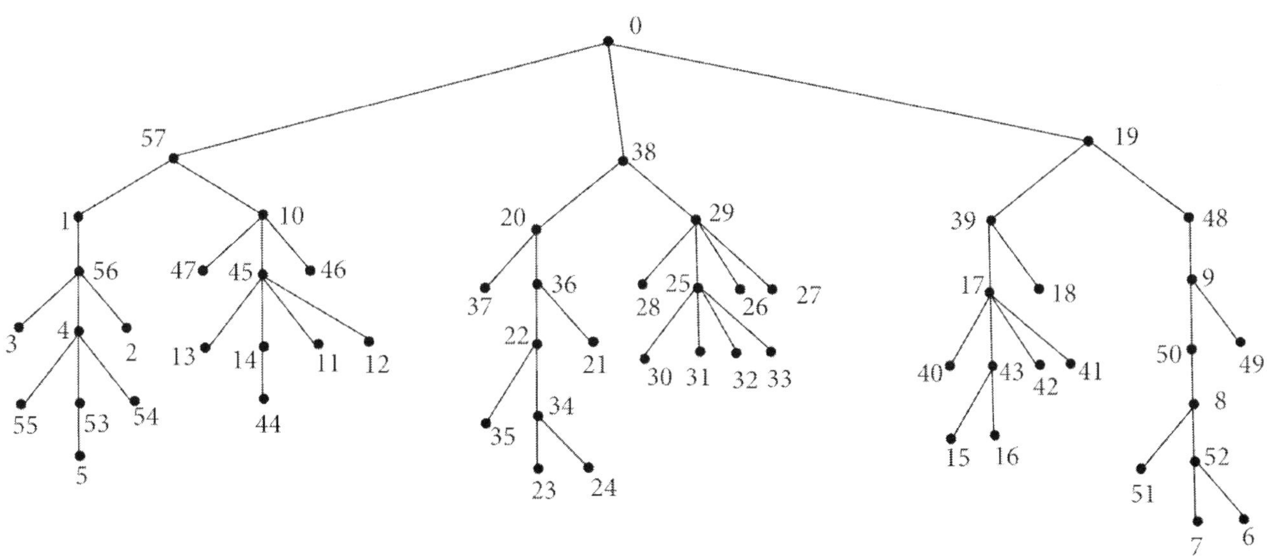

Figure 9: Graceful labeling of an extended super-caterpillar with root at vertex v.

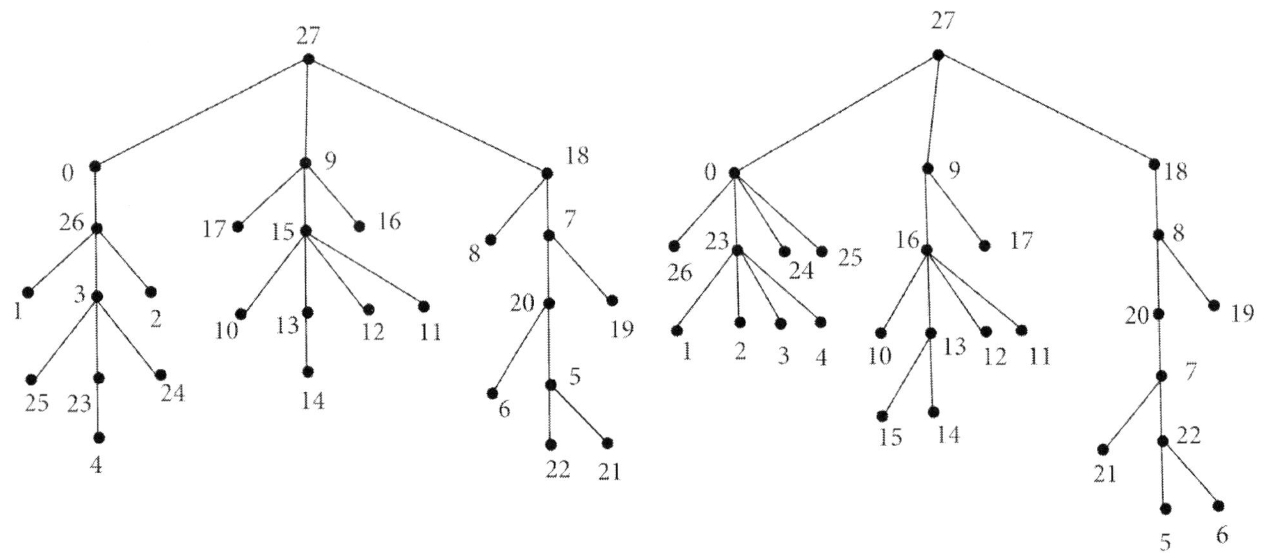

Figure 10: Six graceful caterpillars grouped into two, each containing three caterpillars.

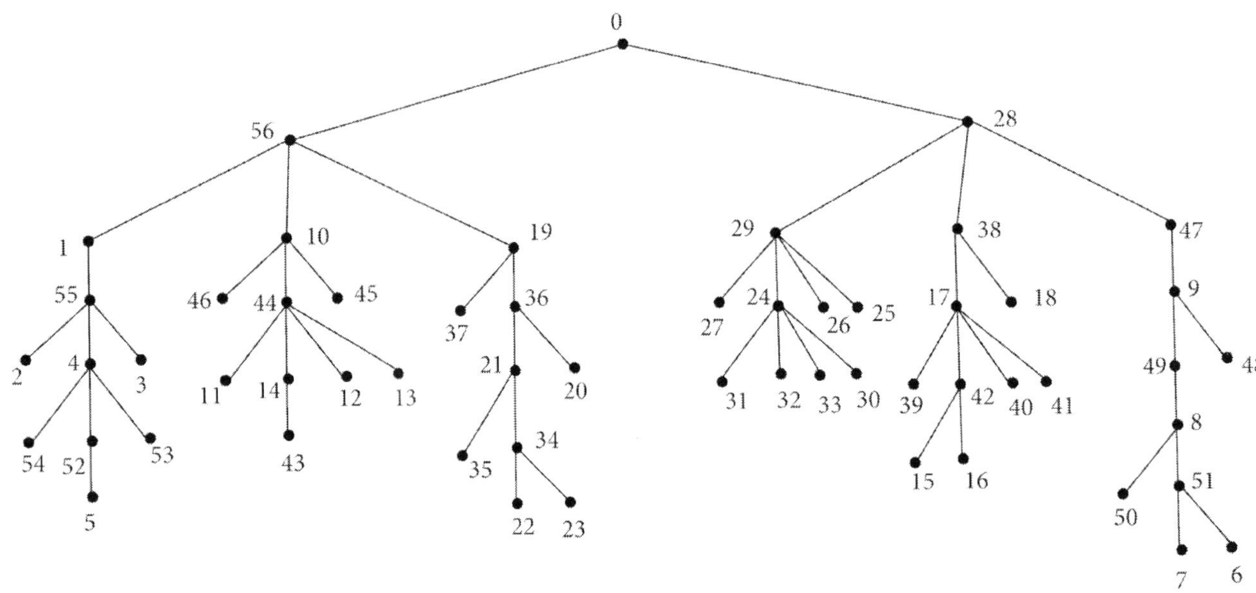

Figure 11: Both groups joined with a single root vertex.

CONCLUSION

We have proved that two fairly general classes of trees are graceful. In particular, if a number of caterpillars have equal number of vertices and total number of vertices in odd levels of each caterpillar are equal, then such caterpillars can be joined to a vertex to obtain a graceful tree. In our future work, we would like to see if more generalized trees constructed from caterpillar can be gracefully labeled.

REFERENCES

1. C. Huang, A. Kotzig, and A. Rosa, "Further results on tree labellings," Utilitas Mathematica, vol. 21, pp. 31–48, 1982.
2. A. Rosa, On Certain Valuations of the Vertices of a Graph, Theory of Graphs, International Symposium, Rome, Italy, 1967.
3. E. Robeva, An extensive survey of graceful trees [Undergraduate Honours thesis], Stanford University, 2011.
4. J. A. Gallian, "A dynamic survey of graph labeling," Dynamic Survey, vol. 6, article 43, 1997.
5. K. Eshghi and P. Azimi, "Applications of mathematical programming in graceful labeling of graphs,"Journal of Applied Mathematics, vol. 2004, no. 1, pp. 1–8, 2004.
6. R. E. Aldred and B. D. McKay, "Graceful and harmonious labellings of trees," Bulletin of the Institute of Combinatorics and its Applications, vol. 23, pp. 69–72, 1998.
7. T. Grace, "On sequential labelings of graphs," Journal of Graph Theory, vol. 7, no. 2, pp. 195–201, 1983.
8. J. A. Gallian, "Living with the labeling disease for 25 years," Journal of the Indonesian Mathematical Society, pp. 45–58, 2012.

9. W. Fang, "A computational approach to the graceful tree conjecture," CoRR Abs abs/1003.3045, 2010.

10. G. S. Bloom and S. W. Golomb, "Applications of numbered undirected graphs," Proceedings of the IEEE, vol. 65, no. 4, pp. 562–570, 1977.

11. G. S. Bloom and S. W. Golomb, Numbered Complete Graphs, Unusual Rulers and Assorted Applications, vol. 642, Springer, 1978.

12. A. Rosa, "On certain valuations of the vertices of a graph," in Theory of Graphs, International Symposium, Rome, July 1966, pp. 349–355, Gordon and Breach, New York, NY, USA, 1967.

13. J.-C. Bermond and J. Schönheim, "G-decomposition of Kn, where G has four vertices or less," Discrete Mathematics, vol. 19, no. 2, pp. 113–120, 1977.

INDEX

K

L

M

N

O

P

R

S

T

U

V

W